Congregation

Congregation

Contemporary Writers Read the Jewish Bible

Edited by David Rosenberg

A HARVEST/HBJ BOOK

HARCOURT BRACE JOVANOVICH, PUBLISHERS

San Diego   New York   London

Requests for permission to make copies of any
part of the work should be mailed to:
Copyrights and Permissions Department,
Harcourt Brace Jovanovich, Publishers,
Orlando, Florida 32887.

Grateful acknowledgment is made for permission
to reprint excerpts from the following:
"Rain Song" in *Modern Poetry of the Arab World,* translated
and edited by Abdullah al-Udhari (Penguin Books, 1986).
Copyright © 1986 by Abdullah al-Udhari.
The Book of Job, translated by Stephen Mitchell
(North Point Press, 1987).
Copyright © 1987 by Stephen Mitchell.

Library of Congress Cataloging-in-Publication Data

Congregation: contemporary writers read the Jewish Bible.

1. Bible. O.T. — Criticism, interpretation, etc.
2. American literature — Jewish authors — Biography.
I. Rosenberg, David. II. Harcourt Brace Jovanovich.
BS1171.2.C65   1987   221.6   87-11972
ISBN 0-15-146350-6
ISBN 0-15-622040-7 (pbk.)

Designed by Karen Savary
Printed in the United States of America
First Harvest/HBJ edition 1989
A B C D E F G H I J

CONTENTS

III WRITINGS

INTRODUCTION

If there is a broad community of American Jewish writers, what subject do they have in common, what challenge would constitute an offer they could not pass up? The Holocaust? Too many are reluctant to approach it as writers. Israel? Many have never been there. The Hebrew Bible, however, is common to virtually all Americans as a cultural heritage. And moreover, the diversity of the American Jewish experience allows all of these writers to acknowledge the original Biblical authors as fellow creators of story and verse.

The Hebrew Bible is written in more than a hundred voices—not counting the hundreds of characters speaking within the narrative. We often overlook this in English, where the idiom of one translator is uniform throughout. Yet in the original, one can discern the different times and places of writing in each book, as well as different portions within most books. The names of these Biblical writers are anonymous; still, their individual personalities are conveyed by the fingerprints of style. While the contemporary American writers who introduce each Biblical book have more distinct voices to us, they too might seem a unity were their essays translated into a foreign language three thousand years from now.

Consider how the Jewish Bible is known to Jews. It is certainly not an "Old" Testament. It is a collection of many different books, falling into three major divisions: Torah (or Pentateuch, or the Five Books of Moses, or Chumash), Prophets (Nevi'im), and Writings (Ketuvim). Taking the first syllable of each of these divisions, Jewish tradition knows them collectively as "Tanach." To scholars they are referred to as "The Hebrew Bible," a phrase as meaningless to religious Jews as "The English Shakespeare." Since the books of the Torah are different from many of the books in Writings and date from many centuries earlier, it is much more common for enlightened Jews to think of Tanach as a collection of authentic books united by their genesis in Torah, by their cultural and religious idiom, their history and shared experience, and, most important, their quality of vision and expression.

If we look at the order of books in the King James Version of the "Old Testament," we find a sequence that mixes up Prophets with nonprophetic Writings, neglecting the Jewish sensibility. In fact, beyond the canon, the Jewish library of holy books does not stop with Tanach; just as the scrolls of Prophets were built on Torah, and Writings often on both, Talmud refers back to all, as late Midrash may refer back to Talmud. Further commentaries extend the library to the modern age, with major stops on the way including the Kabbalah, Maimonides, Rashi, and the holy books of saintly rabbis. Outside this looser canon, but connected to it, run books of mysticism, philosophy, poetry, and translation (from the Aramaic Targumim and the Greek Septuagint to Buber and Rosenzweig's translation of Tanach into German and Steinsaltz's contemporary commentary on Talmud).

Since there is no consensus on how to count the books in the Hebrew Bible, with some divided into parts and the twelve "Minor Prophets" sometimes taken together and sometimes in groups, I decided to let the chips fall where they might. I asked authors to select the three books of the Jewish Bible they would prefer to introduce. When duplications arose, I mediated; when some books went unchosen, I pleaded their case. We have, as a result, essays for several individual books of Minor Prophets, such as Joel or Habakkuk, which are not often treated on their own. Others, equally short, while not individually addressed—such as Obadiah or Zephaniah—are represented by the rich assortment of essays on Prophets. Certain books—Jonah, Daniel, Psalms—were dearly requested by a second writer, though there was no inherent reason for this beyond devotion. In these cases, I allowed second essays which equaled their companions in uniqueness. The canon of Prophets and historical books may have evolved in a similar eclectic manner.

Although many of the contributing novelists read the Bible in the same spirit of intimacy they would bring to a novel, and many of the poets here have bared their innermost poetic instinct in the presence of the Bible's poetry, there were also some whose guard remained up throughout. Their response to my editorial criticism was often a pugnacious adherence to the bagels-and-lox Judaism that may have been all they were familiar with, a refusal to leave the arena of experience they knew best. They did not want to consider the Christian bias of those who infer a "nicer," Christian God; they did not want to tangle with a complex cultural history or confront the depth of religious tradition; rather, they were comfortable with fashionable clichés that relate mainly to minor sects of the contemporary ultra-Orthodox. Yet I learned to appreciate this stubborn response on its own merits, since these writers were saying that what mattered most to them was to resist pretense and the authoritarian airs of academics and clerics. Perhaps more significant, these writers were making the point that they were not satisfied to leave their heritage in untalented hands. Although relatively unschooled, they were bringing to the Bible a freshness of response and a talent for self-expression—and they were bringing it out in the open. More than one author expressed to me the hope that a public response to their views would engender a creative debate. These authors want to learn with their hands on, and perhaps there is something profoundly Jewish in this stubborn refusal to be intimidated, whether spiritually or intellectually.

I found myself wrestling with a few contributors who wanted to read the Bible literally, in a fundamentalist mode—a lively notion, yet easily misleading. When you ignore history and the conventions of ancient poetry and narrative—further distorted by inaccurate or dull translation—you may wind up with imagery that appears absurd if not fully explained. One of the conventions is exaggeration for the sake of poignant contrast; another is the ironic punning of idiomatic Hebrew with ancient officialese. Yet I had to accept that there was a legitimate claim to be made against the way in which the Bible is often taught—as if written last month and in English.

I believe that the concept that best includes all our contributors in a common community narrows down to one of personality, of individual integrity and creative open-mindedness. What we have is an American Jewish Bible that reflects the diversity and imagination of the original Bible itself: there may be some ignorance and some intolerance here, some literary tribalism and some primitive hubris, but there is also a great deal of sympathetic imagination, startling insight, powerful analogy, earned wisdom.

As Ezekiel echoes Isaiah in the Bible, as Isaiah or Psalms echoes Deuteronomy—the reprieve in Esther, Exodus; the cross-cultural love story in Ruth, Genesis—this book itself rings with echoes of shared experience among the various essays. Memories of childhood, of immigrant parents, grandparents, ancestors, of books read and rabbis encountered—all repeat and help to define the personality of American Jewish experience. All the writers here make their own experience of the text personal, and in the same way that their own learning is made accessible to us, the Bible in all its narrative and poetic skill is revealed as surprisingly accessible to everyone. It's the flavor and not just the recipe that is delivered. The rabbis of tradition did all they could to enhance the Bible's personality, ascribing books to beloved authors who were themselves characters, from Jeremiah and Lamentations to David and Psalms. In this book the boldness of individual imagination may remind us of a Moses or an Amos, the creativity remind us of the Job poet or the lover's anguished dream in Song of Songs.

So here, for perhaps the first time, we have an attempt by accomplished writers to characterize their ancient Biblical peers. There is a tendency to admit ignorance that can be disarming—I would like to call it an honest emotional response that the Bible itself inspires. For most, it may be fair to say that the task at hand increased their awareness of human limitations while enhancing their admiration for the scores of original authors.

It is Isaac Bashevis Singer, America's foremost immigrant writer, who best illustrates the cultural matrix in which secular American writers retain Jewish identity. Parallel to the long tradition of Biblical midrash—creative exposition, interpretation, translation—Singer finds in the Bible a metaphorical correspondence to his own experience. In the age of Freud, he brings his personal experience of inner turmoil into an equal relationship with his professional experience as a writer and an artist, using both to illuminate traditional Jewish texts, among which the Bible is primary.

In the introduction to a volume of his stories, Singer writes, "God was for me an eternal belletrist. His main attribute was creativity. God was creativity, and what He created was made of the same stuff as He and shared His desire: to create again. I quoted to myself that passage from the Midrash which says God created and destroyed many worlds before He created this one. Like my brother and myself God threw His unsuccessful works into the wastebasket. The Flood, the destruction of Sodom, the wanderings of the Jews in the desert, the wars of Joshua—these were all episodes in a divine novel, full of suspense and adventure. Yes, God was a creator, and that which He created had a passion to create. Each atom, each molecule had creative needs and possibilities. The sun, the planets, the fixed stars, the whole cosmos seethed with creativity and creative fantasies. I could feel this turmoil within myself."

Following Singer's lead, I asked the contributors to *Congregation* to consider the range of their experience, from childhood to their current professional lives as writers. The resulting portrait of American Judaism today is perhaps more vivid than any previously painted. The majority of American Jews remain unaffiliated with any religious denomination or organization; because most of the authors in this book are part of that group, this is the first time many of them speak for themselves in a Jewish context, rather than bowing to—or turning from—the organized minority.

Since the eclipse of the Yiddish creative community in America, it is only very recently that secular writers have not only written about Jews but addressed a Jewish audience as well. I found that when I attempted to recruit an older generation of American Jewish writers for this book I met with more resistance than with some of the younger ones. Usually the elders begged ignorance, although their Jewish knowledge was more than adequate to the task; it seemed to me that they were either too disturbed by their own ignorance or too alienated from their own identities as Jews. Unlike them, the contributors to this book regarded the assignment as a challenge and even an opportunity to explore and learn more; they were unashamed to present themselves as they are. They had matured to the point where they could rub shoulders with Isaac Singer—not just in the pages of national magazines like *The New Yorker,* but also in a community of writers that is not conflicted about its heritage.

Like Singer, many contributors found themselves contrasting their childhood stereotypes of religion with the more sophisticated art of narrative they were encountering as adult novelists and poets. Yet their responses cover a wide range, from an ironic recoil from religious sensibility to a deep respect for the distilled wisdom and passion that religious tradition further refined.

Exploring ancient Bible translations, I discovered that the most revered Jewish translations, into Judeo-Aramaic, were interpretive paraphrases (Targumim) that were often far from the original—not out of misunderstanding but out of desire to make the translation contemporaneous. One famous Targum completely deanthropomorphizes the deity, angels, etc. It required strong self-esteem to take these liberties, and that strength resided in the knowledge that the original Hebrew was common to all. There is no such text in common for our authors. Although there is wide respect for the King James translation as a classic in English literature, the distance from the original is increased as we lose touch with Elizabethan idiom. And so there is a natural reluctance to match the inventive adaptation that is commonplace to Israeli authors.

Yet there is a need to demystify the cultural clichés that simultaneously idolize and emasculate the text. In fact, this conforms to the intentions of the original Biblical authors: they record a fierce resistance to pagan mysticism, as in the refusal to idolize any man, even Moses. Whereas the Pharaoh he bested partook of monumental burial rites, the grave of Moses was deliberately left unenshrined—so the text would have us believe. Today the Bible's culture-bound idiom of the supernatural can just as naturally be interpreted as mythic without damaging the integrity of the original. Many of the writers in this book respond to the nature of idiom in this interpretive way.

For Americans, Freud may provide the common language for the conjunction between ancient history and myth, on the one hand, and the private myths of our personal lives, the ones we carry forward from infancy, on the other. Consider that the personality of Israel in this century is far more earthy than the stereotype that preceded its rebuilding. In the same way, the realism of character and event in Biblical Israel—no one was permitted freedom from human flaws and limitations—may be more crucial than what is said. It is precisely the quality of portrayal, the concern for the spirit of historical truth, that is close to the heart of the imaginative writer. As Singer notes in his essay, "I am still learning the art of writing from the Book of Genesis and from the Bible generally."

A NOTE ON TRANSLATION AND TRANSLITERATION

The authors used the translations they preferred, in some cases offering their own, original translations. Many refer to the Hebrew, which is transliterated according to the authors' own preferences. A scholarly book may set a standard for transliteration, yet some of the personality in these essays would be diluted by omitting the varying dialects with which the authors are familiar. Some grew up or went to school with Ashkenazic dialect, some with

Sephardic. Some retain the flavor of Yiddish pronunciation, some never knew it. And some, who know Hebrew, have differing preferences for how the spelling should be standardized. Just as I would not change a "Sara" to a "Sarah," if that were a real person's name, I have preserved the personal way in which American Jews hear the Hebrew. Nevertheless, I have standardized spellings whenever I felt it would not disturb the character of the essays.

When it came to spellings of accepted words in English, I sought unity but not neutrality. "Mishnah," not "Mishna"; "Chasid," not "Hasid." Yet what to do when an author purposely spells "Chumash" "Chummish"? I judged this a sweet case of the author's sensitivity to dialect. Spellings that denoted personal preferences were also retained. The Deity is spelled in many ways—"God," "I Am," "the Unnameable," "It," "Yahweh," "Jehovah," "YHVH," "Lord," "the Name," "the Tetragrammaton," "Adonai," etc.—and I did not tamper with them. A rabbi could be "rav," "reb," "rebbe," "rab"—each has its own reason. Capitalization is another area in which I sought to honor the author's intention. When one author uses "Bible" and "bible" in the same paragraph, he is not careless but emphasizing his intention to demystify the term.

There are some words translated and transliterated from languages other than Hebrew or Yiddish—French, German, Russian, Spanish, Italian, Latin, Greek, et. al. Unless it was a flagrant violation, I allowed the author's prerogative.

GLOSSARY AND BIBLIOGRAPHY

There are far more idioms from contemporary Yiddish, Hebrew, and other languages than one would find in a scholarly volume. I decided that if Woody Allen could use them in a movie without footnotes, we might also. *Mishegas, aliyah, yarmulke, kvetch, nudnik, traif,* and *kishkes* remain undefined if the context allows them to be understood.

For the sources, a wealth of definition, commentary, and explication is readily available in English. Many authors refer to specific books. For general information in detail, and for extensive bibliographic background, the *Encyclopedia Judaica* sets a standard. It also proves the best glossary.

ACKNOWLEDGMENTS

I would not have been able to bring this book to publication without the professional advice and concern of Rubin Pfeffer, Marianna Lee, Gary Piepenbrink, and Claire Wachtel. I received invaluable support during the editing of the manuscript from Jody Leopold and Walter Brown. Friendship and enthusiasm from the authors themselves sustained me throughout. Finally, the steady eye of Annabel Levitt helped keep me on course. My gratitude to them—and to the colleagues, friends, and relatives who bore with my sometimes unnerving preoccupation with this book—is considerable.

—*David Rosenberg*

PART I

TORAH

GENESIS

Isaac Bashevis Singer

FOR JEWISH CHILDREN, TO BEGIN STUDYING THE BOOK OF GENESIS WAS always an important event in their lives. Jewish children were brought up with the belief that the Torah was the well of the highest knowledge, given by God to Moses, written on parchment by saintly scribes: in the letters with which God has created the world.

For me, a son and grandson of rabbis, learning the first book of the Pentateuch was the greatest event in my life. I often heard my father recite passages of this book in his sermons to his congregation. I knew already that God had created the world in six days and on the seventh day He rested. It may sound strange, but I began to ponder Creation when I was still a little boy—the problems which in my later years I found in philosophical works such as the *Guide for the Perplexed* by Maimonides, in the *Kuzari* of Rabbi Yehuda Halevi, and still later in the works of Plato, Aristotle, and Kant: What is time? What is space? What is eternity? infinity? How can something be created from nothing? God has created the world, but who created God?

The author's own translation of the Bible used in this essay.

My older brother Joshua had become "enlightened" at about the age of eighteen and began to argue religious problems with my parents. I heard him say, "All religions are based on old books, but these books were written by men and men can lie, distort the truth, or have illusions. If we Jews don't believe in the old books of other religions, how can we know for certain that our books contain the absolute truth?" My parents could never give him a clear answer. All they could do was scold him and call him heretic, betrayer of Israel.

Yes, I began to study the Book of Genesis both with faith and with doubts. In my mind I had formulated many questions for the scribe of this holy book: What did God create first, the earth or the water? Or was the water already there beforehand? When did He create the wind which swept over the waters? And did He also create the 'Tohu and Vohu'? I had heard that the light of day came from the sun. But according to the Book of Genesis, God created the light first and then the sun. And what about time? Did He create time? But how can time be created? And did anything exist before time? My brother Joshua told us that the stars are suns that are larger than the earth and sometimes even the sun. But according to the Book of Genesis, the stars were nothing but additions to the moon. The more I read, the more questions and doubts assailed me. If God could have created Adam by the words of His mouth, why did He have to cast a deep sleep upon Adam to form Eve from one of his ribs? Some ten generations of early men were mentioned in the Book of Creation and there must have been wives, daughters, sisters, but only three females are mentioned. I have always heard from my parents that God is a god of mercy. But why did He accept the sacrifices of Abel and not those of his brother Cain? Didn't He foresee that this would cause jealousy and enmity between the two brothers? And why did He create the serpent to lure Adam and Eve to sin, with the result that God cursed them, drove them out of Paradise, and punished them all with death? Even the fact that God has given the animals to men to be eaten disturbed me. We had a slaughterhouse on Krochmalna Street and I often saw the slaughterers kill chickens, roosters, ducks, geese. And I witnessed how those innocent creatures trembled in the hands of their murderers.

My brother Joshua confided in me that there was no God. The earth tore itself away from the sun, he said, and it took millions of years before it cooled and began to produce bacteria, plants, animals, birds, insects. My brother Joshua used such odd words as "development," "evolution," "accident." He told me that all creatures were born with a survival instinct and had to fight for their existence. The stronger ones were always victorious and brought up new generations, while the weak ones perished and were lost forever. But was this fair? My father and mother always told me that God was a god of justice, on the side of the weak, not only the strong. But I heard my brother remark that nature does not know any compassion; it acts according to eternal laws. He quoted the great Jewish philosopher Benedict de Spinoza, who said that we must love nature with an intellectual love. But how can we love something or someone who knows no pity and perhaps does not love us? My brother told me that initially space was filled with one massive fog. For some reason, a portion of this fog became dense and began to attract other particles, which turned into the sun, the moon, the planets, the comets, myriads of years later. During the time of my growing up, the Yiddish newspapers in Warsaw wrote a lot about Halley's comet. I often saw people come out at night with binoculars, searching for the comet, which supposedly had a huge tail that stretched over half the sky. It was said that this comet could be seen in many countries, perhaps as far as Siberia and America. My father had told me that the sky teems with angels, seraphim, sacred beasts, cherubim. They all worship God, sing His praises. God Himself sits on a Throne of Glory and is so loving and merciful that He spends the nights teaching little children who had died prematurely and He reveals to them the secrets of the Torah. But my brother said that these stories were nothing but legends invented by fanatics. He told me that the sky is full of clusters of stars called galaxies. These galaxies, he said, were so far away from the earth that it takes thousands of years for their light to reach our eyes. He said that God had no plan or purpose in creating the world and He certainly did not do it to please the Jews and give them all the commandments and laws which are found in the Bible, in the Talmud, in the books of the Kabbalah. The world is a product of such powers as gravitation, magnetism, and perhaps electricity.

I was utterly shocked by all these heretical statements. But he told me that he was quoting scholars, scientists.

There was a lot of talk in the Yiddish newspapers about the American scientist Thomas Edison, who had invented the gramophone as well as the electric light bulb. It was written in the Yiddish newspapers that Edison was so diligent he slept only four hours a day, like the Vilna Goan who placed his feet in ice water to keep himself awake in order to study the Torah. For years, the newspapers described the ship *Titanic,* which was designed by foreign scientists; a ship with theaters, restaurants, orchestras, various stores, and luxuries which were unbelievable to the readers and certainly to a child like myself. But later I heard that this fantastic ship had hit an iceberg, the electricity was extinguished, and the passengers sank into the depths of the ocean. This misfortune proved to me that one cannot trust the scientists more than the Torah. Nor could I be convinced that from some cosmic fog emerged gardens, forests, animals, people. And all this happened without any plan, any purpose, just by some senseless accident. My brother said that for millions of centuries the sun shone over the shores of the oceans, rivers, and lakes and that all life sprang from this radiation. It was no less of a miracle to me than the miracles described in the Book of Genesis and in other volumes of the Pentateuch.

While I became as skeptical about science and the scientists as I was about God and His miracles, I acquired a great love and admiration for the stories told in the Book of Genesis. They were more believable and made more sense than many of the books my brother gave me to read. The description of Noah's ark and the way he rescued all the animals and kept them alive in the time of the Flood was a story I never got tired of reading. It kindled my imagination. I don't know where my mother took this from, but she told me that the giant Og, who lived in the time of the deluge, was so tall and so big that he could not enter Noah's ark. In the time of the Flood, he was sitting on the roof of the ark and Noah's wife, or perhaps Noah's daughter-in-law, brought him some food, while outside the waters were raging and erasing all life. Innocent people and little children perished because of the sins of the guilty ones.

I could see before my eyes the people who in later generations had built the Tower of Babel, hoping to ascend to heaven and perhaps take over God's kingdom. I was wandering with Abraham from the city of Ur to the land of Canaan and I could never get enough of the story of Sodom, of Lot and his daughters and his wife, who looked back at the destruction and became a pillar of salt. I walked with Jacob from Beer Sheva to Haran and I looked up at the ladder on which angels were ascending and descending. I was there when the brothers sold Joseph because of his prophetic dreams and because his father made him a robe of many colors.

My brother had begun to write in Yiddish when he was twenty years of age, and I, too, wanted to be a writer. I wanted to write stories like the ones I read in the Book of Genesis, every one of them more interesting than any of the secular novels which my brother smuggled into the house. I would say that although I became disappointed in many beliefs, whether religious or scientific, I was never disenchanted in the wondrous art of these stories. Many years later I read Tolstoy's works, and this great master maintained that the story of Joseph was the best he had ever read and that it could serve as an example in the art of storytelling, where every word, every sentence must be planned to delight the reader and stir his imagination. I lived these tales. (I liked the love stories in Genesis. The story of Jacob and Rachael is a wonderful love story. Here is a man who runs away from a brother who wants to kill him, and falls in love with his cousin. Her father tells him to work seven years so as to be able to get her. He works, seven years. Then the father makes a mistake, or does not make a mistake, makes a mistake willfully, and gives him another woman instead of the woman he loves. He works another seven years. It is a wonderful love story.)

I have heard Bible critics maintain that the Book of Genesis was written not by one person but by many, who pieced various legends together. Yet I am sure it was the same master writer, who knew exactly where his pen was leading him. I feel the same way even now, some sixty or seventy years later. There is perfection in these stories written by a single genius, from whom all writers can and should learn. In our times, Tolstoy was a writer of such caliber, and so was Dostoevsky, and so were—to a lesser degree—such remarkable talents as Sholem Aleichem, Peretz, Knut Hamsun, Strindberg, and many others whose books I read in Yiddish or Polish translation and admired immensely.

I am still learning the art of writing from the Book of Genesis and from the Bible generally. The story of how Abraham's slave went to find a wife for Isaac and brought home Rebecca still delights me today. It is imbued with faith in God and His Providence. I have learned that the great storytellers were all highly religious people, believers that God takes care of every human being, each and every animal, and that everything we do, think, and desire is connected with the Creator of all things.

Whenever I take the Bible down from my bookcase and I begin to read it, I cannot put it down. I always find new aspects, new facts, new tensions, new information in it. I sometimes imagine that, while I sleep or walk, some hidden scribe invades my house and puts new passages, new names, new events into this wonderful book. It is the good luck of the Jewish people, and also of all people, that they were given a book like this. It is God's greatest gift to humanity. The Evil One, too, has written a book: *Mein Kampf.* It is no accident that the writer of this nauseating volume became the vilest enemy of the Jewish people. There is no place for these two books in this world. The Hitlers of all nations knew that if they want to endure, they have to liquidate the people of the Bible or perish themselves.

In my years of literary growth, I had a chance to read Homer's *Iliad* and *Odyssey.* His style was perfect but soulless. Homer's protagonists were wild, cruel, half mad, without any feeling for right and wrong, without any compassion for human life. Their gods were as savage as they themselves. The god of Abraham, Isaac, and Jacob fills the human heart with hope, and gives meaning to our joys and to our sorrows. What is true about Homer can also be said about the scientists of his time, and even those in our time. There is little comfort in the science of today and in its cosmology. It has filled the universe with idols we can never love or even respect. Only the most insensitive can accept the notion that the universe is a result of a cosmic bomb which exploded some twenty billion years ago and continues to run away from itself forever.

No matter how the human brain might grow, it will always come back to the idea that God has created heaven and earth, man and animals, with a will and a plan, and that, despite all the evil life undergoes, there is a purpose in Creation and eternal wisdom.

EXODUS

FROM J TO K, OR THE UNCANNINESS OF THE YAHWIST

Harold Bloom

I

APRIMARY AUTHOR OF EXODUS, THE GREAT ORIGINAL OF THE LIT-
erary and oral traditions that merged into normative Judaism
was the writer whom scholarly convention rather wonderfully chose to call "J". Since Kafka is the most legitimate
descendant of one aspect of the antithetical J (Tolstoy and the early, pre-
Coleridgean Wordsworth are the most authentic descendants of J's other
side), I find it useful to adopt the formula "from J to K," in order to describe
the uncanny or antithetical elements in J's narratives. The J who could have
written *Hadji Murad* or *The Tale of Margaret* was the inevitable fountain-
head of what eventually became normative Judaism. But this first, strongest,
and still somehow most Jewish of all our writers also could have written
"The Hunter Gracchus" or even "Josephine the Singer and the Mouse Folk."
Indeed, he wrote uncannier stories than Kafka lived to write. How those
stories ever could have been acceptable or even comprehensible to the P
authors or the Deuteronomist, to the Academy of Ezra or the Pharisees, let

The Jewish Publication Society's translation of the Bible used in this essay.

alone to Akiba and his colleagues, is a mystery that I have been trying to clarify by developing a critical concept of what I call "facticity," a kind of brute contingency by which an author's strength blinds and incarcerates a tradition of belated readership. But here I primarily want to describe the uncanniness of J's work, so as to break out of facticity, insofar as I am able to do so.

By the "uncanny" I intend to mean Freud's concept, since that appears to be the authentic modern version of what once was called the "Sublime." Freud defines the "uncanny" as being "in reality nothing new or foreign, but something familiar and old-established in the mind that has been estranged only by the process of repression." Since I myself, as a critic, am obsessed with the Sublime or Freud's "uncanny," I realize that my reading of any Sublime work or fragment is always dependent upon an estrangement, in which the repressed returns upon me to end that estrangement, but only momentarily. The uncanniness of the Yahwist exceeds that of all other writers, because in him both the estrangement and the return achieve maximum force.

Of course J himself is considered to be a fiction, variously referred to by scholars as a school, a tradition, a document, and a hypothesis. Well, Homer is perhaps a fiction, too, and these days the slaves of critical fashion do not weary of proclaiming the death of the author, or at least the reduction of every author to the status of a Nietzschean fiction. But J is pragmatically the author-of-authors, in that his authority and originality constitute a difference that has made a difference. The teller of the tales of Jacob and of Joseph, of Moses and the Exodus, is a writer more inescapable than Shakespeare, and more pervasive in our consciousness than Freud. J's only cultural rival would be an unlikely compound of Homer and Plato. Plato's contest with Homer seems to me to mark one of the largest differences between the ancient Greeks and the Hebrews. The agon for the mind of Athens found no equivalent in Jerusalem, and so the Yahwist still remains the mind of Jerusalem, everywhere that Jerusalem happens to be.

I do not believe that J was a fiction; indeed, J troubles me because his uncanniness calls into question my own conviction that every writer is belated, and so is always an inter-poet. J's freedom from belatedness rivals Shakespeare's, which is to say that J's originality is as intense as Shakespeare's.

But J wrote twenty-five hundred years before Shakespeare, and that time span bewilders comparison. I am going to sketch J's possible circumstances and purposes, in order to hazard a description of J's tone, or of the uncanniness of his stance as a writer. Not much in my sketch will flout received scholarship, but necessarily I will have to go beyond the present state of Biblical scholarship, since it cannot even decide precisely which texts are J's, or are even revised by others from J. My attempt at transcending scholarship is simply a literary critic's final reliance upon her or his own sense of a text, or what I have called the necessity of misreading. No critic, whatever her or his moldiness *or* skepticism, can evade a Nietzschean will to power over a text, because interpretation is at last nothing else. The text, even if it was written that morning, and shown by its poet to the critic at high noon, is already lost in time, as lost as the Yahwist. Time says, "It was," and authentic criticism, as Nietzsche implied, is necessarily pervaded by a will for revenge against time's "it was." No interpreter can suspend the will to relational knowledge for more than an isolated moment, and since all narrative and all poetry are also interpretation, all writing manifests such a will.

Solomon the King—nowhere, of course, overtly mentioned by J—is the dominant contemporary force in the context of J's writing. I would go further, and as a pious Stevensian would say that Solomon is J's motive for metaphor. The reign of Solomon ended in the year 922 B.C.E., and J quite possibly wrote either in Solomon's last years or—more likely, I think—shortly thereafter. One can venture that Solomon was to J what Elizabeth was to Shakespeare, an idea of order, as crucial in J's Jerusalem as it was in Shakespeare's London. The Imperial Theme is J's countersong, though J's main burden is a heroic and agonistic past represented by David the King, while his implied judgment upon the imperial present is at best skeptical, since he implies also an agonistic future. J's vision of agon centers his uncanny stance, accounting for his nearly unique mode of irony.

How much of J's actual text we have lost to the replacement tactics of redactors we cannot know, but Biblical scholarship has not persuaded me that either the so-called Elohistic or the Priestly redactors provide fully coherent visions of their own, except perhaps for the Priestly first chapter of Genesis, which is so startling a contrast to J's account of how we all got started. But let me sketch the main contours of J's narrative, as we appear to have it. Yahweh begins his Creation in the first harsh Judean spring, before the first rain comes down. Water wells up from the earth, and Yahweh molds Adam out of the red clay, breathing into the earthling's nostrils a breath of the divine life. Then come the stories we think we know: Eve, the serpent, Cain and Abel, Seth, Noah and the Flood, the Tower of Babel, and something utterly new with Abraham. From Abraham on, the main sequence again belongs to J: the Covenant, Ishmael, Yahweh at Mamre and on the road to Sodom, Lot, Isaac and perhaps the Akedah, Rebecca, Esau and Jacob, the tales of Jacob, Tamar, the story of Joseph and his brothers, and then the Mosaic account. Moses, as far as I can tell, meant much less to J than he did to the normative redactors, and so the J strand in Exodus and Numbers is even more laconic than J tended to be earlier.

In J's Exodus we find the oppression of the Jews, the birth of Moses, his escape to Midian, the burning bush and the instruction, the weird murderous attack by Yahweh upon Moses, the audiences with Pharaoh, the plagues, and the departure, flight, and crossing. Matters become sparser with Israel in the wilderness, at the Sinai Covenant, and then with the dissensions and the battles in Numbers. J flares up finally on a grand scale in the seriocomic Balaam and Balak episode, but that is not the end of J's work, even as we have it. The Deuteronomist memorably incorporates J in his chapters 31 and 34, dealing with the death of Moses. I give here in sequence the opening and the close of what we hear J's Yahweh speaking aloud, first to Adam and last to Moses: "Of every tree in the garden you are free to eat; but as for the tree of knowledge of good and bad, you must not eat of it; for as soon as you eat of it, you shall die." "This is the land of which I swore to Abraham, Isaac, and Jacob, 'I will give it to your offspring.' I have let you see it with your own eyes, but you shall not cross there." Rhetorically, the two speeches share the same cruel pattern of power: "Here it is; it is yours and yet it is not yours." Akin to J's counterpointing of Yahweh's first and last speeches is his counterparting of Yahweh's first and last actions: "Yahweh formed man from the dust of the earth," and "Yahweh buried him, Moses, in the valley in the land of Moab, near Beth-peor; and no one knows his burial place to this day." From Adam to Moses is from earth to earth; Yahweh molds us and He buries us, and both actions are done with His own hands. As it was with Adam and Moses, so it was with David and with Solomon, and with those who come and will come after Solomon. J is the harshest and most monitory of writers, and his Yahweh is an uncanny god, who takes away much of what He gives, and who is beyond any standard of measurement. And yet what I have said about J so far is not even part of the truth; isolated, all by itself, it is not true at all, for J is a writer who exalts man, and who has most peculiar relations with God. Gorky once said of Tolstoy that Tolstoy's relation to God reminded him of the Russian proverb "Two bears in one den." J's relation to his uncanny Yahweh frequently reminds me of my favorite Yiddish apothegm: "Sleep faster, we need the pillows." J can barely keep up with Yahweh, though J's Jacob almost can, whereas J's Moses cannot keep up at all. Since what is most problematic about J's writing is Yahweh, I suggest we take a closer look at J's Yahweh than the entire normative and modern scholarly tradition has been willing or able to take. Homer and Dante, Shakespeare and Milton hardly lacked audacity in representing what may be beyond representation, but J was both bolder and shrewder than any other writer at inventing speeches and actions for God Himself. Only J convinces us that he knows precisely how and when Yahweh speaks; Isaiah compares poorly with J in this, and the Milton of *Paradise Lost,* book III, hardly rates even as an involuntary parodist of J.

I am moved to ask a question which the normative tradition—Judaic, Christian, and even secular—cannot ask: What is J's stance toward Yahweh? I can begin an answer by listing all that it is not: creating Yahweh, J's primary emotions do not include awe, fear, wonder, much surprise, or even love. J *sounds* rather matter-of-fact, but that is part of J's unique mode of irony. By turns, J's stance toward Yahweh is appreciative, wryly apprehensive, intensely interested, and above all attentive and alert. Toward Yahweh, J is perhaps a touch wary; J is always *prepared to be surprised.* What J knows is that Yahweh is Sublime or "uncanny," incommensurate yet rather agonistic, curious and lively, humorous yet irascible, and all too capable of suddenly violent action. But J's Yahweh is rather *heimlich* also; he sensibly avoids walking about in the Near Eastern heat, preferring the cool of the evening, and he likes to sit under the terebinths at Mamre, devouring roast calf and curds. J would have laughed at his normative descendants—Christian, Jewish, secular, scholarly—who go on calling his representations of Yahweh "anthropomorphic," when they should be calling his representations of Jacob "theomorphic."

The "anthropomorphic" has always been a misleading concept, and probably was the largest single element affecting the long history of the redaction of J that evolved into normative Judaism. Most modern scholars, Jewish and Gentile alike, cannot seem to accept the fact that there was no Jewish theology before Philo. "Jewish theology," despite its long history from Philo to Franz Rosenzweig, is therefore an oxymoron, particularly when applied to Biblical texts, and most particularly when applied to J. J's Yahweh is an uncanny personality, and not at all a concept. Yahweh sometimes *seems* to behave like us, but because Yahweh and His sculpted creature Adam are incommensurate, this remains a mere seeming. Sometimes, and always within limits, we behave like Yahweh, and not necessarily because we will to do so. There is a true sense in which John Calvin was as strong a reader of J as he more clearly was of Job, a sense displayed in the paradox of the Protestant Yahweh who entraps His believers by an impossible double injunction, which might be phrased: "Be like me, but don't you dare to be too like me!" In J, the paradox emerges only gradually, and does not reach its climax until the theophany on Sinai. Until Sinai, J's Yahweh addresses Himself only to a handful, to His elite: Adam, Noah, Abraham, Jacob, Joseph, and, by profound implication, David. But at Sinai we encounter the crisis of J's writing, as we will see.

What is theomorphic about Adam, Noah, Abraham, Jacob, Joseph? I think the question should be rephrased: What is Davidic about them? About Joseph, everything, and, indeed, J's Joseph I read as a fictive representation of David, rather in the way Virgil's Divine Child represents Augustus, except that J is working on a grand scale with Joseph, bringing to perfection what may have been an old mode of romance.

I have called Solomon J's motive for metaphor, but that calling resounds with Nietzsche's motive for all trope: the desire to be different, the desire to be elsewhere. For J, the difference, the elsewhere, is David. J's agonistic elitism, the struggle for the blessing, is represented by Abraham, above all by Jacob, and by Tamar also. But the bearer of the blessing is David, and I have ventured the surmise that J's Joseph is a portrait of David. Though this surmise is, I think, original, the centering of J's humanism upon the implied figure of David is not, of course, original with me. It is a fundamental postulate of the school of Gerhard von Rad, worked out in detail by theologians like Hans Walter Wolff and Walter Brueggemann. Still, a phrase like Wolff's "the Kerygma of the Yahwist" makes me rather uneasy, since J is no more a theologian than he is a priest or a prophet. Freud, like Saint Paul, has a message, but J, like Shakespeare, does not. J *is* literature and not "confession," which of course is not true of his redactors. They were on the road to Akiba, but J, always in excess of the normative, was no quester.

I find no traces of cult in J, and I am puzzled that so many read as kerygmatic Yahweh's words to Abraham in Genesis 12:3: "So, then, all the families of the earth can gain a blessing in you." The blessing, in J, simply does not mean what it came to mean in his redactors and in the subsequent normative tradition. To gain a blessing, particularly through the blessing that becomes Abraham's, is in J to join oneself to that elitest agon which culminated in the figure of the agonistic hero, David. To be blessed means ultimately that one's name will not be scattered, and the remembered name will retain life into a time without boundaries. The blessing, then, is temporal, and not spatial, as it was in Homer and in the Greeks after him, who, like his heroes, struggled for the foremost place. And a temporal blessing, like the kingdom in Shakespeare, finds its problematic aspect in the vicissitudes of descendants.

Jacob is J's central man, whose fruition, deferred in the beloved Joseph, because given to Judah, has come just before J's time in the triumph of David. I think that Brueggemann is imaginatively accurate in his hypothesis that David represented, for J, a new kind of man, almost a new Adam, the man whom Yahweh (in II Samuel 7) had decided to trust. Doubtless we cannot exclude from our considerations the Messianic tradition that the normative, Jewish and Christian, were to draw out from those two great contemporary writers, J and the author of II Samuel. But J does not have any such Messianic consciousness about David. Quite the reverse: for him, we can surmise, David had been and was the elite *image,* not a harbinger of a greater vision to come, but a fully human being who had already exhausted the full range and vitality of man's possibilities. If, as Brueggemann speculates, J's tropes of exile (Genesis 3:24, 4:12, 11:8) represent the true images of the Solomonic present, then I would find J's prime Davidic trope in Jacob's return to Canaan, marked by the all-night, all-in wrestling match that concentrates Jacob's name forever as Israel. The Davidic glory, then, is felt most strongly in Jacob's theomorphic triumph, rendered so much the more poignant by his permanent crippling: "The sun rose upon him as he passed Penuel, limping on his hip."

If Jacob is Israel as the father, then David, through the trope of Joseph, is Jacob's or Israel's truest son. What, then, is Davidic about J's Jacob? I like the late E. A. Speiser's surmise that J personally knew his great contemporary, the writer who gave us, in II Samuel, the history of David and his immediate successors. J's Joseph reads to me like a lovingly ironic parody of the David of the court historian. What matters most about David, as that model narrative presents him, is not only his charismatic intensity, but the marvelous gratuity of Yahweh's *chesed,* his Election-love for this most heroic of his favorites. To no one in J's text does Yahweh speak so undialectically as he does to David through Nathan in II Samuel 7:12–16:

When your days are done and you lie with your fathers, I will raise up your offspring after you, one of your own issue, and I will establish his kingship. He shall build a house for My name, and I will establish his royal throne forever. I will be a father to him, and he shall be a son to Me. When he does wrong, I will chastise him with the rod of men and the affliction of mortals; but I will never withdraw My favor from him as I withdrew it from Saul, whom I removed to make room for you. Your house and your kingship shall ever be secure before you; your throne shall be established forever.

The blessing in J, as I have written elsewhere, is always agonistic, and Jacob is J's supreme agonist. But J makes a single exception for Joseph, and clearly with the reader's eye centered upon David. From the womb on to the ford of the Jabbok, Jacob is an agonist, and, until that night encounter at Penuel, by no means a heroic one. The agon, as I've said, is for the temporal blessing that will prevail into a time without boundaries; and so it never resembles the Homeric or the Athenian contest for the foremost place, a kind of topological or spatial blessing. In J, the struggle is for the uncanny gift of life, for the breath of Yahweh that transforms *adamah* into Adam. True, David struggles, and suffers, but J's Joseph serenely voyages through all vicissitudes, as though J indeed intimates that David's agon had been of a new kind, one in which the obligation was wholly and voluntarily on Yahweh's side in the Covenant. Jacob the father wrestles lifelong, and is permanently crippled by the climactic match with a nameless one among the Elohim whom I interpret as the baffled angel of death, an angel who learns that Israel lives, and always will survive. Joseph the son charms reality, even as David seems to have charmed Yahweh.

But Jacob, I surmise, was J's signature, and whereas the portrait of the Davidic Joseph manifests J's wistfulness, the representation of Jacob may well be J's self-portrait as the greatest writer of Israel. My earlier question would then become: What is Davidic about J himself, not as a person perhaps, but certainly as an author? My first observation here would have to be this apparent paradox: J is anything but a religious writer, unlike all his revisionists and interpreters, and David is anything but a religious personality, despite having become the paradigm for all Messianic speculation, both Jewish and Christian. Again I am in the wake of von Rad and his school, but with this crucial Bloomian swerve: J and David are not religious, just as Freud, for all his avowedly antireligious polemic, is finally nothing but religious. Freud's overdetermination of meaning, his emphasis upon primal repression or a flight from representation—before, indeed, there was anything to repress—establishes Freud as normatively Jewish despite himself. "Turn it and turn it, for everything is in it," the sage ben Bag Bag said of Torah, and Freud says the same of the psyche. If there is sense in everything, then everything that is going to happen has happened already, and so reality is already in the past and there never can be anything new. Freud's stance toward psychic history is the normative rabbinical stance toward Jewish history, and if Akiba is the paradigm for what it is to be religious, then the professedly scientistic Freud is as religious as Akiba, if we are speaking of the Jewish religion. But J, like the court historian's David of II Samuel, is quite Jewish without being at all religious, in the belated normative sense. For the uncanny J, and for the path-breaking David, everything that matters most is perpetually new.

But this is true of J's Jacob also, as it is of Abraham, even Isaac, and certainly Tamar—all of whom live at the edge of life, rushing onward, never in a static present but always in the dynamism of J's Yahweh, whose incessant temporality generates anxious expectations in nearly every fresh sentence of certain passages. This is again the Kafkan aspect of J, though it is offset by J's strong sense of human freedom, a sense surpassing its Homeric parallels. What becomes theodicy in J's revisionists down to Milton is for J not at all a perplexity. Since J has no concept of Yahweh but, rather, a sense of Yahweh's peculiar personality, the interventions of Yahweh in primal family history do not impinge upon His elite's individual freedom. So we have the memorable and grimly funny argument between Yahweh and Abraham as they walk together down the road to Sodom. Abraham wears Yahweh down until Yahweh quite properly begins to get exasperated. The shrewd courage and humanity of Abraham convince me that in the Akedah the redactors simply eliminated J's text almost completely. As I read the Hebrew, there is an extraordinary gap between the Elohistic language and the sublime invention of the story. J's Abraham would have argued far more tenaciously with Yahweh for his son's life than he did in defense of the inhabitants of the sinful cities of the plain, and here the revisionists may have defrauded us of J's uncanny greatness at its height.

But how much they *have* left us which the normative tradition has been incapable of assimilating! I think the best way of seeing this is to juxtapose with J the Pharisaic Book of Jubilees, oddly called also "the Little Genesis" though it is prolix and redundant in every tiresome way. Written about 100 B.C.E., Jubilees is a normative travesty of Genesis and Exodus, far more severely, say, than Chronicles is a normative reduction of II Samuel. But though he writes so boringly, what is wonderfully illuminating about the author of Jubilees is that he totally eradicates J's text. Had he set out deliberately to remove everything idiosyncratic about J's share in Torah, he could have done no more thorough a job. Gone altogether is J's creation story of Yahweh molding the red clay into Adam and then breathing life into His own image. Gone as well is Yahweh at Mamre, where only angels appear to Abraham and Sarah, and there is no dispute on the road to Sodom. And the Satanic prince of angels, Mastema, instigates Yahweh's trial of Abraham in the Akedah. Jacob and Esau do not wrestle in the womb, and Abraham prefers Jacob, though even the author of Jubilees does not go so far as to deny Isaac's greater love for Esau. Gone—alas, totally gone—is J's sublime invention of the night wrestling at Penuel. Joseph lacks all charm and mischief, necessarily, and the agony of Jacob, and the subsequent grandeur of the reunion, are vanished away. Most revealingly, the uncanniest moment in J, Yahweh's attempt to murder Moses en route to Egypt, becomes Mastema's act. And wholly absent is J's most enigmatic vision, the Sinai theophany, an absence which culminates in the safe removal of J's too-lively Yahweh back to a sedate dwelling in the high heavens.

II

J's originality was too radical to be absorbed, and yet abides even now as the originality of a Yahweh who will not dwindle down into the normative Godhead of the Jews, Christians, and Muslims. Because J cared more for personality than for morality, and cared not at all for cult, his legacy is a disturbing sense that, as Blake phrased it, forms of worship have been chosen from poetic tales. J was no theologian and yet not a maker of saga or epic, and again not a historian, and not even a storyteller as such. We have no description of J that will fit, just as we have no idea of God that will contain J's irrepressible Yahweh. I want to test these observations with a careful account of J's Sinai theophany, where his Yahweh is more problematic than scholarship has been willing to perceive.

Despite the truncation—indeed, the possible mutilation—of J's account of the Sinai theophany, more than enough remains to mark it as the crisis or crossing-point of his work. For the first time, his Yahweh is overwhelmingly self-contradictory, rather than dialectical, ironic, or even crafty. The moment of crisis turns upon Yahweh's confrontation with the Israelite host. Is He to allow himself to be seen by them? How direct is His self-representation to be? Mamre and the road to Sodom suddenly seem estranged, or as though they never were. It is not that here Yahweh is presented less anthropomorphically, but that J's Moses (let alone those he leads) is far less theomorphic or Davidic than J's Abraham and J's Jacob, and certainly less theomorphic or Davidic than J's Joseph. Confronting His agonistic and theomorphic elite, from Abraham to the implied presence of David, Yahweh is both canny and uncanny. But Moses is neither theomorphic nor agonistic. J's Sinai theophany marks the moment of the blessing's transition from the elite to the entire Israelite host, and in that transition a true anxiety of representation breaks forth in J's work for the first time.

I follow Martin Noth's lead, in the main, as to those passages in Exodus 19 and 24 that are clearly J's, though my ear accepts as likely certain moments he considers only probable or at least quite possible. Here are Exodus 19:9–15, 18, 20–25, literally rendered:

Yahweh said to Moses: "I will come to you in a thick cloud, that the people may hear that I speak with you and that they may trust you forever afterwards." Moses then reported the people's words to Yahweh, and Yahweh said to Moses: "Go to the people, warn them to be continent today and tomorrow. Let them wash their clothes. They should be prepared for the third day, for on the third day Yahweh will descend upon Mount Sinai, in the sight of all the people. You shall set limits for the people all around, saying: 'Beware of climbing the mountain or touching the border of it. Whoever touches the mountain shall be put to death; no hand shall touch him, but either he shall be stoned or shot; whether beast or man, he shall not live.' When there is a loud blast of the ram's horn, then they may ascend the mountain." Moses came down from the mountain unto the people and warned them to remain pure, and they washed their clothes. And Moses said to the people: "Prepare for the third day; do not approach a woman."

Yahweh will come at first in a thick cloud, that the people may hear yet presumably not see him; nevertheless, on the third day he will come down upon Sinai "in the sight of all the people." Sinai will be taboo, but is this only a taboo of touch? What about seeing Yahweh? I suspect that an ellipsis, wholly characteristic of J's rhetorical strength, then intervened, again characteristically filled in by the E redactors as verses 16 and 17, and again as verse 19; but in verse 18 clearly we hear J's grand tone:

Now Mount Sinai was all in smoke, for the Lord had come down upon it in fire; the smoke rose like the smoke of a kiln, and all the people trembled violently.

Whether people or mountain trembles hardly matters in this great trope of immanent power. Yahweh, as we know, is neither the fire nor in the fire, for the ultimate trope is the *makom:* Yahweh is the place of the world, but the world is not His place, and so Yahweh is also the place of the fire, but the fire is not His place. And so J touches the heights of his own Sublime, though himself troubled by an anxiety of representation previously unknown to him, an anxiety of touch and, for the first time, of sight:

Yahweh came down upon Mount Sinai, on the mountain top; Yahweh called Moses to the mountain top, and Moses went up. Yahweh said to Moses: "Go down, warn the people not to break through to gaze at Yahweh, lest many of them die. And the priests who come near Yahweh must purify themselves, lest Yahweh break forth against them." But Moses said to Yahweh: "The people cannot come up to Mount Sinai, for You warned us when You said: 'Set limits about the mountain and render it holy.'" So Yahweh said to Moses: "Go down and come back with Aaron, but do not allow the priests or the people to break through to come up to Yahweh, lest Yahweh break out against them." And Moses descended to the people and spoke to them.

However much we have grown accustomed to J, he has not prepared us for this. Never before has Yahweh, bent upon Covenant, been a potential catastrophe as well as a potential blessing. But, then, certainly the difference is in the movement from an elite to a whole people. If, as I suspect, the pragmatic covenant for J was the Davidic or humanistic or theomorphic covenant, then the most salient poetic meaning here was contemporary, whether Solomonic or just after. The true covenant, without anxiety or the problematic representation, was agonistic: with Abraham, with Jacob, with Joseph, with David, but neither with Moses nor with Solomon, and so never with the mass of the people, whether at Sinai or at J's own moment of writing. J is as elitist as Shakespeare, or as Freud; none of the three was exactly a writer on the left. Yahweh himself, in J's vision, becomes dangerously confused in the anxious expectations of at once favoring and threatening the host of the people, rather than the individuals, that he has chosen. When Moses reminds Yahweh that Sinai is off limits anyway, Yahweh evidently is too preoccupied and too little taken with Moses even to listen, and merely repeats His warning that He may be uncontrollable, even by Himself.

As our text now stands, the revisionists take over, and the Commandments are promulgated. I surmise that in J's original text the Commandments, however phrased, came *after* some fragments of J that we still have in what is now Exodus 24:

Then Yahweh said to Moses: "Come up to Yahweh, with Aaron, Nadab and Abihu, and seventy elders of Israel, and bow low but from afar. And only Moses shall come near Yahweh. The others shall not come near, and the people shall not come up with him at all."

Then Moses and Aaron, Nadab and Abihu, and seventy elders of Israel went up, and they saw the God of Israel; under His feet there was the likeness of a pavement of sapphire, like the very sky for purity. Yet He did not raise His hand against the leaders of the Israelites; they beheld God, and they ate and drank.

This is again J at his uncanniest, the true Western Sublime, and so the truest challenge to a belated Longinian critic like myself. We are at Mamre again, in a sense, except that here the seventy-four who constitute an elite (of sorts) eat and drink, as did the Elohim and Yahweh at Mamre, while now Yahweh watches enigmatically, and (rather wonderfully) is watched. And, again, J is proudly self-contradictory, or perhaps even dialectical, his irony being beyond my interpretive ken, whereas his Yahweh is so outrageously self-contradictory that I do not know where precisely to begin in reading the phases of this difference. But rather than entering that labyrinth—of who may or may not see Yahweh, or how, or when—I choose instead to test the one marvelous visual detail against the Second Commandment. Alas, we evidently do not have J's phrasing here, but there is a strength in the diction that may reflect an origin in J:

You shall not make for yourself a sculptured image, or any likeness of what is
in the heavens above, or on the earth below, or in the waters under the earth.

Surely we are to remember J's Yahweh, who formed the *adam* from the dust of the *adamah,* and blew into his sculptured image's nostrils the breath of life. The *zelem* is forbidden to us, as our creation. But had it been forbidden to J, at least until now? And even now, does not J make for himself, and so also for us, a likeness of what is in the heavens above? The seventy-four eaters and drinkers saw with their own eyes the God of Israel, and they saw another likeness also: "Under His feet there was the likeness of a pavement of sapphire, like the very sky for purity." Why precisely *this* visual image, from this greatest of writers who gives us so very few visual images, as compared with images that are auditory, dynamic, motor urgencies? I take it that J, and not the Hebrew language, inaugurated the extraordinary process of describing any object primarily by telling us not how it looked, but *how it was made,* wonderfully and fearfully made. But here J describes what is seen—not, indeed, Yahweh in whole or in part, but what we may call Yahweh's chosen stance.

Stance in writing is also tone, and the tone of this passage is crucial, but perhaps beyond our determination. Martin Buber, as an eloquent rhetorician, described it with great vividness but with rather too much interpretive confidence in his book *Moses.* The seventy-four representatives of Israel are personalized by this theorist of dialogical personalism:

They have presumably wandered through clinging, hanging mist before dawn; and at
the very moment they reach their goal, the swaying darkness tears asunder (as I myself

happened to witness once) and dissolves except for one cloud already transparent with the hue of the still unrisen sun. The sapphire proximity of the heavens overwhelms the aged shepherds of the Delta, who have never before tasted, who have never been given the slightest idea, of what is shown in the play of early light over the summits of the mountains. And this precisely is perceived by the representatives of the liberated tribes as that which lies under the feet of their enthroned *Melek.*

Always ingenious and here refreshingly naturalistic, Buber nevertheless neglects what he sometimes recognized: J's uncanniness. Buber's motive, as he says, is to combat two opposed yet equally reductive views of Biblical theophanies: that they are either supernatural miracles or else impressive fantasies. But had J wanted us to believe that the seventy-four elders of Israel saw only a natural radiance, he would have written rather differently. The commentary of Brevard Childs is very precise: "The text is remarkable for its bluntness: 'They saw the God of Israel.'" Childs adds that from the Septuagint on to Maimonides there is a consistent toning down of the statement's directness. Surely the directness is realized yet more acutely if we recall that this is Yahweh's only appearance in the Hebrew Bible where He *says* absolutely nothing. J's emphasis is clear: the seventy-four are on Sinai to eat and drink in Yahweh's presence, while they stare at him, and He presumably stares right back. But that confronts us with the one visual detail J provides: "under His feet there was the likeness of a pavement of sapphire, like the very sky for purity." J gives us a great trope, which all commentary down to the scholarly present weakly misreads by literalizing it. J, himself a strong misreader of tradition, demands strong misreadings, and so I venture one here. Let us forget all such notions as Yahweh standing so high up that He seems to stand on the sky, or the old fellow's never having seen early light in the mountains before. J is elliptical always; that is crucial to his rhetorical stance. He is too wily to say what you would see if you sat there in awe, eating and drinking while you saw Yahweh. Indeed, we must assume that Yahweh is sitting, but nothing whatsoever is said about a throne, and J, after all, is not Isaiah or Micaiah ben Imlah or Ezekiel or John Milton. As at Mamre, Yahweh sits upon the ground, and yet it is as though the sky were beneath His feet. May not this drastic reversal of perspective represent a vertigo of vision on the part of the seventy-four? To see the God of Israel is to see as though the world had been turned upside down. And that indeed Yahweh *is* seen, *contra* Buber, we can know through

J's monitory comment: "Yet He did not raise His hand against the leaders of the Israelites; they beheld God, and they ate and drank." The sublimity is balanced *not* by a Covenant meal, as all the scholars solemnly assert, but by a picnic on Sinai.

That this uncanny festivity contradicts Yahweh's earlier warnings is not J's confusion, or something produced by his redactors, but is a *dramatic* confusion that J's Yahweh had to manifest if His blessing was to be extended from elite individuals to an entire people. Being incommensurate, Yahweh cannot be said to have thus touched His limits, but in the little more that J wrote, Yahweh is rather less lively than He had been. His heart, as J hints, was not with Moses, but with David, who was to come. J's heart, I venture as I close, was also not with Moses, or even with Joseph, as David's surrogate, and not really with Yahweh, either. It was with Jacob at the Jabbok, obdurately confronting death in the shape of a time-obsessed nameless one from among the Elohim. Wrestling heroically to win the temporal blessing of a new name, Israel—that is uniquely J's own agon.

III

Martin Noth not only termed the Covenant meal—what I have called a picnic on Sinai—the most original element of the Sinai narrative, but also noted that the silent bystanders who appear alongside of Moses in the E version seem to be competitors of Moses, since they are representatives of the host, not of the elite. But that introduces the largest irony in the relation of J to the normative tradition. Nahum M. Sarna rightly emphasizes the Israelite innovation that marks the Sinai Covenant: there is no analogy in ancient Near Eastern history to the idea "that God and an entire people become parties to the Covenant." If my reading of J is imaginatively accurate, then J himself resisted what is central to his people's vision of itself. I think that returns one to the puzzle of J's Moses, who so clearly is not Davidic or theomorphic, unlike J's grand sequence of Abraham, Jacob, and Joseph.

Though J is, to me, no theologian, I agree with Noth's emphasis when he remarks that "the entire weight of the theology of J rests upon the beginning of his narrative." No writer, fittingly, has ever valued origins as highly as J. For him, to tell how the people were formed is to tell also what they are and what they will be. It is an oddity that J's Moses is a latecomer, while J's implied David, in Joseph, returns to the theomorphic origins. I think that accounts for why Pharaoh, in the J sequence, is so much more formidable in regard to Moses than he is in the received tradition, where he is essentially a stiff-necked despot who at last is compelled to give in. Brevard Childs, in his commentary on Exodus, shrewdly notes the difference in the much more imaginative J writer:

> But to J belongs the picture of Pharaoh who slyly spars with Moses, who passionately confesses his wrong, but with equal speed relents once the pressure has been removed. He can be violent (10:28) and sarcastic (10:10), almost to the extent of getting the best of the argument (10:11). He even seems to know Jewish law! Then when all is lost, the portrayal is not one of tragic despair, but of a sly fox still trying to salvage what he can (12:32).

J's Pharaoh is augmented (and entertainingly so) only because J's Moses is so deliberately less than overwhelming. If we are able to recover that scaled-down Moses, what will the consequences be, not just for how we read what we now call Exodus, but for how we regard what is now called Judaism? I take it that J keenly cared about the Yahweh of Abraham, Jacob, and Joseph (and, through Joseph, of David), but that he felt a certain disinterest in the Yahweh of Moses. What if we were to emulate J? To ask such a question is not to devalue Exodus, or even to back away from Moses. What the question does involve is our freedom, as contemporary Jewish intellectuals, to return to the Yahwist's elitist concerns. Is there a way back to a vision of Yahweh that would set aside the Moses of the Priestly authors, and the Deuteronomist? *That* Moses surged on, to become the Moses of the normative sages of the second century of the Common Era. Is their Judaism the only authentic Judaism that ever will be available to us?

All that is constitutive of authentic Jewish belief must be the Hebrew Bible itself, but what precisely is the Bible? Genesis, Exodus, and Numbers are, for me, the J writer, and *not* the composite text in which the redactors have had the last word, a word they never earned. Unlike J, the other strands are vitiated for me not just because they are tendentious, but because their authors, unlike J, simply were not strong enough writers, not what (following Nietzsche) I would call "strong poets." To adopt Richard Rorty's postphilosophical and pragmatic formulation, they sought to achieve universality by the transcendence of J's contingency, whereas J, with Shakespeare and Homer the strongest of poets, achieved self-creation by the recognition of contingency. J created his own mind by creating his own language, whereas the redactors neither could nor would emulate J, their great original.

It is difficult to read J as J because of the deep nostalgia we feel for the normative tradition. But an awareness of J's strength gradually leads one to the realization that normative Judaism is an extremely strong misreading of the Hebrew Bible that was concluded eighteen centuries ago in order to meet the needs of the Jewish people in a Palestine under Roman occupation. Does it bind us forever as the proper version of the Covenant?

The more deeply I read in J, the more I have the same experience that I have when I read in Shakespeare, which is the revelation of radical originality. The history of J's revisionists is a long march away from J, and so becomes an endless distancing from J's Yahweh. It is a dark paradox that the Yahwist's Yahweh is not the God of normative Judaism, or of historical Christianity, or of Islam. And it is Western culture's largest irony, in our very late time, approaching the year 2000 C.E., that we still need to recover the vision of God that was seen so vividly by the uncanny writer, J, who was our origin.

LEVITICUS

Leon Wieseltier

A RELIGION IS BASED ON A REVELATION: THAT IS THE MOST COM-
mon Western formulation. But this formulation disguises an
interest, that of the managers of revelation; and it disguises a
fatalism, a willingness to settle for something less than experience in a relationship with God. A more precise formulation would be: A
religion is based on a revelation that is over. Of course, that, too, is a
Western platitude. The pastness of God's presence, at least to the senses, is
responsible for the centrality of history in Western theologies. The faith of
the Jew is premised upon the denial of contemporaneity with revelation.
Thus, almost as if it foresaw the fatalism to which such a denial might
abandon the believer, the Jewish tradition has devoted much of its energy
to the re-creation of contemporaneity, most obviously in that theater of the
recovery of experience that is known as the Passover seder.

Coming too late, the Jew detests time. He attempts to abolish it.
Naturally, it is not abolished. At least so far as he remains a believer within

The King James Version of the Bible used in this essay.

the community of believers, and surrenders to the public dimensions of Jewish spirituality, the Jew is never more than a mock contemporary. He is the one who can almost see, almost hear, almost taste. He is a connoisseur of mediation. But opposition is not the only Jewish relationship to time. The ritual abolition of time is, rather, a planned disruption within a highly organized commitment to temporality. The Jew loves time at least as much as he hates it. Coming too late, he has nothing but time. History is oxygen for Jews. It is the essential environment for a faith that calls itself a transmission. You challenge time at the risk of tradition. You may flee time, but alone.

For the Jew, the idea of tradition holds a consolation for the loss of immediacy, or at least of the immediacy of the founding illumination: it ensures that those who come after are also those who come before, that the inheritors are also the bequeathers, that the sons are also the fathers. Finally the logic of progress predominates over the logic of regress in Judaism. Judaism's famous "linear" view of history amounts to an indifference to a fall, to an insistence upon movement. It is not the distance from the beginning that is measured in every prayer, but the distance from the end; the distance from the beginning, though it represents a fall from contemporaneity, has been competently traversed by tradition, to the overwhelming satisfaction of all the generations. (Tradition is an ideology of generations.) Immediacy may no longer be possible, but mediacy is. With respect to the end, however, neither immediacy nor mediacy is possible. All that is possible is desire. Thus the future, not the past, is the term of Jewish desire, and this has the lovely and ironic consequence of restoring the Jew to a position of priority, of coming before. What has been lost in time will be made up in time (hence that Jewish invention, messianism).

The incompleteness of the present, then, is the premise of the Jew's existence. This amounts to the comforting (and, in the moment, challenging) claim that there is meaning sufficient to what has been received; to the claim that separation from the experience of the source is not the same thing as separation from the source itself. The surprise, perhaps, is not Judaism's acceptance of the frustrations of pastness, but its acceptance of the frustrations of futureness. Jewish linearity is not especially hungry. Jewish desire is patient with objects that tarry. Indeed, sometimes it seems precisely like the desire for a tarrying object. The Jew has been taught to stall the completion of the present—that is, to stall eternity. The Jew is supremely willing to wait, to live in the interim. But for certain temperaments, this taste for *nel mezzo del camin* can become spirit-crushing.

In twentieth-century Judaism, certainly, the worship of the interim has flourished. Everything from post-Kantian metaphysics to post-Romantic politics has promoted a celebration of finitude. Realism in history and immanence in theology have captured Jewish intellectuals, and perhaps cowed them. It is nice to be told to love your limits. Of course, the fact of human finitude is incontrovertible, though it is also a little vague and a little banal. And, of course, the catastrophic consequences of heaven-storming in history are plain. But once it is understood (not without a struggle, at this late date in the development of historical consciousness) that history is not the only theater, or even the most important theater, for the single soul, once the distinction between the public and the private begins to make itself felt spiritually, limits may seem less lovable. The line between immanence and complacence is sometimes hard to draw (as, in politics, is the line between realism and complacence). In his aversion to transcendence, the Jew may be too cozy in the world. Why should he not want a larger, more thrilling, more rattling, more fundamental dispensation than indirection? Must the Jew always deny his growing restlessness, always still his rioting soul? Must he starve his hunger?

To the Jew who is discovering the religious utility of impatience, a reading of the Bible is an incitement. But he has been taught to read it precisely not this way, to honor instead a difference that cannot be overcome, a difference in kind between that world and this world. The difference lies in the availability of experience in a world in which the faith was more various, in which there was more (imagine!) than tradition. What separates the young Judaism of the Bible from the older Judaism of the rabbis is not only the simplicity of the one and the complexity of the other. There is, more profoundly, a difference in spiritual quality, in spiritual ambition. In the Bible, tradition was never all there was. There was experience, too.

It should be possible to read the Bible not only for what it tells about tradition, but also for what it tells about experience. This would be a radical, and a presumptuous, and in many cases certainly a delusive, reading. For the purpose of such a reading, an unlearning is necessary—for a start, the unlearning of the look of the traditional edition of the Bible, of that dense, definitive page on which square after square of commentary surrounds (actually, boxes into a corner) a small square of what was revealed. That page stole the shock from scripture; it left the impression, after years of exposure to it, of the absorption of the text into the commentary, of the power of the receiver over the received, of the triumph of a system over a miracle. Anybody who has been raised on those gloss-ridden pages can bear witness to a reduction of divinity by textuality. Of course, commentary is the principal instrument of Jewish development; there is no such thing as a fundamentalist Jew. (Or, to put it differently: Scriptural fundamentalism is a form of decadence in Judaism.) Still, the hegemony of commentary may also be a form of timidity, an arrangement for safety against the agitation of individual desire, against a rapture beyond study.

The simultaneity of experience and tradition, of voice and system, of revelation and interpretation, distinguished only a fraction of the history of the Jews. The Bible is the account of that blessed overlap. It documents the period during which the Jew could dispense with the wager. (Except for the Book of Esther—her "and if I perish, I perish" is the exemplary utterance of a postrevelation world.) It is the record of metaphysical privilege, and it is hard to read without a feeling of metaphysical jealousy.

Metaphysical jealousy is the characteristic emotion of the impatient Jew, not least because of the mundane mystery that sociologists call "collective memory." He comes away from the Bible with nostalgia for a world that he, of course, never really lost. He is reminded of his own lack of proximity. It is a feeling rarely acknowledged in Jewish culture, which generally prefers to tingle with hope. But perhaps the idea of a fall should be given a more substantial place in Jewish culture, certainly in the Jewish culture that has developed since the many effacements of the tradition (by Jews, mainly) in modernity. A fall need not connote sin, as in the Christian construction. It need only connote fate. But fate without sin: that is another way of describing victimization by time. Fate without sin is punishment by duration. You are not guilty, you are merely late; but the effect of exclusion can be the same.

The difference between the Biblical and the post-Biblical may be found in the distinctive relationships of the differentiated to the undifferentiated. The undifferentiated, followed by the simultaneity of the undifferentiated with the differentiated, followed by the withdrawal of the undifferentiated and the triumph of the differentiated: this has been the pattern of metaphysical history in the Jewish view—the sequence "pre-Biblical, Biblical, post-Biblical." Of course, we know nothing of "pre-Biblical"—that is, of the undifferentiated. It "was" before the beginning. But the Bible begins "in the beginning," with the creation of a differentiated world by an undifferentiated God. There follows the narrative of their simultaneity—the Biblical world. And finally, in a fall, the wagering Jewish world emerged, but it is broached within the Bible only by the Book of Esther, the only part of the canon which includes no intervention of immediacy.

The Bible is the record, then, of the period in Jewish history that knew no contradiction between spirit and form, the only period in which there was neither absent spirit nor pure form. (It is when spirit is absent that form is pure, since its referent cannot be found.) Not that there was wholeness instead, or the kind of union that marks a collapse of differentiation: no acosmism is possible after Genesis 1, at least for the Jew. No, there was not wholeness, there was engagement. Form actually received spirit. Spirit actually acknowledged form. Or, to put it differently but no less enviously, the justification of religious form was religious experience.

Perhaps the most remarkable episode of this engagement is the climax of the ceremony of the anointment of Aaron and his sons in Leviticus, 8 and 9. The last verse of chapter 9 tells matter-of-factly, "And there came a fire out from before the Lord, and consumed upon the altar the burnt offering and the fat: which when all the people saw, they shouted, and fell on their faces." Obviously this was not the first communication from God to the Israelites, to individuals, or to the group; and it was not the last. What makes this particular intervention of immediacy so remarkable is the high degree of mediacy that preceded it.

Not only had the burnt offering been prepared according to the detailed requirements, and the fat handled in accordance with God's specific instructions, with which the book began; but the ceremony of Aaron's and his sons' installation, of which this divine fire was the conclusion, was a most extraordinarily detailed and scrupulously staged ritual. "And he slew it; and Moses took of the blood of it, and put it upon the tip of Aaron's right ear, and upon the thumb of his right hand, and upon the great toe of his right foot. And he brought Aaron's sons, and Moses put of the blood upon the tip of their right ear, and upon the thumbs of their right hands, and upon the great toes of their feet: and Moses sprinkled the blood upon the altar round about."

Here, concretely, is an illustration of the Biblical overlap between experience and tradition. Aaron and his sons had been washed; they had been dressed carefully in their vestments; the anointing oil had been sprinkled on the altar seven times, and then on Aaron's head; the sacrifices of the sin offering, the burnt offering, and the offering of ordination had been made according to the laws of sacrifice; those parts of the animals that had to be burned into smoke were burned into smoke, those parts of the animal that had to be placed outside the camp were placed outside the camp; the unleavened bread, the cake of oil bread, and the wafer had been deployed also according to decree; then a second sin offering, then a second burnt offering . . . even in the great strangeness of the priestly cult, the Jew can recognize the universe of the Commandments, of the law, of the ritual—of what would come to be known as the tradition. But then, into this recognizable Jewish universe, into the observance of the Commandments, the action according to the law, the practice of the ritual—into the tradition—there arrives something from outside, something that cannot be mistaken for human work, an intervention—there bursts a fire—not the vision of a fire, or the report of a fire, but a fire—and there appears, to the senses of all those assembled at the altar, what the Jew cannot any longer recognize, what never appears to his senses, what is stranger to him even than these slaughterings and these sprinklings—an acknowledgment.

The Jew reads this, even a modern, Western, liberal Jew who is revolted by the primitivity and the violence of the conditions for this revelation, and he longs. Almost as if to still his longing, to pre-empt his emboldening, the thrilling story of Aaron's fire is followed by the cautionary story of the fire of his sons, Nadab and Abihu. "And Nadab and Abihu, the sons of Aaron, took either of them his censer, and out fire therein, and put incense thereon, and offered strange fire before the Lord, which he commanded them not. And there went out fire from the Lord, and devoured them, and they died before the Lord." Nadab and Abihu have become the personifications of spiritual presumption in Judaism, its classical instances of the Icarian impulse. (In Judaism, the Icarian impulse involves not only a violation of finitude, but a violation of rank, of precept, of structure; according to Rabbi Eliezer, a central figure in the rescue of Judaism from the Roman wreckage at the end of the first century, Nadab and Abihu were punished for propounding the law impudently before Moses.)

We may think of Nadab and Abihu, by virtue of their insistence upon immediacy, as the patron saints—patron sinners, really—of Jewish impatience. Inspired by a fire, they made a fire, and promptly they were destroyed by the inspiring fire. Observe again the magnitude of the gulf that separates that world from this world. In that world, the "strange fire" is not the fire that comes from God. That fire falls within the range of expectation. The "strange fire" is the fire brought by man. And what threatens man is not a deprivation of the divine, but a familiarity with the divine. Intimacy is the corruption of immediacy, in a world in which there is immediacy to be corrupted.

Structure for the reception of the unstructured: this is the subject of Leviticus—indeed, of the Torah. The organization of the world for sanctity proceeded by the increasing specification of ordained structure. Cosmic differentiations (between light and darkness and so on, in Genesis) led to historical differentiations (between the children of Abraham and others, in Genesis and Exodus), which led to the differentiations of holiness (most thickly and systematically in Leviticus). "Chosenness" is the self-congratulatory Jewish formula for the inevitability of separation in the construction of a world hospitable to holiness. In fact, separation *is* holiness. "And that ye may put difference between holy and unholy, and between clean and unclean": that is the characteristic motive for the priestly law provided in Leviticus 10:10. In 19:2, Moses is commanded to address the assembly of Israel with perhaps the most challenging words in the Torah, with the divine dare that "Ye shall be holy." (The Hebrew is more summary by half.) The thirteenth-century commentator Nahmanides insisted that "holy" means simply "apart." The putting of difference, to use the arch-accuracy of the King James Version, is the essential movement that organizes reality into religious order.

The shocking thing about Biblical separation is its specificity, which reached its densest Biblical development in Leviticus. The pettiness of the priestly selections, its disturbing obsession with detail, furnished a great polemical opportunity for the anticlericalism of the eighteenth century.

Those great mockers of the Israelite differentiations, however, might have been pained to learn that they were fastening upon a problem that much perplexed the medieval Jewish philosophers and kabbalists, too. Indeed, it perplexed the rabbis themselves. Why does Sinai bother about *shmita,* they asked about Leviticus 25, which commands that fields lay fallow every seventh year. The question became idiomatic, put by generations of commenting Jews to an expanding tradition that was coming to regulate every corner of life in the name of the revelation at Sinai. What has the technical to do with the sublime? From the standpoint of the sacred, the particulars of religious practice seem like a *non sequitur.*

But it is the premise of Jewish religion that the *non sequitur* is an instrument of the sacred. There is no disjunction of spirit and matter, no embarrassment of the high by the low; there is, rather, a continuum of the spiritual differentiation of the material from the high to the low, with the end of leaving the low in relationship with the high. Spiritually there is nothing unbecoming about ritual precision. Rashi, the master exegete of the Jews, who flourished (who really *flourished*) in eleventh-century France, observes about the appropriateness of *shmita* to Sinai that all the Commandments were, after all, given at Sinai, and adduces a midrashic finding that just as the law of the fallow field was revealed at Sinai in all its general principles and its particular provisions, so, too, were all the other laws that were revealed at Sinai. Revelation originates in detail and circulates through detail. It is given and then infused.

Thus the impatient Jew, for whom detail seems often like an impediment, like the blockage in a beam, like a great taming, must ready himself to be the Jew in the wrong, at least by the terms of the tradition. The tradition can be read rightly, or at least loyally; it has been read thus for centuries. When its institutionalization of awe is belittled by its impatient son (not to speak of the outrageous simplifications of its Christian critics, starting with Paul), he speaks in anger: the tradition is not rattled or routed by the demand for God, though sometimes the community is. The tradition can account for the latter-day whereabouts of inspiration. Its account is, from a certain standpoint, merely unradical.

Leviticus is a manual for the religious organization of reality. The organization is first spatial. Out of the chaos of the camp of the Israelites, Leviticus brings order and consolidates the wandering cosmos of the Jews in the desert—the structures of their sacerdotally dominated society that busy them with a thousand sacraments on Sinai's sands. The first spatial distinction is between the camp and outside the camp, which serve as one set of locations for the pure and the impure. The next spatial distinction is between the camp and the sanctuary, or the Tent of Assembly, in its center, which serve as another and more differentiated set of locations for the pure and the impure respectively.

At the center is the Tent of Assembly, the seat of the cult; around it are the people, the population of the spiritually matriculated, the thronging mass of those whose experience is the substance of sacred history; around them, the unformed, undifferentiated, unillumined netherlands of the others, always scorned, always feared, always of no real relevance to the work of the addressed soul, of the visited group. What is outside the order is erased—perhaps cruelly, certainly cruelly when the erasure took the form of Joshua's wars, but also necessarily for the single-mindedness of the God-engaged.

The differentiations of space are followed by the differentiations of time. The long chapter 23 of Leviticus reports God's instruction to Moses to "speak unto the children of Israel, and say unto them, Concerning the feasts of the Lord, which ye shall proclaim to be holy convocations, even these are my feasts"; and proceeds to the explication of the calendar, from the weekly Sabbath to the festivals commemorating history and honoring nature, to the days of awe and atonement. Then there are the differentiations of people, which are to a certain extent at the heart of the priestly code. The demarcation between Israel and the nations was begun in Genesis and completed in Exodus. Leviticus is more concerned to demarcate within the chosen community itself. The primary demarcation is between the priests and the community, which establishes religious rank, and, more generally, the spiritual stratification of the society. But even more fundamental distinctions are handed down—for example, the thorough proscriptions of incest in chapter 18, which set the bonds of the family into the marble of law. And between the articulations of kinship and the articulations of religious class fall the many articulations of purity and impurity, such as the laws of menstruation or of leprosy, that define the vicissitudes of virtue, the day-to-day spiritual status, of the individuals of the community.

Nor is that all. Chapter 11 sets out, with great taxonomical joy, the animals that may be eaten and the animals that may not be eaten. And the meticulous statutes of the sacrifices introduce differentiations into the bodies of the slaughtered animals, requiring that some organs be disposed sacramentally and other organs be consigned to the oblivion beyond the camp. Moreover, the morphological passion of Moses extends into the world of objects as well, culminating in the extraordinary verse 20 of chapter 19: "Thou shalt not let thy cattle gender with a diverse kind: thou shalt not sow thy field with mingled seed: neither shall a garment mingled of linen and woollen come upon thee."

Nahmanides bridled at Rashi's abandonment of the search for sense in these statutes. Arguing against Rashi's view that these are "the decrees of a king, for which there is no reason," Nahmanides maintained that the prohibition against the mingling of species was designed to preserve the integrity of creation, which had been committed into the free hands of men. In the context of Leviticus, this powerful insistence upon the purity of the species (which is vigilantly observed by pious Jewish tailors around the world) may be seen as something larger: as an apotheosis of alterity. Alterity is the deeper objective of the law; the creation and the regulation of structure are how man imitates God. The dissolutions of identity abhorred in chapter 19 are the exceptions that prove the Levitican rule, which is that separation is the condition of meaning.

May my rabbis forgive me, but it is impossible to study this system of separations without feeling the force of Georges Bataille's analysis of religion. (Bataille would have enjoyed the thought that a reading of his works made a yeshiva boy feel understood.) The priestly code brings "heterology" or the science of differentiation, Bataille's discipline, to mind. The injunctions of Leviticus rupture the inertness of the world prior to revelation; the homogeneity of the unsacralized world is disrupted in favor of heterogeneity, the controlling category of Bataille's theory of religion, which for Bataille is coterminous with "the production of sacred things." The production of sacred things: there is Leviticus.

But with what a twist. In Bataille's scheme, such production is designed to enable orgy and to provide for frenzy. Separation is the instrument of explosion. It is the antithesis of law. Not so in Leviticus: here separation is the instrument of containment. Sacred things are produced for the sake of order, not for the sake of disorder; for social stability, not for individual

release; for continuity, not for completion; for coherence, not for rapture
. . . for tradition, not for experience. In the end, unless God spoke audibly
forever and prophecy never ceased, the Biblical overlap of experience and
tradition loaded the religion in favor of tradition.

"And the Lord called unto Moses," Leviticus begins. (The Hebrew
name for the book is Vayikra, "and he called.") The rabbis in the midrash
comment: "The voice makes its way to Moses and all of Israel does not hear
it." Moses, of course, reported what he heard. It was precisely when the
report of the voice did the work of the voice that tradition was born. Absent
the fire, there is the altar. And absent the altar, there is its successor: the
synagogue. ("So will we render the calves of our lips," said Hosea, establishing the substitution of sacrifice by prayer.) That is why the religion survives.
But it is also why the impatient son chafes in his love, why the obedient
son ponders the withholding of ecstasy.

The priestly code prescribes a religious regime of fearful severity, a
plenitude of requirements and retributions and rewards, all sanctioned by
the sound of God's voice. There is little relief from strictness; the book is
almost completely written in the imperative. But there are interesting
intrusions of the narrative into the imperative, glimpses of the individuals
living within the system. There is the man who comes to the priest and says,
"Something like a plague has appeared upon my house"—who discovers
that there is decay where he dwells, and panics. But happy is the man who
panics but has the priest. And there is the leper who must rend his clothes
and cry, "Unclean, unclean," who must declare that he knows himself to
be no longer pure. But happy is the man who knows himself to be no longer
pure but has the priest.

Most mysteriously of all, there is, in the Yom Kippur service, the man
"that sends the scapegoat to Azazel": "And Aaron shall lay both his hands
upon the head of the live goat, and confess over him all the iniquities of
the children of Israel, and all their transgressions in all their sins, putting
them upon the head of the goat, and shall send him away by the hand of
a fit man into the wilderness." Who is this "fit man" whose role in the most
awesome service is to lead the scapegoat into the barrenness beyond, into
eretz gzerah, or the punished land? In the original he is modestly called *ish
iti,* which is closer to "a timely man" or "an occasional man." This fit man,
this timely man, this occasional man, this anonymous man, this marginal

man, he carries sin away from holiness to the limits of the known. He is the escort of evil to hell. Appointed by the pure to the company of impurity, the timely man must scrub his clothes and wash himself upon his return from the edge of darkness, if he wishes to enter the camp. Surely he is the figure to which a modern imagination, exercised by the darkness that surrounds the light, may kindle most.

Leviticus is the classical text of what might be called hard-core Judaism, the Judaism of religious efficiency and spiritual subordination. (It might also be called precisian Judaism, using the seventeenth-century Puritan term for religious punctiliousness.) Is this Judaism really an incitement? Much of it, obviously, for reasons of history and culture, is also an irrelevance, as those medieval rationalists believed who dissuaded students from the study of the laws of sacrifices. Most of Leviticus is easily read anthropologically, even by an observant Jew, as the survival of an early form of the faith.

But suddenly the historical consciousness of the Jew plays a prank upon its own distance. Irrelevance is transformed into incitement. For has the Jew not been taught to measure the late against the early? And who decides how early is too early, and which portion of the past shall matter for the present? The past is without end. There is no reason not to reach further back, if there is a need. Leviticus may seem strange, but it is the origin. It holds lessons. The zealots in Jerusalem who are preparing for the return to the Temple mount by studying the laws of the sacrifices are learning the wrong lessons, for they mistake the continuity of their own desire for a continuity of history. They fail to appreciate that a past to which God spoke is not a usable past.

The impatient Jew reads Leviticus and thinks: There is where we were, here is where we are. Does he want a restoration? He is not a fool. Does he long for union? Not even when God spoke was there union. There was only—only!—communication. And that is what he dares to dream of. Acknowledgment is the fondest wish of his faith. But he suffers his days in the deprivation of acknowledgment, or, worse, in its commemoration. When the impatient Jew reads of the charged and, in many ways, grotesque beginnings of the tradition, a loss of faith is less the danger than a loss of heart.

NUMBERS

THE REALISM OF NUMBERS
THE MAGIC OF NUMBERS

Geoffrey H. Hartman

THE PLETHORA OF DETAIL THAT OPENS NUMBERS MAKES ONE APPRE-
ciate Maimonides' warning: everything in the Bible is significant, lists as well as theophanies. For mystics that is no news:
the driest can also be the juiciest parts. Behind or within the
soundshape of these enumerations, as behind or within the blueprint for the
Temple envisaged by Ezekiel, there may be glimmers of a hidden sense. Yet
measuring, accounting, or drawing up lists is so basic a way of creating a
semblance of order that any mystical meaning is surely a construction
beyond the call of duty.

The marshaling of the tribes recorded in detail suggests that the children of Israel are emerging from the status of a "mixed multitude" into
something resembling a community. They are growing into the Promise:
Moses is organizing the desert, counting infinite grains of sand. "Who can
count the dust of Jacob, or number the fourth part of Israel?" (Numbers
23:10) The mathematical sublime of "Be fruitful and multiply" begins to

---

The Revised Standard Version of the Bible used in this essay.

manifest itself. In addition to a vertical infinity, a horizontal one is evoked, an endless aggregate that should remain centered on the Tabernacle. Yet, if in this multitude, this potential "nation of priests," everyone is equally near to God, can the center—the focus of authority—hold?

A compromise whose secular genesis is not recorded establishes the Levites as prominent intermediaries between a class of priests, sons of Aaron who stand always in precarious proximity to God, and the common man *(zar)*. Both common man and priest are in special danger of death: Nadab and Abihu, sons of Aaron, died when they offered "strange fire." *(esh zarah;* compare the term for "idolatry," *avodah zarah)* before the Lord (3:4); whereas the commoner who approaches God must be put to death (3:10, 3:38). To "offer" (bring near) and to "approach" (come near) are variants of the root word *k-r-b,* which is also the word used in "Bring the tribe of Levi near, and set them before Aaron the Priest" (3:6). Everything is measured by its distance from the Mishkan or Tabernacle: a fearful symmetry ordains that the Levites occupy a position neither too close to nor too far from that sacred and deadly core. In these first chapters, where the focus is on a division of labor necessary to the formation of a coherent society, it is clear that the Levites are the most stable entity, whose cultic labor *(avodah)* constitutes an alternative to the military service for which the census ordered in Numbers is made. Guarding and servicing the Tabernacle are essential to the tribes as they pass through hostile territory—hostile also in that it is unfruitful (precisely *not* the promised land), so that God must often stand in for nature and provide Israel's nourishment during its long and purgative trek.

Numbers contains some of the best-known incidents of the Bible: the magic appeal of Manna falling from heaven and of water springing from the rock (both also in Exodus); of Balaam setting out to curse the Israelites and instead blessing them; of Miriam (the sister of Aaron) struck down with leprosy; of the rebellion and swallowing up of Korah; and the strange statute concerning the red heifer.[1] Other touches are less magical perhaps, but symbolize clearly and concisely the issue of authority: Moses accepting prophetic speech in others; sharing with the Seventy (so important for the very possibility of a continuous tradition) the burdens of office; and God (through Moses) expanding the blessing from the patriarchs to Israel as a whole, in the benediction of the high priest on each individual of the community. These are but high points, for a great deal of space is devoted to legal and organizational minutiae, rules dry and severe and without narrative luster. But what is generally remarkable in the Pentateuch is this forthright cohabitation of imagination and law.

An imaginative fervor directed toward matters of law not only formed the Jewish people in the first place (if we credit these Books of Moses), but sustained and distinguished them in the Christian era. Imagination and law continue their strange and powerful alliance in the Talmud. There is magic in the law: not as such, but because it is a crucial achievement which the Hebrew Bible allows us to relive by *not* separating apodictic legislation ("Thou shalt," "Thou shalt not") from its concrete and motivational setting. Though laws are promulgated by authority, as having their reason in God, they are accompanied, especially in Numbers, by a chronicle of the birth of a nation, an all-too-human history particular to the Jews and exposing the labor pangs of converting sons *(banim)* into builders *(bonim)*. Christianity, especially in its radical form, when it turns against its own priests, has trouble understanding this love affair with the law, and often attacks what it stigmatizes as an unpurified Jewish legacy: a God of measure and calculation, of stony tablets and jealous laws. Now, it is true that Biblical realism is very different from Christian spiritualism. But since it is better to be offered a choice than a prejudice, let us try to clarify that difference between the two traditions by some further comments on Numbers.

Nearness to a consuming fire is no metaphor in a wilderness that could literally burn up a thirsty people, or activate such cruel and delusive practices as a holocaust of the firstborn, "passing them through the fire."[2] Yet what are we to make of a God who continues to stake out his portion, who claims every firstborn male, including cattle, even if what He settles for is "The Levites shall be Mine" (3:12)? He allows a substitution whereby both Levites and their cattle are counted toward the redemption (i.e., buying back) of His "property" (3:45–51). We are often returned by the Jewish Bible to a realistic transaction that indicates how human rights are not a given, but are established by grant and negotiation. However, to boast of the relative humanity of the Bible in regard to the procedures of redemption or other cultic practices is not enough, for that boast would assign this substitution to a primitive world while suggesting a progressive scheme whereby a later religion (such as Christianity) purifies an earlier religion (Judaism) just as that had modified more primitive cults. No wonder a powerful pathos attends the figure of Jesus, seen as God's only son, sent into the world to "redeem" all mankind.

The spiritualizing of redemption in Christianity is so attractive that many forget its basis in Biblical realism. In the Hebrew Bible, human life does not own itself: like every other kind of life, it is God's property, and if the privilege of ownership passes from the Lord, it does not thereby pass into the hands of feudal kings but, rather, of Israel as a people striving to become a nation. The title, moreover, remains with God: everything is leasehold rather than freehold.

The idea that the earth is the Lord's, or that portions of it are "sacred," is found in other religions, too. The travels of Odysseus are lengthened, they become travails, because of a trespass on divine property, when his men slaughter some of the oxen of the sun. In Coleridge's "Ancient Mariner," the apparent cause of all the woe is trespass: the mariner kills a creature (the albatross) within the guardian territory of the polar spirit—a *lèse-majesté,* or crime against spirit of place, that has to be avenged. Prometheus, too, though a god, takes and alienates divine property, the element of fire that helps mankind to become more divine. To return to the Bible, in Genesis the act of eating from the forbidden tree may also be compared to a theft or a trespass on divine property.

I am suggesting that Biblical realism never forgets the material basis of the social contract, whether concluded between men, or between the people and God. The basis of this contract is a divine legislation that is very specific and down-to-earth. Yet, by setting one Testament's realism against another's spiritualism I do not mean that there are no figures but only *realia* in Hebrew Scripture. Nor do I suggest that the Christian process of spiritualizing is successful: it, too, may be a divine theft, a possessive move that *appropriates* a prior and sacred text. What is clear is that whereas in the Gospels and the patristic tradition the "Old" Testament is considered a blind prophecy, whose *realia* are but figures unconscious of the greater reality they predict (a reality only disclosed through the spiritual force of Christian revelation), in the Jewish Bible, despite its successive redactions, no unmodified triumphalist or progressive claim is found.

Yet something analogous to spiritualizing *is* felt in the Prophets and the Psalms. It remains highly restrained, more like the adaptation or updating of images, their displacement from one context to another: a shift that invests them with an intertextual complexity of reference. The technique does not imply, necessarily, passing from prefiguration to fulfillment. Thus, when we read in the Hallel (Psalm 113), "Praise, O ye servants of the Lord, praise the name of the Lord," it is possible but not crucial to think of the Levites as those servants (*vide* Numbers 3:7f) urged to perform their statutory duties. "Servants of the Lord" seems to refer, rather, to any congregant, and to the community as a whole. Indeed, the very concept of praise may help to erase such distinctions and to move prayer beyond the class-bound petition to a communal, magnanimous thanksgiving. When, similarly, Psalm 119 announces, "I am a sojourner [*ger*] in the earth: Hide not thy commandments from me," we can think of the actual *ger* (resident alien) who approaches the Temple with a formulaic and prescribed petition, for much in the Psalms expresses need related to social types or classes (the barren woman, the sailor in jeopardy, the leader in distress). Yet the phrase I have quoted can hardly be restricted, in context, to a special occasion or group: it looks toward the community as a whole, sympathizes with its various cooperating members, and represents something that lifts singer or worshipper beyond his assigned station. This enlargement holds whether the phrase is uttered by priest or Levite or commoner, or by the stranger dwelling in the community and wishing to observe its laws.

Jewish traditions of exegesis also pursue a mode that enlarges but does not subsume what is lesser in greater. Despite Christianity, or perhaps because of it, there is a resistance to a spiritualizing pattern of fulfillment. Even Philo's hungry allegorical method, though it presupposes the reader's capacity for spiritual progress, is independent of a historical scheme that futurizes Scripture episodes or reaches figuratively (prophetically) beyond events mentioned in the Septuagint. God foresees everything, but not in the mode of transcendence. There is, yes, a moral law (do X, and Y follows), fortified by a principle of hope embodied in Promise or Covenant, one that obliges God to make a nation of Israel and bring it to a land of its own. There is no trace, however, of a family-centered romance which exacts a sacrifice (of the Son) in order to provide amazing grace (redemption) that cannot be measured in contractual terms.

The realism, then, in Jewish exegesis, corresponding to the realism in the Hebrew Bible, is that no event or word can become obsolete through interpretation. Where Christian typology shows every detail of the Old Testament as pointing beyond itself, as signifying the advent of Christ (the red marker placed in the window by the prostitute Rahab to help Joshua's army invade Canaan is understood as a type of Christ's redemptive blood), Jewish countertypology presents words that always fall toward themselves, toward an aspect that is clarified by a comprehensive text rather than by later oracles or acts.[3] The "Oral Law," as Jewish exegesis describes itself, is a second but not a new (modifying or supervening) Scripture. The interpretations of the Oral Law are an original repetition, also from Sinai.

What this means in practice can be seen by how Rashi deals with a problematic verse in Exodus: "And they saw the God of Israel" (24:10). The verse is problematic because Scripture states clearly, "for man shall not see God and live" (Exodus 33:20). So how can they be said to have seen God and yet live? Instead of suggesting a mysterious interpretation, Rashi moves within the text to another difficult verse, Numbers 3:4, which recounts the death of Nadab and Abihu. "They saw and gazed and were doomed to death," Rashi explains, "however, the Holy One did not wish to disturb the joy of [Israel's reception of] the Torah [*simchat haTorah*], so He delayed [the death of] Nadab and Abihu until the day the Tabernacle was dedicated." This move to another place in Scripture coincides with a forward flash that remains within the limits of a moral and motivational probability even realistic writers could delight in. Such temporal or textual back-and-forth is not always so convincing; it can strain the limits of credibility by a synchronic attitude toward Scripture that allows the interpreter to shuttle freely between words very far apart; but it never adds to the text except by using this sort of montage and cross-reference. When we compare Rashi here with the previously adduced example from Psalms, we see that exegesis can respect mimesis, that interpretation can remain attuned to the way the Hebrew Bible depicts human hopes and fears.

Not all exegesis is like Rashi's. There are more extravagant kinds, and they, too, are acceptable. For "In the Desert" (*beMidbar,* the Hebrew designation for Numbers) deals with a subject that calls for miracle and magic, for "strange fire," however down-to-earth its basic concerns. Realism and magic are hard to separate in this epic about the birth of a nation. The magical interventions, in fact, seem often to make a realistic point that elicits from us the right degree of astonishment: how does a mixed multitude ever become a strong nation? This story of an adolescence, of an extended maturing process, grabs us not because of the miraculous parts but because these arouse the same wonder and perplexity we may feel in seeing even ordinary individuals survive and grow up—grow up to separate machismo and maturity. Israel must endure certain tests, form and re-form itself, accept a code of law, accept a degree of political leadership, accept the sense that it has a special destiny, beyond surviving by wandering from place to place. *BeMidbar* evokes, therefore, all the elemental anxieties and wishes that emanate from a state of privation and displacement: emotions for and against strong leadership; for and against anarchic energies of speech ("Would to God that all the Lord's people were prophets!" is the phrase from Numbers used by William Blake as an epigraph for his *Milton*); for and against the stranger in their midst (Numbers 12, the episode of Miriam's leprosy); for and against liberty, or what Kant described so aptly as "enlightenment": "the exodus of humanity from its self-imposed tutelage." (Kant's term is *Unmündigkeit,* the legal condition of being a minor, of not having a voice.) These still translate into the recognizable problems of Israel today, or of any state undergoing birth pangs that do not seem to end: how much democracy, how much freedom of speech, how much rule of law; debates about racism, assimilation, and "manifest destiny."

In his quest for authority, or desperate to maintain the life and hopes of the people, Moses is forced to remain a magician. Yet the charismatic-magical power vested in him is so hedged about that its very exercise seems to disqualify him. He does not use it as a natural attribute, but at risk. He keeps falling from grace in the eyes of the people, and even in the eyes of God after he produces water from the rock (Numbers 20 and Exodus 17)—a "strange water" theme complementing that of "strange fire." Can it really be, though, that he is kept from entering the holy land just because he used the wrong words? Or should we recall Freud's remark that words are a watered-down magic?

Magic, it might be said, does not breach the realism of Numbers but is part of its realistic context. Yet the question remains how to value it, since for many "enlightened" readers such magic is explained, rather than justified, as belonging to the mentality of an older civilization. For these readers it may remain a reprehensible superstition.

Yet most narratives, and most lives, contain residues of magical practices. In a recent and surprisingly powerful movie called *Runaway Train,* the convict-protagonist who has escaped a fortress prison selects impulsively the train he will hijack on his way to "freedom." No sooner does that train, as cold and armored as his previous prison—the scene is an Alaskan winter— roll than its engineer suffers a fatal heart attack, leaving a full-throttled machine speeding out of control down the tracks. The impulsive selection of this rather than that train is "magical" in its resonance; a desperate gamble motivated by an omnipotence fantasy. That the engineer dies is equally magical, a device permitted the author as long as it does not injure beyond repair our sense of probability. Whether it does or not depends, in turn, on how much the viewer is willing to grant a parable that "looks" realistic, though the film stages a fantasy whose uncontrollable impetus is pitted against an increasingly out-of-control series of events. The machine itself, symbol of modern civilization and a triumph of instrumental reason, becomes part of the magic to be appropriated; the battle that develops in this movie between the convict's body, powered by a fantasy, and the machine, which is like that fantasy run amok—as when a space shuttle explodes—results in something akin to a religious chastening.

In many ways the trials undergone by Moses and Israel in the desert are, despite interventions close to magic and miracle, far more realistic than this slick type of fiction. The question, however, that ambushes a mind which recognizes this narrative as Scripture, not fiction, or which remains open enough to consider the distinction, is whether such devices (in fiction) or practices (in life, secular or religious) should be avoided. Does authentic enlightenment, does human autonomy when based on something else than machismo, mean abandoning imaginative resources which are necessary for the achievement of that very autonomy, and which may still be necessary, whatever independence we boast of? Are these fictions not ultimately enfeebling rather than fortifying, like unearned gifts (funny money or magically provided powers) that, as popular wisdom tells us, will exact a delayed price? In brief, are we ever independent, or in control?

If we are not, the question arises of how we should deal with continuing needs, or our consciousness of these, our consciousness of a dependence that could feed a religious disposition. To be honest about our reliance on words, the expectations they arouse, the deceptions they must then confirm, leads to the scrupling science of literary criticism. For words are perhaps the most magical gift of all: though pregnant with promise, they do not clearly show their mortality, as the body does. There seems to be no middle way between inspiring though potentially deceiving speech, and muteness. This is God's problem in the Bible: His word, to quote Jeremiah, is like a burning fire; He is no ironist or doubter; His *davar* tests, and tests again, the stamina of both people and leader. It is Moses' problem, too—Moses, who retails the word of God and perhaps resists it (stutterer that he is) in the water-from-the-rock episode.

I have no idea why just at that moment. But over the Moses cycle of stories—from Pharaoh hardening his heart, to the forty days' tarrying on top of Sinai that results in the idolatry of the golden calf, to the forty years of enforced sojourn in the wilderness, to seeing the Land of Israel only in prospect—there hovers a structure of delay that stands to story as irony to speech, and evokes both the extraordinary directness of divine utterance in the Bible (compared with the deviousness of oracles) and the problem of trusting it while Israel perishes there in the desert.

That the fulfillment of the Promise is delayed—that the patience and pain of secular time come to the fore—suggests that God is anything but a magician. Yet it also introduces a doubt (Israel's unbelief), even if that doubt is shown as the cause rather than consequence of that delay. The Israelites in the desert are ready to stone Moses, and express themselves vividly: "Would that we had died in the land of Egypt!" (14:2–4) Starvation does not breed trust. It is a reasonable cry that is heard, of men afraid not only for themselves but also for their families. They recall the Promise made to them and, instead of its realization, see the opposite: decimation or even destruction, rather than increased numbers in a land of their own. They do not deny God directly, but by impugning the leadership of Moses they imply a deception. "And wherefore doth the Lord bring us unto this land, to fall by the sword? Our wives and our little ones will be prey; were it not better for us to return into Egypt? And they said to one another: 'Let us make a captain, and let us return into Egypt' " (14:3–4). This makes sense, if leaving Egypt behind meant also leaving behind the magic that liberated them from Egypt. If God (or Moses) is not a magician, He (or he) may be a seducer or a deceiver.

Contract or covenant, in short, works only when an accompanying sense of promise and blessing is felt: a balm that mitigates what must be endured. A midrash says: "Not a single word of what the Holy One, blessed be He, had promised Israel fell to the ground," using a word for "fell" *naphal* that resembles the word for "late" *aphal,* to suggest that even when the fulfillment of a promise is delayed it is not "late" (*Midrash Rabbah,* on Numbers 1:1–2). So, too, according to Maimonides, the Messiah may tarry, yet His coming will not be late. The relation between promissory word and fulfillment is the problematic area, one that Christian exegesis handles in a different way from Jewish *simchat haTorah* (joy in the Torah), to fall back on the phrase Rashi uses to explain why God delayed the doom of Nadab and Abihu. Whenever good exegesis takes place, there is a renewal of joy in the reception of the Torah that averts the severe decree.

Rashi's phrase indicates joy in the received Torah: a text applicable and quotable even in the most unexpected contexts, and impossible to supersede. It is as if "Be fruitful and multiply" had also been addressed to Scripture meanings. Magical (fantastic) midrash also continues to rejoice in the Torah as written. Its extravagance or imaginative surge—of an intensity comparable to Christian typology—does not upstage the cited word by positing a division into Old and New (B.C.E. and C.E.). The relation between text and idea, between referent and inferent, is not that of (earlier) figure and (later) fulfillment. The hermeneutic principle, often used by the rabbis, that there is no early or late in the Bible allows no hierarchy among passages, or keeps itself free to reverse any such order. It is the repeated—rejoiced-in—phrases that survive, perpetual angels whose mission is never accomplished. The New Testament, however, depends on seeing in the earlier text an involuntary blessing on its mission. Balaam should be Christianity's patron saint, for he was ordered to curse a holy nation and stayed to bless it. Though Jacob, too, of course, "wrested" the blessing from his brother, then from God, Balaam blessed even his own (Moab's) obsolescence. Precisely so does Christianity treat the Old Testament when it claims to fulfill it.

I want to end with a typical example of *simchat haTorah,* drawn from

Midrash Rabbah's running commentary on Numbers. There seems to have been a tradition that Israel in the desert was accompanied by a well. The midrash on Numbers (see Midrash Rabbah, Soncino edition, vol. 1) reads the initial call for a census, "Take the sum of" (1:2), in the Hebrew "Count the head of," as intending "Raise up the head"—that is, elevate (raise to greatness) all the congregation. In pursuit of this topic, it suggests that God assigned three special tutors, Moses, Aaron, and Miriam, to the people, and specifies the merits of each. The legendary well of waters is Miriam's; this is proved first by aligning Exodus 15:21, "And Miriam sang unto them: Sing ye to the Lord," and Numbers 21:17, "Then sang Israel this song, Rise up, O well, sing ye unto it." Miriam, who led the women in song at the Red Sea, here becomes Israel participating in a magical invocation. A further proof, however, for the connection between Miriam and well is found by an exposition of the words that record her death, *"And Miriam died there, and was buried there"* (Numbers 20:1). And what is written after that? *"And there was no water for the congregation"* (Numbers 20:2). The conversion of a casual, purely narrative, and episodic link into a causal one (Miriam died: the well dried up), is a striking instance of a reading that could join any two passages. That reading method is all the more remarkable since the distance between passages is not measured in this case by a time gap and intervening verses, but resides in the very nearness of an unrelated statement that is taken to be consequential and climactic.[4] A miniplot, focusing on the unmentioned well, is created by joining adjacent segments into a signifying unit as if they were marked by Biblical parallelism. I like this example, both because it shows magic entering the act of reading itself, and because, as Freud says at one point in deciphering a dream, here "dry" means "wet."

NOTES

1. That the ceremony enjoined by the statute seemed close to magic is clear, for example, from Johanan ben Zakki's exchange with an idolater who charged, "These rites that you perform look like a kind of witchcraft." See *Midrash Rabbah: Numbers,* trans. J. J. Slotki (Soncino Press), vol. 2, pp. 757–58.

2. I do not mean to suggest that these practices literally originated in a desert setting. What historical evidence we have indicates that they were associated with urban communities.

3. When there is an *ex eventu* linking of past (Biblical) and later-past (historical) event, it is more often than not a presage of catastrophe. So Jacob's injury in his struggle with God or angel is made to foreshadow the injury inflicted on Israel during the Roman persecutions. Even if, correlatively, Jacob's survival is seen as a type of Israel's survival, the latter appears jeopardized, always still to be assured; it is not yet an event, an *outcome,* and has no text other than Hebrew Scripture to forward it. But the entire issue of reading forward, of how both interpretation and ritual *identify* present with past, or promote the "eternal present" of Biblical story, is too large to be considered here.

4. The forceful conjunction of adjacent verses was a well-known interpretative technique. I am suggesting, however, that this techique is a clue to Midrashic method in general.

DEUTERONOMY

Mordecai Richler

TORAH WAS LITERALLY BANGED INTO ME AND SEVEN OTHER RECAL-
citrant boys in a musty back room of the Young Israel Synagogue, our *cheder,* by a teacher I'll call Mr. Feinberg. If I got
anything wrong, or if I was caught with an Ellery Queen
paperback or, say, a copy of the Montreal *Herald* on my lap open at the
sports pages, Mr. Feinberg would rap my knuckles with the sharp end of
his ruler or twist my ear. However, what all of us feared even more than
his blows was his bad breath. Grudgingly, we attended Mr. Feinberg's classes
after regular school was out—while other boys, who weren't lucky enough
to come from such good homes, were playing street hockey or snooker or
just hanging out, smoking Turret cigarettes, five cents for a pack of five.

Our parents skimped and saved to send us to *cheder* so that we could
benefit from "a good Jewish education." We were to learn the rules and
abide by them and grow up to be a real catch for a girl from an equally
respectable but possibly more prosperous home. Had our parents suspected

---

The King James Version of the Bible used in this essay.

that we were being force-fed poetry and drama in that musty back room, maybe even acquiring a taste for it, they would not have been so pleased.

Years later, when my cousin Fishl registered for a course on comparative religion at McGill, his mother wasn't thrilled. "With you," she said, "the grass is always greener."

Once I came home and told my father that Sean O'Brien's uncle, a teacher, had told me that the Flood was not only a Jewish tale; it was a myth shared by many peoples. What did he mean, *tale? myth?* We had studied it in the Chummish. My father had a short answer for it. "I don't want you to play with Sean O'Brien any more," he said.

Mr. Feinberg told us again and again what an honor it would be, once we had been Bar-Mitzvahed, to be called upon during the Sabbath service to bless a sentence from the Pentateuch, but I wasn't impressed. I had already heard the inside story. Members of the Young Israel congregation bid for the honor of an *aliyah,* starting with the most affluent of their number, notary and city council or "Uncle" Moish Takifman, a.k.a. Twelve-fifty Takifman, who unfailingly opened loud for a big twenty-five dollars, my father squeezing in late with a two-dollar bid. However, my father had revealed that regular members of the congregation were acting as shills, trying to embarrass nonmembers, prodding them into paying heavily for a piece of the Torah action. Bona-fide members, in on the secret, were obliged to pay only half of their declared bid for an *aliyah.*

Yawning, stretching, kicking one another under the long table, we counted the minutes until *cheder* was out. Poor Mr. Feinberg, determined to knock some learning into us, tried to gain our attention with chasidic tales: enchanting tales of the Baal Shem Tov, Menahem Mendel of Vitebsk, Dov Baer of Mezritch. Once he told us of a legendary Lubavitcher rebbe, a prodigy, who could recite the entire Torah from memory. If a pin were put through a page, Mr. Feinberg told us, any page, protruding forty-eight pages later, or sixty-seven pages later, the rebbe, swaying in thought, could tell you exactly what word the pin had pricked. Imagine that.

Alas, a callow bunch, we were more amazed by the feats of Maurice "The Rocket" Richard or Johnny Greco, a local welterweight who was fighting in main bouts at Madison Square Garden at the time. All the same, we certainly preferred Mr. Feinberg's chasidic lore to the logical platitudes of Young Israel's new "modern" rabbi, who was such a big hit with the ladies' auxiliary, if not with the men, who, on Sundays, were now expected to attend father-and-son breakfasts featuring reviews of books by Sholem Asch or Budd Shulberg, who wrote filth about our people. The twinkly Rabbi Bloom, a Brooklyn Dodger fan who didn't even wear a beard, made a pitch for what he called "the kids." Instead of a Sadie Hawkins Day Dance, like *they* were having, how about a Queen Esther Ball with a beauty contest this Purim? He also attempted to appeal to our reason. Pork, he said, was forbidden because it would have spoiled in the heat of Canaan, the children of Israel were enjoined to wear hats to protect them against sunstroke, etc. Suddenly all the magic was gone. All at once there was little to choose between the Commandments of the terrifying Jehovah, vengeful unto the tenth generation, and the Junior Red Cross's Ten Rules of Hygiene. So we argued back, equally tiresome. Now that we have iceboxes, why can't we eat bacon? Who fears sunstroke in this nutty climate? And, come to think of it, where did Cain find a wife?

Released from *cheder,* we collected our sleds and hurried over to Steinberg's supermarket, down the street, hoping to earn a quarter riding a lady's parcels home. While we waited outside in the snow, knocking our boots together to keep warm, we told puerile schoolboy Bible jokes.

—Why was God so angry with Moses?

—Because God asked him to come forth and he came fifth and lost the race.

Another story went that there were originally fifty commandments. God offered them to the Egyptians, the Amorites, the Canaanites, and the Syrians, all of whom, sensibly enough, refused to cut a deal. Then Moses, our father, blundered along and offered to take ten, but no more, and we were stuck with them.

For thou *art* an holy people, unto the LORD thy God: the LORD thy God hath chosen thee to be a special people unto himself, above all people that *are* upon the face of the earth.

In Deuteronomy, the fifth book of the Pentateuch, a repetition with comments on the Decalogue, the children of Israel—the progeny of an evil generation—are discovered this side of Jordan in the land of Moab. After forty years of wandering in the wilderness, they are at last preparing to enter the promised land of milk and honey. Moses, determined that they be bold, reminds them of what they had done unto Si-hon king of Hesha-bon and Og king of Ba-shan, utterly destroying the men, the women, and the children of every city. Or, put in today's sanitized military idiom, he recalled how they had once pacified the countryside.

Before going over Jordan, the Israelites must endure a reiteration of the Mosaic law. They are instructed once more that they are obliged to stone all false prophets, dreamers of dreams, to death. Clearly a case of the poets who wrote the Pentateuch, the most sublime poets we have ever known, advocating that short work be made of anticipated rivals. Or, looked at another way, even the greatest authors are insecure, bad-mouthing the others.

But the same harsh punishment is also due rebellious sons and adulterers and brides whose tokens of virginity fail to pass muster.

Then they shall bring out the damsel to the door of her father's house, and the men of her city shall stone her with stones that she die: because she hath wrought folly in Israel, to play the whore in her father's house: so shalt thou put evil away from among you.

Furthermore, as we have been told by fundamentalists as disparate as Jerry Falwell, the Ayatollah Khomeini, and the Lubavitcher rebbe of 770 Crown Heights, gay pride was out.

The woman shall not wear that which pertaineth unto a man, neither shall a man put on a woman's garment: for all that do so *are* abomination unto the LORD thy God.

If I may digress briefly, Christopher Sykes, in his biography of Evelyn Waugh, writes that during World War II Waugh and Randolph Churchill were parachuted into Yugoslavia as part of the British mission to aid Marshal Tito. Randolph talked incessantly, irritating Waugh no end. Then Waugh discovered that Randolph had never read the Old Testament. Hoping to shut him up, if only for a while, Waugh offered Randolph a fiver if he would read it right through. Randolph only made it halfway before he slammed his Bible shut and exclaimed, "I never realized that God was such a shit!"

I have repeated this anecdote often, though never in an airplane, because, such was my upbringing, the truth is it still scares me to tell it at thirty-five thousand feet. It scares me even as my first furtive taste of bacon frightened me more than my initial puff of pot, which—incidentally—is not forbidden in Deuteronomy, unlike the flesh of the eagle, the osprey, the owl, the night hawk, the swan, and the pelican.

My children are not troubled by such superstitions. They had a different upbringing. Foolishly, we spared them *cheder,* short-changing them with a liberal education. I'm okay, you're okay; no hangups, but no magic, either; too bad. But now, when they sit down with my wife and me to the Passover table, there are many things they want to know. They ask more than four questions. After all these years, I have become their Mr. Feinberg.

But to return to Randolph: his point about Jehovah, albeit blasphemous and more than somewhat smart-ass, is well taken. To be fair, however, the God of Deuteronomy could also be as saucy as Dr. Ruth—an understanding God, not totally terrible.

When a man hath taken a new wife, he shall not go out to war, neither shall he be charged with any business: *but* he shall be free at home one year, and shall cheer up his wife which he hath taken.

Obviously, Biblical draft-dodgers did not light out for Stockholm or Toronto, but instead hastily took a wife, possibly not being too fussy about her tokens of virginity. Mind you, Jehovah, a considerable strategist, did not want conscientious objectors or the chickenhearted in the battlefield.

And the officers shall speak further unto the people, and they shall say, What man *is there that is* fearful and fainthearted? let him go and return unto his house, lest his brethren's heart faint as well as his heart.

More than to any other book ever written, a reader brings his own baggage to the Pentateuch. What you find there depends on your sensibility. There is myth, there is drama, there is poetry. But if what you need is proof of Jewish obloquy, it is also to be found there, in lines precious to anti-Semites everywhere.

Unto a stranger thou mayest lend upon usury; but unto thy brother thou shalt not lend upon usury.

The poetry in Deuteronomy can be vitiated by a nagging reiteration of rules, rules, and more rules, tempered by threats from a God who clearly expects the worst of the people He has chosen to be special unto Himself. In fact, even as they are about to enter the promised land, God seems to be suffering from last-minute second thoughts. Possibly, the children of Israel don't deserve the freehold after all. Maybe, all things considered, He fingered the wrong bunch.

Again and again, Moses reminds the people of all God has done for them, how He delivered them out of Egypt with a mighty hand and an outstretched arm. Their most heinous crimes are recalled. They are assured that the land they are entering will be blessed in

the fruit of thy body, and the fruit of thy ground, and the fruit of thy cattle, the increase of thy kine, and the flocks of thy sheep.

Then Moses, in a rage, lashes out against the undeserving congregation of Israel.

For I know that after my death ye will utterly corrupt *yourselves,* and turn aside from the way which I have commanded you; and evil will befall you in the latter days; because ye will do evil in the sight of the LORD, to provoke him to anger through the work of your hands.

Late one afternoon, released from Mr. Feinberg's *cheder,* I crossed Park Avenue and slipped into Kresge's. I was caught shoplifting. The manager of the store, a Scots Presbyterian, had me into his office. He was not angry, but ashamed for my sake. "I never would have expected such behavior from a Jewish lad," he said. "You come from such a hard-working and law-abiding people. A people I greatly admire because you have always put education, sobriety, and family above all."

Yes, yes, but how did we acquire such a reputation, such habits?

Certainly our forefathers, gathered in Moab, this side of Jordan, were a loutish lot, a bunch of good ole boys, much given to carousing, wenching, pilfering, fighting, and sacking cities. Who knew them better than Moses? Moses, his time short, who warns his flock that they will be cursed if they lead blind men astray, remove their neighbor's landmark, take advantage of widows and orphans, accept pay to murder an innocent person, or lie with their father's wife, or sisters, or beasts.

Moses, Moses.

He served a great God, yes indeed, a mighty and a terrible God, but also a God unforgiving beyond compare. Deuteronomy ends on one of the most poignant notes in the Pentateuch: the death of Moses, Moishe Rabbeinu. A hundred and twenty years old he was when he died, but his eye was not dim, nor his natural force abated.

It has been said that only five leaders of Israel lived exactly a hundred and twenty years: Moses, Hillel, Rabbi Yochanon ben Zakkai, Rabbi Yehuda HaNassi, and Rabbi Akiva. But only of Moses was it written:

And there arose not a prophet since in Israel like unto Moses,
whom the LORD knew face to face.

Moses, of the tribe of Levi, born into captivity, was set adrift by Miriam in an ark of bulrushes daubed with slime and pitch; rescued by Pharaoh's daughter, raised a prince. Moses, who turned his staff into a serpent, made the Nile run red with blood, led his people across the parting of the Red Sea, brought forth water from a rock, smashed the tablets in a rage, and wandered forty years in the wilderness, was sentenced to die without entering the promised land because once or twice he had actually been given to doubts.

And the LORD said unto him, This *is* the land which I sware unto Abraham, unto Isaac, and unto Jacob, saying, I will give it unto thy seed: I have caused thee to see *it* with thine eyes, but thou shalt not go over thither.

Instead he would die on the mount, gathered unto his people, and no man would know his sepulcher unto this day. First, however, the authors of Deuteronomy would have it that the Lord appeared in the Tabernacle in a pillar of cloud and said unto Moses:

Behold, thou shalt sleep with thy fathers; and this people will rise up, and go a whoring after the gods of the strangers of the land, whither they go *to be* among them, and will forsake me, and break my covenant which I have made with them.

Then my anger shall be kindled against them in that day, and I will forsake them, and I will hide my face from them, and they shall be devoured, and many evils and troubles shall befall them.

Say what you like, He was as good as His word. Or so I said to Ornstein the last time we met and got to talking about the old days in the musty back room of the Young Israel Synagogue. Ornstein used to torment Mr. Feinberg. "If," he once said, "as it is written, the LORD your God *is* God of gods, and Lord of lords, than surely this is an acknowledgment that there are other gods. Zeus, maybe. What do you think?"

Ornstein, who broke with the Communist Party long ago, is still opposed to all kinds of religious mumbo-jumbo, any sort of tribalism. A scientist of some renown, he always seems to be heading for or just coming back from an important international conference in Tokyo, London, or Milan. Last year he was in Jerusalem for the first time, and he went to see the Wailing Wall. "And you know what?" he said. "I burst into tears. I wept and I wept."

—

PART II

PROPHETS

JOSHUA

Max Apple

THROUGHOUT MY CAREER AS A WRITER, I'VE MADE IT A POINT NOT to write about the Bible, or even to think about it too consciously. I've done so to protect myself from an old guilt.

Before I was born my grandfather chose a career for me, "Talmud *Chochem*," and why not. He and his brothers gave up a life of study to work in bakeries in America, his only son was killed in an automobile accident, and then a family miracle. There I was, a boy, a male heir, who if brilliant enough might make the chaos and disappointment and tragedy of his own life more bearable.

Easy to see through now, but not then. Before I could read I knew that the big job of my life was to study Torah in order to bring *nachas* upon my grandfather and all those dead ancestors in Lithuania and Poland who contributed their genes and lots of hardship so that I might stand before rabbis in an outpost near Lake Michigan and make everybody proud.

I didn't astound any of them, but I did stand before rabbis. Somehow,

---

The Revised Standard Version of the Bible used in this essay.

my grandfather found them even if they were working undercover as jewelry salesmen or managerial assistants. Wherever he noticed a Talmudic inclination, there he delivered me. I was five or six or seven and already knew that people my age in my grandfather's day spent their lives in happy Talmudic dispute with their elders.

I couldn't read Hebrew and my mind was on toys. I was even too young for baseball. None of this mattered. If I could begin I could succeed. My grandfather had confidence. He also had a high, shrill voice. He would lead me before one of these sages and say, "Do something with him. Teach him. He's growing up like a goy."

I don't know what any of these men might have done. As I think of them now, they were probably bigger disappointments than I was. The itinerant teachers and rabbis who passed through western Michigan in the late 1940s would no doubt have preferred to be elsewhere. How my grandfather found so many amazes me. The easiest were the old men, the *meshulachs*, who appeared before Rosh Hashanah to collect money for widows and yeshivas. They were traveling salesmen, their eyes on richer prey than my grandfather. I had no problem with them: a quick blessing and that was that.

The younger ones made up a kind of circuit, a pony express of teachers, *schochet*s, *moel*s, rabbis, who alighted for a while in the provinces. They would lead a service in Kalamazoo, perform a wedding in Niles, teach a class in Muskegon, all the while doing penance for their mediocrity in the seminary and praying for a better life in a big city. Most of them got their wish, but not before my grandfather brought me in and made his plea. Before they left Grand Rapids there was a big job—me.

Now I see the comedy of it; then it was pure suffering. I would sit beside a Hebrew book and a glass of tea, while a wispy man in his thirties would say, "So we'll begin."

We never did. Nothing penetrated the barrier of my desire to be far from these men and their words. The three or four whom I remember specifically were decent men. They were not very worried about me or my failure. I remember one teacher who quizzed me about apartments in the area, another who drew diagrams of a car in traffic. They were as bored as I was. If they had a choice, and the proper training, they would have preferred to be out killing chickens.

In an hour my grandfather would reappear to claim me, no wiser than when he had left me. No matter how often we enacted that scene, he could not create for me the mood of Vilna in about 1890. It was Michigan in 1948, and my grandfather finally gave up. I was never going to be a Talmud *Chochem.* I might as well go to Hebrew school. My grandfather still loved me and wished me well, but his dream of my special destiny ended. He said he hoped I would still remember him when I had my Bar Mitzvah, and advised me to become a druggist. When I was seven my Bar Mitzvah looked as far away as ancient Egypt. As he delivered me to Hebrew school, my grandfather lingered in the sentiment of his coming death. "Remember me," he said. I did and I do. He lived to be 107 and was full of energy until the last weeks of his life.

When he let go of his hope for my career as a Talmud *Chochem,* I went to a regular Hebrew school. There I was not my grandfather's project, but a boy like the others. Even worse: a wild boy in the back row pulling on girls' pigtails, wrestling in the aisles, making paper airplanes out of the narrow ruled pages of my Hebrew notebook.

My Hebrew-school teacher was a refugee, Mr. Sellinger. When he spoke, the consonants clicked against his plastic molars. His English was almost as difficult to understand as his Hebrew. Against little boys he had no defense, only a ploy. When the chaos got too great, when he could not hear himself over the noise, when there was too much yelling, or now and then bleeding, he went to a white emergency button above the blackboard and let his finger hover over it. He just stood there savoring his ace in the hole. We were not afraid, but when he moved toward the button we did become quiet. It was the one ritual we celebrated with our teacher. At the button we acknowledged his power. He played with those few seconds. Sometimes his thick yellow fingernail actually touched the button. "I'm calling the rabbi," he would say, "I can't stand it any more, I'm calling the rabbi." His swollen knuckle hovered. He stared at us. We looked at our shoes, at the mess we had made of the floor. His finger trembled. He never pushed the button. Of course the rabbi did come in from time to time, unsummoned. In his presence we behaved, but not out of fear. The rabbi was a young man who spoke English, smiled, seemed like a regular public-school teacher. For him it was easy to behave. He was not afraid of us, nor we of him. We behaved because there were rules.

But we must have smelled Mr. Sellinger's terror. Maybe he could not control us because long ago he had given up hope of ever controlling anything. Maybe he could not call for help because he knew there was none. Maybe his finger stayed not at the button but at the void.

During our brief recess we went to the playground, where we imitated Mr. Sellinger's accent and taunted one another with "I'm calling the rabbi." We doubled over in laughter.

Now I recall that line with such shame. How sorry I am that I did not understand what it meant to be a Polish refugee in 1950.

Yet, in the midst of the howling and the chaos, as Mr. Sellinger wrote from the wrong side across the pitted blackboard, I did learn a little. From the private teachers, those pony-express men of ancient ritual, I was as silent as a mummy. What I was supposed to learn I wouldn't. But old Mr. Sellinger in his dark-brown suit, always ready to call the rabbi, moved me now and then to read that strange language. From a little gray book I learned about Abraham in Ur-Chasdim. I learned much about wanderers and refugees in Mesopotamia four thousand years ago, but I did not recognize the one in the front of the room, whistling out the Hebrew cadences.

I tell you this by way of introduction to Joshua, so you will know that I have been preparing for and avoiding this kind of work for most of my life. I tell you so you'll know, also, that the Joshua I see is probably not a Joshua my grandfather or Mr. Sellinger would recognize. The character I see is also a kind of failure, a man who looked across the Jordan hundreds of times, even thousands, probably for decades, and prayed that he might disappear in the masses before he might be called upon to lead his people across the water into the land of their destiny, perhaps.

I think of a Joshua who might have been far greater had he plied his trade nearer the Aegean Sea, circling the thick walls of Troy with Agamemnon rather than leading his desert wanderers to make a great noise on the outskirts of Jericho.

No doubt in the history of another people Joshua might be the chief hero. After all, it is Joshua who leads his army into the land of his enemies and triumphs there, Joshua who leads his people to the fulfillment of the Lord's promise to Abraham, Joshua who is the powerful, unyielding, triumphant general.

Alas, poor Joshua: to him falls the role of warrior among shepherds, soldier among dreamers, servant of the Lord who serves after Moses.

If the Torah was exclusively a record of God's promise to Abraham and the fulfillment of that promise, then the book of Joshua would be the triumphant conclusion of the Torah. Instead, Joshua is the first book *after* the Torah, the beginning of the prophetic books, the book that chronicles the history of the Hebrews after the promise of Abraham is made real. For not even God rescues the Hebrews from history. And in Joshua, they begin their struggle as a united nation, a nation in the realm of history rather than mythology.

In the career of Joshua we can almost see myth begin its transition into history. After Joshua's battles come the division of the land, then the judges and prophets and kings, and the dense, complicated annals of the descendants of those who once walked with God.

Joshua cannot know subsequent history but he can know the past. He does know what it means to follow Moses. He knows that to succeed Moses is more difficult than to overcome Canaanites. Moses talked to God. Moses ascended Mount Sinai and returned with the Ten Commandments. Moses shaped a nation out of slaves, a moral nation, and then, "though his eye was not dim, nor his natural force abated," Moses died. At that dramatic moment the Torah ends. After Moses, in spite of all his accomplishments, everything is still to be done.

Yes, God has promised a land, but that is already an old promise. It will happen in the fullness of time, but there is no rule that tells Joshua he must lead the conquest. Whatever Joshua does will be his own choice, and in choosing he will be hesitant, uncertain. He cannot be otherwise. Joshua's connection to divine wisdom is secondhand. He gets it through Moses. The Joshua who acts so decisively to order the destruction of his enemies is hiding a Hamlet behind the figure of Achilles. Yes, he is a powerful general, but how he wishes for the certainty of Moses, his "father"; how he wishes that the times were not out of joint, that he was still free to roam in the desert, in the great afterglow of the escape from Egypt and the numbing pleasure of the Manna which glistens like the dew and satisfies all hunger; how Joshua still longs to be the young man following orders; how much easier it is to spy out the land than to send in spies; how much easier to be the son than the father.

But Moses is dead, dead without the preparations and failures of old age, dead in the midst of his strength. Moses is dead and the people wait and everyone looks toward Joshua and Joshua gazes across the Jordan and waits. And in the privacy of his tent he must wonder why God and Moses chose him, why among all the miracles there couldn't be one more, a small one that would allow someone else to lead the people.

Moses and God have nurtured these tribes, have weaned them from slavery toward freedom. The forty years in the desert are the extended infancy of Israel. For a forty-year span they do not have to work. All is provided. With Moses as their guide they are learning the new rules of civilized behavior. It may be exile and wandering, but how safe the desert must seem after the slavery of Egypt and the wars that lie across the Jordan. And Joshua knows and understands what it means to cross the borders of dependency. God is patient, but the destiny of Israel lies in the hands of Israel—at this moment, in the hands of Joshua.

Joshua is as certain as anyone can be of the rightness of his actions, and yet he hesitates. The reader can only guess what is in Joshua's mind as he hears the reports of his spies and decides that the years of wandering are now complete. The narrative tells us only: "and Joshua rose up early in the morning and they removed from Shittim, and came to the Jordan, he and all the children of Israel; and they lodged there before they passed over. And it came to pass after three days that the officers went through the midst of the camp."

Three days is a Biblical term that suggests more than waiting. It is an ancient oral formula for internal drama, the anguish that precedes action. When Abraham goes to Mount Moriah, he "lifts up his eyes on the third day." While Joshua waits three days, something happens. The Biblical narrative leaves this out, though to a modern reader the omission may be more intriguing than the details of war and tribal territory.

I think Joshua waits because he is not sure he is the true heir of Moses. He doubts not God, but himself. The people are fickle; Moses must have told him this, and Joshua must have seen it with his own eyes. If they are fickle even in choosing God, how can they ever be sure of their leader? The force of Moses' personality and the intensity of Moses' religious vision kept these desert wanderers united. Joshua does not even have the sign of election in his body. Aaron is the brother of Moses, but Joshua is not a son. He bears an even greater burden: Moses selected him. He is the heir not of the body, but of the task. How deeply Joshua must feel his duty in his bones. How he must loathe it, too, the mess of history after a period of consolidation and rest.

Joshua understands that when he begins the Manna will disappear. A people that can make war is a people that can feed itself. When Joshua acts, Israel's brief protected respite is over. All the dangers and excitements of adult life begin, a life of politics, not myth, a life filled with choices.

The tribes of Israel enter into Canaan as weak and frail and vulnerable as any other Bedouins. The Books of Moses are over, the books of history are beginning. Mythic heroes from now on will be merely soldiers or prophets or judges or kings. The promise of the God of Israel still remains, but His presence is less available.

Because Joshua lives exactly at the tragic moment when myth disintegrates, he may be the first modern man. If he acts, the Manna ceases, the terrible war begins, the tribal squabbling becomes more central than the Ark of the Covenant. If he does not act, he betrays his history and the trust of Moses and God.

Joshua has been hesitating, perhaps far longer than three days. It is possible that he sent those spies into Canaan only to stall for more time. Without the unforeseen intervention of Rehab, the spies might have returned with a warning to wait, or perhaps not returned at all, an even more significant warning.

As Joshua looks across the Jordan he sees the people who inhabit that land, their flocks, their cities, their children. Though the narrator of Joshua has little sympathy for the lives of Canaanites, Joshua did not write this narrative. Joshua the man remembers that the Lord told Moses and Miriam in their joy after crossing the Red Sea that the Egyptians, too, were his people. War is not celebration, and no victory is great enough to erase the losses. Joshua the soldier knows this as he looks at the salty plains around Jericho.

Modern Biblical commentators are quick to point out the necessity for the Israelites to destroy utterly the pagan kingdoms which they conquered, but the Joshua I imagine is too subtle to believe such an argument. Even as he orders the annihilation of his enemies, Joshua must wonder why it is that this holy people fears contamination from idol worshippers. He must wonder, too, why the legalisms of apportioning the land have to be so specifically recorded. Why can't the people live where they choose? Why can't everything be as easy as gathering the Manna? Because Joshua knows that he is now making order, establishing protocol, he is careful and specific about everything. Moses laid the grand framework, the idea of freedom limited by the Ten Commandments. Joshua will settle for the legalisms, the details that come after the sweeping visions. In the specificity of his orders, we can read Joshua's hesitancy. If he fails, it will not be for lack of remembering every symbolic detail.

Before he orders an assault he makes certain that every male is circumcised and that the Passover is observed. He is scrupulous, too, at the end of his life, in reminding the people to pay attention to details. It is the message of his life, the message of a consolidator, the message of a warrior who follows a visionary.

Yet, after all the symbolic and military groundwork is in place, Joshua still hesitates until he receives a visit from a "Captain of the host of the Lord." It is the briefest of angelic visits. Abraham waited upon the angels, Jacob wrestled with his angel until the sun rose, but Joshua makes no significant contact with the "Captain of the host of the Lord." He asks only, "Art thou for us, or for our adversaries?" Mythic beings have already receded. Joshua is ready for war, for history, for reality. An angel is both too awesome and too external for him. Joshua needs assurance not from a messenger but from God. In his "three days" on the lip of history Joshua wants to believe that he is the heir of Moses. He wants to know that the son, for all his shortcomings, can still carry out the task of his great predecessor. Joshua, hesitating before his great work, is an emblem of all sons hesitating after the death of all fathers. The greatness of his own true self is in Joshua. Moses, of course, saw this and selected Joshua because of it. But, on the threshold of lunging into war and history, Joshua feels his insignificance. He has heard the voice of the Lord before and he has still hesitated. Before Joshua can cross the Jordan he needs the confidence of a Moses, and as he listens to himself he hears the Lord.

"This day will I begin to magnify thee in the sight of all Israel, that they may know that as I was with Moses so I will be with thee."

Feeling magnified, Joshua is magnified. He cannot be Moses, but still the Lord will be with him. When he crosses the Jordan, Joshua will do so as Joshua, the best, most magnified version of Joshua, but Joshua still, not Moses, and this Joshua will be sufficient to lead his people and to conquer his enemies. He can do so because he was able to triumph over the myth of Moses.

All sons tremble before their inheritance, but Joshua has the hardest task. He cuts his teeth on history. When Joshua leads the tribes across the Jordan, childhood is over for Israel, but so is their status as refugees. The tribes will take the land and become a people, a great nation. Over the millennia, exile will become the destiny of their descendants, and the longing for return will fill the prayers of a hundred generations.

Even while my grandfather was dragging me from teacher to teacher, that exile was coming to a conclusion. Lesser Joshuas were examining their hearts and crossing other waters. Refugees were everywhere and, even in the cities of western Michigan, people asked visitors, "Art thou for us, or for our adversaries?"

We still wonder how much to trust ourselves and how much to trust our enemies, how to conquer a land and live beside its peoples. There is no Moses, not even a Joshua, only history, most of it tragic, and the memory of our fathers inevitably heroic.

In a way, Mr. Sellinger was a blessing for me. In my grandfather's hopes I was a failure at age seven, and that failure would continue. My tough little *zeyde* fought old age and boredom and despair and cancer almost to a standstill. I could not replace him; nobody could.

But Mr. Sellinger, that symbolic grandfather, the one who did teach me Hebrew, he was easy to defeat. All of us triumphed over him. He was a brown suit, false teeth, an accent—baggage heaved up by a dead Europe. Mr. Sellinger was there to be replaced; it was the only role left for him. He was a wheezy voice, an idle threat.

Seven-year-old boys wrestling on the floor were not ready to replace anyone. But we're grown now, Mr. Sellinger, we're fathers ourselves, filled with our own layers of personal history, our own disappointments. We may even be ready to shut up and learn something. Go ahead, Mr. Sellinger, call the rabbi.

JUDGES

TESTS OF WEAKNESS:
SAMSON AND DELILAH

Phillip Lopate

THE BOOK OF JUDGES COVERS THE MESSY TRANSITIONAL PERIOD OF tribal confederation, after Moses and Joshua had brought their people to Israel, and before the establishment of the Saul-David monarchy. "In those days there was no king in Israel: every man did that which was right in his own eyes" (21:25). Mostly what the Israelites did, it would seem, was backslide and worship the idols of Baal, which made Yahweh furious enough to withdraw His protection and turn them over to neighboring enemies, after which they would pray and moan and promise to be pious again, and the Lord would take pity and raise up a champion in their midst. From tradition and mistranslation, these champions came to be known as "judges," though in fact they operated more like military chieftains than magistrates.

Judges lacks the literary unity of other Biblical books; it is more a parade of large and small characters whose very variety may be intended to give insight into God's process of divine selection. Not only does God

---

The King James Version and the Revised Standard Version of the Bible used in this essay.

make a point of going outside the ruling elite to pick His judges (a woman, a man of the weakest clan, a harlot's son), but He puts forward a wide range of moral types as well. So we get everything from the majestic singer Deborah to the cruel Abimelech, who slays his seventy brothers in order to monopolize leadership; to the diplomatic, resourceful Gideon; to the cunning Ehud, who plunges a dagger into fat King Eglon's belly; to Jephthah the outlaw, who is obliged to immolate his daughter after promising to sacrifice the first thing he saw on returning home victoriously; to the strongman Samson, with his self-destructive weakness for the wrong women.

If I am choosing to focus on this last figure, it is partly because Samson's story seems to me one of the crucial narratives in the Bible (its richness attested to by the many operas, plays, epic poems, and films drawn from it), and partly because I suspect the Samson-and-Delilah dynamic has helped to shape me as a man, like it or not, much more than any of the other stories in Judges.

I grew up in the era of the great Jewish lovers. *Samson and Delilah, David and Bathsheba, Solomon and Sheba* were burning up screens across the land. I never managed to see *David and Bathsheba* (though I knew the coming attractions by heart), because the movie industry in its wisdom deemed that I was too young for this adulterous tale. Inconsistently, they let me into *Samson and Delilah.*

I still remember my excitement when I first saw the poster announcing its imminent arrival in our neighborhood. "See Samson battle a lion with his own hands! See Samson tear down the Temple of Dagon! See Delilah tame the strongman!" I was so crazy about movies that I fixated on everything connected to them as a *promesse de bonheur:* lobby stills, newspaper ads on the entertainment pages, but especially the ten-foot billboards they displayed outside the Commodore, where giants held at bay the encircling, groundless chaos of tempting panoramas.

My tolerance for celluloid had been built up over the long Saturday matinees to which my siblings and I went regularly, and which included a double feature, seven cartoons, newsreels, coming attractions, and a Flash Gordon or Hopalong Cassidy serial. "O dark, dark, dark, amid the blaze of noon!" By the time we had stumbled onto the street, sated with the blood of scalped cavalrymen, the highballs served to Veronica Lake, the dynamite set off by a Bugs Bunny in drag, it was already dinnertime. We would walk under the El past the discount stores servicing our ghetto in Williamsburg, Brooklyn, past Stevens Bakery, which specialized in white icing, past the fish restaurant with its grotesque lobster tank in the window, past the tough shoeshine boys on the corner, past the synagogue, quickly and guiltily because it was Shabbos, and make our way back to the tenement where we lived, debating all the while our favorite scenes.

If you ask me what the Bible meant to me as a child, it signified both those awkwardly drawn comic strips from the Scriptures that the Brooklyn *Eagle* would run next to "Dick Tracy" or "Mary Worth" each Sunday, featuring stern, bearded patriarchs and women with pitchers on their shoulders—and the Biblical spectacles we were constantly told cost "millions" and had "casts of thousands." Whatever possessed Hollywood to turn out all those Biblical/Roman clinkers throughout the fifties? The postwar audience's abandonment of a neorealist aesthetic for the escapist anodynes of costumed bloodshed, the advent of widescreen technologies, which cried out for spectacle, the more conservative political mood, the irresistible formula of having one's cake (sin) and eating it, too (piety), the collapse of the studio system and its replacement by international package deals, all must have contributed to the zenith of this ill-fated genre.

Cecil B. DeMille's *Samson and Delilah* was one of the first of the postwar Biblical spectacles (1949). Watching a VCR tape of it some thirty-five years later, I am struck by how dioramic and artificial (if entertaining in a kitschy way) it looks now, its drama as stylized as Kabuki, its sets like an old World's Fair made of endless lathe and temporary grandeur. The virtues of the Biblical epic—which DeMille had a large hand in shaping—were mainly to be found in art direction, costumes, and special effects. DeMille began in the silent era, and there is an echo of Griffith's Babylonianism in the idol-gargoyled Temple of Dagon.

"Before the dawn of Time . . ." intones the narrator in the opening shot, and we see clouds, and marching feet, and are treated to a little lecture about the struggle between tyranny and freedom. Biblical epics tended to be made mostly after both world wars, when America, as "leader of the free world," had a need to wrap itself in the sanctimonious mantle of previous Chosen Peoples. Curiously, the word "Jew" is never mentioned in the DeMille film, not even "Hebrew" or "Israelite." Samson's people are referred to only as "Danites"—an indication of nervousness about anti-Semitism during the McCarthy era, perhaps?

Samson and Delilah boasted one of those "international" casts: the star (Hedy Lamarr) spoke Viennese-scented English, her leading man (Victor Mature) hailed from Kentucky, and all the Philistine opponents of Judeo-Christianity, in the curious convention of such films, had British accents (George Sanders, Angela Lansbury, Henry Wilcoxin).

A DeMille scholar told me that the director had wanted to make *Samson and Delilah* ten years earlier, but he couldn't get the financing. By the time the deal had come together with the actress he wanted, a certain freshness had gone out of Lamarr: she looked bruised by another decade's strain of holding together her glamour. But her worldly, mocking Viennese air had some of Dietrich's alluring melancholy, especially when she was encountering the younger, oafish Mature: it was the Old World seducing the New World, yet again.

Hedy's basic Delilah costume consisted of a sleeveless halter which stopped just below her breasts, and a long skirt, usually with a slit to show off her nice legs—and, inadvertently, a pair of pumps as well. After she becomes a Bad Woman, she is never seen without a feather-duster plume, which she waves around to make her points, and which is color-coordinated to match her different gowns of silver, turquoise, rose, and sapphire-blue. At times she seems to act mainly with her midriff (midriff eroticism being a staple of these epics, made more piquant by the code rule forbidding umbilicus onscreen), or with her eloquent shoulder blades, as she leans against the wall, thrusting her breasts forward. Even though she seems rather diminutive next to Mature, with her upturned nose, saucy gazes, and spit-curls she is altogether luscious.

Mature responds with a supercilious sneer, like a country bumpkin who knows they are putting something over on him but isn't sure what and hopes his cynicism will distract attention from his slowness. It was about this actor that David Thomson wrote, memorably if cruelly: "It is too easy to dismiss Mature, for he surpasses badness. He is a strong man in a land of nine-stone weaklings, an incredible concoction of corned beef, husky voice and brilliantine—a barely concealed sexual advertisement for soiled goods. Remarkably, he is as much himself in the cheerfully meretricious and the pretentiously serious. . . ." Here, however, he seems bewildered; his eyes look dead when he is called upon to say things like "You—daughter of hell!" He wears a green leather jerkin which leaves most of his chest uncovered, and his broad body, by our more stringent Arnold Schwarzenegger standards of muscular definition, looks fat. (Incidentally, there is nothing in the Bible that says Samson had a brawny, muscular person. Since his strength came from God's spirit inhabiting him, the theological point might have been better made by casting Mickey Rooney or Arnold Stang.)

Yet, by that familiar phenomenon which makes it very difficult to picture a story's characters afterward except in the physical shapes of the actors you saw play them onscreen, however miscast they may have been, the past-her-prime Lamarr and the stalwart ham Mature will always remain in my imagination the quintessential, the *actual* Samson and Delilah.

As a child I was a very forgiving moviegoer. If a picture had one or two scenes that excited my imagination, I would simply evacuate the duller parts from consciousness and concentrate on these privileged images, carrying them around like mental slides long afterward and taking them out solacingly in bad moments. Such a scene was the destruction of the Philistine hall, where the pillars crumbled in sections like gigantic white Tootsie Rolls. For me, Samson was essentially a Superman figure. Just as I would jump off a chair and pretend to fly like the Man of Steel, so I used to play at tying up my hands and ripping the ropes off; eyes closed, I would grit my teeth and fantasize pulling a building down by straining with all my might. I had dreams of toppling P.S. 11, breaking everything I hated into rubble, so that it would be like the newsreels of bombed Berlin. (As it happened, many blocks in Williamsburg already looked that way, torn down to make way for the future Brooklyn-Queens Expressway.)

I prayed to get back at everyone who had humiliated me with one blow, like poor Samson, the blind giant. Not that I had so many enemies; but every child suffers from powerlessness, bossed around by adults, older brothers, classroom bullies. There was one tormentor, Ronald, big for his age, who used to beat me up after school. I would fantasize ways to torture him, a new one each night, like Scheherazade. As I grew older I began to subtilize these revenge plots, sometimes even letting my prisoner go. Curiously, this reprieve gave me a greater *frisson:* I enjoyed the idea of playing cat and mouse with my victim, one day vicious, the next unexpectedly benevolent. Control, restraint, sadism, creativity. I was only a few years from eroticizing this fantasy with a chivalric twist.

In sixth grade, I was attracted to a girl with a Roman nose named Felicia, as were all the boys, since she already had the curves of a woman. She was from a better family than ours, her father was a lawyer, and she carried herself rather haughtily. "She thinks she's Cleopatra—or Delilah!" we would say behind her back, because she knew all the boys fancied her. Secretly I imagined myself drawing daily closer to the beautiful Felicia and impressing her with my intelligence. One afternoon, when I tried to make friendly conversation, she ridiculed me, saying that I wore the same clothes, the same ugly sweater every day. It was true. I had taken no notice of what I had on; neither, apparently, had my parents.

After she had humiliated me, I began to have dreams in which Felicia would knock on my door, completely naked and defenseless: someone had stolen her clothing. Not only did I not take advantage of the situation, but I immediately threw a coat or blanket around her shoulders and escorted her home. This chaperonage would sometimes take us down dank castle steps on which I would have to protect her honor by swordfights. Never did I ask for so much as a kiss in payment—though sometimes she would reward me with a feast of kisses.

The closeness with which dreams of gallantry and revenge were tangled in my brain must be why, even today, when I remember to act in a polite manner (for instance, giving up my seat to a woman in the bus) and she thanks me for being "chivalrous," I instantly feel a twinge of guilty conscience. But, then, I am chronically guilt-ridden about my virtuous side, if you will. "You were always a good boy," my mother has told me so often. "You, I never had to worry about." Even as a baby, before I had any choice in the matter, I was "good": when she was in the maternity ward and all the other babies were wailing from the air-raid sirens, I quietly found her breast.

One of my earliest memories, from about four, is of my older brother and younger sister experimenting with matches. "They shouldn't be doing that," I thought. Sure enough, the kitchen curtain caught fire. There was smoke, flames; my mother came home in the nick of time and doused the fire with pots of water. When it was over she demanded, "What happened?" My brother and sister pointed fingers at each other. "I didn't do anything," I kept telling her. Finally she said, "I know, cookie, I know you didn't." The question years later is, *Why* didn't I do anything? Why was I such a goody-goody? Was I good because I chose to be or because I was too timid, too programmed, to do otherwise?

In an odd way, I was both my mother's favorite and the one to whom she paid least attention, because I didn't cause her trouble. There were rewards for being the "good" boy, but sometimes it was a mixed blessing. By nursery school, I had already developed a reputation for honesty. "Phillip never lies," my nursery teacher said. My mother, pleased to hear it, nevertheless insisted healthily, "Every child lies." "Not Phillip," said this woman, whom I had clearly managed to make fall in love with me.

One day I was jumping up and down on my parents' bed, using their mattress as a trampoline. I was no angel—I wanted to have a good time, to break the rules, to become a real evildoer! (In part 2 of *The Brothers Karamazov,* which Dostoevsky never got to write, the saintly Alyosha was supposed to turn into a great sinner.) In mid-jump I heard my mother coming. "What were you doing? Were you jumping on my bed like I told you not to?" "No, uh-uh," I protested. "I *saw* you do it!" she exclaimed; "don't fib to me." Though I got a beating afterward, we were both relieved: He lies!

In Judges, the story of Samson begins with his mother's barrenness. An angel appears to the woman of Dan and tells her she is going to have a son, but she should drink no wine nor eat anything unclean, and "No razor shall come upon his head, for the boy shall be a Nazarite to God from birth; and he shall begin to deliver Israel from the hand of the Philistines" (Judges 13:5). She runs and tells her husband, Manoah, what the stranger has said, and Manoah gets the angel to repeat these instructions a third time. Then a puff of smoke, flames, and they realize that the stranger is indeed an angel of the Lord; they fall on their faces to the ground. This angelic visitation to a barren woman is a recurrent Biblical formula; only in the context of Judges, with its dense narrative style, does the incident's leisurely redundance surprise us. Why is a whole chapter "wasted" on this business? Certainly no other judge is accorded such preliminary buildup; it is almost as though the whole Book of Judges were taking a breath before launching into the Samson story.

In a way, also, the chapter lets us know that before Samson is even born, he is in God's debt. His body itself doesn't quite belong to him—it's a sacred weapon for God to inhabit with His spirit when He so desires. Moreover, without any choice in the matter, Samson is pledged to be a Nazarite: one who is consecrated, abstinent, separate from others, pure. No wonder Samson acts "bad": he is trying to make a space for his own life inside the one already owed to his parents and God.

So he indulges in skirt-chasing. All of his troubles—but also all his heroic deeds—stem from whoring and womanizing. He falls in love easily, and, it seems, purely on a physical basis. Like Portnoy, he is drawn to *shiksas*. In our very first encounter with the adult Samson, he has just seen a woman in Timnah, the daughter of Philistines, and wants her for a wife. His parents object: "Is there not a woman among the daughters of your kinsmen, or among all the people, that you must go to take a wife from the uncircumcised Philistines?' But Samson said to his father, 'Get her for me; for she pleases me well' " (14:3).

Now, this first time he is exonerated from blame, because the text immediately tells us his romantic entanglement was the doing of the Lord, who "was seeking an occasion against the Philistines." Later, in the Delilah episode, this cosmic alibi is withdrawn, and Samson is made to stand completely alone with his mistake. Everything in the Samson story happens twice, sometimes thrice; repetitions establish his character patterns. Thus, if he had let only Delilah wheedle a secret out of him, that would be one thing; but before that, he gave the woman of Timnah the answer to his wedding riddle, "because she pressed him hard."

Samson is a man whom women nag. For all his strength, he seems not to engender their full respect, much less their obedience. They know how to play on his guilt with tears and reproaches ("You don't really love me or you'd tell me your secret"), to twist him around their fingers. And ultimately they betray him. Not only does the woman of Timnah broadcast the riddle's answer, forcing Samson to pay everyone the betting price, but she even cuckolds Samson by giving herself to "his companion, who had been his best man" (14:20). Delilah does even worse—she ruins him. Sandwiched between these two women is the harlot in Gaza, who also endangers him by keeping him occupied while his enemies surround his house. He escapes by lifting the city gates on his shoulders, but he is clearly tempting fate.

Samson is also a man who seems to enjoy being righteously angry. "If you had not ploughed with my heifer, you would not have found out my riddle," he tells the wedding guests, and kills thirty men and stomps off "in hot anger." Later, when he returns to Timnah and finds his wife has been given to another man, he rejects the offer of marrying her younger sister and says, "This time I shall be blameless in regard to the Philistines, when I do them mischief." So he ties three hundred foxes together, attaches lighted torches between their tails, and lets them burn up all the Philistine orchards and grain. The Philistines retaliate by torching his wife (who had already abandoned him) and her father. And Samson retorts: " 'If this is what you do, I swear I will be avenged upon you, and after that I will quit.' And he smote them hip and thigh with great slaughter." Any destruction, however disproportionate, is "justifiable" if interpreted as retaliation. This way of thinking may partly explain why Samson allows himself so often to be betrayed: it frees him to do what he wants.

I grew up in a household where there was much arguing and yelling, even hitting. But it was necessary, as we learned from imitating my mother, always to lay a groundwork of self-righteousness for any explosion. "I am only doing this to you because you did X and Y to me first." Within the never-ending chain of injured feelings which is family history, it is not always easy to find the beginning of a causal series, which is why the person with the loudest voice or the longest memory is able to make the best tit-for-tat. My older brother, Hal, whose voice is very strong, was for a while the undisputed king of righteous explosions. Fortunately, Hal would fulminate so long on the heinousness of the wrong done him that it was possible to get out of the way of any serious physical harm before he swung into action. We were much more terrified of my father, who was phlegmatic, quiet, and withdrawn for the most part; if he blew up, you had less than a second's warning. When my father got physical the slaps and punches came hard and fast, as in a street fight. He had powerful, bony hands and sharp elbows, and in anger he seemed to lose control, with white spittle foaming at his mouth as if he were a mad dog—or at least that was how it looked to a child. Curiously, he always tried to get out of spanking us; he had no heart for premeditated disciplining, leaving the beatings to my mother.

She would take out her ironing cord—a black-and-white fabric switch, which we thought of as a live creature. What was interesting about the way she beat us was that she would grunt and make awful faces each time she picked up her arm. "You had enough?" she would demand after each blow. "Gonna try that again?"

It is a dialogue; we are supposed to respond correctly so that she will know when to quit. My brother would take his punishment like a man, howling only when he was in pain. I was more of a faker: very early I caught on that it was all symbolic, so I screamed and carried on from the first hand-raise, and she let me go with next to nothing. My sister, Molly, however, would laugh in my mother's face, she would giggle or hum a tune to herself, refusing to concede even when I could see tears welling in her eyes, until finally my mother would stop, baffled, her arm exhausted.

I am struggling to find the pattern among all these pieces. I have the sense that the Samson story and my family story touch in odd ways; I try to put the stencil of one over the other, and although they overlap in certain places, just as often the connection seems farfetched. Nonetheless, I am convinced that at the center of both is the mystery of power relations between men and women. I start to write, "How did it come about that I started mistrusting women, or thought they would betray me?" But then I pause: Do I really? Aren't I often less guarded around women than I am with men? Let us say that a part of me still fears (or hopes?) that women are treacherous creatures. I know that growing up, watching the unhappiness between my parents, watching as my mother disparaged my father every day and he refused to let her go, made me cautious toward the opposite sex. Then, too, my mother was very insecure as a young woman: we would climb in her lap and she would suddenly push us away saying, "Don't start that 'Mommy, I love you' crap, you're only being lovey-dovey because you want something out of me. Okay, what is it this time? an ice cream? a quarter?" Naturally I learned to be skeptical of affection, almost to *want* a barbed hurt to accompany love. As for my father, he had been treated wretchedly by his stepmother, made to wash floors all the time, not allowed to play, so that he was desperate for maternal warmth while suspicious of any feminine softness. When these two hurt, insecure people, the black sheep of both their middle-class families, came together to live in poverty and raise a family, the results were not pretty.

My parents had a bookcase which held a few hardcovers, but mostly Pocket Books whose flimsy, browning pages would crack if you bent down the corners. I can still picture those cellophane-peeling covers with their kangaroo logo and their illustrations of busty, available-looking women or hardboiled men or sometimes solemn, sensitive-looking Negroes, and titles like *Intruder in the Dust, Appointment in Samarra, Tobacco Road, Studs Lonigan, Strange Fruit, Good Night Sweet Prince, The Great Gatsby, The Sound and the Fury.* . . .

Father brought home all the books—it was his responsibility; though Mother chafed at everything else in the marriage, she still permitted him at the time to be her intellectual mentor. I have often wondered on what basis he made his selections: he'd had only one term of night college (dropping out because he fell asleep in class after a factory workday), and I never saw him interested in book reviews. But he seemed to have a nose for decent literature. He was one of those autodidacts of the Depression generation, for whose guidance the inexpensive editions of Everyman, Modern Library, and Pocket Books seemed intentionally designed, out of some bygone assumption that the workingman should—must—be educated to the best in human thought.

My father had an awed respect for the power of good fiction, but mainly when it was able to mirror uncannily the conflicts in his own life. He would often marvel at Kafka's story "The Judgment," in which the patriarch tells his son to jump off a bridge—obviously because *his* father, my grandfather, treated him like dirt. He never stopped praising *The Brothers Karamazov,* which in Brooklyn had the status of the Bible at the time.

Again, I suspect its parricidal theme excited him more than Dostoevsky's philosophy. He did dip into one philosopher, Schopenhauer, and would occasionally read aloud one of the gloomy German's misogynistic aphorisms. These were all to the effect that women had no capacity for ideas, that their only cleverness was in tricking men to perpetuate the species. And my mother gave an odd sort of credence to this theory by boasting that she had "seduced" my father into siring us—finagling away the contraception, I suppose—since he hadn't really wanted children. Four times she tricked him? Whether true or not, it was her way of making us feel indebted to her and opposed to him.

In any event, Schopenhauer's *bons mots* were his single means—a delayed one, at that—of answering Mother's nagging. My father was one of those dependable Jewish workingmen of his generation who regarded housework or any physical task around the house as anathema. (In his case, the phobia may have been increased because of his chore-filled childhood.) He would not "lift a finger around the house, if it killed him!" my mother would say. It was she who had to bang the nails, unstick the windows, lay linoleum, and so on, complaining while my father sat, the soul of passivity, reading a book or napping. It bugged her partly because she had to go to work, too, but also partly because my father was so able-bodied. As a young man he was tall, wiry, and very strong, strong like Samson. In his factory he could lift huge bales; at carnivals he would ring the bell; he triumphed at arm-wrestling. Yet he became a weakling as soon as he arrived home; his kryptonite was family life.

If my mother said something sarcastic to him like "Why don't you get off your bony ass and do something?" or "What do I need you for? You're not married to me, you're married to your easy chair and the goddamn ballgame!" he would merely sink deeper into a defeated shrug. But I believe that behind his stoical, resigned mask there raged a fierce misogynism.

What I would call the *Blue Angel / Of Human Bondage* plot—the educated or sensitive man who is dragged down by a coarse, sluttish vixen—had a particular vogue with my father's generation. One of the books he often touted to us was Ludwig Lewisohn's novel *The Tyranny of Sex*. When I was sixteen and still a virgin I read it, naturally, to find out what was in store. Its lumpy, post-Dreiserian naturalist style disappointed, and I felt the author was weighting the scales a bit too unfairly against the wife. Nevertheless, the luridly compelling story remained with me: a man becomes attracted to a woman, wants to sleep with her, and the next thing he knows he is married, cuckolded, in debt, his dreams for himself have flown out the window, his wife has become a slattern, no longer even attractive, a nagging shrew—in short, woman as swamp, quicksand.

Given the atmosphere in my home, I found the Samson-and-Delilah story the most natural in the world. Already I had imbibed from my father his sense of sexuality as a nightmarish tyranny, robbing a man of his strength, just as I had absorbed from my mother a rebellious, defiantly flirtatious, erotic appetite for life.

My mother had gotten a piano, and she practiced her songs on it, preparing for some far-off day when she would become a professional entertainer. She sang mostly torch songs, the kind Helen Morgan made famous: "The Man I Love," "Just My Bill," "I Must Try to Make the Man Love Me," "Bewitched Bothered and Bewildered," "I Want a Sunday Kind of Love." With her pretty, tremulous voice, she would pour out all her yearning and disappointment into these bittersweet verses. The message was unmistakable, even to a little kid: she was not happy with my father, she was still looking for something better, for "romance."

I loved to listen to her practice, glancing over her shoulder at the sheet music with its rising and falling syllables. All day while I was in elementary school, her songs would go round in my head. At recess I would play tag or punchball to the rhythms of her longing.

One day, when it was too rainy to go outside, the teachers herded us into the auditorium and staged an impromptu Talent Show. Each child was urged to perform in front of the combined second and third grades. There were rampant cases of stage fright; some kids started to entertain, then giggled and hid their faces; others came on and rattled through a comic ditty or radio jingle so fast you couldn't make out the words. I wanted to sing. I faced the group and, hearing my mother's semi-trained voice in my ears, I let her guide me through the melody:

> Some day he'll come along, the man I love
> And he'll be big and strong, the man I love

I could sense the teachers snickering, giving each other looks: We know how *this* one's going to turn out. Kids started laughing. I realized too late that the song was for a girl, they would think me a sissy. I had no choice but to finish. At least I could try to sing on key and with feeling, as she did, and maybe seduce them into liking it.

When the last contestant was finished, the teachers awarded me "first prize," a comic book. I, part Delilah, wondered if I would ever become a real man.

My mother was bawdy: she reveled in calling a spade a spade. She had a store of witticisms about excretory malfunctions, and she would tell smutty Hollywood stories—the scandals of her youth—about Fatty Arbuckle's Coke bottle and Mary Miles Minter, George S. Kaufman ("Oh, he must have been hot stuff!") and Mary Astor's diary read aloud in divorce court. All this was a little hard for me to take. I particularly found it embarrassing when my mother let slip her physical appraisal of men. If we were watching a baseball game, say, on television, and Ted Kluszewski stepped up to bat, she would go, "Look at the shoulders on that guy! That's for me!" or "Boy, that Campy's built like a brick shit house. He's gor-geous." The drama of the baseball diamond would be spoiled, and I would suddenly be forced to see it from a sexual perspective and imagine Mother having trysts with the local butcher, the baker, the ballplayer, whoever possessed a massive physique. (It didn't help that we all knew my mother was having extramarital affairs. Later on I came to see that she had done the right thing for herself in scraping together a little happiness by going outside a marriage that was irredeemably bleak and frustrating; but at the time I sympathized only with my father and thought her "cheap," a Bad Woman.) These comments about male physique made me feel especially inadequate, since I had narrow shoulders and a scholar's untoned body. If being a man meant having a build like Victor Mature or Roy Campanella, then forget it, I would never make it. Fortunately, my mother had another erotic ideal besides the powerful bruiser: the sensitive, poetic "gentleman" with manners and an English accent—Leslie Howard, her favorite, or James Mason. I at least had an outside chance at this ideal. If I speak gently today, to the point of habitually mumbling, it is probably because I am still trying to be Leslie Howard for my mother.

Samson "loved a woman in the valley of Sorek, named Delilah." But nowhere does the text say anything about Delilah's loving Samson back. Indeed, immediately after this first sentence introducing Delilah, the Philistine lords approach and say: "Entice him, and see wherein his great strength lies, and by what means we may overpower him, that we may bind him to subdue him; and we shall each give you eleven hundred pieces of silver" (16:5). In the Bible, Delilah is literally a *femme fatale:* she comes on, performs her treacherous function, and disappears from the narrative, and we are left to guess whether she betrays Samson just for the money or because it is her nature. Virtually all later adaptations soften the harsh functionalism of the Biblical Delilah, both by "humanizing" her with ambivalent motives of love, jealousy, revenge, politics, and by having her visit Samson after he is in captivity. But the first Delilah is the pure Delilah, a dark female force who destroys men with her sex. Like a dominatrix, she is remarkably straightforward about her intentions: "Tell me, I pray thee, wherein thy great strength lieth, and wherewith thou mightest be bound to afflict thee" (16:6).

Fair warning. Samson receives even more evidence of her treacherous intent when, after he has fended her off with a false explanation of his strength, she calls in the soldiers, who had been hiding in her inner chamber, to seize him. Any man with half a brain would leave at this point. But no: three times she entices him to give her his secret, three times he puts her off with fabrications, and three times she summons the Philistine troops to ensnare him. (The fourth time works the charm.)

The mystery is: what happens to Samson's famous self-righteous anger during this period of the three wrong explanations? Either Samson seems to like the danger, or to find it spicy, or perhaps he expects nothing from women other than constant betrayal. Or does he simply overestimate his power to resist her coaxing (which would be foolish, given his past history)?

His hanging around her obviously booby-trapped tent has a comical side. Later dramatizations of the Samson story refrain from showing all four of her questions about his strength and his answers, partly because it would be dramatically redundant, but also because it would get farcical and Samson might lose too much stature. Any man who puts up with that many consecutive betrayals is not a tragic hero but a schlemiehl, a buffoon.

Although not necessarily. In fairy tales, it often happens that someone makes the same mistake three times (for instance, misuses his or her wishes). At the end of each mistake there is no accrual of wisdom. The point is made that human nature keeps screwing up the same way over and over. Seen from this perspective, Samson is Everyman: his continuing to stay with Delilah after he knows she will betray him is no more unusual than, say, a woman's remaining with a husband who beats her or a man's putting up with a wife who continually cheats on him.

One modern interpretation has it that Samson is so sexually fixated on Delilah, like Don José on Carmen, that he can't pull himself away, however much he realizes that she intends to ruin him. And she, for her part, betrays him because that seems the inevitable melodramatic outcome of all fatal passions. But this "fatal passion" explanation, so nineteenth-century (which is why it appealed to Saint-Saëns), seems incomplete. Samson takes too much active pleasure inventing the three lies about his strength for him to be seen as merely a passive moth drawn to the flame. Gradually he himself allows Delilah to get a little "warmer," the third time actually referring to his hair, telling her that to tie up seven locks into a web would subdue his strength. In a way, they are like children playing a game. Each time she notifies him, "The Philistines be upon thee, Samson," it is like calling out a children's-game formula, such as "Tap, tap, Johnny, one two three!"

There is an undeniable playful element in this part of the Samson story. One could say that the strong man is experimenting with disarming himself and seeing how close he can get to being trapped, like a Houdini who ties himself up in order to escape. After all, Samson delivers himself voluntarily into his captors' hands not once but twice: the first time was when his own people betrayed him to the Philistines, and he ended up smiting a thousand with the jawbone of an ass.

The strong would seem to have a need to experiment with the limits of their strength—to experiment, indeed, with their weakness, as though it held a key to self-knowledge. How often in stories the great warrior "forgets" his duty to fight, detained in the arms of a beautiful woman: Ulysses and Circe, Samson and Delilah, Antony and Cleopatra, Wellington and Lady Hamilton. Yet in these trysts isn't the strongman measuring his fortitude against an opponent he recognizes as potentially more dangerous than an enemy general?

The strongman enters the erotic interior of the tent, the boudoir, where he understands that other rules prevail than on the battlefield. Here he hopes to be refreshed, but also tested in an intriguing manner. With a too-docile love slave, there would be no stimulating tension, no edge to the encounter. Yet an experienced wanton like Delilah cannot offer the challenge of conquering her virginity, so there must be another kind of advance-retreat. Like the geisha who are celebrated for their pert replies, wheedling, and jealous tantrums, the woman to whom the strongman surrenders must be in command of a theatrical repertoire of catlike capriciousness.

He enters the dark interior of her body to explore, to reconnoiter like a soldier moving laterally across a field; but by the end he has become soft and feminized, his ejaculated penis small. The strongman enters the tent, secretly, to become a woman. Lovemaking allows him to be tender, to loll about in bed, to be playful and "effeminate," to exchange sexual roles:

> I yielded, and unlocked her all my heart,
> Who with a grain of manhood well-resolved
> Might easily have shook off all her snares.
> But foul effeminacy held me yoked
> To her bond-slave.
> —Milton, *Samson Agonistes*

Afterward, the man resents the woman for several reasons: because she has witnessed his "weakness," because he needs her in the first place, and because she can go much longer than he, sexually speaking—she has no sword to break. Men take revenge for their dependency by projecting their sexual needs onto women, reviving the figure of the insatiable temptress, the castrating Delilah.[1] Proverbs warns, "Give not thy strength unto women," and "The horseleach hath two daughters, crying, Give, give. There are three things that are never satisfied, yea, four things say not, It is enough: The grave; and the barren womb; and the earth that is not filled with water; and the fire that saith not, It is enough" (30:15, 16). The Bible is filled with a sexual-economic fear of women, not unlike that of the general in *Doctor*

Strangelove who practices celibacy so as to hold on to his "precious bodily fluids." The Samson story would seem to admonish us that sex with women depletes the hero of his strength—if not through one "castration" (the postcoital shrunken penis, the depleted fluids), then indirectly through another (the cut-off hair).

Yet, whereas the message of Samson's fall, like Adam's, would seem to be cautionary and misogynistic, underneath we experience his time with Delilah as a liberating fantasy. That is why the story has such continuing claims on us. Don't we secretly rejoice at his having the good sense to follow the route of his desire, to free himself from the "good boy" Nazarite onus by putting himself in temptation's way?

After all, Samson has always been a loner. "If a leader, he was one from a distance. Almost everything he did was as a private individual," writes the Israeli Talmudist Adin Steinsaltz. And Robert G. Boling, in his Anchor Bible commentary, notes: "The whole structure of the Samson segment is different from that of the other judges. There is no participation by Israelites in his elevation to judge and no mention of Israelites taking the field behind him." He is so alone, he might as well be an artist. The first time he comes to grips with another human being and doesn't run, doesn't go off angry or bloodthirsty, but stays—is with Delilah. It is progress of a sort.

The retreat of lovers from the world has always been perceived as both an alluring utopia and a dangerous threat to society, which must be punished—if not by the authorities, then by the dynamic of romantic love itself. In the Japanese film *The Realm of the Senses* by Oshima, a geisha and a bouncer run off together. They become so immersed in making love that they rarely go out, they forget to eat, they become mystics in the pursuit of higher and higher pleasure. But the logic of ecstasy seems to dictate ascending risk; normal intercourse is no longer enough, so they experiment with short strangulations to intensify the orgasmic rush. In the end, the woman goes too far in strangling the man and, realizing he is dead, she cuts off his penis and runs through the streets with it. It is unclear from the film whether the strongman has submitted to her homicidal castrating tendencies, or whether she has merely been the instrument of his suicidal desires. They have reached a point of such fusion, such boundarylessness—the desideratum of lovers, according to poetry—that it is pointless to speak of one "doing" anything "to" the other.

I would like to offer the possibility that a similar sort of collaboration or collusion existed between Samson and Delilah. Not that "she done him wrong," but that together the lovers were able to bring about the desired fatalistic result, which they had been working up to in practice three times. I realize this interpretation is perversely revisionist, with little support in the text. What the Good Book does say is that she pressed him until "his soul was vexed to death." Finally he opens his heart to her. "A razor has never come upon my head; for I have been a Nazarite to God from my mother's womb. If I be shaved, then my strength will leave me, and I shall become weak, and be like any other man" (16:16). The irony is that Samson's great folly consists in nothing more than telling the truth—and telling it to one he loves—which we are usually made to think is ethically desirable.

"And she made him sleep upon her knees; and she called for a man, and she caused him to shave off the seven locks of his head; and she began to afflict him, and the strength went from him" (16:19). She places his head in her lap, that maternal gesture. He is finally "unmanned" by surrendering to his need for mothering. This is at the heart of fear of Woman: that she will touch him in that sore place and open up his bottomless need for mother-love, which he thought he had outgrown, and he will lose his ability to defend himself.[2]

I hated getting haircuts. When my mother took me, it seemed that the barber would pay more attention to her than to me. And when I was big enough to go alone, I still felt invisible in the large barber chair, always imagining that the man must be bored cutting a little boy's head, or annoyed that he would not be getting the full fee, or inattentive because he'd been working all day and wanted to close up early.

One time, when I was around eleven, I went to get my hair cut at a barber shop near the Havemeyer Street markets. I had heard that this particular barber was twenty cents cheaper, and I hoped to use the money I saved for a treat. The barber turned out to be a tiny old man with a *yarmulke* and a palsied shake to his hands—no wonder he was so cheap. His fingers had liver spots on them, like my grandfather's. I was tempted to get up and run, but the cover sheet was already around my shoulders. He brought the scissors close to my head, trembling, stopping at an arbitrary point, where he jabbed them into my temple. As he clipped he made a hundred tentative approximations in the air, like the outlines in a Giacometti drawing, before he landed. When he shaved the nape of my neck, he nicked me. "Oh, did I cut you?" he said. "I'm sorry."

I couldn't wait to escape. The second after I paid him I darted out of the shop and ran several blocks. Finally I stopped in front of a luncheonette. I had twenty cents to spend. I read all the signs above the counter: grilled cheese sandwich; burger and fries; bacon, lettuce, and tomato. . . . I had never tasted bacon. Though my parents did not keep a strict kosher household, we lived in an Orthodox Jewish neighborhood and eating pork was taboo, it just wasn't done. I ordered a bacon sandwich, feeling sinful but defiant, telling myself I deserved to break the rule because I had had to suffer that haircut; I would be "blameless."

I wanted to say something earlier about tests of weakness. Even as a child, I had a strange experimental tendency to indulge a lassitude at the most inopportune moments. Once, when I was about nine, I let myself dangle upside down on a swing and refused, as it were, to exert the necessary muscle traction that would have gripped my legs to the seat. I fell on my head and had to have several stitches taken. Superheroes fascinated me as much for their sudden enfeeblements as for their vast powers. I would picture being in the presence of kryptonite and the voluptuous surrender to weakness. All my childhood illnesses were rehearsals for this crumbling of the will, this letting go of the effort to be a little man.

As an adult, I still often experience the temptation to go weak as a babe, or to let my body get into incredibly clumsy positions, knowing full well that with a little extra effort I could manage the action better. I will forgo putting down one kitchen object before picking up another, and in the awkward maneuvering the food will spill. Or I will go limp as a beanbag when having to extricate myself from the back seat of a car. Or sometimes, when I am helping several people lift a heavy piece up the stairs, I will suddenly become dreamy, forget to hold up my end. It isn't goldbricking exactly, because I'm not generally lazy about work. It's a way of resisting life on the physical plane.

A manly man will pick up a tool and perform a task with just the right amount of energy. I, on the other hand, view all implements as problematic and all chores as a test of manhood which I am half *eager* to fail. My mechanical ineptness is so fertile it borders on creativity. I have no sooner to pick up the simplest can opener than I feel all vigor drain from my hands. I struggle to concentrate my sluggish fingers, to make a go of it; I tell myself, "Even a child can do this." I force myself to grip the can opener and sink its sabertooth into the metal. Then, all too quickly, getting impatient, I bludgeon my way around the circle, starting half a dozen punctures until the whole top is a twisted mess and I am tearing it off with my bare hands. From lassitude to excessive force, nothing in between. I am very good at sacrificing my flesh to cuts, another kind of refusal to pay attention. In all this feigned weakness, one sees a reluctance to leave the boy-man stage, as well as a perverse intellectual vanity, since what is not given to the body must be given to the mind.

Why does Delilah betray Samson? That is the problem all future adaptations of the story sought to solve.

The most complex answer, and the most noble Delilah, are found in Milton's *Samson Agonistes*. She is the secret hero of that great poem. First the poet raises her status by making her Samson's wife. Though this allows Samson's father, Manoah, to quip, "I cannot praise thy marriage choices, son," and the blinded hero to roar when she visits him in prison, "My wife, my traitress, let her not come near me," she herself behaves with sympathy and dignity. She begs his forgiveness several times, offering a spectrum of explanations. The first is that, being a woman, she was subject to "common female faults . . . incident to all our sex, curiosity," and the urge "to publish" the secrets she learns. Then she says they were both weak, so they should both forgive each other. The strongman has very little sympathy for this excuse, retorting that "all wickedness is weakness." Then, more tenderly, she cites the "jealousy of love," having seen his wandering fancies and wanting to hold him near her, to keep him from all his "perilous enterprises." She also swears she was tricked by the Philistines, who assured her that no harm would come to him. He accuses her of doing it for the gold. Delilah vigorously denies this, saying that the magistrates had told her she had a "civic duty" to "entrap a common enemy," and the priest had further appealed to her on religious grounds, asserting that Samson was a "dishonorer of Dagon." He bats this argument away indignantly, saying that she had a primary duty to her husband, not her country. Delilah answers, abjectly, "I was a fool, too rash, and quite mistaken. . . . Let me obtain forgiveness of thee, Samson." She paints a picture of the life they could lead from now on: she thinks she could secure his release; true, he is blind, but "Life yet hath many solaces, enjoyed / Where other senses want not their delights / At home in leisure and domestic ease. . . ." He refuses to be caught again, ensnared by "Thy fair enchanted cup." Delilah: "Let me approach, at least, and touch thy hand." Samson practically jumps out of his skin. The extremity of his reaction, threatening to "tear her joint by joint," betrays how much feeling he has for her still. Sorrowfully, she notes: "I see thou art implacable. . . . Thy anger, unappeasable, still rages." It is a beautiful matrimonial scene; she understands full well the function and operation of his rage. When he tells her that her name will be notorious forever, she allows herself a parting shot: if she is to be infamous among the Israelites, her own people will commemorate her as a heroine. And she compares herself to Jael, who in the same Book of Judges, "with inhospitable guile / Smote Sisera sleeping through the temples nailed."

Indeed, any judgment of Delilah is complicated by the fact that her behavior seems structurally not so different from Jael's, or Judith's decapitation of Holofernes. All three actions occur in a tent, with a guileful woman bringing a warrior down while he sleeps. Yet her "sisters," narratively speaking, are admired and celebrated, whereas Delilah is reviled as the epitome of sluttish perfidy. History is written by the winners.

The Saint-Saëns opera also makes Delilah a Philistine patriot, but adds the dimension that she is the apostle of Love, and is jealous of his primary devotion to God. She carries on like a forlorn Dido about to be jilted by her Aeneas *(Mon coeur s'ouvre à ta voix . . .)*, weeping and arousing his pity.

In the movie, DeMille's scriptwriters introduce another motive by conveniently making Delilah the younger sister of the woman of Timnah (played by Angela Lansbury). The tomboyish Delilah develops a schoolgirl crush on her older sister's fiancé, Samson. When he rejects her as the replacement for the errant Lansbury, she is a woman scorned, and vows to get even by becoming a great courtesan. But her anger fades away during the idyllic period after she has seduced him. Indeed, the scenes of the lovers dallying by the stream and inside her commodious tent are so charmingly playful that it becomes difficult to believe her subsequent betrayal, except as the re-emergence of some innate "Delilah" nature. The Hollywood version has the lovers reunited, and it is Delilah who leads Samson to the pillars, gladly volunteering to die with him!

Why do men want Delilahs? If not in their homes, then in their fantasy lives? Why is the Bad Woman, the deceitful betrayer in all her *film noir* guises, always able to sell movie tickets? Because she is beautiful and sexy? So might be a virtuous woman. Some men want Delilahs because they yearn to be swept away by a passion stronger than their reason—which can only be proved if it goes against their own best interests; because by losing control the man can turn around later and blame her, *She* tempted me, she snatched away my will power; because one never takes her seriously as a partner for life and so there is no threat of having to make a commitment; because, although she may destroy the man, she will not smother him with admiration or doting affection that makes him feel like a fraud; because her treacheries are exciting in an operatic (if ultimately tiresome) way and they keep him feeling alive and angry, and anger is an aphrodisiac; because she confirms men's worst ideas about women; because a man wants to feel alone, to guard his solitude; because she is full of surprises and that keeps men off-balance; because men who have hurt women so often dream of being victims, of being punished for their crimes; because, while Delilah may lack domesticity and compassion, like the woman in Proverbs whose "price is far above rubies," she possesses other arts: the ability to sustain an appearance of glamour, which is a function of the imagination as much as good looks; the ability to control scents, and to manipulate interior spaces; the ability to keep the humdrum everyday world at bay; sometimes the art of dance and playing an instrument; a refreshingly candid lack of decorum; the naughtiness of a young girl or a kitten or anything but a fully adult woman who would serve as reminder of one's own death; the ability to evoke a touch of androgyny when called for; a keen insight into men; and a thorough knowledge of sex.

All my life I have been searching for a woman who will live up to, or down to, this bad-girl archetype. Instead I have met a succession of kind, sweet, devoted women (worse luck), on the one hand, or hassled, self-absorbed, remote women (worse still), on the other hand. I am still waiting to encounter Hedy Lamarr's Delilah, with the headband around her forehead and her many teases.

Actually, I did come close to a Delilah type. She was capricious, sexy, smart, crazy, abusive, pretty, and she tortured me for seven years. We started with a strong erotic spark, which later grew to be rooted in mutual anger—mine at her infidelities, hers at my refusing to take her "seriously." During all this time I was very productive, managing to put her provocations and scenes in the back of my mind and working out of that bottomless pit of creative energy, the feeling of being unloved, *le chant du mal-aimée.* As it happened, Kay was a writer, too, but her work did not get published very often. She would become furious and throw tantrums when she saw my poems in magazines, unless I placated her for half an hour about how much better her poems were—which I rarely did. Once she asked me point-blank: "How are you able to wield so much power in the world? Teach me, how does one get literary success?" I shuddered. It was Delilah's question: Where does your strength come from? I was tempted to say my literary prominence was hardly so grand as to merit envy, but I had to admit that, compared with her, I was "successful." Like many women, she had been kept in the dark about worldly power, and now she wanted to become more like men by sleeping with them. Myself, I was able to do very little for Kay as a poet—not that I tried very hard. She hated me at times with a palpable, shocking openness that was, if nothing else, different: most people like me. My own feelings were a murk of pity, lust, confusion, revulsion at her misconduct, and disgust at myself for staying in the relationship. But I admit that, in a way, it kept me amused.

So Samson is captured and blinded, and made to grind wheat in the prison house, like a beast of burden. "Howbeit the hair of his head began to grow again after he was shaven." Odd that the Philistines, having paid so dearly to learn that the secret of Samson's strength resided in his hair, should let him grow it again. In any event, the foreshadowing detail has been planted and the stage is set for the final catastrophe. The rest we know well:

the Philistines trot him out for sport on their feast day to Dagon, and he tells the lad who leads him, "Let me feel the pillars on which the house stands, that I may lean against them." It is a very satisfying narrative invention, this meeting of architectonics and apocalypse. Samson prays to the Lord for his strength to be returned, "only this once, that I may be avenged upon the Philistines for one of my two eyes." The Lord complies, and the house topples on everyone in it. "So the dead which he slew at his death were more than they which he slew in his life" (16:30).

A good death. To redeem a whole misspent life by the manner of one's dying—to take this inevitable poll tax, mortality, and turn it into a *tour de force* of accomplishment—has been a dream of many suicides through the ages, from Samson to Sydney Carton. However, Samson redeems himself not just by destroying slews of Israel's enemies, which is nothing new for him, but by his self-awareness, contained in his words: "Let me die with the Philistines." He does not pray to God, as he might have, "Let me destroy them in such a way that I can get off harmless." His conscience considers his sins, his follies, his own betrayal of his potential, and logically asks for the death penalty. We tend to forget that Samson was also—in whatever sense we care to take it—a judge ("And he judged Israel twenty years"): his last judicial act is to pronounce sentence on himself. When he says, "Let me die with the Philistines," he also seems to be alluding to his taste for Philistine women: I have eaten *traif,* it is only just that I go down with the *traif*-eaters. With his last noble words, he exiles himself from his own people and joins the Diaspora of the dead: a bitter ending. But he has come a long way from the younger, self-righteous Samson who petulantly said before wreaking havoc: Now am I blameless for the harm I will do them. Like a hero in a Greek tragedy, he has finished his journey from warrior pride to humility, by taking responsibility for violating the tribal laws.

I have said that my father was a physically strong man; this made his inability to deal with my mother or manifest any ambition all the more puzzling to me as a child. It often seemed to me that, in another type of situation, he would have realized a heroic potential. Though he never went into the army (excused from service because he had too many children), he would have made a good soldier. He was intelligent and stoic and did not shirk duty. I am not romanticizing, I hope, when I say that he would have run into a burning building to pull us out, without giving any thought to his safety. I still get shivers remembering one occasion when he risked his neck. We were locked out of our house, someone had lost the keys during a family outing, and my father went next door to see if he could leap from their fire escape to ours. It was no small distance; if he slipped and fell he would hit solid cement. We couldn't see how he was doing because the fire escapes were all on the backyard side, while we waited in the front vestibule. My brother, Hal, started whistling the Funeral March. "Hope you like being a widow. Was that a splat?" he said, cocking his ear. Ordinarily, sarcasm and gallows humor were the preferred family style, but this time my mother chewed her lips and stared through the locked glass door, holding her mouton coat closed at the throat. She had tried to talk him out of it earlier, saying they could call the police to break down the door, but my father wouldn't hear of it. He felt this was his job. I remember my mother's terrified, tear-streaked face while she waited in suspense. Molly said, "Ma, I don't think this is such a good idea," and my mother slapped her across her face, for saying what all of us were thinking. Eventually we saw my father's trousers coming downstairs, and the whole of him shortly after. When he let us in, we kids cheered: "Our hero!" "Don't give me that bullshit," said my father, modestly and gruffly. It did not take my mother long to recover her acid tongue: "Big showoff! You could have gotten killed, dummy!" But her agitated concern during those few minutes he'd been gone was like a revelation to me. Maybe she cared about him more than she let on.

My father is now seventy-six, my mother sixty-eight. Two years ago, she finally gave herself a present she had been wanting for over forty-five years: a divorce. Not that I blame her: she was, as she said, tired of being a full-time unpaid nursemaid to someone she didn't love. She kicked my father out of the house, and he went to live in a less-than-desirable nursing home in Far Rockaway. He has been depressed and emaciated, and he misses the city streets. Recently we heard of the possibility of an opening in a much better old-age home near Columbus Avenue, right in the middle of Manhattan. There is a long admissions procedure, as complicated as getting into an exclusive prep school. My mother brought him to the interview, crowing afterward that the director mistook them for father and daughter. So far his chances look pretty good: my father is not very outgoing, but he is ambulatory and in his right mind. We all have our fingers crossed. So far they've raised only one objection, my mother tells me: they would want him to shave his beard.

NOTES

1. Not that castration fear should be seen solely as a projection of male insecurity. There really are psychologically castrating women, analysts tell us. My mother belittled my father every day of their marriage. She was certainly provoked—he has a maddeningly taciturn, withdrawn, ungiving nature—but she took to provocation like ducks to water: "What are you good for? What do I need you for? You're like a mummy. Get lost, why don't you," she would say, "take a hike." One day he did, and jumped into the East River. Someone fished him out, fortunately, before he could drown. The police brought him home in his wet clothes.

2. Is it only my *mishegas* that associates the Samson story with Oedipus? Both men dealt with riddles, both suffered ruin by sleeping with the wrong woman, and both were blinded. Maybe the two legends came about in the same period or influenced each other.

I SAMUEL

MEDITATIONS ON THE FIRST BOOK OF SAMUEL AND KING SAUL

Jerome Charyn

I

THE FIRST BOOK OF SAMUEL IS ABOUT THE PRESENCE AND ABSENCE of voices, the history of a tribe that has become tone-deaf. The Hebrews have forgotten how to listen. They cannot hear God's voice. The Lord is absent from their lives. They go into battle with the Lord's own Ark and lose it to the Philistines. It's a sad and evil time for the Hebrews. "And the word of the Lord was rare in those days; there was no frequent vision" (3:1).

Enter Samuel. He is God's chosen, the boy who was "lent to the Lord" (1:28). He grows into a prophet, priest, and judge of Israel. Samuel alone of all the Hebrews can hear God's voice. His nearness to God is the one bit of unity the Hebrews have. Samuel *is* the nation. But his own sons are bad priests, and the older Samuel gets, the more that "nation" begins to worry. The elders of Israel say to Samuel: "Behold, you are old and your sons do not walk in your ways; now appoint for us a king to govern us like all the nations" (8:4). Uneasy about the notion of a king, Samuel prays to the Lord,

---

The Revised Standard Version of the Bible used in this essay.

98

and the Lord tells him: "Hearken to the voice of the people in all that they say to you; for they have not rejected you, but they have rejected me from being king over them" (8:7).

And the child of that rejection is Saul. The Lord chooses him as Israel's first secular king. He's handsome and tall. "There is none like him among all the people" (10:24). But Saul hides among his family's baggage when Samuel comes to fetch him. He's an outcast from the moment he's anointed by Samuel. He's the very idea of king as a lonely man. The Bible can't even tell us how old Saul was when he started to rule: the number is missing.

There is something cursed about Saul, something forlorn. The real prince of his army is Samuel, not Saul. When Samuel fails to appear at a certain battle site, Saul grows frightened and offers up in sacrifice sheep and oxen he should have destroyed, as God had dictated to Samuel, and Samuel had dictated to Saul. The Lord will not forgive him. Saul can pray and grovel, but he has become like a dead man. He rules without the word of God. The Lord provides His own king, David, a young shepherd boy who is ruddy and handsome and has beautiful eyes. Yet, though Samuel anoints the boy, Saul still rules the nation.

The Lord torments him with an evil spirit, and it is only young David who can cure it. "And whenever the evil spirit from God was upon Saul, David took the lyre and played it with his hand; so Saul was refreshed, and was well, and the evil spirit departed from him" (16:23). Saul takes the shepherd boy into his service as an armor-bearer and "loved him greatly" (16:21).

Enter Goliath. The giant of Gath challenges the entire Hebrew nation. Saul shivers along with the rest of the Hebrews when Goliath stands in his armor "with greaves of brass upon his legs, and a javelin of brass between his shoulders" (17:6), and says, "I defy the ranks of Israel this day; give me a man, that we may fight together" (17:10). And David agrees to fight Goliath. What does a giant mean to David when David has already destroyed the lions and bears that threatened his flock? The miraculous shepherd boy, with Jehovah on his side, "prevailed over the Philistine with a sling and with a stone, and struck the Philistine and killed him; there was no sword in the hand of David" (17:50). The Hebrews have a new champion, and that champion isn't Saul.

Saul has slain his thousands,
And David his ten thousands.
[18:7]

Thus sing the women of Israel after David destroys Goliath. Saul grows angry and "eyed David from that day on" (18:9). His destruction starts with a heartless song—spiteful *and* joyous. It's meant to belittle Saul and separate him from the boy hero who is adored by God. Saul is unadored. He was flung at the Hebrews, because they had lost faith in Jehovah. And once the Hebrew women sing, Saul is profoundly jealous. He knows that the Lord prefers this shepherd boy. Demons possess Saul. He has to seek out a witch. "God has turned away from me and answers me no more, either by prophets or by dreams" (28:15). The witch summons up the ghost of Samuel, who tells Saul that "the Lord has torn the kingdom out of your hand, and gives it to your neighbor, David" (28:17). And from that moment Saul himself is a ghost, the ghost of a king.

This is why Israel's first king haunts us like no other character in the Bible. He's as bewitched as our own century. Eaten with guilt, isolated, utterly without the Lord, he could have come out of Kafka's parables or Borges' bookish tales. I've lived with that maddened king most of my life. He sticks to my dreams.

I never much cared for David. The little giant-slayer is as competent as any Boy Scout. He has no demons to upset him. Saul's own son Jonathan protects David. He's the darling of the nation, the bringer of song. David is like a musical score. He "civilizes" the Hebrews with his lyre. His house prospers and he begets a whole line of kings. The history of Israel as a unified nation begins with the shepherd king and his lyre. And Saul dies on the battlefield with his three sons. The Philistines overtake him, as the ghost of Samuel had predicted, and the king asks his armor-bearer to "thrust me through" with his sword so that the Philistines will not "make sport of me" (31:4). But Saul's armor-bearer is too frightened to kill a king. And the king falls upon his own sword. "Thus Saul died, and his three sons, and his armor-bearer, and all his men, on the same day together" (31:6). And the house of Saul disappears.

He is a king without issue, a kind of walking shadow, a ghost boy who hides in the baggage. Saul is constantly with the night. Twice in the First

Book of Samuel he enters a cave to "relieve himself" (24:3) while he's hunting down David, and then in order to visit Samuel's ghost in the land of the dead. Saul's constant night turns him into a metaphorical man. He's the king of a "dark" nation that will flower under David. He lives in a dark time, without voices or visions. He serves as a sacrificial bridge that connects a primitive, warlike people with many gods and many tribes to a nation that serves one Lord, one God, with a continuous line under King David. And my own sentiments remain with Saul.

We also live in a time without voices or visions. If Jehovah sings to us, it's hard to hear. We're as deaf as King Saul. "The voice of the turtle is heard in the land, heard in all the arts—in literature, painting, and music—and in the voices of men and women speaking to one another," says John Bleibtreu in *The Parable of the Beast.*

It is not the voice of the dove, that sweet and melancholy sound which the translators of the Authorized Version presumably had in mind; it is the croak of isolation and alienation issuing from within a vault of defensive armor—the voice of the reptilian turtle. This armor we wear—the armor of technology separating us from the rest of the natural world—has created us lately in the condition of exiles. Nature exists within as well as without, and we are become, therefore, exiled from ourselves. The style of the catatonic has become the style of Everyman.

Saul is this catatonic Everyman: godless, alone, with the mocking sound of the turtle in his head. We ourselves are armored like Goliath and Saul. Our entire psyches are clothed "with greaves of brass." Our ears are stuffed. We seek our own witch of Endor in the caves of art. We long for voices—to rediscover our lyric selves. But the melodies are rare.

The Renaissance adored young David. He was Florence's own adopted child. Renderings of David could be found everywhere in that powerful city-state. Michelangelo turned him into a pleasing, handsome giant—a rational Goliath with wonderful loins. But where are the renderings of Saul?

It doesn't matter how many variations, or strands, there are to I Samuel, palimpsests and pentimentos, earlier and later drafts. In none of them is Saul the hero. He's always melancholic, afraid to rule. He is perhaps the first schizophrenic king. Saul's *disease* is the terror of a man who's lost the voice of God. He seeks God and finds only demons. He accuses all his servants of plotting against him (22:8) and protecting David. The voices in his ear gradually darken. He doesn't even have the benefit of David's lyre. The love he felt for David turns to madness and despair. Saul's demons separate him from every other man.

He lacks David's sense of politics and song. Saul is a primitive: there is almost nothing he experiences in I Samuel that isn't related to fear—fear of Samuel, fear of David, fear of God, fear of Goliath and the Philistines, fear of his servants, fear of his son Jonathan. When he fails to destroy the Amalekites, and still spares their king and their cattle, Samuel rebukes him and says: "Though you are little in your own eyes, are you not the head of the tribes of Israel?" (15:17)

Saul *is* little in his own eyes, because he never wanted to become king. What could that first king have been to the tribes of Israel? Half man, half god, prophet, warrior, and magician, a substitute for Jehovah Himself. Saul was much too simple and solitary a man to play at being a god. David can kill Goliath, talk to God, and mourn the dead Saul with an eloquence that borders on the magical:

> Ye daughters of Israel, weep over Saul,
> who clothed you daintily in scarlet,
> who put ornaments of gold upon your apparel.

And Saul has nothing but his rages, his fears, and his own silence. He cannot pull magic out of a sling and kill a giant for his people. Jehovah has cursed Saul by making him king. And perhaps the most poignant and haunted moment in I Samuel is connected to Saul's isolation as a man and a king.

In this one adventure, Saul is preparing to murder David and David's band of men. He enters a cave near Wild-goats' Rocks in order to move his bowels in private. David himself is hiding in that cave with his men, who beseech him to murder Saul. David does something else. While the king squats, "David arose and stealthily cut off the skirt of Saul's robe" (24:4). But David is still the Boy Scout: "And afterward David's heart smote him, because he had cut off Saul's skirt" (24:5). And he will permit none of his men to harm the king.

Saul leaves the cave, and the Boy Scout runs after him with his particular piece of evidence. "See, my father, see the skirt of your robe in my hand; for by the fact that I cut off the skirt of your robe, and did not kill you, you may know and see that there is no wrong or treason in my hands. I have not sinned against you, though you hunt my life to take it" (24:11).

David's words are like his lyre; while he sings them, Saul's madness flees. " 'Is this your voice, my son David?' And Saul lifted up his voice and wept. He said to David, 'You are more righteous than I; for you have repaid me good, whereas I have repaid you evil' " (24:16–17).

There's something oddly touching about that "communion" in the cave: Saul's own secret act of defecation is secretly interrupted by David. But a bonding occurs between the two men. The squatting king is closer to David than he will ever be, and yet he has no sense of this: he is still a king alone in the dark. His madness soon returns; he starts to hunt David all over again, and David hides among the Philistines. Samuel is dead. David is gone. And Saul's divided army destroys itself. The king and his entire house turn to dust.

II

Who will cherish Saul, sing his praises? No one but David. He laments the passing of Jonathan and Saul, who were "swifter than eagles" (II Samuel 1:23). But not even David's lament can rescue Saul. Saul has few echoes beyond his own sad history, while Jonathan is remembered as the beloved friend of David.

> I am distressed for you, my brother Jonathan;
> very pleasant have you been to me;
> your love to me was wonderful,
> passing the love of women.
> [II Samuel 1:26]

And if the Bible is ambiguous about Saul's age and the years of his rule, it is relentlessly clear on the subject of King David: "David was thirty years old when he began to reign, and he reigned forty years" (II Samuel 5:4).

David is a man of many appetites, climates, and roles—lover, father, husband, soldier, poet, musician, king. He woos Bathsheba, Abigail, and Abishag, keeps a harem of wives. He conciliates, cajoles. He dances, sings, and sins. He creates a new capital. We have a city of David, a star of David . . . and nothing for Saul (David had his empire, and Saul had his fits).

And yet it is through this very nothingness that we finally celebrate Saul. He has no Abishag to warm his bed. His son Ish-bosheth succeeds him for a while and is murdered by his own two captains (and David swallows the house of Saul). We have no music to remember him by. He exists in the hollows, in the spaces around his kingdom, in the empty designs of his rule. Negativity and narrowness are his earmarks, the tags of Saul. He is the king who gives way to David, like the howls and birth pangs of a nation. Saul is that ambiguous line where history begins.

While David is in hiding, he establishes his covenant with the dispossessed. "And every one who was in distress, and every one who was in debt, and every one who was discontented, gathered to him" (22:2). And that's how he collects an empire and an army. But Saul consorts with witches, demons, and ghosts. He's king of the impalpable, of those things that cannot be touched. David is the builder of cities and words, the poet-prince. He is rational and sane and devious, the perfect Boy Scout. Saul is insane, or irrational at least. If he could have disguised his own terror, he might have used David as a spear against the Philistines. But the king's at war . . . with himself. He loves David, fears David, is jealous of David, and cannot negotiate among his feelings and moods. He'd prefer to deal with David's ghost rather than David.

After Samuel dies, Saul puts "the mediums and the wizards out of the land" (28:3). But he's afraid of the Philistines. He shucks off the garments of a king and visits the witch of Endor. He enters her "cave." He asks her to bring Samuel up out of the cave, the same Samuel who anointed and abandoned Saul. What good news could a dead prophet bring? Samuel had no love for Saul. Yet the king persists. In a deaf time, he needs to hear a prophet.

The ghost is angry at him. "Why have you disturbed me by bringing me up?" (28:15)

Saul doesn't shiver before this ghost of Samuel "wrapped in a robe" (28:14). He has summoned Samuel so that Samuel can tell him what to do. The ghost answers: "Why then do you ask me, since the Lord has turned from you and become your enemy?" (28:16). "Tomorrow," the ghost says, "you and your sons shall be with me" (28:19).

The king falls to the ground. The ghost departs. The witch of Endor feeds Saul. And the next day, after the Philistine archers surround Saul and wound him, the king falls upon his sword.

Thus Saul's story ends: the reluctant king who fell out of grace with the Lord. "There was not a man among the people of Israel more handsome than he" (9:2). But Saul's handsomeness wasn't enough. His very selection ruins him. He was a little too handsome, a little too tall. And it's the awfulness of his fate—the king as doomed man—that moves the modern reader.

Our own lives seem as arbitrary as Saul's. The blessing of his kingship was only another form of curse. In a century of mass migration and mass murder, of dreamlike poverty and dreamlike wealth, of businessmen-philosophers and pauper-kings, Saul seems as familiar as our own brooding face.

> Saul has slain his thousands,
> And David his ten thousands.

If David is history's darling, then we, all the modern fools—liars, jugglers, wizards without song—still have Saul.

II SAMUEL

Lore Segal

ONE ARGUMENT IN THE MODERN FORESTS OF CRITICISM SAYS THAT no text happens unless a reader stands underneath for it to fall on. As a Bible reader *sans* scholarship, *sans* Hebrew, I'm grateful for what I take to be permission—taking care to keep in mind that I'm missing what I'm missing—to understand what I understand: the Bible happens to me, and writers wrote it. Because writers wrote those lives lived and politics plotted in the alien Middle East at the remove of two millennia, they fall within the imagination of the modern reader. As a writer of modern stories I want to nod to my ancient colleagues: I can tell some things that they are up to, and how they plot their stories and how they manipulate us to understand them.

Finally, because I live, imagine, write, and understand in a different part of the very same forest, I give myself permission to quarrel with some things the stories tell us.

The Second Book of Samuel begins with the raw news of King Saul's

---

The author's own translation of the Bible used in this essay.

death told by the young Amalekite who brings it straight from the morning's battle.

The young man said: It was by chance that I was walking on Mount Gilboa—and there he was—Saul leaning himself onto his spear with the chariot and horse closing in! He looked around and saw me and called to me. I said, Here I am! He said, Who are you? I said, An Amalekite. He said, Come over here and kill me. Pain has got me in its grip but life will not let me go. — So I went to him and killed him, because I could tell that he would never rise again where he had fallen. And I took the crown that he wore on his head and the bracelet from his arm and have brought them to you, my lord!

David treats the story as an account of something that has happened, whereas commentary speculates that the Amalekite might be telling a "story," a fabrication with which he means to manipulate an advantage for himself. We won't worry which is the truth of the matter. Language allows the word both meanings and our purpose need not distinguish between them: telling turns into words what did not happen in words. Event and invention are equidistant from story and require the same arts.

Our young Amalekite has lived inside the history of the First Book of Samuel, in which we have read the stories of David's youth and his lineage that links him, begat by begat, back to very Adam (and will link him forward to Jesus Christ).

The story has insisted on a favorite Bible theme. To show that the Lord shows His favor to whom He shows His favor and His mercy to whom He shows His mercy, He likes to choose younger sons—Jacob over Esau, Menassah over Ephraim—the one of two, according to human organization, not in the line of succession. David has *seven* older brothers and the story parades each before the Lord's king-maker, the prophet Samuel. God explains: "Don't look at his face or his fine tall figure for I have rejected him. Things are not as man sees them. Man looks with his eyes but the Lord looks into the heart."

The Bible likes echoes, and the story of God-favored David calls up the story of God-favored Joseph. Both get attention and do everything right; everyone likes them—king, court, people. At the royal table, young David sits at the left hand of Saul, at whose right sits Jonathan, whose brotherly love for his father's favorite outweighs his love for his father, his obligation to his father's house, and to his own advantage. It drives mad, suffering Saul madder, and he hounds David into an exile.

No wonder the Amalekite thinks he has done David a favor by killing the murderous king and bringing David the crown off the king's head—a mortal error.

David said: And you were not afraid to raise your hand and kill the Lord's anointed? — And David called one of his men and said: Come here and strike him dead! . . . And David tore his clothes, and so did all the men with him. They wept and fasted and mourned seven days.

Thereupon David is crowned king of Judah.

The Bible likes parallel stories with a difference. The two Benjaminites think they have done the king a favor by killing Saul's son King Ish-bosheth and then traveling cross-country all night to bring David the head. David calls his man to come and strike them dead, gives them his lecture on the horrors of regicide, and is crowned king of Israel as well.

Remember the unfortunate Shakespearean kings who have to plant the notion that someone rid them of the lives that stand between them-selves and the throne of England and suffer agonies of blame and guilt? David's obstacles are removed for him without his collusion. He can pi-ously kill the killers (sending a simultaneous warning to any of Saul's people who might be thinking of killing King David) and ascend the throne with everybody's blessing. We have no call to read his rites of public mourning, or his beautiful—and public—elegy of grief for Saul and Jonathan, as insincere. Your sincerest act of mourning turns out to be good policy and good publicity when the Lord plots the outcome. A simpler fiction would have cued us to think David a manipulator or a saint. The subtle story makes him something of both: David is a righ-teous man who has God's grace, meaning the world's good luck, and his luck is running—it will run out in its time.

The two books of Samuel were originally one book and have the scope of a novel whose theme is David's mandate to root the children of Israel in the promised land in which, after four hundred years of slavery and forty years of desert wandering, the Lord has at last planted them.

The story tests government by kingship, a possibly sinful experiment for a people who had the Creator of the universe Himself for its King and chose instead to have Samuel choose them a human one so that they could be like, and could fight like, all the other nations. The Second Book unites Judah and Israel into a single nation with its capital, the City of David, in Jerusalem. It establishes the Ark in its Tabernacle and the king in his luxurious palace, bursting with his wives, his concubines, and apartments for the children. There are chapters that end with the listings of the names, not only of King David's warriors, but of his cabinet, as if the story had brought us to the closure of a civil peace. Turn the page and Israel's hereditary enemies have grown back like Hydra's heads; Abner, the captain of Saul's army, and Joab, David's captain, thicken the plot with their personal ambitions and vendettas; Saul's remnant of half-crazed loyalists continue to throw stones and plot King David's overthrow. Absalom succeeds in ousting his father from the throne for a time, but David has friends and God's election, and counterplots a rare spy operation.

David plays more roles, in more situations, than any modern protagonist: he is boy warrior, musician with healing powers, poet laureate, court favorite; for a while he is the leader of a band of marauders who massacre alien cities. He is monarch, general, diplomat, a natural at public relations, a public man with a private life—a careful son, an irritating younger brother, a loving and faithful friend, the husband of a harem that includes one very angry wife; the father of children who make him howl with grief, an adulterer who plots murder, a penitent, a frequent mourner, and an old man, at last, who meets a new Goliath and can't do anything about it—can't make love, can't keep warm.

It overstates the matter to say the Second Book of Samuel is "about" plotting and manipulation. It is about the events of David's kingship, and the events are full of plots and manipulations. Look at the tale of the rape of Tamar and its consequences.

Prince Amnon puts into practice his cousin Jonadab's plot to manipulate the king into manipulating Amnon's virgin half-sister Tamar into the rapist's house and bed. Her brother Absalom's plot of revenge depends upon manipulating the king into letting the princes come to his sheep shearing. Absalom goes into exile and Joab manipulates the king into bringing him home. Back in Jerusalem, Absalom burns Joab's field in order to get Joab to come and talk to him, in order to get him to go and talk to the king and get the king to talk to Absalom. More anon.

To manipulate is to "handle" other people, purposefully to maneuver their feelings in order to change how they think and what they do.

There are, in the Second Book of Samuel, two central and fully articulated stories with which two of the story's characters set out to manipulate the king, for his own good. Joab hires a wise woman and teaches her a circumstantial fiction of fraternal murder, blood vengeance, and family complication which she tells David to get him to recall the exiled Absalom, something he himself doesn't know that he yearns to do. In the other, the prophet Nathan tells the king the story of the ewe lamb to get David to understand something about himself he would rather not know.

The language does not differentiate between the benevolent and the self-serving act and offers no choice of neutral verbs: to manipulate, to handle, to operate, to contrive, to maneuver, all sound the same disagreeable note. "Scheme," a neutral noun, turns nasty as a verb. Does the nice verb "design" show its true color as an adjective? Our dislike of designing people who act upon our reason from outside our reason goes as deep as language.

But our theme is story, and when we read (or turn ourselves into an audience in a theater or viewers in a gallery of pictures) we hand ourselves over into the artist's hands. I mean the manipulations of the sugar which the baker designs us to read as so "sweet" and no sweeter by the addition of a judicious scraping of rind of lemon only the educated palate of another pro troubles to identify, though its effect combines with, and depends on, every other ingredient as well as the length, calibration, and means of heating learned at Grandmother's oven, modified by subsequent education and experience working upon a native talent that depends on God alone knows what concatenation of personality, history, and happenstance to create an object so inextricably complex that it has a border in common with mystery. It is mystery that falls into the mouth of that other mystery, the one who takes the bite, the one who reads the story: I want to look at some things, this side of mystery, which our Bible story does to this modern reader's understanding.

The Bible's writers might have attended a course in "creative" writing, they tell so little, render so much, use so few adjectives and fewer adverbs. The Amalekite employs one of the Bible's favorite modes, the first-person narrative. An A student and a minimalist, he knows how to pare a story to the essential event, the telling details, and a lot of dialogue. The time is two thousand years in the future in which we writers would have had the reader climb inside Saul's skin to "identify" with the sensations of his mangled flesh.

Bible, myth, and fairy story are not in the business of giving the experience of nerve or muscle. (Unlike our modern tellers and Hellers. I remember Queen Jocasta on a Chicago stage walking over to poor harassed Oedipus and massaging his neck and shoulders for him.)

Nor does the story locate our imagination inside Saul's head to have us look out of his eyes and see what he is seeing: the Amalekite only says he saw "Saul leaning himself onto his spear, and the chariots and horsemen closing in." And, mysteriously and forever, even after King Saul lies dead, after David has recovered King Saul's sacred carcass and given it honorable burial, King Saul still, simultaneously, leans himself onto his spear, turns, sees the young stranger; the trampling enemy horses continue to approach in that same frame of time in which Keats' procession of young Greeks walks forever after its tail end. Whose miracle is it—the reader's? The maker's?

The Bible does not know the formulation "King Saul felt that . . ." or "saw that . . ." or "thought that . . ." except, wonderfully, when we look downward with the eyes of the King of Kings Himself at our own ubiquitous wickedness, before the Flood, and He tells His own heart that He regrets that He ever made us. We're back in His point of view when He rescinds our doom, having judged us to be so aboriginally sinful that even wiping us off the face of the earth will make never a dent in our tendency to wickedness and violence.

If the Bible doesn't use our common modern means to get its story told, how does it tell us what to see and hear and feel?

Roger Fry quipped, "What you don't tell them they don't know," where "you" are the teller and "they" the reader. It follows that what you want them to know you keep telling them. Because the story needs us, for its own purposes, to keep young David's youth in mind, it keeps calling him a shepherd *boy;* because the story does not tell us what David's brothers do around the place, they don't, in our imagination, do anything. The story has made David into the family Cinderella, the boy who stays at home to mind the sheep while the brothers go off to King Saul's wars. The story has taken pains to keep the boy at home so that it can be at considerable trouble to get him, by one means or another, into King Saul's presence.

In chapter 16, Saul's courtiers have prescribed "Jesse the Bethlehemite's son . . . who knows how to play the lyre" for the king's bouts of depression, "when the spirit of the Lord left Saul and the Lord's terror overwhelmed him. . . . And David came and served Saul and Saul grew to love him and he became his armor bearer."

Two chapters later, David is the shepherd boy again, in his domestic role, bringing wine and provisions to his soldier brothers in the field, and the only one in all the army man enough to take the strutting, loudmouthed Goliath on.

The story is refusing to let us not notice the discrepancy. It has us hear the king ask his captain, "Abner, whose son is that boy?" Abner says, "As your soul lives, my king, I've no idea! Why don't you ask him yourself?"

In forcing the reader to accept two mutually exclusive accounts of David's introduction to King Saul, the narrative operates like the Charles Addams cartoon of the skier's tracks bracketing the tree growing in his downward path. Like the account of a miracle, it blows the mind. The mind must imagine the impossible, and can't, and can't let it alone, and keeps trying to argue itself out of its distress. Harmonizing scholarship proposes—and we surely take its word—that we have here an example of two oral traditions both of which the ancient redactor, who doesn't have our hangup with logic, chooses to preserve. It relies on our notion that the ancient reader, not in the habit of realistic fiction, and in the habit of believing miracles, was not made uncomfortable by impossibilities.

But let me suppose that the ancient mind *was,* was meant, was being forced—just like our mind—to *be* uncomfortable. Why would the Lord have given Himself the trouble of making the bush burn, of turning sticks into snakes, of staging those ten special-effect plagues, for minds that were not going to be blown?

Robert Alter proposes that we let the text stand as it stands and receive it as it falls, without worrying whether an editorial or authorial decision is accountable. He teaches us to hold still and use the patient time it would take to argue the text into saying what we are able to understand, to understand what it says.

Let me imagine that the two stories are not erroneously, or innocently, but insistently inconsistent and mean to blow the mind fruitfully. The Lord, who has chosen David against custom and probability, will get him by one means *and* another—by as many means as He chooses to multiply—to where He and to where the story require him to be: into the court of King Saul, into the army of the Lord, into the center of the plot.

Marvel at the means by which the tale of Tamar makes understood a crime, a bad character, and its harvest of grief.

Amnon fell in love with his half sister Tamar and was sick with longing because she was his sister; because she was a virgin, it seemed impossible to Amnon that there was anything he could do to her.

Are we puzzled that her virginity rather than her kinship gives Amnon pause? The Masoretic text (says the note of the Soncino Bible) is punctuated in such a way that it is Tamar's virginity that is understood to inflame her half-brother's lust. Rashi explains that, as a virgin, Tamar would live so sequestered a life it made it impossible for Amnon to get at her. Jonadab's cleverness is to manipulate her out of her protected quarters.

Jonadab said [to Amnon]: Lie down in your bed, as if you were ill. When your father comes to see you, you must say: Let my sister Tamar come and cook some dish that will be good for me, here, so that I can watch her, and she can serve me.

Even if we have not personally lusted for our virgin half-sister, we've longed and sickened enough to put our experience in the place of Amnon's, until the story puts us on notice that we are to feel not empathically but morally. Cousin Jonadab shares with the serpent in the garden the epithet "subtle," meaning clever in the bad way.

Does Amnon start out, like you and me and Eve and most people we know, a reluctant sinner? Amnon becomes ill because Tamar, the healing dish, is forbidden fruit. A virgin is impossible to do anything to. Taboo protects her from hurt and him from hurting her, until the serpent makes the forbidden permissible by making it a possibility. Tamar pleads to reinstitute the taboo: "We don't do things like that in Israel!"

But Amnon . . . overpowered her and took her by force. And afterward he felt a loathing for her that was greater than the love that he had felt for her before. . . .

The story does not explain or comment. It tells us the words Amnon spoke and conveys the tone in which he spoke them. We understand the immediacy and force of his revulsion hideously displaced from his act onto its victim.

. . . and he said, Get up! Go away! . . . And he called his servant and said: Get that woman away from me. Put her out in the street and bolt the door behind her!

The story *names* Amnon's, Tamar's, David's, and Absalom's feelings: ". . . Tamar lived alone and in *despair* in her brother Absalom's house." "When the king heard what had happened he was *enraged*." Absalom says "nothing either good or bad [that is to say, nothing at all] to his brother Amnon because he *hated* Amnon for defiling his sister Tamar."

Absalom waits two patient years plotting his revenge. Amnon's crime ruins Tamar the victim, Amnon the perpetrator, Absalom the avenger, and leaves David grieving for two sons. Cousin Jonadab continues in good health.

The rumor reached the king that Absalom had slain every one of the king's sons and not one remained alive, and the king jumped up and tore his clothes and fell to the ground.

Here is Jonadab, in at the kill that his little scheme has set in motion:

My lord king must not think that all the young princes are dead. It might be only Amnon, for Absalom has had his death in mind since the day his brother raped his sister Tamar. The servant on the look out raised his eyes and saw a lot of folk on the

road coming up the mountain, and Jonadab said: It's just as I said! Only Amnon is
dead.

Like a minor Iago, Jonadab appears to do evil as purely as a saint does
good—for no personal gain except the satisfaction, perhaps, of being in on
things. One commentary notes that he seems in the know of Absalom's
feelings just as he'd been in on Amnon's.

Is the story showing us the characteristic pattern of King David's
grieving?

And David mourned his son [Amnon] every day, and Absalom fled and went to
Geshur and lived there for three years. And King David's soul longed for Absalom for
his grief for Amnon had been comforted seeing he was dead.

Here is David, earlier in the story, grieving for another son—the
nameless baby born of his adultery with Bathsheba, for which the child's
death is to punish him:

The Lord afflicted the child. . . . [I]t became deathly ill. David begged God for the
little boy's life and fasted and came home and slept the night on the floor. The chief
of his servants, who had charge of his household, tried to raise him from the floor,
but he would not be raised, and would not eat. On the seventh day the child died.
David's people were afraid to tell him and said, He would not listen to us when the
child was alive, how can we tell him the child is dead? Who knows what he might
do! David saw them whispering together and knew that the child was dead and said,
Is the child dead? They said, It is dead.
    And David stood up and bathed, and anointed himself and put on fresh clothes,
and went into the house of the Lord and worshipped. Then he went home and asked
for food and sat down and ate.

Now, the story is neither describing nor naming David's feelings.
We observe his behavior as we might observe a grieving friend on the
other side of the room, from the observation point of the king's servit-
ors. They are puzzled, giving the story the opportunity for David to
explain:

His man asked: We don't understand you. You fasted and wept while the child lived
and now it is dead you get up, you eat your food!

He said: While the child lived, I fasted and wept because I thought, Who knows! Perhaps the Lord might have pity on me and let the boy live. But now he is dead, I cannot bring him back again. The time will come when I will go where the child has gone, but the child will not come back to me.

Does the story invite us to speculate? Is David a man of God accepting what God deals out in the way of dead babies and punishments for sin? Is he a veteran mourner who knows that grief is comforted at last? Is he a man who looks the factness of death in the eye, swallows, and gets on with his business—until it's the death of his treasonous and beautiful young son, Absalom?

Admire the interweaving of these stories as we reach back to isolate the thread of Absalom's part in the design: it out-thickens any Dickens plot in sheer complication, obliging us, first, to locate Joab.

Joab—an excellent warrior and general, a man able, when it seems necessary to him, to run his spear into and out the other end of a rival's groin—is the king's lifelong and faithful friend. Careful of his fortunes, observant and tender of his feelings, it is for no ulterior motive, only to ease the king's heart, that he teaches David a portion of forgiveness—enough to bring exiled Absalom home to Jerusalem.

A digression on the subject, still, of the two-step that text and reader perform with one another: would I have advised the Bible writer in my creative-writing class to tidy up the plot, to connect the rape and subsequent murder and exile more strictly with Absalom's treason—have him plot his father's ruin during his exile in Geshur or, better, in the Jerusalem years, while his father refuses to let him see his face? The Absalom in the story spends those years plotting a full reconciliation. It is after reconciliation that he embarks on the demagoguery that plots his father's overthrow. Is the story nodding, or the reader? Our text asks for patience and a determinedly open mind. Have you never wished away, say, a too-red spot from a favorite painting to discover, years after, that the canvas has organized itself around the disturbance? The Bible refuses again and again to be harmonious with itself.

And there is the story of Absalom's demagoguery:

After that Absalom got himself a chariot and horses, and fifty men to run ahead of him. Mornings he would go out and stand on the path to the city gate. If anybody came along with some matter of justice to bring before the king, Absalom would call the man over and say, Where are you from—what town? — The man would say, Your servant comes from such or such a tribe of Israel—and Absalom would say, Your case is perfectly clear and you are in the right, but no one in the king's court is going to listen to you! — And he would say, If I were made judge in this country, anyone who had a case or a dispute could come to me, and I'd see justice done! And if someone approached and was going to prostrate himself before Absalom, Absalom would reach out his arm and draw him close and kiss him, and in this way Absalom stole the heart of the people of Israel.

And so the story takes the art of manipulation head on. Absalom must know the workings of Israel's human heart in order to work upon it. He understands the effect of sheer power and advertises it with chariots, horses, and men. He knows the seduction of power acting humble and friendly and can trust the human heart not to be overly particular, not to notice or care— or to take care not to notice—that it's being conned. And Absalom knows the seduction of the human touch; he handles with hands, embraces, kisses. Oh, designing Absalom! Oh, artful writer! To our primitive pleasure in recognition—yes, that's just how people act!—is added the moral pleasure of indignation: Look at the hateful demagogue, and his stupid patsies! The story moves on to a prompt and canny contrast between the scheming egotism of the son and the father's grace in his crisis, lingering over David's sensitive awareness of the effect of his forced exodus upon his many loving subjects.

When the king saw Attai, the Gathite, marching by he said: You don't have to come with me! Go back and stay with the new king. You are a stranger and have travelled a long way from your home. It was only yesterday that you arrived, why should you leave today and go who knows where? I must go where I can, but you should turn back—you and all your kin—and may faith and kindness go with you!

Attai chooses to go with the king and becomes his trusted general. God's elect is nobody's fool: David makes sure God will have the assistance of a fifth column. He persuades several of his friends to go back and frustrate his son's inner council, which the story returns to Jerusalem to see in session.

We observe Absalom's delight in a particularly neat plan for patricide that will cause a minimal disruption.

The story has insisted on Absalom's heroic beauty, his outward perfection—the things at which we look with our eyes while the Lord looks into the heart.

In all Israel there was no man as beautiful as Absalom, and all Israel praised him. From the sole of his foot to the crown of his head he was without blemish. When his hair was cut—once a year, when it became too heavy—it weighed two hundred measures according to the royal standard.

The story insisted on calling David a "boy" because it meant for us to marvel at the might of the Lord, who can employ a child and his slingshot to fell a giant heathen. What is the story up to when it insists on referring to Absalom, the father of sons, who has spent years in exile and four decades plotting, as a "young man"? I think it is the sheer force of the words "young" and "man" that works upon us, in spite of the logic of mere numbers, to regret that so perfectly beautiful a young man should be so false. It sets us up to grieve with David that a man who is so beautiful and young is dead.

When David sends Joab out against the traitor his concern and instructions are clear to all the army: Make sure nothing happens "to the young man Absalom."

Again we stand with the anxious father, at a gate again, waiting for news of a son.

The king was sitting, waiting between the two gates, and the watchman went up to the roof and looked out and saw a man running alone and called down and told the king. The king said, If he comes alone, then the news is good. The man was coming closer and the watchman saw a second man running and called down: Look at that! Here comes another man running alone! The king said, He brings good news too! The watchman on the wall said, The first one runs like Ahimaz! The king said, He's a good man and brings me good news!

It behooves us to question what we are understanding. We misconstrue often enough the behavior and words of the friend across the room. What makes us think we can read the actions of a God-centered king in ancient

Canaan? The writer who wrote the story is telling us something we know. I've stood, at my Manhattan window, waiting for a son and have thought: If one person comes walking around the corner of Broadway before the count of ten, he hasn't been run over. If two persons come walking . . .

David's anxiety is excruciating. Ahimaz is wanting to give the king news of the triumphant battle, but the king can't listen. "The king said: And is my son Absalom well?" Ahimaz gets cold feet and equivocates. The explanation is mine. The story merely says:

Ahimaz said, There was a great commotion as your servant was leaving—I couldn't see what it was. The king said: Step aside and stand over there. And he stepped aside and stood there. And there came the moor and said, Good news my lord and king. The Lord has justified you against all those who rose against you! But the king said: And is my son Absalom well? The moor said: May all my lord the king's enemies end up as that young man has ended up.

Now the king began to tremble and went up into the chamber above the gate weeping as he went and cried: My son Absalom! My son, my son Absalom! Would to God that I had died for you! Oh Absalom, my son, my son!

This time there is no acquiescence in God's punishment, no facing death as fact, no veteran knowledge of the assuagement of time. Joab has to come and make the king shape up. If he doesn't give over grieving for the traitor and reward his loyal soldiers and get back to ruling the country, he's not going to have a country to rule.

Absalom's wrongdoing is not the kind that brings the Lord thundering down upon the page. The God of the Second Book of Samuel is not the manifest pillar of cloud by day and fire by night that led the community of Israel through the wilderness and who talked to Moses mouth to mouth, seeing wickedness present and to come. The Lord has retired to a largely consulting position. David "inquires" of Him, and He tells David where to move his household and army and gives common-sense instructions in respect to military strategy to the capable king. The Lord has grown civilized, no longer offering to wipe us off the earth or to disinherit Israel, but promising David's descendants appropriate paternal chastisement with simultaneous paternal love.

When David sins with Bathsheba, the Lord "lets him live" and sends

His prophet Nathan to tell him a story that will educate King David's moral and humane imaginations, and ours.

The story of Bathsheba is another tale of lust leading to crime and the punishment visited down the generations.

David has put himself into the way of sin. The time has not yet come when David's people will urge the precious, aging king to stay out of the danger zone. Has King David grown tired, lazy, luxurious? The story does not say that. It only mentions that this is the fighting season and the king has sent Joab and the army out into the field and has stayed home in Jerusalem. What is he doing in Jerusalem? Waking from a nap. "Sleep" operates in the Bathsheba/Uriah story like Buber's notion of a *Leitwort*. The word runs like a thread throughout the story, which depends on who sleeps and where. If King David were out fighting the Lord's battles he would not be waking from sleeping on the roof of his palace, would not be strolling there, would not be seeing Bathsheba at her bath.

The story makes sure to mention that David inquires and is told that the woman is married, and married to a soldier of King David's who *is* out in the field fighting King David's battles. Did Bathsheba want to come? Was she forced or seduced? Did she raise no objection on moral grounds? Perhaps she was not a faithful wife. The commentaries variously speculate that she might have been afraid to say nay to the king, or she might have been flattered to be asked. They do not consider that she might have desired the king's person. We're on our own with our speculations. The story has nothing to say on the subject. It does not raise Bathsheba's feelings or opinions as an issue. The ewe lamb story represents her as a pet lamb slaughtered to entertain a passing guest. Much later her iron will, like Rebekah's, will manipulate her favorite son, God's favorite, Solomon, into the place of succession. The story gives her nothing to say, until she sends the king word that she is with child.

David sends for Bathsheba's husband, Uriah the Hittite, as if to question him about news from the front. David feasts him, makes much of him, and tries, for three successive nights, to get him to go and sleep at home. The witty story never *says* the king is trying a coverup and failing. Unrighteous David, out of God's favor, has no power to manipulate a single soldier into the soldier's own bed to sleep with his own wife. For three nights righteous—self-righteous—Uriah resists his own ease: as long as Joab and David's army sleep in the open field, Uriah will sleep on the ground with David's soldiers, pointing with ineluctable emphasis to the king's laxness in the matter of sleeping around.

David involves Joab in the dastardly plot to send the patriotic Uriah (adjectives all mine) to his death. Joab tailor-makes a battle that gets Uriah killed, and tailor-makes the report that he sends home to prevent the king's forgetfulness from blaming Joab for bad generalship. King David is never going to be allowed to forget any part of what he has just done.

Joab hired a wise woman to teach David to forgive his son and ease his own heart, but when the king's humane and moral education is at stake, a higher agency is brought into play.

He [the Lord] sent the prophet Nathan to David, and he came to him and said: There were two men who lived in the same city. One was rich, the other was poor. The rich man had great herds of cattle and sheep, but the poor man had nothing but one little ewe lamb he had bought and nursed, and it grew up with his children and shared his bite of bread with him and drank from his cup and slept on his lap and was like a daughter to him.

There came a traveler to the rich man's house, but the man didn't want to kill any of his own sheep or cows to serve to the traveler, so he took the poor man's lamb and cooked it and served it to his visitor.

The prophet Nathan explains and comments. He doesn't trust David to understand what he has done wrong, so he adds, "The Lord has forgiven (has put away) your sin; you are not going to die, but . . ." Then he spells out the terrible list of consequences.

Does it puzzle us when the Lord simultaneously "puts away" sin and promises to visit it upon the sinner's children down the generations, according to a formula of the payment of an eye for an eye, a tooth for a tooth, with interest? If David has secretly committed adultery with Uriah's one wife, his son Absalom will commit it publicly with David's many concubines. If David has had Uriah killed with the sword, the sword will rampage among his sons. The story bears out the prophecy. Is it describing the ordinary operations of cause and effect? Violence begets an Oresteia of vengeance for vengeance that looks for all the world, if you like, like divine retribution and includes the slaughter of firstborns and innocents. "You can be sure that the child that is going to be born to you will die," says the prophet Nathan.

We have arrived at our ancient quarrel with the Lord: will He who punishes David for taking Bathsheba and killing innocent Uriah take and kill innocent Bathsheba's innocent baby? We keep waiting for the Lord, who saved us out of our Egyptian slavery, to tell David that it's wrong to enslave the vanquished Philistines and make the Moabites lie on the ground and measure off rope-lengths of them to die and rope-lengths to live. The Jew has one God, so the One who promises Noah that the very animals will be held accountable for the shedding of blood is the Same who disinherits Saul because he fails to massacre his enemy—mind you, let's be very clear about this: if you let them live in your midst they *will* be a thorn in your eye. And Hillel is right: if you don't look out for yourself nobody else will—not today, not ever.

It needed no angel come from God to teach us solipsism. We come by it naturally. The Bible is *about* God's overarching scheme to make Himself a nation out of our Mesopotamian Ur-family: *our* family. It is *our* story, so it's natural for us to be our own protagonist in a world God created on purpose for His purposes for us, not for the Ishmaelites, the Amalekites, the Ammonites, and the Moabites.

Why worry about it? How naïve to hold these ancient tales to account!

We worry because we latter-day Jews find ourselves protagonists in the twentieth-century chapter of our own story, and because it's in our solipsistic blood to worry. We've been quarreling with the Lord since our Ur-father Abraham took Him on before Sodom and Gomorrah: "And will you, the judge of all the earth judge so unjustly and kill the good with the wicked?"

The rabbis have worried down the generations and tell their beautiful stories to justify the way God behaves to men. We cannot, and cannot leave it alone. Believer or not, it blows the mind to imagine an unjust God. Easier to argue all power out of heaven than imagine It capable of fault.

We've tried reforming the Lord into a good liberal and made Him over into a skim-milk God as thin as our own liberal imaginations.

Or we've tried keeping God all good by taking all His faults upon ourselves. We tell ourselves that we have made Him in our image, fathered ourselves a father whose favorite child we are, who will give us the Canaan we need for our very lives, even if the Ishmaelites, the Amalekites, the Ammonites, etc., are living their very lives right on it. Not to worry: the story explains them away. They're descended from our bad older brothers, the ones whose hearts the Lord looked into and rejected. They turned heathen and don't serve the one and only God, who is a jealous God and wants not only to be loved but to be loved alone. In this and in other things He acts as suspiciously human as any Olympian. See how He lets Moses' and David's flattery manipulate Him out of destroying us. He's arbitrary: touch His Ark, and though He, who knows all things, must know that it was courteously done, to keep it from falling, He strikes you dead on the spot. He chooses sides and has favorites among mortals—fortunately they are us.

Job has the solution: Don't think about it. God is not for us to think about. Were we there when He made leviathan?

No, but we were there at Sinai when He taught us the law by which we judge Him. It is we who learned the lesson of the ewe lamb which He sent the prophet Nathan to teach King David.

What is the lesson? King David has sinned against three of the Ten Commandments: he has coveted his neighbor's wife; he has committed adultery; he has caused a murder. That is not what the story takes him to task for. It's not that David has murdered but that (as Joab perfectly understands) he is going to fudge the blame. "It was you," the prophet Nathan tells him, "who slew Uriah the Hittite with the sword of the Ammonite." Nor does the story take up the matter of David's sexual impurity in general or adultery in particular. Why does the Lord send David a story about a man who steals a lamb for a dinner party out of the smallest imaginable sort of greediness? He doesn't want to kill one of his own.

A favorite story in my family annals suggests the sort of thing I think the prophet Nathan means David to understand. My young mother used to go shopping with a young neighboring mother who came over, one evening, to borrow a cup of vinegar. My mother said, "But you bought your own bottle." "I know," said the neighbor, "but it seems a shame to open mine when yours is already open." A minor sin, and a great shabbiness of soul.

The story shows a minor wrongdoing causing considerable grief. It shifts attention from the commission of the sin to the giving of pain. Notice that the story of the ewe lamb is not told with the Bible's usual restraint. It jerks a tear; it nudges the king to care. This is the only lamb in the Bible we get to know personally. It is little, a particular pet, brought up by hand, in the bosom, on the lap, sharing the bite out of that poor man's mouth. The law commands: You shall not steal. But story commands: You shall imagine the feelings of him from whom you steal. Story has the power to manipulate imagination. It makes the king imagine an affection felt by somebody who is not himself in a situation and condition unlike his own.

The king learns two things: to feel someone else's feelings as if they were his own, and to judge himself as if he were someone else. Before the story, David walks inside his sin like poor Pigpen inside his cloud of wavy lines, stinking to heaven and to everyone except himself. Those little black waves emanating from ourselves *are* ourselves. We look and we see ourselves looking just like ourselves, until the story holds the mirror up to our moral nature in the critical moment before we know who that is walking toward us. Remember the witch in the fairy tale who doesn't recognize the recounting of her wickedness and condemns the perpetrator to dance on the hot coals? David is enraged and says, "As the Lord lives, a man who does a thing like that deserves to die though he repays the value of the lamb four times over! He is a man without pity!"

That's when the prophet Nathan says to us, "That man is you."

When Hillel tells us not to do unto our neighbor what we don't want our neighbor to do unto us, he commits us to a truism we don't feelingly believe—that our neighbor feels and minds the same things we feel and mind, and to the same degree. We prefer Hillel's other advice: to look out for ourselves. We do that feelingly. We can feel only our self feeling. We do not, by definition, feel our neighbor's feelings and consequently don't, feelingly, believe that he has got any. That's natural. We naturally feel ourselves to be our story's point of view. There is no way for us not to feel ourselves to be its protagonist, until the creation of story. Story has the power to reverse nature. It surprises us into imagining our neighbor. Imagine if the rich man imagined being the poor! Would he go on taking from the man who has nothing even that which he has? And now imagine something more: imagine what we might do and what we might not do if we imagined the enemy, our brother Ishmaelite, Amalekite, Ammonite, or Moabite. Imagine if our enemy imagined us. It's against nature, but what if we told one another, what if we learned to hear, one another's story?

I KINGS

HARSH, HECTIC, AND FULL OF HOPE

Herbert Gold

I T IS TOLD IN THE BOOK OF SAMUEL THAT THE JEWISH PEOPLE DEMANDED
a king "like the other nations," although God and Samuel, God
speaking through the wisdom of Samuel, warned them of the danger
of tyranny. In a time of clamor and war—what time isn't?—they
insisted on the right to be like the others. The inevitability of fate is no help;
understanding is like a birdwing beating in a hurricane—merely brave.

The Book of Kings is the moving, dangerous, comic, and bloody
chronicle of what happens in history. The tone accepts disaster and stubbornly insists on survival. The lamp of God never quite goes out. Perhaps
it is also not without its tragic fundament. Genius and devotion, when we
wait long enough, lead to power. When power doesn't lead to corruption,
it leads to the failures of mortality, of inexorable time. Kings grow arrogant
and old, or feeble and incapable, even when maidens are put by their sides
to warm their sleep.

The First Book of Kings is violent and political; the telling of it is

---

The Jerusalem Bible used in this essay.

dense, like most of the Bible, except when it is not dense, and is very particular with the detail which brings us out of our distant reverence into the sudden presence of ardor, fear, groaning, suffering, triumph, the grit and sweat of a desert people making its special place in history. Piety gives way (bless poetry) to the passions of silence. The spaces between the words ring with the heavy breath of grief and hope.

Justice is a constant ideal in Kings I. Mercy is also an ideal. Neither one is continually achieved. The tribes lived in the real world of harsh gesture and temptations to treachery and connivance. Tenderness is not exempt from the demands of God and state. Should we look for a lesson? Or should we scale down our moral demands? Perhaps we should merely look for consolation in mankind's constant need to deal with his own character. Harshness and hectic willfulness are like the desert: the life extracted from them is not easy but it is vivid.

The chronicle begins with King David's last days. The sweet singer and hero is now an old man, "and though they laid coverlets over him, he could not keep warm." His servants thought they knew the remedy, the same one traditionally sought by Hollywood moguls and Chicago real-estate millionaires—"they searched for a beautiful girl throughout the territory of Israel." They found Abishag of Shunen; she qualified. "She looked after the king and waited on him, but the king had no intercourse with her."

In other words, he was *old.* But it seems that she kept him alive, because he was still able to foil his enemies, his rivals, the usurpers who planned to steal the succession. Handsome Adonijah, Haggith's son, made his plans and his sacrifices, rallied his brothers for treason—but not Solomon, of course, the rightful heir.

David had chosen his son Solomon. Bathsheba nagged at the old man, asking with rage and sarcasm, "How is it then that Adonijah is king?" This mother fought for her son. The meeting was well orchestrated. When she had finished challenging her allegedly impotent lord and master, the prophet Nathan entered and confirmed what Bathsheba had said. He did more than confirm the idea. He confirmed the rage wrapped in sarcasm. "Is this, then, your decree? Adonijah is to be king after me? He is the one who is to sit on my throne?"

Nathan didn't let David rest. "Is this with my lord the king's approval? Or have you not told those loyal to you who is to succeed to the throne of my lord the king?"

King David roused himself. He brought Bathsheba to him and swore to her that their son, Solomon, would succeed him. He had sworn to God; he swore to Bathsheba. He knew his time was near; he would appoint Solomon that very day.

Bathsheba cried out, "May my lord King David live for ever!"— forever exactly because he was assuring his succession in justice, forever in memory as a good king, which the king surely understood. In the space between her homage and his summoning of advisers, the prophet Nathan and the enforcer Benaiah, one can feel the long look passing between the two old lovers.

"Long live King Solomon!" Pipes played; shouts and rejoicing filled the air. And now they had to deal with the usurper Adonijah. Adonijah's partisans expected a massacre, but the style of Solomon was established with his first act of warning mercy. He did not kill his brother Adonijah. "Should he bear himself honorably, not one hair of his shall fall to the ground; but if he is found malicious, he shall die."

We know that Adonijah will not accept this intelligent mercy. Solomon knew it, too. His act was intended not merely to spare Adonijah but as a sign to the people of how King Solomon intended to rule. "Go to your house," he said to Adonijah, dismissing him.

David finally knew he was dying; now he accepted the end. No more than the Hollywood mogul or the Chicago real-estate millionaire could he alter the fate of all flesh with the most beautiful girl in the kingdom. Abishag slips into the shadows as David attends to his last business, counseling his son about the necessary vengeances in preserving his reign. He commands kindness and prudence; prudence sometimes takes precedence over kindness. The sweet singer had learned to be a ruler. David had promised he would not kill Shimei, but now he tells his son: "You will know how to deal with him."

Adonijah comes asking for trouble, pursuing a strange and fatal course. Presumably this handsome usurper could have his pick of the kingdom's maidens. Whom did he choose? He asked Bathsheba, the mother of his brother Solomon, for the hand of Abishag of Shunen in marriage. He asked his half-brother's mother to give him the last lover of his father. He asked the king to authorize his marriage to the last wife of his father. The usurper did not succeed David as king in Israel, but sought to succeed him as ruler of Abishag. The insult is complicated, subtle, and risky. His behavior made mere incest look banal. Surely he understood that this bland request meant to say that David was impotent when he chose Solomon.

King Solomon has been shown to be merciful; now he is shown to be swift in judgment. The officer Benaiah, whom we have met before, emerges as Solomon's executioner and hitman. "And King Solomon commissioned Benaiah son of Jehoiada to strike him down, and he died."

King Solomon spared Abiathar, at least temporarily, because he had shared David's hardships, but he deprived him of his priesthood. He sent Benaiah to Joab on another killing mission. Benaiah hesitated and asked King Solomon to confirm the sentence; Solomon did so. Benaiah returned and struck Joab down. Since Joab had killed the commanders of the armies of Israel and Judah, justice was done, and for the sake of peace. In filial piety, Solomon exclaimed: "May their blood come down on the head of Joab and his descendants for ever, but may David, his descendants, his dynasty, his throne, have peace for ever from Yahweh."

Solomon cemented his rule. He liked singing and sex; he had an appetite for power, too. While preaching an Aristotelian moderation in violence, he authorized violence. And he appointed his hitman, Benaiah, as head of the army.

There was one more necessary murder before the reign of peace could be inaugurated. Solomon sent Benaiah to punish Shimei. Solomon had promised Shimei that he could live in peace, despite the evil he had done David, if he would keep to his house in Jerusalem. Shimei agreed, and violated his oath, and therefore the obedient Benaiah "struck down Shimei, and he died."

The nation and King Solomon now seemed secure. An era of pleasure, security, justice, and architecture could begin. Solomon begged God for wisdom, "how to discern between good and evil," and this pleased God, because he did not ask for riches or vengeance against the enemies who remained. So of course God decided to give him riches and glory in addition to wisdom and a long life, and other goodies besides. Some of the additional rewards seemed to be entertainments, moral dramas, plays of power and mercy intertwined.

There followed a sunny interlude of piety and empire-building. Solomon married the Pharaoh's daughter—a precedent for many such moments in history, stealing the power of the oppressor. Solomon was doing it right. He bedded down this lady, making the kind of peace a kind of marriage can make.

The incident labeled "the wisdom of Solomon" is one of the best-known dramas in the Bible. Solomon offers two quarreling mothers the chance to retain half a baby each; the one who is willing to cut the child in half in order to assert her rights is clearly not a mother. Solomon's verdict and challenge is a precursor of Dean Swift's modest proposal to nourish the starving in Ireland by feeding them their children. Lenny Bruce might have played Solomon on this occasion. "Hey, you both want him? Get the knife, fellas—you can have a chop, lady, and you over there can have the drumstick."

While he was busy being wise, Solomon was also busy keeping Benaiah by his side as commander of the army. The king composed thousands of proverbs, over a thousand songs, and he knew about plants, animals, birds, reptiles, and fish. He entertained himself. He slept the peaceful sleep of a just man with all the wives he could use. He received gifts from other kings as rewards for his wisdom. And he kept Benaiah near.

He concluded treaties. He built the Temple; he furnished it. The book goes into great detail about architectural plans, decor, art objects. It is specific about the golden altar, the golden lampstands, the golden floral work, lamps, extinguishers of lamps, the basins, knives, bowls, censers of gold, the door sockets. All this work was for the glory of God and the pleasure of Solomon, who said:

> Yahweh has chosen to dwell in the thick cloud.
> Yes, I have built you a dwelling,
> a place for you to live in for ever.

This is not mere architecture, of course. Yahweh dwells in a cloud, but His law deserves embodiment. In his prayer, Solomon begged God to forgive His people, punish the guilty, reward the innocent. The Temple is only a temple. God's spirit is still where the people must dwell.

King Solomon continued with a most important request of God, and perhaps this best defines the Chosenness of Israel. He says: "And the foreigner too" should be granted the favor of God, if he is virtuous. He acknowledges both virtuous foreigners and sinful Jews, "for there is no man who does not sin." He asks forgiveness for the Jews in the light of repentance, favor for the non-Jews, "all the foreigner asks," if he acknowledges God.

As the son of David, Solomon pays homage to his father by carrying on his intention.

We can assume that Benaiah is still with him. He receives the visit of the queen of Sheba with the usual rewards to the man of power. "How happy your wives are!" says Sheba, and he is susceptible to this hint and flattery. He gives her various symbols of hospitality, including his body, which is not merely a symbol.

Riches pour in, just as God ordered—gold, silver, ivory, spices, horses, apes, and baboons. We can hear the usual royal jesting. As he aged, he took seven hundred wives, three hundred concubines, and my computer adds that up to a round thousand bed companions. He grew a little soft. He even allowed his foreign wives to build altars to their foreign gods.

This was not a good idea. God was slow to anger with such a good man, but when He did, He said that Solomon would have to be punished. He promised a Solomon-like punishment. He would lose his kingdom, but not until after his death. And his heirs would not lose the whole kingdom. His son would retain one tribe.

In other words, there was room for posthumous negotiation. God raised other kings and armies against Solomon, and expressed His grief along with His rage. He would humble the descendants of the blessed David, "but not for ever."

When Solomon died, the elders counseled virtue and fairness; during this golden age, the people had learned and would know how to respond. But King Rehoboam listened to rash young courtiers and decided, instead, to beat the people into submission. There were civil wars, religious and political splits; false gods were worshipped. False prophets betrayed the best history of Israel, and so there were wars, disasters, "even men in the country who were sacred prostitutes." Power corrupts, and so does luxury. King Asa of Judah tried to clean things up; he didn't last long enough; other kings continued on the brutal path. I would like to know why the chronicles include this detail about the struggle of Asa: *"In his old age, however, he suffered from a disease of the feet."* It recalls the disease of Philoctetes, whom the Greeks abandoned because of his gangrene until they needed his accurate bow. It's the sort of mysterious detail which makes bearable the recitation of kings, wars, murders, indulgences, this parade of noise and failure after the glory of David and Solomon. The great King Solomon had a flaw; no living man is flawless. God too often becomes angry, shows resentment; jealousy is His privilege.

Finally the time of Elijah came—a prophet who was both wise and efficacious. He kept busy telling the truth, asking favors of God, raising the apparently dead back into life, making eloquence. "How long," he asked the people, "do you mean to hobble first on one leg then on the other? If Yahweh is God, follow him. If Baal, follow him."

When the people stood there stubbornly, Elijah sighed and felt obliged to perform a miracle in order to prove which God is the true one. When the sullen and stubborn people witnessed his miracle, they turned on the false prophets of Baal. "Yahweh is God," they cried, "Yahweh is God." And under the guidance of Elijah, they slaughtered the false prophets in a ravine.

The proof of dominance of the one God is never finally accepted. It must be won in every generation against the temptations of the world. It's a living God; the struggle to believe is also a living thing—that is, susceptible to failure. God's jealousy, His demand of exclusivity, opposes something persistent in human nature. Ahab told Jezebel of the murder— it would be called "execution"—of the false prophets, and Jezebel swore her own vengeance. Elijah's God would not reassure him at once; He demanded the additional sacrifice of Elijah's fear. Elijah wandered in the desert wilderness.

Finally God relented and revealed His deepest nature. There was a shattering wind, there was an earthquake, there was a fire, but Yahweh did not speak out of the wind, the earthquake, or the fire. "After the fire came the sound of a gentle breeze," and here God speaks. He condemns those in Israel who worshipped Baal. He says it differently—*the mouths that have kissed him*—and He will spare the seven thousand who have been faithful.

Wars and treachery are not done. Ben-hadad of Aram says to King Ahab: Give me treasure; I'll spare your wives and children. Ahab consents, but then Ben-hadad demands his wives and children anyway. Ahab declares resistance and promises to destroy Israel. Ahab quotes a proverb: "The man who puts on his armor is not the one who can boast, but the man who takes it off." There was more clangor on the battlefields. Israel was fighting for its wives and children, and made Ben-hadad beg for his life.

The chronicle continues forever. The Kings cannot give up what is Israel's. When they don't do it right, the demanding Yahweh makes them pay and the kings have a gloomy fate. They are forbidden to abandon their wives and children, they cannot abandon their land, they are asked to be better than men in the state of nature. At the same time, their Jezebels tempt them to steal and curse and worship wrongly. God seldom punishes without some negotiation. When Ahab fails Him, yet humbles himself, God rewards him for his virtue and brings the disaster down only on his son. God's mercy is strict (some who love their sons might not think it mercy).

At last Judah and Israel reunite to fight for Ramoth-gilead. Again there are false prophets, raving about the light at the end of the tunnel, and again the nation marches off to conquer. Again there is one—the prophet Michaiah—who is lonely and correct and brings unpleasant news: that the false prophets lie, that Israel should not go off to this war. The messenger Michaiah is beaten and imprisoned. He waits, knowing Ahab's fate.

Ahab not only dies in the battle: the dogs lick up his blood; the prostitutes wash in it; Yahweh has spoken.

Kings continues. Jehoshaphat is pious and good and reigns; Ahaziah worships false gods and leads Israel into ignorance and vanity. History is tireless, and this chronicle tells us that learning from history is not easy. Temptation is stronger than learning, at least for many. When the kings and prophets are eloquent and right, they lead the people; when they are eloquent and wrong, they also lead them.

This may not be an entirely edifying story. Chronicles which are fair to human history hardly ever offer consistent consolation. Yet the entire account of blood and horror, treachery and revenge, does something to the metabolism—it keeps the reader, as it must have kept the ancient listeners, awake and lively. Finally there is forgiveness, because the people in question survives its own failures. Tenderness, both from God and by men, occasionally flashes through all the thrust of struggle. The telling of the story, the poetry and excitement, the lament and energy of its rhythms, persuade us that the worship of falseness will perish against the best genius of a people. Moral intention enlivens the poetic gift.

None of which means that failure and defeat can ever cease. The poets keep their vivid sight and hearing. A people lives by a vision of justice and virtue. Turmoil interrupts the vision. Story here is the ultimate lesson: both the changelessness and the variety of a vigorous history.

While sometimes the chroniclers seem to be preaching a simplified truth—attend to God, attend to Him attentively—they are in fact discovering this conclusion rather than arguing it, and therefore discovering other truths along the way. The book is poetry and drama, not sermon. The truth emerges in flickers out of the history and its rhetoric, with all the clinging meanings and implications beyond the primary duty and privilege. The one unramified God brings a subtle and ramified code. Each flawed hero meets the risks of finding his own right way while the supreme judge waits—and, inevitably, judges.

My own life seems short to me, yet I have been a participant/witness in five wars or revolutions: World War II, the Six Day War in Israel, the civil war over Biafra in Nigeria, the October War in Israel, and a revolutionary overthrow in Haiti. In each case, except for my service in the United States Army, I have met generals, politicians, and heroes who were given trust and an almost religious devotion by their followers. In each case they merited the devotion. They also earned an inevitable consequent degradation of esteem. The American leaders I know by reputation don't seem any different.

The history of Kings shows the wisdom of the chroniclers who learned what we must continually restudy, that generals and prophets are merely human, that the powerful turn vain, that only the ideal is perfect and the ideal exists only in the mind. Our kings are appointed by us and by themselves. But they will be measured in the eternal.

II KINGS

ON THE NATURE OF JEWISH REALISM

Alan Lelchuk

ERTAINLY THE INTELLIGENT GENERAL READER OF KINGS II WILL
quickly despair of seeking an interesting story, finding a sustaining character (despite Elijah), or enjoying the telling of the
history. The whole narrative is too choppy, too crammed with
lists and legacies of kings—some nineteen in the northern kingdom alone—
who reigned over the disunified states of Judah and Israel during the twilight
of the Jewish empire. There are too many wars, revolts, assassinations, names,
and enmities to keep up with—until, of course, the final destruction of the
city of Jerusalem by the Babylonian king Nebuchadnezzar and the painful
exile of the Jews to Babylonia, the grim climax at the end of the chapter.
And through all the jangling chaos and carnage there is no Solomon, as in
Kings I, or David, as in the two books of Samuel, for the reader to focus
on, and grasp on to, while the whole political and social ball of thread comes
unwound.

If the pleasure is not literary, then, is there another value, another

---

The King James Version of the Bible used in this essay.

135

vantage point to the chapter? To use a farfetched literary analogy, why is it that Melville, in *Moby Dick,* spends all of 150 pages, at least, discussing the importance of whaling in nineteenth-century America, and in the process deluges us with endless details and facts about ships, whales, blubber, oil, the whaling industry, etc., until the reader is surfeited with information and longs for the romance of the novel to emerge again? In a book about a crazy captain—the name Ahab naturally has its strong Kings echo, just as Melville's rhetoric has its emphatic Biblical cadences—chasing a white whale of mythic proportion (and semihuman intention), we may ask why it is that the author sees fit to overdose the reader with so many pages devoted to the factual and informational. Is the answer to be found, in significant part, in Melvillean obsessiveness *and* Melvillean realism; in other words, in the great writer's anchoring his larger, mythic text in the nitty-gritty of the actual, the palpable?

Perhaps the analogy is not so farfetched as I suggested, in the sense of Melville's disregarding the interests of the reader for his own purposes of realistic truthtelling. For the Jewish writers of the Bible, of course, were as interested in realistic truthtelling as they were in weaving a fascinating story or entertaining a reader or, even, narrating a didactic religious fable. What was real, no matter how unpleasant the message, story, or character, deserved to be given, described, laid out. Let the reader deal with it. And if part of that realism dealt with the mad and maddening imperfections of the best of kings (Saul, David), or the simple deficiencies of other great ones (Solomon), not to mention the inevitable perfidies of the ordinary kings (Jeroboam or Zachariah), so be it. And if you also had to admit, to acknowledge, that Jews living with Jews could (and did) evolve into a fierce tribe of murderous rivalries and self-destructive factionalism that could go on for centuries, finally leading to agonizing wound and exile, why, that, too, had to be stated, pronounced, confessed. Kings II is a compulsive telling of self-inflicted crippling, as well as a description of external siege, leading to long sorrow and decline.

While truthtelling of history dominates in Kings II, characterization is at a minimum, though we are occasionally reminded of the greats of the last few chapters. The mention of David occurs twice at least in Kings II, both times to allude to the straightforward goodness and glory of the great king. For example, referring to the good king Josiah, it is said in 22:2, "And he did that which was right in the sight of the Lord, and walked in all the way of David his father, and turned not aside to the right hand or to the left." This, in contrast to the evil ways of Josiah's predecessors in chapter 21, Manasseh and Amon, who, instead of following in David's way, built altars to Baal and other false idols. But is not this mention of David homage to only one side of that many-sided figure, that most human king?

For the portrait of David that is given in the Bible is not only a full one—unlike the miniportrayals of character in Kings II of Elijah and Elisha—but it is also a realistic portrait of a man, not the romanticized version of a demigod that one might expect of Jewish historians writing about one of their greatest leaders. (One has only to compare the story of Jesus in the New Testament with that of the Old Testament David to see the differences in realistic conception, and also the different levels of literary appeal.) Just as Kings II portrays a people in power in severe crisis primarily because of their own doing, so the story of David displays a man of enormous gifts constantly warring with himself, with his own public image and personal ideals of self-conduct, as well as with straightforward religious and ethical concepts of virtue and honor. If anything, David is not a straightforward model of moral excellence, or even a straight (or flat) character, predictable or conventional. The realism of the many pulls and twists of his personality, which seeks to reveal rather than camouflage his deep vulnerability and contradiction, makes him an especially interesting figure for us to contemplate.

He is modern—and Jewish Biblical, one might say—in his paradoxes and multidimensionality: his early banishment and yearning for homeland, his unquenchable sensuality and unceasing spirituality, his serious poetic and musical accomplishment alongside his shrewd guerrilla strategies and fierce military inclinations. He displeases his Lord while serving Him steadily, just misses being assassinated by mad King Saul and yet persists in loving his king, crudely takes the wife of one of his most loyal soldiers, and then, to cover up the adultery (and his guilt, perhaps), sends him out to the front lines to be killed. Is he out of control on purpose, this great king, or simply a slave to his passions on the spur of the moment?

A primitive boy he remains, that much is for sure, and it is a tribute to the writers of the Bible that they don't try to clean him up, so to speak, and make him over into something else, someone more "civilized." They allow him his fugitive emotions and primitive instincts, and these all too often dominate his actions, define him. So what if those embarrass his wife (Michal), disappoint his prophet (Nathan), frighten friends, and shame even his nasty general (Joab)? Within the primitive, however, there is plenty of room for cunning—jungle or street cunning, you might say—which, raised to a state level, is nicely called "political diplomacy." The long-feuding Jewish states were unified, and even became an empire, under this young shepherd boy. It did not hurt that he was a great warrior to boot, a man who obviously loved to fight and knew how to fight, from Goliath-killer to guerrilla rebel to chief-of-staff general. This spiritual king had as much instinct for the kill as love for the Lord, as much unfettered passion (for women for sure, and for Jonathan?) as controlled skill for poetical lament and composing. No scholarly wise man, no civilized dandy, no simple or refined king, this loose, lyrical Jewish boy.

The concept of character demonstrated in the portrait of David is a complex one indeed—just as it is with figures like Moses, of course, and Solomon, too, to a lesser degree—and it is enlarged, not reduced, by his acts of wrongdoing. To the dismay of religious purists and moralists, both ancient and modern, David was a bad boy. And he remained so, not progressing upward toward some higher level of morals once he was king, toward some re-evaluation of values and corrective shift in behavior, and maybe in personality. No such convenient setup, his fate or story. His character deepened, rather than changed, as his forty-year reign evolved.

The legendary situation with Bathsheba happens rather early in his royal role, and is emblematic. The paragraphs describing his lust for Bathsheba, his fulfillment of that lust, and his subsequent devilish dealing with the husband (Uriah) he has cuckolded, are blunt and remarkable in revealing his determined, willful sinning. In terms of perverse motive and twisted act, these passages (II Samuel, 11:2ff.) exhibit a realism that is as exacting as it is modern. And as a portrait of passion, passion gone awry and issuing in evil, the picture of David ranks up there with the characters of Shakespeare, Balzac, or Dostoevsky. The taking of Bathsheba is lust in action—no great sinning there, perhaps—but the rest of David's acts fulfill Sonnet 126's dire prophecies about its consequences. For after Bathsheba conceives, David starts turning the screws. His calling down of her husband (and his loyal soldier), Uriah, to see and test the man, is teasingly sadistic enough, and the

Bible writers prove their mettle by having Uriah prove his—namely, by not abandoning his comrades who are still suffering from the anguish of war. His refusal thus to heed David and return to his own comfortable house suits David's wants conveniently, as does his getting drunk. Now the king can fulfill his cruelest intention with rich royal reasoning. And then the vilest deceit, when David has this faithful servant, Uriah himself, deliver (unbeknownst to him) his own death warrant to General Joab, to have him sent to the front line of the battle. Has this king no conscience, no shame? This is not Lady Macbeth driving for power, but King David, the greatest of the Jewish kings, executing his will: a strange, perverse will (and greatness), no?

And it is a strange history to write, concerning one of your most legendary heroes, if you are one of the tribe, one of David's loyal servants probably, in any case a comrade to be sure, and not an enemy. Clearly, then, these Biblical writers had guts, fortitude, literary instinct, plus serious respect for the adult reader—not to mention the adultly religious Jew—and serious chutzpah, to draw so realistic a portrait of one of their finest. The result is a flesh-and-blood protagonist and a spellbinding story, filled with surprise twists of character and sudden turns of plot, not a pious tale of a good king held together by wooden scaffolding and leaden pieties. Historical material lends itself in this case to literary riches, somewhat similar to the uses of Old English history by Shakespeare.

That sense of psychological realism is later on enriched, of course, by the other depths of David, especially seen and felt, perhaps, in the severe anguish of the regal father for his rebel son, once the king discovers that Absalom has been brutally killed—no matter now that the boy had led a military revolt against the father. The death punishes David far worse than any military defeat, one senses: a lament which infuriates his general and embarrasses others ("O my son Absalom! my son, my son Absalom! would God I had died for thee, O Absalom, my son, my son!"). In such moments and scenes, the authors of the Bible raise David to Dostoevskian levels, an ancient hero with Jewish sides and modern depths (whereas, in Kings II, the stresses of reporting history overwhelm and reduce character, and a people's decline and disintegration become the ultimate focus of attention). Not for his rectitude is David to be remembered, though he showed that; not for his military genius, though he displayed that; not even for his brilliant governing abilities, though history records that well; but precisely for those depths.

At least for me, anyway, the attraction started early: when I was a boy of eight or nine and reading Jewish *geshichte* in my Sholem Aleichem school in Brooklyn. There, in that cozy basement room with the small slanting wooden desks, my teacher, Lehrer Goichberg, first introduced me to the vigor and intrigue of that young Jewish shepherd boy who became a king and united the Jewish people. If I was charmed by his slingshot prowess (and immediately made my own out of rubber band and balsam wood, using a round stone for shot against my Goliath, an old rusted oil tank on our vacant lot), I was perplexed by much else. But, curiously enough, I felt an instinctive sympathy with his bizarre relationship with Saul, wanting desperately to have the old king's love and being constantly refused it and even, because of that wanting, put into personal jeopardy. It resembled, in some fashion, my relationship with my own father, who had been kindly toward me until I was five and then seemed to turn against me, in mad, violent spurts. How did the Bible writers understand that? I wondered. And what a complicated fellow this David was, so much more mysterious, I thought, than Moses or Solomon. I remember writing, in my boy's Yiddish, a small essay about David in which I tried to speak about that mystery. And although the Lehrer praised it, he never did know that I kept half of the truth back, about my secret family resemblance.

David as a tribal hero says something to me about the Jewish conception of truth and the Jewish ability to be realistic. The writers of the Bible are impressive in seeking both, weaving in the complex characters and fantastic history amid the weighty pressures of Yahweh theology and religious didacticism. In other words, the Old Testament offers much wider scope and tolerance, displays implicitly much more respect for the intelligent reader, be he secular or religious, than other, more narrowly Orthodox texts (for example, the Koran or the New Testament). Is it any surprise that high literary names inevitably have come to mind here in my consideration?

For me, too, later on as a novelist, the unflinching spirit of David and Jewish realism has meant something significant and suggestive. In my work, I have tried not to shy away from, gloss over, or euphemize the mischievous and confusing realities of our time, our place—pursuing some shard of truth beneath the layers of cultural decadence and detritus, and sometimes coming up empty-handed. No doubt, too, that the problem of the real for the contemporary writer, our truest historian, is also a thorny one, especially, perhaps, in our country, where so much that is real is fantastic and so much that is extraordinary is routine; where trying to trace the path of one invariably leads to the other, though both intersect at the same corner of social upheaval and individual crisis. In two novels, for example, I have portrayed a woman adventurer in the netherworld of American city life who crosses boundaries of reason, good sense, and moral tradition to a land reserved for the daring, the amoral, the innocent. Such leaps of dimension are not always comprehensible or credible to the uninitiated, just as the truths brought back, if any, are not always palatable. But that is the way of literature, and the way of the Jewish Bible as I read it. To shift focus, the writer himself often feels lost today between boundaries, unsure of his place or role, his principles or paths. Indeed, the writer as a protagonist wandering lost in a maze of illusory surfaces and bewildering paradoxes forms the stuff of some of our very best modern novels.

As I said earlier, the climax of Kings II is the destruction of the Temple and the burning of the city of Jerusalem and the carrying away of the Jews to Babylonia. Thus, the hard era of the first dispersion and exile begins, to last fifty years and to presage the next destruction, dispersion, and much more bitter exile—some six hundred years later—which will last nearly two thousand years. This national sorrow is the final outcome of the years of civic strife and internecine warfare, when the kingdoms of Judah and Israel were divided, about 850 B.C.E. Kings II chronicles this fighting between Jews and Jews, though it sacrifices story interest for historical listings. (The chronicling of the next Jewish civil war, leading to the Roman sacking of the city in 70 C.E., is much more effectively told by Josephus, and therefore a far easier lesson to imbibe for contemporary Jews anxious about the situation in Israel today.) The last few chapters, however, dealing with the subsequent sieges by the Assyrians and then by the Babylonians, are powerful reading. The realism here is hard and relentless, the prose style plain and unadorned, and the reader is persuaded, if not assaulted, by the specifics of the tragedy.

I quote at some length to display this realistic, unadorned storytelling:

And it came to pass in the ninth year of his reign, in the tenth month, in the tenth day of the month, that Nebuchadnezzar king of Babylon came, he, and all his host, against Jerusalem, and pitched against it; and they built forts against it round about.

And the city was besieged unto the eleventh year of king Zedekiah. And on the ninth day of the fourth month the famine prevailed in the city, and there was no bread for the people of the land.

And the city was broken up, and all the men of war fled by night by the way of the gate between two walls, which is by the king's garden: (now the Chaldees were against the city round about:) and the king went the way toward the plain. And the army of the Chaldees pursued after the king, and overtook him in the plains of Jericho: and all his army were scattered from him. So they took the king, and brought him to the king of Babylon to Riblah; and they gave judgment upon him. And they slew the sons of Zedekiah before his eyes, and put out the eyes of Zedekiah, and bound him with fetters of brass, and carried him to Babylon.

And in the fifth month, on the seventh day of the month, which is the nineteenth year of king Nebuchadnezzar king of Babylon, came Nebuzaradan, captain of the guard, a servant of the king of Babylon, unto Jerusalem: And he burnt the house of the Lord, and the king's house, and all the houses of Jerusalem, and every great man's house burnt with fire. And all the army of the Chaldees, that were with the captain of the guard, broke down the walls of Jerusalem round about. Now the rest of the people that were left in the city, and the fugitives that fell away to the king of Babylon, with the remnant of the multitude, did Nebuzaradan the captain of the guard carry away. But the captain of the guard left of the poor of the land to be vinedressers and husbandmen. And the pillars of brass that were in the house of the Lord, and the bases, and the brazen sea that was in the house of the Lord, did the Chaldees break in pieces, and carried the brass of them to Babylon. And the pots, and shovels, and the snuffers, and the spoons, and the vessels of brass wherewith they ministered, took they away. And the firepans, and the bowls, and such things as were of gold, in gold, and of silver, in silver, the captain of the guard took away.

. . .

And as for the people that remained in the land of Judah, whom Nebuchadnezzar king of Babylon had left, even over them he made Gedaliah the son of Ahikam, the son of Shaphan, ruler. But it came to pass in the seventh month, that Ishmael the son of Nethaniah, the son of Elishama, of the seed royal, came, and ten men with him, and smote Gedaliah, that he died, and the Jews and the Chaldees that were with him at Mizpah. And all the people, both small and great, and the captains of the armies, arose, and came to Egypt: for they were afraid of the Chaldees.

And it came to pass in the seven and thirtieth year of the captivity of Jehoiachin king of Judah, in the twelfth month, on the seven and twentieth day of the month, that Evil-merodach king of Babylon in the year that he began to reign did lift up the head of Jehoiachin king of Judah out of prison; And he spake kindly to him, and set his throne above the throne of the kings that were with him in Babylon; And changed his prison garments: and he did eat bread continually before him all the days of his life. And his allowance was a continual allowance given him of the king, a daily rate for every day of his life.   [II Kings 25]

So ends Kings II, on the note of distant but intimate pathos. Before that, we have had our closeup view and detailing of a city's sacking and a nation's fall and disorder. What is left unspoken, of course, is the sorrow of the soul of the people. That sort of emotion is left for the reader to experience, and melodrama is avoided. As in other effective narrative moments and scenes of the Bible, where brevity rules, the reader is implicitly summoned to take part, fill in. After the climax of vast communal catastrophe, the focus narrows to the personal, and the time shifts to years later. The intensity of high tragedy has receded, replaced by the poignancy of futile repose. The shrewd strategy of the narrative is apparent here, it seems to me, where national disaster is realistically described, and de-dramatized, as it were, to court the more sophisticated reader. A little like the way Kleist would do it in one of those magical stories mingling the real with the fabulous. So here we are, back to literary resonance even where it seemed, to the present writer, too, most unlikely.

ISAIAH

Robert Pinsky

I

*The vision of Isaiah the son of Amoz, which he saw concerning Judah and
Jerusalem in the days of Uzziah, Jotham, Ahaz and Hezekiah, kings of Judah.*

*Hear, O heavens, and give ear, O earth: for the Lord hath spoken. I have
nourished and brought up children, and they have rebelled against me.*

[Isaiah 1:1–2]

THUS BEGINS THE FIRST AND GREATEST OF THE BOOKS OF THE
prophets: with visionary authority, royal names, proud
genealogy, cosmic scope, and an indictment of the rebellious
children of the Lord.

My grandfather Pinsky's disregard for the practice of Judaism as a
religion was so calm and perfect that he never, to my knowledge, had any
occasion to express his contempt for piety and rabbi-craft—except implicitly, by living his profane and glamorous life. He was a professional boxer
and then a bootlegger, an arrogant young tough born to an immigrant
laborer's family in the coarse, combative America of James Cagney movies.
Maybe his own grandparents had sold vodka to Polish peasants. When I
knew him, he owned the Broadway Tavern, a horseplayer's and downtown
bar on the main street of Long Branch, the New Jersey Shore town where
I grew up. Many of Long Branch's town officials, and all of its senior police
force, had been Grandpa Dave's colleagues during the gangster days of
Prohibition.

The King James Version and the Revised Standard Version of the Bible used in this essay.

He had a Protestant wife, his third. Her name was Della Lawyer, and he lived with her for many years before they were married. At Christmas, his five children—my aunts and uncles, a confusing mix, with different mothers and religions—came, some of them with their own children, to his neat brick house for dinner. He always had a ten-foot Christmas tree. He drove Packards, and when I was very small he introduced me to Jack Dempsey.

If you told Grandpa Dave that he was in any sense not Jewish, or not Jewish enough, probably he would laugh. If you suggested that he was ashamed of being Jewish, he would be ready to punch you in the face. I cannot think of him as "assimilated," still less as a "non-believer." Assimilation suggests protective resemblance to some secure cultural middle, not Grandpa Dave's aggressive ways out on the raffish, sometimes criminal, fringes. Belief is not the issue. Technically speaking, I would define him as an idolator.

His ways are described by the words of Isaiah 2, "they please themselves in the children of strangers," and "they worship the work of their own hands, that which their own fingers have made." His soul was given to the attractions of the world, the world of the senses, the world made by man. Isaiah 2 concludes, with magnificent curtness, "Cease ye from man, whose breath is in his nostrils: for wherein is he to be accounted of?" This is not mere asceticism, which is based on denial, but the transcendence of idolatry. Grandpa Dave stood for the immense beauty and power of idolatry, the adoration of all that can be made and enjoyed by the human body, with breath in its nostrils.

But we—my mother and father and we children—were Orthodox, because of my mother's family. That is, we were nominally Orthodox; we kept kosher, and belonged to the Orthodox synagogue, where I was taught to chant by rote the Hebrew sounds of my Haftorah, the portion from the Books of the Prophets to be read on the Sabbath of a boy's Bar Mitzvah. Mine was a special Haftorah for the conjunction of the Sabbath and the new moon, Isaiah 66: the exalted, terrifying, and punitive concluding chapter, though nobody told me it was Isaiah, or what the words meant.

Laboriously through the hot summer of my final preparation I chanted after the teacher's voice, phrase by phrase. *"Kay aumar adashem, hashawmayim keesee: es bawnehaw."* Thus, in my first encounter with great poetry, I was deaf and blind to it. My Hebrew vocabulary was too small to keep up with the original, and Hebrew school does not use the language of the King James translation, in which my Haftorah begins:

Thus saith the Lord, The Heaven is my throne, and the earth is my footstool: where is the house that ye build unto me? and where is the place of my rest?

    For all those things hath mine hand made, and all those things have been, saith the Lord: but to this man will I look, even to him that is poor and of a contrite spirit, and trembleth at my word.   [66:1–2]

If I have made everything you see, says God in the syllables I studied, then where in the world of the senses could you contrive to build a place for Me? Architecture is futile. Humility, a spirit apt for contrition, and fearfulness will prevail.

    Moreover, worship itself may fail. In fatigue and boredom, I was curious enough to look at the *en face* translation of the Hebrew into the stilted, Victorian English of the Jewish prayer book. In the King James, the next verse of my Haftorah reads:

He that killeth an ox is as if he slew a man; he that sacrificeth a lamb, as if he cut off a dog's neck; he that offereth an oblation, as if he offered swine's blood; he that burneth incense, as if he blessed an idol. Yea, they have chosen their own ways, and their soul delighteth in their abominations.   [66:3]

Autocratic; ardent and monolithic; specific and categorical: this is the voice of Spirit, speaking here in the burning cadences, the harsh monosyllables, and the rolling Latinate inventions of the English language. All forms of worship and ritual uninformed by itself, says that Spirit or voice, amount to idolatry. It is the uncompromising voice of spiritual authority. In Isaiah, that voice is so strong I could hear its powerful demand, though not its beauty, through the muffling translation and the rote learning. If Grandpa Dave represented the allure of the secular world, his adversary was not God—and certainly was not my mother's father, mild Grandpa Eisenberg— but that voice. As soon as possible, I turned away from it toward the larger world, where I eventually heard it again—clearer, and more demanding than ever—in Milton, Blake and Whitman.

    But first of all, it was the voice of Isaiah. And its indictment of failed or unacceptable worship unites the three authors (or compilations) identified by scholarship: First Isaiah, the aristocratic moralist-courtier of chapters 1–39; Second Isaiah, the dark, lyrical Exile poet of 40–55; and the post-Exilic Third Isaiah of my Haftorah. Wrong or misguided worship unites these three writings thematically, a driving force underlying the book's diverse materials—political, visionary, liturgical.

For instance, I was proud that my Haftorah was astronomically distinguished, by the conjunction of the Sabbath and the new moon. And therefore, if I had known what the verse meant, and known that it was the penultimate verse of all Isaiah, I might have relished singing Third Isaiah's "And it shall come to pass, that from one new moon to another, and from one sabbath to another, shall all flesh come to worship before me, saith the Lord."

But, on the other hand, I might have found an ironic indictment of what I was doing in the first chapter of the prophet. There, First Isaiah adumbrates the dog's neck, the swine's blood, the repellent idol of his successor, associating them with the special Sabbath in which I took a little pride of a personal kind:

Bring no more vain oblations; incense is an abomination unto me; the new moons and sabbaths, the calling of assemblies, I cannot away with, it is iniquity, even the solemn meeting.

Your new moons and your appointed feasts my soul hateth; they are a trouble unto me; I am weary to bear them.   [1:13–14]

The hollowness, foppery, or degeneracy of worship is no better here than the haughty daughters of Zion in chapter 3 who "walk with stretched forth necks and wanton eyes, walking and mincing as they go, and making a tinkling with their feet," and whose chains, bracelets, mufflers, bonnets, leg ornaments, headbands, earrings, crisping pins, wimples, hoods, fine linen, stomachers, veils, and tinkling ornaments the courtier-prophet catalogues and denounces, to be punished in commensurate detail with scabs, denuded private parts, baldness, burning rashes, and stinks.

Perhaps empty worship is even worse than those mere worldly vanities. But it also resembles them: I was taught to chant, without knowing the meaning of the words I chanted, a fierce denunciation of hollow worship. The new moons and appointed feasts and hollow oblations make God tired.

His soul hates them. Singing the words of this denunciation without understanding them, I was committing a kind of idolatry, less attractive and more
tiring—to me as well as to God—than the kind practiced by the daughters
of Zion, or Grandpa Dave.

But there is something too obvious, and even heartless, about that
inviting irony. It would be cruel to blame me, cruel to blame the old men
who ran the small-town synagogue. They were immigrants without much
money or knowledge of the world or education among them. Some had
been in concentration camps. Doubtless, they were not very comfortable
with Hebrew themselves. The language they felt at home in was Yiddish,
and I could speak only English. The man these elders paid to teach me was
kind, though sometimes impatient, and he was fighting against the worldly
forces that had entered me—through the air, through our nostrils—two
generations before: the tinkling ornaments, the work of human hands, "that
which their fingers have made," the pleasures of the children of strangers,
the veils and wimples, the secular incense and music of Saturday mornings
outside, in a small town on the ocean. The Saturday-morning service, in the
yellow synagogue on Second Avenue in Long Branch, went from nine
o'clock to some time after noon. Outside, the shadows of idols grew shorter
in the sun. Italian girls in adorable Communion dresses came to Saint
Anthony's across the street, and went.

My teacher, two generations too late for an ardent communal piety,
and a generation too early for the intellectual savor of literature and ideas,
could hardly avoid the blind-rote performance I have called idolatrous,
hateful to God in the very words I was trained to mouth. In Brooklyn, in
a big vigorous traditional Jewish community, boys could—perhaps—learn
the spirit demanded by Isaiah. Or in some affluent, enlightened place Jewish
children of both sexes might be encouraged as part of their religious training
to understand the meaning of sacred texts, in a literary way. In my community, where the old men and young boys conducted the Sabbaths, neither
way was open. The old men had succeeded spectacularly in adjusting to
American culture, in a secular way—the progeny of Long Branch's Jewish
shopkeepers included, in my father's generation, Norman Mailer, the literary
critic M. H. Abrams, the pianist Julius Katchen, the actor Jeff Chandler,
along with doctors, lawyers, business people. But in a religious way, they
could not seem to evade the indictment of the prophet.

The characteristic Jewish falling-away from the faith—a drifting to-

ward the sweets of the world, so different from the tormented process
described by James Joyce, or a Protestant "crisis of belief"—seems to me in
a way to reflect this dogged, passionate, fumbling way of cleaving to the
faith. In both movements, the cleaving and the drifting away, the essence
is something deferred, not present, certainly not in the actual flesh. Its very
name is only named, never uttered. Grandpa Dave and the "Moorish"
synagogue of yellow sandstone (nowadays it houses a Puerto Rican Baptist
church) occupy different spaces in the same void between practice and spirit.
The Book of Isaiah is a great poem of that void, though it is also more.

II

Astoundingly, it is in the very nature of Isaiah's call to prophecy—an
integral part of his first contract with God—that his prophecy will be
spurned. Bad worship and idolatry are Isaiah's dramatic materials. The idea
toward which these materials churn is the inception of God's kingdom on
earth; but the poem's emotion and movement grow with overwhelming
force from the idea that the very words we read have been destined to go
unheeded until the promised end, and that our worship will be false.

The relevant passage is the autobiographical chapter 6, which begins
with a melding of the circumstantial and the marvelous:

In the year that king Uzziah died I saw also the Lord sitting upon a throne, high and
lifted up, and his train filled the temple.

Above it stood the seraphims; each one had six wings; with twain he covered his
face, and with twain he covered his feet, and with twain he did fly.

And one cried unto another, and said, Holy, holy, holy, is the Lord of hosts: the
whole earth is full of his glory.   [6:1–3]

Isaiah's first response to this vision is terror: "Woe is me, for I am undone;
because I am a man of unclean lips, and I dwell in the midst of a people
of unclean lips: for mine eyes have seen the King, the Lord of Hosts" (6:5).
But a seraph places a live coal from the altar upon Isaiah's lips, purifying
him of iniquity and sin, so that when the Lord asks, "Whom shall I send,"
the prophet answers, "Here am I; send me."

Between the circumstantial and the marvelous, in the actual temple with its altar, distraught and "unclean" at the sight of God, purified by an image of pain and muteness, the new prophet receives a strange charge:

And he said, Go, and tell this people, Hear ye indeed, but understand not; and see ye indeed, but perceive not.

    Make the heart of this people fat, and make their ears heavy, and shut their eyes; lest they see with their eyes, and hear with their ears, and understand with their heart, and convert, and be healed. [6:10]

The verbs "hear," "understand not," "see," and "perceive not" are imperatives, the challenge or taunt of God, transmitted by the prophet, to his people. The Revised Standard renders the passage so as to make the imperatives even clearer:

> And he said, "Go, and say to this people:
>   Hear and hear, but do not understand;
>   see and see, but do not perceive.
> Make the heart of this people fat,
>   and their ears heavy,
>   and shut their eyes;
> lest they see with their eyes,
>   and hear with their ears,
> and understand with their hearts,
>   and turn and be healed."

This is supremely strange. The deafness and blindness are not an expectation, nor are they even described here as the strange punishments for past deafness and blindness that logic would make them. Strange retribution: but even stranger as the first charge for a prophet, at the beginning of his career. Isaiah's mission is to prophesy to people who must be made to feel, to see, and to hear in the wrong way, to disregard his message. Heedlessness and bad worship are their destiny.

    This bleak beginning can only be the phase of a process. Isaiah responds to the Lord by asking how long that phase must last:

Then said I, Lord, how long? And he answered, Until the cities be wasted without inhabitant, and the houses without man, and the land be utterly desolate,

    And the Lord have removed men far away, and there be a great forsaking in the midst of the land.

But yet in it shall be a tenth, and it shall return, and shall be eaten: as a teil tree, and as an oak, whose substance is in them, when they cast their leaves: so the holy seed shall be the substance thereof.   [6:11–13]

In the massive, eschatological scale of this answer, invoking the immensity of time as a response to Isaiah's personal mission and fate, lies the difference between truth and prophecy, a difference of degree. The utter strangeness of the six-winged seraphim—dragonflies, griffins, hovering and hiding their legs and faces—encloses in an image the inscrutable moral and historical journey to final things. These are the creatures that bring the searing, paradoxically enabling fire of conscience to the prophet's lips, within the actual walls of the familiar, doomed Temple.

The mighty scale of prophecy, contrasted by Isaiah with the legal exactions, the rituals, the hypocrisies, the political considerations, the vanities, of daily life, was invisible to me, the undiligent student of poor exiles. Only the sensual force of poetry could forge and convey the immensity of that vision; in this sense the prophet had to be a poet. But in Hebrew translation class we limped endlessly through Genesis, without applying our small abilities elsewhere. That eschatological scale, which in Isaiah extends both apocalyptic destruction and the salvation of New Jerusalem to the whole world ("Look unto me, and be ye saved, all the ends of the earth" [45:22]), explains and justifies the obdurate, negative terms of the prophet's charge. Isaiah gives his son the name "A-Remnant-Will-Return," recognizing the immense devastation that must precede the certain, promised end. Though a remnant will return, the final redemption will be universal, global.

The cosmic scope, in a literary way, counterbalances the local, even familial rhythms of indictment and promise, threats and praises. And in a historical way, it is conceivable that Isaiah's vision of "a great forsaking," decimation upon decimation, could offer the imagination a frame for the still-recent Nazi horrors in Europe, indelible but vague nightmare. (Could my attraction to Grandpa Dave's violence be partly a reaction to those unsettling newsreel images of helplessness?) I don't mean the repulsive idea of a just punishment by Holocaust—an idea that also happens to clash with Isaiah's lucid, cosmic fatalism—but something more like a stretching of the imagination to enable it for the dimensions of actual knowledge. This is one definition of poetry.

Certainly, Isaiah offers something like a commensurate poetry of cata-
clysm:

> For wickedness burneth as the fire: it shall devour the briers and thorns, and shall
> kindle in the thickets of the forest, and they shall mount up like the lifting up of
> smoke.
> Through the wrath of the Lord of hosts is the land darkened, and the people
> shall be as the fuel of the fire: no man shall spare his brother.
> And he shall snatch on the right hand, and be hungry, and he shall eat on the
> left hand, and they shall not be satisfied: they shall eat every man the flesh of his own
> arm.   [9:18–20]

This vision underlies and vivifies the idea of the remnant that will return
as a seed. It will return when the wolf lies down with the lamb and the lion
eats straw like the ox. "Their children also shall be dashed to pieces before
their eyes; their houses shall be spoiled and their wives ravished" (13:16).
Chapters 24–27 have been nicknamed by scholarship "The Little Apocalypse." The apocalyptic action within the whole of Isaiah springs first of all
from universal destruction: "Therefore hath the curse devoured the earth,
and they that dwell therein are desolate: therefore the inhabitants of the earth
are burned, and few men left" (24:6).

This destructive movement leads to two nearly opposed themes. First,
God's will is punitive and urgent: "For behold, the Lord cometh out of his
place to punish the inhabitants of the earth for their iniquity: the earth also
shall disclose her blood, and shall no more cover her slain" (26:21). Second,
God's will is ultimately impenetrable and mysterious: "For the Lord shall
rise up as in Mount Perazim, he shall be wroth as in the valley of Gibeon,
that he may do his work, his strange work, and bring to pass his act, his
strange act."

Again, only the conviction of poetry can suspend these two ideas,
God's just retribution and God's impenetrable "strangeness," in a single
action. The idolatrous makers, the smith and carpenter of graven images in
chapter 44, ought to recognize that worshipping the residue of firewood,
their own handiwork, is sacrilege. But they have been blinded: "none
considereth in his heart, neither is there knowledge or understanding to say,
I have burned part of it in the fire; yea, also have I baked bread on the coals

thereof; I have roasted flesh and eaten it: and shall I make the residue thereof
an abomination? Shall I fall down to the stock of a tree?" (44:19). The reason
for this folly echoes Isaiah's call to prophecy in chapter 6: "They have not
known nor understood: for he hath shut their eyes, that they cannot see; and
their hearts, that they cannot understand" (44:18). At the promised end, the
skies will open and pour down righteousness in as universal, sudden, and
"strange" a manner as this terrible blindness and deafness. God will blot out
transgressions, and a remnant will return, in a redemption of horror and
violence on the unthinkable level of the *eschaton,* the end of time. In the
clearest of terms:

I form the light, and create darkness: I make peace and create evil:
I the Lord do all these things.   [45:7]

This God, who will create a new heaven and a new earth, so that the former
will not be remembered, is the God of last things. He can hold the horrors
of history and the abominations of idolatry, lip service, and hypocrisy in
his transcendent gaze. It is prophetic poetry that makes Him possible, in all
His apparent contradictions. The ultimate prophecy requires that it go
unheard. The *eschaton,* the idea of the end of time, seems to require, for
conviction, temporal embodiment. (For some Christians, Isaiah is the Old
Testament book that most clearly presages incarnation and Jesus Christ.)
Apocalypse has its profound meaning in the physical realm of the body, not
that of the Word. The Word is already eternal, the violent end of time will
not transform it; the body, with breath in its nostrils, the inhabitant of time,
will be transformed utterly.

God's glory, in Isaiah, is both unfathomable and also a physical glory.
If this were not so, the ridicule of the idolatrous smith and carpenter,
worshipping leftover firewood, would lose its force. This glory is embodied
by the prophet in many ways—in terrifying visions, in acts of worship, in
the Temple—but most continually in poetry, the physical art of poetry. In
the sense that it is the art that pulls verbal abstraction into its bodily frame,
poetry is the most insistently physical art.

Physical art is precisely what my synagogue lacked. Poor, beleaguered,
displaced, deprived of architecture by history, deprived with one exception
of the physical drama and elegance that depend upon possession of a place,

and deprived even of mere vulgar prosperity, the Jews of Long Branch could supply, in the place of a shining physical glory, only the passionate but colorless light of observance.

The one exception was cantorial singing. Its mournful beauty was indeed embodied, unforgettably, by cantors the congregation hired for the High Holy Days, though the goal was to find a permanent *chazen*. Sometimes a man would come to Long Branch for a few months, until a better position turned up or he was let go for some defect of character or terrible habit. They sang like angels, and carried themselves with the neurotic pride of sickly bullfighters—or of the artists that they were. What they sang was a plaintive courtship between suffering and beauty. Though the congregation liked to criticize and compare their work, the least of them could bring tears to our eyes.

The old men imitated them, praying according to Jewish custom aloud but not in unison, a flamboyant, grotesque howling and muttering, the cantorial dandyism of various parts of Europe aped and distorted. Near the end of the three-hour service they let themselves go wildly in an orgy of competing trills, flourishes, barks, and whimpers. Then they crowded the stairs to the basement, where they pressed and pushed around the postservice Sabbath feast of herring, bread, sponge cake, chick peas and the Seagram's 7 they called "schnapps." Grandpa Dave, in contrast, sometimes showed up in the morning before I left for school, to take me for a day of authorized hooky-playing. He took me to New York for lunch at a good restaurant, and always bought me a new pair of shoes. His capacity for grief did not show. We drove to the city in his Packard, which was the same pearl-gray as his hat. The steering wheel was ivory.

III

There were words in Hebrew of which I did learn the meaning—a central part of the liturgy that was immensely different from the apocalyptic force of my Haftorah in Isaiah. This opposition has a historical parallel which I can only begin, dimly, to understand.

Apparently, historical Judaism—as long ago as the time of the Essenes and early Christians—turned away from the emphasis upon eschatology, upon a God who created light and darkness, whose New World will efface all memory of the old. In *A History of Religious Ideas,* Mircea Eliade describes the replacement of apocalyptic thought by legal thought, the "glorification of the Torah." Eliade quotes the rabbi who maintained that the existence of the world depended on the fact that Israel accepts Torah. In Eliade's words, "The immutability of the Torah and the triumph of legalism together put an end to eschatological hopes." He quotes Hengel's *Judaism and Hellenism:* "Even apocalyptic literature gradually died out and was replaced by Jewish mysticism." This seems an exaggeration, neglecting Jewish mysticism concerned with final things, from the Essenes to the modern period. But even Gershom Scholem, in *Major Trends of Jewish Mysticism,* speaks of a "lack of apocalyptic elements in the Messianic conception of Hasidism." Scholem also refers, in a tantalizing phrase, to "apocalyptic nostalgia" as a powerful motive force in *Merkabah* mysticism.

The words I can remember translating are those of the *Shema,* the liturgical cornerstone of daily observance. The *Shema* is a call, not to the apocalypse or the New Jerusalem, but to daily faith. Its main body is Deuteronomy 6:4–9. In the English of the Weekday Prayer Book:

Hear, O Israel, the Lord our God, the Lord is One. Praised be this glorious sovereignty for ever and ever.

You shall love the Lord your God with all your heart, with all your soul, and with all your might. These words which I command you this day shall be in your heart. You shall teach them diligently to your children. You shall talk about them at home and abroad, night and day. You shall bind them as a sign upon your hand; they shall be as frontlets between your eyes, and you shall inscribe them on the doorposts of your homes and upon your gates.

The power of this is the verbal power of law. These terms describe the force of the reiterated "all" and "all," the uncompromising "shall," the blanketing pairs "home and abroad," "night and day." But I mean also the exacting, intimate legal force of the document's utterance: *These words which I command you this day.* This is a contract to be honored immediately, not a prophecy to which ears and hearts will be made fat.

I think that to a child with even an eye turned toward the secular world, it demands an impossibility. In contrast, the pathos of God's misplaced care, in Isaiah 5, assumes bad worship, and gives it an emotional place:

Now I will sing to my well-beloved a song of my beloved touching his vineyard. My well beloved hath a vineyard in a very fruitful hill:

And he fenced it, and gathered out the stones thereof, and planted it with the choicest vine, and built a tower in the midst of it, and also made a winepress therein: and he looked that it should bring forth grapes, and it brought forth wild grapes.

And now, O inhabitants of Jerusalem, and men of Judah, judge, I pray you, betwixt me and my vineyard.

These lyrical lines are spoken as by one who, stricken with conscience, had his lips cauterized by a live coal, speaking in a transformed and transforming way. The contractual poetry of the *Shema* is like the voice of God, preceding conscience but engendering it. It is a solemn statement of obligation, and the duties it exacts—to love God entirely, constantly, demonstrably—are not exactly impossible. The devout do perform them. But unlike Isaiah's drama of the vineyard, the *Shema* does not admit failure. Isaiah's beloved God expends care, and expects a good harvest, but instead gets wild grapes. Judgment and sorrow will follow; ultimately apocalypse, the one hope, will follow, and the remnant and the New Jerusalem. But the wild grapes have a place in this drama. The *Shema* is immediate: *These words which I command you this day.*

That command engenders not despair, but a kind of shrug, in the less than totally devout. This is a practical matter: one is supposed to pray each day, to bind the literal leather thongs, bearing the black boxes containing sacred words, around one's arm and head while praying. This is a symbol of the mental and verbal devotion that is also a practical matter: *You shall talk about them at home and abroad, night and day.* Such a level of observance, though it omits the role and concept of wild grapes altogether, is bracing, even in a dry way inspiring. It becomes a standard of devotion, saluted and abandoned.

Once one has entertained that harsh standard, a formal or institutional compromise may seem impossible. Our rabbi's frequent sermons denouncing Long Branch's infant but prosperous Reform temple merely reinforced this feeling. We blew the *shofar;* they kept this ram's-horn instrument in a glass case, with a label explaining that their ancestors blew it. I had heard the Reform rabbi, Dr. Tartufkovich, speak at a couple of high-school interfaith assemblies. I judged him unfairly. In line with my family prejudices, I found him slick, self-satisfied, excessively well fed. He and his family made being Jewish seem easy; if my Bar Mitzvah studies had taught me anything, it was that being Jewish was demanding, and if impossibly demanding—*with all your heart, with all your soul*—the more matter for pride. The revamping of that stern formal contract, the diluting of the severe expectation of the vineyard, made Rabbi Tartufkovich and his institutional compromise seem not Jewish: less Jewish than Grandpa Dave, who if he was a "bad Jew" was at least a bad Orthodox Jew.

A more likely compromise is personal. The total demand of the *Shema* is not a power to be fought like an institutional church, or a power to be denied and fled like the threat of Hellfire. It is not the dramatic power of ritual, like the laying on of frontlets itself, nor the poetic power of passages like Isaiah 5's vineyard. It is a verbal power, and therefore one deals with it by interpretation and accommodation. In relation to the legal demands of observance, this seems a shabby, pusillanimous process. But in relation to apocalypse, the immense scale of Isaiah's paradoxical charge, such self-definition takes on more dignity, if not validity. To be wild grapes is not to be merely a malfeasor.

To put it simply, I mean the familiar process in which one decides what kind of Jew to be, decides the degree and nature of one's Jewishness. My father, for example, is a moderate man in most things. A member of the synagogue, he never attended Sabbath services. That is, like many of his friends, he performed a kind of respectable minimum. Partly this is the mild conformity to custom of a small-town boy: my father worked all his life in the town where he grew up, a celebrated local athlete, voted best-looking boy in his graduating class. His characteristic moderation also may be partly a reaction to growing up in Dave's irregular household. Rose, my father's mother and Dave's first wife, a love match, died in her twenties. Molly, Dave's second wife, was supplied by Rose's family as a kind of replacement, to care for the two small children. Though she bore Dave two more children, the marriage was not a success. She went insane. At some point, Dave began living partly in a second household with Della Lawyer, the barmaid. When Molly was institutionalized, Della moved in with Dave and the children of both wives and cared for them. But Della and Dave were not married until after my father graduated from high school. In a small town, these matters must have attracted some attention. They might have made a respectable mildness of personal life seem attractive.

I go into this family history because it sheds an interesting light on the questions of worship, observance, and idolatry. When Dave Pinsky died, I was twelve and my father was about thirty-five, a hard-working small businessman. It is a remarkable fact that faithfully, for the prescribed eleven months, my father—young, pragmatic, preoccupied with worldly concerns—went to the synagogue daily to say morning prayers and the *kaddish* for the dead, for his irreligious father, binding the leather *tefilin* around his arms and head. This meant getting up at perhaps six in the morning, in order to get to the synagogue, pray with the old men, and begin the working day that went from eight or eight-thirty until six; until nine on Thursday nights.

Not long ago, I asked my father why he had performed this remarkably tedious, prolonged observance: eleven months of early rising and bondage to a ritual that I feel sure was not inspiring or sustaining for him. Did Grandpa Dave have an unsuspected connection to Judaism? Well, no, said my father; you know, he was a tough guy. Had Grandpa Dave been Bar Mitzvahed? My father had no idea. Then why in the world say *kaddish* for him, for eleven months, winter and summer?

"Well, he made me do it with him when my mother died."

My father had been a child of seven or eight at the time. Dave's bootlegging activities would have been near their height. There is a sentimental appeal in the picture of the youthful rum-runner, in his sporty clothes, taking his small child with him each weekday morning for nearly a year, to say memorial prayers for his young wife. For one thing, it is a love story. Thirty years later, my father's observance, in turn, seems to express an attractive, dignified piety toward both parents, perhaps toward the love story, and certainly toward the feelings of the small child, his former self.

But in the strict terms of my Haftorah, Isaiah 66, is any of this in the spirit of acceptable worship? Or is it, rather, idolatry? It is idolatry, because it is autonomously defined: "They have chosen their own ways, and their soul delighteth in their abominations." On the other hand, the Lord whose throne is heaven and footstool the earth finds the flaw in even elaborate worship, the incense that is like blessing an idol, the sacrifice that is like cutting a dog's neck. Only the humble spirit, which trembles at God's word, is not idolatrous. "Humble spirit" does not describe Grandpa Dave as most people saw him. Whether it justly describes the spirit in which he said *kaddish* for his first wife, God knows. We can think that when flesh mourns for flesh—parent or lover—it must be humble, having tasted its own end, in its mourning.

The large, prophetic perspective of Isaiah 66 does offer the idea—a forgiving idea, in its way, since it is leveling—that all worship, even the most meticulous or elaborate, may be flawed by the spirit of idolatry. Because we have human breath in our nostrils, it is perhaps even likely—or fated—to be flawed. This tragic idea has a comic counterpart in the tendency of Jews to find other Jews either not Jewish enough, or absurdly too Jewish, in their religious practices. If the pious are too sure that their worship is adequate, then perhaps it, too, is idolatrous. Isaiah himself felt he was "a man of unclean lips," until the seraph touched his lips with the live coal, like a representative particle of the world's end. Such flaws of our "unclean lips" in general can be redeemed only by the actual, unimaginable end of this world, the end foretold in Isaiah 66.

The images associated with this end, at the end of the Book of Isaiah itself, are for the most part terrifying and punitive: "For by fire and by his sword will the Lord plead with all flesh: and the slain of the Lord will be many." Yet the images of the restored Jerusalem are maternal, and the language forges mourning itself into rejoicing:

Rejoice ye with Jerusalem, and be glad with her, all ye that love her: rejoice for joy with her, all ye that mourn for her.

That ye may suck, and be satisfied with the breasts of her consolations; that ye may milk out, and be delighted with the abundance of her glory.

For thus saith the Lord, Behold, I will extend peace to her like a river, and the glory of the Gentiles like a flowing stream; then shall ye suck, ye shall be borne upon her sides, and shall be dandled upon her knees.

As one whom his mother comforteth, so will I comfort you, and ye shall be comforted in Jerusalem.   [66:10–13]

At the end of time, when the chosen of God come "out of all nations upon horses, and in chariots, and in litters, and upon mules, and upon swift beasts, to my holy mountain Jerusalem," such comfort will be eternal.

And corruption will be eternal, too. In the final words of the Book of Isaiah:

For as the new heavens and the new earth, which I will make, will remain before me, saith the Lord, so shall your seed and your name remain.

And it shall come to pass that, from one new moon to another, and from one sabbath to another, shall all flesh come to worship before me, saith the Lord.

And they shall go forth, and look upon the carcases of the men that have transgressed against me: for their worm shall not die, neither shall their fire be quenched; and they shall be an abhorring unto all flesh.   [66:22–24]

The appalling, paradoxical idea of the unending destruction of flesh supplies a suitable image for the climax of the Book of Isaiah, with its recurring disasters and admonitions. They are peculiar words for a child to sing to a watching audience, sealing his admission into a community of worship he more than half knows he will leave. The most peculiar thing about the concluding passage for me is also communal: the eerie going-forth of the chosen to look upon the abhorrent, endless process of corruption. It is a ritual, paradoxically so because time has ended, and a ritual of the flesh, beholding flesh. Just as the worldly idolators must yield up their powers and pleasures because flesh is doomed to corruption, the poetic power of Isaiah, calling his deaf audience to transcend the body and its works, must depend upon images of the maternal, comforting but endlessly dying body, to speak to our mortal ears.

JEREMIAH

THE FOUNTAIN OVERFLOWS

Stanley Kunitz

A
S A TECHNIQUE OF AMBIGUITY AND REVELATION, PARABOLIC
speech is a standard feature of Biblical prophecy, but Jeremiah's utterance is rarely parabolic, its usual mode being closer
to anecdote, personal memoir, and documentary. Although
heroism is of the essence in the day-to-day conduct of his life, he presents
a picture of his world that is intimate rather than heroic in scale. He is a
man of conscience, decent and brave, unconcessive in his passion for social
and political reform, vehement in his exposure of corruption and the breakdown of religion, and altogether reckless of the consequences of his zeal.
In his litany of misfortunes he reminds us, to a degree, of his predecessor
Job, but his story is not really comparable to that of the archetypal man from
the land of Uz who raised suffering to the level of metaphysical drama. In
contrast to Isaiah and Ezekiel, whose spiritual transcendence is overwhelming, Jeremiah appears as an accessible human figure, mostly like us, with a
touch of the God-intoxicated seer.

The King James Version of the Bible used in this essay.

His book, as it has come down to us, is badly organized and chronologically confusing; portions seem to be the work of other hands, interpolated at other times. Nevertheless, Jeremiah emerges out of the textual core as one of the most clearly defined characters in the Old Testament. The rich content of the narrative, with all its incidental references to contemporaneous events and local customs and rituals, invites an exploration of the subtext to see what it reveals.

It strikes me as significant that, after the wonderfully moving report of his first encounter with the divine presence, Jeremiah refrains from depicting God as a physical entity: He is repeatedly a voice, and only a voice. I lack evidence to dispute Jeremiah's automatic assertions that God speaks directly to him ("the word of the Lord came to me," "saith the Lord," etc.), but my inclination is to regard these locutions as a literary device. Let me add that my comments are tentative and fragmentary. I lay no claim to Bible scholarship, nor am I, in truth, much of a believer: I write out of ignorance and sympathy.

Jeremiah was "the son of Hilkiah of the priests that were in Anathoth," not far from Jerusalem, and was a child in the reign of Josiah, king of Judah (ca. 638–608 B.C.E.). Practically all that we know of his early years is that he answered the call to the prophetic office while he was a young man. This was a period when a resurgent pagan idolatry threatened to overcome the teachings of Judaism. Jeremiah's book lifts a corner of the veil that covers some of the unspeakable origins of religion, including the ritual eating of children. In chapter 44 he condemns the burning of incense to the heathen gods, especially to the "Queen of Heaven," called Anath, the ancient Semitic deity whose consort was Yahweh, "Lord of Heaven." Among the places named after her was Anathoth, Jeremiah's town, whose inhabitants were in the vanguard of those who sought to kill him.

Under King Jehoiakim (607–597 B.C.E.), Jeremiah succeeded in making enemies in every stratum of the population, from the idolatrous masses up to the head of state and the palace council of priests and princes. Paganism was not the only target of his invective. He excoriated corruption in high places and the exploitation of labor: "Woe unto him that buildeth his house by unrighteousness, and his chambers by wrong; that useth his neighbour's service without wages, and giveth him not for his work" (22:13). Most dangerous of all was his constant meddling in foreign affairs. In opposition to the king's policy of entering into a defense pact with Egypt, which he denounced as shameful and bound to fail, Jeremiah advocated an alliance with Nebuchadnezzar, king of Babylon, as a means of staving off the fall of Jerusalem to the Chaldean invaders and the destruction of the Temple— catastrophic events that it was given him to foresee.

In the midst of this deepening crisis, God spoke to Jeremiah, saying, "Arise, and go down to the potter's house, and there I will cause thee to hear my words." Accordingly, Jeremiah went to watch the potter at his wheel. "And the vessel that he made of clay was marred in the hand of the potter; so he made it again another vessel, as seemed good to the potter to make it" (18:4).

Whatever God's reason may have been for setting up this demonstration at the potter's house, it was clearly not to applaud the master craftsman for his exemplary perfectionism. God is angry with His people for having abandoned Him in order to commit abominations and whore after false gods. Why should He be patient with sinners who, like the clay in the potter's hand, are mortal clay in God's hand? He will emulate the potter, who is privileged to destroy imperfect handiwork without a shred of compunction. Yet God loves His chosen people, however they betray Him. There is infinite anguish in His cry: "O house of Israel, cannot I do with you as this potter?" (18:6).

Then God instructed Jeremiah to take an earthen jar with him into the valley of Ben-Himmon and there to prophesy the imminence of the vengeance of the Lord. Jeremiah rose to the occasion, speaking with inspired eloquence, as he gave warning of the coming doom of the people and the desolation of the city, in a time of pestilence, when the dead shall be meat for scavengers and the streets become a place of hissing. In the name of the Lord he cried: "Even so will I break this people and this city, as one breaketh a potter's vessel, that cannot be made whole again" (19:11).

Having uttered these words, Jeremiah shattered into bits the jar that he carried with him. The scandal of that speech and gesture made him a marked man. Shortly afterward, he was arrested and put into the stocks. Graver punishments were to follow for the rest of his life: "I am in derision daily, every man mocketh me" (20:7).

Pots and jars, which are traditionally associated with oracles, have a way of turning up at strategic points in Jeremiah's narrative. In his baptismal experience of revelation, when God informed him that he was ordained for prophecy, Jeremiah replied, "Ah, Lord God! behold, I cannot speak: for I am a child" (1:6). Then God put forth His hand to the child Jeremiah and touched his mouth and showed him, in rapid succession, two miraculous visions, like shining toys, the second of which was a seething pot, with its face toward the north (1:13–14). So it was that Jeremiah first learned of the fate in store for Jerusalem when the armies would come pouring out of Babylon.

Just before the fall of the city in 586 B.C.E., while Jeremiah was shut up in prison and the Chaldeans, under King Nebuchadnezzar, were ravaging the countryside, he was visited by Hanameel, his uncle's son, who offered to sell him a field in Anathoth to which he had some claim by right of inheritance. Although Anathoth was then in the hands of the Chaldeans, and he himself, as a prisoner, was in no position to enjoy the fruits of ownership, Jeremiah bought the field for seventeen shekels of silver, then a substantial sum. Since it was even doubtful at this time that the Jewish kingdom could survive, Jeremiah's decision to purchase must have had a symbolic motivation. He was signifying that, despite the darkness of the hour, he did not despair of the future; he was publishing his faith in God's promises and the restoration of the kingdom; he was spelling out the meaning of the land in the long history of the Jews.

On receiving the deed to the land and other records of the transaction, Jeremiah entrusted them to his friend Baruch, who sealed them in a jar of the type we have become familiar with through the recovery of the Dead Sea scrolls. Such depository jars were buried in the ground or stored in caves for safekeeping.

In its entirety, the story of the purchase of the field in Anathoth is an affirmation of the inviolability of the law of contract, a principle stemming from the original sacred Covenant, to which Jeremiah more than once bears witness:

"I will put my law in their inward parts, and write it in their hearts, and will be their God, and they shall be my people" (31:33).

Apparently Jeremiah regarded himself as a better talker than writer, for when the Lord commanded him to put His words into a book, he immediately summoned Baruch, a scribe by profession, to his place of incarceration and began to dictate to him:

"Then Jeremiah called Baruch the son of Neriah; and Baruch wrote from the mouth of Jeremiah all the words of the Lord, which he had spoken unto him, upon a roll of a book" (36:4).

Since Jeremiah was under arrest, he had Baruch go to the synagogue for him with the completed scroll and read from it to the congregation. The news of this aggression soon reached the king, who demanded that the scroll be brought to him and read aloud. After listening for a few minutes, the king took the scroll and tossed it into the fire.

Jeremiah's reaction to this outrage provides an insight into his character: "Then took Jeremiah another roll, and gave it to Baruch the scribe, the son of Neriah; who wrote therein from the mouth of Jeremiah all the words of the book which Jehoiakim king of Judah had burned in the fire; and there were added besides unto them many like words" (36:32).

In my reading of it, that passage ends with a little show of pride, as if to hint that improvements have been made in the script this second try. It is as if we were back again with Jeremiah in the potter's house, where the potter at his wheel makes another vessel and looks at it and sees that it is good.

In the version that we are given, God dictates to Jeremiah in much the same way that Jeremiah dictates to Baruch, transmitting from one to the other the terrible judgments and warnings intended for public consumption. Jeremiah was villified and persecuted because he was the messenger bringing bad news, but Jeremiah did not blame the Lord for his sufferings or beg for mercy.

When the city was under siege and about to fall, Jeremiah was accused of being a Babylonian agent and threatened with death for advocating surrender to the Chaldean invaders as preferable to annihilation. He seemed almost to welcome, because it was just, the downfall of the house of Israel and the dispersal of its inhabitants, even their enslavement. How certain he was of the rightness of his argument! Can one assume he had some inkling that Jewish identity would be verified and consolidated during the bitter years of exile and that the great labor of the Diaspora, the true miracle, would be the reconstruction of the Temple, stone by stone, in Jewish thought and character?

Abandoned to his enemies, Jeremiah was cast into a deep pit (38:6), presumably an old well or cistern, and there, sunk in the mire, he would surely have perished if it had not been for the eventual intercession of a eunuch of the court who came to his help with a rescue squad. Jeremiah was hauled to the surface by means of a rope made of "old cast clouts and old rotten rags."

The bringing up of a prophet into the light, the discovery of a sacred scroll that has been buried in a jar: somehow the two images merge in my mind.

During the nightmare of his immersion in the pit, Jeremiah might well have recalled the words that God had given him years before:

"For my people have committed two evils; they have forsaken me the fountain of living waters, and hewed them out cisterns, broken cisterns, that can hold no water" (2:13).

From Jeremiah, the words were passed on to William Blake, who gave them back to us, modified into one of his ever-shining proverbs: "The cistern contains: the fountain overflows."

EZEKIEL

Elie Wiesel

NO PROPHET WAS ENDOWED WITH SUCH VISION—NO OTHER vision was as extreme. No man has shed such light on the future, for no other light was as forceful in tearing darkness apart. But, then, no one had ever seen such darkness, the total darkness that precedes the breaking of dawn.

It is enough to follow his gaze to be uplifted by the hope it conjures. Look when he orders you to do so, and you will be rewarded by the conviction that hope is forever founded and forever justified. Listen to his words, to his voice, and you will feel strong—stronger than death, more powerful than evil.

Ezekiel: who has not heard of this intriguing and passionate speaker whose visions of dark horror and striking beauty have left an impact on innumerable generations? No messenger has hurt us more—none has offered us such healing words.

When he is harsh, he seems pitiless; when he is kind, his graciousness

---

The author's own translation of the Bible used in this essay.

spills over. In his outbursts of extreme severity, he declares his own nation ugly and repugnant; but, then, all of a sudden, he recovers his compassion, and everything and everybody radiate sunshine and serenity.

He oscillates between the shame of sin and the grandeur of salvation—for him there is nothing in between. Ezekiel is the man of extremes. His visions move from the ecstasy of the chariot to the terror of the dry bones.

And I looked, and behold, a whirlwind came out of the north, a great cloud and a fire unfolding itself, and a brightness was about it, and out of the midst thereof as the color of amber, out of the midst of the fire.

Also out of the midst thereof came the likeness of four living creatures. And this was their appearance; they had the likeness of man. And every one had four faces, and every one had four wings. . . .

What follows is known but rarely understood: in fact, the entire centuries-long tradition of mystical *Merkavah* or *Hekhaloth* literature—the one dealing with the celestial chariot—stems from Ezekiel's description of his first oneiric, fantastic hallucination in his book.

What are those human and animal creatures—both monstrous and divine—that have irrupted in our small orderly planet? What do these extraterrestrial beings try to achieve in our midst? What is the purpose of their visit?

Their feet were straight feet—and the sole of their feet was like the sole of a calf's foot. . . . And they had the hands of a man under their wings on their four sides—and they, too, had their faces and their wings. . . . And their wings were joined one to another. . . .

It reads like a feverish dream, if not a nightmare: all those human and inhuman masks mingled and intertwined. Fragmented images, halting sentences, deafening shouts and soft whispers, words and silences are being used to describe that which lies beyond description: a realm where heaven and earth merge into one element combining fire and crystal, fear and joy, the first and last memory of man facing his destiny.

"The likeness of man, the likeness of lions and eagles, the likeness of the firmament, the likeness of the throne. . . ." Has Ezekiel seen—really seen—all that? Has God really chosen to show him all that He usually conceals from all others? If so: why? Why Ezekiel? What made him so special? All the questions raised with regard to prophecy and prophets—the element of compulsion in the assignment, the unpredictability of the prophet's responses—are even more valid as they pertain to Ezekiel. What had he done to deserve to speak in God's name? Why are his words burning with so much anger, and then with such deep affection?

There are, in his book and in his vocabulary, themes, subjects, expressions that can be found nowhere else. For instance: he "eats" his words; he mentions "heart transplants"—hearts of flesh instead of stone; the poetic term *Ben Adam,* son of man, is used with such frequency that it almost becomes his surname. Also: he is the first prophet to speak of the synagogue as a *Mikdash-me'at,* a miniature, temporary Temple. Has he seen the real one? Only in his imagination—but his description of Jerusalem, far away from Jerusalem, is so real, so factual, so true that it is a jewel in itself. Ezekiel is the prophet of imagination. More than Jeremiah himself, he imagined both exile and redemption in ways that made them both tangible. More important: he was the first to speak of *Kiddush Hashem*—of Israel's privilege and awesome obligation to sanctify the Lord's Name.

No wonder, then, that his narrative seizes the reader with such force. Through years of events and turbulent wanderings, it is his tale that we follow from agony to rebirth. He speaks to us—to us, too—for, more than his own contemporaries, we have witnessed the frailty of social structures and the irresistible power of dreams.

For some of us, once upon a time, did indeed see a desert covered with dry bones. And yes, we could testify to man's power and ability to begin again. No generation could understand Ezekiel as well—as profoundly—as ours. Just read the text and . . .

Vayehi bishloshim shana. . . . And it came to pass in the thirtieth year, in the fourth month, in the fifth day of the month, I was then in exile—or among the exiled, the captives—by the river of Chebar, when all of a sudden the heavens were opened and I saw visions of God. . . .

Clearly, the story opens in the manner of a chronicle. The style is precise. It is the wish of the chronicler that the reader not be confused. We thus know what happened, and where, and when, and to whom.

But, just in case you needed more information—additional details and some name recognition—the chronicler adds that the event occurred during the fifth year of King Jehoiakin's captivity.

Hayo haya dvar adoshem el Yehezkel ben Buzi hakohen. . . . The word of God came to Ezekiel son of Buzi the priest while being in the land of the Chaldeans by the river Chebar. And the hand of God was laid upon him, and *Vaere vehine,* and I looked and behold: a whirlwind came out of the north. . . .

But . . . do not look—not yet. We have not finished with the opening statement, which presents problems. The story begins in the first person—*Vaani*—jumps to the third—*Vathi alav*—and returns to the first—*Vaere,* "and I looked."

Shall we conclude from this that the prophet's knowledge of Hebrew grammar was faulty or that people then already had identity problems? Or did he want to illustrate his own split personality—that the prophet is always both subject and object in his own tale? The answer probably lies elsewhere. The switch may indicate a certain confusion in the mind of the prophet—which would be only natural. After all, we are at the beginning of the story. The prophet has just been contacted by God and he is still shaken from the experience. Most prophets had similar reactions: prophecy was forced upon them. Couldn't God speak more gently to his chosen? Apparently not: prophecy always began with a shock. Is this why Ezekiel, all of a sudden, left reality and moved into a world of fantasy? The historian has been turned into a visionary. Is this why, unlike Jeremiah or Jonah, he did not resist the call? He did not say: Why me? Leaving time and reason behind, he looked and saw chariots of fire, strange beasts, and half-human, half-divine creatures—he looked and saw what exists outside creation.

How is one to explain the quick change of pace? The man who, just one passage earlier, insists on clarity and precision has allowed his mind to wander into delirium—so much so that he forgets to tell us something that may be of essential importance! Didn't he say that "God spoke to him"? Then, why doesn't he tell us what he heard from God? No—he does not tell us what he heard, because he is too busy describing to us what he saw!

And what he saw is so unreal that those of us who dwell in reality are forbidden to follow *his* gaze and look and . . . speak about it.

Listen to the Mishnah in the *Treatise of Hagiga: Ein dorshin baarayot bishlosha*—"One must not debate with three students questions about intimate relations between men and women"; *vlo bemaasse breshit bishnayim*—"nor the mysteries of creation with two students"; *vlo bamerkava beyahid*—"nor the mystery of the *Merkavah,* the chariot, with just one student." This last reference is, once again, to the visions that the prophet Ezekiel had early in his career in Babylon, in the fifth year of King Jehoiakin's captivity.

Merkavah experiences are forbidden territory, dangerous to outsiders. One cannot approach them with impunity. Why should the mystery of Creation be considered less perilous than that of the chariot? Maimonides comments: The first is about Creation, the second about its Creator. Creation is immanent and therefore perceivable; the transcendent forces are, by definition, removed from human perception.

Gershom Scholem quotes ancient texts—of the *Hekhaloth* literature— that warn us against trespassing mystical frontiers: "If a person was unworthy to see the King in his beauty, the angels at the gates disturbed his senses and confused him. And when they said to him 'Come in,' he entered, and instantly they pressed him and threw him into the fiery lava stream. . . . And at the gate of the sixth—of the seven palaces—it seemed as though hundreds of thousands and millions of waves of water stormed against him, and yet there was not a drop of water. . . . But he, the visitor, asked the angels: 'What is the meaning of these waters?' And they began to stone him: 'Wretched, do you not see with your own eyes? Are you perhaps a descendant of those who kissed the Golden Calf and thus are unworthy to see the King in his beauty?' And they struck him with iron bars and wounded him. . . ."

In other words: not only are we not able to understand Ezekiel's chariot visions, but we are not even allowed to make them an object of scholarly analysis. Why? What reason could there be? What is so special about what Ezekiel saw—and why had he, he alone, been permitted to see it?

Well—let us open his file. Who was he? What information is there about his life and work? We know that he was a priest—that he traveled a lot and spoke a lot—that his command of language was both disturbing and enchanting—and . . . what else? We know his mannerisms—his style— his remarkable courage, or was it naïveté, in using repetition. . . . Examples? The expression *son of man* appears a hundred times; *adoshem, adoshem* two hundred times; *vayad'u ki ani adoshem*—"and they shall know that I am the

Lord"—fifty times; *gilulim*—"idolatry"—*only* thirty-nine times. . . . What was his nationality? Was he a Palestinian prophet sent by God to Babylonia? Was he a Babylonian *Yored* (an Israeli emigrant) from Palestine who returned to Palestine? Some sources say he was one or the other; some texts claim he was both, or neither.

From the book itself we gather that he had been exiled, together with his king and the king's court, to Babylonia. We know the exact location of his dwelling: Tel Aviv on the river Chebar.

Babylonian sources tell us that Tel Aviv, or Tel Abib, referred to ruins that remained from before the Flood. In our literature the name fares somewhat better. We are told, thus, that Tel Aviv used to be, was then, the largest Jewish city in the Diaspora. It had the largest Jewish population: ten thousand souls. They spoke Hebrew and observed Jewish laws and attended lectures and, in general, did well.

A midrash tells us of a certain birdwatcher, Hananya ben Menahem, who kept 277 different species at home in Jerusalem. He was so famous that the emperor Nebuchadnezzar himself wanted to meet him—probably to offer him a job. He dispatched an emissary to Tel Aviv, but Hananya ben Menahem refused to go with him, saying: "You forgot that it's Shabbat today, I don't travel on Shabbat." Instead, he traveled to Babylonia one day later, and the emperor gave him a splendid apartment near or inside his palace to keep an eye on the royal birds.

As for Ezekiel, we know that he began to prophesy around six or seven years before Jerusalem's final tragedy and that he continued to be active another twelve to fifteen years. Was he married? Yes. His wife died of the plague, and he saw in her death a prefiguration of the destruction of Jerusalem. He was so affected that, for a while, he lost his power of speech, suffering from aphasia.

Did he have brothers? friends? allies? He had enemies—that has been established. Like most prophets, he was always provoking anger and hostility. Some of his adversaries went so far as to ridicule him, saying: "Who is he, anyway, to talk the way he does? Isn't he a descendant of that woman of ill-repute, you know, Rahav, the harlot who made Jericho famous?" Like Jeremiah, he used pantomime to propagate his views—and fears. When he warned the people of Gilgal of the oncoming exile, he paraded through the streets carrying a knapsack, thus telling them that they, too, would become wanderers. At twilight he would dig a hole in the wall and sneak out into the darkness—like a fugitive, like a refugee. Like Jeremiah, he must have felt that he would not die in the holy land. Jeremiah was buried in Egypt, Ezekiel in Babylon. Iraqi Jews thought they knew the location of his grave and came to pray there, imploring him to intercede in their behalf.

Yes—Ezekiel endured much torment and agony throughout his life. No wonder that God felt the need to give him encouragement and comfort repeatedly: telling him not to worry, not to mind his critics, not to give in to their mockery, but to speak up even if his words were to fall on deaf ears, even if his mission were to bring no immediate results.

As a prophet, he was not free to speak or to remain silent; he was told when to make himself visible and when to remain invisible, clandestine. From the book itself we receive the script God prepared for His emissary Ezekiel. He is ordered to stay seven days under house arrest—to be alone?—to illustrate loneliness. The effect on his character, on his temperament, is obvious: he becomes harsh, demanding, fierce, unbending, unyielding, discouraging human contact. How does he see his fellow men?—in a dream more than in reality. Occasionally he is instructed to act "dumb"—or to be provocative. He is to prepare a model of what Jerusalem would be like under siege, and he is amazingly accurate, always—the halls, the gates, the light, the odors, the sounds, the mood—he describes the punishment of the sacred city, its hunger, its pain, its decline. Lying motionless, he paints the convulsions of a society at war. To symbolize the unclean food people will eat in captivity, he prepares a cake of human or animal excrements. He shaves his head and lets the wind disperse his hair, to illustrate the fate of his rebellious fellow Jews.

Naturally, Ezekiel became a perfect candidate for students and misinterpreters of psychoanalysis. Some term his behavior psychotic, others prefer to call it pathological. Believe it or not, an expert found that our prophet had "catatonic periods" which resulted from his "paranoiac" tendencies. Want to hear more? Listen to more diagnoses: "narcissistic masochistic conflicts . . . fantasies of castration . . . unconscious sexual regression . . . schizophrenia . . . delusions of persecution . . . delusions of grandeur. . . ."

His sermons have the quality and the urgency of eyewitness reporting. Mindful of every detail, he tells us what is going on in God's favorite dwelling place. In short, it reminds him of Sodom. The key word is *Toeva*—"abomination." Physical and moral prostitution, social decadence, intellectual depravation: one could put together an entire encyclopedia of sin just using Ezekiel's chastising vocabulary. He is particularly severe with the leaders: we are informed of what they are saying, thinking, doing, plotting, inside and outside the sanctuary. Are there no good people in the land—no just men left? He speaks of the elders who, in exasperation, began to wonder whether God had not abandoned his people altogether.

Listen: "And the glory of God said unto me: Son of man, look and see what they are doing in my house, to my house. . . . See the great abominations? Look well and you will notice even greater ones. . . ."

Old leaders and priests worship idols. Listen to the language: "Son of man, have you seen what the ancients of the House of Israel do in the dark—or in the secret chambers of their imagination? They say to themselves: anything is permitted, for God cannot see us—He has forsaken this land and abandoned its inhabitants. . . ."

But that is not all, says God to the prophet. Look, and you will see even worse. "Then he brought me to the door of the Temple's gate and behold, there were women weeping for the idol Tammuz. . . ." Wait, says God to Ezekiel. There is worse. "And He took me inside the inner court and between the porch and the altar I saw about twenty-five men, with their backs to the Temple, worshipping the sun."

And then God uses an expression that reminded Ezekiel—and us—of Noah and the flood: *Ki malu et haaretz khamas*—"They filled the land with violence"—and *that* was the worst. As long as people offended heaven, God, in spite of His anger, was willing to wait. But when they ceased to be human toward one another, He had to intervene and punish them.

No prophet has ever spoken with such despair and of such doom. To the inhabitants of Jerusalem, he says that they will be defeated; to those in Babylon, he says that their deliverance is not near. Of course, like most prophets he emphasizes the cycle of sin, punishment, and redemption. But, according to him, redemption is far, far away. While the first two phases are in effect, redemption seems improbable, if not impossible. So much so that one is allowed to wonder: why does the prophet insist with such fervor on Jewish weaknesses and transgressions? Does he enjoy shaming them? One reason may be that, knowing of the catastrophe in the making, he wants the Jewish people to have an explanation, he wants to save them from absurdity. Better that they think their plight represents punishment, rather than gratuitous cruelty. Any answer is better than no answer.

Moreover, the prophet has full power to predict the future. He knows the future because he observes the present. No sin will go unpunished. Collective depravation must result in collective agony. If his perception is right—if disgust, both real and spiritual, dominates the mood of the story—then tragedy is inevitable. Not immediately; later, much later. As in the case of Jeremiah, it will be two decades before Ezekiel's predictions come to pass. But then history itself shuddered.

Now we must ask ourselves the question, Was Israel really that bad, that sinful? Open the Book of History and turn the pages.

Though a vassal state to Babylon, Judah enjoyed internal freedom. After a short reign of some one hundred days, King Jehoiakin and his entourage—together with skilled technicians in the thousands—had been deported to Babylon, leaving behind a newly appointed king, a weakling named Zidkiyahu, or Zedekias. Pressured by Egypt and Phoenicia to rebel against Babylon, Zedekias finally gave up his position of comfortable neutrality and allowed his militant advisers to move the nation into war. The enemy, the emperor Nebuchadnezzar, responded with his army, and thus began the military siege of Jerusalem.

Inside the country, the morale was low. The enemy was strong and the Jews desperate. They could not comprehend God's ways: why had He abandoned His people, who, under King Josiah, had shown such force of character and faith by repudiating idolatry and sin and by undertaking one of the most impressive shows of repentance in history? Despair led to spiritual corruption: since God seemed unjust, why should men be just?

Judea's spiritual leaders, the four prophets—Jeremiah, Uriah son of Shemaiah, Habakkuk, and Ezekiel—tried hard to change the mood, but in vain. Uriah was beheaded, Jeremiah jailed, Ezekiel persecuted and humiliated.

And yet, in the Gentile world, culture was flourishing. Athenians built the Acropolis and celebrated a philosopher named Thales of Miletus, Aesopus' fables and Aeschylus' dramas, and the oracles at Delphi. The

Chinese enjoyed the wisdom of Lao-tse. The Maya built their temples in Mexico. World history was moving forward in waves of abrupt upheavals, the various emperors forever dissatisfied with what they possessed, forever aspiring to enlarge their empires.

Somehow Judea was always in the middle of their political and strategical designs. Egypt and Babylon were enemies—and again both needed Judea. Strange: all the gigantic empires of the times seemed to need Judea. And eventually all would vanish—with the exception of Judea—the Chaldeans, the Assyrians, the Phoenicians, the Persians, the Egyptians, the Romans. What attracted them to Judea? In the end, they all had to withdraw from Judea. Judea alone remained in Judea.

And yet, listening to its prophets you would have thought that Judah's lot would be worse than that of its enemies! Worse? Not entirely. Most prophets found it vital and imperative to address themselves to other nations as well. Just as Jeremiah was called *navi lagoyim*—"A prophet to Gentile nations"—Ezekiel, too, could be classified as a prophet to the enemy nations! For not only did he predict the destruction of Israel, he also foretold the doom of Tyre and Egypt. That was his way of emphasizing again and again that suffering is contagious, as is evil itself. When one people is subjected to humiliation, others are bound to follow. And, ultimately, the destroyer will be destroyed and the victimizer will experience the taste of being the victim of someone else's whims and wishes.

Is this enough to console the victim? I do not think so. That is why Ezekiel came forth with his vision of the dry bones. In the Jewish ethical tradition, one may not rejoice over an enemy's downfall. The enemy's punishment offers no consolation to the victim. The victim's rehabilitation, victory, and redemption must not be linked to other people's suffering. The theme, the purpose, call it the message, in Ezekiel's healing sermons and metaphors is not victory, but repentance. If the sinner repents, he will live; if he does not, he will die.

It is in Ezekiel's book that we find the poignant verse *vaomar lakh bedamayikh hayi, vaomar lakh bedamayikh hayi*—"And I shall tell you: you shall live in thy blood, in thy blood you shall live." In *thy* blood, not in your enemies'.

At one point, God places the sinner's fate on the prophet's shoulders: it is Ezekiel's responsibility to save him. Is it too heavy a burden? Yes, so

God compromises. Your task, He says, is to try. Speak to the sinner, teach him, chastise him, warn him. If he refuses to be saved, at least you will have saved yourself.

Did Ezekiel succeed? He tried—he tried hard. Obeying God's orders to the letter, he went so far as to do supernatural things. While staying in Babylon, he "flew" back and forth to Jerusalem, he inspected the celestial chariot, described events hidden in the future, and subjected himself to humiliation and ridicule, never complaining about his own ordeal.

When he himself enters the story, we are moved by that ordeal. Jeremiah spoke of captives, Ezekiel referred to refugees—and he became one himself. He was always suspected by everyone, resented for being on God's side, for knowing too much, for protesting against false prophets and false comfort. Whatever he predicted to others ultimately happened to him, too.

And yet, and yet. We sense a certain hesitation, a certain reluctance, even a coolness toward him, not only from his contemporaries, but from later generations as well.

One has the feeling that even in Talmudic literature he is treated like a refugee.

His book is the only one—of the Prophets—that almost fell victim to censorship. Indeed, for a while the Book of Ezekiel was in danger of not being published. Why such discrimination? Was it because of his unmitigated criticism of his people? No, others have been as frank and as daring. Why, then? Some Talmudic sages maintain that there are passages in Ezekiel that are in conflict with the Torah. Others reproach him for dealing with forbidden mystical themes. Listen: "It came to pass that, in the house of a teacher, a Jewish child opened the Book of Ezekiel and began studying the story of the fire and the chariot. Soon a fire came out of the fire and burned the child down." So the sages envisaged to suppress the Book of Ezekiel altogether.

Some critics are harsher, but more subtle. They object to Ezekiel's frankness. They would have preferred him to indulge in some kind of coverup. About the sins of Jerusalem? No. About the heavenly secrets. He had visions? Good for him—but why reveal them to others? He saw the heavenly chariot and its strange creatures—why did he have to boast about it? Why couldn't he have locked his impressions in his memory, for later? The fact that Ezekiel could not resist telling the story—and what a story it was!—somewhat hurt his image in certain influential Talmudic circles.

One commentator states, tongue-in-cheek: "Any maidservant saw, while crossing the Red Sea, more than what Ezekiel would see later." In other words: Big deal—visions have little to do with personalities or social categories. Rather, they have to do with circumstances or sheer luck.

A comparison between Ezekiel and a maidservant? Well, that is something he may have shrugged off. But there were other comments of a more serious nature. Said Rava: "All that Ezekiel saw, Isaiah had seen already. And yet, there is a difference between their personalities. Ezekiel could be compared to a villager who happens to come to the city where he saw the king; Isaiah is compared to a city person who is used to seeing the king frequently, even in his own palace, and therefore is not seized by such frantic desire to tell about it."

What is clear from these stories is the resentment in some places toward Ezekiel for having revealed his visions. But, then, isn't he a prophet? Isn't the prophet duty-bound not to keep anything to himself? Isn't he but an instrument of communication between God and mankind? Clearly, nothing in his life is private. All he has, all he is, belongs to both God and His people. His fears and hopes, his joys and depressions, his turmoils and his moments of ecstasy: they are not his alone. A prophet must have no ego, no individual memory. If he hears a voice, he must echo it. If he sees visions, he must share them. Right? Yes and no. Yes, as far as the voices are concerned—when God speaks, the prophet becomes His vessel. But visions—that is something else. God rarely says: Tell them what you see—but, rather: Tell them what you hear.

Then why did Ezekiel choose to go beyond his mission? Mind you, it was no transgression on his part. God had not told him *not* to speak of his visions. But, then, why was his book inexplicably placed in jeopardy? Says the Talmud: "We must remember with gratitude the good Hananya ben Hizkiya—for were it not for his intervention, the Book of Ezekiel would have been put away."

Who was that Hananya ben Hizkiya who fought so valiantly for freedom of expression? It was in his house that the sharpest conflicts were confronted and resolved. The eighteen-point program, which was exceptionally adopted as the students of Shammai outvoted those of Hillel, had been discussed earlier in his attic. He was clearly a man for the impossible mission. When some of his colleagues openly complained that the Book of Ezekiel contained passages that unmistakably contradict the Torah, he ordered enough food and candles to be brought up to his attic—and he did not leave there until all discrepancies were clarified. Characteristically, we are not let in on the secret; we are not told how the scholar managed to reconcile opposites.

For instance: in the Torah it is clearly stated in the name of Moses that *Hashem poked avon avot al banim*—that God is visiting the iniquities of the father upon his children and his children's children. But, says Rav Yose ben Hanina, Ezekiel unashamedly challenged Moses' view by flatly declaring: "Behold, all souls are mine, says the Lord: just as the soul of the father, so also that of the son of the son: only the soul that sins will die. . . ." Moses speaks of hereditary guilt; Ezekiel stresses individual responsibility. Elsewhere, with regard to another matter, we find in the Talmud, not without some exasperation, that *davar ze mitorat moshe lo lamadnu*—"We have learned this not from Moses but from Ezekiel son of Buzi the priest."

Generally speaking, one senses that Ezekiel made them all feel uncomfortable. He disturbed both his contemporaries and their descendants. From the fact that his book was the only one to be subjected to quasi-suppression, we can deduce that our sages had problems with the author as well. His interpretation of Moses' laws is only one element in the equation. There must have been others. Various hints appear here and there in midrashic literature, all drawing a distinction between him and his colleagues. Efforts are made to explain strange things about him, yet some puzzles remain unexplained—"ad bo Eliyahu"—"until the time when the prophet Elijah will come and reconcile all conflicts and solve all mysteries."

Talmudic scholars had problems with Ezekiel, who, apparently, had problems with God. First, he was jealous. Of whom? He was jealous of his fellow prophets. At one point he exclaimed: "Master of the universe, am I not a priest? Am I not a prophet? Why did Isaiah speak for you in Jerusalem, while I must do the same thing here, in Exile?"

But, then, God had problems with him, too. When God asked His prophet, "Hatihyena haatzamot hayeveshot haelu?"—"Will these dry bones come back to life?"—he paused for a while, obviously waiting for an answer; and when it came, it was evasive. Instead of shouting, "Yes, they will—and perhaps they must—for they and we need your miracle," Ezekiel became a diplomat and a politician; he adopted a noncommittal attitude. He was too skeptical.

And that is why, says the Talmud, Ezekiel was condemned to die not in the holy land but in Babylon.

Another legend is even more disturbing. It came to pass that King Nebuchadnezzar ordered all his subjects, in all the lands under his rule, to worship one of his idols lest they all be executed. Three representatives were chosen from each nation to act on behalf of their people. Hananya, Mishael, and Azarya represented the children of Israel. They turned to their teacher, Daniel, for advice. Daniel, in his humility, sent them to Ezekiel, who urged them to reject martyrdom and choose flight instead. They disregarded his suggestion, saying that they wished to die for *Kiddush Hashem,* the sanctification of God's name. Still, Ezekiel persisted in trying to dissuade them from becoming martyrs. When they still refused to listen, he came up with yet another proposal: they should wait with their decision until he received word from God that He would save them through a miracle. God's answer was: No. Nevertheless, the three just men refused to escape or to bow to the king's will. When Ezekiel, in despair, burst into tears, God at last offered him consolation, saying, "Do not worry, they will be saved—I shall save them from the burning furnace." Why couldn't He have told him so beforehand? It was only to allow their faith and their martyrdom to appear even more glorious.

Good for them—but what about Ezekiel? His part in the drama is less enviable than theirs. He is made to sound weak and frightened. Instead of telling the three martyrs to be strong, he wanted them not to be martyrs at all!

However, Talmudic sages have their way of balancing reticence by giving praise to the prophet's wider powers. How? He became instrumental in saving the three just men's lives. Listen: Hananya, Mishael, and Azarya were about to die in the Babylonian furnace when Ezekiel performed the miracle of resurrecting the dry bones. The miracle encompassed more than those directly concerned. Earlier martyrs were also resurrected and rejoined the living community of Israel. Do you know how Nebuchadnezzar learned of Ezekiel's miracle? He had a drinking vessel made of the bones of a slain Jew. He was about to use it, and drink from its wine, when life began to stir in the vessel, and one bone struck the king in the face, and a voice was heard proclaiming, "A friend of this man is right now reviving the dead."

Did he, really? As always, opinions are divided in the Talmud. Some say, Yes, he did—and some go so far as to identify the resurrected, if not by name, at least by origin and category—those Jews, for instance, who, in their impatience, escaped from Egypt before Moses led the whole people out of bondage; or those who, ironically, did not believe in *Tchiat-hametim,* in resurrection; or the young Judeans taken into captivity by Nebuchadnezzar, whose beauty drove Babylonian women mad: under pressure from their husbands, the emperor ordered them killed. Now they were all brought back to life by Ezekiel.

All these possibilities were examined, during a heated session of one of the academies, because of some skeptics who dared to state publicly that, in their opinion, the entire story of the famous dry bones was nothing but a figment of Biblical imagination, or, to use their language, *Mashal haya*— "it was nothing but a parable."

Actually the debate dealt with larger and more general issues. What would happen to *Tzaddikim*—just men—in the long run, after they reached paradise? Would they die again? And, of course, here, too, opinions were divided. Some said, Yes, they will die, but their death will be painless. And they quoted the case of the dry bones: those men whom Ezekiel brought back to life died right away—but they didn't suffer. At which point a panelist got up and said, probably, "What nonsense! The story was fiction...." And thus went the discussion. Said Rebbe Eliezer, "The dead that were resurrected by Ezekiel stood up, praised the Lord, and died." Someone wanted to know the nature—the text—of the praise? Said Rebbe Yeoshua, "They sang '*Adoshem memit umekhaye'*—'The Lord causes people to die and to return to life—the Lord brings them down to the abyss and then lifts them up to the surface.' " A third sage then intervened in the debate with a brief, sweeping remark, "All this *emet mashal haya*—all this was a true parable." Snapped Rebbe Nehemiah, "Really? How is that possible? If it was true, it was not a parable; if it was a parable, it wasn't true. The answer? *Beemet mashal haya*—'It was truly a parable.' " Would you say that thus the debate had exhausted its logical—or illogical—possibilities? That rarely occurs in the Talmud. Hardly had Rebbe Nehemiah finished his linguistic contribution when Rebbe Eliezer, son of

Reb Yose the Galilean, made his own opinion known: he opposed the view that the dead resurrected only to die again right away. "Oh no," said he, "they made *aliyah* to the Land of Israel, they got married and had children." Was this an audacious thought? Rebbe Yehuda ben Beteira's was more audacious: "True," he stated. "They made *aliyah* and I am their descendant, and the *tefilin*—the phylacteries—that I wear are those that I inherited from my grandfather, who was one of them."

Admit it! One does not know what to admire more in those Talmudic sages: their imagination or their sense of humor.

What is clear is that the episode preoccupied them to an astonishing degree. They wanted to understand its meaning, with all its implications, and its place in the life of Ezekiel—and in that of our people.

For, in the text, the story is forcefully and descriptively narrated. It is one of the summits of prophetic literature, perhaps still unequaled in its strange mixture of poetic realism and mystical dynamism.

Remember the location, the setting: the place where Judea's last king, Zidkiyahu—Zedekias—made his last stand against Babylonian armies. The plain is now covered with the mutilated bodies of fallen Jewish warriors. And it is there, in the midst of climactic cruelty, desolation, and mourning, that he has his most glorious and breathtaking vision:

The hand of the Lord was upon me, and the Lord carried me out in a spirit, and set me down in the midst of the valley, and it was full of bones; and He caused me to pass by them round about, and, behold, there were very many in the open valley; and, lo, they were very dry. And He said unto me: "Son of man, can these bones live?" And I answered: "O Lord God, Thou knowest." Then He said unto me: "Prophesy over these bones, and say unto them: O ye dry bones, hear the word of the Lord: Thus saith the Lord God unto these bones: Behold, I will cause breath to enter into you, and ye shall live. And I will lay sinews upon you, and will bring up flesh upon you, and cover you with skin, and put breath in you, and ye shall live; and ye shall know that I am the Lord." So I prophesied as I was commanded; and as I prophesied, there was a noise, and behold a commotion, and the bones came together, bone to its bone. And I beheld, and, lo, there were sinews upon them, and flesh came up, and skin covered them above; but there was no breath in them. Then said He unto me: "Prophesy unto the breath, prophesy, son of man, and say to the breath: Thus saith the Lord God: Come from the four winds, O breath, and breathe upon these slain, that they may live." So I prophesied as He commanded me, and the breath came into them, and they lived, and stood up upon their feet, an exceeding great host. Then He

said unto me: "Son of man, these bones are the whole house of Israel; behold, they
say: Our bones are dried up, and our hope is lost; we are clean cut off. Therefore
prophesy, and say unto them: Thus saith the Lord God: Behold, I will open your
graves, and cause you to come up out of your graves, O My people; and I will bring
you into the land of Israel and ye shall know that I am the Lord, when I have opened
your graves, and caused you to come up out of your graves, O My people. And I
will put My spirit in you, and ye shall live, and I will place you in your own land;
and ye shall know that I the Lord have spoken, and performed it, saith the Lord."

Like all prophets, Ezekiel opened his prophecy with predictions of
doom and closed it with words of consolation. The man who had been sent
by God to speak unto mountains and valleys, objects and human beings, and
warn them of things to come, now felt the need to reassure his people that
there would be an end to suffering and to fear. The visionary who had
foreseen a time when a third of Jerusalem would perish through famine, a
third by the enemy's sword, and a third scattered in the wind, now took
two sticks in his hand and kept them together, to show his listeners that both
houses of Israel would be united again.

Yes—Ezekiel, in many respects, was a prophet, like any other, serving
the Lord with all his heart and soul. Like all of them, he spoke truth to
power, and like them his only power was truth.

And yes—he, too, dared argue with heaven for the sake of his community. Jeremiah exclaimed: *"Tzaddik ata ki ariv imakh"*—"I know that you
are just, and yet I must take exception to some of the things that you do,
or that are being done in your name. At times, when he thought the
punishment was too harsh, Ezekiel would fall to his knees and shout, "Is
this your will? To exterminate the last remnant of Israel?"

Remember: unlike Jeremiah, he had not seen the massacres, had not
witnessed the slaughter. The torment was shown to him only in his vision,
in his hallucinations. But he suffered like Jeremiah. Although he lived the
tragedy from a distance, he agonized over it as if it were his own. His visions
were real to him. The future was present. His exaggerations—both for good
and for bad—offered proof that the impossible, in every domain, is possible.
If the miracle of the resurrection was told by him as a true story—or a story
of a certain immutable truth—it was because the chastisement that preceded
it had also been told with the emphasis on truth. If the children of Israel
could sin that much, they would be saved by miracles that great. Exaggera-

tion of sin must be matched by exaggerated divine rescue. Here Ezekiel disagrees with Jeremiah, who believed in repentance that would generate redemption. Ezekiel believed in redemption that would come outside of repentance. Jews would be redeemed, not because they would deserve it, but because God would choose to be merciful. That is why he insisted so much on Israel's transgressions. He declared that subsequent generations ought never to give up hope. Even if their sins would make them unworthy of redemption, they would be redeemed. In other words, he painted his society in such outrageous colors for a simple reason: future generations would thus be able to think, "We could never be as guilty as his contemporaries were; therefore hope is permitted." After Ezekiel's generation, all others could only become better.

In conclusion, let us return to our initial worry: why the hesitation, in Talmudic literature, why the reservation with regard to Ezekiel?

Was it only because of his harsh words for his people? Were they too harsh? Or was it because of his quick changes of mood? Were they too quick, too abrupt, with no transition whatsoever? Or was it really only because he was too slow to accept God's word that miracles are possible, even those related to the abolition of frontiers between life and death?

It is quite conceivable that all these elements played a role in the situation. Ezekiel *was* an extremist. He did go further than his peers in all his predictions. But what made him totally different, perhaps unique, is something else: in his case, vision and word merged and became one.

A prophet is God's spokesman. The words that he hears are those that he is duty-bound to communicate to his listeners. He repeats what God says, nothing else. If God says, "Be harsh," he must be harsh. If God says, "Be comforting," he must be comforting. It is the voice that matters: the word—the sound—complete sentences—precise thoughts—ideas—principles—ethical injunctions—memories and more memories.

Ezekiel echoed God's words. But he did something else: he used his own. To be more specific, he added his own to those he had heard from God. To put it bluntly, he said things that he should have kept to himself: things that had to do with his visions, things that are part of the *Merkabah* experience.

Remember the passage: *Vaere*—"and I have seen"? God was kind enough to show him the chariot and its mystical creatures. But nowhere is it mentioned that God told him to tell others what he had seen. And yet Ezekiel did not hesitate to reveal *everything* he had seen. *That* was his mistake.

He did not understand that there are experiences that cannot be communicated by words. He did not understand the importance of silence—the occasional necessity for silence.

We do, and so did many Talmudic sages, particularly those who lived in the time of another *Churban,* the second destruction of the Temple and Jerusalem.

Those were the first to elaborate on Ezekiel's *Merkavah* vision. Rabbi Yohanan ben Zakkai and his close disciples taught and studied the story and the lessons of the divine celestial chariot. And we are told that whenever they did, a heavenly fire would surround them. Was it there to shield them or to protect them or to isolate them from reality or to remind them of the fire of Sinai? Perhaps it was there to bring them closer to the fire that consumed the sanctuary in their time—and other living sanctuaries in later generations—or perhaps to teach them the dangers inherent in language, or to teach them that some words have the ability to burn and burn.

With such visions of fire, with such memories of fire, even prophets ought to be careful and remain silent. Then, at least, people would know that their knowledge is doomed to remain their own. What they have seen, no one would ever see. What they know, no one would understand.

Ezekiel should have been more careful. Why wasn't he? Surely he felt compelled to speak, compelled to share, to give others what he had received from God. He refused to let his visions—his memories—die with him.

Prophets are human—and therein lies their grandeur, their sacredness. The greater the person, the more human the person, and the other way around: vulnerable, weak, subject to impulses and temptations—all of these. So what? Ezekiel was too intelligent, too perceptive, too knowledgeable not to know that it is forbidden to transform one's visions into words. But he was too concerned with his fellow human beings' welfare to deprive them of their right to know. He would pay for it? So what? As messenger, he must deliver the entire message, even the parts that could be seen and not heard.

But the question is: Can the message ever be communicated in its entirety? Can we break away from the fire? Can we communicate the fire?

Finally, all the events, and all the prophetic visions in the book, are inserted in their proper calendar. Fourteen dates are indicated to help us place the speaker and his discourse—with one notable exception: the vision of the dry bones, meaning that the resurrection is undated.

And we understand why: that vision, that promise, that hope, is not linked to either space or time.

That vision, that consolation, is offered to every generation, for every generation needs it—and ours more than any before us.

HOSEA

James Atlas

I GREW UP IN A HOME THAT WAS FILLED WITH BOOKS. I SEE THEM ON THE shelf in our living room: an early edition of *Ulysses;* the works of Thomas Mann; the Random House two-volume Proust; translations of Gide, Camus, and Sartre; many volumes of Dreiser, Steinbeck, Hemingway. My father was a physician, but he was devoted to literature—and, once he'd established himself in his profession, he studied it with a zeal that transcended cultural dabbling. Not only had he read *Ulysses;* he was working his way through *Finnegans Wake.* Like so many second-generation Jews, he found in books a solace that had been denied his own parents, working long hours in their drugstore on the Northwest Side of Chicago. And not just the latest selection of Book-of-the-Month Club, either. Our coffee table was piled high with Nabokov and Dostoevsky, André Maurois' biography of Byron, Stefan Zweig's Balzac. *Language and Silence* was a key text; George Steiner was a household name.

So vividly inscribed in my memory is this literary atmosphere that I

The King James Version of the Bible used in this essay.

can recall not only the titles, but the actual books—the dust jackets on the newer volumes, the worn spines and faded lettering on the covers of the old. They come back to me not only as works of literature, but as artifacts, things that denominated a high ideal—culture as a way of life. Need I say that we were Jews? American Jews, assimilated Jews, but Jews nonetheless—and thus avid for the literature our people had produced. Isaac Babel, Sholem Alei-chem, Malamud (Singer we hadn't discovered yet) were more than great writers; they were like members of the family.

Yet, if there was a Bible in the house, I don't remember it. Scanning those crowded shelves again in my imperfect memory, I can't come up with any such book—a book to be found in every motel room in the land. We were secular Jews, militantly so. My grandparents on both sides considered themselves members of the progressive class, the *intelligentsia;* my parents in their youth were vaguely socialist. We had a menorah; also a Christmas tree. Religion was for those of *shtetl* mentality, dutiful boys in their *yarmulkes* bowed over the Torah in freezing classrooms like Saul Bellow's *Herzog,* studying the Old Testament in the cellar of a synagogue in freezing Mont-real, harangued by a tyrannical rabbi, "short-bearded, his soft big nose violently pitted with black." There was no place for such people in the modern world; this was America. While my friends attended Sunday school and prepared for their Bar Mitzvahs, I made my pilgrimage to the Art Institute and worshipped before Seurat's *Sunday Afternoon on the Island of La Grande Jatte.* God was an artist.

It wasn't until I was a senior in college, studying for finals, that I first encountered this marvelous book—and then only in fragmentary form; it was a passage from Genesis in the *Norton Anthology of English Literature.* There was something infinitely mysterious about this passage, an eloquence that was both English and not English, both utterly familiar and utterly strange. I wasn't sure *how* it was familiar: old Hollywood versions of Bible stories on the "Late Late Show," or the Biblical poems of Delmore Schwartz? Nor could I have easily described why it was strange. The sonorous dignity of the language, the sheer orotund grandeur of it, was like nothing I'd ever heard before. *And it came to pass; And there was a famine in the land.* These words possessed a historical resonance that was somehow beyond time. They spoke of events that were formative, epochal. From that came this.

The Bible as literature: that was how I came to know it. And why not? The King James Bible, Steiner argues in *After Babel,* is "native to the spirit of the language, inwoven with the past of English feeling." Opening its pages, we experience what Steiner describes as a sensation of *at-homeness;* the ancient text before us is English—rhetorical, incantatory, full of implausible grammar and locutions, yet English all the same. Like Shakespeare, it offers up in their original form what have since become clichés. A thousand familiar phrases that we recognize without having known their origin, phrases formerly without context, author, source, leap out from every page.

Yet, for all its familiarity, this Bible presents a contemporary reader with immense obstacles. For all its "at-homeness," the text we confront is three centuries removed from us; it plunges the contemporary reader, Steiner cautions, into "a remote, entirely alien world of expression and reference." Reading the opening pages for the first time sixteen years ago, I was instantly lost; it was the sensation I'd had upon trying to make my way through Chaucer and Spenser, of language receding into archaism, threatening to become unintelligible. In my experience, English literature up through the eighteenth century has a patina of strangeness; we read it, if not with difficulty, then with a sense of how much it varies from the language of our own day. Imagine, then, what it's like to read a book of dubious authorship, implausible time shifts, linguistic eccentricities, bewildering narrative leaps—a book that's at once the definitive text of our civilization, the basic source of its myth and history, and so elusive that one often feels, reading it, as if one were reading, with only the vaguest comprehension, a foreign language. We think of the Bible as a book—perhaps the one book—we know; we number it among the books we've read. Only when we turn to it with an eye toward interpretation do we discover how complicated, even incomprehensible it is. "Her rulers *with* shame do love, Give ye"; "now shall a month devour them with their portions"; "Therefore have I hewed *them* by the prophets"—what, in the literal sense, can these words mean? The rhetoric is opaque, obscure; even academic commentators, I note with relief, find passages "bewildering," "ambiguous," "confused." Whole episodes simply elude their comprehension. It wasn't until I followed the advice given by Robert Alter in *The Art of Biblical Narrative* and read them as "prose fiction"—"the imaginative reenactment by a gifted writer who organizes his materials along certain thematic biases and according to his own remarkable intuition of the psychology of his characters"—that I began to get my bearings.

Edmund Wilson, embarking on his study of the Dead Sea scrolls, was surprised to learn that well-educated people he polled were not generally acquainted with even "the most famous Bible stories." In a highly informal poll of my own, I have yet to encounter anyone remotely acquainted with Hosea. I can see why. Even by the standards of a book in which every line, every word, is subject to scholarly dispute, it's conceded to be difficult. According to Francis I. Andersen and David Noel Freedman, authors of the Hosea volume in that indispensable reference work, The Anchor Bible, "the text of Hosea competes with Job for the distinction of containing more unintelligible passages than any other book of the Hebrew Bible." The chronology is unclear; the autobiographical elements of the story are vague; even the speaker—sometimes God, sometimes Hosea, sometimes (possibly) another prophet—is in doubt.

Who was Hosea? Of the eighth-century B.C.E. prophets—Amos, Isaiah, and Micah were the others—he's the one about whom we know the least. Virtually the only biographical documentation is what he reveals himself—and that's not a great deal. As a prophet, he occupied a high position: he was a messenger of God, a sort of exalted foreign-policy adviser mediating between Yahweh and His people. "The word of the Lord came unto Hosea" is the only credential offered—a source high enough to confirm his authority, but it doesn't give us a clue about who he was. Anyway, his patronymic was Hosea ben Beeri.

The Book of Hosea opens with God's advice to go marry a promiscuous woman, "a wife of whoredoms"—"certainly one of the more startling divine allocutions recorded in the Bible," as the Anchor commentators put it. Was Gomer, the wife Hosea chose, a whore when she became his wife, or did she become one later when she tarted herself up—"decked herself with her earrings and her jewels"—abandoned her family and went off with her lovers? There's much discussion on the point. Some scholars argue that the reference to Gomer's promiscuity is proleptic, anticipating betrayals later in the marriage. What's not ambiguous is the nature and depth of the woman's harlotry. The language is explicit—to a contemporary reader accustomed to believing that sexual malfeasance is a twentieth-century invention, surprisingly explicit. Whoredom, adultery, sleeping around:

these are dominant motifs in the Book of Hosea. The prophet's wife is a handful—a ballbreaker in the tradition of Herzog's unfaithful, calculating Madeleine. In this department, as in every other, there's nothing new under the sun.

Not that sordid goings-on are unique to Hosea. In Genesis, Judah "lies down" with his own daughter-in-law, Tamar; Onan beats off; and we know what they do in Sodom. But no other Biblical story depicts so vividly the pathos of adultery. However little we know about the actual circumstances of Hosea's life, the account of marriage and infidelity chronicled here has the feel of autobiography. In the moving passage that opens chapter 2, God addresses Hosea and, through Hosea, his children:

Plead with your mother, plead: for she *is* not my wife, neither *am* I her husband: let her therefore put away her whoredoms out of her sight, and her adulteries from between her breasts;

Lest I strip her naked, and set her as in the day that she was born, and make her as a wilderness, and set her like a dry land, and slay her with thirst.

Eventually Hosea is forced to buy back his wife for "fifteen pieces of silver and an homer of barley." This humiliating gesture restores the family, but with its innocence forever lost. The Book of Hosea is—among many other things—about the ungovernable, destructive force of passion. God, railing against the new evidence of iniquity he discovers in Ephraim and Samaria, compares their adulterous conduct to "an oven heated by the baker, *who* ceaseth from raising after he hath kneaded the dough, until it be leavened." Then, in the hypnotic, repetitive way of this prose, embellishing, expanding, amplifying the original trope:

For they have made ready their heart like an oven, while they lie in wait; their baker sleepeth all the night; in the morning it burneth as a flaming fire.

Passion, once sampled, rages out of control. The description of sensuality is highly evocative: "They are all hot as an oven." Israel—a metonymy for the people of Israel—"hast gone a whoring from thy God, thou hast loved a reward upon every cornfloor" (perhaps a reference to sexual practices engaged in as a part of harvest rituals). Whatever the particulars, the message is clear: debauchery and excess sap the spirit and destroy the fabric of society. "Whoredom and wine and new wine take away the heart." It's not out of piety that He thunders, or some abstract notion of sin, but out of a knowledge of the consequences. Decadence is enervating. It turns men away from their true purpose—the enaction of His will.

But Hosea is more than a story of marital woe. The unhappy marriage chronicled there is a parable of larger events—"a model and metaphor," in the words of the Anchor Bible commentators, "for Yahweh's marriage to his bride Israel." Hedged about by powerful enemies on all sides, the tenuous nation-state of eighth-century B.C.E. Israel bore an uncanny resemblance to its contemporary heir, an Israel surrounded by nations intent upon its destruction. Reading Hosea, I was struck by the parallels; not even the names have changed (for Assyria read Syria; for Egypt, Egypt). Then as now, Israel's fate hung in the balance. Obedience to God's mandate was more than His whim; it was a matter of survival. The years chronicled in Hosea— roughly 755 to 740 B.C.E.—were years of intense political strife. "Loss of the land and the end of the state were not remote and theoretical possibilities but present and impending realities," note Andersen and Freedman. Thus does history repeat itself.

Israel's situation was unique. God had delivered its people from bondage. They were His charges, the Chosen People, and violated their Covenant with Him at their peril. Cults, promiscuity, Baal-worship, assassinations, reliance on armaments, and the many other insidious practices God enumerates with such angry vehemence were a betrayal—a form of collective adultery. "The Lord hath a controversy with the inhabitants of the land, because *there is* no truth, nor mercy, nor knowledge of God in the land," begins chapter 4, wherein He puts before the people His litany of grievances. "By swearing, and lying, and killing, and stealing, and committing adultery, they break out, and blood toucheth blood"—that is, they engage in human sacrifices that violate the sanctity of life. They have broken their vows, "gone a whoring from under their God."

But it's not only the people who are guilty of apostasy; responsibility starts at the top: "Like people, like priest." A nation without leadership is a nation that has lost its way. Those who forsake their God shall themselves be forsaken. "For Israel slideth back as a backsliding heifer," He declares, in one of the more ambiguous passages of Hosea. "Now the

Lord will feed them as a lamb in a large place." This isn't as benevolent as it sounds: not *The Lord will minister to the innocent people,* but *The Lord will henceforth regard the people as helpless, unthinking creatures, an aimless flock.* In a last beautiful and startling image, He predicts: "The wind hath bound her up in her wings. . . ." Having forfeited their claim to God's divine guidance, Israel shall be scattered, dispersed, flung to the ends of the earth. Merciless nature shall have its way.

His cry of outrage rises to a crescendo in chapter 5, where He rehearses his judgment against the people of Israel. Those who abandoned Him shall be abandoned. "They shall go with their flocks and with their herds to seek the Lord; but they shall not find *him;* he hath withdrawn himself from them." Pondering this passage, I was brought to a new awareness of a concept I'd often heard invoked but never grasped before: the Old Testament God. I had only the vaguest notion of this God, whom I supposed a cruel, unforgiving character given to punitive acts of vengeance when He was crossed. Like the oppressive Jewish mother trotted out by standup comedians—*See what I do for you? See the sacrifices I make?*—He was always harping on how much He did for Israel, and what did Israel do for Him? But as I read Hosea, I sensed the desperation of this God, His grief over the frailty of men. The marriage parable became clearer in my mind. Why should He be above anger, vindictiveness, revenge? The people cheated. Even God—I'm tempted to say—is only human.

One of the most astonishing features of Hosea—among the longest books in the Bible—is the modulation of voice from chapter to chapter. The measured historical narrative of chapter 1—*this is what happened, and when*—gives way to autobiography, the chronicle of Hosea's marital crisis; then, in chapter 4, to the prophecies of God, a recital of transgressions that culminates in the minatory "Hear ye this, O priests" of chapter 5; and, finally, in the closing verses—for that is what they are—a rhythmic cadence of redemption. "Come, and let us return unto the Lord," begins chapter 6, "for he hath torn, and he will heal us; he hath smitten, and he will bind us up."

The hope of God's return is announced in a lovely image: "his going forth is prepared as the morning; and he shall come unto us the rain, as the latter *and* former rain unto the earth." Men are fickle; like that of Adam, who betrayed God's word, their faith "*is* as a morning cloud, and as the early dew it goeth away." Nothing humbles them, not even—this is very much my own reading—the prospect of death. Apostrophizing the kingdom of Ephraim, God notes in His bleak, unsparing way: "yea, gray hairs are here and there upon him, yet he knoweth not." Their civilization isn't divine; it's a thing created by men: "the workman made it; therefore it *is* not god." And therefore it can be unmade. The works of man are transient; only the works of God are eternal.

Like so much of the Bible—like so much of literature, like so much of life—Hosea is a lesson in humility. You don't have to believe in God to recognize in the waywardness of Israel a parable of human arrogance. It's not only our sins—whoring, greed, adultery—that condemn us, it's what they represent: a putting of our desires before those of God. "I found Israel like grapes in the wilderness," He rhapsodizes, a fecund and fertile land undefiled by the depredations of man, a second Eden. But the people in their carelessness destroyed it, desecrating their paradisal habitat by claiming it as their own. Even their places of worship reflect their vanity: "For Israel hath forgotten his Maker, and buildeth temples. . . ." Nature is God's creation, not man's.

Hosea is a static book. A reviewer might complain that it's skimpy on plot, the characters are thin. Compared with other incident-crammed chapters in the book, it offers little in the way of action. Hosea remains a murky figure. The main episode—the disintegration of his marriage—is only sketchily described, and the authors devote a mere paragraph, or stanza, to the troubled couple's reconciliation. It's more a diatribe than a story, and—our hypothetical reviewer could argue—a monotonous one at that. Having offered Israel the possibility of redemption, God discovers iniquity in Ephraim and Samaria and once again works Himself up into a lather, denouncing their wickedness and threatening to send them back to Egypt: "For they have sown the wind, and they shall reap the whirlwind: it hath no stalk: the bud shall yield no meal: if so be it yield, the strangers shall swallow it up." (If they do cook it, foreigners will swallow it.)

There is something disturbing about this relentless anger, book after book of punitive judgment. Forgiveness isn't His strong suit. He's like a father disappointed in his son—a comparison made explicit at the beginning of chapter 11: "When Israel *was* a child, then I loved him, and called my son out of Egypt." Boastful, vain, self-righteous, He refuses to recognize that children grow up and go their own ways. I am the Lord, He's always reminding the people, showing off His credentials. I won't destroy Ephraim, He promises: "for I *am* God, and not man." He gloatingly rehearses old triumphs—His "controversy" with Judah, how He got even with Jacob. The God of Hosea is a familiar historical type, the petulant dictator flouting his authority ("I gave thee a king in mine anger, and took *him* away in my wrath"). He can't make up His mind whether to destroy Israel or to save it. In one breath, He's offering to "ransom" Israel from "the power of the grave"; in the next, He's ready to lay it waste. His viciousness—infants "dashed in pieces," pregnant women "ripped up"—is believable after the Holocaust; we've seen everything these Biblical authors can describe. But it's unsettling. He is, after all, He: a God. A God with an ax to grind.

Yet, for all His defiant posturing, a note of self-abnegation, even self-pity creeps in toward the close of His peroration. "I will be thy king," He implores, "where *is any other* that may save thee in all thy cities?" By the last chapter, He's humbler, less wheedling and volatile:

I will be as the dew unto Israel: he shall grow as the lily, and cast forth his roots as Lebanon.

His branches shall spread, and his beauty shall be as the olive tree, and his smell as Lebanon.

They that dwell under his shadow shall return; they shall revive *as* the corn, and grow as the vine: the scent thereof *shall be* as the wine of Lebanon.

Hosea, then, ends with the repentance of Israel and its reconciliation with Yahweh—an event prefigured in Gomer's return to her cuckolded husband. But for a contemporary reader (especially a Jewish reader), the message is more ominous. As I made my way through this gnomic, exalted prose, I kept feeling that I was reading a commentary on current events, a rehearsal in seventeenth-century prose of modern Israel's predicament. How little has changed! I recalled that passage in Bellow's *To Jerusalem and Back* where he enters a quiet flagstone court in the Greek quarter of Jerusalem and finds himself brooding about the history of the Jews. It has been their fate to exist apart, a people unto themselves—a distinction that's had tragic consequences once in our century, and could again. Yet the belief that Jews are different, other, and must put themselves above those who wish to destroy them, continues to prevail. Bellow notes with disapproval George Steiner's argument that Israel must be "more just and moral than others." He talks with an Israeli novelist who insists that Israel "has sinned too much, that it has become too corrupt" to prevail over its enemies—an uncanny echo of Hosea's lament. Israel excites resentment; it doesn't have the luxury of behaving like other nations. But hasn't its uniqueness proved the source of its undoing? Isn't that very conviction of difference a kind of pride?

These questions were new to me. Studying Hosea, I found myself awakened to a consciousness of Jewish identity I'd never had before. Why was the pursuit of culture so ingrained in my family? Where did it come from? Bellow traces this Jewish culture-hunger to the longing of eighteenth-century European Jews newly liberated from the ghetto to claim their place in the society that had excluded them—"its cities, its political life, its culture, its great men, its personal opportunities." Perhaps—or perhaps it goes back further, to their ancient status as—I quote Hosea—"sons of the living god." Whatever its source, this unique identity is both a privilege and a burden. It's with you for life. In the cool courtyard, away from the strife of Jerusalem, Bellow reflects: "The slightest return of beauty makes you aware how deep your social wounds are, how painful it is to think continually of nothing but aggression and defense, superpowers, diplomacy, terrorism." Such worldly preoccupations, he adds, "shrink art to nothing."

Hosea embraces both. Its art, the language as it comes down to us in translation, is transcendent, as eternal as any human thing. Yet the historical situation it describes is charged with grim portent. I was haunted by a passage in 13:3 where God elaborates on His prophecy for Ephraim:

Therefore they shall be as the morning cloud, and as the early dew that passeth away, as the chaff *that* is driven with the whirlwind out of the floor, and as the smoke out of the chimney.

A prophecy that came to pass.

JOEL

Harvey Shapiro

66 THE WORD OF THE LORD THAT CAME TO JOEL THE SON OF
Pethuel." What a way to open a poem. Gives it authority, right? The word of the Lord that came to Harvey
the son of Jacob. What would it take for me, sitting in
Brooklyn, to type those words? Belief in inspiration, I have that. My best
poems, those I wrote in my head on walks, or in my notebook in a rush
of music and feeling, had no source I could name. No, if I began with, was
made to name a source, I suppose I would say "muse." Not even heavenly
muse. Who was that muse I invoked sometimes so directly in my poems?
The ghost of English poetry past, maybe. My way of saying that a Jewish
poet, son of immigrant parents, was writing an English poem. Don't I
remember well that as late as my entrance into college I believed that in
order to write I would have to learn the language of my forebears, which
I insanely thought to be Russian, though I grew up with a Yiddish-speaking
grandmother and knew that Yiddish was the language my mother and father

The King James Version of the Bible used in this essay.

197

both spoke first, and, indeed, was the language I spoke first, according to my mother: the layers of absorbed anti-Semitism in all this confusion and subterfuge.

But whatever I wrote at the insistence of the Muse or muses I claimed as my own, knew as the impulse passed into language that it was my language and finally my voice issuing from that language. And this formula—"the word of the Lord that came to Joel the son of Pethuel"—is demeaning; seen in one light, it puts the poet in a totally passive position: he isn't coming to the word, the word is coming to him. And it's not his word. He's a dummy in a bit of divine ventriloquism. "Hear this, ye old men," Joel begins. One can hear his voice deepen to take on the big bass God. Getting up nerve to say "Hear this," he has to pitch his voice deep in his voice box so that he can address the old men in a manner that will make them listen. And tied to the tail of the formula is his father's name. Would one, of one's own volition, want to be reminded of a father in the act of writing? No, no more than in the act of sex. This poet is destroying himself before he even gets out the first word.

That, I suppose, is being a prophet, the price to be paid for being even a minor prophet. If I had to sign myself, Harvey the son of Jacob, remembering the confusion of that dead businessman who never could figure out what he wanted in the New World but some kind of eminence that he thought would come with money, I would be adding his confusion to my confusion and the words would come out in a kind of pre-Yiddish, a wailing so far from language that only a performance poet could do it justice.

What follows the prophetic formula in Joel is a poem of such violence that it reminds one of the *Iliad* in the pleasure it takes in delineating force. It is a poem of force. The promises of God for peace and plenty scattered through the text come in as grace notes among the bunched cacophony.

"The grey sunken cunt of the world," James Joyce wrote when he had Leopold Bloom think of Palestine, the Dead Sea, the Cities of the Plain. The fructifying force was gone out of it, in his day. To change Joyce's metaphor, it was an empty cradle, disused and tossed on the rubbish heap of history. You might pick it up to point a moral. A dead thing. The stuff of coloring books in Sunday school. But for us the violence of the Old Testament is in the air we breathe. It is the violence of our world and time, and it issues from that strip of land again. So much so that fundamentalists in the churches of Texas, believing in the second big bang that will follow the first big bang of Creation in the short history of the world and will end that short history, bring on the day of judgment, and separate forever the saved from the lost, locate the spark in Israel, no more the grey sunken cunt of the world.

Before the actual description of the battle that is to occupy Joel through the length of his poem, he addresses his hearers directly. He asks the old men and all the inhabitants of the land if what he is about to tell them is anything they can remember happening in their day or in the days of their fathers. A curious question, for what he is about to tell them, describe for them in vivid figures, has happened to them; indeed, if there is any reality to the figurative language that makes up the poem, this must have been the great event in their generation. It's like telling the old men of my generation to remember the Second World War. But the poet assumes collective amnesia. He assumes that what people live through is unreal for them, particularly if they have gone through it as a generation, particularly if it is a catastrophic national event—the assassination of a president, say—unless the poet finds words to make it real. That is what Joel does. These images that we live with—on the television screen, in the movies—have no more reality for us than do our own lives. Reality has to be shoved into words by the poet and then shoved into our faces before we can experience in its fullness a belief in what has happened.

Joel challenges his hearers to understand what it is that they can see for themselves if they have but the vision. And he further commands them: "Tell ye your children of it, and let their children tell their children, and their children another generation." Jewish readers will remember a similar command from their family seders. The Jews are a remembering people; it is what their religion is about. Yet they are always being told to remember something and to tell their children about it, and their children to tell their children. As if the past would disappear if Jews decided to forget it. Is this true? Would the Holocaust be no more without its remembering Jews? When we first left Egypt, to initiate the family seder, we took with us the body of Joseph ("God will remember you if you take me hence" is what he said), so that we would remember our coming into Egypt even as we were departing. So the remembering began then, when there was almost nothing to remember, unless it was the Creation and the desert stars that

Abraham saw. Because if we forget, then God forgets. And in the process of forgetting, He forgets us. And we descend into that nameless void, nameless we descend into it, which is always before us and which is surely before us now. To choose between that history of ours and the void—history stopped, pain forgot—is the choice God gives to us in every generation. Or it is a choice given to us in every generation by whatever agency by which choice is handed out.

What is it that Joel asks his people to remember as if it had happened to them, as indeed it has happened to them? A plague of locusts. But they are figured as a destroying army, though the figure isn't developed until later in the poem. In this first section the agents of destruction named directly by the poet are the palmer worm, the locust, the canker worm, and the caterpillar. There is only one adumbration of the *Iliad*-like descriptions of war that are to follow: "For a nation is come up upon my land, strong, and without number."

In this opening pastoral of desolation, the gathering velocity of the poem is propelled by Joel's vocatives, his direct commands to himself and to the people: Awake; weep; howl; lament; be ye ashamed; gird yourselves and lament, ye priests; howl, ye ministers of the altar; sanctify ye a feast; call a solemn assembly; gather the elders; cry unto the Lord. That is the skeleton of the verse, fleshed with images of the destruction caused by the ravaging locusts. All of these commands and descriptions lead up, mount up, as if in an ascent to Jerusalem, to a cry unto the Lord: because what is prefigured here is for Joel the day of the Lord. Not the destruction we have witnessed but the destruction that is to come: terminal. And "from the Almighty shall it come." This is the land of apocalypse, from the first word spoken by Joel to the last. Every bush in this land is tinder, green though it may be to our present sight. Every hill is a hill of skulls.

Take Allen Ginsberg's "Howl" and transpose the urban images into pastoral, and you have the opening verses of Joel. But in Ginsberg what suffers is man, and in the background is the suffering, blighted urban landscape. In Joel the pastoral landscape is made to suffer up front, and man is in the background. "The field is wasted"; "the corn is wasted"; "the vine is dried up"; withered are the fig tree, the pomegranate tree, the palm tree, the apple tree. The beasts groan; the flocks of sheep are made desolate. And the final image is fire, devouring the pastures, the trees, the animals: "The rivers of water are dried up, and the fire hath devoured the pastures of the wilderness." Dropped into this landscape and always a part of it is man, because he is the key to all this imagery, hidden though he may be, hidden as is this single clause in the midst of these opening verses: "because joy is withered away from the sons of men."

If man is the key and the land suffers because of him, then we turn to the prophet and ask what is it man has done. Allen Ginsberg, in his role of modern prophet—and how much he has lifted from the Bible, Buddhist though he is, and adorned himself with to play that role: the parallel verses, the vocatives driving the verses—is clear and simple about cause. Man is innocent, and what has brought him to this condition, the condition that forces the poet to howl rather than chant, sing, or say, is Moloch, the "fascist national Golgotha"—in other words, the state, industrial civilization, evil as an outside force. In this, Ginsberg is a typical follower of the line romanticism has taken in our century. In Joel there isn't a clue to what specific act or event has caused destruction to come upon the land, though clearly no outside force has victimized man. Man is asked to supply the remedy, so presumably he is the cause. He is bidden to fast, to gather for prayer, to cry unto the Lord. What transgressions of his have brought this plague of locusts? None is stated. What is implied in the injunctions to weep, fast, and cry unto the Lord is that there hasn't been enough of such activities. These aren't sinners in the hands of an angry God; they are people in the hands of a megalomaniac God.

Joel is divided into three sections, and the first section is divided into three parts (let the Christian fathers do their usual). The first part of section one, which ends with verse 12, covers the landscape like the locusts and strips it to a whiteness. There isn't anything left to chew, because "That which the palmer worm hath left hath the locust eaten," through the canker worm and ending with the caterpillar, still creeping but shifting, or prefiguring a shift, into another and perhaps less devastating form of life. If every man is to sit under his fig tree, Joel can't do that; his fig tree is laid waste, as is his vine. It has been stripped down to its bark, and then the bark stripped away to whiteness. Those whom Joel mentions in the first part of this section are husbandmen, vinedressers. In the second part he moves up the social scale to address the priests, "ye ministers of the altar." We know they've been suffering because we've been told that "the meat offering and the drink offering" have been cut off. Now they are admonished by the prophet to gird themselves, lament, howl, fast, and bring everyone into the Temple, "for the day of the Lord is at hand." Gather them in the way you round up a populace before a hurricane. Only this will be worse. We all know what "the day of the Lord" signifies: "And as a destruction from the Almighty shall it come."

The third and final part of section one consists of two short verses, and in these Joel speaks in his own voice; that is, he steps out of the prophetic voice he has used thus far, with the authority coming from God so that he can address priests and expect them to obey. Now, in his own voice, because the situation is urgent, he addresses God Himself, the small voice stepping out of the shadow of the larger one: "O Lord, to thee will I cry; for the fire hath devoured the pastures of the wilderness, and the flame hath burned all the trees of the field." This scaling down of the sound, assuming that Joel writes as a poet and is no more an instrument than Coleridge was a harp, prepares the way for the terrific crescendo opening the second section of the poem.

Here is the heart of the poem. Here it is hard to separate Joel's voice from God's voice, as it is difficult to separate the plague of locusts, which is the subject of this section of the poem, from the figurative army of destruction that Joel describes so tellingly. We are not dealing with tenor and vehicle. We are much closer to Homeric simile. The army has as much rooting in reality as the plague of locusts for which it is ostensibly a metaphor.

The rhetoric is cranked up; the sound is turned up to its highest, acrosonic. Those who hear are to tremble. An alarm is being sounded. We move to a day of darkness, thick darkness. And as the section gathers velocity and sharpness, we begin to see, through the pervasive darkness, the avenging army.

But before the army comes into focus, we are shown the fire and devastation that accompany the army:

A fire devoureth before them; and behind them a flame burneth: the land is as the garden of Eden before them, and behind them a desolate wilderness; yea, and nothing shall escape them.

Then the army appears—first as horses and horsemen; then we are made to hear their approach, as the noise of chariots and the crackling of flame. The verse is very compact at this point, so that we hear and see and feel the terror at the same time:

Like the noise of chariots on the tops of mountains shall they leap, like the noise of a flame of fire that devoureth the stubble, as a strong people set in battle array.

The visual image now is paramount as the army moves closer and we begin to see men who scale walls, men who march. Until finally the terror is brought home and the army enters the city, climbing the walls of houses "to enter in at the windows like a thief."

The army is an antique one, consisting of cavalry, chariots, and foot soldiers, but in its efficiency, in the dread way the men do not break ranks, are incapable of stopping or of being stopped, the army begins to seem almost mechanized, modernized; we are back watching the German army advance into Poland in the opening days of World War II. This is the description of a blitzkrieg, though it be of locusts.

The description of the invading army contains its own terror, but the substratum of the locusts is constant, always adding its element to the accumulating terror. When Joel says of the "great people" who are the agent of the invasion that they resemble horses and run like horsemen, there is a clear, if implied, magnification of the locusts, boosting the individual locust to the size of a horse. Similarly, when Joel in the next verse describes the noise of the approaching army—like chariots leaping down the tops of mountains, like the roar of a brush fire—that noise of destruction holds within it the sound of the mechanical and maniacal chewing of a horde of insects. And this noise seems more terrible than the noise of the army itself.

Why should this be so? Joel's hearers have experienced an invasion of locusts, so one can say this must be a sharp memory, a vivid and direct remembrance. We can only speculate about their experience of invading armies and about the warnings of invasion they must have lived with constantly, being a small tribal power in an area where a great power, Babylon, was building.

For the modern reader the situation is somewhat clearer. He knows the reality of an invading army, if not at first hand then at least at vivid second hand. The invading locusts have not the immediacy of recent history or of an immediately threatened future. But for the modern reader the locust army is still more terrible than the human army because it combines aspects of a science-fiction horror film—enlarged bugs ravaging our planet, grinding us all to bits—and an archetypal terror that indeed this will be so, the smallest particles of moving life that we live among, step on, destroy by the millions when it suits our purposes, when the judgment is finally meted out—and, after all, that's what this poem is about—will be in the saddle (have the appearance of horsemen) and we will be those who flee as before a devouring flame.

The second section has moved thus far from the opening sound of the trumpet, through thick darkness, to the more sharply defined images of fire, horses, chariots, until we come close up and see the invaders as men scaling the walls of the city, climbing the walls of houses, and finally, as the image becomes very close and personal, "entering in at the windows like a thief." The shift to the singular here seems deliberate. This is now one on one: one thief entering one window while one inhabitant awaits his fate.

In this splendid diapason, played on the invading army, Joel reaches the point he wants and then shifts. The shift is from the small, the lifesize (in this poem and in the Bible, lifesize is small), to the tremendously huge:

The earth shall quake before them; the heavens shall tremble; the sun
and the moon shall be dark, and the stars shall withdraw their shining. . . .

After the sharp images of the preceding lines, we move through these vague images of foreboding; they are not visual images, to my way of thinking; they are not meant to sharpen sight. Instead they open up to the threat of total extinction that hangs over the poem.

If there is any visual effect at all in these lines, it is one of darkness. Darkness has been gathering since the section began. In verse 2 it is a "day of darkness and of gloominess, a day of clouds and thick darkness." In verse 6 the faces of those who turn toward the invaders in terror "gather blackness." Indeed, all faces "gather blackness," because of the fire that precedes the army. Facing that fire of destruction, either moving behind it or watching it approach, blackens the features. And now, as the poem shifts, this darkness becomes absolute and universal: the sun and moon and stars are black. And out of this absolute blackness, Joel's setting for the voice that speaks through him, comes the divine voice.

God speaks before the army as if standing before an encampment. So the action of the poem is effectively stopped at this point. That is, the physical action of the poem is stopped, the army still and silent, though the army—an army of locusts, remember—serves in this, as it has throughout the poem, only as an instrument. The locusts are not being addressed; Joel's audience is and we are.

The words uttered by God through His prophet Joel seem to have no real historical setting; they do not seem time-bound in any way. They are sent out into time to travel forever, or until time ceases to exist. A Jew must feel this. The books of the Bible are rotated throughout the year of services, the scrolls turned, until the entire Bible is read, and then the rotation begins again. There is no getting out of the book. That is plain fact, for the synagogue-goer. For the common reader, what places Joel's words on a timeless trajectory is the way Western man has interpreted Biblical text over centuries.

As God speaks, the turning of the poem occurs. "Therefore also now saith the Lord, turn ye even to me with all your heart, and with fasting, and with weeping, and with mourning." The words go on, Joel's voice wrapped around God's words: "And rend your heart, and not your garments, and turn unto the Lord your God: for he is gracious and merciful, slow to anger, and of great kindness, and repenteth him of the evil." The key word here is "turn," which Jews recognize as the turning to God and the right way they are expected to achieve and wish to achieve during the ten days between Rosh Hashanah and Yom Kippur. This is the absolute turning God always demands and man can never accomplish.

The terms of the "turning" are now spelled out for the tribe by Joel, sometimes seeming to quote God directly, sometimes referring to Him in the third person—the original third person. The details are formulaic: Blow the trumpet, sanctify a fast, gather the people.

As the terms for the "turning" come to a close, Joel for the second time in the poem suddenly addresses God directly, through the mouths of the priests, the ministers of the people. Joel's words are what the priests should say as they "weep between the porch and the altar." They have the power of the prophet's cry to God: "Spare thy people, O Lord, and give not thine heritage to reproach, that the heathen should rule over them: wherefore should they say among people, Where is their God?"

This chills the heart of the contemporary Jew, for this is indeed what was said "among the people" during the Nazi terror and as news of the death camps spread like ash-laden smoke across Europe to America. It is no comfort to the Jew to be told that this has happened before, that these words have been said about the Jew and his God before. The Holocaust never happened before. And that reproach—where is their God?—was aimed at us, is aimed at us, and we carry it in our hearts as the bitter portion of our heritage. There is no one to answer the question for us, now that God has set it working in history. History will have to provide the answer. God will have to provide the answer. It is not a question the Jew can answer. He can pray, but it is the semblance of prayer; he can observe the Commandments, but this is a semblance of observance; he can lead the devout life as if his God were there, but when the smoke drifted over the death camps God was not there or appeared to be not there. We are a tribe whose God has seemed to depart, and we must learn to live with that knowledge, which is not to deny the existence of God, nor is it to deny our history and our heritage. Indeed, it is to honor our history and our heritage while knowing in our hearts that our God may have departed.

The Jews Joel addresses directly in his poem are not the Jews who in their lifetime saw the Holocaust; their trial was only a plague of locusts. So Joel can assure them that if the priests say the proper words, and if the people turn, then God will show pity, send them corn, wine, and oil, drive the army of locusts into a barren land where they will die and their stink will come up.

More than that, Joel can turn his poem, for a few verses, into a poem of praise, a hymn, for that is what he does:

Be not afraid, ye beasts of the field: for the pastures of the wilderness do spring, for the tree beareth her fruit, the fig tree and the vine do yield their strength.

The promise of the hymn is a promise of renewal and of the inexhaustible bounty of the earth: "And the floors shall be full of wheat, and the fats shall overflow with wine and oil." And Jews will "eat in plenty" and "shall never be ashamed," because—and here Joel again dons God's voice—"And ye shall know that I am in the midst of Israel."

Along with this promise of plenty and this reassurance of dignity derived from the visible presence of God comes a startling promise of vision, that we Jews will be a visionary people:

And it shall come to pass afterward, that I will pour out my spirit upon all flesh; and your sons and your daughters shall prophesy, your old men shall dream dreams, your young men shall see visions. . . .

Of all the promises made in the poem, this is the one that has come true, though it has yielded us nothing.

In the middle of the hymn of praise, before it turns back to blood and darkness to merge with the rest of this poem of terror, Joel says, speaking for God: "And I will restore to you the years that the locust hath eaten, the cankerworm and the caterpillar, and the palmerworm, my great army which I sent among you." But no one has restored to us the years the locust has eaten. No one has given life back to the dead Jews of our terrible war, and no one has given back to those who survived the camps and the armies those years that the locust ate.

In the last three verses of this second section, the poem swerves back to apocalypse. God, after these promises of peace and plenty, promises also the end of time: "The sun shall be turned into darkness, and the moon into blood, before the great and terrible day of the Lord come." This is the final promise, the destruction of the earth and its inhabitants—except for those who call on the name of God, the saved, that "remnant."

The day of judgment: "Multitudes, multitudes in the valley of decision; for the day of the Lord is near in the valley of decision." The third section of Joel's poem is one long riff, in the mouth of God, on the judgment day. The themes are several: vengeance on the Gentiles who have made the Hebrews suffer and "have taken my silver and my gold, and have carried into your temples my goodly things"; war—presumably the final war:

Proclaim ye this among the Gentiles; Prepare war, wake up the mighty men, let all the men of war draw near; let them come up;

Beat your plowshares into swords, and your pruninghooks into spears: let the weak say, I am strong.

Along with these themes we have the now familiar promise of absolute dark: "The sun and the moon shall be darkened, and the stars shall withdraw their shining" (Joel uses this the way Homer uses "rosy-fingered dawn"). And out of that dark, the Lord "shall roar out of Zion" and will again be "the hope of his people." While the surrounding lands shall be a desolation and a "desolate wilderness," wine and milk will flow for the Jews and "Judah shall dwell for ever and Jerusalem from generation to generation."

The theme of war is right, because this has been a poem of violence from the outset. And the dominant image, though it does not appear in this section, remains the invading army, so carefully and brilliantly described earlier. God's justification for His final judgment, as Joel sees it, and for saving the remnant of Israel after this trial by locusts and by final darkness, constitutes the final verse of the poem:

For I will cleanse their blood that I have not cleansed: for the Lord dwelleth in Zion.

So this poem, this invasion, this final darkness all are part of a necessary blood-cleansing. Cleansing for what reason? Cleansing to eradicate what? It is impossible not to feel the tribal instinct for purity in this divine justification for what has happened and what will happen, and the prophet's appetite for renewal joined with God's. For how else is blood cleansed unless it is first spilled? We are up against the final darkness here.

It is also right to note the one lyric verse in this final section, lovely in its use of nature as a way of suggesting the ease of things when man is at home in his life and his land and his God:

And it shall come to pass in that day, that the mountains shall drop down new wine, and the hills shall flow with milk, and all the rivers of Judah shall flow with waters, and a fountain shall come forth of the house of the Lord, and shall water the valley of Shittim.

Joel, like the Bible, mixes the tribal with the universal. That, finally, is the source of the power of this poem. Yes, there has been a jewellike and terrifying portrayal of a plague of locusts. And there has been that thunder produced by the prophet to invoke deity. And there are other felicities. But consider how tribal revenge, played out in the final section of the poem, contains within it the shattering universal image of "multitudes, multitudes in the valley of decision." Joel's powerful vision of all mankind crowded into the valley of Jehoshaphat to be judged is what has driven this poem from its inception. The cry in verse 5 of the first section, "Awake, ye drunkards, and weep; and howl all ye drinkers of wine," is not only for the wine that has been "cut off," nor is it for what the palmer worm and the canker worm have done to the land, but it is for the fact that man is to be judged, twist and turn as he will. He will finally find himself in the valley of decision with multitudes. This is true on the psychological level for every man and woman. And now how dimly and slowly we begin to see that it may be true for mankind itself. That, along with the palmer worm and the canker worm, man as a species is to be judged, that nothing is guaranteed, and that there is a valley of decision we are hurrying into—as if this Biblical threat and Biblical promise had called into existence a world that knows no other pattern.

AMOS

Howard Moss

MOS WAS THE PROTOTYPE OF THE POPULIST WHO SPRINGS OUT
of nowhere to condemn a civilization. He speaks—and writes,
being the first of the "literary" prophets—both directly and
in symbols, and the sardonic thrust of what he has to say, in
its all-condemning viewpoint, is harsh, unremitting, and without pity. There
is something of Swift in the rigor of his attack, and something of the
innocent who finds himself in the palaces of corruption.

Beyond a few bare facts, Amos' life is one of pure deduction. Born
sometime between 760 and 750 B.C.E. in Tekoa—a desert settlement six miles
south of Bethlehem—he was a shepherd and a farmer with a sizable crop
of sycamore trees that produced an edible fig. No physical reality pervades
the text—no mirror image one can project backward into antiquity to see
him as a man, a face, and a figure dressed in . . . what? White. He is bearded;
with a stick, perhaps a shepherd's crook, or a farmer's walking rod cut from
a tree. (A grove of trees must have been a rare sight in mile after mile of

---

The King James Version of the Bible used in this essay.

sand.) A herder and a farmer both, he knew the animal life of the desert as well as the secrets of the gardener and grower.

Amos seems like a simple man of keen intelligence, but ill-chosen for divine revelation. The morals of the rustic are larded with the generosity (by implication) of the social critic throughout Amos' harangue. Spleen and outrage, and a logic not usually associated with either, are parts of his makeup. Like a yokel arrived in a big city, Amos might well have been startled and revolted by crowds; he has the aura of the radical populist driven mad by the voluptuousness and corruption of cities. A description of him suggests that he descended on Bethel during a festival and walked among the "merrymakers." Whether he disliked merrymaking in general or specific acts committed in its name is hard to tell. There is the unmistakable sound of the countryman, disgusted by sensuality and greed, as well as the undertone of the peasant alarmed by the unfamiliar, orchestrating his disapproval.

Saintliness is beyond his reach, for the Jewish conscience demanded social action. Giddy intemperance colors the invective. Goodness, darkened by temper, seems certain. Wide-eyed, proud, he suggests someone not quite in touch with reality, yet capable of seeing all its flaws. An uncomfortable man, rigidly moral, he can be characterized as a beacon or a spoiler, for in him the puritan and the revolutionary are intertwined to produce a creature we have learned to be wary of: a straitlaced conscience, which, if given power, soon becomes as tyrannical as the forces it opposes.

There was a great deal to oppose in Israel, divided in Amos' time into a southern kingdom of Judah, ruled by Uzziah, and a northern one of Israel, led by Jeroboam II. Both may have been loosely identified under the generic name of "Israel," in the same way that the "United States" and "America" are often used interchangibly. Amos, a southerner hailing from Judah, preached, nevertheless, in the north.

Israel felt itself immune from God's wrath, its populace living under what they believed to be a unique dispensation—the Chosen People. Jerusalem was independent and at its material and social height—one never to be reached again in ancient times—when Amos damned Israel with the news that it was not special, that it would be judged along with its neighbors and by the same standards.

Paying lip service to prayer and the sacraments, the Jews had lost their sense of Biblical values. Imperial and affluent, Israel's leaders believed their country's prosperity to be a sign of God's favor. Amos disabused them of the notion. The Israelites supported official shrines; in fact, the worst oversupported them, as if a hollow gesture could take the place of moral values (in the way a Sicilian Mafioso might contribute handsomely to the Roman Catholic Church). Though the Israelites officially respected the letter of the law, they flouted it; as for the spirit of the law, they showed no understanding of it. Smug in luxury, secure in the false glow of imperial expansion (shades of the nineteenth-century British), they had become hypocrites. Amos, a maverick, denounced a complaisant society for what it prized most: its power.

A prophet was more than someone who could see into the future; he was a seer, a man of wisdom who sees a truth, or to whom a truth is revealed that everyone else misses. There was a long tradition of seers well before Amos. Seers were usually educated men, or those set apart (even in primitive tribes) by instinct, the gift of divination, or training. They were "different," and of a different status from the ordinary citizen. Moreover, the prophet served as a kind of corrective historian, bringing the dimension of justice into his version of history, examining the present as if it were the past, and looking forward to a future in which justice would be a commonplace—a thought often articulated in Chekhov's plays and certainly at the end of *Three Sisters,* where a world far better than the present one is envisioned. Amos is ultimately concerned with clarity and self-knowledge, as opposed to a befuddled intoxication of the senses that can victimize reason with its empty emphasis on the sensuous rewards of wealth and power.

Amos was not educated; he came from none of the privileged sanctuaries a society affords. Angry, forthright, simplistic, and fierce—nothing pastoral tempers his judgment. Rather, the unrelenting heat and spareness of the desert suffuse what he has to say—by his mere existence and presence, he undermined long-held assumptions. Prophets were not expected to rise out of desert rabble, but, rather, from the upper strata—officials, holy men, what we might consider the rabbinate today. A peasant upstart, a minister with holy fire in his eye, Amos was as damning in his origins and his articulateness as he was exacting in his scruples and preaching.

According to the Oxford Annotated Bible in a commentary on the text of Amos, his words fall into three doxologies: "Tirades directed against the neighboring countries of Israel" (by way of examples to Israel of its own courting of disaster), chapters 1 and 2; "an indictment against Israel itself for sin and injustice," chapters 3 through 6; "and visions of Israel's destruction" (exaggerated reminders of the need for moral integrity), chapters 7 through 9. These last were apocalyptic at the time, and so unexpected and severe as to be emotionally and psychologically traumatic. Amos publicly proclaimed the essential evil of a royal house and a self-satisfied theocracy in the name of the same God of the Bible.

Amos' argument is a brilliant circling device that finally narrows and homes in on its true object.

Cleverly, like any demagogue, Amos tells his audience what it wants to hear. He begins by attacking the enemies of the Jewish people, naming them by nation or region: Damascus, Gaza, Tyre, Edom, Ammon, and Moab—places that could be plucked from the headlines of the last two decades. Amos denounces these foreign countries for the crimes of war and violence. And then, being a southerner preaching in the north, he begins to attack the Jewish people themselves, but first only those of the south, Judah, his birthplace. This, too, was pleasing for his northern-Israeli listeners, in the way a South Korean might, with special force, cheer a North Korean stadium audience by reviling South Korea. National prejudice is sharply reinforced by the negative opinion of a native. But then Amos attacks the very audience before him—and this calculated, lengthy buildup of his thesis accounts for its unsettling power. Having led an audience to assent to a condemnation of sin, he held its own sins before it when it was too late to withhold assent. He took a risk; he lashed into his audience with the same spleen he had reserved for its enemies. Just as Antony eulogized Caesar in *Julius Caesar* so that, by the end of his speech, the audience is brought around from its original view to its opposite, Amos, too, lured his listeners (and readers) on to a logically inevitable conclusion.

If Amos was a revolutionary, he was also a conservative. He was out not to change the rules but to have them fulfilled. He wanted to go back to a moral order, not to propound a new one. The notions of overthrowing the sources of power, of specific changes to be made in the social system, are only in the text by way of implication: he is against cheating the poor, against selling the chaff for the wheat, against temple prostitution. He comes with an avenging sword, not a blueprint. The Lord speaks through him, is his dominating muse, and he is merely the mouthpiece, the ventriloquist's dummy through which the truth is uttered.

Being a defender of the poor and the righteous is his chief ethical burden:

> I will not turn away from the punishment thereof;
> Because they sold the righteous for silver,
> And the poor for a pair of shoes;
> That pant after the dust of the earth on the head of the poor,
> And turn aside the way of the meek.

In line 4, even the buried dead are not safe from the greed of the land-hungry rich; even grave titles are endangered.

To elucidate the nature of punishment, God uses symbols four times to illustrate truths to Amos. The symbols are both abstract and specific, and occur in the following order: grasshoppers, fire, a plumbline, and a basket of fruit.

In the first two cases, Amos intercedes for his parishioners:

And it came to pass that when they [the grasshoppers] had made an end of eating the grass of the land, then I said, "O Lord, forgive, I beseech thee; by whom shall Jacob arise for he is small?" The Lord repented for this: "It shall not be," saith the Lord.

And next: ". . . behold, the Lord God called to contend by fire, and it devoured the great deep, and did eat up a part." This, too, ends with a gesture of withheld doom: " 'This also shall not be,' saith the Lord God."

Locusts and fire are suspended sentences, horrors for the time postponed. But the plumbline is different; it is left standing as a threat:

Thus he showed me: and, behold, he the Lord stood upon a wall made upon a plumbline, with a plumbline in his hand. And the Lord said unto me, "Amos, what see'st thou?" And I said, "A plumbline." Then said the Lord, "Behold, I will set a plumbline in the midst of my people Israel; I will not again pass by them any more; and the high places of Isaac shall be desolate, and the sanctuaries of Israel shall be laid waste; and I will rise against the house of Jeroboam with the sword."

So warped from the straight, so crooked and strayed had the Israelis become, that only a plumbline could set a visible moral measure between their current behavior and the true vertical.

The plumbline is the instrument for making foundations straight, angles true, walls secure. The structures of Jerusalem were, literally, to come tumbling down a few years later in an earthquake, as they had in the past. The plumbline is also the sinker that measures the depth of water in a well. Crucial to the discovery and the dissemination of fresh water, the plumbline, as an object *per se,* is a constant reminder of the possibility of drought, the ever-present menace of the desert.

Should Amos' predictions have come to pass—and should the Lord not have revoked them—the natural world would have been put in precarious balance, locusts eating up the land and fire destroying the sea. Only the works of man are left hanging in jeopardy because the plumbline is essential to their construction and use. In the first three symbolic curses, God announces through the voice of Amos that the universe and the world of man are thrown out of kilter.

Finally, God shows Amos a basket of fruit. The fruit is not a vision of what will come, a prophecy, but what *could* have come—a compressed revelation of peace and plenty. Yet, when the Lord shows it to Amos, instead of words appropriate to such a gift, we receive the direst message of all: "The end is come upon my people of Israel; I will not pass by them any more."

"And the songs of the temple shall be howling that day," said the Lord God: "there shall be many dead bodies in every place; and they shall cast them forth with silence." And he decries those "that swallow up the needy, even to make the poor of the land to fail. . . . Making the shekel great, and falsifying the balances by deceit. That [they] may buy the poor for silver, and the needy for a pair of shoes: yea, and sell the refuse of the wheat. . . ."

And there is a further shade of meaning, and possibly the critical one: ripeness is not necessarily all. It is also that state of being that precedes ruin, that moment before flies gnaw through fruit skins to destroy what was, in its prime, edible and bountiful. And so God may have been showing Amos ripeness and the threat ripeness implies, both at the same time. Though the fruits of the earth are a God-given bounty, they must, in time, wither away. Like the pun "spoils," whose noun means "riches" but whose verb means "to ravage," so two worlds of meaning are operative in the same basket of fruit.

But the word "fruit" suggests something else—the end product of a germinating period. The word has the beneficent meaning of "the fruits of one's labor," with nuances of childbirth and good harvests, as well as the malignant one of the serpent's apple, the bad seed. A series of actions eventually bears fruit. Small events do not just culminate in larger ones but determine them, and the larger they become, the more significant. A seed contains the structure of its genes. A basket of summer fruit may be a container of final consequences, as well as a vessel of once-living things now bound to rot.

And so these ambiguities color Amos' words and thought, and they are written words as well as spoken. Amos was not a gifted rabble-rouser, and was the first prophet to put his words on paper, to be a writer as well as an orator, and the precursor, therefore, of a long series of revolutionary writers from Mark to Lenin to Lincoln, Whitman, and Marcuse.

The question of whether Amos was intentionally ambiguous—that is, a writer of more complexity than at first appears—is a real one. The message on its first level is always clear. The complications arise by way of illustration and symbol. But in Amos' case they derive from another fact as well: Amos' prophecies proceed in an inverse order. From chapter 1 on, the punishments become less detailed and the crimes more specific in their cataloguing. Consciously, or otherwise, since the argument is first lulling, then horrifying, the crimes of the Israelites are defined in greater detail than the earlier crimes of the enemies that surround them.

One does not find in Amos the great images, the beautifully phrased cadences of Ecclesiastes or the Song of Songs.

A marked rhythmic drumbeat underlines Amos' voice. Part of the effect, early on, derives from the repeated sounding of place names—a roll call of doom.

> Thus says the LORD:
> "For three transgressions of Damascus,
> and for four, I will not revoke the punishment;
> because they have threshed Gilead with threshing sledges of iron.
> So I will send a fire upon the house of Hazael,
> and it shall devour the strongholds of Benhadad.

> I will break the bar of Damascus,
> and cut off the inhabitants of the Valley of Aven,
> and him that holds the scepter from Betheden;
> and the people of Syria shall go into exile to Kir,"
> says the LORD.

Then there is another kind of effect, a repetition of the same noun building to a climax:

> I will smite the winter house and the summer house;
> and the houses of ivory shall perish,
> and the great houses shall come to an end. . . .

And there is a powerful gift of invective, sometimes combined with the repetition of the same noun or word. Here is Amos delivering his warning to "The wealthy and greedy women of Samaria":

> Hear this word, you cows of Bashan,
> who are in the mountain of Samaria,
> who oppress the poor, who crush the needy,
> who say to their husbands, "Bring, that we may drink!"
> The Lord GOD has sworn by his holiness
> that, behold, the days are coming upon you,
> when they shall take you away with hooks,
> even the last of you with fishhooks.

In "you" and "who"—repeated eight times in a steadily ascending cadence—in the repeated "hooks" and "fishhooks," the victims and the instruments that will transform them into bait are powerfully sounded more than once.

In Amos we find that odd combination of Oriental poetry and democratic agitprop that characterizes Whitman: a curious blend of the image, the catalogue, and the message in a random mixture, united not only by parallel constructions but by the use of contrast. In Whitman, a rhetoric that often suggests the Oriental—

> Loafe with me on the grass, loose the stop from your
>   throat,

Not words, not music or rhyme I want, not custom or
    lecture, not even the best,
Only the lull I like, the hum of your valvèd voice.

I mind how once we lay such a transparent summer
    morning,
How you settled your head athwart my hips and gently
    turn'd over upon me,
And parted your shirt from my bosom-bone, and plunged
    your tongue to my bare-stript heart,
And reach'd till you felt my beard, and reach'd till
    you held my feet.

—works in tandem with the flat statement of the narrative's ultimate point:

All truths wait in all things,
They neither hasten their own delivery nor resist it,
They do not need the obstetric forceps of the surgeon,
The insignificant is as big to me as any. . . .

Amos' image-making faculty exhibits, from time to time, an Eastern echo similar to Whitman's:

And the mountain shall drop sweet wine,
    and all the hills shall melt,

in contrast to the bald statement of crime and the direct threat of punish-ment:

You only have I known of all the families of the
    earth;
Therefore I will visit upon you all your iniquities.

And:

For, behold, the LORD commandeth,
And the great house shall be smitten into
    splinters,
And the little house into chips. . . .

Or:

> And the high places of Isaac shall be desolate,
> And the sanctuaries of Israel shall be laid waste.

Commentators mention Amos' "word play," but of all verbal devices it is the one most easily lost in translation. Yet a slant and certain masculinity of style, replete with natural, primitive images of the desert, make themselves felt, and these images are used extensively as metaphors. A farmer's psyche, a shepherd's vocabulary shape the images and the manner in which they are presented:

> And the shepherd rescued out of the mouth of the
>   lion
> Two legs, or a piece of an ear,
> So shall the children of Israel that dwell in
>   Samaria
> Escape with the corner of a couch, and the leg
>   of a bed. . . .

Childish but chilling, the vividness of this is inescapable, a form of grotesquerie rooted in a harsh world. Surely the word "rescued" is ironic: the lamb is beyond rescue and the shepherd's only motive to prove to the owner of the flock his lack of complicity. A lion was truly on the rampage.

Amos' reiterations, like Whitman's, have a hypnotic, incantatory power. Yet what one misses in the text of Amos is the single quotable line, the poet's line—truth compressed into a memorable phrase—or the descriptive beauty that marks so many Biblical passages, an insight, a turn of phrase, or a moral clue that, withstanding endless repetition, serves for a lifetime.

Amos frightened the establishment. His assault on power did not go unheard in high places. Amaziah, the high priest of Bethel—a temple Amos had sought out for particular scorn—complained directly to Jeroboam, the king of Israel, and Amaziah expressed his personal dissatisfaction to Amos:

> O thou seer, go, flee away into the land of Judah,
> And there eat bread, and prophesy there,

> But prophesy not any more at Bethel.
> For it is the King's chapel, and it is the king's court.

Amos was ultimately banished to Judah, where he wrote down the prophecies he could no longer deliver. Much of their force comes from the single-mindedness of the zealot, the fanatic holy-fire-and-brimstone desert wanderer who becomes authoritative by believing he is and by saying so. That he had a true target is undeniable, but as a man bent on a mission, one who would let nothing stand in his way, he is in many ways as formidable as the forces he attacked. There was no hierarchy above him save One, and therefore none below. He was not a member of the bureaucracy and often took pains to distance himself from the professional prophet. He was directly in touch with the Lord, and his holy messages had the extra force of being passionately delivered by a seemingly common man, a visionary of unshakable fervor with a direct conduit to God.

If history begins with the story of other people, Amos was the first historian, and his importance transcends denunciation. In seeing Israel as a nation among nations, and not merely as the only one, he helped enlarge a tribal consciousness into a broader sense of a world dominated by God's will and by an overall moral view. As if for the first time, the conception of a universal man, an expansion of human purpose, was propounded. It was not, probably, Amos' intention or main focus, but it was an inevitable corollary of his thought. Because of him, local self-images were finally seen as too narrow, too parochial, and no longer fitting the case. A preacher of ethics, Amos unwittingly became a figure who expanded the consciousness of a people. The world suddenly opened—borders that had once held back enemy hordes and warriors now defined lands where people lived and were judged (however negatively), just as the Israelites were.

Almost twenty-five hundred years after this truth was exposed, the irony, the tragedy, is that, in the Middle East, the world at the very center of Amos' thinking should be as torn by conflict as the one he describes. Amos was not so much a prophet of doom, it turns out, at least not yet, as one of repetition. Reading Amos, one feels that little has changed, that for all the lessons, parables, and stories of the Old Testament, history runs its inevitable course.

Amos' leap of the imagination was crucial, however, because his message, though it might be ignored, could never be lost. It is hard to imagine the line of prophets culminating in the Christ figure without him. In Amos, what started out as a moral condemnation ended up as a world view.

JONAH

JUSTICE FOR JONAH, OR
A BIBLE BARTLEBY

Norma Rosen

SHOW ME A TEXT THAT SPEAKS OF GOD'S UNBOUNDED MERCY, AND images of the Holocaust appear before my eyes. It's not anything I can help. *Theology* doesn't help. This is visceral. I don't imagine I'm alone in this. Perhaps my generation will have to die out in the desert before God can appear again on an untarnished mercy seat. Such a return is essential for the healthy nurture of the human religious impulse. I understand that. But I can't be of any help there.

Before the Holocaust it was possible for piety to say, as we read in Lamentations, "We are punished for our sins." After the Holocaust, none but a twisted piety dares say it.

How should someone like me read—as I do with fascination every Yom Kippur—the Book of Jonah? Here, irony of ironies, is the man whose problem springs from his certainty that God will be merciful. Sure enough, when he is sent to prophesy doom to sinful Nineveh, God, as Jonah knew He would, rains down mercy instead of punishment, thus making Jonah a false prophet. Imagine! Jonah's is a theological problem for which the

---

The King James Version of the Bible used in this essay.

twentieth century has devised a complete solution, if Jonah only knew.

Every Yom Kippur I ask myself how Jonah would speak if he could somehow learn what happened to us. Mercy, pity, judgment, punishment: in what proportions might Jonah ascribe those attributes to God if he knew our condition? Is there some way to make a continuum of past and present, as if the Holocaust had not broken its back? Might Jonah study us with the same astonishment as we study him? Let us see what imagination will provide.

Meanwhile, here is Jonah. Thrown overboard. Swallowed by a fish. Brought back to his beginning, a still-reluctant prophet who hates the mercy meted out to a repentant people. God Himself chides Jonah for his mean-spiritedness. Fetches up a vegetable-parable to fetch home the point of brotherly love and fatherly compassion.

Before he entered the Biblical moment recounted in his book, the life of Jonah ben Amittai, the prophet, had been long and illustrious. Over the stormy waters flew the dove (Yonah) with truth (Amittai), the life-giving green of prophecy, in his mouth. Then Jonah stepped into the book of himself—and into the world of sermons, literature, historical anachronism, tall tales and fables, Christian fulminations against the Jews, and cautionary tales for Victorian children.

Other prophets speak to us. Not Jonah. Although he prophesied long and well, no one recorded his words. Only that single sentence to the people of Nineveh: "Yet 40 days and Nineveh shall be overthrown." What's recorded is biography. A scandalous episode in Jonah's life. When God called him to prophesy to Nineveh, Jonah ran away. As if Jonah's read Bernard Malamud's "The Jewbird": "I'm running. I'm flying [in this case, swimming], but I'm also running." Onto a ship that will take him as far from Nineveh as possible. Down to Tarshish, except that a storm interceded.

Why does a seasoned prophet balk at going forth to prophesy again? He is positive God will be merciful, and that he does not want. But in fact he will be hated whether judgment or mercy prevails, this bringer of bad news. "They hate him that rebuketh in the gate," says Amos. "And they abhor him that speaketh uprightly."

Think of the pain of trying to suppress prophecy. "I said, I will not make mention of him, nor speak any more in his name," Jeremiah confesses. "But his word was in my heart as a burning fire shut up in my bones, and I was weary with holding it in, and I could not."

Would any prophet enjoy not speaking? The choice is between fire and water. Jonah chose the sea.

And so Jonah suffers the name of "runaway," an *ad absurdum* satire on every prophet who ever protested unworthiness to carry the divine message. He is called the prophet who cared more for his own image (if, after his doom predictions, God shows mercy, won't Jonah appear to be a false prophet?) and for the image of the Jews (if the pagans of Nineveh repent, won't the stiff-necked Jews appear worse to God?), than for the truth which calls to him by name, and by whose name he is eponymously called.

And that's where Jonah stays stuck. He's the prophet who, according to Christian commentators, illustrates the narrowness and selfishness of the Jews. A few examples suffice:

"The unlovely character of the dour, recalcitrant Hebrew prophet..." *(The Interpreter's Dictionary of the Bible)*. "A narrow-minded Israelite mentality..." (from a high-school textbook, *Teaching the Old Testament*).

Jewish interpreters have not departed much from Christian views, though naturally leaving out the anti-Semitic garnish. One guesses at a reason: though such commentary makes Jews and a Jewish prophet look bad, it makes what Christian commentators call the "Old Testament God" look good. Vindictive judgment, wrath, devouring punishments are banished. In their place, mercy, pity, love. To which Jonah so perversely objects.

Still, the question persists: How can Jonah, who believes in God's omnipotence, expect to hide from God? Is he deficient in understanding? The first in the line of brilliantly perceptive prophets to show dull-wittedness? Not at all. He does not mistake his own powerless position. He surely expects to be found. *Moby Dick* calls up a sermon on Jonah, but Biblical Jonah is closer to Melville's Bartleby, the scrivener, who prefers not to perform the duties for which he's engaged, even though he hasn't a shred of power or an ounce of right on his side. It makes us think that Jonah, like Bartleby, knows something. What that something is, in Jonah's case, I will later try to imagine, by means of a midrash of my own. For now, running away is part of Jonah's Bartlebyness. He, too, has no weapons or defense, but runs on without hope (Bartleby inwardly; Jonah to the sea). When the storm overtakes his ship, Jonah is perfectly unsurprised and unfrantic. He will not pray. He can sleep, knowing that God is in pursuit and will surely find a means to reach him. But Jonah will not acquiesce in his fate.

In this mode, how Jonah has attracted the poets! Robert Frost takes him up in the verse play *A Masque of Mercy,* only to put him down with a New Testament judgment. A character aptly named Paul suggests a cure for Jonah's insistence on justice in "an oubliette, / Where you must lie in self-forgetfulness / On the wet flags before a crucifix. . . ."

In Paul Goodman's play *Jonah,* the prophet is an aging standup comic complete with nagging wife and a shrugging, "Who, me?" attitude. "Jonah," writes Goodman in a preface, "should have a slight Jewish accent throughout." Here he is, then, the original *schlemiel.* When God zigged, he zagged. God wishes for once to send down wholesale forgiveness, no questions asked, and Jonah objects. Not only Jonah, but God also is cartooned. No mystery here about God's intentions, just simple equations: sin plus repentance equals mercy. Like Frost, Goodman nudges Jonah toward a Christological exit from his dilemma. There will one day come good news, an angel confides.

As Jonah called out for justice, so his story calls out to us to bestow justice on Jonah—on this Bible Bartleby, who prefers not to. Since justice, however, is such a perilous matter, let's not approach it pell-mell, but return to other events of the story to see how they sharpen themselves, like Neptune's trident, to pierce Jonah's good name.

Even the pagan sailors on the ship bound for Tarshish behave better than Jonah. When the lot falls on him, he suggests they throw him overboard. The sailors are reluctant to carry this out. First, a midrash tells us, they dipped his feet, then his knees, then his hips. At each immersion the sea calmed, and so, sensible men at last, they relinquished their qualms, and Jonah, to the sea. Now an immense creature of the sea appears, popularly called a whale, but in Hebrew *dag gadol,* "a great fish." It slips over Jonah like a glove, but there's no trauma. Swallowed safe into the fish's belly, Jonah beautifully gives thanks:

The waters compassed me about, even to the soul; the depth closed me round about, the weeds were wrapped about my head.

I went down to the bottoms of the mountains; the earth with her bars was about me for ever: yet hast thou brought up my life from corruption, O Lord my God.

But there is not a word about going forth to prophesy.

Of Jonah's three-day stay inside the fish, nothing else has been recorded in the text—no report from inside the fish. Yet, while the fish's eyes flashed like beacons, refracting light through giant lenses, and Jonah viewed a heaving universe, those two creatures, I believe, conversed. At first they were brief: "Don't cut me," said the fish. "Don't contract," said Jonah. That bargain is kept. Fish and man survive, for three days and nights, in perfect symbiotic balance. The all-important conversations that I believe ensued we will have to leave until later, for the fact is, Jonah was now *too* comfortable. So God (another midrash) sends a pregnant fish to which Jonah is transferred. There he felt the squeeze. There he learned what narrowness is.

Now Jonah goes to Nineveh. Aldous Huxley said that the people in El Greco's paintings look as if they've been inside the whale. We can imagine Jonah looking a little like them, thin and elongated, pressed within and without, stretched taut with anxiety: a touch of Giacometti there, too. Jonah pronounces the single sentence that sentences Nineveh to its doom: "Yet forty days and Nineveh shall be overthrown."

Everyone believes him. For a prophet worried about his credibility, it's simply outstanding. Everyone repents. The people of Nineveh fast and force their animals to fast, too, as if saying to God: If you don't notice suffering in us, maybe you'll notice it in them; or: If *you* won't show mercy, why should we? They put sackcloth not only on themselves, they dress their animals in it also. To the distractable mind this may add a kind of Beatrix Potter note: Mrs. Tiggy-winkle the hedgehog in her apron and mob cap, Peter Rabbit in his elegant vest, all doffed in favor of the new fashion— sackcloth, sackcloth everywhere.

As it turns out, there's shrewdness in this gesture by the evildoers of Nineveh. They know something about catching God's attention. In the final chiding of Jonah, God asks him how he could *not* spare Nineveh when it is so populous with people who "cannot discern between their right hand and their left hand; and," God uniquely adds, "also much cattle?"

Compare and contrast Jonah however we will—to the sailors on the boat, to the fishes in the sea, to the worst abominators of the pagan world— Jonah comes out looking bad. And when in the end he watches from a distance to see what happens, and finds mercy pouring down on repentant Nineveh, Jonah, unregenerate, bursts out in anger: "O Lord, was this not my saying, when I was yet in my own country? Therefore I fled to Tarshish. . . ." God has to talk to him severely, and gets thereby some of the best lines in the Bible, although from Jonah's point of view there is a problem of logic.

I have spoken of calling for justice for Jonah. Yet how take kindly to the idea of a prophet who is so intent on principles of law that he can't unbend himself in the direction of mercy when it comes? To move closer to the goal, I propose we posit two Jonahs. Only one of these two Jonahs will need requitement of justice; the other can remain where we find him, thrown upon the world's mercy. (Though, like Portia judging Shylock, the world, scorning Jonah for his lack of mercy, subjects him to a judgment from which mercy is withheld.)

Still, why two Jonahs? First let me explain what is *not* the answer to that question. Freud posited two Moseses in *Moses and Monotheism,* claiming that the first one was killed in the desert and replaced by a second. Although Jonah's three days and nights in the belly of the fish could be reason enough for the death of Jonah One and replacement by Jonah Two, I don't mean there were actually two Jonahs. Nor do I intend to invoke that other ready response, "Why *not* two Jonahs (especially since there are already two fishes)?" There was really only one Jonah, but so changed by his experience in the fish as to have become practically another. (This seems as good a time as any to mention that certain historical discrepancies exist between the life of Jonah the man, generally located in the eighth century B.C.E., and the Book of Jonah, written probably in the fourth century B.C.E. One such discrepancy is that a later vocabulary appears in Jonah the book that Jonah the man couldn't have known. In this sense, of course, there *are* two Jonahs, the man and the book, but that is a very different sense from the one intended here.)

So: a before-the-fish Jonah and an after-the-fish Jonah.

Who was before-the-fish Jonah One? Not a nice fellow, says tradition, both Christian and Jewish, as we've seen. Before-the-fish Jonah One is narrow, without *understanding* of God's mercy and love, says tradition, but with, nonetheless, unabated faith in them. So much for Jonah One, whose problem, clearly, *stems* from his wholehearted belief in God's unfailing mercy.

After-the-fish Jonah Two was another matter. Here we can attempt some linking of past and present by arranging to have this man, of unshakable faith in God's mercy, see us in our post-Holocaust predicament.

Jonah himself brings us halfway to a solution. Like Bartleby, he knows something that makes him persist in flight against all odds. Whatever that something is (even if it is—*most certainly* if it is—despair), it is powerful enough to make him stand against the inevitable. What is it Jonah knows?

Let us try to imagine our way into Jonah's sojourn in the fish. This fish, Talmud tells us, was prepared at Creation for Jonah. The fish, we might say, is a kind of underwater angel, created to do God's bidding. Now let me posit my midrash. The fish has soaked up the events of the millennia. In those three days and nights in the womb of the deep, here is what must have happened. Like Milton's angel forecasting the future to Adam when paradise is lost, the fish reveals to Jonah what is to come. For three days and nights the fish presents scenes of time that will be. (Perhaps it is the pregnant fish, who, after all, must also have been prepared at Creation—an angel at God's bidding taking on the burdens of ichthyoid sex—who is the communicative one.) First there is the Babylonian exile: how the tongue of the sucking child cleaved to the roof of his mouth for thirst; how the young children asked for bread, and no one gave it to them; how skin was blackened like an oven, because of the terrible famine. "He hath broken my bones. . . . He hath bent his bow, and set me as a mark for the arrow. . . ." The fish's recitation of a few verses from Lamentations wonderfully concentrates Jonah's brain. After that, as in a kind of theater, the fish's cavernous interior fills with scenes from inquisitions and expulsions and ghettos and pogroms and, at last, death camps and crematoria. What the fish teaches Jonah is that, a mere twenty-five hundred years after his boat trip to Tarshish, the civilized world, carrying out with dispatch what gave the pagans pause, would fling six million Jonahs into the depths. The fish, eyes flashing like crystal globes, recounts everything. What the fish's stories tell is that there will be times—incredible as it must have seemed to the man of faith—when there will be no divine intervention, neither judgment nor mercy. Times for which new names will be learned: "eclipse of God," "a turning away of God's face."

Can it be right to say that after-the-fish Jonah wanted only judgment, not mercy? Perhaps he wanted more than that. Consistency. Judgment you could count on. A mercy that was meet. Wanted there never to be a time when there would be no judge and no judgment. If they are lacking, how can there be mercy?

Jonah is guilty of a terrible hubris: he becomes a would-be shaper of the world. Dissatisfied with the endings God provides, he wants to write his own ending to the Book of Jonah.

But God goes ahead with the ending we know.

By the time Jonah got to Nineveh, he was spewing out prophecy the way the fish spewed him. He was stuffed with Jewish history backward and forward the way the fish was stuffed with him. Exhausted, surfeited, he sinks down in his booth to watch the acting out of the last episode. The sun is hot. The desert wind abrasive. After three days in the fish, Jonah's skin is no doubt sensitive. He needs shade badly. God provides a *kikayon,* a gourd vine. Then God withers the vine.

Now comes the strangest bit of God-teasing. Jonah is a man in despair. He wants nothing for himself. A man who has had himself thrown into the sea and lived three days and nights in the belly of a fish who tells him everything there is in creation wants nothing. Except a little shade. Which God destroys, a last link in Jonah's chain of botched efforts.

And then this tease about a gourd. It's the oddest thing, God saying that Jonah *pities* the gourd because it's destroyed. "Thou hast had pity on the gourd, for which thou hast not labored, neither madest it grow; which came up in a night, and perished in a night. . . ." Pity for the gourd? We know what Jonah feels—it's anger at this last-straw loss of a convenience. Then the great point thundered home: "And should I not spare Nineveh, that great city . . . ?"

How shall we understand it—this equating of a gourd, which provides shade, with a people? Is this the *non sequitur* it seems? Or does God require the shelter of human beings against his own creation—good and evil, mercy and justice, reward and punishment, shall and shall not—all the hard edges of a moral world, shadowless, relentless as the blazing desert sun. Without the spreading penumbras of human response to soften that moral construct, does God grow faint?

Happily for Jonah, his glimpse into later centuries has not made of him a twentieth-century man. He is alive in an age of faith and could not conceive of replying in a nihilistic vein, as a twentieth-century being might: Will you destroy the gourd again and again to make a point, as if it were no more to you than human life . . . which you created to make a point . . . which you preserve to make another . . . and permit, now and then, to be destroyed as if there were no point at all?

All the same, Jonah is a monster. Among other monsters. He is sent to prophesy to Nineveh, a monster of a city. When he tries to escape, he is swallowed by a monster of a fish. Jonah himself is a sport, a mutation. A prophet who modestly protests is seemly; a prophet who balks altogether is a monster. "I prefer not to." What ails this Bartleby-prophet? God here is an amiable employer like Bartleby's, a good-natured, Pickwickian fellow who cajoles Jonah, tries to get him to see things reasonably. But no, Jonah prefers not to—against all odds. It will end badly for Jonah, as it ends for Melville's Bartleby. Jonah will go down, as Bartleby went down.

Down, down, down, goes Jonah. Down to Tarshish, instead of Nineveh. Down to the sea in a ship. Down into the sea itself, thrown overboard. Down into the belly of the monster fish. Then farther down, to the bottom of the sea, to the bottom of despair, where the weeds wrap themselves around his head.

And we, too, fall on Yom Kippur, in the late afternoon, when hunger and weariness weight us—down, down, to the bottom of the seas of the soul.

There we encounter Jonah, who has a problem. What is his problem? He is so convinced God will show mercy to sinners, and the moral world will therefore go to rack and ruin, that he wants no part of the transaction, this Yom Kippur Jonah. Unlike the rest of his kind, prophets who plead with God for mercy even while they're warning the people they deserve none—"O Lord God, forgive, I beseech thee," cries Amos, "by whom shall Jacob arise? for he is small"—Jonah prefers to see, in this case, punishment instead. But though the vine under which he is sheltered is destroyed, the city itself is saved.

God then admonishes an angry Jonah, whose problem all along has been his faith in God's mercy, to have more faith in God's mercy.

"I know you are a gracious God . . . and slow to anger," Jonah says. Yet what is swifter than the anger of God? Think of what happened to the worshippers of the golden calf, to Sodom and Gomorrah, and how Abraham had to plead for the release of fifty just men, of twenty, of ten. Abraham Heschell, in his book on the prophets, *stresses* God's anger, in fact, calls it the passion of the Lord's wrath, and finds in it evidence of the warmth with which God confronts His creation. "It is because . . . [God] cares for man that his anger may be kindled against man." Dispassionate punishment—uncaring, detached—is what the *pagan* gods meted out.

Jonah, too, is passionate. If he falls asleep on the ship in the midst of the storm, it's far from indifference. Nothing makes for sleep like depression. Jonah's turning away is full of anger. He's not destroying the relationship between God and prophet with coldness, but angrily, passionately naysaying. No!

Why, then, on a day when Jews beg for God's mercy, should a recalcitrant, disobedient Jew like Jonah be thrust into the forefront of God's consciousness?

The Book of Jonah is meant to teach Jews the power of repentance to earn God's mercy, and to remind them to be merciful. Isn't it also a reminder to God? You, who showed unstinting mercy to the pagan, show it also to us, who do know our right hand from our left but keep getting them mixed up anyway. All of Yom Kippur begs God to forgive. The story of Jonah, in which God chides Jonah into remembering mercy, on Yom Kippur is the very one we cast at the feet of God to stay the death-dealing hand, to stir up a memory of mercy. Nineveh had only 120,000 souls; on Yom Kippur we think of Europe's eleven million who perished in the Holocaust, six million of them Jews, one-third of their number in the world, cut off from the pity of Nineveh.

As for Jonah, whether Nineveh does or doesn't merit mercy is in the end no longer the point. Jonah is dissatisfied with all the endings. He'd rather—in his horrifying hubris—shape his own. How like a writer Jonah is. Between polar opposites, the tightrope is strung. In the tension between the rage to call down judgment on evildoing and the longing for mercy bestowed is the place, the prayer, out of which the writer writes.

Ah, Jonah! Ah, humanity!

JONAH

Leonard Michaels

GOD CALLS JONAH AND TELLS HIM TO GO CRY OUT AGAINST THE wickedness of Nineveh. Immediately Jonah flees to Joppa and boards ship for Tarshish.

Why he would refuse God's call and begin a long, dangerous journey isn't clear, but we are told plainly and repeatedly that Jonah would go anywhere—even "to the bottoms of the mountains"—to escape the presence of the Lord.

He doesn't want to cry out against Nineveh. He doesn't want to be a prophet. In other respects, too, Jonah is a figure of negative dispositions, but this is most largely evident in his effort to flee God's presence.

During the journey Jonah's ship is caught in a "mighty tempest." The sailors throw their wares overboard to lighten the ship, and they appeal to their gods for help. Jonah merely goes down into the hold and sleeps, as if indifferent to the general terror aboard ship, and also inconsistent with himself, a man of action who abruptly leaves home to undertake a journey to a legendary city at the southwestern edge of the ancient world.

The King James Version of the Bible used in this essay.

It must seem that Jonah is so negative that when he is unlike himself, he is like himself. If so, he bears a curious resemblance to God, who is not unknown for inconsistent and paradoxical behavior. Prophets, who tend to be rather unpredictable, perhaps cannot be otherwise. Crazed by the divine presence, some walk about naked, some devour filth, some wear iron horns on their heads, as if their moral vision required frenzied exhibitionism.

Jonah's sleep, neither frenzied nor spectacular, is certainly unpredictable, and it is also pathetic, for he seems to collapse beneath the realization that he has not escaped God's presence. The tempest is made by God. It is His voice—a call of rage.

Like a depressed child, Jonah sleeps, which is a gentle sort of negation, but later he will ask for death and it will be denied him. Not allowed to die, let alone sleep, Jonah suffers the burden of consciousness. This is his sacred affliction, his prophetic calling. Consciousness, for him, is a great power but, since he cannot escape it, a maddening impotence. In the ship's hold, he does not sleep long.

"What meanest thou, O sleeper?" asks the shipmaster. A good question, but Jonah, who is harassed by questions to the very end, doesn't answer. He says nothing until the sailors discover, by casting lots, that he is responsible for the "evil tempest." Then Jonah speaks. He confesses that he is indeed responsible and says he is a Hebrew, fears the Lord, has fled His presence. They ask why. He gives no answer. It isn't that he doesn't know.

Chosen against his will to speak for God, Jonah is unable or unwilling to speak for himself except in this minimal, mechanical manner. He says the tempest is his fault, he is a Hebrew, etc., but he doesn't say it is the fate of a prophet to appall and to thrill the multitudes in spiritual darkness while he, the prophet himself, is never truly understood. A personal residue seethes beneath expression, but, with the tempest screaming all about, it is no time to talk about his feelings. Jonah would sleep if they'd let him.

Nevertheless, he has reasons to complain. There is a dreadful futility in Jonah's calling—nakedness, horns, devouring filth. All prophets are like Kafka's hunger artist; that is, monsters, grotesque illustrations in blood and bone of God's message, yet they can never make its full and exact sense explicit, for that includes the very condition of their being. A prophet would have to tear the mouth out of his face, dig the brain out of his hair. No distinction exists between what he knows and what he is, for God's message suffuses him like an incurable disease, leaving him perpetually beside himself.

The story will end with Jonah's asking for death, then bitterly silent, reduced to a burning and inaccessible privacy, his singular possession, his precious negativity.

"What shall we do unto thee," ask the sailors, "that the sea may be calm unto us?" Jonah tells them to cast him into the sea, as if he were trash—not a person, but a palpable nothingness. In his essay on vanity, Montaigne says, "When I am in a bad way, I grow bent on misfortune; I abandon myself in despair," but this sounds healthy compared with Jonah, who barely even speaks. All he has said so far comes to "This is who I am," "This is what I did," "Kill me." Nobody is more vain than Jonah.

At this point, I believe, the entire opening of the story can be understood, in retrospect, as thoroughly metaphorical.

In Jonah's depressed sleep, he dreamed this tempest into existence. More than his fault, it is his creation. In fact, it begins before he sleeps, but the language intimates that Jonah descends into himself—as when falling asleep—from the moment he hears God's voice. Jonah "went down into Joppa," "down into the ship," "down into the sides of the ship," and later, as he prays inside the belly of the fish, he says, "I went down to the bottoms of the mountains," and more about descending into the deepest deeps of solitude, suffering, and phantasmagoria. His flight from God is a flight from reality toward a wilderness of chimeras within.

Jonah tells the sailors to cast him into the sea, but now it's all the same to him. The sailors, terrified by his advice, try to row Jonah ashore. The sea defeats them. They must then do as he says. It is a murderous concession, or conversion, to the faith of Israel. They do it, however, "and the sea ceased from her raving."

Then the men feared the Lord exceedingly, and they offered a sacrifice unto the Lord, and made vows.

In this moment the sailors enter the prophetic world of Jonah, wherein the metaphorical and the literal are aspects of each other, and everything is savage, magical, and moral. It is perhaps the only world, but the sailors have not lived with the knowledge of it, have not lived with the presence of God. They will henceforth. They made vows.

A great fish swallows Jonah and carries him about for three days and three nights. This is the most famous image in the story. It has numerous applications. To mention one, it renders with striking drama the sickness of self-involution, for the fish is Jonah himself, a man who descended into himself, or swallowed himself, and discovered the animalish abyss into which self-involution leads. It is reminiscent of Freud's discovery of the visceral roots of mind in neurotic devolutionary processes, where, as one grows sicker, one sinks back through time into weird primeval forces of the self. Literally, in the beginning we were fish.

Having established a great distance from God—within himself—Jonah is confronted by nothing less than excruciating intimacy with God. This is deep intellectually, not metaphorically, in the sense proposed by Niels Bohr—that is, in the sense of something of which the opposite can be said to be equally true.

The Book of Jonah, in traditional Judaism, is read during the Yom Kippur service, a solemn occasion. For others, the story is sometimes considered funny. It appears in children's books as a charming little tale, and it has been made the basis for comic routines by professional comedians; the colloquialism "We have a Jonah aboard" further indicates that the story is considered funny. However, all such uses trivialize its implications and effect, as if we weren't actually fascinated by the meaning it seems to represent. Perhaps, in the way it is funny, it touches a certain desperation in what is funny.

At the end of the second chapter, when the fish vomits Jonah onto land, God tells him again to go to Nineveh. Now he simply goes, crying out against the great city, prophesying its doom in forty days. Has Jonah suffered a sea-change? Or does he perform, despite extreme reluctance, in an exultation of bitter obedience? I'd guess the latter, but his feelings aren't examined. He has been saved from death. He is probably grateful, glad to be alive. This is enough to explain his revolutionary obedience to God.

Having been instrumental in converting the sailors, Jonah now effects repentance among the citizens of Nineveh. As a result, "God repented of the evil he said he would do unto them; and he did it not."

But it displeased Jonah exceedingly. . . .

Well it might. Wrenched into performance, Jonah went about the huge city crying, "Yet forty days and Nineveh shall be overthrown." When nothing happened, he must have looked like a lunatic, especially after being so specific—"forty days." But the question here is about God's inconsistency, or negativity, the trait he shares with Jonah. In Jonah's displeasure, he tells God he didn't want to go to Nineveh in the first place, because he knew God was merciful, gracious, loving, and would repent of the evil He intended. Jonah sounds slightly ironical, but if this is really just what he thinks, he might as well have done nothing. He does that now. The man who once fled God's presence and wouldn't go to Nineveh refuses now to leave. In a fit of suicidal petulance, Jonah sits outside the city and waits to see what will become of it, but first he asks God to take his life, "for it is better for me to die than to live." He has been insufferably humiliated by the survival of Nineveh.

Then the Lord said, Doest thou well to be angry?

In its simplicity the question is solicitous; however, it is also ominous, suggesting that Jonah's anger is not justified and not in his best interest. But what can he care about justification or self-interest? He has twice asked for death, and he has been subjected to symbolical death in the belly of the fish. He has gone out of himself, in more than prophetic ecstasy, to speak for God—and look what it has brought him. What, then, is left for Jonah? Mere life? Indeed, his intimacy with God does not spare him a perception of his own mere life, his brute being.

God makes a gourd grow to protect Jonah from the sun, and thus to "deliver him from his grief." By reaching toward him this way, God makes Jonah's grief seem childlike, basically a physical condition. The event, wonderfully fantastic, is very moving in the plainness of the next sentence: "So Jonah was exceeding glad of the gourd."

Then God makes a worm, "and it smote the gourd so that it withered." How sad—not only the fate of the gourd, but also the way it reflects Jonah's pathos. He is not, after all, essentially different from the gourd. He never was. His yearning for death is forgetful of himself, too despising of life. He was "glad of the gourd," but now, very far gone, Jonah cannot learn from his feelings.

And he said, I do well to be angry unto death.

God reminds Jonah of his "pity" for the gourd, the reflection of himself, and says, "for which thou has not labored, neither madest it grow; which came up in a night, and perished in a night." Thus, Jonah fails to appreciate his own existence, which is everything and nothing, or a creation of immeasurable value that even prophets, in the miserable grandeur of consciousness, must acknowledge.

The story ends as it begins, with the voice of God. His words have weight and size, seem virtually to loom, against the silence of Jonah:

And should I not spare Nineveh, that great city, wherein are more than sixscore thousand persons that cannot discern between their right hand and their left hand; and also much cattle?

The story's greatness is in its imagery and the truth from which it issues. Presumably, it is a truth Jonah feels in his silence, his simply being, the condition he shares with more than six score thousand persons of Nineveh and their cattle.

In the final question, which ends the story, God seems almost to plead a case for Himself, and His question seems not entirely rhetorical. It obliges you to wonder about different things, among them the connection between moral behavior and sheer life, and whether prophets are required in a world where spiritual darkness is the prevailing fact—the inability to discern right from left—and whether this darkness, in mysterious ways and degrees, is somehow crucial to the existence of gourds and beasts and persons. It has been taken by some to be a form of grace, this darkness, saving a vast number of us from seeing how bad we sometimes are, or how eerily fortunate it is that we are at all. The gourd came up in a night, perished in a night. "I think, therefore I am," says Descartes. How verbose and smug this appears, when just to say "I" is already an astounding phenomenon.

HABAKKUK

OUR IGNORANCE

Stephen Berg

THE BOOK, THE PENTATEUCH I RECEIVED AT THIRTEEN AS A CON-
firmation gift with my name stamped in gold on the black
leather cover, the endlessly readable, unreadable tome of holy
truths containing God's voice, continues to mystify me. It
remains a text where I believe I may, someday, find *the* passage, *the* sentence,
the vision that will show me the way. In an age of nonprophetic, infinitely
interpretive thought, it's a relief to swim through the columns of future-
tense lamentation and present-tense questioning. In a world where "the stone
shall cry out of the wall" and "the Lord answered me, and said, Write the
vision, and make *it* plain upon tables, that he may run that readeth it," the
conviction expressed in the tone, in the stark, clear rhythms suggesting
absolute knowledge, and in the plain elegance of the diction is consoling.
Although Biblical texts are, to an erratic, unschooled reader like myself, a
deep web that I can only pluck and listen to, here, there, anywhere, it's
always a privilege to listen, and there is always the live voice of men

---

The King James Version of the Bible used in this essay.

badgering, pleading with God, and God answering—a dialogic voice, a voice which is utterly lost to us now.

Although Nietzsche's "God is a sacred lie" has taken the toll Nietzsche hoped it would, the actual King James songs and stories never fail to suggest the possibility of sacred *truth,* the kinds of truth, admit it or not, we all hope to discover. Those are the truths that expect to descend from the mouth of God, often in strange forms.

Habakkuk's primary interest as a minor gem in the dialogue between man and God is in the intensity of its brief vision. It can stand as a model of a moment when a lone man calls out to God and is answered in language which, because of its postrational attitude, seems from the tongue of a far wiser consciousness than ours. The mystery of some of the phrases and the force of the writing make us believe as we listen. Any great poetry will do this, but what great poetry today expresses a situation of mortal danger where "The Lord does not hear . . . ," but then soon speaks: "Write the vision, and make *it* plain upon tables . . . that he may run that readeth it"?

It is not the descriptions of God's power to make rivers and stride the earth or His measureless size that pierce the reader so that he feels he has heard the literal word of God. It is, in particular, sentences like: "Woe to him that saith to the wood, Awake; to the dumb stone, Arise, it shall teach!" This is the passage I want to discuss, without the least shred of scholarly knowledge, as an ordinary reader, a Jew without belief, a Jew nevertheless, a Jew who loves the King James, who would love it whether he were a Jew or not. It is the voice of God I would like to respond to here, though that may sound ludicrous—nothing more than a game played with the imagination and only one player: the reader writing this.

God is giving Habakkuk His helpful vision—a warning to the enemy Chaldeans to mend their ways. Some of His exhortations are indictments of sins: drunkenness, violence, worship of graven images. In these passages He sounds rational, protective, argumentatively limited as you or I would be if we were government officials threatening to bomb a country because it had backed commies while our soldiers occupied the terrain. But those moments throughout the Old Testament when God's voice comes from a different source, a depth of thought that unsettles logic and gives language an intelligence beyond ordinary human powers that forces us to *interpret* and continue interpreting, make us feel we have heard a voice from a strange realm—where truth is located outside us but includes our thoughts, actions, destinies, origins. In other words, it is the territory of heaven, as it used to be called, from which the words "salvation" and "redemption" and "soul" issue and return. Obviously it was men like us who wrote these words. We all know that. Perhaps all we should expect of ourselves in this interpretive dilemma is to imagine ourselves in a crisis imagining God's voice, as perhaps the scribes who wrote these words did. But the words I read were written as words issuing from the mouth of God—as if they were *heard,* not created by men; given, in the heat of that lost art, prayer—orphanlike despair, a man speaking directly to God, demanding response, and getting it. Therefore, I wish to assume what Habakkuk assumed: the existence of God and His ability to speak to me. Is that faith, after all: belief in a voice—not our own inner, audible, conflicted wisdom—a voice simultaneously imbued with past, present, future, so that its logic is, at its most overwhelming, in need of endless interpretation? What other situation would keep us attached to language—but language so difficult to comprehend, so impossible to pin down in its final meanings that each age has to struggle with it until the world itself ends?

Why would God threaten a man with "woe" if he said to wood, "Awake," and to speechless stone, "Arise, it shall teach!"? What difference does it make who or what a man addresses? Who cares? What is the lesson? Near the end of this book, Habakkuk says: "When I heard my belly trembled: my lips quivered at the voice: rottenness entered my bones." To me, the two passages balance each other in intensity, in rhythmical beauty— God's voice a statement of pure, awesome, metaphorical utterance; Habakkuk's a direct and eloquent expression of the power of God's voice to shake a man to the edge of death. This is what we expect, but in these passages the language is perfect. In this song in praise of and in fear of God, the two most linguistically exquisite moments embody, first, God's powers of knowledge beyond man's, and, second, man's perception of his fragility in the presence of that voice, which *is* the presence of God. (The language, in the form of that voice, *is* God.) That language, for me, only becomes God when it takes the shape of mysterious passages like the one I've picked from Habakkuk. Then, and only then, do I feel what Habakkuk felt in his belly, lips, bones. There is the stone and the wood; the belly and the bones. My interpretive first step is to submit that Habakkuk would not have been so moved, so frightened, if God had not said what He did about the wood and the dumb stone. If He had only threatened to drive out the Chaldeans, God's believable existence would not have touched Habakkuk bodily. It is not simply God's voice that is important, but the form of that voice—when the voice suddenly utters oracular phrases, then a man is pierced to his bones and feels death enter them.

Let me try to say what God meant when He referred to the wood, to the dumb stone. When the gulf between what man understands and what God says opens wide in Habakkuk, when what I would like to call *our ignorance of Him* is manifest: that is the moment when a man experiences belief in the existence of God with his very flesh.

In *I and Thou,* Buber defines God for contemporary man as "the moment God," the event of His manifestation between people when the usual I-it relationship becomes I-Thou. This occurs when I perceive you as a subject whose reality is as subjective to me as my own subjectivity is. At such moments one is in touch with God's presence, according to Buber. This idea has always fascinated me, because it makes God's potential existence, his reality, dependent on the intersubjective everyday world, a constant possibility. Thus the ethical, the empathic accessibility of God becomes a portion of our desire to know others, to be known, to be accepted, to be touched by others and relieved of our aloneness, our sense of isolation. It is in his long philosophical lyric, *I and Thou,* that Buber tries to establish a definition of the world of *relation* and to offer it as the only fully realized world, the place where man completes himself, again and again, losing it and finding it, the only place where God can appear to man. In the passage I've chosen from Habakkuk, relation of a special kind occurs, and the passage is immediately followed by: "But the Lord is in his holy temple: let all the earth keep silence before him."

Habakkuk has been listening to God speak to him. God has responded to his prayers by speaking. God's final directive to Habakkuk is silence. What follows in chapter 3, and ends this little book, is Habakkuk's acknowledgment to God of His power. But what matters is how God has made Himself present, how the secular world of Habakkuk's problems is made sacred by the event of His voice, so that Habakkuk knows it as reality, as *actual.*

"Only where all means have disintegrated encounters occur," says

Buber. Is this a definition of our essential helplessness and always partial understanding and of how real relating, I-and-Thou relating, can occur only when that is acknowledged? But in Habakkuk, what goes on is between a man and God. There is no secular man-and-wife or friend-and-friend situation to anchor God's appearance in the ordinary world we live in. Buber's reference to "means" is the key here—when no *way,* no particular approach would suggest an I-it relationship even before the encounter happened, when one does not know any longer how to solve the moment of one's life in speaking either to oneself or to another, then what is said is sincere, unwithheld, and God's response is forthcoming because the speaker's hopelessness—and this is part of the secret—is an admission of his absolute need for God. This is the condition in the mind of man, and in the mind of what is not man, which permits the occurrence of His voice. This is the moment when subjectivity in a man is free of self-defining images, and can unfold *as it is* in the presence of nothing, in the face of probable silence. Out of that hopelessness and silence the kind of sacred voice in the Habakkuk passage I've chosen can be heard. The lost art of prayer as the only response left to a man, I am trying to say, is the precondition for the eruption of certain forms of God speaking.

When Buber writes his hymn to the reality of God between man and man, he is redefining prayer for our age. For him, prayer is the condition of mind, of soul, that makes the I-Thou, and therefore God, possible. All other attitudes are practical, manipulative, and, however necessary, obstacles to this: "But what is greater for us than all enigmatic webs at the margins of being is the central actuality of an everyday hour on earth, with a streak of sunshine on a maple twig and an intimation of the eternal You." A bit later Buber refers to "lived actuality," "reciprocal activity," and "In lived actuality there is no unity of being. The strongest and deepest actuality is to be found where everything enters into activity—the whole human being, without reserve, and the all-embracing God; the unified I and the boundless You." Isn't it in those moments of inescapable prayer to a God who must prove His existence again and again by responding to us that our loss of faith may receive the spark that can turn us in the direction of a new version of knowing?

To any man who addresses the objects of nature as if they could become conscious, like a man, as if they could teach, like a man, I promise grief, woe, punishment, God says. Why? Because nature was created to hold man, to be there behind him and beneath him when he thinks and acts, and although it may embody the laws of birth and death, growth and decay, it cannot pray and it cannot hear God's word. Nature is man before and after his life, his first nothingness and his second nothingness. But when a man lives, although he *is* nature, he is also consciousness, and therefore a witness to God's absolute power. This formula haunts us now as mere possibility; once it emanated from existence. To invoke human powers in wood and stone would be, for a man, to search for truth in the wrong place, however mysterious nature may seem.

The one true mystery is the visible absence and vocal presence of God in the black book with my name stamped on the cover. God's *style,* when He speaks in parables, in the stately, aloof, didactic rhythms of His densest, least finite truths, neither elevates Him nor denigrates us; it changes the location of each: Him and us. It is both His descent and our ascent in a simultaneous moment of awareness in which God and man grasp each other, so that Habakkuk's trembling belly, quivering lips, and ruined bones become instruments that resonate with the fullness of holy speech, while God, who *is* His speech, and the man who hears it (hears Him) has become for just a moment that listening vessel which is absolutely necessary to the manifestation and is, consequently, the vehicle of belief. It is through the "disintegration" of means between man and God that each is made real through the other.

This "disintegration of means" happens when one can no longer use a skill, a mechanism, when one no longer has a way of dealing with the situation. Then one is undefended by his usual means of coping with the world; he is vulnerable and receives the encounter, becomes part of the encounter; he does not execute a skilled handling of the moment that keeps him at a distance from the encounter.

Lately, a memory from my early adolescence has come back. We were living in a tall apartment building in the suburbs of New Jersey. One morning, a sparrow appeared on my windowsill. Even when I came close to the window it stayed there. Soon it was clear that the bird couldn't fly because its wing was broken. I took it inside, filled a shoebox with twigs and grass I had gathered from the garden at the back of the building, and put the bird in it to protect it so its wing could heal. For a few days it sat in the box; then one morning—I had put the box on the windowsill next to the open window—it was gone. I was thirteen. We had just moved to this elegant neighborhood, and the children my age refused to let me play with them. No doubt I lavished the tenderness I felt I needed from them, the acceptance I desired, on the wounded bird. Like a little God I lifted his quivering ounce into the box. But we were two creatures, unlike Habakkuk and God. God's concern for that man was certainly different from my concern for the bird. Habakkuk may be like the bird, but I am certainly not like the God Habakkuk heard. I mention this here because of the aloneness I felt so sharply in those days, and because the coming of the sparrow broke through it. I remember clearly its few introductory peeps on the sill. After that it was quiet. For a few days I had a friend. I helped the bird survive, and in its own unpredictable way it healed me for a time and gave me the power of its need, which dissolved my sense of isolation, *my* feeling of helplessness. The bird's helplessness and mine came together for a while. It was a voiceless encounter, except at the outset, when it called to me before I brought it inside. Then the silence between the creature and me felt sweet and right. We simply glimpsed each other from time to time. When it was gone one morning, I was glad. The bird had come to me because it could not fly and—why not speculate further?—because I had no friends. I was helpless to make those neighborhood kids my friends; the bird was helpless to fix its wing. Neither of us had the means to save ourselves until each one's helplessness encountered the other's, as disguised gods.

ZECHARIAH

David Evanier

I

IN THE FOLLOWING WORK OF FICTION, I ADDRESS THE SUBTLE DIFFERENCES between true and false prophecy, the confusion of a secular with the religious God. I trace the insidious way morality twists into a moral nightmare when men take God's place. I write of a young man who had been a devoted student, a *yeshiva bocher,* on the Lower East Side of New York in the 1930s. This young man, Solly Rubell, would have been well acquainted with the prophet Zechariah, and the promise, he said, God had made to the Jews:

For the Lord will again comfort Zion; He will choose Jerusalem again. . . . [1:17]

> I will restore them, for I have pardoned them,
> And they shall be as though I had never disowned them; . . . [10:6]

. . . I will remove that country's guilt in a single day. In that day—declares the Lord of Hosts—you will be inviting each other to the shade of vines and fig trees. [3:9–10]

The Jewish Publication Society's translation of the Bible used in this essay.

The Lord their God shall prosper them on that day;
He shall pasture His people like sheep.
They shall be like crown jewels glittering on His soil.
How lovely, how beautiful they shall be,
Producing young men like new grain,
Young women like new wine!   [9:16–17]

In those days, ten men from nations of every tongue will take hold . . . of every Jew by a corner of his cloak and say, "Let us go with you, for we have heard that God is with you."   [8:23]

At the age of ten, when Solly "had faith in everything," he would have watched and waited confidently for that day. But it was not only the beauty and pleasure of these images he hungered for. An intensely moral young man, he was even more fiercely drawn to the Lord's predicating this earthly paradise on human ethics and loving kindness, not on fasting and ceremony. The Jews had failed to follow these commands the first time; that is why the Lord had turned His back on them:

Execute true justice; deal loyally and compassionately with one another. Do not defraud the widow, the orphan, the stranger, and the poor; and do not plot evil against one another. — But they refused to pay heed. They presented a balky back and turned a deaf ear. . . . "So," said the Lord of Hosts, "let them call and I will not listen. I dispersed them among all those nations which they had not known, and the land was left behind them desolate. . . ."   [7:9–13]

At the age of eleven, Solly moved with his father to the Deep South and witnessed some of the most wrenching scenes of human compassion turned inside out—some of the farthest stretches of man's inhumanity to man. By the time of his Bar Mitzvah, he "knew the score, and could never go back to what he had been"—especially after he returned north and saw the same cruelty reverberating in Harlem.

How could such things happen in this country? Zechariah had seen a vision of a golden lampstand whose seven lamps were fed through golden tubes by the "gold," the oil, of two olive trees. Through this surreal vision, the Lord had given Zechariah His message to Zerubbabel, the secular head of the repatriated Jerusalem, on how to run the land:

Not by might, nor by power, but by My spirit—said the Lord of Hosts.   [4:6]

In this country, Solly thought, the president did not triumph by God's spirit, but by might and by power. The United States was like Tyre:

> She has amassed silver like dust,
> And gold like the mud in the streets.
> But my Lord will impoverish her;
> He will hurl her wealth into the sea,
> And she herself shall be consumed by fire.   [9:3–4]

II

In the 1930s—while Solly's vision was expanding to take in the world—the death of hope that came with the widespread economic depression in the United States, the rise of Nazism across the oceans, the appeasement at Munich, and the betrayals of the Spanish Civil War had engendered in the poor Jewish community of the Lower East Side (where it had fled from the czar's pogroms) a segment whose yearning for moral and social justice turned it from the God of the Bible to a secular God of the here and now. By Solly Rubell's mid-teens, Jews on the other side of the world were being tortured and slaughtered senselessly by the millions. He thought bitterly of God's words:

. . . I am very jealous for . . . Zion—and I am very angry with those nations that are at ease; for I was only angry a little, but they overdid the punishment. Assuredly, thus said the Lord: I graciously return to Jerusalem.   [1:14–16]

Solly had waited too long for that "graciousness"; the Jews had waited too long. Such gifts would be meaningless now. Either God had broken His promise, or He had no power, or He wasn't there.

What would a sensitive young man do when he had such a collapse of faith, especially one who, as his sister put it, "when he did something, did it with a full feeling"? One day he was handed a pamphlet that brought back the sensation of a shared society in the shade of vines and fig trees. He read more pamphlets, listened to speeches, attended meetings. He stopped reading the Bible.

He had found the concrete embodiment of those ephemeral promises: in the Soviet Union, it seemed, civilization had progressed to the stage of human brotherhood. There the new Jerusalem was being built in the real world, while he and others like him had been blinded by the clouds of religion. And there would be more: workers would rise up in a wave all over the world and throw off their oppressors, after which "the police, jails and army would be abolished, for no soldiers were needed to keep down a liberated mankind." Workers would write poetry in their spare time, and soldiers would lead rich cultural lives. Was this not the *real* meaning of the prophecy:

> Lo, your king is coming to you, . . .
> He shall banish chariots from Ephraim
> And horses from Jerusalem;
> The warrior's bow shall be banished.
> He shall call on the nations to surrender,
> And his rule shall extend from sea to sea
> And from ocean to land's end.   [9:9–10]

It was a rich, exhilarating thought that this "king" was not God, not the Messiah after all, but the people themselves. They had to wait no longer for justice and equality; it was in their hands to achieve it here and now. They could smash the evil in the world with their own hands. They could build a Soviet world, a Soviet America:

> Throw open your gates, O Lebanon,
> And let fire consume your cedars!
> Howl, cypresses, for cedars have fallen!
> How the mighty are ravaged!
> Howl, you oaks of Bashan,
> For the stately forest is laid low!   [11:1–2]

III

Solly Rubell and many of those around him viewed themselves as abandoning dead form and ritual for the true "universal" spirit of Judaism as a religion that cared deeply for the oppressed, the underdog, the helpless, and was doing something about it. What good were prayer and fasting if God never came—was not even there, for all they knew? It was time to take action. God wasn't going to do it. Solly and his comrades would.

This was another current that ran along underneath the torrent of giving, of kindness, of love that Solly felt for all mankind. He didn't look at this other bright thing too closely or too long, but he knew that it made him feel better about himself than he had in all the years when he had been God's humble servant:

And I myself . . . will be a wall of fire around [Jerusalem], and I will be a glory inside it.   [2:9]

The wall of fire around and the glory inside were no longer God; it was just possible that they would be Solly.

He met, fell in love with, and married a girl who also was "going to be different." Then he was ready.

Some of the group I write about would later be accused, and a few convicted, of committing espionage for the Soviet Union.

IV

At their trial, Solly felt oddly sustained by certain words of Zechariah about a God he no longer had faith in. The courtroom seemed to become that otherworldly court where Joshua the high priest stood before the angel of the Lord, and Satan stood at his right, accusing him:

But the angel of the Lord said to the Accuser, "The Lord rebuke you, O Accuser; may the Lord who has chosen Jerusalem rebuke you! For this is a brand plucked from the fire." Now Joshua was clothed in filthy garments when he stood before the angel. The latter spoke up and said to his attendants, "Take the filthy garments off him!"

And he said to him, "See, I have removed your guilt from you, and you shall be clothed in priestly robes."   [3:2–4]

Solly didn't know whether it was by divine power or his own power, but he felt an inner certainty that these words were written about him, that his humanitarian motives would shine through and he would be plucked from the flames like a burning stick.

Solly and his wife were convicted and sentenced to death.

V

Terrorized most of all in the death house by "the dot of doubt," Solly Rubell tried to ignore information that was passed to him about abominations in the Soviet Union that equaled those of Nazi Germany. But he, who had spent his life pursuing certainty, was never certain of anything again in his short life.

If anyone "prophesies" thereafter, his own father and mother, who brought him into the world, will put him to death when he "prophesies." In that day, every "prophet" will be ashamed of the "visions" he had when he "prophesied."   [13:3–4]

When, years later, Howard Fast broke with the Communist Party, he named his book *The Naked God.* The secular God did prove to be naked. But I write of a desperate time, and the fanatical forms that "prophecy" and "moral vision" took for some young Jews in their tragic innocence.

Awake and Sing

"O workers' Revolution . . . You are the true Messiah. You will destroy the East Side when you come, and build there a garden for the human spirit."

—Michael Gold

Whether it happened so or not I do not know, but if you think about it you can see that it is true.

—Black Elk

I: SOLLY, 1954

MORNINGS IN DEEP AUTUMN, WITH THE EBBING OF HIS HOPES, he noticed the leaves and maple-tree seeds blown by the wind descending slowly like helicopters over the death-house wall. The icy Hudson River wind. He began another letter to his children—my precious children—he talked about playing horsie with them and what it was like gathering them in his arms at bedtime—and again, again about his and Dolly's innocence: "All the government had as evidence, children, were those *Freiheit* thimbles. Thimbles your mommy and I gave to our progressive friends for donating to a peaceful world by reading the *Freiheit*. For this, these cunning madmen plan to hang us." He tore the letter up, and began another, telling them he hoped they were taking their piano lessons seriously. He told them their mother (alone in the women's section of the death house) was a diamond, that no amount of government filth could scratch her honor.

The guards led him out into the yard again in the afternoon. The wind stung his ears. He watched a seagull sail upward in wide circles, lifted by the wind, and fly into the wide-open sky until he could no longer see it. And he saw Delancey Street and Columbia Street, the crowd surging by the pushcarts, the chickens in their wooden boxes cackling, the merchants shouting and fighting, and Solly felt himself hurrying home to Dolly and the kids. Rocking them all in his arms, crying out, "It's over. Everything's hunky-dory." His legs almost buckled. He looked at the white streaks of calcium carbonate running in broken lines from brick to brick along the wall. He thought of coal and iron ore dug from the earth, trucks carrying it to the mills, iron and steel pouring from furnaces, parts sent to the prison. Mechanics molding them into an edifice, a death house . . .

What could he tell his children to make them understand? One parable, one picture. Peekskill, the Scottsboro boys, Gastonia, *Kristallnacht,* Fuchik's letters, Spain, Dmitroff's speech to the Nazi court . . . And he remembered something that said it all. The American captain who had told Solly of being on the outskirts of Dusseldorf in early 1945. The captain was preparing with his men a siege to liberate the city from the Nazis. A German worker, a printer wearing an apron, approached the captain. The German had asked the American captain for permission to hold a meeting of his communist club, the first that would be held since Hitler took power. He handed the captain the written announcement of the meeting for his approval. It contained the date, time, and place, and the words: Those who fluttered with the breeze are not invited.

Only a communist—no, Solly would have to write "progressive"—could have the perspective to call twelve years of Nazism "a breeze." He sat down to write the letter. My precious children, do you now understand why your parents are dying?

And again Solly could breathe.

II: DOLLY, 1936

Dolly Stern would walk from Seward Park High School with her friend Sylvia Packman to the Jefferson Street Library, across from the Educational Alliance and near the *Daily Forward* building. The two girls often saw the old black woman seated on the bench by the library. She was in her forties, wrecked. Straining forward on the bench toward the sky, crying out, "Hurry, sundown . . . hurry, now . . . oh, *hurry,* sundown . . ." with different inflections and emphases, louder and softer, cutting through the afternoon dusk.

How differently such a woman would be treated in the Soviet Union, Dolly would say, and her friend would nod her head in agreement.

They hurried up the library staircase to the third floor, where their club, Pindar's Children, was located. There they read and wrote poetry.

Afterward they slowly edged their way home. They walked along dark and cluttered Delancey Street, the elevated subway roaring by above them. Men sold apples at the corner. At the market, a *schochet* stood by as a truck unloaded crates of chickens. Feathers landed in the girls' hair, and Dolly tried to pick the feathers out.

At Rivington Street, peddlers passed them, returning from their day's work, their pushcarts smelling of rotting fish and vegetables. The girls looked up and saw quilts, mattresses, and feather beds made of goosefeathers hanging out of windows.

Dolly wore a steel brace because of a recurrent back problem. She stood erect. She would cock her head when she spoke and held it up high. Sylvia thought it made her look stiff and stuffy, but couldn't tell her so. With her pale, small face, her black curly hair, her frailness, her silence, Dolly was almost like an invisible person.

But she was really pretty, too, she loved poetry and singing, and was really a good Joe when you got to know her. She had a beautiful singing voice and was a member of the music club.

The kids called her "Dictionary."

Sylvia and Dolly did not go to Hebrew school afternoons like the other kids. They studied together, at the East River Pier on Houston Street when it was hot, other times at the Jefferson Library or the Hamilton Fish Library on Houston Street.

They sang together, walking across the Williamsburg Bridge. The girls in front of them giggled as the boys, waiting on the bridge, pounced on them. But no one bothered Sylvia and Dolly. And they pretended it was the last thing that mattered to them.

They would go camping with other friends in the Palisades. Dolly's pancake, that's what they called it. They would lie under the blanket and try to sleep. If someone wanted to turn over, she would signal, and they all turned. The blanket just wasn't long enough otherwise.

Friendship for the two girls meant they could sit for hours, reading separately, not speaking. Staring through the windows of the dazzling Paramount Cafeteria on Delancey Street, where the vaudevillians and musicians from Loew's Delancey gathered. Dolly confided to Sylvia that she was afraid to go inside, that she might not use her knife and fork the right way.

It was something to be the star of the school assembly. After rehearsals, the girls would stroll down Rivington Street in the soft spring night. The tugboats' whistles sounded from the river. Dolly was radiant. She recited a poem by the people's poet, Sol Funaroff:

> The poet, in his nightcap,
> descends the stairs of the dark,
> and holds a flickering candle.
>
> There are always bugaboos and drafts.
>
> His magic cap makes him invisible.
>
> But the flame he carries reveals him.
> Here in the streets of life,
> His bright body walks.

They didn't want the night to end. Sylvia would walk Dolly home. Then Dolly walked Sylvia. Back and forth.

"I'm not getting married," Dolly said. "Spending my life shopping, cooking, and cleaning.

"I'm going to be different," she said.

She got the part in the school play, *The Valiant:* the sister of a man facing execution. She recited the lines from *Julius Caesar,* her fist clenched, sweat appearing on her brow: "Cowards die many times before their death. The valiant never taste of death but once."

Dolly refused to take a typing course. She dreamed of and waited for college.

In winter Dolly's parents sat in the cold kitchen with their feet in the oven. A tub on high legs with an enamel top stood in the kitchen. The front of the unheated flat was a store and workshop for Dolly's father, a dental technician. The flat was long and narrow. There was a toilet in the hall shared by three apartments.

In a windowless bedroom slept Dolly, her brother, Joe, two single aunts, and a bachelor uncle, Moshe. Moshe was a survivor of a famous lost battalion of World War I.

The backyard had a wooden fence around it. Dolly's brother and his friends played handball against the fence, punch ball and stick ball, ring O'leaveo, kick-the-can, Johnny-on-a-pony, and running bases. They swam in the East River at Jackson Street, opposite the Brooklyn Navy Yard. On very hot days the boys opened the fire hydrant and placed a barrel over the pump to get a shower of spray.

The boys hung out on the street in winter, building fires to keep warm. To earn money they collected scrap or stole large milk containers from Ratner's restaurant. They built a fire around the container and lid, and melted off the lead used to solder the joints. A can and lid contained a pound of lead, which they sold for seven cents.

When Joe celebrated his Bar Mitzvah, Dolly's mother, Ruth, treated his friends to the movies at the Cannon Theater. It cost three cents to enter, or two admissions for five cents. Kids would go in the mornings, bring their lunch, and stay until evening. Mothers were allowed to come in and search for their children.

Molly called her daughter, Dolly, "Miss Smarty Pants." She smiled when she told Dolly she could not go to college. "You want to do something? Make slipcovers, like I do."

Dolly slammed the door. In the backyard, she whispered to herself, Here in the streets of life, his bright body walks. Her pounding heart gradually quieted. A pigeon hopped along the pavement.

III: STREET SCENES, 1932

When he was eight, Solly Rubell sold lollipops for a penny apiece on the roof garden of an apartment house on Stanton Street and at street corners. He would not take the penny for the lollies he sold on Friday nights because it was the Sabbath, but would return for it the next night.

A skinny boy, he stood on the roof, waiting for customers. Then, dressed up in a black suit and stetson hat, Solly went to *shul* with his father, sister, and cousins.

It was the thick of the Depression. At night, after work, his father cut lace to make a little extra money. Everyone did it, even though it was against the labor laws. If strangers entered the building, people went running from floor to floor calling out, "Lace inspectors!"

Solly and his family lived on the top floor. It was a coldwater flat. Water dripped from the roof, and the toilet in the hall had no light. In winter the wind swept through the rattling windows. But in summer they kept the front door open so a breeze would waft through the apartment, and put bowls of ice in front of the fan.

The candy stores were cool, dark, and dank, with their smells of pretzels, malteds, lime rickies, and sawdust. Baseball cards with gum, pink candies, and watermelon slices cost a penny. A big chunk of ice surrounded the sodas in a metal box; on the floor around it was a growing puddle.

Solly and the other boys caught fireflies and bottled them. He tried to read "The Motor Boys Under the Sea" by the fireflies' light.

At ten in the morning, the junk peddler with his horse and wagon rang his cowbell and called: "Old clothes, old rags, old newspapers, old springs, old junk." Later a singer in a top hat appeared in the courtyard. Pennies fell from windows, rolled in small packets of paper.

When the cool sheets hanging on long ropes in the laundry were drying, Solly and his friends ran through and hit their steaming faces against the wet sheets.

IV: SOLLY'S SISTER, 1986

"Solly moved to Alabama with my father. Solly was eleven. He loved our father so much. Mama died when Solly was four, and he did not remember her very well. I stayed with a relative on Pitt Street while they tried to make ends meet. Then, two years later, our father's business failed and they came back to the Lower East Side. Something happened to Solly. He became a radical. It was a wrench for our father. Solly went to an extreme. He kept shouting against any unjust factor; he came right out with it. He was just blowing his top about it. In the yeshiva—he went afternoons after school—he had been a hundred percent religious. Took a keen interest in Hebrew. Put his whole heart into it. When Solly did something, he did it with a full feeling. He was a prone leader, a brilliant boy.

"Solly had faith in everything at ten, just like young girls who haven't reached maturity or gone out into the world yet. But he lost all his faith after a while. I think Dolly was his first girl friend. He was her first and she was his first. These boys were so pure. these Yiddish *boyeles*.

"We had culture from my father. He was a self-educated man. He educated himself to read the *Forward*. My mother didn't have an education, she couldn't read, but she knew to *dovenn,* which amazed me. In *shul,* the way she *dovenned*! You'd think she was reading from the book, but she knew it by heart.

"My father told us stories about his childhood. His parents died from hunger in Biayłstok. They had eleven children. Eight died. The three survivors were sent to America, my father and his two brothers. He told us stories, how they discriminated against Jews, the hardship they went through. I couldn't believe these things; I was American-born. We didn't see this in America.

"Welfare came to investigate us when my father was out of a job. They refused us. But we got along. My mother used to make a hardboiled egg, divide it, and we'd share.

"We lived first on Stanton, then Hester, and then Delancey. A step upward—you had hot water and steam. The radicalism was so common among the poor children.

"Solly's children. After the arrest, I took them to the park, bought them candy, ice cream. When I'd leave, the little one—he was afraid, you could see the fear—he'd jump up at me. With his little shortie pants. He was only four years old.

"Dolly was a super-duper person. She won't talk against anyone. I was with her when a man undercharged her for some merchandise. She said, Mister, you didn't charge me enough. She couldn't afford to pay that extra two or three cents, but she paid it. That was Dolly. And they were so in love with each other.

"I would come into her cell. Her apple would be on the metal window, a round of toilet paper, pictures of the children. She was short. Without shoes, she was even shorter. Everybody said they were supposed to have money from the Russians. But my brother and Dolly were so poor. If my father didn't give Solly money to fix his soles, he would go without shoes. They ate dinner at my father's house and he took a roll from my father to take home. They didn't have anything. I mean, they were *shleppers*.

"Imagine, the very last day, I went to see Dolly, then I went to see

Solly. The stay had come through. They were so happy. She had a little can of chicken she set aside to celebrate; they shared it. But we didn't know the stay had been suddenly overturned that day. Solly evidently got wind of it over the radio. I was with Solly. Papa was with Dolly. And Solly said to me, 'Take Papa home, take Papa home.' He cut it short. He didn't want to see his father, because my brother would break down. But I didn't know what was happening. 'Just take Papa home,' he kept saying. 'I don't want Papa to come here this afternoon.' That's all he said to me. So I took my father home. When I got home, I heard the news.

"This here was my brother's Hebrew book from the yeshiva. June 12. Twelve o'clock. Four o'clock. Room 7. Five o'clock. He was a little boy then. Written by Sol. That's his handwriting. Upside down. Why did he write it upside down? No, wait, Sol's right. This is the way to hold it. I forgot, this is the way it goes; he was right! My brother's Hebrew book . . . held in my brother's hands.

"I had envelopes addressed by him to their friends. I kept them. Where did I put them? Goddamn it. I'll find them. . . . I'll find them. . . ."

V: THE SATURDAY-AFTERNOON PARADE

Solly and his father moved to Mitchell's Dam, Alabama, when Solly was eleven. Solly's father opened a workclothes store on the railroad track from Red Mountain. His father had done everything from loading pig iron on railway cars to selling tombstone insurance. They lived in one big room behind the store. The mountain was thirty miles long, with solid iron ore. The track from the steel plant went straight on a level past the highway crossing where they lived, straight on down the track.

Behind the store was the large shanty area called Niggertown. The store became the Jewtown corner of Niggertown. The white community lived on the other side of the tracks.

Most of Solly's new friends were black: Ray, Louie, Smitty, and Ronnie. Their mothers fed him at lunchtime. They called him their honey. A little Jewish boy. He could not insult them by refusing and telling them he was kosher.

At a crossing point of the tracks, Solly would hop the freights from the steel mill with the other kids. They fished and swam in a rock quarry. They shot marbles. Pitched horseshoes. Chased water moccasins, cottonhead rattlers, down the creek together in the running rapids. At the base of the mill, where the water came through the sluice, there were huge rocks. The water moccasins lay under the rocks. Solly and his friends would run barefoot on the rocks, holding clubs in their hands.

Solly's friend Ray was always writing (his mother had taught him). Ray wrote out a sheet in pencil which he distributed weekly to the other kids: "The Journal of the Sleeping Hollow Home for Blind Mice." The journal dealt with the problems of the blind mice trying to cope with life in a civilized world, trying to get attention for their special problems.

At night, when the mill was closed, the slag that had been poured into the huge slag pots all day had to be emptied. It was still red hot. The slag pots were on enormous hangers. When the six pots were tipped over, the hot slag would light up the sky like a volcano. Solly loved to watch it at night from his bedroom window.

In school, the first exercise was to recite the Pledge of Allegiance. About everyone being equal. The words were odd to him. His black friends were not starting school. Then the teacher asked each student to tell the class about himself or herself. Solly didn't say very much. The teacher asked him who his friends were. He said, Smitty, Louie, Ray, and Ronnie.

At recess, the kids formed a tight little circle around him in the yard. The tallest of them took him by the shirt and said, "Hey, Slopbucket, Slopfuckit, your friends ain't Smitty, Louie, and Ray. Your friends ain't got no names. Your friends is Niggerbaby, Tarbaby, and Smokerack. They're dirty and stupid and they smell of rat shit. That's why there's no school for 'em. We're gonna beat you up, niggerlover."

They knocked Solly to the ground and jumped all over him. They rolled him over and jumped on his back. They kicked him and spat on him. When the class bell rang, they ran back to the schoolroom, laughing and shouting.

Solly's teacher, a pretty young woman named Bessie Stuart, came out looking for him and saw what had happened. She touched him and said, "Now you know, Solly: niggers are just dirty and ignorant and stupid. That's why there's no school for them, and that's why you got no business playing with them." She put her arm around him and walked him back to school. She said, "I'm sure the boys and girls are sorry for what they did to you. But now you know why they did it."

A month later, some of the kids followed him home. One boy told him to knock the chip off his shoulder. Solly refused. Another boy said, "Well, I'll show him what we do with cowards." He twisted Solly's arm and threw him into a ditch.

The next day, Solly went back to the school, smiling. He was scared, but he smiled. He didn't tattletale, but he didn't play up to them, either.

In the afternoons, he still played a little with his black buddies.

And on the Sabbath, he didn't play with anyone.

The work week in the town stretched until Saturday noon. Saturday was payday. There was drinking, whoring, blackjack, and poker, and a movie house for whites. Gambling was off limits for blacks.

On Saturday afternoon, the sheriff would pick a half-dozen cronies, appoint them deputy sheriffs, give them revolvers, which they jammed in their pockets, pin badges on them, and head with them for Niggertown.

In Niggertown, the men fanned out, looking for a crap game. Every crap game had a pot on the ground with a large sum of money in it. The sheriff would spot a big pot among a bunch of blacks and shout, "All right! Fan out. Get away from there." He confiscated the money, which he shared with his deputies, and aimed his revolver at the blacks. "Now march," he shouted.

The Saturday-afternoon parade had begun. The sheriff and his men marched the blacks who had been involved in the game—men, women, and children—down the railroad tracks to the crossing down a rampway in the dirty road into a large open enclosure beside the jailhouse. It had a barbed-wire fence around it and a locked gate.

They opened the gate and herded the blacks inside. They locked the gate.

The blacks would remain there until they could get a dollar somehow and buy their way out. They huddled in the heat, without sanitation.

The Saturday-afternoon parade took place year-round.

The Declaration of Independence was celebrated in Brightwood Park on July 4. It didn't take place in Niggertown.

There were many contests, including watermelon eating. The white participants wore aprons. The watermelon was sliced for them.

The nigger show came next. Blacks were hired for the day. In the watermelon-eating contest, the black men would have to bury their faces in half a melon to scoop it out. No aprons were provided. Their hands were tied behind their backs.

Foot races were held. Whites were tied at the feet and had to hop. Blacks were tied hands and feet.

The next contest was never engaged in by whites. It took place in the creek. Two blacks would have a boxing match with bare fists in a barrel. They could hardly fit in it together. The barrel would tip over in the water. The two men would have to keep beating each other to a pulp until the whites said it was enough. Then the two bleeding men were rescued.

In Mitchell's Dam, blacks were permitted to walk only on the dirt road, not on the paved sidewalks. They were allowed to cross the sidewalk only to enter a store. The saying went, "The color of their money is the only good thing about them."

But if blacks were in one store and wanted to go to the store next door, they had to go out, cross the sidewalk, walk down the dirt road, and cross the sidewalk again. They were not to walk across on the sidewalk.

One Saturday, Solly was standing in the movie line, waiting for the theater to open.

From the line, he watched the black people shopping for groceries. They were jammed into the narrow dirt roadway.

The pressure of the crowd suddenly pushed two black men up onto the sidewalk. By chance, they jostled the sheriff, who was standing by Solly.

"What are you, a couple of smart niggers?" the sheriff said.

They did not say a word.

He took his revolver out, aimed it at each man's head, and pulled the trigger.

Their bodies lay in a red puddle in the ditch.

He aimed his revolver at two black men in the dirt roadway. "You two niggers," he said, "come over here."

The shaking men approached him. He pointed to the two bodies in the ditch. "Drag them over there and leave them there all day. This will show you niggers your place."

VI: AWAKE AND SING

He knew the score, and he could never go back to what he had been.

Shortly after his Bar Mitzvah in Alabama, Solly returned to New York with his father. The price of cotton, which had been thirty-six cents a pound, dropped overnight to six cents. Solly's father had paid for his stock with cash. He was wiped out. Solly's sister, Ruth, who had been living with relatives on Pitt Street, rejoined Solly and his father at a coldwater flat on Delancey Street.

He was in his junior year of high school. Solly's father wanted him to return to yeshiva study afternoons after school. He told his father he could not go back. Society was collapsing all around him, and at the yeshiva they discussed what happened when you cut open a pregnant cow: was the baby a dairy or a meat product? He still believed the saying in the Talmud, "Words which come from the heart penetrate the heart."

He could not consider the 613 laws of the *Halakhah* while capitalism was reaching its final stage: fascism. One day on Rivington Street, a man in a red beret had handed him a Communist Party pamphlet. Solly stayed up all night reading and rereading it. So this was why there was so much suffering all about him in the face of so much plenty. Fascism was imperialism gone mad. He had always been moved by the vision of the prophet Elijah coming and the hearts of the fathers returning to the sons and the sons' hearts returning to the fathers: the time when there would be love in the world, when people would be compassionate and their hearts would turn toward one another. And here was a way of reaching that reality.

Solly found work as a clerk at a grocery store on 125th Street in Harlem. One morning he saw a truck run over a Negro woman and escape from the scene. The woman, her arm severed, was carried into the store. He frantically called for an ambulance, and tried to bind her bleeding body. When the ambulance arrived an hour later, the woman was dead. He felt the furious helplessness and anger in the pit of his stomach.

In Harlem he had seen the overcrowding, the rancid slums, the high prices for inferior goods, the rotten meat. All the stores on 125th street were white-owned, and the workers were all white until Adam Clayton Powell, Jr., led picket lines of protest.

Solly's father desperately looked for a job and finally found work on a production line. Some of the other workers baited him for being Jewish, stealing his chisels, putting glue on his tools and on his good clothes. A foreman railed against the Jews and told Solly's father, "I'm going to make you quit." The foreman placed him on a rapid production line on which he was the only man hand-sanding cabinets. His father would come home at night with his fingertips raw and the skin partly rubbed off. Solly would bathe his father's fingers and put ointment on them. His father always went back to work the next day, never complaining.

In the New York streets, there was no work to be had. Now he began to understand capitalism's artificially induced storms, its need for constant crises and colonial wars of oppression and expansion. He understood why food and clothes were burned or dumped into the ocean while millions were starving and freezing.

When Solly joined the party, he learned that under capitalism the profit motive governed everything, that the human being counted for nothing. He sat quietly, overwhelmed to be accepted as a comrade at party headquarters, staring at the wallpaper with drawings of brawny working-men in overalls and upraised fists, and capitalists with fat cigars and huge bellies sitting on piles of coins.

He understood that capitalism was doomed—that was obvious—that he would help to smash the legacy of endless wars, racism, and white chauvinism. He understood, he understood everything; he shouted down his father at the dinner table as a Jew who buried his head in the sand. He had gained confidence: in his unit the comrades had become still when he talked of his experiences in Alabama and the Saturday-afternoon parade, and looked at him with liking and sympathy. The *Freiheit* and *Daily Worker* editorials filled him with certainty, and there was no subject, no country, no area of the globe that was outside his comprehension.

Mussolini had invaded Ethiopia, and the fascist generals had staged an uprising in Spain. In Harlan, Kentucky, the coal miners were shot down in cold blood by the capitalist pirates because they struck for a few more pennies in their paychecks. When his father cursed the communists, Solly told him, "Look what's happening in Kentucky. All the miners want is a few pennies so they can live, Papa. What happens? They're shot down by the ruling class in cold blood. Do you really think the workers can take over the means of production without a violent revolution when even for a few pennies they're dropping blood?"

He struggled to keep up with it all: the Scottsboro boys, Tom Mooney, Munich, the unemployed councils, the hunger marches, the Group Theater, everything that had happened and was happening, the Peter Cacchione and Ben Davis campaigns, all the books and pamphlets at the Jimmy Higgins bookshop: Clara Weatherwax's *Marching! Marching!*, Lenin's *Left-Wing Communism: An Infantile Disorder*, *Seaman and Longshoremen under the Red Flag*, William Z. Foster's *Toward a Soviet America*.

Solly could quote the pamphlet by Stalin *The Soviets and the Individual*, his address to the graduates of the Red Army Academy, by heart: "Of all the valuable capital the world possesses, the most valuable and most decisive is people," and the intriguing passage: "We pushed forward still more vigorously on the Leninist road, brushing every obstacle from our path. It is true that in our course we were obliged to handle some of these comrades roughly. But you cannot help that. I must confess that I too took a hand in this business. . . . *(Loud cheers.)*"

He steeled himself in the struggle; he gained the political maturity of knowing all the phrases and slogans. He learned he had to throw away all his old values about life and people, adopt a world view, a long-range state of mind, a calmness, the firmness that was the character of a good communist—the new man—what they called the capacity of mind to dominate matter, a strong political consciousness instead of an intensely subjective state of mind. "Once the test has been passed," they told him, "the new steel can be tempered." Solly was thrilled. The instructor at the Workers School— tweed suit, pipe, mazes of smoke—said, "The more active you become, you will see that experience proves again and again the correctness of our theories. Lenin always starts with first principles and hammers on bigger and better polemics against foes and adversaries." Solly patterned his behavior on how he imagined Stalin would act in social situations.

He learned about deviationists and social fascists and Trotskyite vermin. He learned better than anyone else, for he believed, he believed, he stood up now and shouted, "Comrades, let's not be bashful about the trials of the Trotskyite and Bukharin wreckers and spies. Let's hail the death of the twenty-one traitors and the findings of Soviet workers' justice with gusto and joy. We must as never before take the offensive to convince our brothers and sisters about the need to clean out the Trotskyites from our ranks. When they realize the full meaning of the schemes against peace and democracy of this scum, we'll be ever more successful in strengthening and consolidating our struggle and smoothing the grid for the coming advance of peace and solidarity." Standing on a soapbox at City College, it was Solly who answered a heckler by declaring, "Stalin brought Russia into the twentieth century."

Solly's face was aglow, sitting in Madison Square Garden, watching Earl Browder, the quiet man from Kansas, mumble, "We're living in the rapids of history and a lot of folks are afraid of being dashed on the rocks. But not us, comrades!" After the cheering, Browder mumbled, "Our ideological struggle has to be conducted as a concrete struggle arising from unfolding events. It should be carried out in a fresh language and in forms that the workers can understand and in terms of their own experience. The correctness of this perspective will be tested by life itself. If we project a correct perspective," the foremost people's leader droned on, never looking up from his text, "we will defeat those who spread pessimism and despair (and we all know who they are), confusionism and obscurantism, adventurism and recklessness, and thus establish unshakable ideological ties with the workers and the peasants. As the great, the wondrous Stalin says, 'We will abolish underripe fruit and overripe fruit and quench our spirits with fresh fruit forever!' All hail to the Union of Socialist Soviet Republics, the first land of Socialism! All hail! May Stalin's example be a fresh twig forever, for his leadership in the liberation of peoples from centuries of oppression continues to take on ever greater clarity! All hail our Party! Deeply rooted in theory, we know that only through struggle will anything come to pass! We will root out petit bourgeois influences, eliminating the final vestiges of right-opportunism and left-adventurism, never adopting a middle-of-the-road policy, steering a firm course at this critical crossroads. At this juncture we must particularly stress the next immediate stage of progress for the people which is inseparably bound up with, and requires the crystallization of a broad democratic front coalition."

Browder drew a breath, smiled, and finished reading: "Comrades, it's no accident that we are here today. It is no accident, furthermore, that ours is the Party that combats left-sectarianism, right-opportunism, and philistinism of all sorts. We shall continue to develop correct tactics adopted to the concrete situation!"

VII: A SOVIET AMERICA

There shall yet be old men and women in the squares of Jerusalem, each with staff in hand because of their great age. And the squares of the city shall be crowded with boys and girls playing in the squares. . . . Thus said the Lord of Hosts: I will rescue my people from the lands of the East and from the lands of the West, and I will bring them home to dwell in Jerusalem. . . .
—Zechariah 8:4–8

In Solly's favorite pamphlet, *Happy Days for American Youth in a Soviet America* by Max Weiss (the cover a smiling young worker in beret holding a sledge hammer over his shoulder), he read of the death of the spirit in the United States: "how many Shakespeares and Miltons are buried together with their talents beneath a sea of poverty! . . . Not so the youth of Soviet America! For them, the world would for the first time open itself wide, to be rebuilt, to be changed, to be written about. . . . There would be no mute, inglorious Miltons in Soviet America! . . . Undoubtedly a workers' and farmers' government in America would be of a Soviet form."

It was the Soviet Union that informed his hopes and his dreams. There was the concrete reality, where civilization had progressed to the stage of human brotherhood. The Soviet Union, whose constitution declared anti-Semitism a crime punishable by death. Small wonder that the workers' fatherland was bearing the brunt of the war against Nazism while the West practiced appeasement. And that antifascists from every country in the world were finding sanctuary there.

And as soon as that final battle against fascism was won, the police, jails, and army would be abolished, for no soldiers were needed to keep down a liberated mankind. Time would no longer be wasted on military drills and tactics; soldiers would lead rich cultural lives.

Even at this early stage, there was free education, free medical care, treehouses for honeymooners, the elimination of prostitution and crime and homosexuality and venereal disease and mental illness; so soon the elderly were living to a hundred and 120 and even more because they (and children, of course) came first in the society. Yiddish was spoken everywhere by many workers and by many soldiers in the Red Army as well—but, in the spirit of proletarian internationalism, Yiddish was only one choice; all the nationalities were free to practice their customs as they saw fit. Yet he was acutely aware of how the Yiddish theater and Yiddish books were flourishing.

Tears would come to Solly's eyes as he contemplated the reality, and he grew lyrical talking about it at meetings and on soapboxes.

He repeated all the information he'd received in his unit: the end of racism and exploitation; the vitamin-filled food the workers received on the job; the poetry they wrote in their spare time in the clubrooms and libraries attached to their factories, mines, and mills; how they played chess and checkers, sang, danced, played. The factories themselves, so sunny and spacious, all the machinery made safe and reliable. The infant stations at each factory where mothers happily left their children for glorious days.

This was the end of the dark ages; this was where history was tending. A new age—he would live to see it, he would live to see the end of sharecropping and peonage and sweatshops and Jim Crow and limbless soldiers returning from wars of capitalist conquest. He was a red hot; he wanted to implement his beliefs with actions. He wanted to fight with all his heart for the day when his own country would reach that level, and he felt ennobled with the joy and the hope and the humanity of it. Every child he saw in the street, so innocent, so trusting—so soon to be trampled on by capitalism's uncertainties and insecurities, mortalities, and endless cycles of war and depression—made Solly vow to fight even harder to bring the day sooner when a Soviet America would end the needless suffering of all children. And he thought always of his people, herded off in freight cars to deaths in gas chambers all across the Nazi continent, deaths that were slow and filled with the newest, most ingenious tortures ever devised by man. Practiced by creatures who prided themselves on their anticommunism. Yes,

Solly knew where he stood and why. Brecht: In Praise of Communism. They say that it is evil. *But we know it is the end of evil.*

Solly was the first to arrive at his unit's headquarters, and he was almost always there when the others had left. He seemed to the others never to go home. Sometimes he acknowledged to himself his loneliness, but it was always with the realization that his feelings were unimportant compared with the objective situation.

Of course it was true he yearned to be holding "a dear one" (as he put it to himself) when he watched the Almanac Singers at hootenannies, or the Jewish People's Philharmonic Chorus at Lewisohn Stadium in summer, or the Freiheit Gesangverein, a Yiddish choral group that sang workers' songs at Webster Hall, or went to Soviet films at the Stanley Theater. Of course he wanted to share the struggle with someone who had a correct perspective. Among his subjective feelings were questions about what it felt like to hold a girl in his arms, what a breast felt like (he often stroked his pillow, and thought the softness must be a little like that), and he wondered what a kiss felt like, how you did it, how much pressure you applied, what you did with your tongue, and with hers.

In the deserted unit, at night, he suddenly heard his pounding heart.

VIII: PUT DOWN YOUR FORKS, COMRADES

Solly was squashed into his seat at the Paramount Cafeteria on a Saturday night at eight-thirty beside the other comrades from his unit.

Leon Pepstein, who always wore a tweed scarf draped over his shoulder, was talking about the coming abolition of the army in the U.S.S.R.: "Why waste time on military drills when you have close ties with the workers?" he shouted. No one disputed him. "None of this blind obedience to bullshit orders! No class distinctions! As the masses become social beings, as the economic basis for crime and other antisocial acts is removed, police won't even be necessary."

Leon suddenly pounded on the table and they all sang out the City College song against President Robinson. Robinson had welcomed the fascist students from Italy and suspended student protesters who had objected as "guttersnipes," pointing his umbrella at them.

> We're all fed up with Robinson's rule
> We're sick of high-priced knowledge
> To get the 19 back in the school
> Strike City College!

Solly, in a mischievous mood, took his knife and fork and the silverware of the other comrades and stuck them in his jacket. "This place is already rich from the workers it exploits," he declared.

"No, Comrade Solly," a little voice piped up. It was the pretty new comrade who had recently joined the unit. The only girl at the table, she had been eating her food very carefully, her eyes glued to her plate. Solly couldn't bring himself to look much at girls anyway. She had looked at her plate, and he had looked at his.

Now he gazed directly at her.

"Remember," she said, "what Lenin wrote: to steal less than the state is petty thievery. When the Bolsheviks took the Soviet Union, comrade, they took a state. If you fight, you fight for a country, for important things. For principles." She took a deep breath. Everyone was silent.

Solly grinned. He dropped the silverware back on the table with a little crash and leaned toward her.

"My name, in case you're wondering, comrade, is Dolly. Dolly Stern."

IX: THE DEATH HOUSE, 1954

If he were asked if he was sure of what he had done—on one level he would proclaim his certitude. But—on another—yes, there was terror of dying. But the deepest terror was the dot of doubt. Some Trotskyite scum—some social fascist—*Who?, Why?*—had mailed him that week the Fred Beal book, *Proletarian Journey*—and Solly had been taken off guard. After all, a Gastonia defendant, the leader of the strike, fled to the Soviet Union. But then! He had to keep reading, until the world seemed to be turning upside down and he wanted to burn that book page by page, but he couldn't keep the faces out of his headaches at night.

Starving Soviet men and women, peasants and workers—gathered at garbage cans looking for food during collectivization. Rounded up, protesting, by guards with whips and guns. The stoned pavement scraping their bare feet, sores oozing from their faces and feet, tossed like sacks of flour or bales of hay into freight cars, screaming for help and weeping. Taken to areas where they would starve unseen because a delegation of American progressives from a union—*Solly's* union—he'd almost gone on that trip—were coming to visit.

He tried to tell Dolly. She rose up, proclaiming, "What? You, too? Methinks you're beguiled by their offers of forty pieces of gold!" Solly stared ahead. She told him to leave her cell.

She never spoke to him again.

MALACHI

Francine Prose

READING THE BOOK OF MALACHI FEELS RATHER LIKE EAVESDROP-
ping on the end of a long family quarrel. In this last book of
Prophets, God speaks to Israel through Malachi in the voice of
the irascible, exasperated, but ultimately loving parent—the
voice of the father who, after so many estrangements and reconciliations,
has finally had enough. The God of Malachi is precise, demanding, difficult
to fathom, and harder still to please—the Father whose perpetual disappointment has driven Him to sarcasm and mockery, to imitating His children, mimicking both their questions and their responses. He is, one
imagines, a great deal like Kafka's father—not the real Hermann Kafka, the
rail-thin specter haunting those last photos, but the father Kafka dreamed
and experienced, that fierce and implacable patriarch to whom he wrote,
"All my writing was about you."

In Malachi, the prophet who has nearly dispensed with personality
reveals to us a God who has nearly abandoned poetry. The word Malachi

---

The King James Version of the Bible used in this essay.

means "my messenger"; it is not, strictly speaking, anyone's proper name, so that these four brief chapters are generally assumed to be the only anonymously written prophetic book. Yet our sense of Malachi's anonymity extends beyond considerations of credit and authorship to those of voice and tone. Here, there is no talk of ecstasy, or of song. One finds none of the personal anguish which led Jeremiah to curse the day he was born, or of Jonah's heartfelt confession of his own tortuous coming to God. Malachi has not been granted Zechariah's vision of black and white horses stalking the earth, or Isaiah's awe before the Lord's anger, or the intensity of his longing to comfort and console.

Just as it is nearly impossible to read Jeremiah without learning much about the prophet's complex relation to prophecy and to God, it is almost impossible to discover anything at all about Malachi, who not only says nothing of personal history but never once speaks of himself in the first person. In that way, he may well be, in a dual sense, the ultimate prophet— the purest conduit for God's will. The prophet himself has all but vanished from the work, or anyway has grown very quiet, so that mostly the voice we hear in these chapters is God's.

And God, it seems to me, has never spoken so plainly—not straightfor-wardly, for that is not at all the case, but, rather, without adornment. The flashes of poetry—"the Sun of righteousness . . . with healing in his wings" that Malachi promises—are luminous, but rare. It is almost as if the Lord of Hosts has grown impatient, grown tired of His children's repeated failure to extract meaning and learn from the gorgeous, impassioned language of an Isaiah or a Jeremiah. Having lost faith in metaphor and poetic strategy, the God of Malachi—like many fathers who feel themselves to be embat-tled—resorts to the bitterest and most biting of ironies.

This irony is the basis of Malachi's formal structure. For, unique among the prophetic books, Malachi advances its argument almost entirely through dialectic. God makes a pronouncement, then asks a question. But the ques-tion is Israel's question, God's ironic mimicry of Israel's question—the ignorant, self-justifying whining of a stubborn, ungrateful child. Then, as if the answer weren't evident in the mockery itself, God and the prophet attempt to address that which deserves no reply. And what is the Father talking about? The Father is speaking of love.

After a brief superscription, the book begins: "I have loved you, saith the Lord. Yet ye say: Wherein hast Thou loved us?" And now the God of Malachi cites, as proof of love, the story of Jacob and Esau—surely one of the quintessential family nightmares. Here, the evidence of God's regard for Jacob (Israel) is His hatred of Esau—the rival brother—and the harshness with which He continues to deal with Esau's descendants, the Edomites. Could the drought-stricken Hebrews of Malachi's time have been much consoled to hear that the (admittedly hostile) Edomites had it worse? Perhaps, and yet one cannot help thinking again of Kafka's dismay at seeing his father war with his sisters—even with the "abhorrent" Elli—and of how closely the irony God employs in Malachi resembles that which, Kafka claimed, his father used constantly on his children:

You put special trust in bringing up children by means of irony, and this was most in keeping with your superiority over me. An admonition from you generally took this form: "Can't you do it in such and such a way? That's too hard for you, I suppose. You haven't the time, of course?" and so on.

The theme of parents and children, of honor and fear is continued in the next verses of Malachi: "A son honoreth his father, and a servant his master: If then I be a father, Where is mine honor? and if I be a master, where is My Fear?" But now God turns His scorn against His priests, whose laziness and laxity inspire the ironic dialectic which continues throughout this first chapter:

Ye offer polluted bread upon mine altar; and ye say, Wherein have we polluted thee? In that ye say, the table of the Lord is contemptible.

And if ye offer the blind for sacrifice, is it not evil? and if ye offer the lame and sick, is it not evil? offer it now unto thy governor; will he be pleased with thee or accept thy person? saith the Lord of hosts. . . .

Ye said also, Behold what a weariness is it! and ye have snuffed at it, saith the Lord of hosts; and ye brought that which was torn, and the lame, and the sick; thus ye brought an offering: should I accept this of your hand? saith the Lord.

The sarcasm here is unremitting and unsparing; its harshness and relentlessness begin to awaken in me a discomfort I cannot deny. I cannot help sympathizing with Malachi's audience, nor can I imagine a section of prophecy more perfectly tailored—or crueler—to its listeners. Surely the priests must have heard themselves in the lame excuses and equivocations parodied here. In these mocking questions, I hear echoes of modern voices, the voices of nonobservant Jews, of my own voice explaining why we no longer practice old rituals, laws formulated before the advent of refrigeration and indoor plumbing, observances which now seem purely formalistic, rules for the sake of rules.

But that formalism, the God of Malachi would say, is precisely the point. Though ultimately the soul of worship is reverence and love for God, the only way to demonstrate this faith is through strict observance of the proper forms. The issues here are neither convenience nor common sense. If ease and expediency were the criteria for acceptable sacrifice, then the lame and sick and damaged stock would be the most pleasing to God. The point is not our comfort but God's will; the only purpose is His purpose, and His demand that we honor Him. Why? says the tyrannical parent. Because I say so. A dictum to which the priests might well have reacted like any disobedient child—guilty, resistant, and craving, above all else, that overwhelming comfort and love, the promised reward for absolute submission.

I recognize these feelings, for they are the ones I wrestle with when, from time to time, I consider changing my life—keeping the Sabbath, a kosher home, providing my children with some kind of meaningful religious education. What stops me, on the shallowest level, is the same things which Malachi mocks in the priests—the difficulty, the inconvenience, the daunting personal expense. But beyond that, and far more disturbing, is some profound hesitation about the God I would be serving, the God of Malachi—a Father with so little patience or tolerance for His children's missteps, for the ordinary run of human failings.

In that way, I suppose, the Old Testament must always come as a bit of a shock to those of us who do not live with it on a daily basis. For the God we had in mind—the God who'd taken up residence in our imaginations since the last time we read the Bible—is not this God at all. Our God is a "nicer" God, more forgiving and just, less arbitrary, primitive, and demanding. A friend who has taught the Old Testament in college literature courses speaks of her students' almost predictable dismay at the Bible's brutality, and of coming to realize that, though she and most of her class are Jewish, they are all, in a sense, Christian—that is, their concept of the divine is closer to the Christian than to the Hebrew. What seems to be at issue here is ethics, and our expectation that the Highest Power will behave with the highest ethic. But what cannot be overlooked is the relation between social ethic and social necessity, and the vast differences between the necessities of tribal existence and those of the industrial state. Biblical culture is based, in ways we often forget, on survival, on the precariousness of life itself, and on the tribal needs for identity, security, protection. What hardly needs saying is that the parent who perceives his children to be in mortal danger is less inclined to reason, persuade, explain, cajole, is far more likely to storm and rage and threaten. And so we find the God of Malachi making the extended, terrible threats which dominate the book's second chapter:

If ye will not hear, and if ye will not lay it to heart, to give glory unto my name, saith the Lord of hosts, I will even send a curse upon you, and I will curse your blessings; yea, I have cursed them already, because ye do not lay it to heart.

Behold, I will corrupt your seed, and spread dung upon your faces, even the dung of your solemn feasts; and one shall take you away with it.

I find I cannot go on, cannot continue to write this essay honestly, without confessing that I find this last image not only off-putting but even slightly ludicrous. I find it simply beyond me to subscribe to the notion of a God who would rub His priests' faces with dung, who would chastise His children like a modern dog-owner attempting to housebreak a pet, who would, in short, make threats I would be horrified to hear my children make.

I can only imagine how Malachi and Malachi's God would mock both my squeamishness and my arrogance, would ask who am I to predict what God would say or do, or to attempt to separate His meaning from His prophet's redaction? Nonetheless, I am tempted to suggest that, in transmitting the words of God, Malachi may have allowed some literary considerations to enter in here: that is, the writerly instinct to dramatize and intensify God's threat so that the promise and reassurance that ends the book—the "Sun of righteousness"—will seem to shine even brighter, will stand out in greater relief: a version of the narrative principle which consigns Job to the ash heap before he can be redeemed.

It may also be true that Malachi was here re-creating God, not in his own image but, rather, in the image of that enraged and impossible, demanding, primitive patriarch. Once again let us listen to Kafka on the subject of the threatening and—so it seemed—almost divinely omnipotent father:

You reinforced abusiveness with threats, and this was applied to me too. How terrible was for me that, for instance, "I'll tear you apart like a fish," although I knew, of course, that nothing worse was to follow (admittedly, as a little child I didn't know that), but it was almost exactly in accord with my notions of your power, and I saw you as being capable of doing this too. It was also terrible when you ran around the table, shouting, grabbing at one, obviously not really trying to grab, and Mother (in the end) had to rescue one, as it seemed. Once again one had, so it seemed to the child, remained alive through your mercy and bore one's life henceforth as an undeserved gift from you.

Reading Malachi and Kafka's "Letter to His Father" in concert is, it seems to me, enormously revealing. For not until I chanced to read the former and reread the latter, around the same time, did I understand how closely, how deeply the Hebrew God follows the paradigm of the impossible, unknowable, autocratic paterfamilias. Indeed, the thoughts which Kafka attributes to his father near the start of the letter sound astonishingly like the sentiments which Malachi expresses on God's behalf.

. . . you have worked hard all your life, have sacrificed everything for your children. . . . You have not expected any gratitude for this, knowing what "children's gratitude" is like, but have expected at least some sort of obligingness, some sign of sympathy. Instead I have always hidden from you, among my books, with crazy friends, or with extravagant ideas. . . . I have never come to you when you were in the synagogue. . . . And what is more, you charge me with it in such a way as to make it seem my fault . . . while you aren't in the slightest to blame, unless it be for having been too good to me.

The God of Malachi reminds one, too, of the father in Bruno Schulz's fiction, more terrifying certainly, and crueler, but no less mythic, marvelous, ineffable, larger than anything we could imagine of life. Seen in this way, the mood of Malachi is almost entirely familial, the tone one of harsh and untempered paternal rebuke, so that when God leaves off His threats and speaks of the good priest with whom the Covenant was created, the one who has not broken His law ("The law of truth was in his mouth, and iniquity was not found in his lips; he walked with me in peace and equity, and did turn many away from iniquity"), it is rather in the manner of the father describing another, better child, the ideal brother, the Jacob who exists partly as a standard against which Esau can forever measure his fall from grace.

There follows a verse, "Have we not all one father? hath not one God created us?," which is frequently cited—wrongly, it seems to me—as an expression of universalism, of a kind of spiritual brotherhood transcending religious and cultural divisions. My own sense of these lines is that they are yet another series of ironic questions, another mock justification-in-advance for the "abomination" which God censures next—"Judah hath profaned the holiness of the Lord which he loved, and hath married the daughter of a strange God"—the crime of intermarriage, which Israel endeavors to justify, as lamely and futilely as ever, by arguing for a common origin, a universal Father and Creator.

Once more I am uneasy, though perhaps my discomfort stems from the fact that, yet again, I hear my own voice in these weak protestations, these thin attempts to defend myself against the implicit accusation of having married the son of a strange God—as the distant, well-mannered, and somewhat detached God of my husband's Episcopalian parents would certainly have seemed to Malachi. Of course I can cite special cases—Abraham, Esther, the Moabite Ruth's almost forgotten husband—exceptions in the Bible itself; I can almost convince myself that God, in this instance, hardly has me in mind. But my conviction of this wavers when I hear of the fate which God has in store for these transgressors: "The Lord will cut off the man that doeth this, the master and the scholar, out of the tabernacles of Jacob." Reading these words, I feel the same sense of exile, of isolation, I felt not long ago at an Orthodox family wedding—knowing that these were my people, my blood, envying them their solidity, their community, but also knowing that for me to join them would mean undoing a series of decisions made throughout my life, perhaps even before my birth.

This dual sense of belonging and exclusion is confusing—a confusion, I would think, shared by many assimilated, nonpracticing Jews of my generation. We feel ourselves to be Jews and treasure whatever aspects of self and identity we consider particularly Jewish—a certain kind of humor, intelligence, a common language, as it were, an earthy common sense. We fear the label "cultural Jew" even as we know it to be partly true. I remember a Sunday last fall: I walked around the Lower East Side, excited by the crisp autumn air and by the crowds of Chasidic families shopping rather manically for their Succot *esrogs*. I remember asking the religious-bookstore owners for a book I needed and having them address their replies to my husband, and how hurt I was by this, until, by the time we got to the dairy cafeteria, the—admittedly even-handed and impersonal—rudeness of the waiters seemed a metaphor for rejection, for my alienation from my own kind.

A modern Malachi, one imagines, might curse the religiously lax not with dung or blasted seed, but, rather, with a certain kind of loneliness which seems almost endemic in the population. Again I turn to Kafka, if only for the peculiar comfort of knowing that even this has its precedent in Jewish history. At that Orthodox wedding and earlier, on East Broadway, I experienced the same duality and ambivalence that caused Kafka to write in his diary, "What do I have in common with Jews? I have hardly anything in common even with myself," and, in a letter to Milena, "Had I been given the choice to be whatever I wanted, I would have chosen to be a little Eastern Jewish boy in the corner of that room, without a worry in the world." That longing for community and faith—and the sense of what the loss of it entails—is expressed perhaps most movingly in this letter to Felice:

> You go to the synagogue. . . . And what is it that sustains you—the idea of Jewishness, or the idea of God? Do you feel—and this is the essential point—an unbroken tie between yourself and some reassuringly distant, possibly infinite, heights and depths? He who always feels this is not forced to roam about like a lost cur with a mute plea in his eyes, nor yearn to slip into his grave as though it were a cozy sleeping bag and life a frigid winter night.

Yet even in Malachi there are passages which make one feel as if birthright alone were a guarantee of inclusion, as if God were, to put it simply, looking out for us, too—safeguarding our future. For after the interdiction on marrying the "daughter of a strange God" comes a section in which God rebukes the kind of man who, as he grows older, "deal[s] treacherously against the wife of his youth"—that is to say, divorces her and marries someone younger. Such verses provide us with one of those moments which seem a bit like time travel: zooming back through the millennia to discover how much remains unchanged. However distressing it is to realize that one of the more regrettable aspects of human social behavior should be among the most persistent, I must say I quite like the notion of a God who looks out for no-longer-young married women—our future selves—and who considers their fate to be of primary importance.

And yet, at the risk of sounding once more like a spoiler, I must also add that one of the functions of passages such as this is to remind me that God and His prophet seem to take for granted an audience of men. It is only the men He chastises for marrying outside the tribe, for "putting away" their spouses; the priests He addresses for much of the book were also, it hardly needs pointing out, male. And I cannot help thinking of that same Orthodox wedding, the one at which I felt so estranged, and of how my wish to belong was confused and confounded when the Sephardic rabbi—in a gloss on the wedding ceremony I hadn't heard in years and thought somehow I would never hear again—explained that, in signing the marriage contract, the bride had declared herself to be the groom's property.

And then, just as these doubts and frustrations threaten to topple one's faith entirely, we find ourselves—as if by an act of grace—in Malachi's last two chapters. Here the raging, distant Father becomes the merciful and eternally present one. For, though these verses are couched in the vocabulary of judgment and apocalypse, they exist, I would argue, chiefly to bring us the promise of protection and redemption. The tone changes and becomes more lyrical, less scolding. The pacing speeds up, driven forward by a sort of eschatological momentum. Irony and dialectic give way to poetry and exhortation, and even the perpetual mock-questioning—except for brief recurrences in verses 7, 8, and 14—all but disappears.

These chapters, which in certain versions of the Bible are combined into one, begin and end with prophecies, in the most literal sense. The first of these concerns the arrival of God's messenger, to be followed swiftly by the coming of the Lord Himself.

But who may abide the day of his coming? and who shall stand when he appeareth? for he is like a refiner's fire, and like fuller's soap:

And he shall sit as a refiner and purifier of silver: and he shall purify the sons of Levi, and purge them as gold and silver, that they may offer unto the Lord an offering in righteousness.

Such judgment, we are told, would go hard against the sorcerers, adulterers, false swearers, "those that oppress the hireling in his wages, the widow, and the fatherless," and yet, in contrast to the preceding chapters, these verses seem less of a threat than a promise, less a curse than an offer of rapprochement (". . . and fear not me, saith the Lord of Hosts. For I am the Lord, I change not; therefore ye sons of Jacob are not consumed"). Indeed, the context is almost entirely one of reconciliation ("Return unto me, and I will return unto you, saith the Lord of hosts"). The language here is that of the Father who, however frustrated and disappointed in His dealings with His children ("Even from the days of your fathers ye are gone away from mine ordinances, and have not kept them"), has not for one moment stopped loving them. And along with this love comes the desire to protect ("And I will rebuke the devourer for your sake, and he shall not destroy the fruits of your ground"), to restore, and even to glorify: "And all nations shall call you blessed: for you shall be a delightsome land."

These themes—judgment, repentance, reconciliation—reappear, with variations, throughout the concluding verses of Malachi. There is more of the ironic dialectic so characteristic of the prophet, yet now it is followed by the suggestion that there are others who do not plead ignorance or question God in this way, who fear the Lord and think upon His name, and who will, in return, find their names inscribed in a "book of remembrance." Once more the metaphor of parent and child appears, yet now the reference is to the righteous, obedient son: "And they shall be mine, saith the Lord of Hosts, in that day when I make up my jewels; and I will spare them, as a man spareth his own son that serveth him."

In these concluding verses the diction becomes rhapsodic, the language more lyrical and more intensely poetic than anywhere else in the book:

For, behold, that day cometh, that shall burn as an oven; and all the proud, yea, and all that do wickedly shall be stubble: and the day that cometh shall burn them up, saith the Lord of hosts, that it shall leave them neither root nor branch.

But unto you that fear my name shall the Sun of righteousness arise with healing in his wings; and ye shall go forth, and grow up as calves of the stall.

And, finally, there is the prophecy which had been widely interpreted as the most unequivocal promise of Messianic salvation to appear anywhere in the Old Testament: "Behold, I will send you Elijah the prophet before the coming of the great and dreadful day of the Lord." And what will this

Messiah do? Given what we have come to expect from Malachi, it is hardly surprising that the post–Messianic era should be envisioned in terms of familial harmony ("And he shall turn the heart of the fathers to the children, and the heart of the children to their fathers"), or that the Lord of Hosts should, in the very last words of the book, prove unable to restrain Himself from making one last threat: ". . . lest I come and smite the earth with a curse."

And yet, somehow, we have come full circle, so that now even this threat has come to seem like further evidence of love. For, I would suggest, no matter how strong our doubts and misgivings, it is ultimately almost impossible not to be reassured and comforted by what we come to learn of Malachi's God, a God who "change[s] not," who, despite everything, still tells us, "Return unto me, and I will return unto you." The ways this love is expressed, the raging, the curses, the impossible demands, seem finally less important than the fact of its eternal endurance. For where is there a religion which permits its worshippers to tell God how to love them? This sense of a higher presence, permanent and unchanging, is finally what offers us, for the taking, the reconciliation Kafka sought in vain: the sustaining conviction of an "unbroken tie" between us and "some reassuringly distant, possibly infinite, heights and depths," the certainty and comfort which—to quote the words with which Kafka ended his "Letter to His Father"—cannot fail to make "our living and our dying easier."

PART III

WRITINGS

PSALMS

Allen Mandelbaum

F OR MANY READERS, SPEAKERS, PRAY-ERS, SOME TEXTS GROW WITH time, some diminish. But *Tehillim* (Psalms) is one text that, I now can see, has had a strange constancy for me. In the distant weather of a *mitnaged**** childhood, study superseded prayer (or, more hyperbolically, prayer "interrupted" study). But even then, the Great Hallel (Psalm 136), the Egyptian Hallel (Psalms 113–18), the *shirei hamaaloth* (the Songs of Ascent, of Degrees, of Zion—Psalms 120–34), and the Little Hallel (146–50, to which I should add 145) echoed the implicit fulfillment of "I end—but am still with You" (Psalm 139:18—*hekitzoti v'odi imach*) with the explicit end of *Tehillim:* "the blasts of the horn . . . harp and lyre . . . timbrel and dance . . . lute and pipe . . . clashing cymbals . . . clanging cymbals." These—*shofar, navel, kinor, toph, machol, minim, ugav, tziltzilei shama, tziltzilei teruah*—have never been stilled for me.

[*See the note at the end of this essay.]

The Jewish Publication Society's translation of the Bible used in this essay.

And even when I became, with time, a devotee of cantorial cadenzas (and they need not be on the level of a Rosenblatt or Mordechay Hershman to compel me), the essential song of *Tehillim* was sung by the Hebrew text itself when uttered, in however unimbellished fashion, by a *minyan* (prayer group) or by oneself.

That constant inner cantilena has, of course, through time, been accompanied by lateral voices, some accordant, some discordant. Chrysostom's and Jerome's deep feelings for Davidic Psalms, the massive *Ennarationes in Psalmos* of Augustine (one manuscript of which is included in a gift to Petrarch in Milan from Boccaccio in Florence), the metrical paraphrasts and imitators (not least among them Petrarch, Aretino, Wyatt, Surrey, Milton, and some three score French poets from Marot to Malherbe dealt with by Michel Jeanneret in *Poésie et tradition biblique au XVIᵉ siècle*)—these spoke to me. And if Robert Pfeiffer's hefty manual did not find me of accord with his assertion that "with rare exceptions the Psalmists excelled in religious fervor rather than literary genius," I do not think that I was so unaware of blemishes that, even as a journeyman, I would have disagreed with his assessment of Psalm 119 as "the most dreadful example of Old Testament versification" (though I would and do disagree with his reference to Tanach as the Old Testament).

What accounts for that constancy, the long-sounding resonance of those instruments? One aspect, surely, is the comprehensiveness of *Tehillim,* not only as an inventory of states of soul, but as a historical inventory that, speaking of (and derived from) the Jew in bondage in Egypt and the pre-exilic Jew, also contains the Jew in his first Exile and in his return—and, implicitly, in the long *Golah* (Exile) and the Second Return. (If anything, recent philology has weighted things more heavily toward the pre-exilic than would have been thought opportune just decades ago.) And even the illicit attributions/superscriptions of almost half of *Tehillim* to David are more than an astute redactional ploy. Behind the lyric sequence lies a master narrative: the densest biography in the Tanach (and perhaps unique in antiquity in tracing a life from boyhood to death), the only life that contains so many varied and so many naked instants. And the most telling superscriptions are those that expand the simple annotation "Of David" with "when he fled from his son Absalom"; "when he sang to the Lord, concerning Cush, a Benjaminite"; "after the Lord had saved him from the hands of all his enemies and from the clutches of Saul"; "when he feigned madness in the presence of Abimelech"; "when Nathan the prophet came to him"; "when the Philistines seized him in Gath"; "when Saul sent men to watch his house in order to put him to death"; "when he was in the wilderness of Judah"—or the one that was always dearest to me, the laconic "while he was in the cave" of Psalm 142 (the same psalm that Francis of Assisi is said to have sung on his deathbed).

That cave was the chief counter I had to withstand the force of Plato's cave. And, for me, David's cave joined his later, less beleaguered quarters, where, at his bedside, a lyre was suspended. There, "at midnight, the northwind came, and as it blew, it played upon that lyre, waking David, who rose at once and studied Torah until daybreak" (*Berachot* 3b*). As it stands, the tale balances the demands of song and study; though that same page of *Berachot,* some lines earlier, ascribes—following Rav Ashi—a different order to those pursuits of David: "Until midnight he was occupied with matters of Torah; from midnight on, song and hymns of praise engaged him."

But whether song preceded study, or study song (and their parity was, in any case, a useful lesson for any *mitnaged* boy), it was that northwind, which of itself could play upon a lyre, that entranced me. At first, it deeded two things to me: the sense of a determined metrical module that, when in-spired (by the *north* wind—the chill wind that does not lie or cozen, waft or beguile), can sing—with the module as *vehicle* for song, but not yet song—and then the sense that the very act of song, even if in despair and supplication, was already *some* answer to what is prayed for. And, finally, the transpersonal wind and the unattainable experience of David became exemplars of the signal way in which the prayer uttered by a nameless author can escape the gnawing dilemma of the devotional poet.

Early on, that dilemma found its indelible statement for me in Marvell's "The Coronet." There, in Marvell's garland of praise to his Lord, lies the "serpent old . . . with wreaths of fame and interest." Confronted with his possible pride in his song, Marvell asks that his floral offering, in which the serpent is intertwined, may "wither so that he [the serpent] may die," even though the garland is "set with skill, and chosen out with care." And earlier in that same poem, Marvell had condensed the problem of poets' pride in one of the most pathos-ridden parentheses we have: "I gather flowers (my fruits are only flowers)"—with an *only* that diminishes the value of the fruits, but, at the same time, implies that there is no *other* offering he can make; his verses are his *only* possible offering. The psalmists' use of David is one way to anonymity—the anonymity that can elude the snare of pride—and if David's lyre is seen as played upon by force beyond himself, then even he, David, becomes not the singer but the sung.

There *is* one narcissistic note in all of *Tehillim,*[1] one contemporary turn of the singer to his own scribal self: "my tongue is the pen of a fluent scribe" (or—for *sofer mahir*—the JPS translation's "expert scribe" or the King James' "ready writer," in Psalm 45:2, the only secular poem in *Tehillim,* a song of love, an epithalamion for a king's wedding). But the dominant tone of *Tehillim* is surely: "Singers and dancers alike [will say]: 'All my fountains [or "springs," "sources"] are in You' " (Psalm 87:7). (And here the gloss in *Midrash Tehillim*[2] seems to call on the Song of Songs: "The Rabbis . . . took the verse to mean that even as the men will sing songs, so will the women," for the word for "springs" [or "fountains" or "sources"—*maayani(m)*] is used in Song of Songs 4:12 for woman: "A garden barred is my own, my spouse; a fountain barred, a sealed-up spring." [This is a text that the *Yalkut Shimoni**—portions of which were later incorporated into the *Midrash Tehillim*—cities for other reasons, as it cites *Piska* 11 of *Pesikta de-Reb Kahana* for still other reasons. Whatever the reasons, the constellation "garden-spouse-fountain" invited commentary.])

It is indeed "All my fountains are in You" that serves as central epigraph for the immediacy of *Tehillim* and the nearness of the God its sentences invoke. There are angels in *Tehillim,* but they are infrequent, secondary bystanders. The actor is God: it is He "who sent redemption to His people" (Psalm 111:9), "who raises the poor from the dust" and "lifts up the needy from the refuse heap" (Psalm 113:7), "who will guard your going and coming now and forever" (Psalm 121:8), who inclines His ear "to champion the orphan and the downtrodden" (Psalm 11:18), "who is near to all who call Him" (Psalm 145:18). That explicit awareness echoes, too, in the *Haggadah*'s gloss on His delivering the Jews from their bondage in Egypt "not by means of an angel and not by means of a seraph and not by way of an emissary—but He the Blessed One Himself with His presence."

But if the You is one, the fountains of *Tehillim* are many—not only the many songs, but the sometimes contradictory burdens of the songs: "You do not desire sacrifice and meal offering; You do not ask for burnt offering and sin offering" (Psalm 40:7), standing prophetically against the more priestly refrain, "You will want sacrifices offered in righteousness, burnt and whole offerings; then bulls will be offered on your altar" (Psalm 51:21).

And, often enough, the fountains of philology are not complementary but contradictory. The JPS Masoretic text sees the *la-merchav,* "the wide expanse," of Psalm 18:20 as "freedom," with "He brought me out to freedom." Dahood, in the Anchor Bible, reads that *la* as "from," not "to," and derives "He brought me out of the wide domain," where *merchav* is not "freedom" but, pejoratively, the vast expanse of the netherworld—on which Dahood insists so often in his edition.

But whether *la* is "to" or "from," surely for the young Jew reiterating *Tehillim,* Sheol and afterlife were very indistinct: hardly the defined and Dantesque realm that haunted the Catholic imagination for centuries and, early in our millennium, added purgatory to hell and paradise. (Of course there are the afterlife and resurrection of the dead elsewhere in the long line of Jewish texts and credos, not least in Saadya's scholastic-like queries and the queries attributed to Rabbi Eliezer ben Hyrcanus, Rabbi Eliezer ben Yaakov, and Rabbi Maier. But *Tehillim* was not a pillar in that edifice: what animates eternity in *Tehillim* seems to be the succession of generations: "No man is more than a breath" [Psalm 40:13] but faith is kept "forever" with David and his "offspring" [Psalm 18:51] "for all generations" [Psalm 145: 13].)

Some contradictions, then, and—above all—much variety in the gamut of soul-states: despair and supplication, awaiting, gratitude, percussive praise, and pensive praise, and the acknowledgment, immediately after the anthropomorphic reference to God's "hand" or "palms" (Psalm 149:5), of His being "beyond my knowledge; it is a mystery; I cannot fathom it" (Psalm 139:6). And Dahood's *"your* knowledge" as "too overpowering for me . . . too towering, I cannot master it," however different, does leave the incommensurability of God and man intact.)

At least for me, the bridge between the many "fountains" and the one "You" has been the saliency in *Tehillim* of *shir chadash,* the "new song" (Psalms 40:4, 96:1, 98:1, 144:9, 149:1). The very act of reutterance is a new song in the one who speaks psalms now, or in the maker of "new songs."

And perhaps the fullest midrash on *Tehillim* is the *siddur* (weekly prayer book) itself, the continuity of *piyut* (liturgical-devotional poetry) from generation to generation—though there the Sephardic line is longer and less unbroken than the Ashkenazic.

Piyut, of course, can be less direct, more subject, in later centuries, to philosophic pressures that are not more profound than those we find in Job or in Psalm 139:1–18, but are more technical. Witness the thirteenth-century collection *Shir ha-Yichud,* where the *piyut* for the fifth day enumerates Aristotle's-via-Saadya's ten categories, Averroes' seven quantities, Aristotle's six kinds of motion, and the three modes of predication, the three tenses of human time, and three dimensions. But then that *piyut* returns, as if remembering the psalmist, with: "In the Creator, not one of these exists, for he created all of them at once. / They all will wither and suffer change; they will be lost and be no more. / But You will stand and see them all vanish, for You live and endure everlastingly." (And there is something *Tehillim*-like, too, in the *Shir ha-Yichud*'s being, if not anonymous, then nearly so—with some four possible candidates for its authorship.)

And after the *siddur* and *piyut,* "new songs" can extend (even on the Ashkenazi side) not only to the quarrels with God in the poetry of Yankev Glatstein, but to the *danken und loyben,* the "gratefulness and praise," of Glatstein's lines to his aunt Zipporah with her *Tehillimel mit greizen*—the pack (the haversack?) of garbled psalms that was her mouth (and just as "heart" in *Tehillim* can mean "mouth"—see below—so, too, can "mouth" mean "heart").[3]

All along that line of "new songs" there lies the directness of *Tehillim,* God's accessibility to those "who call," even if only to declare *to* Him His unfathomability, with the certainty that He will hear that declaration. And in *Tehillim* itself, that accessibility of God is evident throughout—through all the vicissitudes of form, all the layerings of styles that range from purest utterance to later, more ornate diction. I had always wondered at Pascal's simple, very unsophisticated use of *coeur.* But then I remembered the ways in which *Tehillim* invokes *lev* again and again: as *levavi*—"my heart" (Psalm 73:13)—and *levavo*—"His heart" (Psalm 77:72). These are simple warrants for the vocative and the declarative (reinforced, were that needed, by the JPS's translation note on the frequent use of *leb* to designate "the organ of speech," "the source of speech" in Ecclesiastes 5:1, Psalms 19:15 and 49:4, Isaiah 33:18 and 59:13, and Job 8:10).

I remember that and, like every Jew, remember the *chesed* of *ki l'olam chasdo,* for "His *chesed*—love, lovingkindness, mercy, pity, or steadfast love [this last, the JPS solution]—endures forever," and so many other chimings on *chesed* in *Tehillim.* That remembering of *chesed,* its constant presence, involves, I know now, some forgetfulness, some censoring of some psalmists' will to see foes punished, even gruesomely. There *is* smashing and shattering and vengeance, the militant will in *Tehillim.*

And my forgetfulness may have been abetted by the tone of *Midrash Tehillim,* where vengeance is qualified by: "Lest you suppose that vengeance will be executed upon the common people, the Holy One, blessed be He, says: No! Only upon kings"—and, more drastically, by one of the glosses in *Yalkut Shimoni* on the "two-edged sword" of that same psalm (149), where the two edges of the sword are the written Torah and the oral Torah (Rabbi Yehuda).

And that same last page of the *Yalkut,* reaching beyond my earlier descant on the psalmists' anonymity, notes that it is said that David, over-proud at his completion of *Tehillim,* asked the Lord if there were "anything in the world that has matched me in song." At which a frog passed and cautioned David against his arrogance, for he (the frog) sings more copi-ously than David, and "on each song I sing I can mount three thousand parables-exegeses."

I was mindful of that fraternal, ecumenical frog as I looked at the distant, sharp, plunging, sheer profile of one of the mountains beyond Valbonne in the maritime Alps. It was past that mountain, so I was told, that the Huguenots fled for refuge northeast to Piedmont. And they called the mountain—as in exegesis 3001 on the Songs of Ascent in *Tehillim*—Jerusalem.

NOTES

* Some inevitable Hebrew lexical items that may need glossing: A *mitnaged* is, literally, "one who opposes"—that is, who countered the force of Chassidism with a more intellectually centered orientation (here it is used as rapid and approximate shorthand for a study-centered environment, one that also incorporated *Maskilic* [Enlightenment] elements, with modern Hebrew literature and "general" learning much present). *Berachot,* "Blessings," is a tractate of the Talmud. The *Yalkut Shimoni* is a comprehensive midrashic compilation/haversack.

1. There is one other self-reference to the singer in *Tehillim,* but though it carries pride, it does not bear the freight of a craftsman's narcissism: "My mouth utters wisdom, my heart is full of understanding. I shall turn my ear to a theme, set forth my teaching to the music of the lyre" (Psalm 49:4–5).

2. In the tangled tale of *Midrash Tehillim,* the first printed edition (Constantinople, 1512) of that midrash "proper" covers all of the first 118 psalms except 96, 97, 98, 115. The second edition (Salonika, 1515) draws on an unknown manuscript for Psalms 119–21 and 138–50, and draws on the *Yalkut Shimoni* for the midrash on 122, 124–30, 132–37 (there is no *Yalkut* on Psalms 123 and 131). The Salonika pattern is followed by all later editions, beginning with Venice (1546). Solomon Buber's 1891 edition used a miscellany to fill Psalms 123 and 131. William G. Braude translated *Midrash Tehillim* into English (with Buber as his base): *The Midrash on Psalms* (New Haven: Yale University Press, 1959), 2 vols. And this present note follows Braude's untanglings on pp. xxx and xxxi of volume one; but while Braude does have brief fill-in texts for Psalms 96, 97, and 98, he has nothing for Psalm 115. The *Yalkut Shimoni* on *Tehillim*, except for those portions used to fill in *Midrash Tehillim*, has not been translated.

3. Or one might cite, as a "new song" even more recent than Glatstein's, these lines from a poem of Anne Arikha that reached me while I was writing these pages: "A scrap from Psalms, come like a guest, sat down / within my chest, chanting till dawn drew near / praise in Hebrew rhyme for the more-than-none."

PSALMS

John Hollander

FOR A LONG TIME THERE WAS ONLY ONE PSALM. I CAN STILL HEAR THE tones of my father's voice identifying a puzzling string of utterances: "That's the *twenty-third* psalm," stressed just like that. It seemed the name of only one thing, and since I didn't know what the set "psalm" comprised, the poem remained *sui generis*. By then I was just beginning to learn that what in the world was called "The Bible" existed, in its Jewish part, in Hebrew (which I wasn't beginning to learn just yet). It would be some years before I could put together the cadences of the English Bible (the King James Version [KJV], sections of whose Psalms and Proverbs were still read aloud in public schools, to the unwitting profit of many of those who were bored by their recitation) with what went on in synagogue, occasionally "on Sabbaths" and always "on festivals." Even though the language of the part of the liturgy that was recited in English (my family attended Conservative services) was usually a corrected pastiche of KJV English (whether translations of Torah, of *piyut*-liturgical-devotional poetry, or whatever), it would be decades before I would come

---

The King James Version of the Bible used in this essay.

to grasp the complex relations between the Hebrew Bible, the strange and powerful tendentious reading of it called the Old Testament, and the various vernacular translations.

For a modern reader, the language of KJV is inherently poetic primarily because of the relation between its high, condensed diction and the impenetrability of so much of its language, caused by semantic change since the early seventeenth century. I suppose that a poetic childhood consists in misunderstanding a good bit of what one hears and sees, in being too reticent to ask for the solution to puzzles of pattern and meaning which adults must know are silly, and in then resorting to one's own private versions of what was meant. (Mis*construings* and re*constructions:* these verbs for analysis and building are from the same Latin one.) And I suppose that the inability to put away such childish things may attune the attention to the still, small tones of a vocation. "My knowledge was divine," wrote a seventeenth-century English poet and parson; "I knew by intuition those things which since my apostasy I collected again by the highest reason." He was speaking of childhood's innocence generally, but with just enough of a specific epistemological interest to seem pre-Wordsworthian. And so it is, particularly with objects of language. The child in the American joke who innocently deforms Psalm 23's penultimate verse, assuring her adult listeners that "Surely good Mrs. Murphy shall follow me all the days of my life," will only learn with "a later reason," as Wallace Stevens called it, that she was getting *something* more profoundly right about the line, the psalm, and poetry in general than any of her correctly parroting schoolmates. For the "mistake" personifies the "goodness and mercy"—the *tov vachesed* of the Hebrew—as a beneficent pursuer (the Hebrew lines imply that they are the poet's only pursuers, dogging one's footsteps, perhaps, but never hounding). Good Mrs. Murphy following the child about like a beneficent nurse is a more viable, powerful homiletic reconstruction of what had otherwise faded into abstraction than any primer's glossing. The child rightly attended to the trope set up by the intense verb "follow me" and supplied an appropriate subject for it, thereby turning mechanical allegory into poetic truth. Losing, in mature literacy, the ability to make such mistakes can mean being deaf and blind to the power of even the KJV text, let alone that of the Hebrew. One's reading slides over the figuration, and thereby over the force of the line of verse. Thus in Psalm 85:10, "Mercy and truth are met together;

righteousness and peace have kissed each other" (KJV), the state of affairs being described (for all sorts of reasons, it might well be translated with verbs in the future tense—it is not our state of affairs now) points up sharply what is wrong with the present relation of the paired concepts in each case: mercy (again, *chesed,* translated "lovingkindness" or however) and truth *(emet)* do not, in fact, meet together. Nor do righteousness *(zedek)* and peace *(shalom)*—in our lives, each is usually achieved at the expense of the other or the other's terrain. They are zealous warriors against their particular enemies. But in their zeal they must necessarily compromise their fellow active virtues, revelations of truth frequently being merciless, acts of mercy involving the comfort of falsehood, peace being attained only at the expense of some wrong being righted, and the righting of wrongs requiring strife. Not getting the equivalent of the "good Mrs. Murphy" out of these lines is not getting the poet's moral point, namely that when "glory may dwell in our land" (Psalm 85:10), then virtues will not conflict, but that *they do now,* and not to notice this is moral torpor.

My own initial childhood contacts with Psalm 23 were full of small good-Mrs.-Murphys. "I shall not want"—the intransivity wasn't a problem so much as learning from this clause alone the older meaning "lack" or "need," instead of the more colloquial American "desire." But perhaps the contemporary reader, who may not have these precise phrases and cadences by ear (is "by heart" better?)—given that young persons are no longer required to memorize verse and prose at school, and that various insipidly "corrected" versions have replaced KJV in all public institutions save those devoted to the study of literature—might be reminded at this point of the text:

A PSALM OF DAVID

1 The LORD is my shepherd; I shall not want.

2 He maketh me to lie down in green pastures: he leadeth me
    beside the still waters.

3 He restoreth my soul: he leadeth me in the paths of righteousness
    for his name's sake.

4 Yea, though I walk through the valley of the shadow of death, I
    will fear no evil: for thou art with me; thy rod and thy staff
    they comfort me.

5 Thou preparest a table before me in the presence of mine
   enemies: thou anointest my head with oil; my cup runneth over.

6 Surely goodness and mercy shall follow me all the days of my
   life: and I will dwell in the house of the LORD forever.

Simply having the memorized text, possessing it without fully understanding it, allows one's attention to caress its frequently opaque locutions and cadences. I suppose that I was introduced to trope by this psalm, as much as by any other poem: I knew that the authorial "David," the young harp-playing shepherd from my illustrated *Stories from the Bible,* didn't mean to say that he felt comfortable partially *in that* his cup was spilling onto the floor (a dreaded commonplace of the nursery). I knew that the line about the table and the enemies meant *something* beneficent, but couldn't figure out what. I didn't know what "the house of the LORD" actually was (churches were "houses of God," but I knew synagogues weren't—I'd been taught that a *shul* was a place of assembly, a *bet haknesset*), but I fancied that it designated something very general. The "paths of righteousness," the "valley of the shadow of death," the "house of the LORD"—I began to savor the rich ambiguity of those constructions which can indicate so many syntactic relations, possessive, instrumental, causative, attributive. It would be many years before I knew both enough Hebrew and enough about English to understand that the KJV's peculiar way of translating the Hebrew construct state led to all sorts of latent allegorizing. The paths of righteousness, what were they? Were they the paths that led to a place—alas, somewhat distant—called Righteousness? Were they the paths someone called Righteousness used to take, striding along on business or taking his ease, and where, with proper guidance, one might get to walk, too? Were they the paths he still patrols? Were they paths across Righteousness's property or territory? Will these crooked, difficult paths, if one is led along them properly, make one righteous?

All these ambiguities characterizing that "the X of Y" construction in the English came to *feel* Biblical for me. As I grew older, it kept appearing everywhere in the fabric of the poetical grammar of the English language. (It is amusing to note now how I could not know then that "green pastures" and "still waters" in that beautifully rhythmic couplet were moments of correct translation of the original, the *benot deshe* and the construct state of the *mei mnuchot*, "grassy pastures" and "tranquil streams," which would ordinarily have become "fields of verdure" and "waters of tranquillity," had the usual strategy been adopted.)

Again, the "rod" and the "staff" simply blended into some notional shepherd's crook for me (I didn't realize that the pastoral conceit had vanished by the third verse). Only after I knew the Hebrew—and knew something of the mysterious ways of the parallelistic line of Hebrew poetry, and how it works in far more than mere decoratively varied repetition— could I realize what the slight archaism of the English words had veiled. The "rod" of "spare the rod and spoil the child," a proverb acquired a bit later on, and the staff (as "cane," "alpenstock," "staff" of Father Time and of life, as bread in another commonplace) eventually did diverge into the complementary sticks of weapon and prop or support. Likewise, the cadential phrase "for his name's sake," which seemed only to make sense in its more usual role of expletive (often of parental annoyance—"For God's sake, can't you . . .") combined with "What in the name of God have you done with your . . ."), here played a strangely quiet, though darkly forceful, role. And again, only later learning would allow the less mysterious but conceptually plausible "as befits his name," for the *lma'an sh'mo* of the original, to operate. But, as in any riddle, the solution effects a loss even as it enables gain, and the "explanation" or "answer" explodes fiction created by the enigma, and the literal triumphs in the end. So it is with the vanishing of all the good Mrs. Murphys with the coming of the dawn of learning.

Coming to linguistic terms with the half-understood English text, then, marked the growth of my inner ear for poetry. Even the rhythmic component of the KJV psalm was fecund with incomprehensibles. Nobody had ever explained the principles of Biblical verse to me, and I construed the unrhymed but closed lines as versions of accentual metrical schemes. The rough pentameters, frequently dactylic, of "Yea, though I walk through the valley of the shadow of death" (with the assonantal pattern of the last phrases pointing up the stresses), of "thou anointest my head with oil; my cup runneth over," and the final couplet made of lilting fourteener and pentameter: "Surely goodness and mercy shall follow me all the days of my life: /

And I will dwell in the house of the LORD forever"—these cadences were always alive in the language for me. And puzzlingly so: why did what sounded like the beginning of a stanza (or, in my childhood vocabulary, a "verse") then break away from its scheme into something uncountable by ear? Was that part of the strangeness of the language? The three hemistichs of 2 and 3a seemed to make up a little stanza of their own, for the ear, at least:

> He maketh me to lie down in green pastures,
> He leadeth me beside the still waters,
>   He restoreth my soul.

Doubtless, the anaphora in all three lines, and the rhythmically identical (and grammatically similar) pair "lie dówn in gréen pástures : besíde the still wáters," as well as the undeniable effect of the "pastures . . . still . . . restoreth" sequence, all were bolstering my ear's little misreading of the metrical scheme, on the basis of the unintended and *ad hoc*—for the Jacobean translators—occasional rhythm. What my ear took in and remembered I could not, of course, have explained in this way at that time. But there always remained for me this singular rhythmic presence, underscoring all the memorable phrases that I subsequently acquired from the rest of the Book of Psalms like familiar melodies.

Thus, for example, with the resonant opening of Psalm 24, which for a long time I knew by opening alone: it sounded as if it scanned in a half-quatrain—

> The earth is the LORD's, and the fulness thereof,
>   the world and they that dwell therein

—as if implicitly to continue—

> In oceans below and in mountains above,
>   the tall and short, the thick and thin

—or something like that. And then, having teased one out of prose, as it were, the psalm's voice abandoned one's expectations again. Actually, the phrase "the fulness thereof" had its own rhythm of mystery: my ear took it in as designating the stuffed, filled quality of the well-fed ground, something like Yeats's "mackerel-crowded seas," which I wouldn't encounter for a good many years. I could not yet realize that the words mean not *plēroma* (as, indeed, the Septuagint Greek has it), not the condition of being filled, but, rather, that which does the filling—the stuff, not the stuffedness. But the engimatic beauty of the phrase haunted me much more than the palpable strangeness of gates being called on to "lift up their heads" later on in the psalm (not once, but twice).

And so it would be with all of the constantly quoted, re-echoed, half-revised phrases from the KJV psalms that kept emerging in all my reading. They seemed to be part of the very idiom of written English, along with the folk proverb and the occasional bits of Shakespearean tag. That so many of these words have lived a strange but long life, out of their context and themselves the product of the English translators' own inadvertent good-Mrs.-Murphy-making, was of no matter. There they were: "Out of the mouths of babes and sucklings hast thou ordained strength" (Psalm 8:3) and, a few verses later, the wonderful "What is man, that thou art mindful of him? and the son of man, that thou visitest him?" (Here the puzzling beauty lay in the loss of the older meaning of "mind" = "remember," preserved colloquially only in proverbial admonition to mind p's and q's and manners. The Hebrew, of course, has the verb *zakhar*, "remember.") "The apple of the eye" is paired with "the shadow of thy wings" in Psalm 17:8: the literal "eyeball" yields a figure so compelling as to be used to denote, out of context, some cynosure, some lovely prize of the eye, rather than the prized organ itself; the second phrase being so ubiquitous in the psalms (e.g., 36:7, 57:1, 61:4, 63:7, 91:4). The "fire and brimstone, and an horrible tempest" shall be for the wicked "the portion of their cup" (Psalm 11:6). The "strong bulls of Bashan" which "beset me round" (Psalm 22:13) are also familiar. The opening simile of Psalm 42:2, with its mistranslation of male deer for the female that the Hebrew verb requires, gives the naïve listener some of the same punning flavor ("hart"/"heart") that was so dear to the early seventeenth century: "As the hart panteth after the water brooks, so panteth my soul after thee, O God." We so often refer to the longed-for "wings like a dove" of Psalm 55:7 and the whole reverberant opening of Psalm 90—

LORD, thou hast been our dwelling place in all generations.

Before the mountains were brought forth, or ever thou hadst formed the earth, and the world, even from everlasting to everlasting, thou art God.

Thou turnest men to destruction; and sayest, Return, ye children of men.

For a thousand years in thy sight are but as yesterday when it is past, and as a watch in the night.

Thou carriest them away as with a flood; they are as a sleep: in the morning they are like grass which groweth up.

In the morning it flourisheth, and groweth up; in the evening it is cut down, and withereth . . .

—and the later, sadly canonical "the days of our years are threescore and ten" (Psalm 90:10). These all underline the purported authorship in the rubric of this remarkable poem, "A Prayer of Moses the Man of God," which has its legacy in Isaac Watts' "O God our help in ages past," so ecumenical as to seem almost secular. The mapping of God's dominion "from sea to sea, and from the river unto the ends of the earth" in Psalm 72:8 seemed, when I first encountered it, to be quoting from its figured paraphrase by Katharine Lee Bates ("From sea to shining sea"), until I thought for a bit.

And so many more: the mention of them "that go down to the sea in ships, that do business in great waters" (Psalm 107:23); "sing unto the Lord a new song" in Psalm 96:1, itself an old song, perhaps a quotation from Isaiah; "they that sow in tears shall reap in joy" in Psalm 126:5; the "two-edged sword" of Psalm 149:6; "my days are like a shadow that declineth" in Psalm 102:12, a haunting trope of a shortening life; "in thy light shall we see light" in Psalm 36:10, which I would encounter in the Vulgate on my university's seal while at college ("*In lumine tuo videbimus lumen*") and in paraphrase in the college song ("In thy radiance we see light"); the "green bay tree" whose spreading is like that of the wicked (Psalm 37:35); the canonical statement in the psalms, as in Isaiah 50, of the herbal *topos,* in Psalm 103:14–16 (itself seeming to echo the passage from Psalm 90):

For he knoweth our frame.
He remembereth that we are dust.

As for man, his days are as grass;
As a flower of the field, so he flourisheth.

For the wind passeth over it, and it is gone;
And the place thereof knoweth it no more.

The opening four verses of Psalm 114, the Exodus poem, became familiar to me early because of its role in the Hallel sequence of the Passover seder:

When Israel went out of Egypt, the whole house of Jacob from a people of strange language;

Judah was his sanctuary, and Israel his dominion.

The sea saw it, and fled: Jordan was driven back.

The mountains skipped like rams, and the little hills like lambs.

Growing up literate in English, one could not avoid encountering these and so many other tags of psalms, so that reading through the Book of Psalms itself as I got older meant encountering many commonplaces in their uncommon original. Along with the variety of the psalms, their inconsistencies of length and degrees of familiarity, their range of tone, their problematic ascriptions of authorship, all made "The Psalms" a very strange sort of Biblical book. First of all, there were the mysteries of the title. "Psalm," from the Greek word for a song sung to a plucked string instrument, better translates the Hebrew *mizmor* or "accompanied song," a word used only in the subtitles of many of these poems to further specify something like their genre, or occasion for performance. I think that as a child I made some kind of vague connection between "psalms" and "psalteries." It was only at eleven or twelve years of age, when, during the synagogic *longueurs,* I would search through the *siddur* or *machzor* for bits of lore in the annotations, that the Hebrew title began to bother me. *Tehillim*— praises. Before I knew enough grammar to catch the *hallal* root prominent in Hallel and "halleluya," I could still wonder why *tehilla,* a feminine noun, should have a masculine plural, rather than *tehillot.* In any event, it seemed a strange title for an anthology of hymns of praise, songs of personal lamentation and national mourning, odes of thanksgiving and royal lyrics (like the marriage song of Psalm 45, subtitled *al shoshanim*—probably "to the tune of The Lilies"—and *shir ydidot*—a song of loves). The midrash on psalms starts out by asserting a parallel of ascriptive authorship—"As Moses gave five books of the Torah to Israel, so David gave five books of psalms to Israel"—and it goes on to list the five divisions, each book ending with a doxology, although only the first two (up through Psalm 72) contain "psalms of David." The subtitles themselves were so enigmatic: what was a *maskhil?* a *shiggaion* (Psalm 7)? What, indeed, did the grammar of the frequent *mizmor ldavid*—a song of David—mean: a song about, or by, or to, or for David the shepherd and/or king? "Song" was itself a strange term, for what I encountered in Hebrew was itself sometimes sung, although the cantillation of psalms, of the Pentateuch, and of parts of the liturgy, including blessings and prayers, all ran into one another for me as a generic kind of unaccompanied *shul*-singing—unaccompanied because we were a Conservative congregation with no organ. (Today I should venture that our word "lyric," still echoing with the name of the Greek musical instrument, manages to indicate that the word *mizmor* has a similar resonance.)

And here again the psalms were beginning to lead a mysterious life for me in their variety of musical identities. The actuality of Biblical song is mostly lost to us, and all of the liturgical cantillation observant Jews encounter is of relatively recent origin (medieval). It is also itself unaware, as setting, of the structural principles of the verse it set, and on the basis of which one can be fairly sure that the original levitical performances of the psalms had been composed. And what about the elusive instruments mentioned in the Bible, the *kinnor* and *nevel,* both usually translated as "harp"? Was one small and private, like the Greek *lyra,* and the other large, public, and used to accompany choral song, like the Greek *kithara?* "Lyric" means solo song, and so, I should guess, does *mizmor,* and yet the musical life of the psalm texts has been in liturgy, Judaic and (now taking the Psalter as part of the Old Testament) Christian. But all those layers of interpretation of the poems, their use in the second temple, their refigured role in the religious practice of the realm of the synagogue, turn the solo song into public chorale.

Overhearing (and then, when I was older, beginning to participate in) this choral singing was part of my preliterate introduction to Hebrew. But, again, this was as problematically fraught with variation as all the other aspects of the psalms themselves. My father made Friday night *kiddush* or prayers in his own Ashkenazic and with one kind of *niggun* or melody. Our synagogue used Sephardic, which was how my mother pronounced Hebrew, and when I finally learned to read a little, it was that Sephardic pronunciation I was taught. Fragments of the psalms I first heard sung without knowing the meaning of the words returned to me in their context only later in life. At school I might have sung, to the "Old Hundredth" tune of the Geneva Psalter,

> O, enter then his gates with praise,
> Approach with joy his courts unto;
> For why, the LORD our God is good,
> And it is seemly so to do . . .

or verses 4 and 5 of Psalm 100. (Separatism would not have allowed the doxology, usually sung in American Protestant churches to that tune, into the public-school music class. It was with some surprise that I discovered, only when slightly older, that its text was more canonically associated with the melody than even the metrical version of the psalm for which the melody had been composed.) I had no idea at the time that the last two lines were, in Hebrew, so full of commonplaces that even my limited vocabulary could grasp them—*ki tov adonai l'olam chasdo / v'ad dor vador emunato*—and that, perhaps the following week, I would uncomprehendingly be singing at a Passover seder the opening of the so-called Great Hallel, Psalm 136, *hodu ladonai ki tov / ki l'olam chasdo* (the latter three words repeated as a refrain twenty-five times), finding it strangely domesticated from its role in the morning synagogue service. Or my mother's voice—I still remember it—singing the opening words of the first of that mysteriously named group of fifteen psalms starting with number 120, *shir hama'alot / 'l adonai*. I did not know, even as the words and melody sank into my memory, that these words were not lyric praise, but some editor's parenthetical subtitle, "A Psalm of Degrees," as the KJV gives it. (Actually, that mystery remains one, there being no scholarly agreement about what "ascents" or "degrees" refers to. The term is an open trope, like the whole body of the psalms: are these the fifteen psalms that were—or were written to be—sung by the Levites standing on the fifteen steps that the Mishnah was assured led up part of the temple? Are they lyrics of the sublime? Do they embody a spiritual ascent of some kind—as one reading of Psalm 121:1 in KJV, "I will lift up mine eyes unto the hills, from whence cometh my help," might suggest?)

The Passover *Haggadah*, the ritual book, was, in general, a wonderful scene of discovery, providing some elementary commentary and significant identification of texts at the very scene of musical intonation. I knew that the *hallel* were a sequence of psalms (113–18, the so-called Egyptian Hallel) started before the seder meal and finished after it. I had heard the exultant 114th (which I quoted earlier) sung before I could linguistically and conceptually put the left- and right-hand pages, the English and the Hebrew, together, as it were. For in the cases of the psalms that were at all familiar liturgically (29, when the Torah scroll is returned to the ark; 92, read responsively in English in Saturday-morning service at summer camp; 30 at Chanukah; 95; 99), they occupied a different corner of my inner library and record cabinet from many of the others, which were themselves repositories of memorable phrases.

Meanwhile, however, the musical versions of these poems came at me from all directions. Nobody can know and love Western music of the sixteenth through the twentieth centuries without being drenched in settings of the psalms. My very first contact with the ubiquitous Vulgate versions was, again, at grade school, where the same music teacher who taught us "Old Hundredth" gave us the Elizabethan canon on the lines that I would not for many years be able to put together with those that followed on the filling of the fourth cup of wine at seder: *lo lanu adonai lo lanu / ki-lshimkha ten kavod / al hasdkha al-amitekha.* What we sang at school in the Latin I had not yet learned any of was its translation: *non nobis domine, non nobis / sed nomini tuo da gloriam* (Psalm 115:1). By the time I reached college, the Vulgate Psalter was ubiquitous in my musical world. Vivaldi's *"Beatus vir"* setting of Psalm 112—*Beatus vir qui timet dominum / in mandatus eius volet nimis*—which I read through and wrote liner notes for while at Columbia; all the motets I ever remembered any part of; the texts in Stravinsky's *Symphony of Psalms,* which I sang often in a college chorus: all these texts were as new ones, each was a *shir hadash* or new song. I think particularly of just those lines from Psalm 40 in Stravinsky's setting:

Exspectans exspectavi Dominum: & intendit mihi. Et exaudivit preces meas. . . . Et statuit supra petram pedes meos, & direxit gressus meos.

These were sung slowly and calmly, up through *preces meas,* the patience of "I waited patiently for the Lord; and he inclined unto me and heard my cry" expressed in the reduplication of *exspectans exspectavi* just as it is in the *kavo kiviti* of the Hebrew. The fugal texture gets denser and denser, the singers' own feet get "set upon a rock," and the music, as well as the Lord, are "establishing their goings." And then, after an instrumental interlude, the percussive force of the now homophonic texture at the words *Et immisit in os meum canticum novum. . . .* The familiar, old formulaic *shir hadash* of the Hebrew had never meant this, and any singer of the Stravinsky literally feels the presence of some kind of new song in his or her mouth at just that point in the setting. The composer's translation of the Latin has turned it into a praise of singing, even as the last section, with its setting of the *laudate eium in chordis et organo,* develops undertones of self-reference. But generally it was *singing* the Latin psalms, rather than listening to them, which brought yet another psalter into my possession.

Nor should I neglect my strange but nonetheless telling outsider's sense of the chanted psalms in the Book of Common Prayer. When young, I courted a young lady who sang in the choir of the college chapel, whose denomination was acutely Established, and I would often "to church repair / Not for the doctrine, but the music there" (as Alexander Pope disparagingly puts it, but which for me is always authenticating, the only true "doctrine" being music). I thus got to know yet another version of the psalter, the psalms in Miles Coverdale's wonderful early-sixteenth-century English (the Prayer Book of the English Church antedating the KJV, of course, by three-quarters of a century). Psalm 47 begins "O clap your hands together, all ye people: O sing unto God with the voice of melody," the *kol rina* or resounding-cry voice of the Hebrew getting nicely interpreted as "voice of triumph" in KJV, but more rich and strange, and off the mark in a relevant direction (given the etymology, probably) in the original. Later on, in verse 5, we have "God is gone up with a merry noise: and the Lord with the sound of the trump," for the more sober exultation of "God is gone up with a shout" of KJV. For British schoolchildren who would brood over what they had half heard, the corners of the church must have re-echoed, over the centuries, with good Mrs. Murphys. But knowing and singing Thomas Weelkes' marvelous polyphonic anthem on this text, for example, gave me "God is gone up . . ." on an ascending fifth in the bass part, and imprinted the translation as if I had been taught it at school. On the other hand, when, at sixteen, in a blaze of literary piety, I committed vast acres of *The Waste Land* to memory, the allusion of line 182, in "The Fire Sermon," "By the waters of Leman I sat down and wept," to Psalm 137 was one I heard. But the mystery of why it was the *waters* and not the *rivers* of Babylon which were being refigured bathetically (and with no gloss in the celebrated and evasive notes) was only resolved when I could conclude that the English Church's Prayer Book provided the canonical text for Eliot: "By the waters of Babylon we sat down and wept: when we remember'd thee O Sion. / As for our harps we hanged them up: upon the trees that are there-in." The Coverdale psalms are full of treasures, not of quaintness but of true power, and almost any familiar text will blaze forth anew in it. I might only add the beginning of Psalm 19 (a psalm I propose to discuss for a bit in a moment). In the Book of Common Prayer it goes:

> The heav'ns declare the glory of God;
>   and the firmament sheweth his handy-work.
>
> One day telleth another:
>   and one night certifieth another.
>
> There is neither speech nor language:
>   but their voices are heard among them.
>
> Their sound is gone out into all lands;
>   and their words into the ends of the world.

These poems, then, spawned versions of themselves, and gradually coming to terms with them all, and putting them into poetic perspective, has been something of a synecdoche of my life as a reader and writer. To have been able to repossess the *ars poetica* of the original, coming back from all the misconstrued good Mrs. Murphys of English to realize that the original is itself full of them, has been to grasp something essential about Biblical poetry in general—namely, that it exists in and for its interpretations, and that some archaeological reduction is all the authenticity one needs. By the poetics of the psalms, I mean not merely the structural wonders, say, of Psalm 42, with its patter of five verses plus refrain, five verses plus refrain (and with Psalm 43, a supplement, confirming this), or of the word play in the original. That word play is usually displaced in translation anyway—for example, in Psalm 122:6, "Pray for the peace of Jerusalem: they shall prosper that love thee" (KJV; more properly, "let them prosper"), there is a fortuitous, faint pattern of alliteration in the English, but the Hebrew is denser: *sha'alu sh'lom yrushalam / yshlayu ohavayikh.* The first four words, seemingly connected semantically, are all quite distinct in meaning, and it is as if the name of Jerusalem were derived from the words for "ask," "peace," and "prosperity"—such is the momentary etymological fiction set up by the word play. Sometimes the effect is more fleeting, as in Psalm 102:12, mentioned earlier—"My days are like a shadow that declineth; and I am withered like grass" (KJV)—where, in the second half-line, *va'ani ca'eshev ivash,* the last two words ("like-grass," "dry-up") are made to sound inevitably connected in the Hebrew.

In short, losing the mysterious poetry engendered by mistranslation, or even by distance from the English usage of a much earlier text, is compensated for many times over by re-entry into the original. Confronting the psalms in yet another identity, decked out and bejeweled by linguistic and homiletic commentary, has been an activity of my later life. More and more mysteries open up in these versions as well. For example, back in Psalm 23:4, the famous crux of "the valley of the shadow of death" comes from a tendentious repointing of the word *tzalmavet,* which could mean either "deep shade" or "death shade," and probably the former. In any case, the line means "dark valley": the two construct states piled on each other— "valley *of* the shadow *of* death" in the traditions of English—pile near-allegory on near-allegory. It is not usual in the psalms to find "shadow" a menacing notion; and although only in Hebrew, among languages I know something of, does morphological ambiguity provide any glimpse of "dead" lurking in "shade," only in this psalm did the early editors conjure it up. (This reading is there in the Septuagint, and must have been there before.) But knowing all this in no way makes the poem shed its outer garments for the sake of a naked linguistic truth, and the various translations and versions and misprisions all coexist, and inhere in every phrase.

Whole poems of various genres from the Book of Psalms, such as the storm ode of Psalm 29 and the terse, powerful personal lament of Psalm 130—with its famous *incipit* in the Vulgate, *De profundis clamavi,* "Out of the depths have I cried unto thee, O Lord"—the splendid sequence of Psalms 102–4, the brooding over the ruins in language which some scholars feel to be akin to that of the Book of Lamentations, of Psalm 74, all continue to call up possible applications in Judaic tradition alone. The reinterpreted Psalms of the Christian Old Testament add more; and even the kind of liturgical use to which these versions have been put—for celebratory or congregational use in various traditions—have in another sense constantly been reinterpreting, reallegorizing, the nature of the "I" of the psalmist. To that extent, all the different kinds and occasions of musical setting have become as much part of the surrounding frame of annotation as any scholarly conjecture about a single dot of vowel-pointing.

The great Psalm 137, *al naharot bavel,* "By the rivers of Babylon," is for me one of the very greatest. It has suffered an ironically amusing metamorphosis in English tradition, not merely in the translation—this is a minor matter—but in the adaptation, in the seventeenth and eighteenth centuries, in the versified versions, growing out of the so-called metrical psalters used for congregational singing in the English Church, written by so many English poets. The famous opening (KJV) speaks of a condition of exile:

> By the rivers of Babylon, there we sat down, yea, we wept, when we remembered Zion.
>
> We hanged our harps upon the willows in the midst thereof.
>
> For they that carried us away captive required of us a song; and they that wasted us required of us mirth, saying, Sing us one of the songs of Zion.

The power of the refusal to perform for the captors grows during the subsequent verses. Hanging the harps, *kinnorotenu,* on the trees, abandoning familiar and consoling music, is hardly anything but a violent gesture—it is a slamming down of the piano lid, say, or a closing of the instrument case. With the memory of the lost home that follows, the almost violent power continues:

> If I forget thee, O Jerusalem, let my right hand forget her cunning.
>
> If I do not remember thee, let my tongue cleave to the roof of my mouth; if I prefer not Jerusalem above my chief joy . . .

(The KJV "forget her cunning," for the Hebrew *tishkach,* "let forget," is one of those wonderful glossings—suppose it had the form "forget [e.g., her cunning]"?—which seem forever to inhere in the poetic text of the psalm *for* English.)

The violent conclusion of the psalm with its curse against *bat-bavel,* the "daughter of Babylon" (meaning the city itself, not one of its wretched and synecdochic inhabitants), has been generating throughout the poem. But in English Protestant tradition, the opening image became more and more languorous, and the memory of Jerusalem engendered by the scene more and more nostalgic. Thomas Campion, around 1614, versifies the lines about the harps hung on the trees as

> Aloft the trees that sprang up there
> Our silent harps we pensive hung . . .

with a lovely and delicate attention to the etymon of *pendere,* "to hang," in "pensive," but making it poetically and deliberately ambiguous whether the harps or the hangers of them were pensive, and in what sense. Richard Crashaw, in 1646, has

> On the proud banks of great Euphrates' flood
> There we sat, and there we wept:
> Our harps that now no music understood
> Nodding on the willows slept. . . .

And Thomas Carew, around 1655, talks of

> Our neglected harps unstrung,
> Not acquainted with the hand
> Of the skillful tuner, hung
> On the willow trees that stand
> Planted in the neighbour land.

Sir John Denham wrote, sometime before 1668, "Our harps to which we lately sang, / Mute as ourselves, on willows hang." The unfolding theme of abandonment and neglect, rather than positive, outraged refusal to perform, is far from the point of the Hebrew poem, but moves toward the generation of a new trope, the association of the instrument and the singer: they become each other. Such a version could only occur to poets.

I should like to close these remarks with a look at what may be the greatest psalm of all, and one whose greatness resides not in spite of but within and because of its deeply problematic character. It is the heavenly hymn 19, so celebrated in paraphrase (Addison's "The spacious firmament on high / With all the blue Etherial Sky"; "The Heavens are telling the glory of God, / The Wonder of his work displays the firmament" in the text of Haydn's *The Creation*). It starts out with a vision of the animate coherence of the created heavens, starting from 2 (KJV):

> Day unto day uttereth speech, and night unto night sheweth knowledge.
>
> There is no speech nor language where their voice is not heard.
>
> Their line [should be "call"—a mispointing of *Kavam*] is gone out through all the earth, and their words to the end of the world. In them he hath set a tabernacle for the sun,
>
> Which is as a bridegroom coming out of his chamber, and rejoiceth as a strong man to run a race [*orach,* should be "track"].

The Hebrew has the *yom l'yom, vlaila l'layla,* which Jerome's Latin *(Dies diei eructat verbum: & nox nocti indicat scientiam)* and all the good English versions until such as the New English Bible ("One day speaks to another") retain. Since the point of the lines is that the communication is soundless and, indeed, nonlinguistic, the effect in English of the "day unto day / night unto night" is to underline the unmediated quality of the connection.

But the really deep problem comes with verse 7. Following on the little allegory of the sun as hero, picking up after the last part of it (6),

> His going forth is from the end of the heaven, and his circuit unto the ends of it: and there is nothing hid from the heat thereof.

we get,

> The law of the LORD is perfect, converting the soul: the testimony of the LORD is sure, making wise the simple.

> The statutes of the LORD are right, rejoicing the heart: the
> commandment of the LORD is pure, enlightening the eyes.
>
> The fear of the LORD is clean, enduring forever: the judgments of
> the LORD are true and righteous altogether. . . .

The leap from the matter of the heavens to the perfection of the Torah *is* the story of the poem. And yet, originally, these were two different texts, yoked together not by violence but by interpretive connection. That is, if the first part, about the heavens, is made part of a parable, then the other part is the remainder of the psalm, up to and including the final verses of what one might call prayer and metaprayer, the psalmist concluding with a supplication, and then a supplication *in re* that supplication:

> Keep back thy servant from presumptuous sins; let them not have
> dominion over me: then shall I be upright, and I shall be innocent
> from the great transgression.
>
> Let the words of my mouth, and the meditation of my heart, be
> acceptable in thy sight, O LORD, my strength, and my redeemer.

Even the pairing of the more concrete *words* and the heart's *musing* (with its punning overtones in English of silent *music,* also perhaps lurking in the Hebrew *hegyon,* used at this point) seems to recapitulate the relation between the two parts of the combined poem: what's out there, communicating without text, what's down here, communicating by text.

The consciousness in rabbinic tradition that these may indeed have been two separate poems is manifested, as frequently is the case, by the mode of its repression: I have heard that Psalm 19 was often set as an exercise for interpretation, the injunction being to read over the seam, to assert the unity of the psalm. That parabolic unity—the relation between the wonders of the sky and the wonders of Torah—*is* the psalm. Once established as an agenda, it lights up points in the text. For example, rabbinic commentary might draw attention to the word used about "the commandment of the Lord" in verse 9, *mitzvat adonai bara,* the word *bara,* "pure," showing that it is used of the sun in Song of Songs 6:10. The poem's lyric action could be shown to be that of a movement from looking *out* to looking *in,* or from up to down, "The matter of the starry skies and / The great Word they

entail / As eyes lower in praise / / Toward textual ground, or turn inward":
Immanuel Kant, evidently meditating on this famous psalm, produced his
(in turn) famous assertion about the connection in wonder between the
starry heavens above us and the moral law within us.

Such textual assimilations, separations, revisions, occur throughout the
Hebrew Bible, and interpretive tradition, in general, tendentiously tropes
the resulting text with the impolitic injunction to consider it as having been
revealed/composed in just that way. It results in the final and monumental
good Mrs. Murphy, and Psalm 19 is a superb instance of this. Every reader
has to put Psalms 1–6 and 7–15 together in a new way, making his or her
own kind of sense out of it, in a larger instance of having to come to terms
with the KJV locutions like "night unto night" or even the now largely
revised-out "their line is gone out through all the earth" (Coverdale and
the Vulgate get "call" right). This requires an *ad hoc* trope of a "line" of
communication—some pretechnological telephone to make sense out of.
The layers of misreadings and rereadings are part of the poetry of the text
itself in the poetic portions of the Bible. And the problems and puzzles of
the psalms will remain eternal occasions for the reader's negative capability
as well as for the interpretive wit that turns every reader into a poet, if only
momentarily.

PROVERBS

David Shapiro

I N MY FAMILY, THE BIBLE WAS INEXTRICABLY BOUND UP WITH MUSIC, with the singing of my grandfather, the cantor Berele Chagy, whose sweet tenor voice in performance and recording gave me my first sense of Kafka's comfortless spiritual world. It is no surprise to me to find in Hebrew a lack of words for poetry but an abundance for music, nor was I surprised that, when my grandfather died while singing, the grandchildren were told that this was the best death: to sing until the end. It is always with some wonder that the commentaries I read on the poetics of the Tanach delete this sense, though I am aware of the difficulty of importing it to our discussion. But it is a personal impossibility for me to think of the "Scriptures" as writing without tones, without utterance, and without the improvisational pathos brought by the great singers. While reading even the most austere of the prudent counsels of our book, I hear always the elegiac embellishments of the golden *chazzanim* (or cantors): Chagy, Sirota, Rosenblatt. If Kafka speaks in his diaries of the "unjust Judges" and of how the

---

The Revised Standard Version of the Bible used in this essay.

pages do not flutter for him, yet for me they move most with the sense of a singing performance, not ethical discursivity, but the real chamber music of the synagogue.

There is a dazzling note in Kafka that reminds us of his sudden pietistic twinges, not unlike our own: "The Polish Jews going to Kol Nidre. The little boy with prayer shawls under both arms, running along at his father's side. Suicidal not to go to temple." This is the correct beginning for the student's sense of Proverbs in our time: the distance and nearness from the children the writer feels, the destructiveness in our ironic interval from ritual, our need for a temple, and the comical theme of its exoticism in those fluttering prayer shawls. Just as there is passionate hesitation in the interpretation of Kafka—Scholem finding in Kafka all allegory and, recently, Deleuze admonishing us to look for nothing but social surface—so the Proverbs remain as a constant problem. On the one hand, for many they seem to be a scribal textbook plagiarized from Egypt, or a textbook to be plagiarized by even later Egyptian clerks; however, for others they are the most explicit binding together of allegories, explicit and concealed, and of Wisdom—and not merely prudential understanding, but the Wisdom that initiates worlds, the Wisdom that presides over the irreducible evils of Job. Coming to the Proverbs, most contemporary writers are disturbed by their conservative norms, and such a penetrating reader as Northrop Frye suddenly calls a strophe on discipline one of the most harmful of sentences. No allegorist will be likewise stopped by the theme of discipline, a constant in all mystical literatures. Is this an anthology like Benjamin Franklin's bourgeois success stories, or is this a garland of enigmas?

More than one author has suggested that the book has sunk in reputation in our century because of its confident tone and its lack of doubt. Yet this is particularly annoying as a view of Proverbs, since students of the so-called Wisdom movement have been led to see aspects of it as essentially an antipietistic movement, if not of doubters then of international sages instead, who stood apart from the priest and prophet. There can hardly be a formulated skepticism without the kind of resolute attempt at principle exfoliated at such a scale in *Mishlé* (Hebrew for "Proverbs"). Just as Kafka confines his most fideist dreams to some marginal reflections despite what seem to be the labyrinthine doubts of his novels and tales, so the proverbs here speak of a tension with skepticism. Embedded in many resolute adages is a remarkable realism: "Scoffers set a city aflame. . . . A fool gives full vent to his anger. . . . If a wise man has an argument with a fool, the fool only rages and laughs, and there is no quiet" (29:8; 11; 9). "He who robs his father and mother and says, That is no transgression . . ." (28:24). The first wave of this last horrifying phrase is enough to convince the ephebe that moral perversity exists. Principle alone and quotation by itself are not sufficient: "Like a lame man's legs, which hang useless, is a proverb in the mouth of fools" (26:7). One does not expect a fideist collection to announce that it must be used wisely and with a sense of humor, but *Mishlé* repeats itself on this point: "Like a thorn that goes up into the hand of a drunkard / is a proverb in the mouth of fools" (26:9).

Here is a book without covenant, history, or revelation, but a book that teaches us how to read: "to understand a proverb and a figure, the words of the wise and their riddles." The world is to be decoded by the most strenuous deciphering, and the beginning is reverential anxiety. Immediately there is a picture of a violence that destroys all codes: "Like Sheol let us swallow them alive and whole, like those who go down to the Pit . . ." (1:12). The structure of this book concerns receptivity: "Making your ear attentive to wisdom" (2:2). All utterance must conform to this ideal, deriving from divine speech: "Put away from you crooked speech, and put devious talk far from you" (4:24). In a sense, the search for a perfect language begins and concludes with the admonition to "pay attention." The world is broken into fragments like these many proverbs, but the hidden spark-gatherer is Wisdom, since it alone seeks such unities as are possible. The wilderness of worldly proverbs baffles the imprudent reader, who loses his way among such badly infinite perspectives. But Proverbs relies on a resolute envelope, as at the conclusion: "Every word of God proves true, he is a shield to those who take refuge in him. Do not add to his words . . ." (30:5). Reading is an activity that makes a difference, and this difference cannot be minimized or foreshortened: "Like a madman who throws firebrands, arrows and death, / is the man who deceives his neighbor, and says, I am only joking" (26:18). The ethical life is not a dream, it is barbed like the arrow of time and rushes forward with a mortal tempo.

A simple hypothesis concerning *Mishlé* is the possibility that it was performed in schools, with one line sung out by a teacher and the couplet oratorically finished by a student. Certainly this approach could account for some of the "literary" embellishments of the proverbs, where folk sayings are famous for their savage unity; by contrast, our collection is replete with more "writerly" forms. What is significant for Proverbs is not simply that the book was meant in part to be performed, but that the performance is in strict accord with the theme of the book, which is familial unity with the divine. The ephebe is constantly addressed, and mother and father are unified in the most drastic sense. "There are those who curse their fathers and do not bless their mothers. There are those who are pure in their own eyes . . ." (30:11–12). The Lord is to be feared like a father, and not, as one psychoanalyst has admonished, because without such fear He will castrate like a father. The Lord is to be shown reverence because He has created the multiple perspectives of a miraculous world, the world in which the "Good Wife" can be conceived and the world in which the industrious ant reproves all sluggards. Meaninglessness is not a problem here, nor in Job, but, rather, the proliferation of meanings is a problem. Merleau-Ponty was right: we are condemned to meaning; and Proverbs at its darkest condemns us to language, meaning, and the "comfortless" spiritual world that Kafka reflected.

There is an extensive anthropological and linguistic literature that has developed on Proverbs, and we have learned much from it that might be of use in our reading of the canonic texts. Joyce Penfield, in her extensive studies of the Igbo peoples, who are much given to quotation and proverbs, has discovered in the field, and with the help of the Prague formalist Mukařovský, that the proverb is essentially a device of depersonalization, of distance and control, of a contextual indirectness. She has discovered in the proverb a route toward "group conscience," a means to control violence and shame with the most condensed means of prestige in formulation. The metaphorical proverbs force the listener into acute "processing," and yet are specific despite all ambiguities as recipes. As a matter of fact, David Robertson, who argues for a non-Aristotelian reading of Proverbs, also suggests this sense of situational specificity. A proverb in our text seems to float above and beyond situations. But really, as Robertson suggests when trying to dissolve the knot of a famous contradiction—whether to answer a fool according to his folly or not, and our book suggests doing both—the scandal of the proverbial method is its worldliness, its ineluctable link to surface despite metaphor and ambiguity. The anthropological suggestion is to read this encyclopedia of formulations with all due attention to its fractures, indications of a wilderness of eruptive contexts. Proverbs demand places.

When we think of proverbs as demanding persons and places, we realize the scandalous difficulty of reading this seemingly ahistorical book without history. And yet the archives of archaeology are not that potent here. Despite beautiful parallels found in James Pritchard's extraordinarily useful anthologies of Egyptian and other Near Eastern texts, there is no certainty in Wisdom scholarship as to whether we are dealing with an essentially Egyptian text "collaged" onto a Solomonic frame, or whether Israeli Wisdom was diffused into later Egyptian scribal forms. At the least, however, the parallels, including the too-congruent use of the number thirty in organizing one section of our text, remind us that universalism here finds both form and content interfused. The proverb is a cosmopolitan form, though one anthropologist has discovered that urbanity tends to threaten the form. Still, we may find in Proverbs a truly Solomonic urbanity, and the howl of Wisdom takes place "at the entrance to the city gates" (1:21). We are impressed that more than one student has remarked on the relation of the condensed proverb to the establishment of the alphabet. The proverb is as much early science as ageless prudence. It stands with Solomonic architecture as a tectonic vehicle: the building up of character in an ambiguous school.

The poet Wallace Stevens is said to have collected volumes of proverbs in much the way Walter Benjamin is said to have searched for collections of psychotic world-systems. Our book does have a problem at its core: the massing of the microcosmos. Yet to us, reading this fractured so-called list of lists, we are surprised at the unified power of this disunity. The book announces itself with a mighty framing device:

> That men may know wisdom and instruction,
>   understand words of insight
>   receive instruction in wise dealing,
> righteousness, justice and equity;
> that prudence may be given to the simple . . .
> the wise man also may hear and increase in learning. . . .   [Proverbs 1:2–5]

And the ode to the "Good Wife" stands as the other ferocious framing of this book. To begin at the beginning, instruction in the reading of all codes, and to end with the "fruit of her hands," suggests that the late editor of this text knew how to make a recipe book seem intently focused. The last acrostic, since the "Good Wife" is organized by the alphabet and its mystical resonance, seems to make a whole poem into a proverb, if we recall that *Mishlé* comes out of a matrix of words for "analogy," "metaphor," and "figure." In a book in which the ephebe is to learn how to decode life's wilderness, it is fitting that the last figure is the powerful wife who "opens her mouth with wisdom / and the teaching of kindness is on her tongue" (31:26). The maximum affirmation is made through the minimum alphabetic technique.

The book has been decried for its repressive constancy, its fidelity to fidelity. No doubt the wise man reads the Book of Proverbs and turns to Job, where we have a rather skeptical indictment of false comfort. It would seem too easy to describe Job as the inversion of Proverbs, and the false comforters as those who have learned our book too early and too well. Here it is significant to recall that our Proverbs contains a tremendous worldly darkness: the world of panic to those who have refused wisdom, but also the simple strictness of the relative world itself, where a woman is charming but leads to an accessible abyss. Those who have seen in Proverbs a fear of desire, a fear of woman, a misogyny at the core, must be corrected. The book does have some of the great representations of the slipperiness of desire and its discontents, but in that it shows the moral realism that releases us to a new knowledge of woman and her stature. There is a fundamental finding of the Other here, the wife evaded by both Kafka and Kierkegaard, and both adulteress and householder are seen and fully revealed as forms of divine power glimpsed within the ordinary companionate dream. Proverbs contains a loud psalm to woman—divine, thus terrible—and what is refused is the "rehearsed response," as if we knew how to read her. The adulteress is portrayed as a demon as glidingly powerful as any girl of Avignon. On the other hand, the "Good Wife," charitable, working and loving, is a finale, radiant as a fundamental eulogy—I still recall the effect of the rabbinic recitation at my grandmother's funeral. Woman is the key to our seemingly opaque allegory.

S. R. Hirsch gives a fundamentally sound, if pietistic, reading of the meanings of *Chochmah* (Wisdom) in our Wisdom text: "The terms . . . are found also as applied to God. In fact, they can be applied in their truest, deepest and fullest sense only to God. The share that people get from this spiritual essence of wisdom, understanding, and knowledge—emanating from it and made possible by it—is merely an infinitely faint echo of the Divine. . . ." The Book of Proverbs may be said to be divided into those passages that give worldly advice as to the conduct of business, politics, matrimony, friendship, affairs of state and heart, and those maxims that most stringently concern the spiritual rapports. But the book attempts to create an inescapable self-reflexiveness: "The beginning of wisdom is this: Get wisdom, and whatever you get, get insight" (4:7). There is a link between the high and the low, between world and spirit: "Prize her highly, and she will exalt you; she will honor you if you embrace her" (4:8). "It is the glory of God to conceal things, but the glory of kings is to search things out" (25:2). This is a cunning counterfoil to Einstein's remark on God's subtle lack of malice. *Deus absconditus* might indeed be the first and final incitement to all science and all poetry. We find in mundane suggestions simply the arithmetic for the conduct of a life tied to the divinity, hidden like gravity and as constant. Just as Walter Benjamin dreamed of a book entirely of quotations that would reveal a whole city, so Proverbs in multiplicity reveals the divine city, a place in which the good woman's "works praise her in the gates" (31:31).

The Proverbs are a constant reminder of the inclusivity of Judaism, an inclusivity Freud discovers in linking Moses to the universalist vision of Akhnaton. The Proverbs begin with prudence and end with happiness: they are a poem to the earth in the ethical dimension as much as the Song of Songs is the earthly ode in the aesthetic and erotic dimensions. There is little of the tribalist in our text, and yet for all those who have seen this collection as internationalist, it is also important to think of it as yielding a national collection, a group anthology that fosters unity through memory. Here analogy is more significant than chronicle, and the book foregrounds a constant present tense. It is the present tense of these shocking analogies that functions as such a contrast to the epic past of the great histories: "Like a gold ring in a swine's snout / is a beautiful woman without discretion" (11:22). The analogy is correct and is always correct, like gravity or the alphabet. And the future tense is not one of prophecy but, rather, is one announcing the exact causalities: "He who trusts in his riches will wither." The prophet may find himself quoting a proverb, as Ezekiel does (16:44), but the condensation of the proverb functions much more like a rule than like a warning or revelation. It is the man-made scientism of the rules that gives them so much modern force in the aphorisms of Ludwig Wittgenstein and Karl Kraus.

The French negative theologian par excellence, Jacques Derrida, has remarked in a dialogue that the theological motif is always *homogeneity*. If this were indeed so, one might profitably think of Proverbs in its eclectic "collage" state as part of the Jewish critique of idealism. One's face is rubbed in *the near,* as Leo Baeck has put it—the nearness of the divine, the nearness of the world, the nearness of the uncanny fusion of world and divinity. There is no wisdom without the fear of God, but also no wisdom without the fear at home, the fear of home, since we are those who may be exported in haste to a dim underworld, as materialist an underground as has been conceived, a world called Sheol, derived etymologically from the small cramped grave. *Mishlé* is a heterogeneous text and obdurately so, because it bears upon its "speaking" side the scars and fissures of all the contexts that make its demands so exigent. Proverbs is a cadenza of prudential severity, and it may indeed be misconceived as the authoritarian necklace, chain, or crown to which it refers. Actually, it may come to seem closest to a book of dreams or jokes, with the kind of prudence we feel in Freud when he suggests that children should not be sent to the Arctic with summer clothing and maps of the Italian lakes. Proverbs, said to be the most sublimating book in the Bible, is, rather, an eruptive text of a restless shrewdness that does more than balance the idealism of priests and prophets with the cunning of the "elders." Commandments are finite; the Proverbs are infinite and remind us that attention must be so.

The Book of Proverbs is not simply the site for craftsmanly counsel on cunning, though some have analogized it with the effluorescence of the arts under the imperial Solomon. Like the so-called Wisdom psalms, this book contains a tone of strenuous searching that links it with the pre-Socratics. It is true that there is an overwhelming worldliness in some of the chief topics, such as avoiding violence and adultery and drunkenness, but we also note, as in chapters 8 and 9, another theme, so grandly stated as to force the mundane, as it were, into allegory: the theme of a personified Wisdom. "Wisdom has built her house, she has set up her seven pillars" (9:1). One does not need the traditions of Zohar and other hermeneutical vehicles to enjoy the multiple perspectives of this allegorical architecture:

"She has slaughtered her beasts, she has mixed her wine / she has also set her table" (9:2). This is a wisdom that can only be described at the risk of the most drastic revisionism, as in a new genesis: "The Lord created me at the beginning of his work / the first of his acts of old" (8:22). This "wisdom" seems as if it would appeal to the latest neo-Platonisms of the Wisdom of Solomon, most probably written under Hellenic influence. A series of idealizing odes forces the inner collections to be read through their irradiation. Although one might agree with Mark Van Doren that the Song of Songs is "merely" human and erotic, *Mishlé* here offers a tremendous rebuke to any reductive reading.

Let us accept that many of the inner collections in our canonic text emerge from an international matrix of prudential counsels. Let us even accept that these inner collections function as modest and moderate rote learning for a new civil servant: "To impose a fine on a righteous man is not good; to flog a noble man is wrong" (17:26). Those who have seen this book, like Robertson in a recent essay on its "syndetic" quality, as being without beginning or end, miss the fundamental insistence on Wisdom as Beginning. I do not think it improper to share my sense that those who have called this work a collage mistake or misconceive the nature of collage or even *bricolage,* as Northrop Frye has called the whole Bible an ingenious *bricolage.* The collage has its own unity and is particulate despite ruptures in texture and changes of density and direction. A collage is not, moreover, beginningless or endless. The Book of Proverbs has many recipes, it is true, and Robertson is right in suggesting that we must learn how to apply our little directives. But the book also has some enormous principles and pressures, and these cannot be mistaken even if the form is turbulent and the punctuation of the form is restless, anomalous, asymmetrical. The book that is said to end nowhere concludes with woman as language and happiness. The book that is said only to accumulate begins with a proliferation of absolute oppositions between wisdom and folly. It is a modernist misreading to conceive this book as "accretion without development." Wisdom signifies development.

It is fitting for the melancholy poet of disunity, the Jewish Catholic Hugo von Hofmannsthal, to have written a prose poem on chapter 30 of Proverbs and the mysterious figure of Agur. Here we have a sudden skeptical darkness that seems to yield an endless undertow to our book:

"I have not learned wisdom, nor have I knowledge of the Holy One. / Who has ascended to heaven and come down? Who has gathered the wind in his fists?" (30:3–4) This is the fabulous cadenza of answerless questions that we have heard in Job's whirlwind encounter. Here it initiates the great numerological poems on the wonders of the world. Like the great choral ode in *Antigone,* it foregrounds the wonder of man himself, and yet it does this with the constant Near Eastern decorative zeal of linking the whole animal kingdom. How much the lyric poet Antonio Machado was to learn from the modest singing tones of this mystical numerology: "Three things are too wonderful for me; four I do not understand: the way of an eagle in the sky; the way of a serpent on a rock; the way of a ship on the high seas; and the way of a man with a maiden" (30:18–19). Machado in his "proverbial poems" speaks of things that are not useful at sea: one, rudders; two, anchors; and three, the fear of shipwreck. This prudential and uncanny lyric could not exist without the wonders of Agur. And Agur's erotic underlining of the way of man and woman speaks against those who find Proverbs' prudence antierotic. Prudence leaves space for wonder.

Just as a proverb may seem a humble or mean or quotidian form but turns out to be a focusing of attention that is in itself a delight, there is a congruity in the imagery of Agur with the focus on the seemingly insignificant. The ants are a humble people—one might say, a comically tribal bunch—but they are also rationalists for us to stare at. The badgers look fallible and frail, but they invade mountains. The locusts may look anarchic without a king, but they are Prussian in their orderliness. And, in the last insidious image of paradox and strangeness, Agur yields the immortal image of eruptive power: "The lizard you can take in your hands, yet it is in king's palaces." These are not proverbs, but extended numerological miniatures that remind us that Proverbs is *not* simply a collection of proverbs, but an anthology of diverse forms. And it is diversity that Agur celebrates, a diversity of power that encounters the worst without blinking: "Under three things the earth trembles, under four it cannot bear up: a slave when he becomes a king, and a fool when he is filled with food; an unloved woman when she gets a husband, and a maid when she succeeds her mistress" (30:21–23). There is a Shakespearean tone of the aristocrat's privilege here, but what is most available to us is the sense that some tolerance is paralyzing.

One cannot tolerate one's own negation (as my own mother used to remark about the limits of pluralism).

This is the one text that can make contradiction explicit, as in the famous, scandalously opposing advice on answering fools (26:5–6), because the world is presented as a wilderness for wise men to garden. The cultivated reader is not provoked by a contradiction, but understands that the symbols will be applied tactfully to the situation as it arises in the murk of multiplicity. The Wise Man, like Joseph, decodes dreams like brothers and becomes a ruler by such decoding. And brothers are indeed a theme: "Better is a neighbor who is near / than a brother who is far away" (27:10). Charles Peirce went so far in his semiotics as to say that man himself is a sign, and that would be acceptable to Agur among his wonders. A wonder, a sign, a figure, an analogy are methods and means for an encyclopedic text on the subtle but not maliciously designed world: "Faithful are the wounds of a friend; profuse are the kisses of an enemy" (27:6). Prudence is not the stairway to a Machiavellian *Realpolitik;* it is a means of avoiding the falser Machiavellis who surround the wise man like hidden snares. It is relationship, in reading, friendship, and speech, that is the canonic Buberian hero of our nonstory: "Iron sharpens iron, and one man sharpens another" (27: 17). The proverbs in mosaic sharpen one another, as later the fragments of a *Minima Moralia* are sharpened with Theodore Adorno's juxtapositions.

Our book is not concerned with success so much as it is concerned with health itself. Emerson was influenced by this book to become a great aphorist on the theme of health, and yet few have noted, despite Emerson's essay on prudence, that we cannot have our strongest native transcendentalism without a grappling with the problem of prudence. The inconsistency and the eruptiveness beloved of Emerson, as of Whitman, were not an infantile discontinuity but one founded on an attention to the divine as a focusing device. *Mishlé* counsels us in a myriad of ways to avoid infantile paradises and to grow up toward the difficulty of "real life" seen in almost penological perspectives. There is no easy way to avoid the theme of punishment, because this book tries to become "equipment for living," and it would be a saccharine collection indeed if it refused the perspective of punishment. "A wicked man earns deceptive wages" (11:18). At the least, the book concerns itself with our illusions, and for those who think *Mishlé* is not worldly enough to note the success of the unrighteous, we might add the

Freudian note that money does not guarantee happiness, since it does not reward an infantile desire. "He who troubles his household will inherit wind" (11:29) seems to suggest that the book is a constant critique of infantilism. If there are no constants, there is the drive toward constancy. The book may, at least, be seen as an anthology of utopian and, paradoxically, materialist idealizations. These ideals, as William James has said, create the real. The real world depends upon a comparison.

Throughout our century there has been a positivist desire to search for a perfect language. One has only to think of the tension in the master of *figura,* Ludwig Wittgenstein, who sought for a language whose propositions could be laid next to reality like a ruler. This pursuit in Wittgenstein finally cracks into his later, mature mode, which revels in the anthropocentric infinitude of so-called language games. We might say that *Mishlé* is already ruled by the tension between the pursuit for a perfect language—the divinity, seen allegorically as Wisdom, the Sage, the Good Wife—and the resolute acceptance of the shattered world of forms—glimpsed in the multitude of prudential adages. Proverbs insists, as a text, that metaphor cannot be escaped, though there remains the immortal desire for an escape from metaphor. Metaphor, with its compacted insistence on difference as much as identity, is the single method for attaching word to object, man to thing, and person to divinity. We might say that the Tanach, with all its aniconic zeal and the anti-idolatrous urge, could not help being negative toward the metaphor as eidolon. Yet Solomonic glory resorted to a decorative architecture, and this late book (sixth century B.C.E.?) is a Bible of metaphors. God speaks in metaphors: "I also will laugh at your calamity; I will mock when panic strikes you, when panic strikes you like a storm, and your calamity comes like a whirlwind" (1:26). Out of the whirlwind come questions and metaphors. Those that would purge us of analogies would purge us of architectural models to which we must cling. Just as the word "metaphor" is metaphorical, the very word for "proverbs" is a compacted figure of figures. Borges speaks of a book of analogies which splits into infinite pages, and so the form of this book is purposely of its monotonous magnitude. The scale itself is an allegory of the extent of wisdom: Solomonic numerology.

The Wisdom movement is usually viewed by scholars as polarized, so that the skeptical authors of Job and Ecclesiastes seem to admonish the repressed conservator of Proverbs. But again and again there are flashes of a dazzling darkness in our book that rival the darkness of those "strange books." One does not merely want to create a rudimentary contrast of pessimism versus optimistic faith, but since this is a theme so harped upon in the commentaries, I would like to remind the reader to remember these gloomy adages: "When the wicked rule, the people groan" (29:2). Of course, this is only the last part of the dystich "When the righteous are in authority, the people rejoice." But the undaunted realism of the groaning people remains and stains the whole dystich. Elsewhere, the entire adage is Hobbesian and brutish and short: "If a ruler listens to falsehood, all his officials will be wicked" (29:12). A lack of receptivity is death itself, the final disunity, seen in the most corporeal of images: "He who is often reproved, yet stiffens his neck / will suddenly be broken beyond healing" (29:1). All the comical inelasticities that Henri Bergson speaks of at the heart of wit are summoned in the images of excess and psychopathology: "A miserly man hastens after wealth, and does not know that want will come upon him" (28:22). Rashi speaks in a commentary about the sexual intercourse that is discreetly summoned in this infuriatingly sly image of the impure: "This is the way of an adulteress: she eats, and wipes her mouth, and says, 'I have done no wrong' " (30:20). This portrait, with its unbending mimetic punch, is an example of a realism beyond hope or despair. These things are so because the earth and the emotions are laid out with the geometrical zeal which will appeal later to the lensmaker in Amsterdam (Spinoza): "Wrath is cruel, anger is overwhelming: but who can stand before jealousy?" (27:4) Rather than repression, sublimation, or conservatism, we find in Proverbs a contempt for illusions: "A continual dripping on a rainy day / and a contentious woman are alike; to restrain her is to restrain the wind . . ." (27:15).

Boris Pasternak's freshest collection is called *My Sister Life;* I know of no one who has drawn attention to the great Biblical figure parallel to this: "Say to wisdom, You are my sister, and call insight your intimate friend" (7:4). This is how the peculiar narrative on the impure woman is initiated, and it leaves us with a less embittered sense than without it. Robert Alter has spoken of the extended power of this little secular poem, and we are amazed at its spatial precisions, its rhythmic finesse (both in Hebrew and in the King James translation, moreover, a translation to be wondered at, unrivaled, in itself untranslatable—though for my discursive purposes, I cite here from the Revised Standard Version), its tremendous forward motion and tragic close. "For at the window of my house / I have looked out through my lattice / and I have seen among the simple, I have perceived among the youths, a young man without sense . . ." (7:6). The repetitions are horrifying and they deepen the turbid atmosphere like glazes: "in the twilight, in the evening, at the time of night and darkness" (7:8–9). The woman is dominant: "She seizes him and kisses him, and with impudent face she says to him: I had to offer sacrifices, and today I have paid my vows; so now I have come out to meet you, to seek you eagerly, and I have found you." Like Pharaoh's wife in the Joseph story—perhaps written in Wisdom circles, as current scholarship has it—this woman unites a false aestheticism with ethical betrayal: "I have decked my couch with coverings, colored spreads of Egyptian linen. . . . Let us delight ourselves with love. For my husband is not at home" (7:19). And the victim follows, like an ox, a stag, and a rushing bird. So much for those who cannot decode the Other and the others.

Proverbs may seem to be the greatest case of what Hermann Broch once referred to as "I"-suppression. It should be noted, however, that the collection is constantly pierced by the dialogic tone of father to son, and thus is not the tedious string of decontextualized adages it may seem to be to those who plunge into its midst. Theodore Reik has spoken of Jewish wit and its idiosyncratic self-lacerating tones, and he suggests that a "powerless" people may develop the signs of pathology that Freud speaks of in his essay on "The Exceptions," those who behave as if early suffering gave them antinomian privileges. But our book is the least antinomian and has about it the most empurpled sense of doom and mortality: "A little sleep, a little slumber, a little folding of the hands to rest, and poverty will come upon you like a vagabond, and want like an armed man" (6:6). Perhaps it is the concreteness in the condensed majesty of these lines concerning the absence of all control that goes to making the "personism" of Proverbs. Because we come to see teaching itself as something bound physically upon our hearts and necks, we do not find the book sepulchrally impersonal in any late-Romantic sense. This physicality is present everywhere: "Can a man carry fire in his bosom, and his clothes not be burned?" (6:27) "The words of a whisperer are like delicious morsels, they go down into the inner parts of the body" (18:8). We understand by the indirect admonition against slander that the book is to become part of our body. Reading is vascular or nothing.

Robert Alter is correct in pointing out how much of the pithiness of the Hebraic proverb is lost in the smooth unraveling of the English mistranslations. Alter understands that the authors of this book regarded linguistic facility as the gateway to Wisdom: "If we are not good readers we will not get the point of the saying of the wise" (Alter, page 168). And he is most adept at calling attention to the morality of the "smallest verbal movements" in the precepts and riddles of our text. His analogy with Alexander Pope, moreover, is correct, if one recalls the true ferocity of that great satirist. This book is not one of elegance alone, but of the sanity that derides false luxuries and none-too-subtle adulteries. Elsewhere, Alter derides some of the formulations for having the hackneyed predictability that could be expected in schools of rote devices. But note that a poetry of prediction and predictability is not so far from a poetry of fate and causality. The smoothness of the road to adultery slips into unsurprising doom. In many ways, the music of law—indeed, of predictability—is a resonant one here. If a modernist is mostly attracted to adages with stippled surprises or sudden reversals, it is also true that wisdom demands a stern regularity: "A just balance and scales are the Lord's; all the weights in the bag are his work" (16:11). Proverbs demand patience.

There are many things for a poet to learn from Proverbs, even that perverse pleasure in condensation and *non sequitur* that appears in the "perverbs" of our contemporary Harry Matthews, who with delight takes canonic maxims and deranges them. What is extraordinary in *Mishlé* is, however, the scale of its *extended* narratives, as in the extended homage to the Good Wife, where the woman becomes anagrammatically the whole language. "She rises while it is yet night," and becomes a constant like a sun. "She is like the ships of the merchant," and effectively annihilates space and time, like wisdom. But it is always wisdom that is being praised in the elongations of *Mishlé,* as in the final tribute: "Charm is deceitful, and beauty is vain, but a woman who fears the Lord is to be praised" (31:30).

Drunkenness, too, receives its opposing extended and physical fugue: "Who has woe? Who has sorrow? . . . Those who tarry long over wine, those who go to try mixed wine. Do not look at wine when it is red, when it sparkles in the cup / and goes down smoothly. At the last it bites like a serpent and stings like an adder (23:29–32). There is an eidetic physicality to the rush of this vertigo: "Your eyes will see strange things, and your mind utter perverse things. You will be like one who lies down in the midst of the sea, like one who lies on the top of the mast" (23:33). Such self-violence is the opposite of reading.

The drunkard antihero cries from within this vertigo as one who is indeed simple, simplified, and, etymologically speaking, wide open: "They struck me, you will say, but I was not hurt; they beat me, but I did not feel it. When shall I awake? I will seek another drink" (33:35). There is a grave circular comedy being enacted here and by the "intimate yell" that another poet has discovered in great Russian admonitions. Here the intimism is intense and relentless; the ephebe is caught up in the repetitive folly of a minor ecstasy. Note how difficult it would be for the Hasidim to reverse the enormous canonic weight of these admonitions against immoderate states.

One does not want to call this book merely Apollonian in its calls to order and sobriety, but surely there is a parallel to Greek wisdom in its rebuke to excess and its parallel call to self-knowledge. It might be part of the glory of the tragedians and the authors of *Mishlé* that self-knowledge is seen exactly within boundaries, relations, and balances, as opposed to any infantile Rimbaudien *dérèglement de tous les sens*. All the senses are to be part of the ruled world, a world created in number, weight, and measure. Thus the drum beat of the measured proverb is like a genesis of its own, dismaying to drunkards, a web woven in honor of exigent Wisdom.

What remains for us today of Proverbs is perhaps surprising in its abundance. We do not think of its fideism as part of a slothful false comfort known to Job's friends, since nowhere is there counsel that the promises of rewards are calculated as insults to the suffering. As a matter of fact, we might cite a host of proverbs that speak of kindness, empathy, tact: "A poor man who oppresses the poor / is a beating rain that leaves no food" (28:3). Job's friends give the right cliché at the wrong moment, but the whole lesson of Proverbs concerns the tact of utterance and rapport. Ecclesiastes, too, that "strange book," is not more strange in its distressed materialism than the abundant materialism of our book: "As a door turns on its hinges, so does a sluggard on his bed" (26:14). And as for Blake's proverbs of drastic desublimation, there remains the exuberant: "Better is open rebuke / than hidden love" (27:5).

Freud speaks in his *Moses and Monotheism* of the soaring abstractions of Egyptian thought and the savage particularities of the volcano god of later tribal tradition. In Proverbs, we have both the soaring particularities of a late, cosmopolitan universalism, and the fundamental monism of the Wisdom allegory. We may be moved by the sweep of this book, as by the great analyst's most labyrinthine case histories, where a rage for order and a tolerance for concreteness support one another. The analytic wisdom tradition includes the imperturbable doctor of our shattered Soul.

No contemporary reader has much problem with the so-called moral realism of Proverbs, as when the melancholy Agur summons up images of greed and infantile fantastics:

> The leech has two daughters;
> Give, give, they cry.
> Three things are never satisfied;
> four never say "Enough.":
> Sheol, the barren womb,
> the earth ever thirsty for water,
> and the fire which never says
> "Enough."   [30:15]

What is more difficult for some is the sense of pietistic hope in the seemingly simple theodicy: "He who walks in integrity will be delivered but he who is perverse in his ways will fall into a pit" (28:18). To this, the simple reader asks, Isn't this simply refuted by experience; is all this, as it were, pre-Job? Is it not this that Ecclesiastes and Job were written to refute?

But I do not think it is so. A reading of the Psalms will show how often the great national songs include in them constant promise of reward for righteousness: "Blessed is every one who fears the Lord, who walks in his ways! You shall eat the fruit of the labor of your hands; you shall be happy, and it shall be well with you" (Psalm 128:1). The link of Psalms and Proverbs in these seemingly naïve counsels is the tone of pathos and desire. Both Psalms and Proverbs are stating the counsels of the wise as the dream of righteousness. It is obvious from the darker maxims of Proverbs, as from the dark exilic hymns, that the wise men knew quite well of the triumphs of the wicked; many formulae sketch this perverse triumph. The theme of righteous reward is not in contradiction to the suffering of a Job. Job himself is crowned with a final reward, if only *ex machina*. Is this unsatisfactory? (My mother used to say, with some "moral realism," that Job never got back his original children. This I take to be the height of the prudential tone in contemporary Jewish wit.) Reading Psalms and Proverbs together, one learns how often a proverb is a song.

We conclude that David Robertson is wrong in suggesting that *Mishlé* is a *syndetic* book, mainly involved in creating, like libraries and museums, a nondeveloping accumulation of recipes in random order. It does develop, it is synthetic, it does indeed reconcile opposites. I think no reader of poetry can miss the sustained and alarmingly tense opposition of Wisdom and Folly, of the Adulteress and the Good Wife. This volume is an extended homage to Wisdom in its perpetual militancy against sluggard inattention. The longest and most seemingly random of the collections has at its heart the sense of prudential insight as reaping reward and being its own self-reflexive joy. The climax in the acrostic poem clearly underscores the idea that the logocentric universe is indeed well ordered, like the family in its true dialogues. Whatever is minimal in the prudence of *Mishlé* is accompanied by the Tremendum: "Better is a little with the fear of the Lord / than great treasure and trouble with it" (15:16). I think it is straining to modulate from the early interpretations of this book as being a conservative scribal textbook to the new vision of it as a whimsical collage of popular art. The folk sayings are indeed derived from popular sayings, but are transformed into a unity of supernal power. It is not a unity easily glimpsed, but it is a delirious mistranslation to seize in it only disunity. For its exemplariness Coleridge might well have yielded us his neologism, "Multeity." The radical multitudinousness of Proverbs always points to a vision, and a vision of vision: "The eyes of the Lord are in every place." It is because these eyes are everywhere that the book may seem to some to be bursting with everything. It is a strange recipe book that supplies the food.

JOB

Leslie Fiedler

Almost exactly forty years ago—with all the brash assurance of a neophyte teacher—I tried for the first time to say in public what the Book of Job meant to me. I had been reading and rereading and rereading it ever since I was thirteen or fourteen—in the King James Version, of course, in all of whose magnificent inaccuracy I will remember it, I suppose, until the day I die. Certainly I am not prepared to trade the haunting cadences of "Yet man is born unto trouble, as the sparks fly upward" for the more "correct" rendering of the scholarly text before me: "A man is born for trouble / As the sons of Reshef fly upward"—whoever or whatever "Reshef" may be. I could, I know, solve that small mystery by consulting the footnotes. But I am reluctant to do so, having learned over four decades that such information is irrelevant to the solution of larger mysteries at the heart of Job, finally comprehensible, if ever at all, to one not learned but wise—in any case, "full of days."

The King James Version of the Bible used in this essay.

At some level, I must have been aware of this even when I was very young; but it did not trouble me, because there is much in the text easily available and instantly appealing to readers of that age, consumed with impotent rage against a world which seems a conspiracy against *them*. Obviously this does *not* include the speech of resignation with which Job accepts the first series of catastrophes that befall him at Satan's instigation, as he never for a moment suspects—and, as he never for a moment doubts, the permission of his God. No more does it include his initial bland acceptance of the second. Though—or perhaps, rather, because—I knew that the instant clichés with which he responds to both ("The LORD gave, and the LORD hath taken away; blessed be the name of the LORD" and "What? Shall we receive good at the hand of God, and shall we not receive evil?") were especially prized by pious adults, they seemed to me abjectly craven. I did not then suspect—irony being alien to the young—that there might be something ironical, even implicitly subversive, in Job's apparent retractions. Nor can I quite make myself believe even now that, however attractive such a reading may be to modern, post–"Death of God" sensibility, it is a true one.

Back then, at any rate, I dismissed the narrative frame story of Job, the prose prologue and epilogue, as a naïve anthropomorphic fable beginning with an incomprehensible wager between God and Satan and ending with a pat, all-too-comprehensible "happily ever after." What I found especially unsatisfactory, however, was Job's unruffled piety in face of the unmerited suffering he endured in between, his infamous "patience." To the self-righteous anger which is the *Leitmotif* of the enclosed verse dialogue, on the other hand, I (responded) sympathetically. That anger has, to be sure, already erupted even before the prologue is quite over, when Job ferociously turns on his wife, whom God and the Adversary have in their, to me then, still-incomprehensible collaboration strangely spared, as they have not Job's children and his worldly goods. "Curse God and die," she advises him, yielding to the hysteria and despair which he has resisted despite all his suffering; and for the first time his equanimity is shattered, so that he screams back at her, "Thou speakest as one of the foolish women speaketh."

At this point, she, anonymous from start to finish, disappears from the book forever, quite as Satan does, after tempting God into the wager whose final settlement we are not permitted to know, and Elihu, the fourth "comforter" of Job, will do after speaking his final unanswered condemnation of Job. Before her disappearance into the silence of the text, however, she has triggered the wrath of her husband, suggesting that her response to the monstrous succession of disasters which have befallen him is not just one more calamity, but the last straw. It is a convincing scene, rendered with the utmost economy, though I did not fully understand it until I had lived long enough to learn at first hand that perhaps the worst effect of seemingly gratuitous household calamity is turning the survivors against one another; as they project the guilt they cannot help feeling for having survived onto whomever they most dearly love, or whoever merely happens to be closest at hand. I find it now, therefore, inevitable that what began with the destruction of Job's livestock and servants, and then climaxed in the death of his seven sons and three daughters, does not end there. Instead, it descends into the anticlimax of a husband-wife quarrel. But this means, too, that it edges toward, without ever quite slipping over into, burlesque: maintaining an unconsummated flirtation with the comic, which I have come slowly to realize is typical of the comic-tragic work as a whole.

Of all this, however, I was not at first aware; perceiving and relishing not the multiple ironies everywhere present in the Book of Job (the chief of which is his unawareness throughout of what we as readers know from the start, the scandalous wager in heaven), but the explicit rage which dominates the dialogue with the comforters and finally with God Himself. Even before he utters his first words to the three Sages who have come from afar, presumably to sustain him in his grief, but who begin a little inauspiciously by mourning for him as if he were already dead, he has exploded: cursing not his Creator, to be sure, but the day he was born—which is to say, the gift of life itself.

Then he cries out with mounting vehemence against the injustice of his own unmerited suffering, the inherent evil of the entire created world, especially the plight of humankind: doomed, whatever good or ill may befall them in their brief span of existence, to die forever. His most venomous invective, however, he reserves for his pious "comforters," who, finding his insistence on blaming not himself but God for his plight blasphemous, respond in kind.

Eliphaz, to be sure, who answers him first, begins by trying—or at least pretending—to speak sympathetically. But his patience soon runs out, as Job maintains his "integrity" and insists on his right to quarrel with his Maker; and he ends by railing against Job as vituperatively as his companions, Bildad and Zophar, who are enraged from the start by Job's "unorthodox" contention (with which, to be sure, God has in the prologue agreed) that humankind, and he in particular, sometimes suffer "for nothing."

They grow even more furious as Job's anger, mounting in response to their own, is directed at the sanctimonious platitudes with which they, immune to pain, try to explain away the injustice he is experiencing in his own rotting and pain-ridden flesh. His suffering, they explain, is—like all human suffering—a punishment for sin, a discipline that purifies the soul; to deny this, they go on, is to compound sin; but to confess it and repent will bring in the end recompense and reward. They do not, however, speak reassuringly, but in reproach and exasperation.

Finally, what was begun as a theological argument in verse becomes a screaming match. Never has poetry been made at a higher decibel level or a steeper pitch of acrimony, which is further raised when a fifth participant in the debate appears out of nowhere, his intervention unmotivated and unprepared for. He is, we are almost immediately informed, younger than Eliphaz, Bildad, or Zophar, and presumably Job as well. Certainly he is—as perhaps befits his age—angrier than the rest, his anger directed not just against Job, who has still not ceased to argue his case, but against the other three, who have stopped contending with him. Even before we learn what he is called, we learn of his anger. "Then was kindled the wrath of Elihu, the son of Barachel the Buzite . . . ," the introductory tag in the text reads, "against Job . . . because he justified himself rather than God. And against his three friends . . . because they found no answer. . . ."

He is an oddly shadowy figure, this Elihu, despite the fact that (ironically once more) he is called by a Jewish name, the name, in fact, of the great prophet of Israel. He represents, I am convinced, an afterthought, a last desperate attempt on the part of the poet who gave the Book of Job its final form to defend orthodoxy against Job's subversive challenge, which that poet, like Elihu, apparently believed had not yet been satisfactorily confuted.

Yet, though he has seemed problematically present to all readers and commentators ever since, that metatextual kibbitzer is invisible and inaudible to the rest of the *dramatis personae,* who neither respond to him nor acknowledge his presence. Even Job, whom Elihu, unlike the three other sages, calls by name over and over in an almost comically vain attempt to attract his attention, ignores him. Moreover, so also does the Lord, whose thunderous Voice out of the whirlwind drowns out the last echoes of Elihu's peroration, as if to make clear that it is to Him the final word belongs, rather than to that presumptuous upstart who has tried to pre-empt His privilege.

He does not, even in His all-encompassing righteous wrath (for Him, too, anger seems the chief motive for discourse), deign to condemn Elihu, as He does Eliphaz and his fellows, for "not having spoken of him the thing which is right." Nor does He address him in an attempt to bully him into silence, as He does Job, whom, indirectly and backhandedly, He indicates has spoken of Him truly. But what this means remains unclear. Does it amount to a confession—extorted from Him who will not even reveal the scandalous wager that began everything—that He is indeed, as Job contends and his "comforters" deny, one who "destroyeth the perfect and the wicked" and "will laugh at the dismay of the innocent"? But He does not finally destroy Job, whom He has described as perfect, or laugh at his plight; He restores him at the poem's end to health and prosperity.

We are confronted again with an apparent contradiction between what is said in the enclosed poetic dialogue and what we are told in the framing prose story. In the latter, God proves finally to be a God of mercy, who "blessed the latter end of Job more than the beginning." But in the theophany which concludes the former, He manifests Himself as a God of wrath, the creator of all in the natural world which is hostile to and unconquerable by man: Behemoth, the phallic monster, the nerves of whose testicles are intertwined and whose penis is like the lofty cedar; and the leviathan, that fiery engine of destruction who makes the very deep boil like a pot. At this point Job declares, "I have heard of thee by the hearing of my ear; but now mine eye seeth thee"—suggesting he has learned at last what his long suffering had not taught him, not merely that God is beyond good and evil, but that He reveals Himself only to one willing to maintain this unpalatable truth over the objections of the pious.

At age fourteen, at any rate, I identified myself with Job thus understood, though, alas, unlike him, I did not believe, or at least I *believed* I did not believe, in God. I had, therefore, no one to blame for my own misery and the palpable injustice of the world around me (it was the time of the Great Depression) except "society," "history," "heredity," and "environment"—dumb abstractions incapable of answering anything. Nonetheless, I persisted in speaking what I hoped were Jobean truths that the pious of our own time, my parents and teachers, considered blasphemous; and, in spite of all, dreaming that a Voice from Somewhere would somehow declare that I had spoken the thing which was right.

When I reached the age of thirty, however, I had come to believe that I believed in Job's God—just in time to blame Him for the near-annihilation of East European Jewry, through which, to be sure, I had lived at a safe distance, but in which every member of my family still in the Old World died. So also I cried out against Him for the horrors of World War II, which I had experienced at first hand: surviving the Battle of Iwo Jima and (the final horror, perhaps) rejoicing when, as a Japanese interpreter assigned to monitoring Radio Tokyo, I heard the news of the dropping of the bomb on Hiroshima. But of this I was not ashamed then and am not now, since it meant the end of the mutual slaughter I could no longer abide. Of the role which human error and villainy, including my own, played in these events, I was aware; but they seemed too petty to explain away disasters so cosmic in scope. Such suffering "for nothing" only a God of the cosmos, omniscient, omnipotent, but vindictive or indifferent, a Hangman God, could have, *must* have—for reasons unknowable and unthinkable to mere humans—instigated or, in any case, permitted.

Consequently, I took the first opportunity afforded me to cry out against Him, like Job, challenge Him to justify Himself. As if I were some unconvincing counterfeit of the role I sought to play, however, an Elihu pretending to be Job, He did not answer me—not out of the whirlwind, or even inside the silence of my troubled head. Yet what could I have expected? When I was at last able to speak out on Job's behalf in public, I was no lonely sufferer on a metaphoric ash-heap, but a Ph.D. hired by the state to lecture to freshmen at the University of Montana.

It was, to be sure, a setting no more remote and improbable than the land of Uz—another Edom, in fact. Moreover, the spiritual descendants of Job's scandalized "comforters" had gathered together to confront me. Indeed, as soon as the word went out that I, a Jew from the urban East (which is to say, a "communist" and "atheist" until proved otherwise), was going to expound the Scriptures to good Christian children, fundamentalist preachers came from far and near to monitor what I said.

To make matters worse, the course in which I was lecturing was called "Introduction to the Humanities," suggesting to them that what I was about to teach was "humanism," "secular humanism": dread words even then to those who had not yet begun to speak of themselves as the "moral majority." That I considered myself not a skeptical secularist but a Hebrew of the Hebrews, an apostle to the Gentiles, mattered to them not at all. In any case, I was the enemy, to be watched as warily as I in turn watched them, sitting side by side at the very back of the auditorium, where they scribbled notes on my "blasphemies" that they then duly transmitted to the chairman of my department and the president of the university.

What offended them from the start, confirming their worst suspicions, was my insistence that my Job, *our* Job, was not "patient" at all, though in *their* tradition he had become a proverbial example of that presumably Christian virtue. In the main body of the dialogue, I contended, he refused to submit in silence to the will of God, but instead impatiently challenged Him in ever-increasing rage. But, I assured my listeners, this ongoing quarrel with their Maker whenever He seemed to infringe the law He had given to His people is an essentially Jewish tradition. So the prophets and the psalmist cry out in indignation because the race is not to the swift or the contest to the strong, and ask angrily why the wicked prosper. So, too, we are told, Abraham risked divine wrath by protesting against the destruction of Sodom, and Jonah sulked and grumbled at the last-minute salvation of Nineveh.

Equally "Jewish," I further argued (not troubling to make clear that this was only true in prerabbinical times), is Job's rejection of the doctrines of the resurrection of the body and the immortality of the soul, his insistence that when we die, as we all must, we die forever, and that therefore justice must be done us, if God is just, here and now. Or perhaps, I went on to speculate, what the redactors of the Old Testament and especially the author of Job meant to suggest is that we must act *as if* there were no life after death, so that our righteous demand for justice in this world not be undercut by the (perhaps delusive) hope that in the next the wicked will be punished and the virtuous be rewarded. In any case, I concluded—even more offensively, I guess—that Job could in no sense be considered, as the fathers of their faith had argued, a prototype of Jesus, who had gone without a mumbling word of protest to the sacrificial death decreed for him by his "Father in heaven."

Paradoxically enough, however, I reminded the goyim before me, Job had been a goy like them, apparently quite unaware of God's Covenant with Abraham or the giving of the law to Moses on Mount Sinai. Certainly neither he nor his "comforters," whose very names, except for that of Elihu, indicate that they are Idumeans, Edomites, betray any knowledge of the special laws and rituals which separate YHVH's Chosen People from the Gentiles. Even in his "negative confession" in chapter 31, Job declares himself guiltless only of those "sins" forbidden in the Noachite Code, injunctions, the rabbis believed, known to all men without special revelation. Moreover, throughout the poetic center of the book, the four-letter Hebrew cult name for the Lord is avoided in favor of nonspecific designations like "Shaddai," "El," "Eloah," and "Elohim."

Jesus, on the other hand, was, as Job presumably was *not,* circumcised on the eighth day and, though finally found heretical by the high priest, seems always to have thought of himself as a Jew, promising his followers that not one *yod* or tittle of the law would pass away. Nonetheless, in the prologue, God Himself, called at that point YHVH, disconcertingly describes Job as "perfect," and in the epilogue, again in that Name, declares the rightness of all he has said. Yet, despite this, both Orthodox Jews and Christians have accepted the Book of Job as canonical. But why, I asked, *why?;* and none of the watchdog clerics answered. Indeed, none of them ever rose to challenge me face to face, unwilling to re-enact their archetypal roles in the mythological script I felt myself to be re-enacting.

Maybe it was because they felt embarrassed by my show of scholarship. During the years between the war's ending and my return to teaching, I had (fumbling tentatively back toward the faith of my ancestors) studied Hebrew at the Harvard Divinity School. There I had learned enough of the holy tongue to plod through the simple prose of the frame story of Job, and in a class on "Exegesis of the Prophets," taught by Robert Pfeiffer, I had acquired some of the jargon and simpler techniques of the "higher criticism"—enough, apparently, to cow into silence the fundamentalist clergy of Missoula, Montana. Or perhaps they were only bored when I began—more than a little pretentiously, I fear—to throw about words like "hapalogomena" and "theodicy." In any case, as I abandoned the open language of myth for the hermetic abstractions of the academy, they drifted away one by one.

Finally I was left alone with my students, who of course did not argue back, either. They were too busy taking notes in preparation for the upcoming midterm examination really to listen as I attempted to "justify God's ways to man," or, rather, to present what I took to be the Job poet's attempt. For the atheist, I explained, the presence of gratuitous human suffering in a world produced by blind chance and mindless evolution is no problem at all. Nor did it seem one to the ancient Greeks, who thought of men as the playthings of amoral immortals, often at odds with one another, and always at the mercy of fate. Still less were the Manichees troubled, since they believed the universe to be ruled by two eternally contending principles of light and dark.

As for the Hindus, I went on remorselessly, they were able—believing as they did in reincarnation—to explain the suffering of any individual, however blameless, in terms of "bad karma" inherited from moral failures in an earlier existence. A similar way out was available to orthodox Christians, who had somehow managed to derive from the myth of the Temptation in the Garden the doctrine of "original sin": the notion that "in Adam's Fall we sinned all," and that therefore we all of us, guilty from birth, deserve whatever calamaties befall us. Unless, to be sure, by believing in Jesus as the Christ, we are saved. That even such true believers (indeed, Christ himself) are sometimes martyred for that belief, the fathers of the Church could scarcely deny. But there was always the fallback doctrine that amends would be made after death: transient earthly suffering rewarded with eternal heavenly bliss.

But this cop-out of "pie in the sky," I insisted (trying to use the dialect of my auditors, as I noticed some of them beginning to nod and doze), was scorned by the author of Job, who was convinced that "as the cloud is consumed and vanisheth away; so he that goeth down to the grave shall come up no more." Consequently, his protagonist demands of his God—whom, enlightened pagan that he is, he believes to be One, omniscient, omnipotent, and above all just—justice *here and now*. It never occurs to him, moreover, that evil might be, as later philosophers argued, the mere absence of good, much less illusory, unreal. One can imagine the incredulity with which he would have greeted Socrates' assertion that in some sense, the highest sense perhaps, "No harm can befall a good man, living or dead." Job knows he is a good man and that the suffering inflicted on him is temporally and *sub specie aeternitatis* real; and he asks, hoping for no other recompense, to be told why.

He therefore requires of his God, whom he desperately hopes is *answerable,* the answer that mere men cannot give; certainly not the sages who seek to alleviate his discomfiture with bland platitudes to which that very discomfiture gives the lie. Nor will he be silenced when that God—improbably, unexpectedly—appears to him, speaking out of the whirlwind. We seem to tremble for a moment on the verge of his desired Happy Ending, the resolution of the problem of unmerited suffering. But (in another typically ironic turn of the screw) what the answerable God answers in wrath and exasperation is that there is no answer—at least none understandable to a mere human, who does not even understand the monstrous in the created world. Yet this anticlimatic nonanswer Job seems to find satisfactory, subsiding, at any rate, into silence more like one who is truly satisfied than one who is merely cowed or subdued, as I had believed when I was very young.

Certainly this must be the meaning of Job's final explanation for his capitulation: "I have read of thee by the hearing of the ear; but now my eye seeth thee; / Wherefore I abhor myself and repent in dust and ashes." Understanding these verses, we understand that Job was given not less but more than he had asked for, more than he had known how to ask for. He sought only to be enlightened in his own grieving heart and to be justified in the sight of his fellows, to understand and to be understood. He was granted instead a moment of mystical transport, a glimpse of the divine essence. In that dazzling moment, it is suggested that precisely for this reason the *tam,* the perfect, are chosen for egregious and gratuitous suffering, which alone can deliver them from the pious lies with which the orthodox seek to euphemize the mystery of evil and God's terror at its heart—thus enabling them to see Him face to face.

This, back then in Missoula, I took to be the final solution to the problem of the theodicy offered by the Book of Job. In fact, even now, as I approach three score and ten, I consider it still to be crucial to an understanding of that enigmatic work. I have come to realize, however, that it is a partial reading only which, by concentrating on the framed poetic dialogue, ignores the two framing mysteries of prologue and epilogue that qualify such a solution: the mystery of the wager and the mystery of restoration. It seems to me now, indeed, that the dialogue, though (or because) its participants are portrayed as ignorant of the wager throughout, represents an attempt to translate the mystery it embodies in *haggadic* form into abstract terms more congenial to its latter-day theologian-poet. But, like all such attempts at translating multivalent mythos into univocal *logos,* this attempt turns out to be not merely reductive but sufficient only unto its own day. Later abstract thinkers have, therefore, felt compelled to *re*translate it again and again into the theological or scholarly jargons fashionable in their own time.

God knows there have been many of them, Jewish, Christian, Humanist, Positivist, Existentialist: ranging from Moses and Maimonides to Martin Buber, from Gregory the Great and Calvin to Kierkegaard and Reinhold Niebuhr, from Thomas Hobbes and Immanuel Kant to Josiah Royce and Paul Weiss. However dialectically subtle, their interpretations twice removed, reductions of reductions, are lacking in archetypal resonance. Whatever light they cast on their own authors and their era, I find them consequently not very helpful in coming to terms with the work they pretend to explicate, much less to the triune mystery at its core. Still less helpful are the scholarly commentaries, recent and contemporary, through which I have felt compelled to slog my weary way in preparation for writing this, my last word on Job. Though they solve certain lexical and textual problems in the dialogue, suggesting meanings for rare and difficult words, and reordering rationally such obviously garbled and lacuna-ridden passages as chapters 24 to 27, they do little to illuminate the tantalizingly ambiguous frame. Nor should they, since its ambiguity is not accidental but essential.

More useful in this regard—since they preserve that ambiguity—are the more properly *haggadic* interpolations into and extensions of the ancient folk tale, of which there are also, thank God, numerous examples. As is characteristic of all truly archetypal narrative, the core Job-fable has survived, for simpler readers at least, outside the interpretive contexts in which the redactor of the Book of Job and his successors have tried to enclose it. Indeed, it has, as it were, insisted on being told and retold *as a story,* ever growing and changing—or, rather, seeking to complete itself, to find its entelechy, its final form. Such accretions and transformations began as early as the Testament of Job, and the not-very-faithful "translation" of the Septuagint; continuing on in Muslim holy texts, the rabbinical midrashim and the interpretive parables of the Zohar. Closer to our own time, the body of Judaic legend spawned by the archetypal substrate of Job has been gathered together for readers of English by Louis Ginzberg, and richly reimagined in *Messengers of God,* that midrash of midrashim, composed by the Nobel laureate Elie Wiesel as he meditated on the Holocaust.

Nor has it been absent from the secular literature of the goyish West. Both its form (he considered it the prototype for the Brief Epic or Epyllion) and its content profoundly influenced John Milton's *Paradise Regained;* and Goethe palpably adapted its *mythos* in the "Prologue in Heaven" of *Faust.* In our own century, it has been retold in an updated version in H. G. Wells' novel *The Undying Fire;* and Robert Frost has recast it, with oddly feminist overtones, in his poem "A Masque of Reason." It was, moreover, turned into a strange little playlet by Thornton Wilder, called *Hast Thou Considered My Servant, Job*; and in 1955, Archibald MacLeish's verse drama, *J.B.,* starring Christopher Plummer and Raymond Massey and directed by Elia Kazan, became a smash hit on Broadway.

In the process, the Book of Job itself has come to be regarded by many not as "scripture" but as "poetry"; in the words of Tennyson, "the greatest poem of ancient and modern times"; which is to say, no longer a work to be read as a guide to wisdom and salvation but one to be preserved in libraries and taught in classes in "literature." Rereading it, therefore, we find it harder and harder these days to hear in our inner ear the storyteller's voice, spinning a tale never heard for the first time or the last, always different though always the same: "A man there was in the land of Uz, his name Job. . . ." Yet even the most secular versions send us back, at least, from the analytic dialogue to the oneiric frame, which signifies as dreams do: its images overdetermined, polysemous, finally inexhaustible. Most useful in this regard are the midrashim, for whose inventors "literature" had not yet been separated from "scripture."

Primarily through them, in any case, I have been led back to the prologue and epilogue I had so long ignored; though, to be sure, much that troubled the rabbis who created them does not much interest me. Some of them sought, for instance, in their addenda to resolve ambiguities in the original fable about whether Job was a Jew or a Gentile, and whether in either case he was circumcised—born without a foreskin, perhaps, as befits one called *tam*. Others tried to make clear his marital status, some insisting that he had had one wife, some two, and in neither case naming those spouses. I am, however, convinced that he was an uncircumcised goy, and remain indifferent to whether he begot his second family on the woman who bore his first or on someone else. Yet I must confess that I am a little intrigued by the notion that, after the death of his first wife, he married Dinah, the daughter of Jacob who was terribly raped and revenged; so that quite properly, if rather ironically, he could on his deathbed warn the children she had borne him against intermarrying with Gentiles. I could not care less, moreover, whether, after his death, he, who denied the immortality of the soul, was granted a share in the life to come, as some rabbis insisted he was *not*.

What chiefly interests me are the attempts of the rabbis to suggest, by filling in lacunae in the original tale, reasons why blameless Job of all men had been Chosen by the Adversary to suffer, and especially why God had assented. In several often-repeated midrashim, he is portrayed as having been, before the time of his testing, a counselor to the Pharaoh of the Exodus story. Consulted, along with those other Gentile prophets Balaam and Jethro, as to whether the midwives of Egypt should be ordered to kill the newborn sons of the Jews, he refused to answer or equivocate. Therefore, unlike Balaam, who strongly urged their slaying and is damned, or Jethro, who argued against it and is blessed (becoming, indeed, grandfather to the children of Moses), Job is destined to endure both good and evil, turn and turnabout. Other traditional Jewish tales, however, portray him not as a moral equivocator but as a guiltless scapegoat whom God offered up to Satan in order to distract him from inflicting harm on his own Chosen People, less innocent than he. So, for instance, we are told, God used him to save Abraham, whom the Adversary had rightly accused of infringing the law by substituting one sacrifice for another on the altar; or else to preserve from drowning the children of Israel, whom, at the moment of their crossing the Red Sea, the Enemy of Mankind charged (once more justly) with having bowed down to strange gods in Mizraim.

Other midrashim sought to explain, not so much God's apparent complicity in Job's unmerited tribulations, as Satan's having chosen him in the first place. Job had, such stories inform us, in his time of prosperity, desecrated a shrine set up in Satan's honor; thus demonstrating (at least so the Zohar interprets it) an unwillingness to pay proper respect to "the Other Side," which, the writers of that mystic book insist, the Torah itself enjoins. What else does the Holy Text mean, they argue, by urging us to worship "with all our hearts," except that we must serve him also with the *yetzer-ha-ra,* the Evil Impulse as well as the Good? And the "Evil Impulse" is, they further teach, another name for Satan.

Nor is their subtle and disturbing charge against Job without foundation. Neither in the fabulous frame story nor in the enclosed poetic theodicy of the Book of Job does its protagonist ever allude to Satan by any of his names, as if he were not merely unwilling to give the devil his due, but could not even conceive of his existence. When his multiple calamities befall him, Job does not attribute them to the natural catastrophes or human enemies whom the narrative tells us are their proximate cause; but still less does he fix responsibility for them on a supernatural Adversary. For him God is the sole author of all that befalls humankind, evil as well as good.

Nor does anything in the text call this assumption into question. Indeed, God Himself, in His final appearance, seems to verify it: confessing nothing about the wager in heaven and saying nothing to imply the existence of its instigator. But why? Is He who speaks out of the whirlwind (as a few embittered modern commentators have dared to suggest) ashamed to admit to the frail human being who has successfully passed His terrible test that He Himself has failed an earlier one? Or is He thus revealed as a hoakster, a cheat, in this black comedy's last and blackest joke? Before answering, we should pause long enough to note that the narrator, too, is silent at this point about Satan, who does not even appear to be discomfited and cast out—as we might well expect in approaching the tale's happy ending.

It is as if (or at least so I read the encrypted text, paying attention to its silences as well as its statements) what it suggests is that Satan finally does not exist except as a metaphor for what can be understood once God is fully revealed as an aspect, a projection, an emotion of the One who alone really is forever. All the more is this true of those surrogates for Satan, Job's wife and the egregious Elihu, who at this point also disappear from the book;

having been, like the *yetzer-ha-ra* itself, assumed into the Divine Unity. But at this YHVH has already hinted in his parabolic speech about the Behemoth and the leviathan. "These things of Darkness," he has declared in effect, "I acknowledge mine."

Surely here is the final clue to the meaning of the mystery of the wager with the Adversary, to whom we were first introduced standing at ease with his fellow *b'nai elohim* before the heavenly throne. It is with Himself that God is betting: with His own "Other Side," from which He cannot otherwise exorcise the suspicion that no man, not even Job, His "perfect" servant, does good "for nothing." It is this nagging doubt which entices Him into making the cruel test whose outcome, we tell ourselves, He surely knows from the start. But, then, like Him perhaps, we remember how Adam, similarly tempted, fell. Certainly, ever since that mythological event—which is to say, since mankind first knew good from evil—we have been haunted by doubts about our own virtue, which we project in fear and trembling upon our Maker.

After all, Job is a work written by man and not God, as even the rabbis taught, attributing its composition to Moses, but insisting that, unlike the Pentateuch, it was not the product of divine inspiration. Moreover, one or two of them also insisted, it was to be read as a *mashal*—a myth or parable rather than history; and read, so it seems to me, as a revelation, psychological rather than theological, that we *want* to be thus tempted by God, *want* the doubt about ourselves which we attribute to Him to be resolved in our favor. Only after this, in the wish-dream which constitutes the true heart of Job, comes the long-awaited happy ending. At this point, however, we pass from the mystery of evil to the even greater mystery of restoration, which, I must confess, I have as yet barely begun to understand. I suspect, indeed, that I never shall, unless, like Job (but God forbid that I pay the price), I am granted a double three score years and ten in addition to those I have already lived. Until then, therefore, I am moved, like him, "to lay my hand upon my mouth" and to repeat his penultimate vow of silence, which finally, to be sure, he did not keep: "Once have I spoken . . . yea, twice; but I will proceed no further."

THE SONG OF SONGS

LOVE IS STRONG AS DEATH

Grace Schulman

I
N A MAGNIFICENT PASSAGE, "MY BELOVED SPAKE" (2:10–16), A WOMAN,
who is the dominant character in the Song of Solomon (so-called in
the King James or Authorized Version), recounts her lover's rousing
words: "Rise up, my love, my fair one, and come away." The six
verses, taken as a unit, are characteristic of the Song as a whole, which is
concerned with a man and a woman who, with heightened sensations of
sight and smell, taste and touch, celebrate each other's beauty just as they
praise the hills and animals, the trees and flowers of Israel in spring.

The section prefigures the Old French *reverdie,* a poem that glorifies
new love and the green earth. Here the device of parallelism strengthens the
amorous plea, as in the lines

The flowers appear on the earth; the time of the singing of birds is
come, and the voice of the turtle is heard in our land.   [2:12]

The King James Version of the Bible used in this essay.

in which a series of phrases with like images amplify spring's return, the last illustration locating the subdued birdsong in the country of the man and the woman, emphasizing the growing relationship between them and the landscape.

The passage ends with a refrain, or "distant" repetition, "My beloved is mine, and I am his: he feedeth among the lilies," a verse that introduces a shift in tone and imagery, in the time of day, and in the emotion. Throughout the Song, lines that recur with variations set off such changes.

"My beloved spake" and the Song as a whole tell of awakening to a rising green world in its fullness, with renewed hope. The tactile yet transient figures of birds, vines, figs, and lilies, and the repeated verb forms in the present tense, call forth a creation story, a genesis, a tale of new beginnings. Often the imagery is unmistakably sexual, with emphasis on smell and taste ("Let my beloved come into the garden, and eat his pleasant fruits" [4:16]; "thy breasts shall be as clusters of the vine" [7:8]; "let us see if the vine flourish, whether the tender grape appear" [7:12]). The physical imagery, though, however graphic, is rendered generative by a vulnerable, even animallike, manner of discovery. The earth is burgeoning; people and animals are coming into themselves and into one another's love.

At the same time, the book is built on an alternating pattern of ecstasy in daylight scenes and loss at night. "My beloved spake" immediately precedes one of the dark passages, in which the joyful address, early in the poem, "O thou whom my soul loveth" (1:7), is repeated and varied as "I sought him whom my soul loveth: I sought him, but found him not" (3:1). Strengthening the repetitive wish for love that is genuine, but that may be transitory, are the strategic refrains or distant repetitions ("Rise up, my love, my fair one," "Arise my love, my fair one" [2:10, 13]); the epanaleptic repetitions, in which words are taken up again after intervening words ("let me see thy countenance, let me hear thy voice; for sweet is thy voice, and thy countenance is comely"), and the acervate clusters of detail that focus attention on the characters' longing.

Passion and danger are the terrifying polarities of the Song. Passages such as "My beloved spake" are balanced by verses that intimate devastation, as one that recurs, with variations:

> Who is she that looketh forth as the morning, fair as the moon,
> clear as the sun, and terrible as an army with banners?   [6:10]

and death:

> Set me as a seal upon thine heart, as a seal upon thine arm: for love is strong as death;
> jealousy is cruel as the grave: the coals thereof are coals of fire, which hath a most
> vehement flame.   [8:6, 7]

In the first of those verses, the final phrase comes as a surprise, the woman's power changing to destruction in the eyes of the man, who utters the lines. In the second verse, also spoken by the man, the parallel phrases are doubled: assertions and amplifications are qualified, each term having two parts, resulting in lines that are crowded with strong images.

Although passion is fierce, love is strong as death and will triumph despite fears, ambivalence, and life's decay. Love, tenacious as death, conquers the inevitable; passion, harsh as death, simultaneously terrifies and endures. Seemingly opposed, love and death have, in fact, one name. Although the Song's characters salute life and love, the work does not iterate life's mutability. Those grim lines, at the climax of the poem, convey the startling truth that love is only apparently transient, but actually eternal.

One of the shortest books in the Bible, second only to the Book of Ruth in its brevity, the Song has inspired libraries of comment. For centuries scholars have debated the date of composition, which ranges from Solomonic times to the fifth century B.C.E.,[1] the allegorical interpretations, the question of plot, and other considerations. The Hebrew title, שיר השירים אשר לשלמה, translated as "The Song of Songs, which is Solomon's," is a superlative, as in "king of kings" or "vanity of vanities." The book is also called Canticles, which comes from the Latin Vulgate rendering of Canticum Canticorum.

Erotic as it is, the Song is the first of the Five *Megillot,* or Scrolls, preceding Ruth, Lamentations, Ecclesiastes, and Esther, and is read on the eighth day of Passover. Although the book has no explicit mention of God, and has neither overt theological doctrine nor apparent national theme, it was taken into the canon largely because of its allegorical interpretation, that of the lover-bridegroom as God, and the Shulamite-bride as Israel. This level of meaning, which is accepted even today by many serious readers, was defended near the close of the first century C.E. by Rabbi Akiba, who cursed anyone taking the words literally, but who, on the other hand, called the Song of Songs the "Holy of Holies."[2] Just why he did so is uncertain: he may have been referring to the Song's mystical connotations, or to his conviction that marital love was sacred because it awakened a more profound love of God. His phrase seems ironic now, for it echoes the superscripture, and presents as religious the love songs that scholars, centuries later, have deemed profane. Still, the Synagogue received the Song of Songs early, if not without debate. The Christian Church accepted the allegorical interpretation as well, understanding the symbolic meaning to be Christ and his Church.

Marvin H. Pope's intriguing conviction is that the origins of the Song are in the sacred sexual rites of ancient Near Eastern fertility cults, which celebrated, often with eating, drinking, and copulation, the life in death and the continuity of life.[3] He refers often to the Tammuz cult, or, in Babylonian religion, the worship of a young god loved by the moon goddess, Ishtar, who kills him but restores him to life. His festival, commemorating the annual death and rebirth of vegetation, corresponds to that of Adonis. This cultic view, likening the woman to Ishtar, Aphrodite, and Anat, does clarify her role in the Song as the initiator, whose viewpoint, even when distorted by pain or by passion, compels us to see things as she does.

In literary terms, the Song is not, strictly speaking, allegory, since the other *(allos)* meaning is not implicit in the text, and because there are multiple levels of meaning. Allegory, as distinguished from ambiguity, is a structural principle and depends upon a continuous use of imagery that refers to a set of ideas.

The question is important here because it governs language. The woman declares, for example, that her love "shall lie all night betwixt my breasts" (1:13). There, allegorical and eclectic readings might be at variance if, as we learn in Midrash Rabbah, the image refers to Abraham's head clasped between the Divine Presence and the angel, or, as in the work of an early Christian expositor, the image presents a man's head enclosed by the Hebrew Bible and the Gospels. On the other hand, words such as "garden," "vines," "tender grape," "myrrh," "rising," "navel" bear religious and sexual connotations, in addition to their denotative meanings as natural objects. The difference between the two kinds of images is, in fact, one small fissure in the vast chasm between allegory and ambiguity.

Nor do I mean to dismiss an allegorical purpose in a work that has carried varied readings so gracefully. New interpretations have increased the fascination of a book whose prevailing tone is wonder: the lovers marvel at the intensity of their passion and at the splendor of the natural world. As though in sympathy with their mystification, scholars and critics have questioned incessantly the origin of the book, the identity of the characters, and the unity.

The theories range from the Song as a protest against the urban life of the early Israelites to a text for modern psychological dream-interpretation. Although some readings seem irrelevant to the Song's aesthetic impact, a few are worth noting. To begin with irrelevance, a theory involving a coherent plot, with a shepherd and a royal bridegroom competing for the bride, has been discarded, by and large, because there is no allusion to rivalry in the text, and because there is no structural progression that would support that reading. Although Solomon is named in the title, it is unlikely that he wrote the book, and he is not an active character in it. Instead, the references to him are probably invocations of a royal ideal of beauty.

The "wedding-week theory," proposed in the last century by J. G. Wetstein with respect to Syrian villagers and by von Kremer regarding Lebanese people, holds that the Song rests on ancient Syrian-Palestinian marriage customs. Although the proposals have been disputed, because those traditions were not found to exist earlier than the nineteenth century and because parts of the Song, notably the reverie chants (three and five), are hardly wedding pieces, the notion does bear on the Song's style. One custom is that the bride, on her wedding eve, performs a sword dance, which would be a likely accompaniment for chant seven ("How beautiful are thy feet"). The book's royal imagery suggests the nineteenth-century—but not earlier, apparently—practice in which the couple, during the wedding week, are celebrated as "king" and "queen," with village maidens attending the bride, and townspeople forming a regal procession singing praises to the physical radiance of the bridal pair.

The concept of recent decades is that these are secular verses, concerned only with human love. Although that perception ensures a compelling reading, it does not account for the godlike stature of the man ("his countenance is as Lebanon, excellent as the cedars" [5:15]), or the goddess quality of the woman ("I am the rose of Sharon" [2:1]), or the woman's unquestioning generosity with regard to others who worship her man ("therefore do the virgins love thee" [1:3]); nor does it explain the religious meaning it has had for early and modern readers. In reading the Song as literature, I regard the allegorical and cultic elements as allusions that expand or enlarge the central human characters, radiating out from them. When the woman, in chant one, speaks of her lover as "the king," she praises a man with allusive shadows of Solomon, YHWH, Christ, the Syrian bridegroom, Tammuz, Adonis, Baal. When the man sings, "Thou art all fair, my love" (4:7), he worships a lady with qualities, real or imagined, that are allusions to those of Ishtar, the Shekinah, Mary, Aphrodite, Anat, Astarte, and, of course, the people of Israel. The reading I find most relevant to the poem's great achievement is that the mythological and religious figures heighten, rather than become, the central characters.

The man, primarily, sings in fantastic images that objectify his happiness and veiled fear ("Thy neck is as a tower of ivory" [7:4]; "Thy neck is like the tower of David" [4:4]). The luminous, hyperbolic images are reminiscent of conceits bearing antithetical elements, which are common in love poetry and in devotional verse, as in, for example, "A Description" by Lord Herbert of Cherbury, in which the lover compares his lady's neck to an atlas; or in "The Odour" by George Herbert, in which the speaker perceives the divine voice as a fragrance.

In the Song, though, the outlandish images are equivalents for inner perceptions of what is the purest, the strangest, the most glorious. I am reminded of the Gedullat Mosheh, a small midrash devoted entirely to Moses' journey to heaven. In it he sees streams of water, celestial windows marked "war" and "peace," angels with seventy thousand heads, and seraphim with calves' feet. In the highest heaven, Moses finds two angels, each five hundred parasangs tall (one parasang equals three miles) and forged out of chains of black fire and red fire.[4] The outsize images have affinities, also, to those in the *Hekhaloth* books that cover a period of one thousand years, from the first century B.C.E. to the tenth C.E.[5] Vividly recorded there are journeys of *Merkabah* mystics, a group that included the Song's early defender, Rabbi Akiba (Akiba ben Joseph).

The mystic attained, through fasting and prayer, a condition of self-oblivion. Then, actually seated, head between knees, but inwardly ascending to the palaces in the highest of seven heavens, he had to fend off hostile demons opposed to the soul's liberation. The journey was splendid in its promise of perfection, frightening in its dangers, and terrifying in the underlying knowledge that the traveler must fall to earth. Such are the heights and falls of the Song.

Another kind of imagery in the poem is based on the form of the Arabic *wasf,* a descriptive song in praise of the beloved. Usually the poem has an affirmative introduction, as in the *wasf* of chant four ("Behold, thou art fair, my love"); comparisons, as in the anaphoral lines that follow ("Thy teeth are like. . . . Thy lips are like. . . . Thy neck is like . . ."); and clusters of detail that control passion by objectifying it. The maiden's sword dance in chant seven is performed to a *wasf* that is sung by the man.

Although the *wasf* is very old, it has survived to our day. I think of a *wasf* in a recent anthology called *Modern Poetry of the Arab World,* translated by Abdullah al-Udhari. The poem "Rain Song" by Badr Shakir Al Sayyab (1926–64) opens:

> Your eyes are palm groves refreshed by dawn's breath
> Or terraces the moon leaves behind.
> When your eyes smile the vines flower
> And the lights dance
> Like the moon's reflection on a river
> Gently sculled at the crack of dawn
> Like stars pulsating in the depth of your eyes
> That sink in mists of grief like the sea
> Touched by the evening's hands. . . .[6]

Modern Israeli love songs, on the other hand, often incorporate present-day displacements of tradition, making ironic use of the Song. In Yehuda Amichai's poem "Love's Gifts," the lover declares:

> I comforted you with apples, as it says
> in the Song of Songs,
> I lined your bed with them,
> so we could roll smoothly on red apple-bearings.[7]

The Song's unity is a major achievement in itself. It is the structure that reveals larger concerns, such as the gift of consciousness, the power of love, and the complexities of joy. In fact, for those who believe it is a collection of popular ditties, it is necessary to add that the unknown scribes who arranged the songs were actually editors with a redactorial genius that is rare, and even unwanted, in times of evident authorship. By studying it, verse by verse, line by line, the reader can find its symmetry, unity and scope.

The Song is a great love poem, an extended lyric whose structure is determined by musical amplifications and variations. Its chapters, sequences of verses, are actually "chants" or rhythmic divisions. The poem modulates from theme to theme, one image suggesting another, which in turn leads to a new statement.

The structure is also psychological and is built on the emotional progress of the two characters. The joyful scenes, like the call to spring in chant two, are set in daylight, with vivid colors (green figs [2:13], the chariot's purple cover [3:10], the scarlet thread [4:3], ivory belly [5:14], pomegranates throughout). The sorrowful sections are set in twilight states and are in the diction and imagery of reverie, as in chants three ("By night on my bed") and five ("I sleep, but my heart waketh"). They are characterized by distorted dreamlike imagery, and by sudden, surprising leaps in tone that are associational rather than logical. Between those opposite states are happy daydreams, again marked by brightly colored images, such as the scenes that open chants two and eight, and contain the recurrent lines "His left hand is under my head," "His left hand should be under my head" (2:6, 8:3).

The poem is profoundly concerned with consciousness, and the psychological progression includes a movement from awareness to daydream to reverie, to awareness to deeper reverie, to awareness to daydream, and back to full consciousness. Waking is central to the action: the lovers call each other to "Arise!" and to "Awake!" In a blissful scene, when the senses are acute, the woman alludes to wine "causing the lips of those that are asleep to speak" (7:9). And in the recurrent lines "I charge you, O ye daughters . . . that ye stir not up," she warns Jerusalem girls not to rouse love until it comes of its own accord. (Although some translators interpret the phrase as "my love," it is more likely that the word *ahabah,* used without the article in 2:7, 3:10, 5:8, 7:7, 8:6, and with the article, *ha'ahabah,* in 3:5, 8:4, 17, means "love" itself.)

The poem is unified further in that changes in awareness are the very shifts set off by refrains, or distant repetitions, spaced widely over the eight chants. Usually those recurrent lines vary in one or more words, altering the meaning slightly, and assisting the emotional or narrative progress. They have effects similar to incremental repetition in stanzaic verse, a device found as early as in ancient Chinese poetry. One of the Song's distant repetitions is "My beloved is mine, and I am his," "I am my beloved's, and my beloved is mine," "I am my beloved's, and his desire is toward me" (2:16, 6:3, 7:10), all spoken by the woman. The first, ending the passage "My beloved spake," indicates a change from daylight and rapture to night and loss; the second sets off the transition from a man who is absent to a man who returns but is apprehensive ("Thou art beautiful . . . comely . . . terrible as an army with banners"), and the third precedes his peaceful resolution ("Come, my beloved, let us go forth into the field"). Another of the distant repetitions is "My beloved is like a roe or a young hart," "Be thou like to a roe or a young hart upon the mountains of Bether," "Be thou like to a roe or a young hart upon the mountains of spices" (2:9, 17; 8:14). First the image appears as an inquisitive animal; next it calls forth a rapid shift to night in lines that introduce the first reverie, with its pain of loss; in the third instance it closes the book.

Also patterning the long poem is the device of repetitive parallelism, or the use of lines that recur without intervening text. Some verses are both repetitive parallels and distant repetitions, such as "Behold thou art fair" (1:15, 16; 4:1, 7). The first of these verses leads into the woman's daydream in chant two; the second introduces the man's disquieted courtship; the third ushers in his call to flee to the mountains.

Another unifying principle is the depiction of one leading character throughout. It seems remarkable, too, that an active woman is the chief suitor of this ancient love song. Her yearning is the most poignant. She calls, beckons, cajoles, pursues. The Song opens and closes with expressions of her desire: "Let him kiss me with the kisses of his mouth," and "Make haste, my beloved." (Incidentally, the enallage, or shift in persons, in 1:2 makes her love appear godlike, at least to the woman; actually, though, the usage occurs frequently in Biblical verse.) Boldly she expresses her longing: "Comfort me with apples: for I am sick of love" (2:5; or, I faint for love), she exclaims. Proudly she declares: "I am a wall and my breasts are towers"

(8:10); "I am black, but comely" (1:5); "I am the rose of Sharon, and the lily of the valleys" (2:1), a verse whose erotic implications are amplified by the recurrent image of lilies among which her lover feeds. She courts the man: "Let my beloved come into his garden, and eat his pleasant fruits." In the night reverie chants she leaves her bed to find him (chant three), then leaves her bed to find him gone (chant five).

Complementing her development in the poem is the progress of the man, who, in contrast, is acted upon. Although both declare their longing, she is the braver, he the more timidly withdrawn. He is baffled by his own response to her beauty, complaining, "Thou hast ravished my heart with one of thine eyes" (4:9). He pictures her and their love in images of combat. In chant four, depicting his lady as the ideal beauty, flawless, with perfect teeth and lips, he presents her also in images of defensive weapons at rest: shields, "the tower of David builded for an armoury" (4:4). In his vision, distorted by terror, his beloved is cool, aloof, "a spring shut up." When he disappears, the young women of Jerusalem, who may be bridesmaids according to the "wedding-week" theory or simply companions, join their friend in her quest, asking, "whither is thy beloved turned aside? that we may seek him with thee" (6:1).

Because of her beauty and mastery, the woman evokes curiosity. More details are provided, but they are all the more intriguing for their ambiguity. The woman's assertion "I am black" has prototypes ranging from the black madonnas in churches of Europe to the Indian goddess Kali, whose name means "black" and who is carnal but violent. Robert Graves observes that many statues of virgins in Spain and southern France are black because the Saracen occupation during the Middle Ages taught local Christians to consider blackness wise.[8] I believe these are best regarded as allusions that radiate from the central figures, elevating them and intensifying their plight. In terms of the Song's pattern of imagery, though, the statement distinguishes her as being uncommon, rare, out of the ordinary. On the other hand, her lover is fair and ruddy, with raven-black hair.

Her song, "Look not upon me, because I am black" (1:6), rises and soars, sent aloft by a double parallel structure, the second and third phrases amplifying the first assertion, and the fifth and sixth phrases clarifying the third, "my mother's children." Displeased with her, those children made her "keeper of the vineyards; but mine own vineyard have I not kept."

Throughout the Song, vines, gardens, foliage are sexual, sometimes flagrantly so, and procreative, when preceded by "my" and "her." The woman has been deprived of love ("sick of love"), and, thus far, of the opportunity to continue the life cycle.

The portrait of the woman, which awakens attention from the beginning, acquires depth in chant three, the first of the passages in the mode of psychic experience that involve for the woman and for the reader the whole of the sensibility. Her inner struggle here and in chant five, both set at night, are characterized by the "rhetoric" of consciousness, which is conveyed by sudden leaps in thought, by irony, and by expanded, dreamlike images. Her arousal ("I will rise now" [3:2]) is presented in ironic contrast to the awakening in "My beloved spake" ("Rise up, my love, my fair one, and come away"). In the later episode, the woman, alone in bed, yearns for her love. Her desire is compelling, although it is probably based on fancy, rather than experience, for the law forbade premarital fulfillment.

The woman's lament in chant three, in the diction of reverie, is reinforced by a beautiful repetitive parallel that has a distant repetition as well: "By night on my bed I sought him whom my soul loveth: I sought him, but I found him not," and "in the broad ways I will seek him whom my soul loveth: I sought him, but I found him not," and, recurring in the second night chant, "I sought him, but I could not find him" (3:1, 2; 5:6). The two night pieces enclose the *wasf* of chant four, sung by the man to his distant beauty, and the woman's seductive proposal. The scene moves rapidly from day to night in chant five, as well, and the woman deplores her loss: "I sleep, but my heart waketh" (5:2).

The imagery in both night scenes is extended beyond waking logic, but is precisely in keeping with reverie's exaggerated dimensions: "Who is this that cometh out of the wilderness like pillars of smoke, perfumed with myrrh and frankincense, with all powders of the merchant?" she asks in three (3:6). Describing Solomon's wedding bed, she pictures servants with swords that protect against "fear in the night" or the bad dreams she knows well. To be sure, there are historical theories for this imagery, such as the explanation that the smoke is incense from a wedding cortege that is guarded against bandits. Such reasons, though, fail to account for the vitality of the two scenes built on images that move by association and that present, in their dislocation, the panic of loss.

A deeper level of consciousness distinguishes the diction and imagery of chant five, the second night section. Here the woman, alone, undressed, hears her love knocking at the door, his hair filled with dew. She rises to greet him, her hands wet with myrrh. He is gone. He does not answer her quietly desperate call. She describes her absent love in magnified proportions: "His legs are as pillars of marble, set upon sockets of fine gold: his countenance is as Lebanon, excellent as the cedars." The hyperbole recalls the queen's dream of her lost lover, in Shakespeare's *Antony and Cleopatra*, V, ii:

> His legs bestrid the ocean; his rear'd arm
> Crested the world; his voice was propertied
> As all the tuned spheres. . . .

As in chant three, the action here is symbolic of waking behavior. The woman, who behaves frequently with the audacity of a goddess, is given to moments of reserve, and these occur dramatically in the night scenes. In chant three, she asks the city watchmen for help, then finds her beloved and grasps him firmly, but not without self-reproach. Her recurrent admonishment to the maidens, imploring them to let love follow its own course, is based on her own anguished restraint. In the second night chant, where the imagery is hallucinatory, her wish for discipline is intensified. Unexpectedly for the diction of waking narrative, but appropriately to the rhetoric of consciousness, the watchmen strip her and beat her: "the keepers of the walls took away my vail [sic] from me." She is, in her own estimation, a temple prostitute. The lady's directness, her sexual frankness, call for control: the watchmen are agents of her wish for protection against her own ardor.

The uncommon musical symmetry of this long poem is illustrated by chants six and eight, both composites of images and refrains that acquire momentum from their repetitions throughout the Song, either in repetitive parallels or in distant recurrences. In chant six, set in daylight and sung by the man, the woman, and the Jerusalem girls, we hear again, variously altered, "My beloved is gone down into his garden," "I went down into the garden," "I am my beloved's, and my beloved is mine," "Thy teeth are as a flock of sheep," "Thy hair is as a flock of goats." Again the tremulous man speaks of his love in battle images, varying the "tower of David" imagery of chant three. In lines whose destruction is emphasized by distant repetition, with variation, he asks: "Who is she that looketh forth as the morning, fair as the moon, clear as the sun, and terrible as an army with banners?"

Another sharp turn occurs with the *wasf* in chant seven, sung by the man. Often reserved, he speaks openly of his craving, without fear. He acclaims his lady's navel, comparing it to an empty goblet; her belly, likening it to wheat; and her breasts, associating them with twin roes.

Chant eight, containing the climax of the poem, begins with another of the abrupt changes in tone, this time from ecstasy to withdrawal. The woman, now cautious, wishes her love were a brother, that she might kiss him without being scorned. Just as she shrinks from boldness, the man's fright returns. Here he utters those ringing lines at the Song's climax ("Set me as a seal upon thy heart") and sings out the somber but assuring truth known to the ancients, to the gods, to the religious, and to sculptors of erotic figures on stone sarcophagi: "For love is strong as death; jealousy harsh as the grave." Love, mighty as death, is, therefore, immortal. Following that statement, the image of the little sister embodies the continuity of life and love. Like six, the chant is plangent with refrains that bind the poem together; it ends with the distant repetition that closes chant two.

Although I read the Song as a long poem concerned with human lovers and with allusions to divine and mythological figures, the literal level of this work is iridescent with ambiguity. There is the obvious analogy (not allegory) between the passion of the Song and that of any religious experience of going beyond the self to find God. The resemblance between sexual desire and divine worship is a venerable concept. For example, in Judaism as early as the twelfth century C.E. Maimonides asserted that love of God should be accompanied by constant nervous tremors, such as a man feels when he is lovesick for a woman.[9]

On the other hand, it seems a pity to miss the Song's wider implications by regarding it as being either religious or secular, without entertaining simultaneously sacred and erotic interpretations. I think of a Passover seder guest who was disconcerted by the Haggadah, illustrated by Saul Raskin, with a scroll whose Hebrew letters spelled out the first verses of the Song: "Let him kiss me with the kisses of his mouth. . . ." The page was decorated with tropical flowers, a long-necked doe, and a princess whose eyes were shaped like the animal's fluent head.

I recall, too, a listener who was baffled by Henry Purcell's "My Beloved Spake," a setting of that passage. Sung by an alto, a tenor, and two basses, the polyphonic anthem had varying high and low phrases that reinforced the poem's blend of happiness and pain. The listener objected to the end of the piece, a strong round of "Hallelujahs" which is not in the text and which struck him as an abrupt tonal shift in music and language.

Actually, the Haggadah and the anthem are appropriate, according to traditional views: they are, in the first instance, the Song's prominent inclusion in the *Megillot,* and, in the second, its concern with divinely inspired human love. Apart from that, many deeply religious works are to be read with the whole of our sensibility, including physical love, and great love poems call for a spiritual reading as well. For that matter, whether we adore with our hearts or souls is a matter for endless speculation. We do not know how we cherish, but only *that* we cherish. And the Song, with its great affirmation of love's immortality, is a love poem that calls upon our deepest responses, on every level. The more its authors sing of love, the more they whisper of God.

NOTES

1. The third century B.C.E. is favored by H. L. Ginsberg, "Introduction to The Song of Songs," in *The Five Megillot* (Philadelphia: The Jewish Publication Society, 1969), p. 3. Scholars are still divided, however, on the date of composition. As recently as 1973, Professor Chaim Rabin presented evidence assigning the date to Solomonic times, in "The Song of Songs and Tamil Poetry," *Studies in Religion,* vol. 3, pp. 205–19. Proponents of the later dates often ascribe the "songs," or lyrical passages, to earlier times. A comprehensive discussion of the dating is found in Marvin H. Pope, *Song of Songs: A New Translation with Introduction and Commentary,* The Anchor Bible (Garden City, N.Y.: Doubleday, 1977), pp. 22–34.

2. Tosephta Sanhedrin 12:10, and Yadayim 3:5.

3. Pope, *Song of Songs,* pp. 145–53.

4. The Gedullat Mosheh exists, at this writing, only in an Arabic version. However, a description exists in Louis Ginzberg, *The Legends of the Jews,* trans. Henrietta Szold (Philadelphia: The Jewish Publication Society, 1979), pp. 304–9.

5. Gershom G. Scholem, *Major Trends in Jewish Mysticism* (New York: Schocken, 1941), p. 52. Also pp. 40–79.

6. *Modern Poetry of the Arab World,* trans. Abdullah al-Udhari (New York: Viking Penguin, 1986), p. 29.

7. *The Selected Poetry of Yehuda Amichai,* trans. Stephen Mitchell and Chana Bloch (New York: Harper and Row, 1986), p. 90.

8. Robert Graves, *The Song of Songs: Text and Commentary* (New York: Potter, 1973), p. 15.

9. Maimonides (Moses ben Maimon), *Mishnah Torah, I, The Book of Knowledge,* 10:3, "Laws Concerning Repentance."

RUTH

Cynthia Ozick

*For Muriel Dance, in New York;
Sarah Halevi, in Jerusalem;
and Lee Gleichman, in Stockholm*

I. FLOWERS

HERE WERE ONLY TWO PICTURES ON THE WALLS OF THE HOUSE I grew up in. One was large, and hung from the molding on a golden cord with a full golden tassel. It was a painting taken from a photograph—all dark, a kind of grayish-brown; it was of my grandfather Hirshl, my father's father. My grandfather's coat had big foreign-looking buttons, and he wore a tall, stiff, square *yarmulke* that descended almost to the middle of his forehead. His eyes were severe, pale, concentrated. There was no way to escape those eyes; they came after you wherever you were. I had never known this grandfather: he died in Russia long ago. My father, a taciturn man, spoke of him only once, when I was already grown: as a boy, my father said, he had gone with his father on a teaching expedition to Kiev; he remembered how the mud was deep in the roads. From my mother I learned a little more. Zeyde Hirshl was frail. His wife, Bobe Sore-Libe, was the opposite: quick, energetic, hearty, a skilled *zogerke*—a women's prayer-leader in the synagogue—a whirlwind who

The Jewish Publication Society's translation of the Bible used in this essay.

kept a dry-goods store and had baby after baby, all on her own, while Zeyde Hirshl spent his days in the study house. Sometimes he fainted on his way there. He was pale, he was mild, he was delicate, unworldly; a student, a melamed, a fainter. Why, then, those unforgiving, stern eyes that would not let you go?

My grandfather's portrait had its permanent place over the secondhand piano. To the right, farther down the wall, hung the other picture. It was framed modestly in a thin black wooden rectangle, and was, in those spare days, all I knew of "art." Was it torn from a magazine, cut from a calendar? A barefoot young woman, her hair bound in a kerchief, grasping a sickle, stands alone and erect in a field. Behind her a red sun is half swallowed by the horizon. She wears a loose white peasant's blouse and a long dark skirt, deeply blue; her head and shoulders are isolated against a limitless sky. Her head is held poised: she gazes past my gaze into some infinity of loneliness stiller than the sky.

Below the picture was its title: *The Song of the Lark*. There was no lark. It did not come to me that the young woman, with her lifted face, was straining after the note of a bird who might be in a place invisible to the painter. What I saw and heard was something else: a scene older than this French countryside, a woman lonelier even than the woman alone in the calendar meadow. It was, my mother said, Ruth: Ruth gleaning in the fields of Boaz.

For many years afterward—long after *The Song of the Lark* had disappeared from the living-room wall—I had the idea that this landscape (a 1930s fixture, it emerged, in scores of American households and Sunday-school classrooms) was the work of Jean François Millet, the French painter of farm life. "I try not to have things look as if chance had brought them together," Millet wrote, "but as if they had a necessary bond between them. I want the people I represent to look as if they really belonged to their station, so that imagination cannot conceive of their ever being anything else."

Here is my grandfather. Imagination cannot conceive of his ever being anything else: a melamed who once ventured with his young son (my blue-eyed father) as far as Kiev, but mainly stayed at home in his own town, sometimes fainting on the way to the study house. The study house was his "station." In his portrait he looks as if he really belonged there; and he did. It was how he lived.

And here is Ruth, on the far side of the piano, in Boaz's field, gleaning. Her mouth is remote: it seems somehow damaged; there is a blur behind her eyes. All the sadness of the earth is in her tender neck, all the blur of loss, all the damage of rupture: remote, remote, rent. The child who stands before the woman standing barefoot, sickle forgotten, has fallen through the barrier of an old wooden frame into the picture itself, into the field; into the smell of the field. There is no lark, no birdcall: only the terrible silence of the living room when no one else is there. The grandfather is always there; his eyes keep their vigil. The silence of the field swims up from a time so profoundly lost that it annihilates time. There is the faint weedy smell of thistle: and masses of meadow flowers. In my childhood I recognized violets, lilacs, roses, daisies, dandelions, black-eyed Susans, tiger lilies, pansies (I planted, one summer, a tiny square of pansies, one in each corner, one in the middle), and no more. The lilacs I knew because of the children who brought them to school in springtime: children with German names, Koechling, Behrens, Kuntz.

To annihilate time, to conjure up unfailingly the fragrance in Boaz's field (his field in *The Song of the Lark*), I have the power now to summon what the child peering into the picture could not. "Tolstoy, come to my aid," I could not call then: I had never heard of Tolstoy. My child's Russia was the grandfather's portrait, and stories of fleeing across borders at night, and wolves, and the baba yaga in the fairy tales. But now: "Tolstoy, come to my aid," I can chant at this hour, with my hair turned silver; and lo, the opening of *Hadji Murád* spills out all the flowers in Boaz's field:

It was midsummer, the hay harvest was over and they were just beginning to reap the rye. At that season of the year there is a delightful variety of flowers—red, white, and pink scented tufty clover; milk-white ox-eye daisies with their bright yellow centers and pleasant spicy smell; yellow honey-scented rape blossoms; tall campanulas with white and lilac bells, tulip-shaped; creeping vetch; yellow, red, and pink scabious; faintly scented, neatly arranged purple plantains with blossoms slightly tinged with pink; cornflowers, the newly opened blossoms bright blue in the sunshine but growing paler and redder towards evening or when growing old; and delicate almond-scented dodder flowers that withered quickly.

Dodder? Vetch? (Flash of Henry James's Fleda Vetch.) Scabious? Rape and campanula? The names are unaccustomed; my grandfather in the study house never sees the flowers. In the text itself—in the Book of Ruth—not a single flower is mentioned. And the harvest is neither hay nor rye; in Boaz's field outside Bethlehem they are cutting down barley and wheat. The flowers are there all the same, even if the text doesn't show them, and we are obliged to take in their scents, the weaker with the keener, the grassier with the meatier: without the smell of flowers, we cannot pass through the frame of history into that long ago, ancientness behind ancientness, when Ruth the Moabite gleaned. It is as if the little spurts and shoots of fragrance form a rod, a rail of light, along which we are carried, drifting, into that time before time "when the judges ruled."

Two pictures, divided by an old piano—Ruth in *The Song of the Lark,* my grandfather in his *yarmulke.* He looks straight out; so does she. They sight each other across the breadth of the wall. I stare at both of them. Eventually I will learn that *The Song of the Lark* was not painted by Millet, not at all; the painter is Jules Breton—French like Millet, like Millet devoted to rural scenes. *The Song of the Lark* hangs in the Art Institute of Chicago; it is possible I will die without ever having visited there. Good: I never want to see the original, out of shock at what a reproduction now discloses: a mistake, everything is turned the other way! On our living room wall Ruth faced right. In the Art Institute of Chicago she faces left. A calendar reversal!—but of course it feels to me that the original is in sullen error. Breton, unlike Millet, lived into our century—he died in 1906, the year my nine-year-old mother came through Castle Garden on her way to framing *The Song of the Lark* two decades later. About my grandfather Hirshl there is no "eventually"; I will not learn anything new about him. He will not acquire a different maker. Nothing in his view will be reversed. He will remain a dusty indoor melamed with eyes that drill through bone.

Leaving aside the wall, leaving aside the child who haunts and is haunted by the grandfather and the woman with the sickle, what is the connection between this dusty indoor melamed and the nymph in the meadow, standing barefoot amid the tall campanula?

Everything, everything. If the woman had not been in the field, my grandfather, three thousand years afterward, would not have been in the study house. She, the Moabite, is why he, when hope is embittered, murmurs the Psalms of David. The track her naked toes make through spice and sweetness, through dodder, vetch, rape, and scabious, is the very track his forefinger follows across the letter-speckled sacred page.

II. MERCY

When my grandfather reads the Book of Ruth, it is on Shavuot, the Feast of Weeks, with its twin furrows: the text's straight furrow planted with the alphabet; the harvest's furrow, fuzzy with seedlings. The Feast of Weeks, which comes in May, is a reminder of the late-spring crops, but only as an aside. The soul of it is the acceptance of the Torah by the Children of Israel. If there is a garland crowning this festival of May, it is the arms of Israel embracing the Covenant. My grandfather will not dart among field flowers after Ruth and her sickle; the field is fenced round by the rabbis, and the rabbis—those insistent interpretive spirits of Commentary whose arguments and counterarguments, from generation to generation, comprise the Tradition—seem at first to be vexed with the Book of Ruth. If they are not actually or openly vexed, they are suspicious; and if they are not willing to be judged flatly suspicious, then surely they are cautious.

The Book of Ruth is, after all, about exogamy, and not simple exogamy—marriage with a stranger, a member of a foreign culture: Ruth's ancestry is hardly neutral in that sense. She is a Moabite. She belongs to an enemy people, callous, pitiless, a people who deal in lethal curses. The children of the wild hunter Esau—the Edomites, who will ultimately stand for the imperial oppressors of Rome—cannot be shut out of the family of Israel. Even the descendants of the enslaving Egyptians are welcome to marry and grow into intimacy. "You shall not abhor an Edomite, for he is your kinsman. You shall not abhor an Egyptian, for you were a stranger in his land. Children born to them may be admitted into the congregation of the Lord in the third generation" (Deuteronomy 23:8–9). But a Moabite, never: "none of their descendants, even in the tenth generation, shall ever be admitted into the congregation of the Lord, because they did not meet you with food and water on your journey after you left Egypt, and because they hired Balaam . . . to curse you" (Deuteronomy 23:4–5). An abyss of memory and hurt in that: to have passed through the furnace of the desert famished, parched, and to be chased after by a wonder-worker on an ass hurling the king's maledictions, officially designed to wipe out the straggling mob of exhausted refugees! One might in time reconcile with Esau, one might in time reconcile with hard-hearted Egypt. All this was not merely conceivable—through acculturation, conversion, family ties, and new babies, it could be implemented, it *would* be implemented. But Moabite spite had a lasting sting.

What, then, are the sages to do with Ruth the Moabite as in-law? How account for her presence and resonance in Israel's story? How is it possible for a member of the congregation of the Lord to have violated the edict against marriage with a Moabite? The rabbis, reflecting on the pertinent verses, deduce a rule: *Moabite, not Moabitess.* It was customary for men, they conclude, not for women, to succor travelers in the desert, so only the Moabite males were guilty of a failure of humanity. The women were blameless, hence are exempt from the ban on conversion and marriage.

Even with the discovery of this mitigating loophole (with its odd premise that women are descended only from women, and men from men; or else that all the women, or all the men, in a family line are interchangeable with one another, up and down the ladder of the generations, and that guilt and innocence are collective, sex-linked, and heritable), it is hard for the rabbis to swallow a Moabite bride. They are discomfited by every particle of cause-and-effect that brought about such an eventuality. Why should a family with a pair of marriageable sons find itself in pagan Moab in the first place? The rabbis begin by scolding the text—or, rather, the characters and events of the story as they are straightforwardly set out.

Here is how the Book of Ruth begins:

In the days when the judges ruled, there was a famine in the land; and a man of Bethlehem in Judah, with his wife and two sons, went to reside in the country of Moab. The man's name was Elimelech, his wife's name was Naomi, and his two sons were named Mahlon and Chilion—Ephrathites of Bethlehem in Judah. They came to the country of Moab and remained there.

Elimelech, Naomi's husband, died; and she was left with her two sons. They married Moabite women, one named Orpah and the other Ruth, and they lived there about ten years. Then those two—Mahlon and Chilion—also died; so the woman was left without her two sons and without her husband.

Famine; migration; three deaths in a single household; three widows. Catastrophe after catastrophe, yet the text, plain and sparse, is only matter-of-fact. There is no anger in it, no one is condemned. What happened, happened—though not unaccoutered by echo and reverberation. Earlier Biblical families and journeys-toward-sustenance cluster and chatter around Elimelech's decision: "There was a famine in the land, and Abram went down to Egypt to sojourn there, for the famine was severe in the land" (Genesis 12:10). "So ten of Joseph's brothers went down to get rations in Egypt. . . . Thus the sons of Israel were among those who came to procure rations, for the famine extended to the land of Canaan" (Genesis 42:3, 5). What Abraham did, what the sons of Jacob did, Elimelech also feels constrained to do: there is famine, he will go where the food is.

And the rabbis subject him to bitter censure for it. The famine, they say, is retribution for the times—"the days when the judges ruled"—and the times are coarse, cynical, lawless. "In those days there was no king in Israel; everyone did what he pleased" (Judges 17:6). Ironic that the leaders should be deemed "judges," and that under their aegis the rule of law is loosened, each one pursuing "what is right in his own eyes," without standard or conscience. Elimelech, according to the rabbis, is one of these unraveled and atomized souls: a leader who will not lead. They identify him as a man of substance, distinguished, well-off, an eminence; but arrogant and selfish. Even his name suggests self-aggrandizement: *to me shall kingship come.* [*] Elimelech turns his back on the destitute conditions of hungry Bethlehem, picks up his family, and, because he is rich enough to afford the journey, sets out for where the food is. He looks to his own skin and means to get his own grub. The rabbis charge Elimelech with desertion; they accuse him of running away from the importunings of the impoverished, of provoking discouragement and despair; he is miserly, there is no charitableness in him, he is ungenerous. They call him a "dead stump"—he attends only to his immediate kin and shrugs off the community at large. Worse

---

*Latter-day scholarship avers that Elimelech is a run-of-the-mill name in pre-Israelite Canaan, "and is the one name in the Ruth story that seems incapable of being explained as having a symbolic meaning pertinent to the narrative" (Edward F. Campbell, Jr., *Ruth*, The Anchor Bible Series, vol. 7 [New York: Doubleday, 1975], p. 52). The rabbis, however, are above all metaphor-seekers and symbolists.

yet, he is heading for Moab, vile Moab! The very man who might have heartened his generation in a period of upheaval and inspired its moral repair leaves his own country, a land sanctified by Divine Covenant, for a historically repugnant region inhabited by idolators—and only to fill his own belly, and his own wife's, and his own sons'.

Elimelech in Moab will die in his prime. His widow will suffer radical denigration—a drop in status commonly enough observed even among independent women of our era—and, more seriously, a loss of protection. The rabbis will compare Naomi in her widowhood with "the remnants of the meal offerings"—i.e., with detritus and ash. Elimelech's sons—children of a father whose example is abandonment of community and of conscience—will die too soon. Already grown men after the death of Elimelech, they have themselves earned retribution. Instead of returning with their unhappy mother to their own people in the land dedicated to monotheism, they settle down to stay, and marry Moabite women. "One transgression leads to another," chide the rabbis, and argue over whether the brides of Mahlon and Chilion were or were not ritually converted before their weddings. In any case, a decade after those weddings, nothing has flowered for these husbands and wives; fertility eludes them, there will be no blossoming branches: the two young husbands are dead—dead stumps—and the two young widows are childless.

This is the rabbis' view. They are symbolists and metaphor-seekers; it goes without saying that they are moralists. Punishment is truthful; punishment is the consequence of reality, it instructs in what happens. It is not that the rabbis are severe; they are just the opposite of severe. What they are after is simple mercy: where is the standard of mercy and humanity in a time when careless men and women follow the whim of their own greedy and expedient eyes? It is not merciful to abandon chaos and neediness; chaos and neediness call out for reclamation. It is not merciful to forsake one's devastated countrymen; opportunism is despicable; desertion is despicable; derogation of responsibility is despicable; it is not merciful to think solely of one's own family: if I am only for myself, what am I? And what of the hallowed land, that sacral ground consecrated to the unity of the Creator and the teaching of mercy, while the babble and garble of polymyth pullulate all around? The man who throws away the country of aspiration, especially in a lamentable hour when failure overruns it—the man who promotes egotism, elevates the material, and deprives his children of idealism—this fellow, this Elimelech, vexes the rabbis and afflicts them with shame.

Of course, there is not a grain of any of this in the text itself—not a word about Elimelech's character or motives or even his position in Bethlehem. The rabbis' commentary is all extrapolation, embroidery, plausible invention. What is plausible in it is firmly plausible: it stands to reason that only a wealthy family, traveling together *as* a family, would be able to contemplate emigration to another country with which they have no economic or kinship ties. And it follows also that a wealthy householder is likely to be an established figure in his home town. The rabbis' storytelling faculty is not capricious or fantastic: it is rooted in the way the world actually works, then and now.

But the rabbis are even more interested in the way the world *ought* to work. Their parallel text hardly emerges *ex nihilo*. They are not oblivious to what-is: they can, in fact, construct a remarkably particularized social density from a handful of skeletal data. Yet, shrewd sociologists though they are, it is not sociology that stirs them. What stirs them is the aura of judgment—or call it ethical interpretation—that rises out of even the most comprehensively imagined social particularity. The rabbis are driven by a struggle to uncover a moral immanence in every human being. It signifies, such a struggle, hopefulness to the point of pathos, and the texture and pliability of this deeply embedded matrix of optimism is more pressing for the rabbis than any other kind of speculation or cultural improvisation. Callousness and egotism are an affront to their expectations. What are their expectations in the Book of Ruth? That an established community figure has an obligation not to demoralize his constituency by walking out on it. And that the Holy Land is to be passionately embraced, clung to, blessed, and defended as the ripening center and historic promise of the covenanted life. Like the Covenant that engendered its sanctifying purpose, Israel cannot be "marginalized." One place is not the same as another place. The rabbis are not cultural relativists.

From the rabbis' vantage, it is not that their commentary is "implicit" in the plain text under their noses; what they see is not implicit so much as it is fully intrinsic. It is there already, like invisible ink gradually made to appear. A system of values produces a story. A system of values? Never mind such Aristotelian language. The rabbis said, and meant, the quality of mercy: human feeling.

III. NORMALITY

I have been diligent in opening the first five verses of the Book of Ruth to the rabbis' voices, and though I am unwilling to leave their voices behind—they painstakingly accompany the story inch by inch, breath for breath—I mean for the rest of my sojourn in the text (perforce spotty and selective, a point here, a point there) to go on more or less without them. I say "more or less" because it is impossible, really, to go on without them. They are (to use an unsuitable image) the Muses of exegesis: not the current sort of exegesis that ushers insights out of a tale by scattering a thousand brilliant fragments, but, rather, the kind that ushers things *toward:* a guide toward principle. The Book of Ruth presents two principles. The first is what is normal. The second is what is singular.

Until Elimelech's death, Naomi has been an exemplum of the normal. She has followed her husband and made no decisions or choices of her own. What we nowadays call feminism is of course as old as the oldest society imaginable; there have always been feminists: women (including the unsung) who will allow no element of themselves—gift, capacity, natural authority—to go unexpressed, whatever the weight of the mores. Naomi has not been one of these. Until the death of her husband, we know nothing of her but her compliance, and it would be foolish to suppose that in Naomi's world a wife's obedience is not a fundamental social virtue. But once Naomi's husband and sons have been tragically cleared from the stage, Naomi moves from the merely passive virtue of an honorable dependent to risks and contingencies well beyond the reach of comfortable common virtue. Stripped of every social support,* isolated in a foreign land, pitifully unprotected, her anomalous position apparently wholly ignored by Moabite practices, responsible for the lives of a pair of foreign daughters-in-law (themselves isolated and unprotected

---

*The rabbis' notion of Elimelech as a man of substance is no help to his widow. She has not been provided for; we see her as helpless and impoverished.

under her roof), Naomi is transformed overnight. Under the crush of mourning and defenselessness, she becomes, without warning or preparation, a woman of valor.

She is only a village woman, after all. The Book of Ruth, from beginning to end, is played out in village scenes. The history of valor will not find in Naomi what it found in another village woman: she will not arm herself like a man or ride a horse or lead a military expedition. She will never cross over to another style of being. The new ways of her valor will not annul the old ways of her virtue.

And yet—overnight!—she will set out on a program of autonomy. Her first act is a decision: she will return to Bethlehem, "for in the country of Moab she had heard that the Lord had taken note of His people and given them food." After so many years, the famine in Bethlehem is spent—but since Naomi is cognizant of this as the work of the Lord, there is a hint that she would have gone back to Bethlehem in Judah in any event, even if that place were still troubled by hunger. It is no ordinary place for her: the Lord hovers over Judah and its people, and Naomi in returning makes restitution for Elimelech's abandonment. Simply in her determination to go back, she rights an old wrong.

But she does not go back alone. Now, willy-nilly, she is herself the head of a household bound to her by obedience. "Accompanied by her two daughters-in-law, she left the place where she had been living; and they set out on the road back to the land of Judah." On the road, Naomi reflects. What she reflects on—only connect! she is herself an exile—is the ache of exile and the consolations of normality.

Naomi said to her two daughters-in-law, "Turn back, each of you to her mother's house. May the Lord deal kindly with you, as you have dealt with the dead and with me! May the Lord grant that each of you find security in the house of a husband!" And she kissed them farewell. They broke into weeping and said to her, "No, we will return with you to your people."

But Naomi replied, "Turn back, my daughters! Why should you go with me? Have I any more sons in my body who might be husbands for you? Turn back, my daughters, for I am too old to be married. Even if I thought there was hope for me, even if I were married tonight and I also bore sons, should you wait for them to grow up? Should you on their account debar yourselves from marriage? Oh no, my daughters!"

In a moment or so we will hear Ruth's incandescent reply spiraling down to us through the ardors of three thousand years; but here let us check the tale, fashion a hiatus, and allow normality to flow in: let young stricken Orpah not be overlooked. She is always overlooked; she is the daughter-in-law who, given the chance, chose not to follow Naomi. She is no one's heroine. Her mark is erased from history; there is no Book of Orpah. And yet Orpah *is* history. Or, rather, she is history's great backdrop. She is the majority of humankind living out its usualness on home ground. These young women—both of them—are cherished by Naomi; she cannot speak to them without flooding them in her fellow-feeling. She *knows* what it is to be Orpah and Ruth. They have all suffered and sorrowed together, and in ten years of living in one household much of the superficial cultural strangeness has worn off. She pities them because they are childless, and she honors them because they have "dealt kindly" with their husbands and with their mother-in-law. She calls them—the word as she releases it is accustomed, familiar, close, ripe with dearness—*b'notai,* "my daughters," whereas the voice of the narrative is careful to identify them precisely, though neutrally, as *khalotekha,* "her daughters-in-law."

Orpah is a loving young woman of clear goodness; she has kisses and tears for the loss of Naomi. "They broke into weeping again, and Orpah kissed her mother-in-law farewell." Her sensibility is ungrudging, and she is not in the least narrow-minded. Her upbringing may well have been liberal. Would a narrow-minded Moabite father have given over one of his daughters to the only foreign family in town? Such a surrender goes against the grain of the ordinary. Exogamy is never ordinary. So Orpah has already been stamped with the "abnormal"; she is already a little more daring than most, already somewhat offbeat—she is one of only two young Moabite women to marry Hebrews, and Hebrews have never been congenial to Moabites. If the Hebrews can remember how the Moabites treated them long ago, so can the Moabites: traditions of enmity work in both directions. The mean-spirited have a habit of resenting their victims quite as much as the other way around. Orpah has cut through all this bad blood to plain humanity; it would be unfair to consider her inferior to any other kind-hearted young woman who ever lived in the world before or since. She is in fact superior; she has thrown off prejudice, and she has had to endure more than most young women of her class, including the less spunky and the less amiable: an early widowhood and no babies. And what else is there for a good girl like Orpah, in her epoch, and often enough in ours, but family happiness?

Her prototype abounds. She has fine impulses, but she is not an iconoclast. She can push against convention to a generous degree, but it is out of the generosity of her temperament, not out of some large metaphysical idea. Who will demand of Orpah—think of the hugeness of the demand!—that she admit monotheism to the concentration and trials of her mind? Offer monotheism to almost anyone—offer it as something to take seriously—and ninety-nine times out of a hundred it will be declined, even by professing "monotheists." A Lord of History whose intent is felt, whose Commandments stand with immediacy, whose Covenant summons perpetual self-scrutiny and a continual Turning toward moral renewal, and yet *cannot, may not, be physically imagined?* A Creator neither remote and abstract like the God of the philosophers, nor palpable like the "normal" divinities, both ancient and contemporary, of both East and West? Give us (cries the nature of our race) our gods and goddesses; give us the little fertility icons with their welcoming breasts and elongated beckoning laps; give us the resplendent Virgin with her suffering brow and her arms outstretched in blessing; give us the Man on the Cross through whom to learn pity and love, and sometimes brutal exclusivity! Only give us what our eyes can see and our understanding understand: who can imagine the unimaginable? That may be for the philosophers; *they* can do it; but then they lack the imagination of the Covenant. The philosophers leave the world naked and blind and deaf and mute and relentlessly indifferent, and the village folk—who refuse a lonely cosmos without consolation—fill it and fill it and fill it with stone and wood and birds and mammals and miraculous potions and holy babes and animate carcasses and magically divine women and magically divine men: images, sights, and swallowings comprehensible to the hand, to the eye, to plain experience. For the nature of our race, God is one of the visual arts.

Is Orpah typical of these plain village folk? She is certainly not a philosopher, but neither is she, after ten years with Naomi, an ordinary Moabite. Not that she has altogether absorbed the Hebrew vision—if she had absorbed it, would she have been tempted to relinquish it so readily? She is somewhere in between, perhaps. In this we may suppose her to be one of us: a modern, no longer a full-fledged member of the pagan world, but always with one foot warming in the seductive bath of those colorful, comfortable, often beautiful old lies (they can console, but because they are lies they can also hurt and kill); not yet given over to the Covenant and its determination to train us away from lies, however warm, colorful, beautiful, and consoling.

Naomi, who is no metaphysician herself, who is, rather, heir to a tradition, imposes no monotheistic claim on either one of her daughters-in-law. She is right not to do this. In the first place, she is not a proselytizer or polemicist or preacher or even a teacher. She is none of those things: she is a bereaved woman far from home, and when she looks at her bereaved daughters-in-law, it is home she is thinking of, for herself and for them. Like the rabbis who will arrive two millennia after her, she is not a cultural relativist: God is God, and God is One. But in her own way, the way of empathy—three millennia before the concept of a democratic pluralist polity—she is a kind of pluralist. She does not require that Orpah accept what it is not natural for her, in the light of how she was reared, to accept. She speaks of Orpah's return not merely to her people but to her gods. Naomi is the opposite of coercive or punitive. One cannot dream of Inquisition or jihad emerging from her loins. She may not admire the usages of Orpah's people—they do not concern themselves with the widow and the destitute; no one in Moab comes forward to care for Naomi—but she knows that Orpah has a mother, and may yet have a new husband, and will be secure where she is. It will not occur to Naomi to initiate a metaphysical discussion with Orpah! She sends her as a lost child back to her mother's hearth. (Will there be idols on her mother's hearth? Well, yes. But this sour comment is mine, not Naomi's.)

So Orpah goes home; or, more to the point, she goes nowhere. She stays home. She is never, never, never to be blamed for it. If she is not extraordinary, she is also normal. The extraordinary is what is not normal, and it is no fault of the normal that it does not, or cannot, aspire to the extraordinary. What Orpah gains by staying home with her own people is what she always deserved: family happiness. She is young and fertile; soon she will marry a Moabite husband and have a Moabite child.

What Orpah loses is the last three thousand years of being present in history. Israel continues; Moab is not. Still, for Orpah, historic longevity—

the longevity of an Idea to which a people attaches itself—may not be a loss at all. It is only an absence, and absence is not felt as loss. Orpah has her husband, her cradle, her little time. That her gods are false is of no moment to her; she believes they are true. That her social system does not provide for the widow and the destitute is of no moment to her; she is no longer a widow, and as a wife she will not be destitute; as for looking over her shoulder to see how others fare, there is nothing in Moab to require it of her. She once loved her oddly foreign mother-in-law. And why shouldn't open-hearted Orpah, in her little time, also love her Moabite mother-in-law, who is as like her as her own mother, and will also call her "my daughter"? Does it matter to Orpah that her great-great-great-grandchildren have tumbled out of history, and that there is no Book of Orpah, and that she slips from the Book of Ruth in only its fourteenth verse?

Normality is not visionary. Normality's appetite stops at satisfaction.

IV. SINGULARITY

No, Naomi makes no metaphysical declaration to Orpah. It falls to Ruth, who has heard the same compassionate discourse as her sister-in-law, who has heard her mother-in-law three times call out "Daughter, turn back"—it falls to Ruth to throw out exactly such a declaration to Naomi.

Her words have set thirty centuries to trembling: "Your God shall be my God," uttered in what might be named visionary language. Does it merely "fall" to Ruth, that she speaks possessed by the visionary? What is at work in her? Is it capacity, seizure, or the force of intent and the clarity of will? Set this inquiry aside for now, and—apart from what the story tells us she really did say—ask instead what Ruth might have replied in the more available language of pragmatism, answering Naomi's sensible "Turn back" exigency for exigency. What "natural" reasons might such a young woman have for leaving her birthplace? Surely there is nothing advantageous in Ruth's clinging to Naomi. Everything socially rational is on the side of Ruth's remaining in her own country: what is true for Orpah is equally true for Ruth. But even if Ruth happened to think beyond exigency—even if she were exceptional in reaching past common sense toward ideal conduct—

she need not have thought in the framework of the largest cosmic questions. Are we to expect of Ruth that she be a prophet? Why should she, any more than any other village woman, think beyond personal relations?

In the language of personal relations, in the language of pragmatism and exigency, here is what Ruth might have replied:

Mother-in-law, I am used to living in your household, and have become accustomed to the ways of your family. I would no longer feel at home if I resumed the ways of my own people. After all, during the ten years or so I was married to your son, haven't I flourished under your influence? I was so young when I came into your family that it was you who completed my upbringing. It isn't for nothing that you call me daughter. So let me go with you.

Or, higher on the spectrum of ideal conduct (rather, the conduct of idealism), but still within the range of reasonable altruism, she might have said:

Mother-in-law, you are heavier in years than I and alone in a strange place, whereas I am stalwart and not likely to be alone for long. Surely I will have a second chance, just as you predict, but you—how helpless you are, how unprotected! If I stayed home in Moab, I would be looking after my own interests, as you recommend, but do you think I can all of a sudden stop feeling for you, just like that? No, don't expect me to abandon you—who knows what can happen to a woman of your years all by herself on the road? And what prospects can there be for you, after all this long time away, in Bethlehem? It's true I'll seem a little odd in your country, but I'd much rather endure a little oddness in Bethlehem than lose you forever, not knowing what's to become of you. Let me go and watch over you.

There is no God in any of that. If these are thoughts Ruth did not speak out, they are all implicit in what has been recorded. Limited though they are by pragmatism, exigency, and personal relations, they are already anomalous. They address extraordinary alterations—of self, of worldly expectation. For Ruth to cling to Naomi as a daughter to her own mother is uncommon enough; a universe of folklore confirms that a daughter-in-law is not a daughter. But for Ruth to become the instrument of Naomi's restoration to safekeeping within her own community—and to prosperity and honor as well—is a thing of magnitude. And, in fact, all these praiseworthy circumstances do come to pass, though circumscribed by pragmatism, exigency, and personal relations. And without the visionary. Ideal conduct—or the conduct of idealism—is possible even in the absence of the language of the visionary. Observe:

They broke into weeping again, and Orpah kissed her mother-in-law farewell. But Ruth clung to her. So she said, "See, your sister-in-law has returned to her people. Go follow your sister-in-law." But Ruth replied: "Do not urge me to leave you, to turn back and not follow you. For wherever you go, I will go; wherever you lodge, I will lodge; your people shall be my people. Where you die, I will die, and there I will be buried. Only death will part me from you." When Naomi saw how determined she was to go with her, she ceased to argue with her, and the two went on until they reached Bethlehem.

Of course this lovely passage is not the story of the Book of Ruth (any more than my unpoetic made-up monologues are), though it might easily have been Ruth's story. In transcribing from the text, I have left out what Ruth passionately put in: God. And still Ruth's speech, even with God left out, and however particularized by the personal, is a stupendous expression of loyalty and love.

But now, in a sort of conflagration of seeing, the cosmic sweep of a single phrase transforms these spare syllables from the touching language of family feeling to the unearthly tongue of the visionary:

"See, your sister-in-law has returned to her people and her gods. Go and follow your sister-in-law." But Ruth replied, "Do not urge me to leave you, to turn back and not follow you. For wherever you go, I will go; wherever you lodge, I will lodge; your people shall be my people, and your God my God. Where you die, I will die, and there I will be buried. Thus and more may the Lord do to me if anything but death parts me from you."

Your God shall be my God: Ruth's story is kindled into the Book of Ruth by the presence of God on Ruth's lips, and her act is far, far more than a ringing embrace of Naomi, and far, far more than the simple acculturation it resembles. Ruth leaves Moab because she intends to leave childish ideas behind. She is drawn to Israel because Israel is the inheritor of the One Universal Creator.

Has Ruth "learned" this insight from Naomi and from Naomi's son? It may be; the likelihood is almost as pressing as evidence: how, without assimilation into the life of an Israelite family, would Ruth ever have penetrated into the great monotheistic cognition? On the other hand: Orpah too encounters that cognition, and slips back into Moab to lose it again. Inculcation is not insight, and what Orpah owns is only that: inculcation without insight. Abraham—the first Hebrew to catch insight—caught it as genius does, autonomously, out of the blue, without any inculcating tradition. Ruth is in possession of both inculcation *and* insight.

And yet, so intense is her insight, one can almost imagine her as a kind of Abraham. Suppose Elimelech had never emigrated to Moab; suppose Ruth had never married a Hebrew. The fire of cognition might still have come upon her as it came upon Abraham—autonomously, out of the blue, without any inculcating tradition. Abraham's cognition turned into a civilization. Might Ruth have transmuted Moab? Ruth as a second Abraham! We see in her that clear power; that power of consummate clarity. But whether Moab might, through Ruth, have entered the history of monotheism, like Israel, is a question stalled by the more modest history of kinship entanglement. In Ruth's story, insight is inexorably accompanied by, fused with, inculcation; how can we sort out one from the other? If Ruth had not been married to one of Naomi's sons, perhaps we would have heard no more of her than we will hear henceforth of Orpah. Or: Moab might have ascended, like Abraham's seed, from the gods to God. Moab cleansed and reborn through Ruth! The story as it is given is perforce inflexible, not amenable to experiment. We cannot have Ruth without Naomi; nor would we welcome the loss of such loving-kindness. All the same, Ruth may not count as a second Abraham because her tale is enfolded in a way Abraham's is not: she has had her saturation in Abraham's seed. The ingredient of inculcation cannot be expunged: there it is.

Nevertheless it seems insufficient—it seems askew—to leave it at that. Ruth marries into Israel, yes; but her mind is vaster than the private or social facts of marriage and inculcation; vaster than the merely familial. Insight, cognition, intuition, religious genius—how to name it? It is not simply because of Ruth's love for Naomi—a love unarguably resplendent—that Naomi's God becomes Ruth's God. To stop at love and loyalty is to have arrived at much, but not all; to stop at love and loyalty is to stop too soon.

Ruth claims the God of Israel out of her own ontological understanding. She knows—she knows directly, prophetically—that the Creator of the Universe is One.

V. UNFOLDING

The greater part of Ruth's tale is yet to occur—the greater, that is, in length and episode. The central setting of the Book of Ruth is hardly Moab; it is Bethlehem in Judah. But by the time the two destitute widows, the older and the younger, reach Bethlehem, the volcanic heart of the Book of Ruth—the majesty of Ruth's declaration—has already happened. All the rest is an unfolding.

Let it unfold, then, without us. We have witnessed normality and we have witnessed singularity. We will, if we linger, witness these again in Bethlehem; but let the next events flash by without our lingering. Let Naomi come with Ruth to Bethlehem; let Naomi in her distress name herself Mara, meaning "bitter," "for the Lord has made my lot very bitter"; let Ruth set out to feed them both by gleaning in the field of Elimelech's kinsman, Boaz—fortuitous, God-given, that she should blunder onto Boaz's property! He is an elderly landowner, an affluent farmer who, like Levin in *Anna Karenina*, works side by side with his laborers. He is at once aware that there is a stranger in his field, and is at once solicitous. He is the sort of man who, in the heat of the harvest, greets the reapers with courteous devoutness: "The Lord be with you!" A benign convention, perhaps, but when he addresses Ruth it is no ordinary invocation: "I have been told of all that you did for your mother-in-law after the death of her husband, how you left your father and mother and the land of your birth and came to a people you had not known before. May the Lord reward your deeds. May you have a full recompense from the Lord, the God of Israel, under whose wings you have sought refuge!" Like Naomi, he calls Ruth "daughter," and he speaks an old-fashioned Hebrew; he and Naomi are of the same generation.*

---

*"Boaz and Naomi talk like older people. Their speeches contain archaic morphology and syntax. Perhaps the most delightful indication of this is the one instance when an archaic form is put into Ruth's mouth, at 2:21—where she is quoting Boaz!" (Campbell, *Ruth*, p. 17).

But remember that we are hurrying along now; so let Naomi, taking charge behind the scenes, send Ruth to sleep at Boaz's feet on the threshing floor in order to invite his special notice—a contrivance to make known to Boaz that he is eligible for Ruth's salvation within the frame of the levirate code. And let the humane and flexible system of the levirate code work itself out, so that Boaz can marry Ruth, who will become the mother of Obed, who is the father of Jesse, who is the father of King David, author of the Psalms.

The levirate law in Israel—like the rule for gleaners—is designed to redeem the destitute. The reapers may not sweep up every stalk in the meadow; some of the harvest must be left behind for bread for the needy. And if a woman is widowed, the circle of her husband's kin must open their homes to her; in a time when the sole protective provision for a woman is marriage, she must have a new husband from her dead husband's family—the relative closest to the husband, a brother if possible. Otherwise what will become of her? Dust and cinders. She will be like the remnants of the meal offerings.

Boaz in his tenderness (we have hurried past even this, which more than almost anything else merits our hanging back; but there it is on the page, enchanting the centuries—a tenderness sweetly discriminating, morally meticulous, wide-hearted, and ripe)—Boaz is touched by Ruth's appeal to become her husband-protector. It is a fatherly tenderness, not an erotic one—though such a scene might, in some other tale, burst with the erotic: a young woman, perfumed, lying at the feet of an old man at night in a barn. The old man is not indifferent to the pulsing of Eros in the young: "Be blessed of the Lord, daughter! Your latest deed of loyalty is greater than the first, in that you have not turned to younger men." The remark may carry a pang of wistfulness, but Boaz in undertaking to marry Ruth is not animated by the lubricious. He is no December panting after May. A forlorn young widow, homeless in every sense, has asked for his guardianship, and he responds under the merciful levirate proviso with all the dignity and responsibility of his character—including an ethical scruple: "While it is true that I am a redeeming kinsman, there is another redeemer closer than I"—someone more closely related to Elimelech than Boaz, and therefore first in line to assume the right—and burden—of kinship protection.

In this closer relative we have a sudden pale reminder of Orpah.

Though she has long vanished from the story, normality has not. Who conforms more vividly to the type of Average Man than that practical head of a household we call John Doe? And now John Doe (the exact Hebrew equivalent is Ploni Almoni) briefly enters the narrative and quickly jumps out of it; averageness leaves no reputation, except for averageness. John Doe, a.k.a. Ploni Almoni, is the closer relative Boaz has in mind, and he appears at a meeting of town elders convened to sort out the levirate succession in Naomi's case. The hearing happens also to include some business about a piece of land that Elimelech owned; if sold, it will bring a little money for Naomi. Naomi may not have known of the existence of this property—or else why would she be reduced to living on Ruth's gleaning? But Boaz is informed of it, and immediately arranges for a transaction aimed at relieving both Naomi and Ruth. The sale of Elimelech's property, though secondary to the issue of marital guardianship for Naomi's young daughter-in-law, is legally attached to it: whoever acquires the land acquires Ruth. The closer relative, Ploni Almoni (curious how the text refuses him a real name of his own, as if it couldn't be bothered, as if it were all at once impatient with averageness), is willing enough to buy the land: John Doe always understands money and property. But he is not at all willing to accept Ruth. The moment he learns he is also being asked to take on the care of a widow—one young enough to bear children, when very likely he already has a family to support—he changes his mind. He worries, he explains, that he will impair his estate. An entirely reasonable, even a dutiful, worry, and who can blame him? If he has missed his chance to become the great-grandfather of the Psalmist, he is probably, like Ploni Almoni everywhere, a philistine scorner of poetry anyhow.

And we are glad to see him go. In this he is no reminder of Orpah; Orpah, a loving young woman, is regretted. But like Orpah he has only the usual order of courage. He avoids risk, the unexpected, the lightning move into imagination. He thinks of what he has, not of what he might do: he recoils from the conduct of idealism. He is perfectly conventional, and wants to stick with what is familiar. Then let him go in peace—he is too ordinary to be the husband of Ruth. We have not heard him make a single inquiry about her. He has not troubled over any gesture of interest or sympathy. Ruth is no more to him than an object of acquisition offered for sale. He declines to buy; he has his own life to get on with, and no intention of altering it, levirate code or no levirate code. "You do it," he tells Boaz.

Boaz does it. At every step he has given more than full measure, whether of barley or benevolence. We have watched him load Ruth's sack with extra grain to take back to Naomi. He has instructed the reapers to scatter extra stalks for her to scoop up. He has summoned her to his own table for lunch in the field. He is generous, he is kindly, he is old, and in spite of his years he opens his remaining strength to the imagination of the future: he enters on a new life inconceivable to him on the day a penniless young foreigner wandered over his field behind the harvest workers. *Mercy, pity, peace, and love:* these Blakean words lead, in our pastoral, to a beginning.

The beginning is of course a baby, and when Naomi cradles her grandchild in her bosom, the village women cry: "A son is born to Naomi!" And they cry: "Blessed be the Lord, who hath not withheld a redeemer from you today! May his name be perpetuated in Israel! He will renew your life and sustain your old age; for he is born of your daughter-in-law, who loves you and is better to you than seven sons."

Only eighty-five verses tell Ruth's and Naomi's story. To talk of it takes much longer. Not that the greatest stories are the shortest—not at all. But a short story has a stalk—shoot—through which its life rushes, and out of which the flowery head erupts. The Book of Ruth—wherein goodness grows out of goodness, and the extraordinary is found here, and here, and here—is sown in desertion, bereavement, barrenness, death, loss, displacement, destitution. What can sprout from such ash? Then Ruth sees into the nature of Covenant, and the life of the story streams in. Out of this stalk mercy and redemption unfold; flowers flood Ruth's feet; and my grandfather goes on following her track until the coming of Messiah from the shoot of David, in the line of Ruth and Naomi.

LAMENTATIONS

Stephen Mitchell

RABBI JUDAH, RABBI ELAZAR, RABBI SIMEON. THEY ARE SITTING IN the backyard on an afternoon in early spring. Redwood fence and furniture; the sharp smell of eucalyptus. The yard is planted with azaleas, geraniums, forget-me-nots. On a table, beside the lemon tree, a platter of apple and tangerine slices and cellophane-wrapped sesame candies.

Rabbi Judah begins: "How inclusive the Bible is when seen from a distance! There is every kind of event in it, from the glorious to the horrible, and every kind of expression, with praises and lamentations following one another like moods. Even the somber moods remind me of the verse from Ecclesiastes, 'He has made everything beautiful in its time.' "

Rabbi Elazar: "Surely not the horrors of siege and famine."

Rabbi Judah says: "No, what I mean is the poet's grief, which is so full and impersonal that it can speak for the whole nation. 'God has made everything beautiful in its time, and has put the whole world in our heart.'

The author's own translation of the Bible used in this essay.

Grief as well as joy, lamentation as well as praise. One might even say that it is a joy to hear grief so deeply expressed."

"Hmpf," Rabbi Elazar says. "I have never particularly cared for Lamentations myself. The emotion seems too raw for a poem. The *reality* is too raw. It dwarfs the expression. It's impossible to make such laments valid for us. If we translate them into our history—as we should, if we want to test their impact—they become merely obscene. 'By the waters of Bergen-Belsen. . . .' "

Rabbi Judah: "But with grief, don't we have to start somewhere? And who can deny the genuineness of this poet's emotion? His words hardly qualify as literature. Even the form of Lamentations—a series of alphabetic acrostics—seems like a way of setting an arbitrary limit to a sorrow that is limitless. A way of saying 'I will stop after verse 22, otherwise I would go on forever.' But perhaps you like the poem better as it is chanted in Hebrew. As you know, it has its own, most beautiful cantillation. You might even keep the melody and toss out the words."

Rabbi Elazar: "Yes, I like the chant. And its lovely setting in the last movement of Bernstein's *Jeremiah* symphony."

Rabbi Judah: "What *I* admire about the poet is his refusal to be consoled. Grief pulls him into himself like the force of gravity. It lies upon his heart with such a weight that it crushes out his music. Whereas joy breathes its music like a flute."

Rabbi Simeon says: "It is all so mysterious, these events and emotions that appear out of nowhere, that are given to us, perhaps without our consent. Which of them are good, which are bad? Which should we receive, which not? I woke up this morning with a verse on the tip of my tongue: 'Wisdom opens her gate.' (I couldn't track it down in Proverbs. Did I dream it?) But grief, after all, like joy, comes to us as a passing guest. We ought to treat it with courtesy, as Abraham treated the angels. Who knows what disguises our angels take?"

Rabbi Judah: "There is such desolation in this poem. We've all seen pictures of the famine in Ethiopia. Here, too, the agony of the children is at the center, and is heartbreaking. Add to that, rape, mayhem, mothers so insane with hunger that they eat their own infants, the city burned to the ground. And lost in the rubble is the belief in God's special protection. The poet is left clinging to a single idea—that God has punished Jerusalem for her sins—as if to a plank after a shipwreck."

Rabbi Elazar: "And yet, as grim as the siege was, there is worse to come in Jewish history. Almost unimaginable cruelties, both Jewish and Gentile, that make you feel you are suffocating in horror and shame. One incident in Josephus made me, for a couple of hours, want to hand in my membership card in the human race. There was a Jewish king, Alexander Jannaeus, a descendant of the Maccabees. In about 100 B.C.E. he crucified eight hundred Pharisees, political opponents of his. It was the entertainment for his feast—for his orgy, rather, because he and his courtiers and their women were turned on by the crucifixions. For dessert, hanging there, the Pharisees had to watch their wives and children being killed, one by one. Long live the king!"

"My God," Rabbi Judah says. "How can such horrors be given a religious meaning, or any meaning at all, without devaluing what is most precious? But that's what happens when you make history into parable."

Rabbi Elazar: "History is the absence of God."

Rabbi Judah: "I would put it another way: You need more than a magnifying glass to find an electron."

Rabbi Simeon: "But isn't the meaning as plain as the nose on your face? Isn't it what the prophets were always warning? The more I open my heart to the light, the more I am filled with light; but if I give my heart to power, I'm liable to become a demon, like this Alexander. At the least, I will be caught in the realm of force, and subject to the laws of force—just one more billiard ball, striking and being struck. The exceptions, the righteous men, like our American Founding Fathers, appear in history with the impact of miracles."

Rabbi Elazar: "There is one way of reading Lamentations that does satisfy my sense of history. And that is to see Jerusalem as a symbol for *all* cities captured and destroyed. After all, we have no words handed down to us from the agony of Troy. Silence from Herat, which Genghis Khan obliterated with its million and a half inhabitants; silence from Montezuma's Tenochtitlan; silence from ten thousand African villages whose existence we don't even know about. And from the Canaanite cities, Jericho, Hazor, Ai, and the rest, where our own exemplary Joshua, for the greater glory of God, 'butchered every creature in the city, all the men and women, all the babies and old people, all the oxen and sheep and donkeys': a terrible silence. Only these words of lament for the destruction of Jerusalem remain. Why shouldn't they be given to all the other cities as well? We Jews are rich in words. We can afford to be generous."

"And why not give them to planet earth, in provisional mourning?" Rabbi Judah says.

"Yes, since in the end she is the same figure—Jerusalem, Gaia, Virgin Mother—and her undoing must come, someday, as surely as one plus one equals two. I can imagine some far-off, perhaps still-human descendant of ours, millions of years from now, when the sun has begun to die and the earth is as desolate as the moon—I can imagine him looking back and chanting, *'Eikháh yashváh vadád,'* 'How solitary she sits, she who was once filled with living things.' "

Rabbi Judah: "The intensity of love that the old Jews had for their holy city! 'The perfection of beauty,' our poet calls it. 'The joy of all the earth.' "

Rabbi Elazar: "A fierce love. And it still exists, in all its fierceness."

Rabbi Judah: "You can see the momentum of that love through the centuries. In the Diaspora, Jerusalem becomes the receptacle for all the people's pain and spiritual longing. They imagine that her very stones are radiant with God's presence. The only paradise, as it's said, is a paradise lost. And the momentum of that longing made Jerusalem the heavenly city for the whole Western world. I once heard the account of an Israeli woman—a professor of economics, I think—who was attending a conference in Rio de Janeiro. One morning she got into a conversation with the young girl who made up her room. 'Where do you come from?' the girl asked. 'From Jerusalem.' The girl's jaw dropped open. She pointed to the sky and said, 'You mean from up there?' "

Rabbi Elazar: "Ah, that Diaspora love, that Christian love. They leave me as little impressed as I am by Dante's love for his insubstantial Beatrice. Give me a real, flesh-and-blood, *achieved* marriage any day. Give me the modern, earthly Jerusalem, with her pockmarks and traffic and garbage problems, and *then* let's see how passionately I can embrace her."

Rabbi Simeon shakes his head. "Ultimately, it is a form of idolatry."

"What is?"

"That fierce love for Jerusalem. Idolatry means putting what is relative on the level of the absolute. It makes one's love of God dependent on outer events. The patriarchs, after all, had no holy city or holy land. All Abraham possessed was his attention. He listened so acutely that he could hear the still, small voice that answered his deepest needs. And there was no holy city for

Isaac or Jacob or Moses, not until David conquered the Jebusites. By that point the religion had become cluttered. It's like this: A young couple fall in love. They live in a one-room apartment, they need practically nothing, they are overflowing with each other's presence. After a while they acquire a large house, a vacation home, two cars, books and records, silverware and jewelry, fine clothes, paintings. Now, suppose they lose everything and have to return to the bare, one-room apartment. Are they devastated? Or are they still happy? It depends on how dispersed they have become: on the quality of their love."

Rabbi Judah: "I like the way Simone Weil expressed it. 'Every time that we say *Thy will be done*,' she writes, 'we should have in mind all possible calamities added together.' Piety isn't protection money, as Job found out. There are no deals that we can make for our future. And being too attached to something is like looking at God through the wrong end of a telescope. The result is that when hard times come, God seems cruel. So according to our poet, 'The Lord has become like an enemy.' How terrible it must be to suffer under such an illusion!"

Rabbi Simeon: "Not that we should withdraw from the world. The world is our learning-place, our mirror. But there is a difference between dearly loving our wives and children, our country, our planet, and loving with all our heart, soul, and might. Another way of saying this is that ultimately nothing matters. We can ultimately afford to lose everything, because God is all in all."

"I have always been moved but also slightly repulsed by this love of Jerusalem," Rabbi Judah says, "just as I am both moved and repulsed at the sight of grown men and women kissing Herod's stones at the Wailing Wall. The image doesn't have to be graven for it to qualify as an idol. Anything holy is an idol."

Rabbi Elazar: "In Psalm 137, 'If I forget thee, O Jerusalem' is uttered with a passion that seems to me appropriate only for justice or mercy. The obverse of that kind of love is the murderous hatred that appears at the end of the psalm: 'Blessed is he who takes and dashes your infants against the rock.' I can easily forget Jerusalem. I do it every day. But rather than be cut off from what I know is right, I would have all my limbs amputated, not just my right hand."

Rabbi Judah: "And then, we Jews learned a thing or two, if I remember correctly, by the waters of Babylon; we stayed there for a thousand years, farmed, prospered, built our academies, wrote the Talmud. And by the waters of the Guadalquivir, where fortunately we *didn't* hang up our harps on the willow trees. And by the river Hudson."

Rabbi Elazar: "The problem with spiritual idolatry is that it necessarily becomes political. Group A has to prove the superiority of Idol A, which can only happen at the expense of Group B's Idol B. So the issue of Jerusalem is a particularly dangerous one. I am not worried about secular Israelis; they are sensible people, and their nationalism has been, relatively, benign. But when that old-time religion gets mixed in, the issue becomes truly frightening. Because the proof-texts are right there in the Bible, which is, among its more admirable qualities, a document of propaganda. And the ghost of Joshua, that fierce spirit, is alive and kicking. The last time I visited Jerusalem, I was told that some of the Orthodox parties are actively planning to rebuild the Temple. Which means tearing down the Mosque of Omar. I shudder to think of the result."

"May I take a different approach?" Rabbi Simeon says. "For the past few minutes, I've been looking at this little lemon tree. It is so graceful and full of light. It doesn't seem to mind that its fruit is sour enough to set our teeth on edge. Maybe trees are the only angels."

Rabbi Elazar: "Well, I wouldn't be surprised to learn that they're the most spiritually evolved life form on our planet. What will a truly advanced civilization make of our Voyager probe, with its message of 'I Can't Get No Satisfaction' and its words of peace recorded in the voice of . . . Kurt Waldheim. Won't it see through our pretensions? I can imagine a UFO landing and the emissaries not even bothering to talk to us—going right to the trees."

Rabbi Judah: "Since they are intimate with the depths and the heights, trees can be immovable and at the same time yielding. I love it when our old poets pay attention to them. Job says,

> Even if it is cut down,
>   a tree can return to life.
> Though its roots decay in the ground
>   and its stump grows old and rotten,
> it will bud at the scent of water
>   and bloom as if it were young.

Then, later,

> And I thought, 'I will live many years,
>   growing as old as the palm tree.
> My roots will be spread for water,
>   and the dew will rest on my boughs.'

In Hebrew the same word, *yashar,* means 'standing straight up' and 'righteous.' So trees are a symbol for those who embody God's will, as in Psalm 1:

> Blessed are the man and the woman
>   who have grown beyond their greed
>   and have put an end to their hatred
>   and no longer nourish illusions.
> But they delight in the way things are
>   and keep their hearts open, day and night.
> They are like trees planted near flowing rivers,
>   which bear fruit when they are ready.
> Their leaves will not fall or wither.
>   Everything they do will succeed."

Rabbi Simeon: "There was a willow in my grandparents' backyard. We children used to sit under it, play hide-and-seek in its shadows, climb on its lower branches; it felt to us like a huge, good-natured sheepdog. I have never thought that 'weeping' was an appropriate adjective for willows. They seem to lean over more like women drying their long hair in the sun. And if they *are* grieving, it is with a kind of serenity at the core."

Rabbi Judah: "No wonder they were there by the waters of Babylon. I hope some of the exiles recognized them through that disguise."

Rabbi Simeon: "The *first* exile, the bitterest one, is the soul's. *'Eikháh yashváh vadád,'* 'How solitary she sits.' Why is the soul imagined as a woman?"

Rabbi Elazar: "Because women are more present in their bodies."

Rabbi Judah: "Because women are more intimate with birth."

Rabbi Simeon nods his head. "And because they know how to receive more gracefully than we do. Therefore they are less under the compulsion to control."

"But why is she solitary?" Rabbi Elazar says.

"That is a necessary stage in her progress. She has grown accustomed to so much clutter. It all has to be taken away. She must sit alone in a bare room, with nothing but grief for a mirror. Or, to change the metaphor, she must penetrate to the place where there is no consolation. Any kind of comfort would only distract her. It would take away her pain, but, like the lotus-eaters in the *Odyssey,* she would never arrive home."

Rabbi Judah: "Once, when I was still a disciple, I came to see my teacher after a few days of anguish when I couldn't bear to face him. I was suffering over a girl, as I remember, though it's not important why, because I used to spend a lot of time in the depths. My teacher saw my face and, very gently putting his hand on my shoulder, said, 'It will be all right. You are just homesick for your original home.' "

Rabbi Simeon: "That home is where God is sunlight and water, and the soul feels the serenity of a tree. She feels completely at peace, for all time, as if she is being rocked in someone's arms. Her mother's arms? Her own? She couldn't tell the difference even if she tried. It is a place described in Psalm 131, one of the shortest and most beautiful of the Psalms:

> Lord, my mind is not noisy with desires,
>   and my heart has satisfied its longing.
> I do not care about religion
>   or anything that is not you.
> I have soothed and quieted my soul,
>   like a child at its mother's breast.
> My soul is as peaceful as a child
>   sleeping in its mother's arms."

Rabbi Judah: "Later, in my early thirties, I happened upon a painting by Vermeer. It was an astonishing experience. I had never seen such a lucid, such a luminous, imagination of grace. For a while I used to go see it at the Metropolitan Museum every day when I was in New York. I would sit in front of it for an hour every day. Looking at it became a form of prayer. The art historians call that painting *Young Woman with a Water Pitcher,* but I came to call it *Portrait of the Soul: At Home.*"

Rabbi Simeon: "We all recognize that place—if one can call it a place—where the soul sits in *blissful* solitude, and is nothing but the light. We see it in the faces of our children. It is a state of being we all knew as children and have lost and will all someday want to find again. We visit it every night in deep sleep. If we are totally deprived of these visits, we go insane or die. All longing is the longing for God."

Rabbi Elazar: "Please, let's find another name for God. I keep having to brush away thoughts of the old king in the sky."

Rabbi Simeon: "I call God 'the Unnamable.' It isn't an it or a thou, though we may have to refer to it that way. 'My name is I AM,' it said to Moses. 'Tell them I AM sent you.' It is infinitely close to us, closer than our own breath or heartbeat, and yet we imagine it to be distant. The soul longs for it as a girl longs for her beloved. 'He is so far away,' she sighs. 'When will he return? If he doesn't come soon I will die.' God is bitterly absent—at least, to the soul, at this point in her learning, it *seems* that way."

Rabbi Elazar: "And comfort would be a distraction."

Rabbi Simeon: "Anything that she could recognize as good or bad would be a distraction."

Rabbi Judah: "That reminds me of a story. One day, outside the garden, Eve met her old friend the serpent. 'Good morning,' said the serpent, 'Nice skirt you've got on. How are you doing?' 'It's kind of you to ask,' Eve said. 'Actually, not so well.' 'Ah, yes,' said the serpent, 'aftereffects of the fruit. It does taste rather sour. Pretty color, though, that bright yellow.' 'But how can we get back inside the garden?' Eve said. 'Good question,' said the serpent. 'For me it's easy, of course: I just burrow under the hedge. Straight through the roots. In fact, I've *become* a sort of movable root. But I'll give you a hint: go back the way you came.' 'Thank you,' Eve said. 'You're still welcome,' said the serpent."

Rabbi Elazar: "Hmm."

Rabbi Simeon: "A nice hint."

Rabbi Elazar: "His point being that they don't return because they don't think they can?"

Rabbi Simeon: "They think themselves into a lot of problems."

Rabbi Judah: "Aftereffects of the fruit."

Rabbi Elazar: "And the cherubim with flaming swords who guarded the path to the Tree of Life? I bet they were redwoods, with sunlight glittering in their branches."

Rabbi Judah: "Perhaps. Perhaps if Eve and her husband could fully give themselves to a lament, they would find praise on the other side of it."

Rabbi Simeon: "Jeremiah, to whom Lamentations is traditionally ascribed, modulates into a prophecy that seems to me the most important of them all. 'The days are coming, says the Unnamable, when I will make a new covenant with Israel.' "

Rabbi Elazar: "Not only with Israel, I hope, but with all humanity. We could certainly use a more effective rainbow."

Rabbi Judah: "Israel, you know, on another level, means anyone who, like our father Jacob, has had the courage to wrestle in the night with the mysterious Other. *Yisra-el:* 'he who has struggled with God.' Or, as I prefer: 'he who has defeated God.' "

Rabbi Simeon: "And this is how Jeremiah continues his prophecy: 'I will put my truth in their innermost mind, and I will write it in their heart. And no longer will a man need to teach his brother about God. For all of them will know Me, from the most ignorant to the most learned, from the poorest to the most powerful.' "

Rabbi Judah: "And every fruit that they eat, apples and tangerines, will be from the Tree of Life."

"Because we already know that condition beyond time and space," Rabbi Simeon says. "The verse you quoted before, from Ecclesiastes, 'He has made everything beautiful in its time, and has put the whole world in our heart'—I would translate it more intimately, and close the circle: 'He has made everything beautiful in its time, and has put eternity in our heart.' "

ECCLESIASTES

A READING OUT-OF-SEASON

Daphne Merkin

I

ECCLESIASTES, OR AS IT IS ALSO KNOWN BY THE *NOM DE PLUME* OF its author, *Koheleth*, opens with a great sputter of protest, an exhaust fume of indignation let off against the motoric insensateness of life: *"Havél havalim,"* intones Koheleth, *"Havél havalim, hakól hevel"*—"Vanity of vanities, Vanity of vanities, all is vanity." The Hebrew is remarkably sonorous in its repetitiveness, but it is nonetheless grim; there is no denying the opening message of raging futility. We read on and discover that this message runs throughout the text, pumping its sentences with the strange sense of invigoration that sadness can bring.

I cannot imagine what it is like to read Ecclesiastes on a sunny day under a clear sky. It is, however much the pious commentators bustle in with their ready assuagements, a depressive's lament—perfect reading for a gray day. I began to explore Ecclesiastes on such a day, on a wintry afternoon,

The Jewish Publication Society's translation of the Bible used in this essay.

and immediately found myself colored by its plangent melancholy: *Kol ha'devorim yegayim* ("All words fail through weariness") (1:8); *V'ayn kol chadash tachat ha-shemesh* ("There is nothing new under the sun!") (1:9). Of course, it is precisely from such a miscomprehending reader as myself that the sages wished to protect this slim book, potentially the most subversive of the thirty-three in the Biblical canon. Midrashic literature (those disparate, post-Talmudic interpretations of the Bible known collectively as "midrash") resounds with anxieties about the heretic influence of *Koheleth,* quoting a Rabbi Benjamin who declared that the sages originally wished to conceal the text, and a Rav Samuel ben Isaac who maintained that its reading could easily lead to unbelief. That Ecclesiastes got in under the wire of religious censorship at all is due to its alleged authorship at the hands of King Solomon—a construction now discarded by most Biblical scholars— and also to a somewhat startling elasticity of spirit on the part of those who dictated the shape of the Tanach, or Bible. But its negative power was certainly not lost on those who decided in favor of its inclusion.

For a Jewish text, Ecclesiastes is almost unconscionably jaded, brimming over with the most romantic and sophisticated sense of *Weltschmerz.* Cyclical time—time looped back in on itself, like an eternally replaying tape—is no longer seen as an assurance of God's revelational hand. Whereas religious life seeks to deflect the ennervation insisted on here by rendering time continuous, Koheleth experiences seasonal circularity only as evidence of the entropic impulse in nature: "Blowing toward the south and veering toward the north, ever circling goes the wind, returning upon its tracks. All the rivers flow continually to the sea, but the sea does not become full; whither the rivers flow, they continue to flow" (1:6–7).

Koheleth, who takes for himself the *persona* of the wealthiest of Jewish kings, is at ease among the glitterati. (The midrash rather cunningly points out that, had a poor man uttered the words *havél havalim,* we would have scoffed at him, but since they come from King Solomon, whose vessels were all of gold, we pay attention.) No withdrawn, ivory-towered observer he, Koheleth is someone who vies with competitive zeal and has tasted of excess: "I bought slaves and slave girls, in addition to my household retainers; my possessions of cattle and sheep also were greater than those of all who had preceded me in Jerusalem, I amassed also silver and gold, such private treasure as kings and satraps have. I provided myself with male and female singers, and with the pleasure of the flesh, concubine after concubine. As I became greater than any who have been before me in Jerusalem . . ." (2:7–9). And yet nothing suffices for this acquisition-happy malcontent, this Biblical character blessed with the dazzling "life style" of a corporate raider but burdened with the wrong soul—the soul of a Flauber. Like that other great connoisseur of *ennui,* Koheleth is acutely aware of the "boredom and ignominies of existence," and would, I suspect, agree with the nineteenth-century writer's calibrated assessment: "I admire tinsel as much as gold: indeed the poetry of tinsel is even greater, because it is sadder."

Although the corpus of Ecclesiastes is carefully appended with a statement of religious exhortation (generally thought to have been composed by a later, uneasy editor)—"The sum of the matter, when all is said and done: Revere God and observe his commandments!" (12:13)—its twelve segments contain little in the way of homiletics or even of the platitudes of Jewish faith. God, insofar as He is a presence in the book at all, seems mainly to be suffering from a repetition compulsion: "I realized, too, that whatever God has brought to pass will recur evermore: Nothing can be added to it / And nothing taken from it . . ." (3:14). Similarly, the idea of an afterlife, in which the good are rewarded and the bad punished, is questioned—"Who knows if a man's life-breath does rise upward and if a beast's breath does sink down into the earth" (3:21)—and specifically contradicted: "But the dead know nothing; they have no more recompense, for even the memory of them has died. Their loves, their hates, their jealousies have long since perished; and they have no more share till the end of time in all that goes on under the sun" (4:5–6). So much for the consoling childhood images we carry with us—those neatly polarized depictions of heaven and hell, golden-haloed angels and pitchfork-wielding devils.

More interestingly still, Koheleth proposes that as far as *this* life goes, moral stature and earthly status not only don't necessarily follow on each other practicably—"Sometimes an upright man is requited according to the conduct of the scoundrel; and sometimes the scoundrel is requited according to the conduct of the upright" (8:14)—but also they may not bear any but the most oblique relation to divine will: *Ki le'odom shetov lephanav natan chachma v'da'at v'simcha*—"To the man, namely, who pleases Him He has given the wisdom and shrewdness to enjoy himself" (2:26). The phrase *shetov lephanav* ("who pleases Him") is, to my mind, a provocative one, for it suggests that God may be seducible by an attractiveness of aspect—a *simpatico* quality—that has nothing to do with inner probity, and may be entirely arbitrary. The progression is clearly spelled out: *first* one finds favor, *then* one merits His bounty. Given the almost Calvinistic preselection of the process, how are we to know if God might not indeed stand up for (attractive) bastards after all—fall head over heels, that is, for the wrong man?

Known as "the most modern book in the Bible," Ecclesiastes is undeniably the most heterodox. Even the least cautious of critics is quick to point out that Koheleth's skepticism is only the topmost stratum of his core identity as a monotheistic Jew. Still, there is no getting around the fact that the ideas he espouses, in a pithy and proverb-based style that has been called "Oriental," are informed by the pressure of nullity. Koheleth comes to us having faced down the existential void, the hollowness at the heart of the getting and spending that is the human enterprise: "The race is not won by the swift, / Nor the battle by the valiant; / Nor is bread won by the wise / Nor wealth by the intelligent, / Nor favor by the learned" (9:12).

No wonder it is the Old Testament text most cherished by secular readers, by non-Jews and even by those who are faintly anti-Semitic in their sentiments. Tennyson proclaimed it "the greatest poem of ancient or modern times," and so unlikely a reader as Havelock Ellis suggested that you could spare yourself some unhappiness in the world "if, before hand, you slip the Book of Ecclesiastes beneath your arm." Even more sweepingly, there is the verdict of Ernest Renan, the French historian and critic, for whom *Koheleth* is "the only charming book ever written by a Jew."

There is, to be sure, a bracing—even healing—aspect to the stark realism of the writer's vision, a way in which his resolute emphasis on the transience of all things human can be said to be a cloud-chaser. Still, the "charm" of Ecclesiastes is a tonic charm, a somewhat bitter-tasting dose of our own dust-to-dustness. (For some readers, the atmosphere of skull-rattling verges on the lurid, like those Elizabethan revenge-tragedies where Death puts in an appearance as a character on stage: "The book has indeed," mused one Biblical exegete, "the smell of the tomb about it.") But the appeal of this work stems primarily, I think, from its tone of mercurial intimacy—from the narrator's almost defiant credo of personalism. The stakes here, unlike the stakes set by the "other-directed" Prophets, are very private ones: What is the formula for achieving success? Do or don't I find happiness in this life? What use is *carpe diem* if disaster may strike as readily as good fortune?

In his abiding pragmatism, Koheleth makes frequent use of a Hebrew term, *yitron,* which literally means the surplus or profit remaining from a transaction. The word occurs ten times in all, and first appears early in the text: "What profit hath man of all his labor / Wherein he laboreth under the sun?" (1:3) Commentators have pointed out that the word appears nowhere else in the Bible. Along with the use of two words of Persian origin—*pardes* ("grove," "orchard") and *pitngam* ("judgment," "sentence")—it is a clue to the historical dating of the book, generally believed to have been written in the second to third century B.C.E. But the term is also of intrinsic interest for what it suggests about the limitations of the writer's philosophy, entrenched as it is in the mercantile culture of the early Hellenistic period and bounded by rationalist, egotistic considerations.

The cornerstones of Koheleth's philosophy seem to be the concepts of consolation *(menachem* or *nachas),* futility or vanity *(hevel)* and profit *(yitron).* Within this triad of possibilities, consolation is at best fleeting, vanity is a constant, and profit is difficult to show. Ultimately, the reader is presented with the cunning collapse of two of the terms into the third, and we find ourselves with the triumph of contingency over forethought. (In diagram form this system would reveal an upside-down triangle, with the vectors of consolation and profit meeting at the inverted apex of vanity and futility.) Like the stock market at its most dismally unpredictable, a potentially profitable angle is rendered null and void by events undreamed of in our calculations: "If a snake which has not been charmed bites, what is the use of having a snake charmer?" (10:11) There is no solace to be found.

Of course, with his healthy respect for money and his palpable indifference to the idea of community, Koheleth seems to be talking far more than the usual Biblical protagonist for the *real* rather than the *ideal* self in all of us. If, as recent psychological research indicates, personal happiness derives less from how close we come to our idealized inner selves and more from how content we feel with ourselves as we are, it is perfectly understandable why Ecclesiastes has been embraced in all its cold and gnomic comfort. "Wedged in among resplendent priests, ecstatic psalmists and implacable prophets," as Robert Gordis so aptly described him, Koheleth cuts a less than imposing, recognizably human figure. Shamelessly inconsistent in his reasoning, though always a bottom-liner, with what relief we fall upon him!

It must be fairly noted, however, that a lonely perusal out of season is not what the sages had in mind for this pickled dish of a text. Such a reading can only lead away from the larger ritual purpose, the instructive calendrical context, that the rabbis who agreed to include Ecclesiastes had presupposed. As is true of so much of Jewish life, the specific occasion designated for its reading—the festival of *Succot*, or Tabernacles, which falls, in our hemisphere, in the brilliant days of early autumn—evokes a dialectic and therefore a deliberate state of tension. It is part of the constant righting of balances that is at the heart of this religion's approach. Set against the gaiety and plenty of the holiday, which commemorates the ingathering of the harvest, the shadows cast by the book of Koheleth lengthen and darken.

II

Succot is an eight-day festival during the course of which Ecclesiastes is read aloud in the synagogue. It stands out in my mind as the favored holiday of my childhood. The Biblical injunction concerning its practice stresses enjoyment (*v'samachta b'chagecha*—"and you shall be happy in your festival") over decorum. Following as it does upon the heels of Rosh Hashanah and Yom Kippur—those sober, prayer-inundated, and self-abnegating Days of Awe—*Succot* struck my youthful imagination as decidedly and atypically carefree. Given that my attitude toward the minutiae of Jewish observance was an admixture of resentment and a not wholly unappreciative compliance, I had a perhaps overdeveloped sense of the prohibited (what I wasn't allowed to do on *yontiv,* or "good" days, as they were called: turn on lights, write, listen to music) and not enough of the celebratory as a factor in religious life. *Succot,* with its light touch and cheery tone, was just the right corrective for me—nearer, or so it seemed, to the Christian ideal of holiday than to the Jewish.

For starters, the holiday is deeply sensual: aromatic with the branches of *s'chach,* the pine or evergreen that crowns the makeshift dwelling of the *succah* (a reminder of the portable huts the Jews built while wandering the desert), and pungent with the scent of the *etrog,* the ritual citron resembling nothing so much as a wrinkled and obese lemon. Then there were the decorations within the *succah* itself: the painstakingly lettered and curlicued drawings, like Hebrew versions of kitchen samplers, that my siblings and I had worked on for days. These were hung on the thin wooden walls of the *succah* next to ancestral photographs, alien-looking relatives who stared out from their frames with mournful sepia gazes. In between the branches of *s'chach* nestled vivid touches of fruit—apples, oranges, and an occasional banana. If one looked more closely, one glimpsed the tiny glass bottles of oil, flour, and wine symbolizing the harvest (and which my mother packed away from year to year) that stirred in the breeze, catching the light.

Although both the holiday itself and its representative text constitute a warning against being too at home, too comfortable in the material universe, *Succot* is also very much about the aesthetics of improvisation. True, we may die or lose everything at any time, but we can dance rings around that fact, festoon it with all manner of ingenuity. In a family where the spiritual impulse often seemed to get buried under layers of German formality and propriety, *Succot* drew on my mother's strengths—her genuine love of beauty, her pleasure in tasteful adornment. It is more curious, therefore, that when I think of the message of Ecclesiastes I think not of myself or my family but of Teddy, the Irish handyman, who fixed leaking ceilings and faulty plumbing. It was he who, within the course of a single afternoon, put up the *succah* in the space allotted for it in the driveway—just under the basketball hoop.

With nothing more than a mouthful of nails and four planes of green-painted plywood, Teddy worked the sort of magic my brainy but impractical brothers and father could never have managed. He built us a house, one with curtained windows and a plastic roof that could be raised and lowered over the fragile covering of *s'chach* in case of rain. It was a real house, with room inside to seat twelve or fourteen, but one that also partook of the meta-real—a house appearing suddenly in the woods in a fairy tale, providing shelter from storms both metaphorical and actual. Teddy, whose face was always slightly ruddy—from wind or from drink, or a bit of both—seemed to understand the implication of Ecclesiastes deep inside his bones: Everything that happens, has happened, will happen again. Alone among us, he seemed to take the world precisely as it came, caught up in a race against no man or clock. Free of the morbid self-consciousness that marked the members of my family, he was satisfied with his own inner synchronism.

Of course, my setting the mantle of Koheleth on an Irish laborer is not entirely fanciful. Ecclesiastes is one of the five *Megillot* (the other four are Ruth, Esther, the Song of Songs, and Lamentations) contained in the third part of the Tanach known as *K'Tuvot* ("the Writings" or "Hagiographa"). Along with the Book of Job and Proverbs, it belongs as well to that body of work within the larger Biblical tradition known as *chochmah,* or "Wisdom literature." Radically divergent from the rest of the Old Testament, this literature has been called "a kind of third force" in the cultural life of the people, texts that address individual rather than institutional needs.

Among Wisdom literature, both Job and *Koheleth* are strikingly independent-minded and secularist, with more than a trace of apostasy. They are thought to have been written by teachers of the *chochmah* school (*Koheleth* in Hebrew means "teacher" or "one who addresses an assembly"), whose upper-class members were immersed in both Jewish scholarship and the Greek culture around them. Fittingly, the original reference of *chochmah* was not to intellectual learning but to trained craftsmanship—mechanical rather than book knowledge—and only later did it evolve a more erudite connotation. In a quite literal sense, then, our Irish carpenter can be thought of as embodying the spirit of *chochmah* out of which *Koheleth* emerged. Like the Biblical jewelry designer, Bezalel, in connection with whom the term "wisdom" was first used, Teddy was gifted with his hands, and this practical intelligence makes him eligible, as it were, to bear the message contained in Ecclesiastes.

Who was Koheleth? Who was the person behind the *persona,* the man behind the philosophy? Although as contemporary readers we might wish to psychoanalyze his malaise—to make guesses about his temperament and upbringing—there is too little to work with. The paucity of personal allusions in this self-revealing yet elusive document spares him. We deduce that Koheleth is an older man, looking back on his life from a position of material success as well as spiritual disappointment. From his casual reference to attendance at sacrificial rites, scholars have presumed that the Temple was nearby, and that he probably lived in Jerusalem. Ancient Jerusalem appears to have been no easier a country for old men than Yeats's modern Ireland— "an aged man" there, too, "but a paltry thing." In one of the last and more lyrical passages of the book, the writer describes the humiliations of senescence so vividly—with an almost Yeatsian intensity—that it suggests his own biography.

"So appreciate your vigor in the days of your youth," opens chapter 12, "before those years arrive of which you will say, 'I have no pleasure in them. . . .' " Then follows an allegory composed of a series of startlingly beautiful metaphors in which the slow deterioration of the parts of the body is likened to the closing down of a once-bustling village: "When the guards of the house become shaky" (i.e., the arms); "And the men of valor are bent" (legs); "And the maids that grind, grown few, are idle" (teeth); "And the ladies that peer through the windows grow dim" (eyes); "And the doors to the street are shut" (ears). This terrifying vision of decrepitude and impotence concludes with the painful reminder: "And the dust returns to the ground / As it was, / And the life-breath returns to God / Who bestowed it" (12:7). Like "the old, old men" in Yeats's poem—titled, with grim humor, "The Old Men Admiring Themselves in the Water"—Koheleth flashes before us a mirror in which is reflected an image of our eventual fate: "one by one we drop away."

There are other traits we can adduce about this Biblical *cahier*-keeper, habits of mind and intellectual biases (although any critical theory constructed about this most protean of texts immediately produces a countertheory: Greek influences have been equally asserted and denied, and one lone scholar claims to see a Buddhist influence). Deeply skeptical as he may be, Koheleth is a political conservative, a believer in the sovereign power of the state as reflected in the king. *Hakesef,* he says at one point, *ya'ane et hakol*— "Money answers everything." He is a man for the eighties, a private-sectorite. But being a personality who wears contradictions without discomfort, he has another side, one that suits another realm—the realm of the artist, where a restless spirit of inquiry soars beyond the walls of the *status quo*.

Like Voltaire and his *Candide*, the author of Ecclesiastes engages in an exercise of constructive fantasy. The book has scarcely any narrative to hold on to; it offers little of the systematic construction of Job. What it offers instead are the squiggles of an implied quest, a classical quest that can also be put in the most contemporary of terms: If you were rich as Croesus—as Kashoggi—how would you choose to live? Through the reversals and inconsistencies of Koheleth's paradoxical reasoning (examples of sloth in chapter 10, for instance, are followed by examples of too much caution in chapter 11) emerges the curve of a critique, a testing of the standard notions of pleasure. The consolations Koheleth remains with have mostly to do with the actual producing of Wisdom—the making of however pessimistic a philosophy. Then, too, it is possible to find a dim comfort in the thought that catastrophe itself is part of the experiential spectrum: "For there is a time for every experience, including the doom; for a man's calamity over-whelms him" (8:6).

But even these small victories snatched from the jaws of despair cannot be granted without qualification. Given his acute awareness of the role hubris plays in human affairs, Koheleth is convinced of the ultimate useless-ness of intelligence, its tragic lack of effect: "For as wisdom grows, vexation grows; / To increase learning is to increase heartache" (1:18). Later in the text, describing an underpopulated city which might have been spared its ransacked fate had anyone thought to seek the counsel of a wise but poor inhabitant, he concludes: "A poor man's wisdom is scorned / And his words are not heeded" (9:16).

Thinking about who the author of Ecclesiastes might have been and who scholars historically perceive him to have been brings me to an even more literal-minded linking of the figures of Teddy and the writer of the book. Although my mother used to quote a phrase from *Koheleth* as an argument in favor of getting married—*tovim ha'shnayim min ha'echad* ("two are better off than one")—I now realize she did so slyly and knowingly out of context. For one thing, the reference is to business and not marital partners; for another, Koheleth was probably a bachelor, a very early case of what today we might call the uncommited male. Although he commends matrimony in the abstract—"Enjoy happiness with a woman you love, all the fleeting days of life" (9:9)—his distrust of women's wiles verges on virtual misogyny: "Now, I find woman more bitter than death; she is all traps, her hands are fetters and her heart is snares. He who is pleasing to God escapes her, and he who is displeasing is caught by her" (7:26). Who can say what circumstances in his own life led to this extreme position: Was Koheleth perhaps thrown over by a woman he loved for someone less implacably dark-natured? Or was he the son of a dominating mother whose clutches he felt even in old age? One can only guess.

But what I, as a female reader, cannot help being especially struck by, more than his probable bachelorhood, is the *childlessness* of the narrator. For a Jewish text, Ecclesiastes is remarkably and singularly devoid of the urge to perpetuate. The sense of futurity and continuity—both familial and racial—that the idea of posterity guarantees is wholly absent in Koheleth. Always conscious though he is of his own mortality, he never succumbs to the allure of having children as a means to ensure one's *im*mortality. When Koheleth speaks of "the case of the man who is alone, with no companion, who has neither son nor brother," one can reasonably speculate that he is talking of himself. And "the case of the man who is alone" brings me back willy-nilly to Teddy. For in a childhood where all the grown men I encountered were married, and often saddled with kids, Teddy was single. It must be said in his behalf that he didn't begin to share in Koheleth's rampant hostility; he seemed to like women, albeit from a safely flirtatious distance. But Teddy certainly hadn't been inspired to tie the connubial knot; nor, so far as I knew, had he sired offspring. As an unprocreative male, he was spared one of the prevailing anxieties in Ecclesiastes: the fear of lineage and its attendant decline, of "toiling for the wind."

In the years that have intervened between then and now, Teddy has aged imperceptibly. He has never married—he is, I think, proud to have abstained from so routine a decision—and he appears to be childless. Although I connect him with my childhood, he still comes around to painstakingly repair windows and stop up leaks. The present has caught up with him, as it has with me, but in a sense it will never overtake him. He will not witness the fruit of his labor despoiled by future generations, a son who builds houses on shaky foundations, or a grandson who scoffs at his way with a piece of wood and nails.

As a daughter in an Orthodox household, I had no text to call my own. In contrast to Jewish sons, who are raised with a proprietary relationship to the Bible, Jewish daughters have at best an oblique connection to the sacred volumes of their heritage. When each of my three brothers turned Bar Mitzvah at the age of thirteen, they recited the weekly Torah portion as well as the selection from the *haftorah* Shabbos morning in *shul*. The arduous months of preparation—the bearded teacher who sat with them, ceaselessly going over the *"trop,"* the half-chant, half-melody in which the lines of the text are sung—paid off handsomely in that hour of glory up on the *bima*, before a jam-packed congregation that hung on to every syllable uttered. When I turned Bas Mitzvah, at the age of twelve, my family went out to dinner at Lou G. Siegel's, a kosher restaurant. I wore a light-blue dress that had belonged first to my sister, and I recited nothing of greater consequence than a litany of thank-you's.

In a sense, it was already too late: by the age of twelve I cast a cynical eye on the whole religious arena. Two years before, I had stopped believing in God—mostly on the basis that I couldn't see where the bad (my mother and father and my many siblings) were any worse off than the good (myself). I was, if I had only known it, a young follower in the steps of Leibniz, a ready believer in theodicy, except that *I* had given up on finding a divine vindication of evil in my lifetime. In retrospect, I think that, as a young girl with a marked tendency to depression and no great conviction about the particulars of the faith in which I was reared, I would have warmed to Ecclesiastes. I might even have chosen it—its antifeminist aspect notwithstanding—as my text, my very own out-of-season *haftorah*, to be recited before an admiring public not on *Succot* but on my birthday, which fell in May.

The message I take from *Koheleth* is that sadness flows under the skin of things, like blood. It is a part of life—Freud's "ordinary unhappiness," what we are left with even after "neurotic misery" is cured—not to be avoided, but to be recognized and understood. Once understood, it becomes possible to contain the sadness within circles of light: orbs of warmth against the encroaching chill. When I look back on the *succah* of my childhood, it stands out in my memory as one of those circles, a confining but also cozy haven. If it makes me somewhat wistful to realize that I am now irrevocably outside the radius of the *succah*—that I have moved away from its green smell and flickering candles, its food and conversation—I also realize that for me it was a necessary, liberating step. Still, who knows if there won't come a day when I will once again step inside under the canopy of *s'chach* and inhale the complex religion of my upbringing as it wafts by me?

If the news the sober, immensely clear-eyed writer of this book brings us is that there are no second acts, even in Jewish lives, who is to say what twists and turns the first and only act holds in store for us? *Ayn chadash tachat hashemesh* is perhaps the single most famous sentence in Ecclesiastes: "There is nothing new under the sun." What else can this mean except that possibility is recurrent; nothing is surprising, nothing is absolutely unprecedented. In our leavetakings are the stirrings of return.

ESTHER

APART: HEARING SECRET HARMONIES

Richard Howard

THESE STORIES WERE TOLD US—VERY YOUNG CHILDREN, DISAF-
fected Jews in a Midwestern suburb—before we read them,
before we could read at all. At first they were told as *Bible
Stories for the Young,* but very soon they were read to us from
the Authorized Version. Greek myths and Shakespeare could be diluted
almost indefinitely, but the Old Testament—like the tales of Andersen and
the Grimm brothers—soon came to us in what passed for original strength.
It never occurred to us that such things were translations.

And out of the stories, as they were told, as they were heard, loomed
a sort of wandering wonder we associated with any telling—it could be
Alice, it could be Artemis—a cloud of conjecture inseparable from its source
in "ancestral voices prophesying. . . ." There was always the implication,
of course, that eventually we would be reading—for ourselves, as it were—
that we would bestow upon all such received matter the resolved and
rectified attention which *reading* inveterately signified. I think we under-

The King James Version of the Bible used in this essay.

stood, even in our passive condition, even in our delight, that a time would come when we would be reading *on our own,* that we might at that time *correct* the promiscuous and irresponsible suppositions of hearing by a more severe indoctrination. We would leave off the appropriate response to telling, which was speculation, and take up the appropriate response to reading, which was acquiescence. No wonder, then, that we were encouraged to learn how to read for ourselves, which meant for others, whereas when we listened to others telling, we heard—and hypothecated—for ourselves.

Indeed, in the ensuing years I was informed and sometimes admonished that my own excessive bookishness was evidence of my Jewishness. I was one more bespectacled child who had learned to read "too soon"; my literacy was a symptom of my lineage. Were we not—as ignorant of Islam as we were knowing about the *Arabian Nights—the* people of the Book? But as I loiter more inquisitorially over my early experience with these stories, with the histories and apocrypha of the Bible as I heard them, I must acknowledge that we were the people, initially, of the Tale. Telling, and hearing, came first, and the process was marvelous, metamorphic, meant. We were beguiled by, and brought together upon, narratives which in their recounting allowed for—indeed, which compelled—all kinds of speculation as to their outcome and as to their ongoing likelihood. The Scroll of Esther was merely a characteristic wonder as it unwound in the telling. Perhaps because of the doubleness of its method it was more resonant than the others, more resplendent, and could lead more easily, by the very contrast of the eponymous half of its substance with the rest of its matter, into the auguries of imagined life.

In the largest, cloudiest apprehension, I knew that Esther was about my mother, and that Mordecai was about the world—about my stepfathers and the struggle for survival. Esther was magic, Mordecai was management. Exactly apprehended, the process was accounted for by Michelet, though neither a Jew nor a child, in *The Bible of Humanity* (1864):

The history of the Jews, at whatever level of seriousness, transpired against a fictive background—the arbitrary miracle, in which it pleased God to choose among the lowest, indeed among the unworthiest, a liberator, a savior, an avenger of His people. In the Captivity or in Court intrigues, sudden fortunes cast imaginations on the path of the unexpected. The splendid historical novels of Joseph, Ruth, Tobit, Esther, Daniel and many more appeared. Always based on two figments: *the good exile* who, by the interpretation of dreams and financial astuteness, becomes minister or favorite; and *the woman beloved of God* who makes a great marriage, attains to glory, seduces the enemy and (astonishingly enough, in contrast with Mosaic notions) becomes a deliverer of her people. But it is precisely the unexpected choice which fiction seizes upon: God makes the woman a snare, utilizes her seductiveness, and through her brings about the downfall of a man he has doomed. There is the essence of the novel: it is the contrary of history, not only because it subordinates great collective interests to an individual destiny, but because it does not favor the ways of that difficult preparation which in history produces events. The novel prefers to show us the lucky throws of the dice which chance occasionally produces, to flatter us with the notion that the impossible frequently becomes possible. By this hope, this interest, this pleasure, fiction wins its reader, spoiled from the start, who will pursue it avidly—to the point where he foregoes talent, even skill. The chimerical mind is interested in the story, in the *affair,* wants it *to turn out well.*

Esther (and, scarcely to a lesser degree, Susannah and Judith) was the heroine in whom, as soon as I had heard her story, I invested *that hope, that interest, that pleasure,* for she was less arbitrary than Alice (after all, from my perspective she was a grownup) and less absolute than Artemis (after all, she was a mortal). And if, as Michelet so uncannily perceived, I was spoiled from the start, it was not just because I wanted the story to turn out well (though I did, I did—I lingered over every seductive detail likely to establish Esther's invincible appeal; or, rather, I did not linger, I ran ahead, I devised every possible allurement out of whatever lay around the house, out of anything I deemed likely to move the Ahasuerus of South Park Boulevard, my imminent stepfather), but also because I entertained (sic) so many fears of its turning out otherwise, because there was so wide a margin for error. Only the story of Scheherazade—not the stories she told, but *her* story, her situation, her discovery that silence was death and *telling* was life—could rival the enchantment of "Bible stories," and, indeed, the reason for that rivalry, for that equivalence, would become apparent to me as I marveled over Esther.

My amazements here began at the beginning, began with what narratologists would call the prologue: the repudiation of Vashti. For, in order to produce Esther, in order to bring on the heroine, if there was to be a heroine at all, place must be made for her. And was there a hero? Why was

Mordecai given such minor billing? His was a position comparable to Joseph's—obviously Joseph's story had exerted a strong influence on the writer of Esther—and indeed in the *Book of the Chronicles of the Kings of Media and Persia* referred to at the end of Esther it is "the greatness of Mordecai" that is proclaimed, not the greatness of Esther. Emphasis in the early sources on Mordecai rather than on Esther suggests that there were indeed two stories, two *affairs:* the *history* of Mordecai, engaged in court intrigue, jealousy, and persecution of the Jews in Susa, and the *story* of Esther, who won her king's favor and prevented the persecution of her people: *i.e.,* the *tale* of Esther, the *book* of Mordecai. The heroine must replace the old queen. Who was no such thing, this offstage Vashti: she was young and lovely—so lovely that her extravagant and impulsive lord commands her to exhibit her beauty to the people and princes at a feast, wearing the royal turban or *Megilla.* (*Megilla,* in our house, was not known to be the Hebrew word for "scroll"; it was the word assigned to anything complicated or intricate.) Here was a story, or at least a circumstance, which I could commit to speculation, for I knew it already; I had heard it already, as I had heard of Artemis and Alice. I had been told a Greek story of King Candaules, who was so proud of his queen's loveliness that he contrived to have his servant see her naked. . . . I knew how that story ended, if it was allowed to end. But in the story of Ahasuerus (which scholars in Göttingen as recently as 1958 related to the story in Herodotus through an original Persian New Year festival), the ending was altered. The story changed. For the lovely queen, whether or not she must appear naked at the feast (some rabbis actually suggest that Vashti was commanded to attend the feast clad in the *Megilla* and in nothing else), was but demonstrating decorum in refusing to appear before a crowd of drunken men. Indeed, was she not asserting her royal prerogative? For when the drinking began at a feast, that would be the signal for concubines and courtesans to join in. If Vashti appeared at the feast then, she would no longer be queen, but would by her mere presence be degraded to the status of a concubine. And were there not some commentators—they were Christians, but even so—who recognized in such reluctance a propriety so pervasive that they declared Vashti to be the only admirable person in the entire tale, precisely by virtue of her refusal to accede to her giddy husband's perverse and perilous command? ("I am so hostile to Esther," Luther remarked in his *Table Talk,* "that I could wish she did not exist at all; for Esther and Maccabees judaize too greatly and contain much pagan impropriety.") Thus Vashti became, to my obstinate hypotheses, one of those haunting, secret figures in literature, like Lot's wife, who make one decisive negative gesture, who violate a commandment and then vanish forever, leaving only a symbolic transgression for memorial.

Here the story diverged from the Candaules theme and braided itself into another, one equally familiar to the ears of childhood: the story of Scheherazade. If we were to have Esther, Vashti *had* to be deposed. And the king, after half a year of feasting in his winter capital (which the Greek geographer Strabo declared to be so hot that snakes and lizards trying to crawl across the roads at noon were burned to death), his anger having subsided and his appetite revived, upon sober reflection *had* to be supplied with a new queen, "better than Vashti," to be chosen not just out of the harem of existing wives, concubines, consorts, and courtesans, but out of all the virgins of the realm. Certainly Memucan's suggestion of a nationwide search presented a much more exciting prospect to the king than the quotidian selection. It was easy to understand that the splendid postal system of the Persian empire ("nor snow nor sleet can stay these messengers from the swift completion of their appointed rounds": Herodotus' words were on the post-office cornice), later invoked to such purpose in this very story, would be employed in making sure that the *irrevocable decree* against Vashti was publicized. Those advisers would hardly want to confront the displeasure of a reinstated queen! But disobedience for disobedience—a subject of consuming interest to myself and my coevals in those days, when we were also told stories about the insubordinations of Brunnhilde and the last Mrs. Bluebeard—it seemed to me that Vashti, in refusing to appear, was no more refractory than Esther would later prove in refusing to stay away. But perhaps I had already learned, with regard to kings and fathers and husbands, that there were *degrees* of transgression, and that one violation of the rules provokes anger, and another may elicit, just as readily, mercy. . . .

Now, what happened, I wondered, to this wife who had been put away? Where had she gone? Deposed . . . Repudiated . . . Was it like "divorced," as I identified such abjurations in my own family, in Cleveland? My mother had already been divorced—twice. And I knew her to be a vivid figure, still, in the world of those discarded—and discarding?—figures. Was Vashti still accommodated somewhere in the palace, despised perhaps but not altogether disposed of? I knew of households, no grander than our own, in which some awkward aunt, some senile grandmother, had separate quarters at the top of the house, visitable but not receivable. After all, the virgins whom Ahasuerus condescended to inspect (I could imagine that the king's servants were eager to smooth away his discontent), and to whom he eventually preferred Esther, were not eliminated in the manner of Scheherazade's predecessors. Following a night with the king, apparently an unsatisfactory one, such women were not beheaded but merely relegated to a "second" harem, where they would wait—apparently the rest of their lives—for the king to summon them, to call them by name. Of course, I had some clues as to why Esther had been preferred to these women, and what mistakes the others had made—beyond sexual incompetence, which I failed to take into account, though I was fascinated by the notion of a year's preparation to please the king: six months of massage with oil of myrrh and six months with balsam and other unspecified cosmetics. Each virgin, the story went, on her way to the king was permitted to take with her anything she desired. Esther alone, it would seem, required nothing, and obtained favor by requiring nothing. Evidently the compunctions of Cinderella were in force here, and I recognized the merits of modesty and an unassuming demeanor, even one that had been massaged and perfumed for twelve months.

Esther herself was only called "queen," of course. She did not rule, once the king set the *Megilla* upon her head and threw her a party ("even Esther's feast"). And later, though she had been acknowledged queen for five years, she occupied a precarious position still, at least in her own mind. She did not put herself forward in any way, therefore, and made no claim upon her lord, but remained all that time in the harem, waiting. And if all the concubines and even the wives who did not find favor in the king's eyes were confined along with the approved "queen" to that world of women which the word "harem" signified to me (and where, after all, "to die" might have meant nothing graver than not to be alive in the king's imagination, not to be present in his thoughts), did Esther and Vashti never meet there? What might such an encounter be like—the confrontation at the well, or in the baths (I had seen reproductions of Ingres' uterine fantasy of the women's baths as well as Gérôme's)—between the new queen, still unfamiliar with Ahasuerus, and the once-favored queen, who had been so arbitrarily thrust aside? As yet Esther had not "showed her kindred nor her people." Universally popular in the harem and elsewhere, Esther must have eaten, dressed (and undressed), and behaved like a Persian harem-girl, rather than like an observant Jewess. What, then, would she and Vashti say to each other? What precepts might be passed on, what experience shared? This was not a situation Scheherazade was ever obliged to contend with—rather, it was one that could crop up only in a thoroughly modern harem. I pondered the relationships—marital, divorced, adulterous, matronly, and virginal—which I could identify in the society around me (Cleveland 1936, say, as opposed to Susa 500 B.C.E.), and I marveled at Esther's *astuce* in beguiling the king's impulses rather than expressing her own, in showing the docility and submissiveness so notably lacking in her predecessor. Though perhaps—and here I began my own embroidery, my own affabulation—with the wisdom of hindsight, it was Vashti who had advocated such attitudes in her successor. I could imagine the scene all the more readily for having witnessed analogous encounters between present wife and "ex," between *maitresse en titre* and old flame: deprecating or implacable, as the case might be. The story of Esther, as I mused upon it, was one that transpired in an astonishingly alien world of sultans and viziers, as in the *Arabian Nights,* and yet in a world of reassuring familiarity, as in Hollywood movies and at our own dinner table. The Oriental despot who would hand over an entire people to his cruel vizier without even inquiring as to that people's name was the same tyrant who had just repudiated his wife on a whim and who would shortly execute his vizier on a new wife's word. As one ancient Jewish commentator put it, Ahasuerus sacrifices his wife to his friend and later sacrifices his friend to his wife. Even the names of the (ultimately Jewish) hero and heroine were instructive as to this doubleness, this ambiguity: Esther and Mordecai bear not only non-Hebraic but even idolatrous names (so that Esther, a Daniel in reverse, must be given a second name, the Hebrew name Hadassah, which is interpreted to mean "myrtle—for as the myrtle spreads fragrance in the world, so did she spread good works"). Ishtar and Marduk are pertinently proposed as the Babylonian gods whose ritual became a historicized Jewish myth, "a Jewish adaptation of a popular Persian novella."

Certainly, with the introduction of the second story, the story of Mordecai, a history of manipulation and intrigue, it was clear to me that Hadassah was the heroine's appropriate name when she figured in the

Mordecai tradition, and Esther was her appropriate name when she belonged to the magical tradition. Once Vashti had been spirited away (as in so many apocryphal harem tales), there was every indication that the Scroll of Esther was no more (no less?) than a conflation of two texts. Indeed, one French scholar, Henri Cazelles, found evidence for this duplicity in the pervasive "twoness" of episodes and situations in the tale: two banquets; two lists of seven names, one the reverse order of the other; the second house of the women; the second contingent of candidates for the king's favor; Esther's two dinners; Haman's two discussions with his wife, Zaresh, and his friends; Esther's twice risking her life by appearing before the king. One text, Cazelles asserts, was "liturgical" and concerns Esther/Ishtar, the provinces of the empire, and non-Jews at the time of the Persian New Year (so that Purim is to be identified with a bacchanalian Persian festival—this, of course, is also Frazer's reading of the story); and the other text is "historical" and concerns Mordecai the Jew, the persecution of Jews in Susa, and the working out of Court intrigues.

Even on an early hearing—before *reading* taught me to conflate, to correct, and to revise rather than to remember, before I learned even to glimpse what Professor Cazelles and his like might be suggesting by the operations of higher criticism—I knew that there was a difference in the kind of interest I might invest in the Esther who exposed herself for her (as yet unacknowledged) people, and the interest I was expected to take in Esther/Hadassah, Mordecai's "daughter," the instrument of political manipulation. I know now what the difference was, for I have learned that in all cultures what is known as Wisdom literature is another thing altogether from law and history and prophecy. Wisdom literature is not Jewish, of course—it bubbles up out of Egyptian and Mesopotamian sources—and it is primarily concerned with happiness and success in this world. As Dr. Moore tells us in The Anchor Bible (Esther, volume 7B, where I have found so much grist that I can barely persuade my mill to grind), it is noncultic and detached in spirit, "prudential and pragmatic." It is what stories depend on. The story of Esther—the Esther we are asked to regard as a heroine, the Esther for whom the scroll is named, though it is Mordecai who outstrips her in all the earliest sources—is a Wisdom narrative, the kind I must also have recognized in the attitudes and even in the costumes of those other women, the conspicuously attired or abluted Susannah, Jael, Judith, all the way to Salome, perverse echo of these heroic ladies. In the Cleveland Museum of Art, and in books of art reproductions, I had pored over the magic effects of their appearance: Susannah observed in her bath by the elders, Judith adorning herself to beguile Holofernes. And I had watched my mother getting ready for those evenings with those men, one of whom would become, I knew, another of my stepfathers. I also knew (I *learned*) what significance might be attributed to the proper placing of a jewel, the right choice of a perfume: secrets of the harem! In them was to be discerned, to be discovered, why it was that Esther was a heroine, why she was so brave and so brilliant. *The toilette of Esther* was a subject for mannerists and the Baroque masters, for Tintoretto and Veronese, Rubens, Poussin and Claude Lorraine. It was what appeared to be her particular heroism: preparing herself to appear, unasked, before the king.

There was a detail here that always held me fast in the hearing, a ritual detail which I felt I understood in a secret way. Until this moment I have never sought to confirm my understanding, but was not Esther's decision to broach the king's presence unasked (an apparition which jeopardized her life) a form of sexual violation, a reversal of male and female roles which would dangerously suggest autonomy in a woman and submissiveness in a man, at odds with the orthodox view? Was this not the sense of the scene's climax? "When the king saw Esther the queen standing in the court, she obtained favor in his sight, and the king held out to Esther the golden sceptre that was in his hand. So Esther drew near and touched the top of the sceptre." Is this not an expression of a certain sexual understanding between suppliant and sovereign? The condign phallic recognition which is granted to the "inadmissible" woman, and which is responded to by her dumb show as well: the king extends the golden scepter (it is licit that she rouse his desire) and the queen touches its top (she acknowledges phallocracy). Then they can talk. Then she can ask a favor, can ask anything, even unto half the kingdom. This, I remembered, was what Herod offers Salome to forestall her demand for the head of John the Baptist. But no one ever wants half the kingdom. Esther, in fact, wants the whole kingdom for her people, to whom she then and there reveals herself as belonging.

Though I had realized, as the Mordecai themes of the story were brought closer home by the developments of world politics, that it was cunning of the author to have managed to braid the two narratives together, there were still discrepancies. Why had Esther not heard about the edict which Haman had persuaded Ahasuerus to let him issue against the (unnamed) Jews? Had Mordecai taken up his lamentations in the king's gate so quickly that word had not yet reached the harem? Was Esther so isolated there that she had heard nothing? Or was she so indifferent to the problems of the outside world and of her people that she did not care? No, I think I understood even then that Esther simply had no part in *that story,* that Haman does not even mobilize royal forces against the Jews—he marks them as outlaws. The king's protection is withdrawn from them: they may be killed and plundered by anyone with impunity. Whereas Mordecai's edict grants the right of self-defense to the outlawed Jews, who may "stand for their life" and with impunity kill those who would kill and plunder them. In other words, in the Mordecai story, parity is established between the Jews and their enemies. These enemies are never named, we do not know who they are, and Haman is isolated so that his decree against the Jews is really a decree against Mordecai, an act of personal vengeance. As far as Jews in general go, the city of Susa is said to be *perplexed* (grieved) when Haman's edict is published, and the same city rejoices in Mordecai's appointment as vizier in Haman's place. And Esther only returns to the story here, having passed up two splendid opportunities to intercede for her people, the king in each instance having committed himself to granting her even half the kingdom.

Esther's return to the story is part of her fascination—her fascination with regard to that preliterate audience of which I was such an impassioned member. For her "action" is a passion, indeed a passivity. "Had we been sold for bondmen and bondwomen, I had held my tongue," Esther says, "but we are sold to be destroyed, to be slain, and to perish." Whereupon, once she has named Haman, Esther's part in the story is eliminated, or, rather, is emphasized: she lies upon her couch, unmoving, as Haman falls upon it ("upon the bed whereon Esther was"), permitting the king to reach the most damaging interpretation possible. As with Vashti, it is essential that Ahasuerus be removed from the room. Commentators have offered a long list of explanations for the king's tempestuous withdrawal and return ("the king arising from the banquet of wine in his wrath went into the palace garden . . . then the king returned out of the palace garden into the place of the banquet of wine"). The story comes to its magical (as opposed to managerial) conclusion with a tableau of retributive justice: Haman—who should have sought mercy from the king, not from his revealed racial enemy—at Esther's feet, was actually *lying on her bed,* and either seizing her feet or kissing them. And Esther simply allowed her position (in every sense of the word) to do the rest. For, according to harem regulations, even if Haman had prostrated himself a foot away from the queen's couch, the king's reaction could still have been justified—though many scholars have characterized that reaction as excessive, unreasonable, or just plain drunk. Esther's *petition* is no such thing, of course—it is an admission. She has not so much unmasked the villain as she has unmasked herself. Esther's heroism is self-revelation—the rest is politics. *Tout commence en mystique,* Péguy says, *et finit en politique.* Certainly that is the arrangement arrived at in the Scroll of Esther.

Furthermore, the response of world literature to this theme has been similarly doubled, similarly divided. The tale became a preferred subject of miracle plays and of the religious theater, from Spain to Moscow. *La Hermosa Ester* is Lope de Vega's version, and the first play in Russian, produced in 1672, is based on the same tale. Racine's version complicated the magic, for the court of Louis XIV recognized Vashti as Madame de Montespan, the Hebrews as Huguenots or Jansenists, and of course Esther as Madame de Maintenon! Handel's oratorio—whose words were long thought to have been written by Pope and Dr. Arbuthnot—restores the tale to a less clearly keyed articulation, and thereby both Voltaire and Tom Paine found Esther "execrably cruel" and the book "fabulous." How appropriate that Jefferson, our most inexorably political Father, should advise reading such books "as you would read Livy or Tacitus," historians—not as you would read Ovid or Virgil.

Just as I knew that human beings, not Jehovah, delivered the Jews, so my delight in the Scroll of Esther, by the time I could read, was a delight that there was a power disparate from that of politics, a power that inheres in Wisdom literature, though that literature might well be called the literature of folly. For that power is merely and magically that of showing forth, apparition, epiphany of the person, of the poor, defenseless, and, as I could determine now, invincible human body. Mordecai and his machinations enabled the Jews to escape Haman and to meet his wicked enmity with a countervailing force. They had nothing to do with the story of Esther as

I had *heard* it, as I immediately and inwardly understood it, the story of the revealed mystery of presence. That story was a much cruder, much earlier, much more primal one. It was no longer the matter of the deliverance of the Jewish people through a brave woman. It was a reminder, urged as by a tidal undulation from an unacknowledged depth, of the body's power, beyond argument, beyond art, to beguile. Michelet was right about the kind of attention, of allegiance the story required: only it was not the "chimerical mind" which was at stake, for that mind was the reader's; it was the substantial body, and that body was the listener's.

DANIEL

Lynne Sharon Schwartz

Jerusalem was burned, and even the Temple was left a mass of smoking ruins. Some of the people were sent to Egypt, some to Babylon, some to the lands of the Medes and Persians, far, far away from their beautiful city where they had not remembered to live in peace and goodness.

Now a new life began for the Jews. . . . They began to wish themselves back home again in their own lovely country. They understood how wicked and cruel they had been to each other, and here in the lands where only foolish idols were worshipped, the Jews remembered the beautiful Temple of Jerusalem, and the wise teachings of the one true God. . . .

They tried harder and harder to live good pure lives, and they always hoped that some day God would find them worthy and would allow them to return to their own Kingdom of Judah.

WHEN I WAS SIX, AND SEVEN, AND EIGHT, I WAS ENTRANCED by these words. Not only the nostalgia and longing and remorse, which I tend to find irresistible, but the assumption that good behavior would be rewarded, in the longest of runs, and evil punished. Was that taught to me in the cradle, I wonder, giving me so willing an ear for the chapter in my *Bible Tales* called "The Fall of Jerusalem," or was it the *Bible Tales* themselves, which I read over and over as eager child readers do, that taught it? Either way, it is one of the hardest lessons to unlearn. The will to see good or bad fortune as controllable is prompted by the deepest, most infantile needs, and, in the case of the peripatetic ancient Jews, vies with a cultivated, almost cherished despair.

So, in telling of the sixth century B.C.E. disaster and subsequent exile in this manner, the author of my *Bible Tales* was not being careful with her

---

The King James Version of the Bible used in this essay.

young readers, imposing order on wayward, baffling events. The incessant uprootings and dispersions, wanderings, defeats, and occasional triumphs of the Jews are, throughout the Bible, presented as the material reflection of their behavior and the responses of a God whose notions of morality and whose flashing messages are as predictably fixed as a computer is electronically programmed.

The Israelites were not the only nation swirled in the savage power struggles of the first millennium B.C.E. As one commentator puts it, "Israel's history is a minor sideshow in the larger history of the ancient Near East."[1] Moabites, Ammonites, Philistines, and many more were shoved about by the great powers—Babylonians, Persians, Greeks—for no reason other than the usual lusts for dominion and land. Only the odyssey of the Israelites became a parable of the enactment of divine purpose, a morality tale. The Jews were not Everyman, however. They were chosen. Did they choose to be chosen? That is a riddle for metaphysicians and insomniacs. For a writer, the more fruitful matter is that they wrote it all down and left it for us, as a testament. Even at six and seven, then, I knew two crucial things about the Jews: we were the chosen people, a sentence too stony to penetrate; and we were the people who chose to make stories out of our sufferings.

I have been trying to go back to that child who loved the Book of Daniel in volume II (Joshua to the Maccabees) of Edith Lindeman Calisch's *Bible Tales*, and see to what it was that she loved. This entails a narrowing of self—all the things I have learned and seen since—and also a stretching, like working unused muscles, because the visions and imaginings of childhood are vast and know no borders.

"When the Kingdom of Judah was broken up, many of the people were taken far across the plains to the city of Babylon, where ruled a king called Nebuchadnezzar." A fine opening sentence, in more than obvious ways. For one thing, "where ruled a king" opens intriguing vistas of how sentences can be made to turn somersaults. And what a name. The king with the funny name had frightening dreams, and the only one who could interpret them was the young Jew with a "bright face and great wisdom," Daniel. Like Nebuchadnezzar, Daniel was a dreamer too; also a visionary. He dreamed and he interpreted. His dreams, sent by God, were redemptive: whatever their fantastic vagaries, they always meant that someday the punishment of the Jews would end, and they would return to the beloved land.

I was a dreamer, too, and a visionary, and I was happy to find another, though he dreamed in more orotund language and in a far-off time and place. I began to write stories that were like visions. One was about the creation of the earth by a kind scientist. One was about the freeing of prisoners. One was about where people go when they die—a place full of flowers. They were, I can see now, written under the influence of the Book of Daniel. They were written with a blue ballpoint pen in a composition notebook with black-and-white mottled covers and a white rectangle in the center of the front cover for the writer's name. I wrote them at night, and once or twice in the morning I showed them to my father while he was shaving. He was not a dreamer, to my knowledge, but he read them and approved them. Nodding sagely, draped in a white towel like a garment of yore, the lower half of his face bearded in rich lather, he resembled the drawings in the *Bible Tales.*

Daniel and the rest of the Jews were in exile, strangers in a strange land, adapting as best they could, even finding favor with their overlords, but all the time dreaming and longing for their own place and life. I felt in exile, too, although there was nothing particularly oppressive about my childhood except the commonplace oppression of being a child in a world of adults who believed that good and bad behavior would win their just deserts, and the oppression of being a dreamer in post–World War II Brooklyn. The fact that most of my overlords, at home, at school, on the street, were benign made no difference to this elusive, obscure sort of oppression. My *Bible Tales,* too, ever attuned to its delicate readers, acknowledged that "The king was kind to the captive Jews, and very few of them were made to work as slaves." School was a form of slavery. What I was exiled from, I know now, was my future, which would be totally different, I knew even then, from what I was living as a child. How, I could not have said. Only it would be my own. It would come eventually, I was promised, as Daniel was promised. But how long the waiting seemed. . . .

Well, how do such exiles manage? Besides dreaming, they serve their masters in good faith, with their special kind of divided integrity—a contradiction in terms. Certain things, things of the spirit, they do not, cannot compromise. What they hate most of all is coercion. The flesh they permit to be coerced, but not the spirit. What they believe, they cling to with fortitude, and with an unearthly tenacity that both saps their strength and replenishes it. They will not worship false or frivolous gods, for then they would no longer be who they are; if they are thrown into the lions' den for their stubbornness . . . that is the risk.

King Darius, who was fond of the honorable, highly placed Daniel, was tricked by a group of "jealous governors" into sending him to a gruesome ordeal. Flattering royal vanity, the jealous governors persuade Darius to pass a law requiring that anyone who does not pray to the king alone for thirty days be cast into the lions' den. As in any fairy tale, the plot needs some key stricture: "In those days, when a law was once made not even the king could change it." Naturally Daniel prays to his God as always; who could wish him otherwise?

"Daniel was not the least bit afraid. He put his faith in God, and calmly and quietly entered the den of the lions. A great stone was rolled before the mouth of the cave." But Darius tosses all night, and in the morning rushes to the cave and cries, "Daniel, my friend, have you died, or has your God been able to save you?"

The sense of joy and validation I felt, of pure aesthetic rightness at Daniel's words, is indescribable: "Oh King, here am I, safe and well. For I put my trust in the Lord and He has saved me from the lions." Not "Here I am," but "Here am I." That transposition makes all the difference. To a writer, where the ear is seduced, the heart follows. "Great was the joy of Darius," but no greater than mine. The power of God did not interest me much. Unaware of any sacrilege or poetic adjustment, I was certain it was Daniel's own power that had saved him. Fortitude, tenacity, integrity—they could be a charm, a spell: even lions were cowed.

That was not all Daniel's power. There was still better.

One night a prince of Babylon by the name of Belshazzar had a costly feast for a thousand of his friends. All night long they ate and drank and made merry, and suddenly Belshazzar cried to his servants: "Bring forth the cups and vessels of gold and silver that we brought from the Temple of Jerusalem, the city of the Jews!"

. . . Belshazzar and his friends filled them with wine, and passed them from hand to hand, and laughed to think that they were drinking from the vessels that had never been used before except in the service of the Lord.

Soon dawn began to break, and a shaft of early sun stole through a window. Belshazzar watched the ray of light as it shone upon the high white wall. What was that? A hand, writing giant words on the stones? Belshazzar rubbed his eyes! Yes, there on the wall were strange letters, showing clear and black in the dazzling light. Belshazzar trembled and grew pale.

"What mean these words?"

Only Daniel could read the writing on the wall.

I had seen writing on a wall, too. When I was three and a half, Eileene, the eleven-year-old girl who lived downstairs in our two-family house on Midwood Street, stood me in front of a large blackboard in her narrow hallway and wrote with chalk: first my name, then letters, words. Every day, after Eileene came home from school, we would stand in front of the blackboard and her big hand would write giant words, till they came clear and the world was unsealed. In the beginning, the word: I knew my life would be lived in words and moved by them.

The words Daniel reads foretell of Belshazzar's downfall, for he has "mocked at the Lord. . . . That very night, Belshazzar's enemies came upon him, slew the proud, wicked prince, and divided his lands among them just as Daniel had said they would." Words are proved powerful, as I suspected. Daniel did not simply read; didn't he, indirectly, make it happen? And to my mind it was a just punishment for one too dense to read for himself.

My *Bible Tales'* version of the story of Daniel taught two supreme things: that freedom is a quality of the inner spirit and not of the body's circumstances, and that events move purposefully—if mysteriously— toward just and meaningful conclusions. Many of us who have grown to maturity amid the brutalities of the twentieth century find these beliefs impossible to sustain. But they are powerful ideas nonetheless, and occasionally true (just often enough to keep them going), and maybe always necessary for human endeavor. Anyway, they won my heart at seven years old; if they cannot abide with me through adulthood, at least they were good enough to get me there. And more than good enough was the prose of those precious two volumes, a most faithful translation. For a young reader, there is no resisting the lure of:

"Read me the words on the wall," he begged, "and tell me what they mean, and I will clothe you in scarlet and put a chain of gold about your neck."

Then Daniel looked at the great letters, and he said to Belshazzar: "Give your gifts to someone else, for I do not want them. But I will tell you the meaning of the writing on the wall."

Nor of:

Morning came, and Darius hastened to the lions' den. All was quiet! The king was sure that the savage beasts had slain his good friend. For a moment he stood before the stones at the entrance to the cave, then his sorrow overcame him, and he cried aloud: "Daniel, my friend, have you died, or has your God been able to save you?"

At once, there came the voice of Daniel, saying: "Oh King, here am I, safe and well."

Decades later, I discover all sorts of unsuspected things about the Book of Daniel. Some fortify my childhood vision and version, some undermine them. Daniel purports to take place between 586 B.C.E., the time of the destruction of Jerusalem by the Babylonian king Nebuchadnezzar, with the resulting dispersion and exile of the Jews, and 539 B.C.E., when Cyrus overran Babylon, established Persian rule, and sent the Jews home to reclaim their land and rebuild the Temple. Cyrus has a reputation for enlightened benevolence: one of his good deeds was returning to the Jews the holy vessels defiled at Belshazzar's feast.

It seems to be true, according to historians, that the exiled Jews were not too badly off in Babylon. For one thing, Nebuchadnezzar skimmed off only the cream,

certain of the children of Israel, and of the king's seed, and of the princes;

Children in whom was no blemish, but well favoured, and skilful in all wisdom, and cunning in knowledge, and understanding science, and such as had ability in them to stand in the king's palace, and whom they might teach the learning and the tongue of the Chaldeans.   [Daniel 1:3–4]

Thus the dispersion had the effect of "transferring the real centre of Judah's life to Babylon."[2] In "the City of Merchants," as Babylon was called, the Jews enjoyed some social freedom and a degree of self-rule, were permitted to maintain their family and tribal groupings and manners of worship, and to take advantage of economic opportunities—in short, they could pursue, though as foreigners, their accustomed way of life. As they had always done and would have ample opportunity to do again, they adapted to the surrounding customs and culture. At the same time, the exile became a period of group solidarity and spiritual renewal, a time of gathering and preserving the literature and codes of law. Surely the Jews in defeat would take more seriously the prophets' tireless reminders that their misfortunes were a punishment for turning away from God. Several of the psalms were written during the Babylonian period, while the memory of Jerusalem was fresh and plangent and wounding, yet threatened by the possibility of a too-comfortable assimilation. It was as if, with Judah no longer a true nation but, rather, a community of the spirit, its cohesion was strengthened.

This is the situation the Book of Daniel purports to be about. In truth, as unearthed by research and archaeology and linguistic analysis, the author of Daniel was of another, later time, another place, and obsessed with other events entirely. He was indulging in a clever and now familiar tactic, using the Babylonian exile to illuminate the destiny of Israel in his own day, just as Arthur Miller used the seventeenth-century Salem witch trials as an emblem for the McCarthy purges of the 1950s, or as Swift used Lilliput and Brobdingnag to illustrate the fatuities of the English court, or as contemporary Latin American novelists clothe their political indignation in the costumes of never-never lands.

We might as well indulge, too, then, and, before unveiling the political realities, or what modern critics would call the subtext, savor what we can of the story. For six of Daniel's twelve chapters are just that, pure vigorous narrative, with more things and wonders than I dreamed of, reading the child's version. The first violation to befall the exiled Daniel and his three friends, Hananiah, Mishael, and Azariah, who are being groomed as advisers, is having their names changed. Daniel becomes Belteshazzar; the other three become Shadrach, Meshach, and Abednego (of jukebox fame in the 1940s). So it was with slaves brought here from Africa, so it has probably been with slaves everywhere: make them forget who they are; remake them by renaming them. A name in the Bible is no small matter, if we recall that early privilege of naming the beasts of the field and the fowls of the air: the Lord "brought them unto Adam to see what he would call them: and whatsoever Adam called every living creature, that was the name thereof" (Genesis 2:19).

Food is next, ever a touchy issue for the Jews. Daniel and his three friends refuse to defile themselves with the king's meat and wine. They will eat only "pulse"—legumes, beans. Miraculously, after ten days they are "fairer and fatter" than those who gave in. Vegetarianism works; with God's help everything works. Once they are thus made presentable, Nebuchadnezzar meets the four and finds them "ten times better than all the magicians and astrologers that were in his realm" (1:20).

Nebuchadnezzar dreams a frightful dream and, his usual magicians failing, summons Daniel. But this is no ordinary task of interpretation. The king has utterly forgotten the dream! He needs to have it restored before it can be explained. As one of the confounded Babylonian seers protests, "It is a rare thing that the king requireth" (2:11). Even Daniel must go home and wait till God reveals it to him in a "night vision." The dream was of a great statue—head of gold, breast and arms of silver, belly and thighs of brass, legs of iron, feet of clay—eventually shattered by a stone "cut out without hands," which grows to cover the earth. From top to bottom, reports Daniel, the statue represents a succession of empires to come, each one to be shattered in the end by the kingdom of God, which, like the stone, will supersede all others, for all time.

As before, the glories of God interest me less than the glories of the dreamer. What does this mean, that Daniel not only interprets the dream but virtually invents it, intuits it? It means he is no mere sociologist, taking meaning from mores; he is an artist. First he tells people what they dream, re-creates for them what they know but cannot call forth or articulate; then he finds their destiny in the dream.

Perhaps under the influence of the dream, the unsubtle Nebuchadnezzar has a huge golden image made and commands all the nations in his domain to worship it. When the renamed Jews, Shadrach, Meshach, and Abednego, refuse, the king, "full of fury, and the form of his visage . . . changed" (3:19), orders them thrown into a fiery furnace, heated seven times hotter than usual, so hot that the men who throw them in are consumed. But Shadrach, Meshach, and Abednego, tossed in bound, can be seen walking "loose" in the midst of the fire, with a fourth, "and the form of the fourth is like the Son of God" (3:25). They are released, and everyone gathers to see "these men, upon whose bodies the fire had no power, nor was an hair of their head singed, neither were their coats changed, nor the smell of fire had passed on them" (3:27). The king, for the moment convinced, decrees that no word be spoken against the God of Israel, for "there is no other God that can deliver after this sort" (3:29). Never mind those unchosen who were burned in order to prove the point, or that thousands of years later, when his chosen people were consumed in a newer fiery furnace, he chose not to deliver in this sort. Even to raise the question is blasphemous. That is what being beyond question means.

Another night Nebuchadnezzar dreams of a tall tree reaching to heaven and spreading to the ends of the earth, laden with leaves and fruit, shading the beasts of the field and sheltering the birds, till a voice from above decrees that it be cut down, the leaves shaken off, and the fruit scattered, with only a stump remaining. Daniel is loath to tell what it means but Nebuchadnezzar encourages him: the king will lose his reason, be cut down like the tree. "Let his portion be with the beasts in the grass of the earth: Let his heart be changed from a man's, and let a beast's heart be given unto him" (4:16). Daniel warns the king to curb his pride, to "break off thy sins by righteousness, and thy iniquities by showing mercy to the poor" (4:27), but evidently to no avail, for the next words from Nebuchadnezzar are prideful ones: "Is not this great Babylon, that I have built for the house of the kingdom by the might of my power, and for the honour of my majesty?" (4:30) The words are scarcely off his lips when he is "driven from men, and did eat grass as oxen, and his body was wet with the dew of heaven, till his hairs were grown like eagles' feathers, and his nails like birds' claws" (4:33). It is the archetypal language and imagery of madness.

Lunacy, erupting inexplicable and wild even now, must have been terrifying to witness then. The Jews, with their everlasting compulsion to dissect and explain—that salient flaw of Job's comforters—would naturally be swift to seek a reason as comfort. And given their particular relation to God, it is not surprising that madness was seen as chastisement, one more demonstration that "none can stay his hand, or say unto him, What doest thou?" (4:35)

After seven years as a beast, Nebuchadnezzar looks up to heaven, humbled, and understands where all power comes from: "the most High ruleth in the kingdom of men, and giveth it to whomsoever he will" (4:32). This acknowledged, he gets his reason back, along with his kingdom, his "honour and brightness." A strange fashion of justice, distressingly neat.

Belshazzar's guests who drink from the gold and silver goblets taken from the Temple turn out to be not simply his "friends," as my book said, but "his princes, his wives, and his concubines" (5:2). When he sees the handwriting on the wall, Belshazzar does not merely rub his eyes and grow pale. No, "the joints of his loins were loosed, and his knees smote one against another" (5:6). The writing is an enigma till the queen, the only woman mentioned in this stern and hard, unrelenting book, remembers Daniel, "in whom is the spirit of the holy gods" (5:11). Daniel reminds Belshazzar of how his father paid for his pride, dwelling with the beasts and eating grass, a lesson obviously lost on the son. Then he reads: *Mene, Mene, Tekel, Upharsin.* "God hath numbered thy kingdom and finished it. Thou are weighed in the balances and art found wanting" (5:26, 27). This is the moment of deepest satisfaction. That there will be a time of weighing in the balances, of ultimate judgment against absolute standards, is an atavistic fantasy I suppose I will never entirely root out. It rests, only half asleep, with other childhood fantasies. So, while I balk at the vengeful deeds, I am willingly snared, and quickened, by the great and mysterious words, bearers of truth and justice. More wishful thinking: since they appear by magic, the one who can read them must be a magician.

The lions' den is the last of the stories. The curious thing about it, which makes the actual book less personal than the *Bible Tales* version, less the story of a hero than a fable of gritted teeth, is that we are never with our hero overnight in the den. All Daniel reveals is that "My God hath sent his angel, and hath shut the lions' mouths" (6:22). We can only imagine, if we care to, what it was like. A modern, subjective writer would have to do it differently, would stay with Daniel and chart his blood pressure as the stone was rolled against the door, bringing darkness, and the lions approached, growling. What really did happen in the lions' den? That might tell me what I want to know about this "God" character. Did he cast a spell over the lions right away, so that their eyes closed, as did their mouths, the dread jaws locked? Or had he created for them, the hour before, more delectable meat, so that they had no interest in human flesh? Or had he taken away their appetites? Surely he could manage that. Was Daniel in a panic, did his knees also smite one against another? Or did the angel speak to him and reassure him?

I have a terrible suspicion, from what I know of the "God" character, that he waited till the very last minute, exactly as he did with Abraham and Isaac—one second's distraction (if we can imagine him distracted) and it might have been too late. I have a feeling that the lions (how many, anyway?) leaped to within an inch of Daniel, and Daniel's heart leaped to his throat as he despaired of ever seeing his native Jerusalem again and felt the teeth piercing his skin and tearing at tissue before it ever happened, before it didn't happen, and was made by the insatiable God to cry out his faith one more time, one last test, which he did, frantically, and then . . . after an eternity, the mouths were shut and the beasts sidled away.

Then again, maybe not. Maybe in private, dealing with his chosen, he is kinder and more civil than I know.

As an afterthought, the king casts into the lions' den those men who had accused Daniel, and with them their wives and children. The lions "brake all their bones in pieces or ever they came at the bottom of the den" (6:24).

The last six chapters of the Book of Daniel fall in the genre of prophecy, or, to be more precise, apocalyptic writings—prophecy impelled and shaped by the imminence of judgment: visions of the end. Scholars distinguish Daniel from other such writings by its greater scope and comprehensiveness; its view sweeps through centuries of changing rule and shifting borders to the final, triumphant establishment of the kingdom of God, a theocracy. It demonstrates, says one commentator, a "conception of the unity of history as controlled by divine purpose."[3] Prophetic writings generally contain symbolic acts and are informed by a sense of personal contact with God, while in apocalyptic writings the acts are replaced by elaborate imagery, animals, angels, bizarre supernatural visions, and God is not personal but at his most administrative. This is what happens in the latter half of Daniel.

The Book of Daniel was actually written in the second century B.C.E., over four hundred years from the fall of Jerusalem and the start of the Babylonian exile; scholars place it shortly after the Maccabean rebellion against the Syrian king Antiochus IV in 165 B.C.E. It was written during one of the worst persecutions the Jews had ever known, at a time when Syria's policy of forced Hellenization had gone so far that possessing a Torah was a capital offense. For the ultimate blow, Antiochus had placed an altar to Zeus and sacrificed pigs in the Temple of Jerusalem, demanding that all Jews do likewise, which "abominations of desolation" led the village priest Mattathias to lead an armed guerrilla-type revolt. So the book is a call to arms, to defiance, and to faith. What Daniel and his three friends did, the second-century Jews, many of them already Hellenized, are exhorted to do: resist and pray and hold fast. It makes manifest "the theology of the Maccabean revolution," and in fact has been called "the Manifesto of the Hasidim."⁴ ("The Chasidim" means "the Pious," and though the Chasidim of today are doubtless equally pious, they arose out of altogether different historical circumstances.) The Pious, of whom the author of Daniel is believed to be one, were rural people isolated from the prevailing Hellenization, who undertook to defend the faith amid the ubiquitous pressures of Greek culture.

How did we get from the tolerable atrocities of Nebuchadnezzar to the intolerable ones of Antiochus? While Belshazzar pondered the writing on the wall, the Persians were growing in power, till Cyrus conquered Babylon in 539 B.C.E. and restored the Jews to their homeland. In Jerusalem, the rebuilding of the Temple was fraught with internal struggles as well as disputes with the Samaritans to the north; nevertheless, it continued under Cyrus' successors, Cambyses II and Darius I (not the Darius who was Daniel's admirer). Over the next century, the Jewish community solidified still further under the leadership of Nehemiah and Ezra. Nehemiah is credited with imposing a policy of strict exclusivity, distinguishing the Jews sharply from their neighbors and defining the standards of birth and background that make a Jew. And the rigid conformity to the letter of the law that characterizes Orthodox Judaism as we know it is said to have begun with Ezra.

For about two hundred years the Jews lived in relative security under Persian rule, until the rise of Alexander of Macedon. By 326 B.C.E. Alexander had overcome Persia and conquered all of the Near East, and though he wept that there were no more worlds to subdue, he could still dream of spreading Greek culture wherever he held sway. At his death in 323 B.C.E. the empire was divided into four parts, but it was mainly the Egyptians and the Syrians, with their centers at Alexandria and Antioch, who inherited the fruits of his labors. While Palestine was ruled by the Egyptian Ptolemies, Hellenization was not thoroughly or brutally enforced, although many Jews embraced Greek ways. Only when the Syrian Antiochus III defeated Ptolemy V in 198 B.C.E. did persecution begin in earnest: the Syrian kings were fanatic Hellenizers, more for political and economic than for cultural motives. It was Antiochus IV, called Antiochus Epiphanes because he claimed to be Zeus manifest, who instituted the "abominations"—death for mothers who had their children circumcised, death for observance of the Sabbath, enforced sacrifices to Zeus—precipitating the Maccabean revolt and the austere fervor of the zealot who wrote the Book of Daniel.

The stories in the first half of Daniel may have been legendary accounts of heroic resistance, in circulation for centuries. Daniel himself seems to have been a known figure and is mentioned in Ezekiel, twice in the esteemed company of Noah and Job (4:14, 20) and once for his famed wisdom (28:3). Wherever they came from, the stories have been shaped to allude to the persecutions of the Syrian kings, and to instruct the victims on how to respond. The command to worship a golden statue, the fiery furnace, and the lions' den are no merely fanciful scary images. They are analogues to real abominations and reprisals, just as the book as a whole stands for an enduring, or recurring, truth in the history of the Jews.

For the long period when Daniel was assumed to have been written during the Babylonian exile, its latter, prophetic half must have seemed truly miraculous. Both the king's dreams and Daniel's visions foresee with uncanny accuracy the rise and fall of specific empires over the centuries. In Nebuchadnezzar's first dream of the colossal statue, for instance, the dream Daniel is good enough to remember for him, the head of gold represents the Babylonian empire, the chest and arms of silver the Median, the belly of brass the Persian, the legs of iron the rule of Alexander, and the feet of clay the Hellenistic kingdoms of Egypt and Syria.

We know now that this is not inspired prophecy but history, and, like much of history seen from four centuries away, it has its share of errors. There was no Median empire between the Babylonian and the Persian; the gourmet Belshazzar was not Nebuchadnezzar's son but the son of a later and more disliked king, Nabonidus (555–39 B.C.E.); Darius the Median who lost sleep over Daniel in the lions' den is an unknown figure; and so forth.

Moreover, Daniel's visions in those last six chapters—grotesque beasts overthrown, a grappling goat and ram, immense armies and battles—are, frankly, tedious to read. At once telescoped and cinematic, they compose a kind of special-effects *tour de force* that might appeal to fans of *Raiders of the Lost Ark* or *Star Wars*. They are narrated in code, a sealed book, and require step-by-step translation. Thanks to historians, we know that the lion with eagle's wings is the Babylonian empire; the leopard with four wings and four backs the Persian; the goat is the Greek empire and its great horn Alexander, broken into four horns as his empire was broken. And so forth, again, down to the most minute vicissitudes of four centuries of dynastic upheaval.

To Jews of the second century B.C.E., however, the visions must have been accurate enough, and hardly tedious or obscure. On the contrary, they were the most forceful Biblical expression of history as the enactment of God's will, culminating in the establishment, when he is ready, of his eternal rule, the vast stone covering the earth. "Prophecy and history have here met together," a critic early in our century writes; "the eternal righteousness of God and the final peace of his people have here greeted each other."[5]

At the very end of Daniel, chapter 12, the tone of the prophecies changes: "The point at which the vision, from being veiled but generally accurate history, passes into vague prediction (end of xi), is precisely that of the Maccabean revolt."[6] This is the point at which the writer could not have known what happens next. And once the book extricates itself from history and moves back to poetry, it soars again. A time of great trouble is to come, when the angel Michael will appear,

and at that time thy people shall be delivered, every one that shall be found written in the book.

And many of them that sleep in the dust of the earth shall awake, some to everlasting life, and some to shame and everlasting contempt.

And they that be wise shall shine as the brightness of the firmament; and they that turn many to righteousness as the stars for ever and ever.

But thou, O Daniel, shut up the words, and seal the book, even to the time of the end.   [12:1–4]

To the multitudes being yoked into obedience, such a conclusion must have been a welcome catharsis, exalting and sustaining. They certainly would not have shrunk at the burning of the men who led Shadrach, Meshach, and Abednego into the fiery furnace, or at the children of Daniel's accusers being thrown to the lions, for these would have been read as Antiochus' soldiers and future persecutors.

The oppressed Jews would have remembered, too, how Ezekiel was led by the hand of the Lord to the midst of a valley full of bones, dry, hopeless bones, and was asked by God, Can these bones live?, and how before Ezekiel's eyes, muscles and flesh and skin covered the bones and the wind blew breath into them and they arose, and how God promised that just that way he would breathe spirit into Israel and bring its people home (Ezekiel 37).

The Book of Daniel is hard to cherish today as I did when I was seven. It is written out of terrible and long despair; there is no gentleness in it or magnanimity of spirit—how could there be? It breathes not with any mellow quest for deliverance, but with a fierce compulsion to make history turn out right, a compulsion for justice and meaning and purpose that is both enormously seductive and chillingly repressive in its tensed grip. It wills and forces history, lassoing events into teleological order with the stubborn tenacity that has always been the Jews' greatest strength and tightest limitation, good for survival but not for spontaneous inquiry. It is an inevitable trait in a people who long ago defined itself in opposition, in contradistinction to, and became destined to be defined that way by others in perpetuity.

How to get back to the closeness again? It must be through the language and the stories. One critic writes of the original Hebrew (and Aramaic, in the case of Daniel): "It is a language in which every other word is a concealed metaphor . . . ; there is no room in it for niceties of relation expressed by subordinate conjunctions. The thoughts are flung at you in succession and you are left to relate them for yourself."[7] This sounds dangerously like the dry bones of contemporary minimalist fiction, yet the offerings of the Book of Daniel are maximal. Its rhythms and tonalities open outward; the vast arch of its poetic vision gives the mind space to stretch, and the ear magnificent music to luxuriate in. The courage of the dreamer-hero is fathomless, his patience is without bounds, and his insight unfailing. When the tough-hearted author lets Daniel address us directly, he speaks so close to our ear and in a voice so true that, whatever we believe, we come away shaken:

And I heard a man's voice between the banks of Ulai, which called, and said, Gabriel, make this man to understand the vision.

So he came near where I stood: and when he came, I was afraid, and fell upon my face: but he said unto me, Understand, O son of man: for at the time of the end shall be the vision.

Now as he was speaking with me, I was in a deep sleep on my face toward the ground: but he touched me, and set me upright.

And he said, Behold, I will make thee know what shall be in the last end of the indignation: . . .

And I Daniel fainted, and was sick certain days; afterward I rose up, and did the king's business; and I was astonished at the vision, but none understood it.   [8:16–27]

It is no wonder that God calls him "greatly beloved" and lets him see and talk with angels.

The unique timbre of that voice, its conviction and self-knowledge, are what one can return to at any age. The book's magic does not reside in the ideas or the history, important as they are. In fact, Daniel suggests that ideas do not make history but history makes ideas: the band of wanderers that became the nation of Israel was not born piously stubborn and committed to moral rigor, but got that way in history. Maybe they were born tellers of tales, though, worshippers, from the beginning, of the word. The genius of Daniel is in the stories, which remain the same, pure and entrancing, no matter what I know about their allusions or their author. Daniel, in exile, dreamed dreams of regaining his true life, if he would only hold fast to the truth. He told those around him their lost dreams and their life stories. He had to go into a dark, savage place, and came out unhurt, telling no one of what he felt or did there. He read the writing on the wall and saw what it meant and told it. Above all, like most dreamers, he performed his necessary, difficult work, and he waited, trusting God's words, "Blessed is he that waiteth" (12:12).

NOTES

1. Bernhard W. Anderson, *Understanding the Old Testament* (Englewood Cliffs, N.J.: Prentice-Hall, 1957), pp. 4–5.

2. H. Wheeler Robinson, *The Old Testament: Its Making and Meaning* (Nashville, Tenn.: Abingdon Press, 1927), p. 87.

3. Robinson, *Understanding the Old Testament,* p. 33.

4. Anderson, *The Old Testament,* p. 515.

5. Robinson, *Understanding the Old Testament,* pp. 131–32.

6. Ibid., p. 131.

7. Ibid., p. 12.

DANIEL

Mark Mirsky

THE BOOK OF DANIEL IS THE MOST FARAWAY AND THE CLOSEST OF the Biblical books—a fairy tale and a book of contemporary political instruction. Within the Book of Daniel is hidden another Book of Daniel, being revealed and sealed in the same moment for the prophet and his readers.

Scholars assert that Daniel, while having a historical kernel of truth in the sixth, fifth, and fourth centuries B.C.E., is really a book addressed to the problems of the second, that the prophecies which end it make reference to the bitter disputes of the Jews with their Seleucid overlord, the Greek tyrant Antiochus, whose defilement of the rebuilt Temple in Jerusalem and persecution of religious Jews led to the revolt of the Maccabees. Whether or not this is so, it does not explain why Daniel would have survived its value as propaganda in the second century C.E. Or, indeed, since it counseled not revolt but patience and faith in the sure vengeance of the Holy One upon His enemies, why was it credited at all in the wake of the successes

---

The author's own translation of the Bible used in this essay.

of the aggressive Maccabees? The Book of Daniel, as the voice of the angel clothed in white linen cautions the author, is a book "sealed up until the time of the end." It is not ranked in the Jewish Bible within the books of the prophets, despite its forecasts. Yet Louis Ginzberg has noted, "the writing of a prophet is not necessarily a prophetic book."

Was Daniel a prophet? The Talmud seems to answer yes and no. This skillful interpreter of portents and dreams, whose own head was crowded with images of apocalypse, is essentially ambiguous. His dreams do not speak to a specific king or time. Many years after the book was composed, whether in the sixth century, or in the second from the hand of an inspired redactor of earlier traditions, Daniel's example was to be prophetic. Roman emperors would declare themselves gods and demand the worship of their subjects. The notion of man rather than the Holy One as the object of petition, prayer, was to regain its grip on human imagination. It is then that the serene steps of Daniel to his open window, to address the mysterious God of Israel, knowing that an earthly king's writ demanded death for it, would give heart to Jews in the Holy Land and in Diaspora.

Who is this Daniel, whose character is as important as his utterances? In Hebrew the name means "God has judged" or, alternatively, "My judge is God." Was his own name prophetic to him? For he must have known that there were ancient stories in the Syrian and Palestinian world about a wise man bearing this name. All of us given names which speak a message or which have gone before us in glory know that they summon us to tasks like cryptograms sent from the past. And names are important in Daniel. The king, Nebuchadnezzar, is careful to give Daniel a name in Aramaic which will attach him closely to the Babylonian dynasty—Belteshazzar, which seems to mean "O Bel protect the king!" (However, the Biblical scholar Edward Greenstein suggested to me an alternative meaning, *Belti-sar-usur,* "O My Lady [the goddess Ishtar], protect the king!" remarking that "this is the difference between Belshazzar and Belteshazzar." The androgynous moniker provokes me to wonder about how the Babylonian court saw the Jewish princes they co-opted for service as courtiers. Was there laughter or a memory of a threat to make them eunuchs in the name?)

The fact that Daniel accepts a name containing that of Bel, one of the leading deities of Babylon, expresses a certain humor, tolerance, and even worldliness. How strange that Daniel, whose story is the very paradigm of the successful courtier and was a well-known tale in the Middle East of antiquity, should be the figure by whose example the rabbis quietly fix the schedule of Jewish prayer outside the Temple. Even stranger that the courtier's story begins with his tactful but firm diplomacy for kosher food. This is ironic narrative. Daniel is a book of secrets, and the rabbis of the Talmud maintain ambiguity in their attitude toward its author: "Rabbi Nachman said: If he [the Messiah] is of the living [today] it might be one like myself, as it is written, *And their nobles shall be of themselves, and their governors shall proceed from the midst of them* [Jeremiah 30:21]. Rab [Rabbi Nachman] said: If he is of the living, it would be our holy Master, if of the dead, it would have been Daniel, the most desirable man" (T.B. *Sanhedrin* 98b). On the other hand, in *Baba Bathra,* 4a, of the Babylonian Talmud, it is said, in the name of the same rab, that Daniel was thrown into the lions' den as a punishment, "only because he gave advice to Nebuchadnezzar." For the rabbis observed that Daniel's advice to Nebuchadnezzar to *"atone thy sins by righteousness and thine iniquities by showing mercy to the poor, if there may be a lengthening of thy tranquility"* (4:24) had won the king a twelve-month reprieve from the madness which Daniel has prophesied would come down upon him. Such commentary is more than a shrewd reading of the text. It speaks to an understanding of the paradoxical position of the Jew in exile: even in the highest position of power, helpless. Daniel shone in the exile like Messiah, but his very position made him an abettor of that villain Nebuchadnezzar, and he was cut down from power in the end. The rabbis hold his name synonymous with that of "Hatach" in the Book of Esther, a name which they derive from the word *chetach,* "to cut down." According to commentary, to those who argue that it is to be vocalized *chatach,* or "to decide," since "all matters of state were decided [*chatach*] according to his counsel, what answer can we give?—That he was thrown into the den of lions" (*Baba Bathra* 4a). Yes, for all Daniel's pre-eminence at court, his advice was certainly not asked in the decree of idolatry which led to his being cast into the lions' den. On the other hand, the trial among the roaring lions is what shows to the Persians the hand of the Holy One and marks Daniel as his chosen vessel. Sin, tribulation, salvation, is this the meaning of the Exile?

Daniel is the essential text of the Diaspora. I realized this at a *shir* (lesson) of Rabbi Joseph Soloveitchick where I heard him speak of the book,

saw him become Daniel. According to Rav Soloveitchick's midrash, Daniel
was about to leave the Exile and return to Jerusalem as a prince of the
Jews—in fact, the principal Jew of Babylonia, when he understood that he
must stay behind. "More than any of the Jews in captivity, Daniel wanted
to return. This is what he had hoped for, prayed for. Through his sagacity
and services to the Median and Persian thrones, he had helped bring it about.
Yet he was told to remain.

"Why?"

It was not only for mighty deeds, for advice, counsel, to protect the
Jews in Israel and abroad through his patronage, for his paramount influence
with the throne of Persia, his weight in the role of the court Jew (of which
he is one of the prototypes). "No," said the Rav, he was told to remain "for
what seems like small things. He gave gifts to the poor, he showed charity.
When there was a Jewish wedding, he went. To cheer the bride, he did a
little dance." And I watched the Rav, who had had to be assisted by the
shoulders of his students entering the lecture hall at Young Israel in Brookline, Massachusetts, rise in his chair and do the dance of Daniel before the
bride in the streets of Shushan as he spoke the last phrase. A man already
a legend and so crippled with age and infirmity that he could not bend that
day to tie his shoelaces, I saw the merriness of the bridal party flicker on
his face and understood something of the secret Daniel whose mild demeanor fashioned the heart of the Babylonian exile, the Diaspora of teachers
to whom the direction of Judaism was to be given.

The Book of Daniel is one of the sources for the tradition of the three
times of Jewish prayer: the morning devotion, *shachris;* the afternoon,
minchah; and the evening, *maariv,* facing toward Jerusalem.[1] Daniel did not
bother to protest in the wake of the proclamation instigated by the jealous
courtiers of King Darius that no one petition for thirty days to any god but
the king. "But when Daniel knew that the writing was signed, he went into
his house—now his windows were open in his upper chamber toward
Jerusalem—and he kneeled upon his knees three times a day, and prayed,
and gave thanks before his God, as he did aforetime" (6:11). Daniel's order
of prayer, institutionalized, was to sustain the Jewish sense of the Holy One's
closeness in the aftermath of His sanctuary's two destructions.

My first reading of Daniel was in Hebrew school. A miserable experience, my childhood in classes at the Beth El in Boston, the consonants of

Hebrew buzzing faster and faster, like fiery bees about my ears. I slunk away to the library one morning in a recess and discovered comic books of the Bible in English. There were the three Jewish princes, Hananiah, Mishael, and Azariah, subtitled Shadrach, Meshach, and Abednego, walking around in the fire with an angel under the amazed eyes of the cruel Nebuchadnezzar. A few pages later I found the ghostly handwriting on the wall, and then the lions, caressed under Daniel's patient fingers. These images are still alive to me today. And for most readers they represent the book, and rightfully so. It is the promise of a miracle in return for faith that gives Daniel its hold over the popular imagination, the promise to an unbelieving world of a visible sign of the bond between the Holy One and those who hold fast to belief. Some years ago, in helping to edit the translation of a text, *The Alphabet of Ben Sira,* I returned to Daniel for a serious reading. I had realized, following the references in the former text, that *The Alphabet of Ben Sira* was essentially a commentary, a comic embroidery upon Daniel. I felt the Messianic trumpets of Daniel, the cry for the "end of days." But I was also led into the Babylonian Talmud, where one could locate some of the outrageous phallic jokes of the *Alphabet* in the stories about the wickedness of Nebuchadnezzar. The secrets of Daniel, I believe, are partly to be unraveled through the Talmud's perspective. As I reread *Daniel* now, it is in the context of books to which it is very close kin: Esther, Ezra, Nehemiah, Jonah, the prophets Malachai and Zechariah, all of which constitute a world, are chapters in the tale of exile and return. And despite minor inconsistencies lodged in the book, from the very beginning its narrative suggests an underlying unity to the whole. In deciphering the pattern of the whole of Daniel, I find some answers to the mysteries of its parts.

Daniel begins amid a sea of woe, the carrying of the Jews into exile, and so the detail that a "part of the vessels" (1:2) taken from the House of God were brought with King Jehoiakim, were deposited in the "treasure house" of Nebuchadnezzar's god, goes almost unnoticed. Yet the word used to denote "part of," *miktzoh,* is echoed exactly in the expression used to signify the "end of the days" of preparation of the young men Daniel, Hananiah, Mishael, and Azariah in their presentation before the king a few verses on (1:18). The reason for this peculiar repetition, and for the use of a word with a double meaning (a word that recurs four times in the Book of Daniel, but only in one other place in the Bible, in the Book of

Nehemiah, which is one of Daniel's sister texts), is not immediately apparent. Many years and verses later, the son of Nebuchadnezzar, Belshazzar, has the temerity to summon the holy vessels out of the treasure house for the lips of royal concubines and courtesans to sip from at a pagan feast. The hall rings with the praises of the pantheon of gods toasted with the sacred Temple utensils. At this moment the reader is reminded of the detail in the second verse which begins the story. And, following the hand which writes of the end of the Babylonian royal house on the wall of Belshazzar's feasting hall, one realizes the doom the holy vessels were sure to spell for the line of kings when they were entrusted to Nebuchadnezzar's care. It is easy to understand that this small portion, *miktzoh,* of holy vessels would undo the greatest kingdom the world had yet seen. But there is a deeper echo to that word, *miktzos,* and it is signaled by its deliberate employment in Daniel the second time it is found, in its other sense: "And at the end of the days which the king had appointed for bringing them in [the four Jewish princes], the chief of the officers brought them in before Nebuchadnezzar." *Ool'miktzos* is the expression used for the phrase "and at the end." At the time it is read, the repetition may seem haphazard. What can a "remnant" or "part" of the holy vessels have to do with "the end" or "conclusion" of days? It is at Belshazzar's feast that Daniel's earlier warnings about the "remnant," or "conclusion" or "end of days," become apparent, in the apocalypse that overtakes the Babylonian empire. The book itself will "end" on that somber note. "And you, go to the end, you will rest and stand up to your lot at the end of days" (12:13). Those words, repeated in the strong rhythm of the Hebrew, in the final verse, "end" *(kaytz)* and "the end of days" *(kaytz ha-yomin)* cannot help recalling the *Ool'miktzos ha-yomiim* ("at the end of days") of Daniel's presentation before Nebuchadnezzar (1:18). Both are derived from verbs which mean "to cut off." There is a similarity of sound between their roots in the Hebrew. (It is possible that they come from a common original root.) But these verbs connote more than just the cruel "cutting off." They carry the meaning of fixing boundaries, borders, of separation, and so in this case of the boundary between life and death, between the Messianic future and the present. Daniel, "that desirable man," is brought to the "end of his days" of preparation (1:18) in sanctity, like a vessel of the House of God in Jerusalem, a holy thing, for precisely the reason that the Holy One intends to use him, to speak through Daniel. His colleagues, similarly prepared, ritually pure because of their insistence on diet, are indestructible against the fire, as Daniel will later be proof against the lions. (The Talmud elaborates on this: "What is meant by *in whom there is no blemish* [1:4]—R. Hama b. Hanina said 'They did not even bear the scar made by bleeding.' What is the meaning of *and had the ability to stand in the king's palace?* [Ibid.]—R. Hama B. Hanina said 'This teaches that they restrained themselves from levity, conversation, and sleep, and suppressed the call of Nature out of royal respect!" [*Sanhedrin* 93b]) Daniel stresses to the kings that the prophecy and interpretation of dream are not in him but in the Holy One. Well may he insist on this, for his predictions are hardly reassuring, either to Nebuchadnezzar or his son Belshazzar. The Jewish reader of the sixth or the second century B.C.E., hearing that the sacred vessels are to be profaned, will remember the story of I Samuel 5, when the idol of Dagon falls into pieces because of its proximity to the Ark of the Holy One. The identity of men, "representative Jews" (to paraphrase Emerson), as vessels of sacred holiness is something that carries a silent message for the nation in Exile. Neither his beautiful vessels nor his "desirable ones" will the Holy One allow to be put to sordid use in the Exile. Further, the "remnant" of the vessels, like the "remnant" of the nation, is linked to the "remnant or end of days." The immanence of final judgment sounds throughout the book. Scholars have noted that, before interpreting Nebuchadnezzar's dream, Daniel is careful to state to the king why he has received it: "It is that Nebuchadnezzar may know *what is to happen in the last days*" [2:28], i.e. at the end of the present era. The vision is eschatological, to reveal the ultimate destiny of the world.

"But you, go to the end!" (12:13) The book is full of voices, the autobiographical "I" of Daniel, Nebuchadnezzar, the Aramaic of the Chaldean necromancers, and moves from third to first person and back to first again. The most compelling voice in my ear is that of the man dressed in white linen, eyes "like torches of fire," who declares the prophecies to Daniel and speaks the word to which the book is sealed, the Book of Daniel and the book of life, man's life. This voice mingles assurance of the end of the present Jewish troubles with deliberate ambiguity, a new beginning with a far more distant note which refuses specific prophecy. Prophecy, according to tradition, ends with the generation of Daniel, with the Book of Ezra, his younger contemporary.

The timbre of this angelic authority strikes in Daniel's voice as well.

It speaks to a theme which resounds from the drum of Daniel throughout, the necessity for humility in power. Nebuchadnezzar, ruler of the world visible to the Hebrews in captivity, is reduced in a second to a beast wandering the wet fields eating grass. His son will be reft of throne and life in a single night for forgetting the warning given to his father, proudly lifting up the Temple vessels, praising gods of gold, silver, iron, brass, stone, and wood with their lips. (The stuff of these idols echoes the dream of his father, Nebuchadnezzar, who has seen an idol of gold, silver, iron, brass, and clay, which Daniel interpreted as prefiguring the fate of the world's empires.)

Yet Daniel, despite its apocalyptics, is gentle in contrast to Ezra and Nehemiah, texts contemporary to the momentous events of the return from captivity, books which may seem harsh to the contemporary imagination in their uncompromising denunciation of foreign marriage, ritual backsliding, their focus on racial purity and the emerging details of the law. Perhaps for these reasons, they have never been popular books among the Jews. They are of the here and now of the mundane, the tasks of nation- and temple-building. It is Daniel and its sister Esther which have been taken to the Jewish bosom. Whereas the Scroll of Esther concerns the saving of a people and is a gay, topsy-turvy tale, the Book of Daniel at first glance is the opposite. No nation is saved. No national holiday is celebrated in its wake. Four individuals experience a miracle of personal salvation. Daniel is an introspective book, a scroll of dreams and ethics. It tolls the salvation not only of Jews but of all men. Its Gentile kings acknowledge the power of the Holy One, and the verses of its last chapter sound the horn of the hereafter in a voice of such solemn assurance that readers touched with a fear of death have trembled ever after. "And many of them that sleep in the dust of the earth shall awake, some to everlasting life, and some to reproaches and horror everlasting" (12:2).

Why was the Book of Daniel to become such an important part of the dream life of the Diaspora? From its first lines, the book spoke of the carrying away of the holy into the profane, the Gentile world. Yet it also addressed the coexistence in Diaspora of the sacred—the holy—with the profane—in this case, the Gentile world. A part of the Temple vessels have been entrusted to the care of this wider empire as well as to the Jewish people. And here a phrase which the secular commentators do hear the echo of joins the ambiguous *miktzos* to point to the subterranean stream of Daniel. The young princes of the royal seed are "youth in whom there is no blemish" (1:4). This is the language which is used to speak of the animals selected for sacrifice in the House of God. The drama unfolds, first through fire, then through the lions' den, but not as a story of martyrdom, for first the three princes, then the fourth, are saved. Daniel is the very opposite of a martyrology. It is like the Akedah, the sacrifice of Isaac, a test of faith. It is a demonstration that the Akedah, which took place on Mount Moriah, the Temple Mount, thus hallowing it for the site of the House of God, has now shifted to Diaspora—"in part." That word becomes crucial: not all, but only a part of the holy vessels have left Jerusalem. The first sacrifice the princes make is like the first mention of the Temple vessels, understated, a detail of diet. This question of diet, which might be perceived as an over-meticulous notion of the princes, is the crux of the drama. It verifies their description as being "without blemish." Nor is it a question, as in Ezra or Nehemiah, of priestly purity, but is, rather, the purity of the secular princes and, by extension, of the Jew in the street who must ensure the survival of Judaism.

This is a message which few generations heard with more skepticism than my father's. He came from the center of what seemed, in contrast to America, an absolutely Jewish world, a city in Eastern Europe, Pinsk, with a Jewish majority, where the holidays and the Sabbath were the dominant features of the social landscape and dietary laws were only part of a larger whole. In the speedily assimilating America which I inhabit, I have come to believe that the fabric of Jewish life begins to unravel around the individual by not doing something specific, taking on a part of the respon-sibilities of *halakhic* or legal regulations of inherited Jewish law, until there is nothing to hand on to children, the next generation.

In return for observance, the Book of Daniel promises a miracle. The voice of prophecy can speak in Diaspora and, more important, *to* Diaspora. Holiness, the very sanctity of the House of God, the holy vessels themselves carried into Diaspora, do not lose their powers beyond the Temple Mount. And, on the contrary, their abuse leads to the catastrophic punishment of a worldwide empire. Daniel, however, is not a narrowly Jewish book. Throughout there are portraits of righteous, understanding Gentiles. Perhaps the most impressive of them is met in the first verses, the anonymous chief of the officers and his steward who agree to let Daniel and his friends try a kosher table. Even the kings of Babylon and Media are brought to hymn the glory of the Hebrew Holy One seen as the transcendent power in the world. Whether these are later interpolations or not is almost irrelevant in the perspective of the book as it was read. Daniel holds out the hope of a world in which the Gentile kings will take their place among the Temple singers and the psalmists. It offers the overwhelming vision of the prophet held contemporary to its events, Zechariah: "And it shall happen in this day, that from Jerusalem living waters go forth, half to the Eastern, half to the Western sea, in summer and winter it will be—and the Lord will be as king over all the earth in this day, the Lord will be one and His name one" (Zechariah 14:8–9).

Daniel seems serious in contrast with Esther, its consort. The image of the beautiful Jewish girl in bed with a foolish Persian king invites an obvious buffoonery, an upside-down attitude toward the sacred. It may be somewhat of a surprise that the sages of the Talmud had a twinkle in their eyes in speaking of Daniel and its cast of characters. "When Hananiah, Mishael and Azariah emerged unscathed from the fiery furnace, all the nations of the world came and smote the apostate Jews [who had bowed to the idol] upon their faces, saying to them, 'You have such a God, yet you worship an image!' Immediately the apostates opened their mouths and confessed, 'To You O Lord, [belongs] righteousness, to us confusion of face, as on this day!'" (9:7, quoted from *Sanhedrin* 93b) What happened afterward to the three princes, Hananiah, Mishael, and Azariah; why did they disappear from the story? " 'They died from an evil eye,' said Rab. 'They drowned in the spittle,' said Samuel. 'They went up to Palestine, married and begat sons and daughters' " *(Sanhedrin* 93b). According to the laconic remark of Samuel, the poor princes drowned in the sea of spittle spat on the Jews who had apostasized when the nations saw the three princes who refused to do so triumphantly emerge from the furnace. And where was Daniel during the trial of his three friends? Why was he absent? "Rab said, 'To dig a great spring at Tiberias.' Samuel said, 'To procure animal fodder.' R. Johanan said, 'To obtain pigs from Alexandria of Egypt.' " In the breath of the last, a dig at the Jews of Alexandria and the meticulous *kashruth* (observance of the kosher laws) of Daniel, we may certainly hear the rabbis laughing. Why are they laughing? Is it because they wish to leaven the notion of miracle in the Book of Daniel? It is important to understand that Daniel, like the princes associated with him, is just a man—a righteous man, one who can interpret dreams, it is true, but finally human, vulnerable. The passage above in *Sanhedrin* goes on to state, "Three were involved in the conspiracy [to keep Daniel from the furnace]. The Holy One, blessed be He, Daniel and Nebuchadnezzar. The Holy One, blessed be He, said, 'Let Daniel depart from here, so it won't be said that they were delivered through his merit.' Daniel said, 'Let me go from here that I be not a fulfillment of [the verse] *the graven image of their gods shall ye burn with fire*' [implying that Nebuchadnezzar had elevated him to the status of a deity]. While Nebuchadnezzar said, 'Let Daniel depart, so people won't say he [Nebuchadnezzar] has burnt his god [Daniel] in fire.' And whence do we know that he worshipped him [Daniel]. From the verse, *Then the king Nebuchadnezzar fell upon his face, and worshipped Daniel*" (2:46). In Daniel's reason for absenting himself, and Nebuchadnezzar's for not including him, there lurks this apprehension of a confusion between the Holy One and His messengers. The laughter of the Talmud in this regard is a way of assuring that the reader will understand the division between man, who is always the butt of circumstances, and the Holy One.

If the rabbis' storytelling tweaked the ear of sober Daniel and his associates, one can expect that when they came to Nebuchadnezzar, they would not restrain themselves. The text of Daniel, with its tale of a king on all fours eating grass with the beasts of the field, is an invitation. There is no evidence that the Nebuchadnezzar who took Jerusalem suffered from insanity. But the narrative demands that the king responsible for the cataclysmic end of the Jewish kingdom should suffer the fate of being degraded to the lowest of the low. That a Persian king should get sick several generations down the line requires a narrative much longer than Daniel. (Although we may regard the punishment of Belshazzar in the lyric of Daniel's narrative as such a movement toward the epic, it is also the kind of long-suffering justice that the modern novels of Faulkner and Marquez at their best declare.)

The image of the idol in which Daniel announces the kingdom is surely ironic. Nebuchadnezzar is an idolator. He receives a vision of an idol smashed to such fine bits that it is in the power of the wind. Since "wind," "spirit," is a synonym for the Holy One, the image of chaff on the threshing floor has a double force. The rabbis, as we saw, were wary of the strong image of Nebuchadnezzar falling on his face and worshipping Daniel. Yet it is a perfect expression of the king's benighted state, which will lead to his dream of a golden idol.

The editors of the Anchor Bible Daniel (to which a reader wishing to know the scholarly opinion of the Book of Daniel might well resort) deny any correspondence between the idol that Nebuchadnezzar makes and the one he is told about in the vision. It seems to me that some correspondence exists. For the idol created by Nebuchadnezzar has its authority from the king's decree. Therefore, it represents the king. In the dream, only the head of the idol is gold, and Daniel announces, "Thou art the head of gold." The idol Nebuchadnezzar makes is entirely of gold. Is this idol meant to frustrate the dream, which describes a vulnerable idol of brass, iron, and clay, which will be broken by the unhewn stone? (The unhewn stone is a symbol of the Jewish altar.) Of course, it is laughable, because gold is no more proof against destruction than any of the other ingredients of the idol. Yet it may be Nebuchadnezzar's attempt to forestall the kingdoms that will follow him and to identify himself with an immortal kingdom. When the king stares into the fiery furnace and sees the fourth figure accompanying the angel, he exclaims, "The appearance of the fourth is like a son of the gods!" This is what Nebuchadnezzar has aspired to be. A year after the warning from Daniel "to break off your sins by almsgiving and your iniquities by showing mercy to the poor" or else be abased to a beast of the field, it is his vaunt which dunks Nebuchadnezzar in the soup. The pratfall is almost comic. "At the end of twelve months he was walking upon the royal palace of Babylon. The king spoke and said: 'Is not this great Babylon, which I have built for a royal dwelling-place, by the might of my power and for the glory of my majesty?' While the word was in the king's mouth, there fell a voice from heaven: 'O King Nebuchadnezzar, to you it is spoken: the kingdom is departed from you.' "

First Nebuchadnezzar falls on his face before a human being, Daniel, then he dreams of others falling on their faces before an image of him. A melancholy obsession links his dreams to his downfall.

And the same accusations against the Jews are passed down from one house of kings, the Babylonian, to another, the Medes: the demand that they bow down before the idol, then before the king (in prayer), thus the same idolatry. In the story of Esther one recalls the refusal of Mordecai, its hero, to bow down before the minister of the king. (If Daniel stood in the gate in the court of the king, from the reign of Nebuchadnezzar through that of Cyrus, we know that Mordecai was standing there, too.) Bowing before earthly kings—is there a certain laughter in the phrase, "they learned to stand before the king"? The euphemism, evidently, for holding their urine through long court sessions will also serve for their uprightness. The issue is the king's divinity. In this sense, the formula "O King live forever," in the mouth of the evil magicians the Chaldeans, has a determined ring; it is idolatrous. Alas, even Daniel emerging from the lions' den speaks it to a worshipful Darius. Yet this phrase, which has been bandied about by the magicians and repeated to an earthly king by the prophet (though in a moment which makes it clear that Darius has subordinated himself to Daniel's God), is heard at the very end of Daniel in a very different context. In the mouth of the angel who "sware by Him who lives forever" (12:7) it is given its proper echo, because it is uttered at the moment when the Biblical promise of resurrection is given to man. It is through Daniel, that most beloved and desirable of men, that the promise comes. And this, as scholars point out, is the first "unambiguous" statement of a general resurrection, though echoes of it have been heard before in the prophetic books like Ezekiel. If the promise has been handed down, mouth to mouth, from a distant time in the tradition of the Jews, it is now, just before the closing of the canon, that it is given to Daniel to hear and record it. This alone would make the book and its hero momentous.

But Nebuchadnezzar, his clowning, his pretensions, and even his successor, Darius, must exit the stage before the drama can turn to its metaphysical concerns.

This leads me to wonder about all the curious absences in the Book of Daniel. At the very first test I notice it. Daniel does not rush to stand before the king when the call is issued for the magicians, sorcerers, and Chaldeans. The fact that previously he used to stand before the king is emphasized in the word *ohmdoo* ("they stood"), both for the magicians and for Daniel with his associates. Why are they absent from the roll call the first time? Their advice is supposed to be as good as, if not better than, the rest of the king's counselors'.

More puzzling is Daniel's absence when his friends are put to the test.

We have seen the rabbis speculate humorously about this. And again, when the decree about prayers to anyone but the king is promulgated (which again implies the divinity of the king, in this case Darius), Daniel deliberately absents himself and provokes the test in the lions' den by going to his room, though leaving the door conspicuously open. The absences are in part a necessity of the narrative. If Nebuchadnezzar had declared in the presence of Daniel, "Who is the god who will deliver you out of my hand?," it would have been impossible for the latter not to answer.

"The one who showed me the meaning of your dream"—the fact that Nebuchadnezzar has forgotten this shows that he is forgetful to the point of buffoonery. If absence of mind defines the king, a form of absence, circumspection, describes the character of Daniel. Daniel is almost too considerate. The sages of the Talmud faulted him for showing Nebuchadnezzar a way to avoid the decree of insanity for almost a year. Yet tact is the way of the Jew in Diaspora, at least in the moral instruction in Daniel. He speaks by diplomatic indirection from the very beginning. We watch Daniel work on the officer of officers, then on the steward to find a way to preserve his dietary laws. It is always obliquely that Daniel works his will, showing the powers of his God. We can assume that he and his fellow princes have received a conditional no from the officer of officers, though in a kindly voice. Daniel cleverly finds a loophole in the no and exploits it with the officer's underling, the steward in charge of the boys (or perhaps only in charge of him and his three companions). There is almost a threat of a hunger strike implied in those lines, "Give us vegetables and we will eat, water and we will drink," although couched in an obsequious sweetness, "as you see, do with your servants," that appeals to the steward's intelligence, vanity, and, quietly, possibly, his pocket. All these were to be well-understood lessons for the Jew wishing to survive in Diaspora. It leads to the quietism of the end of the book, the Jew in Exile who stands patiently while the superpowers slug it out. Yet, for all that, Daniel is not a suffering servant. Like Joseph, he is a man of great power and, at the opportune moment, he thunders in the voice of the Holy One, which echoes through his, the uncompromising judgment from on high. This play of opposites in Daniel give him a complexity that makes him more than a match for the Babylonian, Median, and Persian kings.

The book mirrors this complexity, and not only in its narrative structure. It is a text whose historical meaning for the Jewish people has been profound, speaking as it does to "the notion of martyrdom, of being ready to die, *ahl kiddush hashaym* [for the sake of sanctifying the name of God]." (A friend, reminding me of this, adds, "A theme we see alive and well—but not well enough?—in the secular army of Israel more than anywhere else.") In this century of the furnace from which so many did not walk safely out, Daniel's riddles are more appreciated than its miracles.

Let us admit it—the reader who seeks the solace of narrative, its entertainment, will find in Daniel many tedious stretches toward the end. It is precisely in this obfuscation that the power of Daniel for the religious reader lies. And as a writer I am bound to admire the way the drama of those final riddles is prepared. First in the dream of the king, then in the vision of Daniel, the miracles of the fire, the lions, the mysterious fourth figure seen by Nebuchadnezzar in the furnace, the smoke of the altar has gone up from the holy vessels, a part of them, and it is in this haze that the end of days is announced, the cutting off of imperial glory, empire after empire. The drama of Daniel speaks to its unity.

I argue for the unity of the book, not to enter the fray of scholars who see interpolations throughout, but because it was as a book, not a collection of sources, that the rabbis "published" it, authorized its inclusion in the canon. As a book it influenced writers who came after it. Here is the first mention of the angel Gabriel, *Gavri Ayl,* "My man/sir is God," and of the angels, *melachim,* having wings. A stream of angelology was to flow from under the throne of inspiration found in Daniel. A writer in English who has been moved by Milton can not afford to ignore his sources in Daniel. Poets or prose narrators to whom Dante's *Commedia* is important, in repeated meditation on the Florentine will come to discover the presence of the Book of Daniel in the drama.

In Nebuchadnezzar, both Daniel and the commentary that followed on it give expression to a strange figure of the Biblical narrative and the rabbinic traditions. Like Balaam or the Pharaoh of Egypt who opposed Moses, Nebuchadnezzar is by virtue of the role he plays more than an archvillain. He is the chosen, almost sacred instrument of the Holy One's anger. The attitude of the Biblical text toward Nebuchadnezzar is divided. This is the king who destroyed the first House of God and brought the princes of Judah into exile. This is the king who had the intelligence and foresight to educate the Jewish princes to be his counselors. He is not forced to utter praise like Balaam, nor is he a hardened evildoer like the Pharaoh. But the task of serving as instrument of divine retribution is too great for him. He is not "without blemish." Since he cannot rise in understanding to a role which is superhuman, he must fall in understanding to the subhuman, the bestial. He relapses into vile idolatry, which brings about the miracle of the three princes cast into the fire. Yet Nebuchadnezzar is a witness to the miracle, and we hear, in the first person, his psalm of praise. (The Talmud, in *Sanhedrin* 92b, tells the story of how, when Nebuchadnezzar threw Hananiah, Mishael, and Azariah into the furnace, the Holy One ordered Ezekiel to resurrect the bones of the Jewish exiles slain on the plain of Dura. These bones came and "smote the wicked man upon his face. 'What kind of bones are these?' he exclaimed." Learning of the miracle, he "broke into utterance. 'How great are His signs, and how mighty are His wonders! His kingdom is an everlasting kindom and His dominion is from generation to generation' [3:23]. R. Isaac said: 'May molten gold be poured into the mouth of that wicked man [Nebuchadnezzar]! Had not an angel come and struck him upon his mouth he would have eclipsed all the songs and praises uttered by David in the Book of Psalms.' ") A few moments later, in this same compelling autobiographical "I," we hear the king describe his second dream. (Note the contrast of this with the first dream, which he commanded the magicians, and then Daniel, to describe to him.) Not only does Nebuchadnezzar have in this second vision a vivid apprehension of the degradation Daniel will forecast, but he is also made to abuse himself, speaking of "the watcher and the holy one" who "came down from Heaven" to cry, "Know that the Most High ruleth in the kingdom of men, And giveth it to whomsoever He will, and setteth up over it the lowest of men" (4:10, 14). The seven-year insanity of Nebuchadnezzar may well be the expression of his impossible role, which causes a form of nervous breakdown. The narrative, its twists and turns, compels in me an interior belief. Yes, it is so: Nebuchadnezzar will go mad, mad in the particular way of imagining himself a beast.

There is much of what I admire about Kafka in the Book of Daniel. The transformation of the king into the lowest of the animals smacks of the *Metamorphosis* of the Jewish fabulist of Prague. And there is not just one metamorphosis in Daniel. In chapter 7, which has been described as the "core" of the book, a procession of beasts appear; the mighty kings of the earth had been transformed into them. The beast of the apocalypse, "teeth like iron to it," an earthly king and tyrant, is opposed to the vision of Messiah, when indeed, in "Dominion taken away from the beasts" (7:12), we are promised a better world.

Details offered by Biblical scholars of historical antecedents are important clues to the book's mysteries: the skin disfigurement of a Babylonian monarch, Nabonidus; his absence from his royal capital in an Arabian oasis, Teima. As Professor Edward Greenstein cautioned me, "Scholars are concerned with what Daniel meant in its earliest Biblical context. . . . It is a great discovery to be able to read Daniel 1–6, in the context of 305 B.C.E., and Daniel 7–12, in the context of the mid-second century B.C.E." The danger is that some readers will hold only the pieces in their hands and not see the shape of the whole. It would be sad to have in place of the Biblical narrative Daniel an awkward piece of patchwork without grandeur or fear, and consequently without meaning. I have read the Canaanite text in which a wise man named Daniel appears. It is a curiosity, an archaeological find. I can reconstruct for myself an idea of the Canaanites from it, but it doesn't speak to me of the holy as Daniel does. Something overrides the specifics of the prophecies in the latter. Is it a sense of a general apocalypse in which the admonition to us is to seal up the book and look to our own rest? Not what Daniel is told, but how he is told it, the meeting of man and angel, is what has lingered in the ears of men and women who have caught sight of the banks of the river, glimpsed the world to be and the world to come. The Book of Daniel speaks to the desire to look into the future, to greet the end of days, of frustration with the world as we know it. Yet it encourages man to live in the world in such a way that he may wake beyond death to a better one. Daniel is an open door through which Biblical man looks into the afterlife, not in the *persona* of the prophet, divinely inspired, but in the less imposing but more accessible character of a righteous judge, a character in reach of all.

Time has elevated the Hebrew language of the book. The "Anointed One," who contemporaries of Daniel and the centuries before the destruction of the Second Temple may have understood as a recognizable heir of the line of Davidic kings in exile, has walked into a distant, glittering future endowed with the glow of angels. We await him in the guise of Messiah.

If indeed the figure of evil referred to at the end of the prophecies in chapter 11 is Antiochus IV, then he bears a curious resemblance to Nebuchadnezzar in his overbearing manner. But he stands as a type, the earthly king who dreams of displacing the hosts of heaven. This king, who in self-deification forgets even the gods of his father (11:37) and mother (evidently Tammuz, who was known as "desire of women") to vaunt his own divinity, reminds us of Nebuchadnezzar's idol. The worldly laughter of Daniel scorns a king who can not even worship his own deities properly.

As we close Daniel, we hear that the reading of the book is an act of sacrilege. It is sealed against the end of time. We are in a labyrinth of Jorge Luis Borges. The latter kings who have been metamorphosed into horns and beasts are nameless. I am returned to Nebuchadnezzar and the beginning of the scroll. And since the first seals were broken, the oral traditions surrounding Daniel mean that a knowledgeable reader hears not only the sound of strife between Seleucids and Ptolemies, but also the beast tale of the Talmud. For in this Daniel Nebuchadnezzar's descent does not stop among the beasts roaming the world like wild oxen, eating grass. The king of kings is also the beast of beasts. He is carnivorous and lecherous. As king he tried to sodomize the prophet Zedekiah, who caught him eating a rabbit and reported it. Only a miracle saved the prophet from this outrage. "Rab Judah said in Rab's name. When that wicked man [Nebuchadnezzar] wished to treat that righteous one [Zedekiah] thus [submit him to sexual abuse] his membrum was extended three hundred cubits and wagged in front of the whole company [of captive kings]." In revenge for this insult, Nebuchadnezzar during his metamorphosis is himself abused by all the beasts of the field. In the "fabulous" text *The Alphabet of Ben Sira,* a commentary on this Daniel, its antihero, Nebuchadnezzar, is returned to the stage of Jewish literature to match swords with a younger generation.

It seems as if there is not one Book of Daniel but many. There is the Book of Daniel which is about Daniel himself, the gentle, studious judge. That book I received from the hand of the Rav. For, after that lesson at a Young Israel study hall in Brookline, Massachusetts, in which he stressed the decision of Daniel to remain in Diaspora, one of the students who had journeyed from Jerusalem to hear him speak walked up to his table, after the formal session had ended, to ask, not about the rebuilding of the Temple in the sixth century B.C.E., but about the Jewish obligation to rebuild the Temple today, in the twentieth.

"How about the shining of the Cohen Ha-Gadol's [High Priest's] face, when he came out of the Holy of Holies?" cried the man, a student in his forties. "Isn't that important for us Jews today to recover, the actual Temple and the spirituality it brought to Israel?"

"The shining of the Cohen Ha-Gadol's face?" the Rav repeated slowly, an edge of amusement in his voice as he faced the reddening cheeks of the insistent student. "You know, many of the Cohen Ha-Gadols were not distinguished men. Let us not be romantic," he drawled. "Some of them, we know, paid for the position. They were not always learned. Several were quite ignorant. Even their meticulousness in observance was suspect. Scholars had to be appointed to help them and, in certain cases, to keep a sharp watch over them. They were not *perfect,* by any means, these Cohen Ha-Gadols," he sighed.

His eyes within his thick glasses seemed to look inward. "When I was a boy, I used to study *mishnayot* (chapters of the Mishnah) with my father." In the lenses there floated a shadow of joy, which spread over his face. "And the way my father used to study *mishnayot* with me—that was *perfect!*"

At this moment, the expression of the Rav glowed through the dark room at Young Israel, shining.

The Book of Daniel has become dear to me for many reasons, but above all because, as the text of the Diaspora without peer, within its light there shines a glimmer of explanation for the long Exile, the continued Exile, that finds me writing, in my forty-sixth year, not in Hebrew but in English. And, as if to reassure us in the very marrow of the text, it carries half its sacred message in the tongue of that first Diaspora, Aramaic. (In a noncanonical version of Daniel, a portion of the book is in Greek.) The Book of Daniel reaches out from the wide spaces of time and geography, from the Jewish root in all the lands and provinces of the earth, and from the Gentiles, the history of man, toward the narrow ark lodged on a hill in Jerusalem which carries the dream of a universal human being who exists beyond death as we know it, a human being whose ethical will will deserve the gift of eternity. Ezekiel mentions Daniel with two other Biblical figures,

Noah and Job. It is significant that they are all figures who stand outside the Jewish world as such and appeal to the wider world of the non-Jew as well. Daniel, like his predecessor Joseph, has been sent in slavery to a foreign land, rises to become a chief counselor of kings, and shows by his moral example a way to personal salvation. Finally, it is Daniel, the type, "the most desirable man," who stands like Ralph Waldo Emerson's "representative man" as the measure of the book. Daniel is kin to Jonah, who is forced to announce salvation to the non-Jew, and Esther, who is consort to a Gentile king, and Joseph, who is counselor to Pharaoh, and Job, a righteous Gentile who will experience the Holy One as an overwhelming riddle and stand the test of faith.

The Book of Daniel has become a personal reassurance. As I read it this time, working on a novel in the same breath, I found myself dreaming an old dream. It was a vision of the last moment in which I find myself in a room, to pass out of which is to pass into the other world. I write in my chapter, "If I were to evoke the suffocating horror of that room between life and death, it would be the space in which the couples of Jean Paul Sartre's *No Exit* face each other." But that is a final room. What is more frightening here is the sense of a looming horror to stage left—one has come into the bedroom, the sheets are mussed, dirty, and inevitably one has to pass on into that wing where death and extinction lie. The curtain, if there is a curtain, the lights, if there are lights, the moment in which the play is over, is encroaching steadily. One will exit left to death; that is a certainty. And each time I dream the dream, I know that the final time I will not wake up and be rescued by finding myself in the audience. It is such a hopeless dream.

And what do we know of death but such dreams? It is for this reason that the voice of the angel in the Book of Daniel has such authority for us. It seems to speak out of the soft assurance of a parent, my mother bending over the bed, singing in her lovely, throaty voice, "Close your eyes, / And you'll have a surprise. / The sandman is coming. / He's coming, he's coming." It is the voice which urges one down into sleep in the hope not of extinction but of joy. To hear that voice one second after death would redeem all earthly pain.

NOTES

1. Since so little has been published of the thought of Rabbi Soloveitchick, I have taken the liberty of including my hastily jotted lecture notes of his remarks that morning.

   "Daniel was in the chambers of the Kings as a proud Jew. He practiced *Gemillat Chesed* [doing acts of loving-kindness]. He was close to the king—he got quite a few concessions from the king. He had more opportunities for *Gemillat Chesed* than in Eretz Yisroel. *Gemillat Chesed* is more important than the Temple Service. He helped the people.

   "The Almighty advised Daniel not to rush his trip to Eretz Yisroel. Apparently *Gemillat Chesed* is at least as important.

   "[And what did it consist of—his *Gemillat Chesed*?] There was a young girl there with no friends. He used to dance. Simple services—this had more preference than the Beyt *Ha-Mikdash* [Holy Temple].

   "Apparently Chazal looked upon his *davening* [praying] as having surprising quality. *Tfillah* [prayer] is actually a *Gemillat Chesed*. For *tfillah* is not only for myself but for all Israel.

   "That's what Daniel used to do. That's why the *Kodosh Boruch Hoo* [The Holy One Blessed be He] needed him. If he left, it would take away the sources of help, comfort, that people needed."

EZRA

A SAMARITAN AT CAMP WINSOKI

Jay Neugeboren

"Now when these things were done, the princes came to me, saying, The people of Israel, and the priests, and the Levites, have not separated themselves from the people of the lands, doing according to their abominations. . . . For they have taken of their daughters for themselves, and for their sons; so that the holy seed have mingled themselves with the people of those lands: yea, the hand of the princes and rulers hath been chief in this trespass. And when I heard this thing, I rent my garment and my mantle, and plucked off the hair of my head, and of my beard, and sat down astonied."

—Book of Ezra   [9:1–3]

"Camp Winsoki is dedicated to the spirit of youth, the love of nature, the development of good comradeship, and the fostering of the ideals of our American and Jewish heritage."

—Camp Winsoki Memories

BETWEEN THE AGES OF ELEVEN AND NINETEEN, FOR EIGHT WEEKS each summer, I lived in exile among Jews. During the school year, in the section of Brooklyn where I grew up—three blocks from Erasmus Hall High School, a fifteen-minute walk to Ebbets Field—I was the most Jewish of my Jewish friends: the only one who kept kosher at home and away from home, the only one who went to synagogue every Saturday morning, the only one who chanted directly from the Torah at his Bar Mitzvah, the only one who went to Hebrew High School, the only one who put on *tefilin* each morning. But at the end of

---

The King James Version of the Bible used in this essay.

each school year I would journey north to Camp Winsoki, on Triangle Lake ("cradled in a mountain top, Triangle Lake is the second highest lake in the state of New York"), where I was one of the few campers who did not come from an Orthodox home, who did not go to a yeshiva.

My mother, a registered nurse who often worked double and triple shifts to enable our family to survive financially (my father, a jobber in the printing business, was endlessly failing, forever in debt), came to camp with me and my brother, trading her services for our tuition. Some years she worked as the camp nurse, but more often she was something called "camp mother," the woman who tended day and night to the needs of several hundred Jewish children: their allergies and their homesickness and their bed-wetting, their fingernails and toenails and scalps and hair and diets. The camp was owned by my cousin Shelley, a rabbi married to my father's niece Marilyn (my father's side of the family was Orthodox, my mother's was not), and, except for the fact that its staff and clientele were Orthodox Jews, it was a camp like any other American summer camp: we played baseball and volleyball and basketball and tennis; we made ashtrays and lanyards and photo albums in arts and crafts; we went on raids to the girls' bunks in the middle of the night; we swam and we hiked and we sang and we had campfires and we put on productions of *Carousel* and *Oklahoma* and *South Pacific;* and at the end of each summer we divided into two teams and went at each other ferociously in four days of a quasi-military and fanatic competition called Color War.

We were all Jews at Camp Winsoki, most of us fleeing the heat and concrete of New York City, but among Jews who prayed three times each day and observed the Sabbath scrupulously and studied Torah and Talmud and Gemarrah after softball and basketball games, I felt ignorant and inadequate and impure, an outcast and a reject.

One summer, I fell in love with a wonderfully intelligent and beautiful dark-haired girl (when she smiled shyly from under long dark lashes, she looked, I would realize a few years later, like Joan Baez), and though I felt confident that she liked me as much as I liked her, I was tentative in my approaches to her, afraid to risk ruining a precious friendship by letting her know how I *really* felt. At socials, which took place in the canteen after the evening activity, I danced with her often, holding her as close as possible, loving the feel of her warm cheek next to mine, closing my eyes when her thumb would gently rub the back of my hand or her fingers would graze my neck. I would hum along to our favorite songs—Tony Bennett's "Cold, Cold Heart," Nat "King" Cole's "Too Young"—her body warm and unresisting when she felt me grow hard.

Walking her back to her bunk one night in July, I ached too much not to take a chance and do what I had been longing to do—to kiss her, to tell her how much I liked her. But when I leaned toward her, she pushed me back firmly, and looked down, embarrassed. She liked me *very* much, she said—she wanted me to know that, and she didn't want to hurt my feelings—but, given where I came from, she just couldn't allow herself to become involved with me, no matter what she felt. Would I forgive her?

We stood at the side of the dirt path, in the neutral zone that divided the line of boys' bunks from the semicircle of girls' bunks, and I pleaded with her as best I could. Was there something wrong with me? Had I said or done something to offend her? I really did like her a lot and I thought she liked me; since we lived within walking distance of each other's homes we could keep seeing each other back in Brooklyn after the summer. . . . What did she mean when she talked about where I came from?

But of course I knew exactly what she meant and, her large brown eyes watering, she put my knowledge into words: it was just that her family would not approve of her going out with a boy who went to a public high school. "It's just"—she said—"it's that you're not Jewish enough for me."

Though we remained friends, I never stopped desiring her, I never stopped hoping things would change, I never stopped being enraged at the circumstances—beyond our control, not of my making—that kept us apart. That summer I played ball with maniacal fury, ate like a starving madman (I was voted both best athlete and biggest eater in the annual poll at summer's end), and dreamed day and night of the abandon with which, overwhelmed by feelings she could control as little as I could, she would one day give herself to me. I did not, for the rest of that summer, try to kiss another girl. In my own nonreligious way, I was ever as pure and absolute as the most observant of those who were denying me.

All through my adolescence, then, I led a double life that I resented deeply: I was the least Jewish of my friends during the summers, the most Jewish of my friends during the school year—a Samaritan among Jews for two months, a Jew among Samaritans for ten.

One of my best friends' mothers would often fry up a pan of bacon when I visited, then hold the shimmering ribbons of crisp Manna in front of my nose and urge me to try a piece. Would I die if I ate some? Didn't it smell wonderful? Didn't I want to know what the forbidden food tasted like? She laughed at me for my adherence to what she saw as a silly Old World superstition she was American enough to have left behind. When, after I made the JV baseball team at Erasmus as a pitcher during my sophomore year, some of the guys came to me and asked me be on their team during the off season, in the Ice Cream League at the Parade Grounds, I sneaked out of the house one Saturday morning to practice with them; the following Monday I quit the team I had barely joined: my mother had spent the weekend (without, I later learned, discussing the matter with my father) pointing out to me just how much it would hurt him if I played baseball on Shabbos morning instead of accompanying him to *shul*.

During July and August at Camp Winsoki, and during the one summer of my teen years when I did not go there but worked, instead, to earn college tuition as a busboy at the Pioneer Country Club, a Borscht Circuit hotel for Orthodox Jews, I came, often, to hate many of these Jews for what I perceived as their bigotry, their narrow-mindedness, their arrogance, their mean-spiritedness, their venality, and—most of all—their hypocrisy.

If they prayed so much and observed so many of God's laws, I sometimes screamed in the silence within my head, why weren't they better and more moral human beings? Why did they cheat in business, and lie to their friends, and hate and exploit blacks and Puerto Ricans? If they were so close to God, where in their lives was His light, His generosity of spirit?

And why did my mother, on visiting days during the summer, and at the bus station at the end of each summer, have to go around sucking up to these Jews—fawning on them about how much she adored their children, smiling at them so that they would remember to give her their two- and five- and ten-dollar tips? What right did they have to treat her like a servant and a beggar when she worked harder than any of them? From a distance, and without letting anyone know how I felt, I fumed.

I had lived closely with Orthodox Jews and I knew that they masturbated and teased and cursed and played around as much as my Jewish and Gentile friends at Erasmus—that they were at least as greedy and vain and cowardly and unscrupulous. (They could also be as kind and fair and generous; what, then, was the relation—if there was any at all—between religious observance and moral behavior?) Why, then, did their endless praying and their unthinking observance of absurd and mindless rituals entitle many of them to act and feel, as it seemed to me they did, so superior to those unlike themselves? And why would young women I lusted after soul-kiss and dry-hump and screw in the woods with Jewish boys from yeshivas, but not with a Jewish boy like me? Perhaps, I mused in lighter moments, all that praying helped, after all.

The Book of Ezra, written by Ezra the scribe, tells the story of the rebuilding of the holy Temple in Jerusalem in the sixth century B.C.E., and of what happens when, sixty years after the completion of the Temple, the Jewish people fall into evil ways. It is a fascinating and compelling tale of exile and redemption, told in a voice that is individual and passionate and exacting—a voice that mingles passages of the deepest personal feeling with passages that might have been set down by an earnest CPA; it is filled with lists and decrees and genealogies and catalogues and inventories and memoranda, with the most direct and impassioned accounts of a great man's doubts and reflections and acts.

Ezra tells the story of how the Jewish people came up out of the Babylonian exile, bearing the gifts and good will of the kings of Persia, to rebuild the holy Temple in Jerusalem, and while he does his focus is not primarily on the renewal of the national and religious life that occurs seventy years after the destruction of the Temple but, rather, on how this renewal is continually being sabotaged, from without and from within: by the enemies of the Jewish people (the Samaritans), and—more dangerous and deadly—by the corruption and immorality of the Jewish people themselves.

The Book of Ezra is not so much a hymn to the rebuilding of the Temple—to one of the most glorious moments in Jewish history—as it is an accounting of how the Jewish people respond to adversity, to the attempts to hinder the rebuilding of the Temple as they work to re-establish the Jewish community in the Holy Land. It is a narrative that is obsessed with purity and impurity; thus, in the second half of the book, when Ezra sets out with a commission from Artaxerxes I authorizing him to reorganize the

Jewish community in Jerusalem sixty years after the Temple has been rebuilt (the book is mysteriously silent about what happened during these sixty years), the great enemy against which he must marshal the Jewish people is intermarriage.

> Now when these things were done, the princes came to me, saying, The people of Israel, and the priests, and the Levites, have not separated themselves from the people of the lands, doing according to their abominations, even of the Canaanites, the Hittites, the Perizzites, the Jebusites, the Ammonites, the Moabites, the Egyptians, and the Amorites.
>
> For they have taken of their daughters for themselves, and for their sons; so that the holy seed have mingled themselves with the people of those lands: yea, the hand of the princes and rulers hath been chief in this trespass. [9:1–2]

The problems then are the problems now: How are the Jews to live among the nations? And if and when, in the course of history, the Jewish people come out of bondage and prosper and are blessed with the freedom to live and to worship as they please, how do we, *without external adversity,* sustain our faith and our will and our singular identity?

Ezra's response is clear: the Jewish people must be as wary of assimilation as of the Samaritans; we must keep ourselves separate and pure, morally, religiously, physically. Although, of course, as modern Jews, we may try to gloss over the literalness of the injunctions against mingling with the Gentiles and choose to interpret the text metaphorically (we should keep ourselves separate only from the abominations and evil *ways* of the Gentiles, of impure and immoral Jews), the text itself is unequivocal: if we Jews are to be true to our Covenant with God as His chosen people, we must guard always against the slightest physical or moral union with those unlike ourselves, with those not chosen by God. To judge from Ezra, this includes not only Gentiles, but also those Jews who are corrupt because their lineage or faith is questionable. The young women who spurned me at Camp Winsoki would have been as praised by Ezra as by their parents.

Though enumerating all those thousands who journeyed to Jerusalem out of exile ("The whole congregation together was forty and two thousand three hundred and three score, Beside their servants and their maids, of whom there were seven thousand three hundred and thirty and seven: and

there were among them two hundred singing men and singing women"
[2:64–65]), Ezra also records, in detail, the lists of impure Jews:

And these were they which went up from Tel-melah, Tel-harsa, Cherub, Addan,
and Immer: but they could not shew their father's house, and their seed, whether they
were of Israel:

The children of Delaiah, the children of Tobiah, the children of Nekoda, six
hundred fifty and two.

And of the children of the priests: the children of Habaiah, the children of Koz,
the children of Barzillai; which took a wife of the daughters of Barzillai the Gileadite,
and was called after their name:

These sought their register among those that were reckoned by genealogy, but
they were not found: therefore were they, as polluted, put from the priesthood.
[2:59–62]

In the most dramatic moment in the first half of Ezra, the Samaritans,
who live in the Holy Land and worship the God of Israel even as do the
Jews (though they also serve graven images), discover that the Jews have
laid the foundations for the Temple in Jerusalem. They offer to join with
the Jews and assist in the rebuilding of the Temple, but their offer is rejected.
Now the Samaritans, descended most probably from non-Jewish colonists
and, perhaps, from those Israelites who escaped the captivity at the time of
the exile in Babylon, seem to have been more scrupulous about observing
the ordinances of the Pentateuch than the Orthodox Jews of the time. They
consider themselves to be Jews.

But they are not Jewish enough. When they are first introduced into
the story, Ezra will not even call them by their name; they are, simply,
"adversaries":

Now when the adversaries of Judah and Benjamin heard that the children of the
captivity builded the temple unto the Lord God of Israel;

Then they came to Zerubbabel, and to the chief of the fathers, and said unto
them, Let us build with you: for we seek your God, as ye do; and we do sacrifice
unto Him since the days of Esar-had-don king of Assyria, who brought us up hither.

But Zerubbabel, and Jeshua, and the rest of the chief of the fathers of Israel, said
unto them, Ye have nothing to do with us to build an house unto our God; but we
ourselves together will build unto the Lord God of Israel, as king Cyrus the king of
Persia hath commanded us.   [4:1–3]

Rejected because they are judged impure ("Ye have nothing to do with us to build an house unto *our* God"), the Samaritans become embittered, and work to destroy the rebuilding of the Temple.

> Then the people of the land weakened the hands of the people of Judah, and troubled them in building,
>
> And hired counsellors against them, to frustrate their purpose, all the days of Cyrus king of Persia, even until the reign of Darius king of Persia.
>
> And in the reign of Ahasuerus, in the beginning of his reign, wrote they unto him an accusation against the inhabitants of Judah and Jerusalem.   [4:4–6]

The Samaritans succeed in hindering the construction of the Temple for twenty years, during which time the prophets Haggai and Zechariah urge the people to continue the work. The Jews deal with the obstructive tactics of the Samaritans by appealing to the Persian officials, who make inquiry, discover the original decree of Cyrus, and bring it to Darius. Ezra narrates the events straightforwardly, interpolating the texts of actual documents with brief historical commentaries. The Persian officials, sympathetic to the Jews and to their just claims, convince Darius of their views; a new royal decree is issued, once again authorizing the reconstruction of the Temple by the Jews:

> And the God that hath caused his name to dwell there destroy all kings and people, that shall put to their hand to alter and to destroy this house of God, which is at Jerusalem. I Darius have made a decree; let it be done with speed.
>
> Then Tatnai, governor on this side of the river, Shethar-boznai, and their companions, according to that which Darius the king had sent, so they did speedily.
>
> And the elders of the Jews builded, and they prospered through the prophesying of Haggai the prophet and Zechariah the son of Iddo. And they builded, and finished it, according to the commandment of the God of Israel, and according to the commandment of Cyrus, and Darius, and Artaxerxes king of Persia.   [6:12–14]

The first part of Ezra ends joyously, with the completion and dedication of the Temple and the celebration of the Passover.

> And the children of Israel, which were come again out of captivity, and all such as had separated themselves unto them from the filthiness of the heathen of the land, to seek the Lord God of Israel, did eat.

And kept the feast of unleavened bread seven days with joy: for the Lord had made them joyful, and turned the heart of the king of Assyria unto them, to strengthen their hands in the work of the house of God, the God of Israel.   [6:21–22]

The problem of immorality and intermarriage that now beset the Jews, however—their own "filthiness"—requires more than the intervention and decrees of outsiders such as Cyrus and Darius; it requires leadership from within their own house. And this is what, in the second half of his story, Ezra provides. "When the Torah was forgotten in Israel," the Talmud says, "Ezra came up from Babylon and established it."

What we have, then, in the Book of Ezra is the story of two efforts to renew national and religious life, and though the first (the rebuilding of the Temple) seems of greater worldly moment, the second has greater issue, for it contains within it those elements that possess the possibility of sustaining the Jewish people in *all* circumstances—with or without the existence of the Temple, in exile or in the Holy Land.

What Ezra does is not merely to carry out his mission to reorganize the Jewish community in Israel and purge it of immorality and heathenish ways, but in so doing to teach, by his example and his word, that the survival of the Jewish community and way of life depends not upon the generosity of others, but upon the preservation of those things within the Jewish religion that make it distinctive and holy.

Although Ezra is at pains to trace his own lineage back to Aaron the high priest, he himself, as governor and high priest in Israel, abolishes priestly privileges. Henceforth and down to our own time, due to his acts, the Torah becomes, not the exclusive possession of the priestly class, but the common property of all Jews. "If Moses had not preceded him," say the rabbis, "Ezra would have received the Torah."

Ezra halts the decline of the Jews into heathenism not by decree, but by appealing to the conscience and memory of the nation—by saying to the people of Israel that they must take individual responsibility for their acts and for the consequences of those acts. The Jewish people can be redeemed, now, not by an act of a foreign king, or even of God, but by instilling within one another the will to change.

Ezra is able to cause his own tender love of God to spread to others because he is not afraid to love fully and because he is not afraid to enter and reveal the depth of his own despair. As with public personalities in our own time such as Martin Luther King, Jr., Gandhi, Bishop Tutu, or Anatoly Shcharansky, it is not merely the intensity of Ezra's religious experience that makes him a leader of nations, but his ability to bring his personal experience into the light of day for others—to tie the personal to the political, the individual need to the national need.

Ezra shows the Jewish people that, in the world, hope lies not just in the love of God, but in the ability to act upon that love. This is what allows the transformation of darkness into light, despair into hope, hope into change.

And at the evening sacrifice I arose up from my heaviness; and having rent my garment and my mantle, I fell upon my knees, and spread out my hands unto the Lord my God,

And said, O my God, I am ashamed and blush to lift up my face to thee, my God; for our iniquities are increased over our head, and our trespass is grown up unto the heavens.

Since the days of our fathers have we been in a great trespass unto this day; and for our iniquities have we, our kings and our priests, been delivered into the hand of the kings of the lands, to the sword, to captivity, and to a spoil, and to confusion of face, as it is this day.

And now for a little space grace hath been shewed from the Lord our God, to leave us a remnant to escape, and to give us a nail in his holy place, that our God may lighten our eyes, and give us a little reviving in our bondage. [9:5–8]

What is remarkable about Ezra is his ability to move—both in his life and in his work—from the most personal to the most practical. Just as the Book of Ezra moves from long lists and genealogies to intense passages of private grief, so in Ezra's life he moved from impassioned speeches to the people of Israel concerning purity and impurity— speeches that cause the people to weep, as Ezra himself weeps—to the most specific and practical measures. He is able to bind the large historical and spiritual imperatives to the most ordinary, immediate and essential human needs.

Throughout—and this is the genius of the narrative—he is wonderfully aware of how history and memory mingle and move within our separate lives and hearts.

But many of the priests and Levites and chief of the fathers, who were ancient men, that had seen the first house, when the foundation of this house was laid before their eyes, wept with a loud voice; and many shouted aloud for joy:

So that the people could not discern the noise of the shout of joy from the noise of the weeping of the people: for the people shouted with a loud shout, and the noise was heard afar off.   [3:12–13]

Ezra seems to have understood that Judaism would survive only if its laws, teachings and ways were reinforced by the regular practice of rituals that were adhered to and sanctioned by the entire community. Not only did Ezra democratize Judaism from within by giving the Torah to the people, but he also laid out the specific ways that would allow the people to have that Torah, to study it, and to know it.

He ordained that public readings from the Torah should take place on Mondays and Thursdays as well as on the Sabbath. He established schools, rewrote the Bible in an alphabet that was more accessible and more distinctively Jewish, compiled (with five others) the Mishnah, established the body known as "the men of the Great Synagogue," enacted the ordinances known as "the ten regulations of Ezra."

By his acts and example, then, he showed the Jewish people that henceforth they would have to rely not upon prophecy, but upon themselves—they would have to derive the basis for their communal life not from the Written Torah, but from the Oral Torah—from study and analysis and prayer and deed.

Thus the Book of Ezra opens by telling us how God works through *others* to save the Jews:

Now in the first year of Cyrus king of Persia, that the word of the Lord by the mouth of Jeremiah might be fulfilled, the Lord stirred up the spirit of Cyrus king of Persia, that he made a proclamation through all his kingdom, and put it also in writing, saying,

Thus saith Cyrus king of Persia, The Lord God of heaven hath given me all the kingdoms of the earth; and he hath charged me to build him an house at Jerusalem, which is in Judah.

Who is there among you of all his people? his God be with him, and let him go up to Jerusalem, which is in Judah, and build the house of the Lord God of Israel, (he is the God,) which is in Jerusalem.   [1:1–3]

And it ends, almost anticlimactically, with Ezra sitting down with other Jews to work out, detail by detail, the problems—mainly that of intermarriage—that beset the Jewish people:

> And Ezra the priest, with certain chief of the fathers, after the house of their fathers, and all of them by their names, were separated, and sat down in the first day of the tenth month to examine the matter.   [10:16]

Ezra and the others list the names of those who have taken non-Jewish wives, after which the book closes, not in moral exhortation or prayer or rejoicing, but with a simple and blunt sentence that states an unpleasant fact:

> All these had taken strange wives; and some of them had wives by whom they had children.   [10:44]

The Temple was destroyed, the rabbis teach, because the Jews were honest in their study of Torah but dishonest in business, in their dealings with other men. Ezra's mission was to inspire the Jews to be true to their study of Torah—to be separate from the other nations—and to be true and ethical in their dealings with others. "For Ezra had prepared his heart to seek the law of the Lord," his story notes, "and to do it and to teach in Israel's statutes and judgments" (7:10).

I lived in exile among Jews all the summers of my teenage years because, in truth, my way of life and theirs were incompatible. From an Orthodox point of view, there was no such thing as being a little bit Jewish. Although I have, in my adult life, been actively involved in the Jewish community, I live, like most Jewish Americans, more in America than in Judaism, taking from Judaism, along with some rituals and customs to which I am attached by memory, belief, and feeling, mostly those moral teachings and values that any fair, generous, and thoughtful human being, Jewish or not, might take.

Ezra redeems the Jewish people from their slide into corruption and assimilation not by teaching *general* ethical concepts ("Do unto others . . ."), or by promulgating the laws and systems of the nation under whose protection the Jews live ("We hold these rights to be self-evident . . ."), but by teaching *Israel's* statutes and judgments, by reminding Jews of those specific laws and practices pertaining to prayer, marriage, study, food, and family that really do set them apart from others. He makes them give up their very wives and children and families so that the Jewish nation might draw into itself and, as a specifically Jewish nation, survive. In no way does he advocate the kind of democratic and ethnic pluralism upon which most of us in America have been raised.

As a Jew growing up in the United States in the middle of the twentieth century, I wanted to be accepted and loved for being myself—that was what my schools and my parents and my favorite movies and even my rabbis taught me was my inalienable right—and so I was, of course, deeply indignant and enraged at being treated *unfairly,* at having the happenstance of my birth and my parents' sins (their lack of Orthodoxy) visited upon me.

Yet I was also by birth and upbringing Jewish, I took pride in being Jewish (more, as a boy, in Hank Greenberg and Sid Gordon than in Freud or Einstein), and so I could not understand, given all I knew, how one could be considered, especially by Jews, not Jewish enough.

Although, when I think back to my years in Camp Winsoki, I do so with more affection than bitterness—I did make friends and have good, even wonderful times there—the memory of how miserable I felt when I was rejected by the girl I yearned for, how insanely jealous and unhappy I was when she began going out with an Orthodox boy, remains tangible. I never stopped desiring her shy and loving smile, the feel of her mouth on my mouth, her hand in mine. Although her decision may, I like to think, have caused her as much frustration as it caused me, it occurs to me now that her parents, like Ezra, were, from an Orthodox point of view, correct, even if, somehow, un-American. The Jewish community is, in fact, as history shows again and again, imperiled by assimilation and intermarriage, both of which are usually brought on by secular freedom.

The kind of freedom the Jews enjoyed under Cyrus and Darius and Artaxerxes I, like that enjoyed by Jews in France and Germany in the nineteenth century, or by American Jews in this century, even if such freedom is conditional, seems to lead inevitably to a weakening of the traditional Jewish community—to a diluting of its daily and seasonal observances, to a destruction of its separateness.

Reading the story of Ezra, I found myself taking pleasure in the woes that befall the children of Israel and cause Ezra to journey to Jerusalem to save them from their own iniquity; I could, that is, redeem the vestiges of my own bitterness by reading Ezra's tale as a parable, one in which the haughty Jews are punished for having rejected the innocent Samaritans. Because the Jews reject the Samaritans for not being Jewish enough, they are plunged into a state of corruption in which they themselves choose to join with those even less Jewish (and more pernicious) than the Samaritans. It is their pride, then—their rejection of Jews to whom they feel superior— that brings them low. For their action they suffer the loss of their wives and children and families, and nearly lose all that is most dear to them: their Temple, their nationhood, their distinctive and separate way of life.

But such a reading (leaving aside, here, historical and scholarly issues as to the actual and/or true motives of the Samaritans, the true nature and authorship of Ezra, of its relation to Nehemiah, and so forth), is not merely self-serving. It is also false to the thrust of Ezra's narrative. Although I would like to believe, for example, that the strength of Judaism lies not in things negative—the prohibitions and injunctions (thou shalt not intermarry, thou shalt not work on the Sabbath, thou shalt not mix meat with dairy)—but in things positive (the belief in study, the belief in certain ethical and judicial teachings, the belief in the value of acts of lovingkindness, the emphasis on this world and not on an imagined afterlife), history seems to indicate, in Ezra's time as in our own, that if Jews are to preserve their specific identities as Jews, they need to guard as much against Samaritans as against their own natures. If Jews abandon those rituals and laws that make them a separate people because the practices seem outdated or irrelevant or silly, will they also lose those humane and specifically Jewish teachings—those that have to do, for example, with how we should treat one another—that have more than transient value? Ezra, clearly, believes that they will, and the force of his life and work is to make such a belief the reality upon which not merely the Temple, but the entire Jewish way of life, is built.

The double life I led in the world during my childhood had its parallel in the double life I led at home. My father believed in and practiced an Orthodox way of life, while my mother hated all religions and would go on tirades in which she proclaimed that without different religions people would have loved one another more, warred against one another less.

I was born between two worlds, one old (and Jewish) and one new (and American), my parents' conflict vividly present at my birth: for the first two days of my life I was "Jacob Mordecai" (named for my father's father); but on my birth certificate, on the third day of my life, the names "Jacob Mordecai" were crossed out, the words "Jay Michael" written in above. And thirty-seven years later, when my father died at the age of seventy-one, my mother's first act upon coming home from burying him in the Jewish cemetery was to mix the meat and dairy silverware and dishes, thereby unkoshering a kitchen she had kept kosher for thirty-nine years.

Her own mother and father had fought each other savagely, setting their six children against one another in ways that seemed to me, when I was young, somewhat exotic—as if I were living within a mad Russian family from a novel by Tolstoy or Dostoevsky. Her parents fought brutally, physically—her mother throwing her father down the stairs, the police being summoned to the house to break up their battles—and the children, taking sides with one parent or the other, would go for years without speaking to each other. My mother's mother, eldest sister, and only brother did not come to my Bar Mitzvah; my mother's mother, in fact, did not talk to her for the last eight years of my grandmother's life.

My father, one of nine children, came from a warm and loving Jewish family whose father was the spiritual leader of their community both in the old country (Ryminov) and in the new (East New York), a man honored for his generosity, knowledge, and wisdom. By marrying my mother—a girl who felt she was not Jewish enough for his family (his family always treated my mother as one of them)—he cut himself off from his family for most of his adult life. We saw his brothers and sisters and nieces and nephews rarely, spent most weekends and holidays with aunts and uncles and cousins from my mother's side.

The humiliation and devastation that were visited upon the Jews in the world seemed to me, as a child, to be visited upon my father daily, and he had no wherewithal to fight back, no Ezra to lead him out of the darkness and unhappiness and failure of his own life. It was not, then, merely that

I lived in exile among Jews each summer, but that I often felt I lived in exile within my own home.

One of the rare occasions upon which my father seemed to me to be a man was when he was, in fact, a Jew: at least then he knew things my mother didn't know, at least he could lose himself in a world she had no entry to, a world tied for him to that part of his life that contained rich memories of the reasonably coherent and sane family life he had known as a boy. At Camp Winsoki, when he visited on weekends, he could do what I feared I could never *know* enough to do: he could lead the Jewish community in prayer.

A few days after his death—three days after my mother had unkoshered her home—at the afternoon *minyan* during the week of *shivah*, praying among the kind of Orthodox men who had always, in my feelings at least, mocked me for not being as Jewish as they were, for not knowing what a Jew should know, I walked to the front of the congregation and, trembling as much as I ever had before going on stage, or before running onto the field or court for a ballgame, or before leaning forward to try to kiss a young woman I feared would spurn me, I led several dozen Jews in the evening prayers.

When I was done and was walking back to my mother's apartment, I smiled and talked with my father about many things, telling him what I had done, and how pleased I was, how pleased I hoped he would be. We had earned a small victory together—more emotional than religious, surely, but in that moment which seemed to exist out of time, I also felt as if I had, by my ordinary performance of a daily ritual, allowed myself to begin to emerge, in part, from a state of exile that had been with me all the days of my life. Perhaps I might still, in a troubled and difficult and complicated life, find ways to put to rest those deeper fears that made me, too often, feel that I was living in exile within myself—an exile caused not so much by worldly adversaries or circumstances as by my own inability to let go of past fears and wishes, feelings that persisted and terrified me, feelings that had the power to sabotage all those parts of my self and life that ached still—not with bitterness, but with desire—to be born, to be renewed, to change.

I was, then as now, deeply drawn to the way of life my father had once known, and though I could not, by temperament or belief or habit, join myself to that life in more than peripheral ways, I wondered, then as now, how what was beautiful in it—not just the customs and laws, but those attitudes toward life that seemed to me essentially valid and singularly Jewish—could be mine in this life, could be passed on to my own children, if the structure within which these rituals and beliefs flourished was allowed to die.

NEHEMIAH

Anne Roiphe

THE BOOK OF NEHEMIAH: IT IS A GENERAL'S DIARY, A GOVERNOR'S report, a man's plea to be given credit by his God, to be remembered for his good works, a mixture of recordkeeping and plea bargaining, of nationalism and piety, a tale of good management, courage, skullduggery, of moral and physical renewal, a memoir. Perhaps it is the first historical memoir to praise friends, to accuse enemies, to name names, to seize immortality by writing the text. This is a book whose bravado, whose matter-of-fact accountings, whose religious assumptions twist today's heart, wringing out pity and reluctant recognition.

In Nehemiah's record of the rebuilding of Jerusalem we view Ben Gurion, Golda Meier, Begin and Ariel Sharon, Dyan, Rabin, Peres, Shamir, their faces frozen in this ancient mirror. We see the Israelis today divided between civilian and army duty, just as Nehemiah describes: "the basket carriers were burdened doing work with one hand while the other held a weapon." We can be sure that Nehemiah's words echo through the Knesset

The Jewish Publication Society's translation of the Bible used in this essay.

473

and affect today's decisions; thus Scripture is the not-so-secret sharer of Jewish response. We can be sure that the redemption, the promise made to the people of Israel, is echoed now in every political crucible, in the annexing of territories, in the questions: who is a Jew, what is to be done with the Arabs, is the state a special state or is it a normal nation like the other nations against whom it so fatefully jostles? Nehemiah believed that the rebuilding of the nation was a sacred commitment, at one with the spiritual destiny of the Jewish people. We modern Jews, whether religious or secular, whether Zionist or anti-Zionist, communist, socialist, capitalist, cannot help reading the words of Nehemiah as blueprints of today's action, as a prologue in a history that may be moving forward but does so in a peculiarly cyclical manner, so that the past becomes the pattern for the present and casts us as members of a Messianic search party, whether we like it or not.

We read in Nehemiah's account of ancient hostilities antagonisms that still threaten, rivalries and jealousies and alliances that even now undermine the modern state. Nehemiah rebuilt Jerusalem after an exile, a captivity, a humiliation. But today's Israel exists after a second disaster and then a *Shoah* (holocaust) of such immensity that our thinking has changed, our confidence, our pieties have been altered. We know too much. As we read Nehemiah now, the history to follow falls backward onto each page and each verse. As we rejoice in the rebuilding of the walls of Jerusalem and the society within, we who are reading the book in this century know that all the work, all the planning, all the rectitude of those who gave their goods and pledged faith to the nation, who renewed the Covenant as it was given at Sinai, proved ephemeral, unequal to the storms of history, to the powers of other nations. Nehemiah is like a child building a sandcastle near the ocean's edge. We know that the tide will come in again, so, as we watch the child hauling his water pail up the beach, our pride mingles with a tenderness that strains all the bounds of reason and brings with it a fear: are we perhaps that child?

After Nehemiah, with the aid of informers and a stockpile of arms, has warded off the immediate enemy who had threatened to attack, he begins the harder work of reconstituting the social and religious order of his nation. He begins to renew the moral fiber of his citizenry. As he re-creates order among his people, he protests the common practice of intermarriage. He discovers that Jews had married Ashdodites, Ammonites, and Moabite women. He realizes that some children speak the language of other nations and do not speak Judean. He acts with unconflicted directness. "I censored them. I cursed them. I flogged them. I tore out their hair . . . and adjured them by God, saying . . . 'You shall not give your daughters in marriage to their sons or take any of their daughters for your sons or yourselves.' They were breaking faith with God by marrying foreign women." Here is a thorn bush that bleeds us even in this modern moment.

Assimilation and intermarriage will weaken the piety and the order of the community. They will crumble the shape of the nation, permitting Easter eggs on Jewish tables, children who go to movies on the Sabbath, and men and women who disobey the Commandments. It undermines the Covenant. It threatens the mission with which the Jewish nation has been entrusted. It offers to destroy us from within as we could never have been routed from without.

But wait. Nehemiah tells us how he scolded, how he sent away a valued aide who had married a foreign woman. He tells how he insisted on pure lineage and followed through by sending the stranger out from the Jewish city, exiling him from the Jewish nation. We who have heard the Nuremberg Laws, who have suffered the edicts of medieval cities, we know that despising the stranger, outlawing marriage between groups, setting up one as racially or religiously correct and the other as corrupt is digging a well right into the geyser of human cruelty which then will come, will inevitably come, rushing to the surface, destroying everything in its path. What was our Deity doing when He said that "No Ammonite or Moabite might ever enter the congregation of God"? In this matter perhaps our God suffered an ethical lapse, did not transcend the local habits of thought, the all-too-human patterns that set group against group. All over the ancient world the tribes drew bloodline distinctions and treated the outsider with brutality. All over the modern world the story remains the same, Tamil against Buddhist, Bahai against Muslim, Sikh against Hindu, Catholic against Protestant, and everyone against Jews. Brilliant cultures, moral and aesthetic religions, industrious and ethical societies are created and maintained in separatist glory, in tribal pride, in self-conscious distinction against the other. Jews carried out of Egypt the moral ideal of treating the stranger kindly, but even they have not always done so. It is this contradiction that we struggle with today. Just as Nehemiah was concerned about the attrition of his people, the loss to assimilation in Babylon, to death and slavery, we, too, worry about our numbers. But how can we best maintain ourselves and still undo, weaken, discover a cure for this terrible human disease, this catalyst for pogrom, the ideal of group purity? The painful paradox is that the soul of a society and its need to segregate itself from others seem bound together, like mind and body, like male and female. What God designed this ironic human condition?

Beneath the text of Nehemiah we can hear the children of the exiled wives calling for fathers who have disowned them. We can hear the women who brought their dowries, who disrobed and gave their bodies in trust, alone in the night, wandering in the no-man's-land between the nations, betrayed and abandoned because of an accident of birth. Nehemiah has no question that this is what God intended. We have to wonder. At least we must tremble at the ugly side of the continuance of the people, the strengthening of the nation. With our twentieth-century eyes, the problem of intermarriage, of group isolation and concepts of nationhood, of racial right and wrong, becomes more complicated, and the implications of such a position cannot so easily be pushed away. We cannot shut our ears to the weeping.

The problem is a real one. If we are not to betray our history and abandon the idea of the nation, we must keep a form, a purpose, a destiny that are ours alone and are related to our shared history and our religion. And yet, if we insist that the stranger is to be shunned or exiled, then what are we, what have we done to our finest ethical teachings? How can we make our separateness one among the other virtues, rather than an excuse to despise or be despised? How can we increase the tolerance of one group of people for another, a tolerance on which our safety also depends, which our Jewish tradition encompasses, and still keep ourselves for ourselves?

The problem is underlined for us today because each Jewish birth replaces one of the six million, because our numbers are small, and because our survival depends on sufficient population, so that our enemies cannot overrun us and our friends cannot forget us, so that we can continue to be whatever thorn in the side, inspiration, muse, critic, light unto, that we have always been. We have to find a way to be with the stranger that is not demeaning, is not so harsh as to exclude or cut off, but is nevertheless firm enough to allow for a continuing people. Perhaps we can finally accept our own injunctions to remember our times of slavery, our own stranger-ness, and through empathy and imagination find a path toward others. We can try—although it seems clear that no other people on earth have managed— to make such fine ideals reality. We can try, but we will not succeed. We will not succeed because the natural rage, the perfectly normal human rage we feel at suffering so long from the unkindness of others, makes us unlikely to grow into the first nation among the peoples of this exhausted planet to break the chains of mistrust and abuse.

Nehemiah makes certain assumptions about the value of the nation that block out concern for specific pain. This is the way generals and governors always think. Those who sound the trumpet for war have the collective in mind, never the individual. This is as true of Sharon moving into Lebanon as it is true of Nixon sending bombers into Cambodia. But today, we who are not generals must keep reminding one another that individual destiny, particularly human suffering, is also a religious matter, a matter of state concern. We know too well where it all leads when the state becomes an idea, the nation becomes an idol at whose feet one throws the blood of citizens and noncitizens. Our problem is far more complicated than Nehemiah's, because we know that nationalism is a rock and if you pick it up and look at its underside you see murder and torture and villany of all kinds. Here is another paradox we cannot yet resolve. We live private lives, and each death and each life casts its own light. But simultaneously we belong to a larger group that can suffer and inflict suffering without regard to individual need or worth. Our contemporary story has made us painfully certain that we need collective strength. But we also understand that human beings can become *figur*, "stuff," and states can become monsters whose religion has turned malignant. If we wish to preserve ourselves as Jews, we must remember that nation-building is a dangerous activity and if a Jewish nation destroys its ethical traditions, its morality, it can no longer exist: it becomes a contradiction that will wear itself out. But at the same time we remember that when we had no material nation, when we had no army listening to the radar at our borders and no airplanes patrolling above our homes, we were abandoned. We must find a way to be ourselves without insulting, excluding, inflicting unnecessary pain on any human being. We must do this in order to preserve ourselves. How can we hold on to our uniqueness without making our separateness a wall, like the walls of Jerusalem, which never did withstand the siege of a determined enemy, allowing only the briefest illusion of safety?

After Nehemiah has taken care of the practical matters, he begins to take a census. He writes down the names of the families, the priests, the sons, and the list goes on, paragraph after paragraph. This listing, this census, is without plot; it drones on and on, and one's attention easily wanders. However, it is in these pages that Nehemiah, echoing the genealogies in Genesis, pays his deepest respects to the people of his nation. They are not simply a mass folk, they are not a nameless remnant, they are individuals. And here he follows the tradition that makes of each life the whole, each birth a sacred matter, each son like a star in the heavens. Each has a name, and in recording that name before history, before God, Nehemiah gives recognition to each hand that worked, that bore arms, that offered tithes, that sang at the festival, that belonged. Here is the precedent that explains the work of the archivists of the pogroms, those who kept records of the murdered, displaced citizens of the *shtetl*s emptied during World War I. Here is the precedent of Yad Vashem, of the YIVO institute in New York, so important to us all. Each name is recorded; all the villages and all the towns of the murdered are inscribed. We keep the names of the families, now too numerous to be written in our scriptures, but not too numerous to be saved. We keep them within the pages of some book in some library, where the record is clear: who lived and who died and where they died. This is man's sad echo of God's writing in the Book of Life on Yom Kippur. After all that has happened, we have taken the responsibility for recording into our own hands. It's after the fact: the record is only of disaster, but we have no choice. The dead belonged to the people, and we have refused to let them go without note, without name, as much as is possible, as best we can. We have served notice on the world that you cannot murder a single Jewish baby without this nation's remembering. In our vast existential universe, God no longer leans down and collects the names of the righteous as He might have in Nehemiah's time. So our compilations, our maps, and a census of our villages, our ghetto lists, are saved for their own sakes, to remind ourselves of the sanctity of life, even if we alone endow life and death with holiness, even if sanctity is no more than another human opinion. Even in an empty universe we keep the lists of the nation as Nehemiah did in the days of the rebuilding of the city. Our list rises like a fist into the sky. It changes nothing, but remains a brave and holy gesture.

Nehemiah writes of sons and of fathers, of men, and only rarely are Jewish women mentioned. Once, on the ramparts, when he lists the names of those who are repairing a section of the wall, he speaks of Shallum, son of Halohesh, chief of half the district of Jerusalem, and his daughters. Again we fleetingly see women and children as they celebrate the dedication of the walls and the opening of the Temple. Nowhere is a Jewish woman mentioned by name, and that is natural enough for a leader of state, a man of those patriarchal times. We assume that poor Shallum, son of Halohesh, had no sons and so had to build with his daughters. We assume that the mothers and the sisters of all the priests and the Levites and the singers and those included in the census who are mentioned by name took credit for their role in building the nation—secret, silent credit, unheralded, uncelebrated credit. But nevertheless we imagine that they shared in the general happiness and knew that they counted, knew that they had fed and washed and clothed, they had carried and buried and tended and worried and worked and loved and lived, even if, sadly enough, the author of the memoir did not have the vocabulary to mark their days.

There is one important mention of women. It appears when Ezra reads to all the assembled in front of the water gate. Here women are counted. Here, as at Sinai, the word was brought to the men and the women, and the ears and the soul of the Israelites were not segregated by gender. It is to this assembly that we wish to return and from there forge a Judaism that names the female as often as it names the male. Because, as Nehemiah understood, "Oh my God, remember me favorably for this and do not blot out the devotion I showed toward the House of God and its attendants": to be without record, to be without name, is to be diminished in the eyes of the future and in one's own hopes.

Nehemiah refers several times to the singers. "The priests, the Levites, the gatekeepers, the singers, some of the people, the temple servants and all Israel took up residence in their towns." At the dedication of the wall, "the singers built themselves villages in the environs of Jerusalem." How good to know that, immediately after building the wall, the artists were recalled:

they were needed again to aid in the worship, in the sacrifice, to sanctify both God and state. The mention of singers here in this ancient text might make our modern dictators nostalgic for the past. Here they can find reason to believe that the singers will glorify the political enterprise, will play their part properly. We have cantors today, but we no longer have a special class, a whole group devoted to voicing appreciation of God and state. Nowhere does this exist in the modern world. Our singers have strayed. They turned to criticism, to carping, to singing about disharmony. They sign petitions, they march against the house of government waving signs and chanting songs that invite new policies. In most countries they are no longer given villages to live in. They are not allotted part of the general resource on which to sustain themselves. They sing but do not praise, and some countries view them as enemies to be imprisoned, their tongues removed, to be discredited. When the Temple keys were finally returned to God's hands, the singers began to sing a different song. Possibly they had discovered that all the singing to the glory of God and His state did not avert the breaching of the walls, and so they decided to sing against the order, to point out weak spots in the gates of state, as a reminder of obligations. Perhaps the prophets, tired of ignominy in the desert, tired of being scorned by an unheeding populace, have taken the form of singers, appearing to amuse, to soothe, rather than to scold. In this disguise our prophets have stayed with us through the centuries—novelists, poets, dissidents whose ancestors were once singers camped outside the gates of Jerusalem. Nehemiah, who was so decisive, so filled with plans and commandments and good clear management, would never have understood what has become of his singers.

Nehemiah describes the injustice, the oppression, that afflicted the less fortunate among the Jews in the country. To his distress and anger, Nehemiah hears the complaints of the people whom the wealthy Israelites have placed in great debt, the poor whose daughters have become slaves, who are losing their land and their livelihood. He says, "abandon these claims, give back at once their fields, their vineyards and their olive trees." He insists that one group should not exploit another. He himself does not use his governor's allowance, meaning that he does not further tax the people for the upkeep of his own considerable household. He does ask credit for these good deeds, and if the highest form of charity is anonymity, as our rabbis have said, Nehemiah, who hardly cherishes oblivion, will not rank as high in the eyes of heaven as he had hoped. However, as a statesman, as a leader, he imposed a morality, a halting of greed, a concern for the public weal. This is the act of a wise leader as well as a righteous one, because the poor were in such distress that they could not contribute to the state and thereby could not be counted on as loyal citizens. Nehemiah understood that his country would flourish as the ethos of the greatest good for the greatest number created a citizenry ready to serve the state. Nehemiah was always concerned that evildoing among the citizenry would again bring down the wrath of God, leaving the city vulnerable to all its enemies. Given a chance, a little chaos, a loose leadership, difficult conditions, the strong will prey on the weak and the goods of any society will gather in the hands of a few. That story has not changed in two thousand years. We, who have seen the coming and going of Marxists, Keynesians, Trotskyites, Leninists, supply-side economists, Maoists, free-market worshippers, etc., know that the system has yet to be devised that will control the urge of one to take from the other, to have more than the other. We need Nehemiah to come roaring into our midst and by decree, by fiat, by New Deal, restore the social order. The only trouble is that the Nehemiahs of the world seem always to be passing through—twelve years here, a little time there. Then they return to their kings or to their Maker. We accept their leadership for a while and then we turn back to what we have always done best. Is this because Eve was so willing to share the apple in the garden or because Cain was so eager to have his offering win the prize, or is it simply the gene for aggression that Freud teased out of our biological matter? Nehemiahs come and go, leaving their portraits hanging over the bedposts of the poor, but the order they create is as quickly carried away as a cookie left on the porch, devoured before noon by the garden ants.

Nehemiah's great task was to bring healing to the walls of Jerusalem. "Jerusalem's wall is full of breaches and its gates have been destroyed by fire." To rebuild the wall is both a physical act and a political one. Sanballat the Horonite, Tobiah the Ammonite, Geshem the Arab watch the rebuilding with apprehension, jealousy, and anger. They fear another strong nation will come among them and take power over them. Sanballat mocks the workers as they dig among the sun-bleached ruins. "Can they raise stones out of these dust heaps, burned as they are?" Tobiah says, "That stone wall they are building—if a fox climbed it he would breach it." But the work went on

until the sheep gate, the fish gate, the dung gate, the broad wall, the horse
gate, east gate, all were built and the city was enclosed.

Because Nehemiah was clever and because the people worked hard for
fifty-two days, the wall was built and watchmen were set out on the towers.
There were intrigues, of course. His enemies tried to trick him into blas-
pheming by hiding in the sanctuary. They tried to frighten him by threatening to send word to the king of rebellion in the provinces. The matter of
Jerusalem, then as now, had international repercussions. He managed all
difficulties with skill, and the victory was his. Today, however, the smallest,
most inferior of missiles can breach any wall. Today the watchmen need
intelligence information borrowed from the American government, as well
as electronic communications on the far edge of the Golan Heights. Today
intrigues and the pressure from distant rulers and their Cabinets cannot be
ignored. The arms buildup that Nehemiah encouraged, the draft for the
wall-building and defense unit, served to stave off the enemy for a few
generations. The timber that King Artaxerxes gave to Nehemiah is like the
aid of the United States to the fledgling Israel, a necessary beginning but
not enough for security. Now that we have been intimate with destruction
on more than one occasion, we may begin to look for a way to protect
ourselves that goes beyond the building of walls, the holding of weapons,
the readiness of the army. This is not to assume that prayer can stand in the
place of human effort, nor can we believe any longer that Jerusalem will
fall because of the spiritual crimes of its citizenry. Prayer has proved an
inadequate protection for our children, and if Noah had built his ark out
of rabbinic commentary he would have swiftly sunk. Waiting for the
Messiah to bring us back to the land of milk and honey would have left
us dangling, fragments of a nation. Quite likely, on his arrival the Messiah
would have found no Jews to greet him—all murdered, vanished like the
ichthyosaurs, glorious creatures in their time.
    After Nehemiah has built the walls he says, "The nations around fell
very low in their own estimation; they realized this work had been accomplished by the help of our God." It is very dangerous to have neighbors who
have fallen low in their own estimation. The hatred and the bitterness this
evokes does not drain with the waters down to the sea, but stays and pollutes

all the streams, including those that bring water to your city. Nehemiah says to Sanballat and Tobiah, "The God of Heaven will grant us success and we, His servants will start building. But you have no share or claim or stake in Jerusalem." With these words he guarantees their enmity. With these words he makes it harder for accommodation to be found. He taunts them with the power of his God and with the strength of his nation. When neighbors are humiliated, when they are ridiculed, they will not slink away and disappear. They begin to plan for another siege.

Nehemiah reminds us that with God's help the Jews of the Exodus "captured fortified cities and rich lands, they took possession of houses filled with every good thing, of hewn cisterns, vineyards, olive trees and fruit trees in abundance." So the history of this small oasis in the Middle East is one of siege and casting out, of taking what has not been yours and defending it against all claims. It is a benighted, blood-filled history that we in the twentieth century cannot see as an expression of our God's success against their God or Gods but as a misfortune for us all, as a calamity of human misunderstanding, cycles of woe and broken pride. One group's victory is another's lamentation. While children are dying and learning hatred, today's rulers are tilting swords in far-off courts, creating schemes that have little to do with the people whose olive trees and cisterns keep changing hands at great human cost. When Nehemiah returns to Jerusalem after an absence of some years, he finds that Tobiah has been set up in one of the storage rooms of the sanctuary. He throws him out immediately. He reports the episode of communal backsliding with righteous indignation. We have not heard Tobiah's side of this brief episode, but surely it is full of humiliation, of aspirations thwarted, of mounting hatreds that have left a strong smell of fear and the threat of revenge in every cranny of the most beautiful city in the world. Perhaps it would have been better if Nehemiah had invited Tobiah to tea, had found out what he wanted and how it would be possible to give him some of what he needed, to make a friend and an ally in the place of a mortal foe. Nehemiah describes this episode so curtly that we can barely sense the animosity that must have existed even within the city, a part of the politics of the moment, the backstabbing and the grasping for power and goods. Nehemiah was a fine general, but he was better at vanquishing than at making alliances. We can see now, having endured the effects of defeat, that defeating the physical enemy is never enough. He comes back again and again and disturbs one's sleep, assassinates one's children, attacks on sacred holidays, remembers just as you do all the injustices that have ever been done him.

It seems that the walls of Jerusalem will only be secure when there is no longer a need for walls, for defenders, for watchmen of the day or night. If we have a chance to avoid another turn of the historical wheel that will send us flying into new Diasporas, new lamentations, new territories, perhaps new planets, we will have to secure the peace the only way that will make it hold: that is, to reach across the low esteem of others, to heal not the wall but the hurt of human beings, and come to terms, some terms that do not betray the self, but do give others a chance to live with dignity in a land and place of their own. We must return the territories before we become the cruel Pharaohs we have always despised. Let the enemies be men with pride of their own and they may become friends, allies. We must repair the broken cosmos, make whole the divisions of the peoples, risk friendship, and build alliances in the place of hatred. Jewish history holds echoes of itself, it has themes that recur, it has ancient passions that animate the present. But it is not a circle, it is not a calendar year, it is not a primitive system of sun and moon. Jewish history moves forward, and we can put an end to the destructions and the persecutions if we are brave enough to risk peace. The other approach historically has proved ineffective. We have not won permanent victory in any physical battle, whether our weapons were spears or Uzis. We have not won a permanent victory through endless prayer, through submission or passivity. We must now be strong enough to win through an inventive strategy that includes knowing our enemy, inviting him to discuss the issues with us, to stop his scheming and his attack, and to discuss with us his grievance, to know us and our human face as we get to know his.

Nehemiah believed that the Jews had been wicked and had been punished and that that was why he found himself in a foreign country bringing wine to an alien king. He says, "Surely You are in the right with respect to all that has come upon us for You have acted faithfully and we have been wicked." He adds, "On account of our sins it yields its abundant crops to Kings whom you have set over us." He urges the populace to keep the Sabbath, to "Make an oath to observe carefully all of the commandments of the Lord our Lord. His rules and laws." He hopes to avoid future punishment by insisting that the people obey God, and at the same time he reminds God of His promises of redemption if the people return to His ways. For Nehemiah history was the result of God and man responding to each other as Father and son, as Master and servant. His was a universe where moral cause and moral effect were connected. God had given rules and would punish the Jews if they rebelled. Nehemiah prays, "Be mindful of the promise you gave to your servant Moses; 'if you are unfaithful, I will scatter you among the peoples, but if you turn back to Me, faithfully keep My commandments, even if your dispersed are at the ends of the earth, I will gather them from there and bring them to the place where I have chosen to establish my name.' For they are Your servants and Your people whom You redeemed by Your great power and Your mighty hand." It is here that as modern readers we turn our faces away from the page and our hearts grow stony cold and we shiver with envy for Nehemiah, who saw guilt and penance and redemption where we see only disorder, death, and confusion.

In this century, many of us can no longer speak of God's punishing, and if we cannot speak of God's punishing we cannot speak of redemption, renewal. Those causal links have been smashed. We do not have a language in which we can speak of avenging ourselves on God. Instead, we live with absence. Nehemiah modeled himself after his image of a powerful, masterful, righteous God. Whom are we to model ourselves after? The modern reader has to see Nehemiah as a man whose delusion of guilt and redemption enabled him to build, to accomplish, to restore order. It was a spectacular idea. It placed the blame for disaster on the self, on the community, and it kept intact the concept of a benevolent Deity who would take care of, bring to power, gather the scattered peoples, lead out of slavery, save those who followed the rules. It was an idea that kept order in the society and for centuries kept at bay our recognition of loneliness, of vulnerability, of our transient lives that last for no more than a moment beneath the falling stars, on top of the turning earth, under the Einsteinian sun, the Freudian winds, the Darwinian waves. In our modern world even our delusions are no longer coherent. We know that if there was a betrayal, a broken word, a covenant cracked, it was not, could not have been, the fault of the Jewish nation. We can no longer believe that our unfaithfulness to God is greater than His unfaithfulness to us. With this change of assumption, history spins, its certainties fall away, and even though the walls in Jerusalem are built again we are shadows of our former selves, perhaps.

There are advantages to losing Nehemiah's certainty. We can reshape our identity and admire ourselves for our creations, more remarkable still if they were not given at Sinai but were the product of particular human minds struggling with the cruelty of man and nature. We can value the nation for its own sake, for its tradition, for its history, for its bravery and its poetry, its civilization, its drama, its courage as a David who sometimes defeated Goliath and sometimes did not, its dreamers and its mystics, its lovers of God and its lovers of politics, its legal minds, its philosophers, its generals and its judges, its battle to remain distinct in the whirling cultures that passed through and by and over its faithful core, its sons and daughters who struggled against persecution and exclusion into the modern world and gave to the host ideas, stories, political systems, and science and music and math, all born at the rubbing edge between ancient Judaism and the modern mind.

We can see ourselves as masters of our own destiny. We do not have to implore or praise or beg for our safety. We do not have to sacrifice or fear for the world to come. If we are the children of Isaac, bound on the mountain in Akedah, waiting for the ram to appear, we need wait no longer. We can jump up. We can bless our father Abraham for his piety, for his poetry, for his loyalty. We can promise that we will carry his words and his ways with us forever, but we don't have to remain on the altar, our eyes searching through the thickets for the first sight of the horn that will free us. We do not have to suffer guilt for crimes we did not commit. We can love the Jewish nation without feeling that we must bend our backs in sorrow for collective sins. Look how the idea of a collective Jewish sin snaked its way into the Christian world and left its bloody tracks. Let us never again speak of Jewish sin: a particular sin, a human sin, a political sin, a military sin, a personal sin, of course, but not a collective sin for which group punishment is accepted. Now we can see our own face in the mirror, marked as Cain, covered with boils like Job, fearful as Jonah, but still stand like Joshua before the walls, ready to make history, to do better, to try again, a nation like all the other nations—but not quite. Because we have survived the exile, because of the unique ethical, literary, and tragic dimensions to our tale, we will always have a special place, as originators, as bearers of the moral impulse, as a people watched by others. We have believed in ourselves as Chosen, and even if we conclude that we elected ourselves, so much more the honor in our accomplishments, so much more the luminosity of human spirit that shines through our traditions, our memories, our stories that we tell one another, our holidays that tie us backward and forward into history. In our living, generation after generation we will make our own purpose, unfold our own meaning onto the map of human events.

We can take pride in ourselves for having moved mankind forward, away from idols who fractured morality, toward a better ethical, legal knowledge. And we can continue to find ourselves as a light unto the nations, as a special flower in the field, while following the moral precepts of our ancestors, not because we were bound at Sinai to do so, but because we have survived and have more work to do, more to write, to think and invent, to build and create, efforts that will be a gift to an astonished and unworthy world.

It is true that when you remove the conviction that all our moral acts are being judged by God, when you no longer believe as Nehemiah did that military routs, massacres, pogroms, inquisitions, are the deserved punishment for a wicked people, the world changes radically, and with this change comes the sadness that affects us when we read Nehemiah. His belief was so clear, his actions so simple, and his direction so purposeful, whereas ours are cloudy, haunted by events beyond lamentation and beyond restitution. We almost seem like other kinds of humans, as if we were birds without wings, lions without teeth, horses without legs.

But if we think of all that would not have been if Nehemiah had never convinced King Artaxerxes to let him return with the proper letters and the right amount of timber, if the people had married the Babylonians and the Moabites and the Ashdodites, and the Torah had been swallowed in the shifting sands of the Middle East, then we can read Nehemiah with awe, approving his stern actions, his decisive military decisions, his fine governorship. We can forgive him a little credit-seeking and a hunger for immortality. He was only human, and one of us at that. We can be thankful for all the fences that protected the traditions, and the laws themselves and the scribes and the rabbis and the students and their students and the communities that held together in times of stress and desecration. We can be thankful that the Torah and the *Kethuvim* (Writings) were preserved for us to quarrel with, to serve as a looking glass that enables us to focus on ourselves and our grim times, again and again. In a God-abandoned universe it is a sweet thing to remember how it was when generals knew that the force of good was with them, that righteousness would be rewarded and evil undone. And with such bitterness in our mouths, we need the taste of simplicity: we need it for our sanity.

Nehemiah reports on the temporary loss of morale among the people. "The strength of the basket carrier has failed. And there is so much rubble; We are not able ourselves to rebuild the wall." But they were, and they did, and so have we, despite the doubters, the shirkers, the deserters. If we continue to think of Nehemiah as having built his fort too close to the incoming waves, as a child with pail and shovel working till dusk at the shore's edge, then we may see the tide coming in and crumbling all the carefully shaped turrets into the froth of the lapping water. If that happens to us, if we, too, are Nehemiahs, then we will have to try again, yet again, to make a city last against the siege of regents and the wear of human corruption. In the work of building we celebrate ourselves. If permanence should elude us, then persistence will have to content us.

CHRONICLES

Gordon Lish

I HAVE AS MY ASSIGNMENT (IT COMES TO THAT FOR ME, YES) WHAT IS taken to be the last book of the so-called old testament, or Jewish bible. But I have to say, before I say even worse things of the kind, that it troubles me to see those two words side by side. I hate it—the "Jewish bible"—and I should like to use my time with you to speculate why. My daughter Jenny, no small thinker, I assure you, takes the view that the difficulty I have with these two words being set side by side is evidence of the kind of Jew I am. But she means not Jew enough, whereas I would argue that I am all the Jew that one can be—and that my distaste for the foregoing pairing proves it. I would—since I am not unwilling to be combative on this score—even go so far as to suggest that those who welcome the pairing of these words are not Jews at all. Such persons may not in fact be Christians, but, to my mind, they are what Christians are.

I have to say this—I was so happy when I was offered the chance to air my thoughts on the subject that has assembled certain writers here. For

---

The King James Version of the Bible used in this essay.

I have been collecting thoughts on the matter of the Jews and the bible for the longest time. Well, "thoughts" says more for what presses at me than its nature really is—I do not have thoughts on this subject, I have feelings on it, and I am glad to have been brought to an occasion where these feelings might be made present to something like a forum. If I give offense, then please know that I am doing so only in my effort not to give a pretense, not to give a lie.

I chose the last book of the Jewish bible because no book of the Jewish bible would mean any more to me than any other book of the Jewish bible would. The books of the Jewish bible are all one thing to me. The bible, Jewish or otherwise, is all Christian to me—an alien object, uncongenial to me at its least, pestilential at its worst. It is the Christians who own all of the parts of this book, from whichever sources its gorgeous sentences may have once issued. Try this sentence of mine: The Christians owned the bible even before there were Christians.

Don't you know that the Christians have title to all the objects of the world?

They even own, as they could any instant prove, my body and probably yours.

My spirit (what do you want me to call it? you have a good word?), this they cannot get their hands on. Ditto the speech that was the bible before rhetoric became the bible; ditto the ludic, the vatic, the fluid, the crazed, the oneiric, the gnomic, the numinous; ditto all that was the word before it became the Word. Not that, as a reader, I have anything against the Word. But as a Jew? As a Jew, I tell you that in my heart I have my whole heart against it—for the Word is canon, and canon is totem, and totem is just as far from Jewish as you can get.

Am I thinking of the side-curled whose scholarship totemizes a text?
The answer is yes.
Then I must be asserting that they thereby Christianize that text.
The answer is yes, I am asserting it.

I have to make an admission. I did not really choose Chronicles. I chose nothing. I said, Assign to me what's left over, what no one else elects to speak for. It mattered not at all to me which element of the bible I would end up with—since I would scarcely want to use my time to waste yours. I have nothing to say about the bible as a place where certain sentences might be read. But I should certainly like to say a thing or two about the bible as an object that I do not feel safe being in the world with. Listen, I am no enemy of those sentences; I know that they can fetch the heart right out of your chest; I know that there is no felicity of language that they do not, for my own good, offer me a model of. But the realm wherein those sentences have their life is one whose ether seeks to suck away my breath.

I have a Jewish history. This Jewish history that I have I say is all posterior to my Jewishness, but I am going to tell you about it, anyway, this so that I will not leave behind me an absence of clarity. Listen, all of my days I have been a Jew; there has not been in my life a day, an hour, an instant, when I was any the less alert to myself as a Jew—indeed, as a Jew first and foremost. This is how it has always been for me and how I know it will always be for me—no time off, right up to the hole in the ground that I am going into.

I used to think I might profit from some time off.

I do not think that any more.

But not to make the mistake of seeing me as a fellow who grew up with side-curls. Because I grew up with no side-curls, and far from the company of those who had them. Mine was a well-to-do Jewish family where at least some Yiddish was spoken every day, where at least some synagogue was gone to every year, but where all the wind that we moved in in our comings and goings was always uniformly and pungently Jewish. I want to say this this way: We were in the world as Jews. Being Jews was our angle of insertion into existence. We would never have thought to budge one inch off plumb with that angle—change a name, change an address, change a friend, change a way of being.

All right, I was Bar Mitzvahed.

I sang my haftorah.

No one said to me, "Gordon, you realize this is the Jewish bible you are singing these words from?"

I am glad no one said that to me.

I liked the idea that my heart had just invented what I sang.

I am also glad that I stopped going to temple right afterward. After years and years of *cheder,* and after my Bar Mitzvah, I stopped making myself a participant in ceremony. I am glad of that. I grew up in that. I grew up as a Jew in that. I grew up as a Jew in coming to such a quitting. I claim I was all the more the Jew for doing what I did. That is what my feeling was. You can laugh all you want, but you will never laugh me out of my feeling.

I have not been back to a synagogue since—and you know what? The mere fact of such nonattendance has, to my mind, enforced my claim to complete Jewishness. Listen again: My apprehension of myself as a Jew is so complete that I would sooner be deprived of my name than to misplace one particle of that apprehension. I mean by this that I would dissolve, come apart, be Buck Rogers without his space belt. A Jew is not what I am, it is who I am—first.

Everything else is second.

I cannot fix the time when this feeling overtook me. I can only tell you that I do not think it was the yield from my fear of Germany. Even before I knew that Germans wanted to kill Jews, I knew that people wanted to kill Jews—and yet I am not certain how I came to know such a thing, although I am entirely certain that every Jew does come to know such a thing and that he thereafter, loudly or silently, comes to live his life in relation to that knowledge. I would tell my daughter Jenny that the knowledge is—what? Preverbal? Extracted from the vapors? Like Chomsky's idea of a genetic disposition to a grammar, coded into some kind of metabiology? Yes, I think I would say to Jenny that there is something fishy about all of this, about how the mechanism moves into place, what the fuel is to get it there, how we know we're going to be killed for being Jews even if they never get around to doing it.

Who said this?

Who said that after the Diaspora the very rocks hated Jews?

Me, I would amend the sentence to omit its mediating adverb.

Going back, going way, way back, going back to little playmates in backyards, I had the feeling: *Gordon, you are going to die for this.*

You cannot tell me that I did not have that feeling. Nor can you tell me that you did not have that feeling. We still have it. Our having it is what makes them want to kill us. But even if they do not kill me, my being a Jew will still be the reason for the finish of me—this is the feeling I am trying to get down onto the table between us—the feeling that, one way or another, whatever you die from, you die for being a Jew.

Such knowledge does not exert itself in fractions. It is total. I am in this sense, I say, as totally Jewish as are the side-curled. But here's the thing—in refusing to allow the propriety of a Jewish bible, I say that I declare myself to be more totally the Jew than the side-curled are (if you will allow the mathematics of excess to go to work on you—and of course I would urge the view that you are no Jew at all if you won't).

So now this: They come to me, the editor and the publisher, and they ask me to turn my mind to what they tell me is an object of a Jewish kind, and I, in reply, must say that my heart knows otherwise, that it is no Jewish object at all, that however many of the side-curled lift themselves into transport on its sentences, no bible is Jewish, not even the Jewish one.

Let me tell you what this Jewish bible of yours makes me feel in my Jewish heart—fear, jumpiness, the pressure of an angry object, a thing that conspires against me for my Jewishness. Nothing can ever change that. The massive wrestlings of Harold Bloom cannot change that. No Jew can wrench this thing from the goy. The bible, all of the bible, is Christian property—first, last, and always. And that's just fine, that's just exactly as I think it ought to be. However powerful the hermaneutics of the thinker, however illuminated the scholia of the side-curled, Jews have no bible, nor should have. Read Kermode, for shiningest example, alongside great Bloom, and then come and tell me which of them is out wandering and which other is hugely at home. Oh, the belatedness is all ours, even if they only steward what we devised. But I say cherish the belatedness: it is what preserves you in the glory of the Jewish condition of a heart.

I just thought of something.
We have a bible here.
We have a bible in my home.

It is my wife's bible. She brought this bible to our marriage. She owned it. I do not know if she feels she still owns it to the extent that she once did. At all events, it is a large first- and second-testamented volume with gold stamping on its spine. It has never mingled with our things. I won't let it. In fact, I think I want to tell you what I have done with this bible—because if you gave me yours, I would do the same.

But I want first to tell you what I did with the bible that was in the home I had when I was a boy. That bible was like this one, a large thing, and in that instance it was my parents who were the owners of it, and they, in turn, kept the thing stored in a bookcase in my room. When I was around twelve, I think it was, I would get that bible down from there from time to time, just to read something to get hot from reading and then to beat off on it. Oh, it wasn't just the words. Like this bible that is in my house now, the one that was in my house then had pictures in it, too, and I thought those pictures very sexual, I think: the figures of women, of the pious no less than of the impious, always with their gorgeous Y's visible through raiment that was just as wonderfully scanty and as translucent for the blessed as it was for the damned. (One has to say that it all came to the same thing in the end, the piety and the impiety; it was all sexy, meant to be sexy, maddeningly sexy—as Leo Steinberg has so persuasively observed in his famous essay on the officially sanctioned representations of the madonna and the child; one now waits to hear Steinberg on Jesus on the cross, a subject susceptible to even nastier jeopardies.) Anyway, I got a lot of that bible that we had back then read back then, this in that berserk early adolescence of mine, such was—since believing is seeing—the encouragement I kept getting in my pursuit of the dirty parts. I loved that bible. Crazily (but now I realize not so crazily), it proved, as an inspired text, even more serviceable to me in my needs than did *Forever Amber*.

(I now see that I must have been a spiritually adept child.)

But, getting back to this bible, the one that is right here with me in this room now, let me tell you how it is used: for it goes in a place where whichever book goes in that place it is going to be hidden from view. In other words, my wife's bible goes where it goes so that a book whose spine I want to show off will not have to go there in that place.

I mean, see the room this way, shelving from floor to ceiling on all of the room's walls and books on all of these shelves. Now, since the table I am sitting here at and writing this at stands pushed up against a certain section of these shelves, the legs that hold this table aloft will hide from view whichever books are behind them.

So now you have it.

That is where we have this bible.

That is where I have this bible.

I just bent over and looked and saw that the gold stamping I was talking about says *The Holy Bible.*

Ah, God, to my Jewish heart, those are such unfriendly words.

I do not want to see them.

I know that they are in the world, but I do not want to see them in it.

I just remembered something about that other bible. In fact, I read it through and through twice, once for the lively purpose that I have already made known to you, and then, a second time, on a business of a much less authentic kind. Three years later, still in my adolescence, it happens, I again went from cover to cover through the bible, this time in an effort to pass myself off (principally, I'm sure, to myself—since I cannot imagine who else might have been the least interested) as a young fellow of a certain high-minded nature. I mean that I had seen some piece in the *Partisan Review* (I also cannot imagine what I thought I was doing looking in the *Partisan Review,* except that my theatricality—I often played these parts strictly for myself— had taken a more costly turn against me) extolling the bible for its poetry, and so I fixed for myself the task of reading all of the bible, this by way of producing for myself an impressively exhausting elevating experience.

Point being that I twice read the bible in its popular entirety and twice felt myself a Jew—for reasons mysterious to me though agreeable to me in their mystery—sinning. In my heart of hearts, I felt myself somewhere where I did not for the life of me belong—but not, I insist, only because I was in search of a sexual aid in the first instance and of a moronically exalted opinion of myself in the second. In my bones I knew; down there where that metabiology is, I knew: *A Jew does not do this, Gordon.*

Consider with me. How was it that, although I was going to Sunday school and to Hebrew school, and in both contexts receiving Jewish instruction in the so-called Jewish bible, I nevertheless felt, both when confronted with the bible there and in the grammar school that I was going to: *Gordon, you have to preserve yourself against this, this is no friend of the Jew in you*? How was it that, even then, even with all of the meliorating activity of Jewish bible study, something Jewish welled up in me in revulsion? I knew: *This bible of theirs is a disrupter of my Jewish well-being! I am not safe in the world with this bible in it! This bible is their official violence!*

Without willing it, without wanting it, it came to me not at my bidding; I resisted, I was resisting; the Jew in me was making me do it, I could not help doing it, it was the very Jew in me which was doing it; *The Holy Bible* wanted to be my undoing, and if they called it *The Holy Jewish Bible,* then, I'm sorry, that made it, to me, no less the menace.

Listen to me: I am proposing a prior sensation, an energy that enters in at an early opportunity of the consciousness; I am proposing a sensation too swiftly registered in the *kishkes* for you to be able to head it off with any of your noble ratiocinations. I am proposing that they can have *our* bible right along with *their* bible, that no Jew should want any part of any bible, that you are no Jew if you cannot get along without every bible very nicely.

Listen to me: We have no business in the company of such an object; it belongs to those to whom things can belong—whereas you, a Jew, do not want to belong even to yourself—but, good God, only to God.

So, Jenny, were you listening?

CHRONICLES

Herbert Tarr

WHEN I MENTIONED TO A NOTED BIBLICAL SCHOLAR AND historian that I was writing an introduction to Chronicles, he threw up his hands and exclaimed, "That whitewash!" That characterization is true enough—but not the whole truth, which we shall now explore.

Though the Chronicler repeats much of what was recorded earlier in the Books of Samuel and Kings, sometimes almost verbatim, he indeed so whitewashes his glorious heroes, King David and his son Solomon, that not only do their failings and sins disappear, but also much of what has made them for some three thousand years fascinating, understandable, appealing, if at times appalling. The Books of Samuel and Kings read like a magnificent historical novel, with personalities so human and alive they fairly leap off the pages. What the Chronicler presents, however, is two professional saints, unconvincing in their perfection. One might call this the stained-glass view of history.

The author's own translation of the Bible used in this essay.

Gone are all events leading up to the enthronement of David (ca. 1005–965 B.C.E.), the two-year reign of Saul's son Ish-bosheth as king, and David's battle with him for the throne. Gone, too, are accounts of David's family, vital to his kingdom as well as to him. Bathsheba, with whom David committed adultery and for whom he had her husband killed, isn't even mentioned. Gone, too, are the revolts of David's beloved son Absalom and of Sheba son of Bichri. And there is no mention of the great David in his dotage: sick, impotent, easily manipulated. Chronicles depicts Solomon's succession to the throne as the will of God; the Book of Samuel ascribes it more to the wiles of his mother, Bathsheba.

Likewise with Solomon (ca. 965–25 B.C.E.), all is wartless. There is no mention of his supplanting his half-brother Adonijah as David's successor, of Solomon's marriages to countless foreigners and building them pagan shrines, his own turning to foreign deities, the political and military troubles at the end of his reign, or any hint that Solomon's policies may have resulted in the dismemberment of his kingdom immediately after his death.

Surely, no king who is portrayed as being as wise as Solomon would have conscripted all males to serve four months each year in the army or labor batallions in addition to taxing his people so heavily to feed his enormous bureaucracy and to support his public works (roads, buildings, copper mines, a refinery), a navy, cavalry, chariot cities. Solomon expanded David's fortress of thirteen acres, Jerusalem, into a teeming metropolis with a magnificent royal palace (which took thirteen years to build) and the Temple (which, though larger, was completed in seven years) and a vast government bureaucracy—but at what cost! The king's extravagance drove shepherds and small farmers off the land and into the cities in search of jobs, while enriching government officials, landowners, and merchants. Upon Solomon's death, therefore, the northern tribes seceded from the united kingdom. Alas, the people Israel never recovered from the glory that was Solomon's.

The Chronicler is also silent, for the most part, about the history of the northern kingdom of Israel (which disappeared two centuries after its secession). It is mentioned only when it impinges on the history of the southern kingdom of Judah or when two virtuous Judean kings try to woo the remnants of the northern kingdom back into the fold with invitations to worship at the Temple. The Chronicler evidently figured: Why bother with an apostate kingdom that is illegitimate? History for him is the history of God's loyalists. He considers Judah the *true* Israel: he often refers to the southern kingdom as "Israel" or "all Israel."

Yet, if he were reproached for all these significant omissions (even the sages of the Talmud regarded Chronicles with its fantastic numbers as a midrash or creative exegesis, rather than history), I can imagine hearing the Chronicler retort: "There is no such thing as an objective history, only what individuals report as of significance to them. *All* histories are highly selective. Any historian who simply records one fact after another should be faulted for lack of interpretation, no point of view. My perspective is theological, not merely historical, certainly not personal. I've chronicled not all that actually happened, but what truly mattered. The world is drowning in facts, suffocating in statistics. What's needed is *meaning*."

Chronicles, which covers Biblical history from the Creation to the end of the Babylonian Exile (ca. 536 B.C.E.), can be divided into four sections.

The first nine chapters are a highly abridged history from Adam to Israel's first king, Saul: history so instant that often the Chronicler merely lists genealogies, apparently to demonstrate the continuing favor granted by God to His people and to legitimize the upcoming reign of the House of David. Such is his haste to get to his ideal, David, that the Chronicler scants Abraham, Isaac, and Jacob, as well as Moses and the Exodus from Egypt.

In the overwhelming number of begats, the mother is never mentioned—not even Eve. Since daughters, too, are rarely mentioned, a reader might well wonder whom all these men married. And it's the father's lineage that determines whether his progeny is reckoned a priest, a Levite, or an Israelite.

(Only two women stand out—and that's toward the end of Chronicles. One is Queen Athaliah of Judah—daughter of the wicked queen of the northern kingdom of Israel, the murderous Jezebel, a full-blooded Phoenician—who slew all but one of her grandsons and usurped the throne for six years. The other is the prophetess Huldah, whom Judah's good King Josiah consults about the Book of Deuteronomy.)

The second section of Chronicles, or the narrative proper, begins in chapter 10 with a description of Saul's defeat by the Philistines and his suicide, concluding with the chilling judgment: "Saul died for the transgression he had committed against the Lord. Also, he had consulted a ghost for advice and did not seek advice from the Lord. He therefore had him slain and the kingdom transferred to David son of Jesse."

A cruel, ungrateful summing up of Israel's tragic first king, who had never sought the crown. From ca. 1020 to 1005 B.C.E. Saul had struggled valiantly to unify the twelve tribes and rally them against the invading Philistines. Despite many successes, he was finally defeated by the more sophisticated Philistines, who were far better armed.

Saul is treated in a far kindlier fashion by the midrash, which has God saying to His angels: How brave is this mortal Saul! Instead of fleeing for his life, he chose to lead his army into battle, despite knowing that he and his three sons would be killed. For he also knew that, without his leadership, the army would suffer far worse.

Clearly, the Chronicler was less interested in doing Saul justice than in introducing his thesis that whoever breaks faith with God is punished instantly and severely. Not even the king was immune to this immutable law. *Especially* not the king, for he is God's collaborator in His theocratic rule.

The next nineteen chapters focus adoringly on David, who founded the dynasty and is portrayed as the spiritual father of the Temple and its service. Such considerable attention is devoted to the Levites and their choir (much more so than to the priests and their sacrifices), one assumes the Chronicler himself was a Levite, probably a chorister. For, according to him, no important task, including warfare, was undertaken without the singing of hymns.

David's first acts as king are bringing the Ark into Jerusalem, erecting a tent for it, and arranging religious services, then asking God's permission to build a Temple to house the Ark. Permission was not granted: the reason given is that as a warrior David had shed blood (it was not that he was far too busy warring to construct anything so elaborate). Nevertheless, the king concentrates on getting the Temple built: choosing the site, conscripting craftsmen, importing materials, having blueprints drawn up, and fund-raising—also, organizing the administration of the Temple, the priests and the Levites and the choirs and musicians and the gatekeepers. The only reason the Chronicler stops short of having David himself erect the Temple, it would seem, is that everyone already knew that Solomon had done so.

Yet, for all his idealization of David, the Chronicler never attributes to him any aspect of divinity. In the pagan world of Egypt, Canaan, Mesopotamia, Asia Minor, the common practice was to deify their king. He was a god or a son of a god, for whom death was only a temporary state: he would soon rise again. But there are no such traces of mystery religions in Chronicles. No matter how exalted his position, the king of Israel never takes on supernatural elements. "They transported the Ark of God . . . and David and all Israel danced before God with all their might." Clearly, David was one of the people, not worshipped by them—all Israelites being equal before the Covenant and in the sight of God.

If no deity, David could be what's almost as difficult to achieve: a *mensch*. When he expressed a craving for a drink of water from the cistern at Bethlehem's gate, three of his officers broke through the Philistine army to get the well water and brought it back to him. "David would not drink it, but poured it out. . . . For he said, 'God forbid I should drink this! Can I drink the blood of these men who jeopardized their lives?' " This is entirely in character with the David of the Book of Kings, who twice had the chance to kill Saul, who was out to kill him, but refrained from doing so.

And one can forget for the moment the king's complicity in the murder of Bathsheba's husband while reading David's magnificent prayer:

Yours, O Lord, is the greatness and the power and the glory and the victory and the majesty—all that is in the heaven and in the earth is Yours. Yours is the kingdom, O Lord, and pre-eminence above all. . . . Who am I and what are my people that we should make this free-will offering? All things come from You; what we have given to You is Your own gift. For we are sojourners before You, transients like our fathers: our days on earth are like a shadow, and there is no abiding. . . . I know, my God, that You search the heart and desire uprightness.

In the third section, of the nine chapters about Solomon more than six are devoted to the building of the Temple, its decorations and furnishings, its dedication and the organization of its affairs. In those days, just as in modern times, there was a need for a center wherein to worship the Deity. Saints may be able to live on faith alone, but ordinary people require outward symbols and sacred forms, ceremonies and living institutions. Without them, it would be difficult if not impossible to preserve religious truths and transmit them to future generations. Cut flowers, however beautiful, generally do not reproduce.

At intervals the Chronicler records testimonials from leading Gentiles of the day: the king of Tyre and the queen of Sheba. Curiously, hers comes immediately after a passage emphasizing not Solomon's wisdom, but his wealth: "When the queen of Sheba saw how wise Solomon was and the palace he had built, the food of his table, the seating of his courtiers, his butlers and their apparel, and the procession with which he ascended to the House of the Lord, it took her breath away." Continues the Chronicler: "King Solomon surpassed all the kings of the earth in wealth and wisdom." (Note that wealth precedes wisdom.)

The impression conveyed here is that opulence is not only good, but also Exhibit A of wisdom. Indeed, the Chronicler seems preoccupied with Solomon's gold, recording his two hundred shields of beaten gold, 210,000 gold shekels, three hundred gold bucklers, his ivory throne overlaid with pure gold, complete with footstool of gold, then adding, "All of King Solomon's drinking vessels were of gold, and all the utensils of the Lebanon Forest House were of pure gold; silver counted for nothing in Solomon's days."

Whence all this affluence? In the power vacuum that existed in the Near East during that particular period, Solomon took full advantage of Israel's central location to become the greatest of merchant princes. He bought and sold goods to his neighbors, monopolizing the horse and chariot trade, and levied tolls on all shipments passing through Israel. And his enormous military buildup consolidated the conquests of David; Israel now controlled all the territories from Kadesh on Syria's Orontes River to the Gulf of Akabah, as well as Transjordan as far as the Arabian desert on the east and the Mediterranean coast on the west, except for Phoenicia and small sections of Philistia. So powerful was Israel then, and so weak its foes, that nearly all of Solomon's forty-year reign was peaceful.

All this is not achievement enough for the Chronicler, however. He offers this pious excuse for Solomon's building his chief wife, the Egyptian princess, a private palace: "For Solomon said, 'No wife of mine shall dwell in the palace of King David of Israel, because that area is holy, the

Ark of the Lord having entered it.' " (There is no mention of the pagan altars which Solomon built for her as well as for his scores of other foreign wives.)

Happily, the Chronicler records some of Solomon's exquisite prayers:

But will God really dwell with man on earth? Even the heavens in their uttermost span cannot contain You—how much less this House that I have built! Yet . . . hearing the supplications that Your servant and Your people Israel offer toward this place, heed them in Your heavenly abode—give heed and pardon. . . . When they sin against You—for there is no person who does not sin—and they repent and make supplication to You, saying, "We have sinned, we have acted perversely, we have acted wickedly," may You hear their prayer and supplication in Your heavenly abode, uphold their cause, and pardon Your people.

This prayer, it should be noted, also includes a plea for non-Israelites as well: "Moreover, concerning the foreigner who is not of Your people Israel and comes from a distant land . . . when he comes to pray toward this House, may You hear in Your heavenly abode and grant whatever the foreigner asks of You."

Significantly, contained in this section is a restatement of the Covenant:

As for you, if you walk before Me as your father David walked before Me, doing all that I have commanded you, keeping My laws and rules, then I will establish your royal throne over Israel forever, in accordance with the Covenant I made with your father David, saying, "You shall never lack a descendant ruling over Israel." But if you desert Me and forsake My laws and commandments, which I set before you, and go and worship other gods, then I will uproot them from My land which I gave them, and this House, which I have hallowed for My name, I shall cast out of My sight and make it a proverb and byword among all peoples.

Chronicles' final twenty-six chapters, its fourth section, are the roller-coaster history of the kings of the southern kingdom of Judah, starting with Solomon's son and successor, Rehoboam (ca. 925–908 B.C.E.). There is no idealization here. The omissions of material recorded earlier in Kings are not of failings, sins, or crimes. And the Chronicler's additions regarding economics, politics, the judicial system, and the military flesh out the royal portraits in Kings and enhance our understanding of that era (though such was not his primary purpose).

Rehoboam is presented in all his witlessness, reaping with alacrity the whirlwind sown by his father. When Solomon's rebellious commander Jeroboam and a delegation of northern elders come to Rehoboam saying, "Your father, Solomon, made our yoke heavy. Now lighten the harsh labor and the heavy yoke which your father laid on us, and we will serve you," Rehoboam retorts: "I will make your yoke heavy, and I will add to it. My father flogged you with whips, but I will do so with scorpions."

Thereupon, to no one's surprise but Rehoboam's and his cronies', the northern tribes split off from the south of the large tribe of Judah and the small one of Benjamin. This schism permanently crippled the people Israel, for the north was larger, more populous, and wealthier than the south, which now had to battle continually to withstand its foes. (The north fared even worse: two centuries later it would vanish from history.)

So, for example, "In the fifth year of Rehoboam's reign, King Shishak of Egypt attacked Jerusalem. . . . He captured Judah's fortified cities and entered Jerusalem and took away all the treasures of the House of the Lord and the treasures of the king's palace. The Pharaoh carried off everything that Solomon had wrought." Only decades before, remember, the united kingdom of Israel had been so powerful that an earlier pharaoh had given his daughter in marriage to Solomon to curry favor with him.

However, so convinced is the Chronicler that everything that happens is God's will, even catastrophes, that he reports God as saying to Rehoboam, "This thing [the schism] has been brought about by Me." Not by foolish policies or intransigence or bad advisers or stupidity, but by the omnipotent Lord Himself. And why did Egypt's King Shishak attack Judah? "For Rehoboam and his people with him had abandoned the teaching of the Lord." Foreign nations, no matter how mighty, are always seen simply as rods of chastisement employed by God to punish Israel for breaking the Covenant.

Because of his interest in religious reforms, the Chronicler expands on the reigns of Jehoshaphat (ca. 869–48 B.C.E.), Hezekiah (ca. 715–686 B.C.E.), and Josiah (ca. 639–608 B.C.E.), adding details unrecorded in Kings.

Jehoshaphat purged the old administration and appointed Levites, priests, and eminent laymen to administer both the civil and the religious law. (This probably enabled the high priest to replace the king as chief judge of Judah after the return from the Babylonian Exile.)

Following the wicked reign of Ahaz, Hezekiah cleansed the land of pagan worship and revived the neglected celebration of Passover. Dispatching couriers to the northern tribes, he invited those brethren, too, to make the holiday pilgrimage to Jerusalem and rejoin the Judean kingdom.

The good King Josiah completed the purging of paganism in Judah, cleansed the Temple of all idolatrous rites and objects, and reinstated dismissed priests. He also sponsored the greatest Passover celebration ever for all Israel, abolished all shrines outside Jerusalem, and centralized worship in the Temple. While repairing it, he accidentally discovered within the Temple "a scroll of the Lord's teaching given by Moses"—evidently the Book of Deuteronomy. "Josiah read to [all his people] the entire text of the Covenant scroll . . . and solemnized the Covenant before the Lord." Thus, it became the law of the land, its constitution.

Nevertheless, the strivings of these righteous kings are outweighed, alas, by the manifold transgressions of lawbreaking kings like Ahaz, Manasseh, and Zedekiah:

All the officers of the priests and the people transgressed very greatly, following the abominations of the nations, and they polluted the House of the Lord which He had hallowed in Jerusalem. The Lord God of their fathers had warned them repeatedly through His messengers, for He had compassion on His people and on His dwelling-place. But they mocked the messengers of God, scorned His words, and scoffed at His prophets, until the wrath of the Lord rose against His people. . . . He therefore brought upon them the king of the Chaldeans.

Babylonia conquers Judah, destroys the city, burns the Temple (ca. 586 B.C.E.). All, the Chronicler underscores, because the kings of Judah and their people turned away from God. There is no evil that befalls them that is not punishment for their lawbreaking. No king of Judah, no matter how great his armed forces, can win a battle without turning to the Lord, just as nobody turning to God can lose.

Here, it would seem, ends the history of the Judeans, just as it ended in ca. 721 B.C.E. for the northern kingdom of Israel when Assyria conquered her, exiled many of her inhabitants, and populated the land with foreigners, resulting in the disappearance of those tribes through assimilation.

But no: whether written by the Chronicler himself, or tacked on by the ancient rabbis (who were so loath to have any Biblical book conclude on a negative note that they would sometimes repeat an earlier, positive verse from the same book), Chronicles ends with this coda (ca. 536 B.C.E.): an edict by the benevolent King Cyrus of Persia, conqueror of Babylonia:

The Lord God of heaven, who has given me all the kingdoms of the earth, has ordered me to build Him a House in Jerusalem, which is in Judah. Any one of you of His people, may the Lord his God be with him and let him go up.

Hence the name Jews: all of them today are descendants of Judeans—or Jews, for short.

It's fitting for the Jewish Bible to conclude with the Book of Chronicles (which was probably written during the fourth century B.C.E.). Not only does it review the history of Genesis through Kings, but it reiterates the central contractual theme that runs throughout the Jewish Bible and foreshadows the Talmud, which focuses on the rule of law and its application. For it was the people Israel and their Bible—not classical Rome, a Johnny-come-lately to the ancient world—that gave mankind the concept of law as well as monotheism.

Since Pauline Christianity dismissed the legal contract that is the Jewish Bible and proclaimed in its stead a *new* covenant (the New Testament), Christians regard the Jewish Bible as a small library of individual books—an amalgam of history, Wisdom literature, narratives, laws, psalms, rituals, biographies. Not so: the entire Jewish Bible is essentially one extended lawbook that delineates the Covenant into which God and Israel entered voluntarily. If Israel is the Chosen People, she is also—this is equally important—the *choosing* people. Without Israel's concurrence, there would have been no deal—and no Bible.

This legal contract obliges each party to be mutually faithful, excluding all others: the people Israel would serve only God, and He would guard and prosper them. That's why the Jewish Bible spotlights only God and

Israel, its costars, as they cleave to this contract—or fail to do so. Other nations—Egypt, Amalek, Philistia, Assyria, Babylonia—are only supporting players who are directed by God to punish Israel for lawbreaking.

This theme is introduced at the Bible's very beginning: in Genesis, God enters into a personal covenant with Abraham, saying: "Go forth from your motherland and from your father's house to the land that I will show you, and I will make of you a great nation, and I will bless you. I will make your name great, and you shall be a blessing—I will bless those who bless you and curse whoever curses you. In you shall all the families of earth be blessed."

This contract is renewed with Isaac and with Jacob (Israel). Then, at Mount Sinai, the personal covenant is broadened to include their descendants, the *entire* people of Israel. Thereafter, every event in the Bible that involves the people Israel or an individual Israelite and God occurs within that contract's purview. To fulfill their part, they must serve God alone and, equally important, mete out justice to their brethren.

Sacrifices and prayers are never enough; they are worthless unless accompanied by deeds of righteousness in daily conduct. Lip service is no substitute for upright living. Salvation by faith alone is found nowhere in the Jewish Bible. What counts are *acts*. And so, cheating in a business transaction, for example, is no mere civil crime, but a breach of the Covenant as well and therefore condemned by God Himself.

It is when the king or people Israel breaks this contract that a prophet appears to castigate them. The Covenant is the legal basis for his indictment. Acting as God's messenger (a forthteller or preacher, *not* a forthteller or predictor), the prophet appears during every reign to transmit the word of God, berate Israelites for their misdeeds, warn of God's wrath, and urge repentance. Indeed, *every* Biblical writer insists that it is impossible to serve God while at the same time mistreating one's fellows. To love God is to practice justice.

In fulfillment of His part of the bargain, God redeemed the Israelites from Egyptian bondage, shepherded them during their wanderings through the wilderness, gave them the land of Canaan, installed leaders to help them flourish. Moreover, He will continue forever to observe this contract, which is legally binding on each Israelite.

Time and again the Chronicler stresses God's reaction to Israel's actions:

immediate punishment for breaking the Covenant and reward for carrying it out. It is her fidelity alone, not the deeds of outsiders, that determines Israel's fate. The Chronicler hammers at this theme with a very heavy hand indeed, oblivious to the fact that enough is miraculous in the history of the people Israel without making each and every event in it a miracle—that is, the result of divine intervention. For example, in the war against Amon and Moab, "King Jehoshaphat positioned singers to the Lord praising His majestic holiness as they preceded the army, saying, 'Give thanks to the Lord, for His steadfast love endures forever.' As they began their cries of joy and hymns, the Lord set ambushes for the armies of Amon, Moab, and the hill country of Seir, who were attacking Judah, and they were routed!"

Now, this is not history, it is grand opera.

As for the monstrously evil King Manasseh, who "shed much innocent blood until he had filled Jerusalem from one end to another," he ruled Judah for *fifty-five years*. Where was *his* instant punishment? Well, the Chronicler lamely posits a religious conversion for Manasseh during his brief imprisonment in Babylonia—a born-again experience, if you will.

But this is not theology, it is *reductio ad absurdum*.

Completely disregarded as factors in Israel's fate are her geography and the might and malice of neighbors. (Some things never change.) Located at the crossroads of the ancient Near East, Judah was a buffer region—with a small population and meager defensive capabilities—between superpowers always eager to subjugate Judah, or to use her as a highway to get at another superpower. Even the most virtuous of Judean kings would have found it infinitely difficult to withstand the empires of Egypt, Aram, Assyria, Babylonia. To the Chronicler, however, victory in war never depended on the numbers of soldiers and arms, but upon the king and his people's asking for divine aid and heeding His laws.

Would that life were that simple! Does it indeed always follow, as night does day, that virtue is immediately rewarded and evil punished? This one-note theology flies in the face of universal experience. And what of the supposedly pious who reason backward that those beset by troubles must have transgressed, or that wealth is a sign of God's rewarding merit? Or, grotesquely, that it was because of their sins that the Six Million were murdered? (The Chronicler ascribes to God a plague that killed seventy thousand as punishment for a supposed sin of *David!*) Such pseudo-religious views are enough to drive sensitive, intelligent people away from religion and leave it in the hot hands of zealots and fanatics.

Happily, the Chronicler's isn't the last word on the subject. In their great wisdom, the rabbinic compilers of the Biblical canon granted the sanction of divine revelation to the Book of Job, which portrays the ineffable suffering of a good man who is entirely blameless. For that reason, that he has not sinned and therefore deserves no punishment, Job demands God be brought to court. It is on strictly legal grounds that he wants God put on trial: He has broken His own contract. Hasn't Israel been prosecuted whenever she broke her contract with Him? Now Job demands to be vindicated legally and declared in the right, and his infuriating friends— with their traditionally pious, conventional views about suffering always resulting from sin—declared in the wrong. Clearly, then, to a Job and his legion of sympathizers, the Chronicler grossly overstated his case.

And yet one must concede that sermons like the Chronicler's, extreme though they are, have proved to be strangely energizing. The people Israel are the only ones in history who always blamed themselves for whatever calamity befell them. Everyone else (not unlike today) invariably blamed everyone and everything *but* himself: enemies, society, fate, circumstances, minorities, majorities, the devil, etc. Not so the Jews, who must have invented guilt.

Paradoxically, guilt, which can be crippling, proved liberating for the people Israel when they wedded it to acceptance of responsibility for misdeeds and trust in God's favorable response to their repentance. This magical mixture granted an enormous sense of power to the powerless. All Biblical writers taught that God does not desire the destruction of the sinner, but his reformation. Certain, therefore, that their own actions could determine their fate, the Jews never fell into permanent despair or lost the will to persevere. If they would return to the Lord and their Covenant, they believed, He would surely requite them for good—never mind external circumstances or malevolent foes. So time and again throughout history the Jews lost everything, but never hope.

(It's no accident that the name of the Jewish national anthem, which antedates the State of Israel, is *Ha-tikvah,* "The Hope." And during the horrors of the Warsaw ghetto, Jews sang, "I believe in the coming of the Messiah. And even though he tarries, nevertheless, I still believe.")

So the devastating Babylonian conquest, the destruction of the Temple, and the exile of Judeans to Babylonia were followed by an unparalleled phenomenon—a miracle wrought by the Judeans themselves. They were the only people in antiquity exiled from their homeland and national religion who maintained their religious and social identity in captivity. All other exiled peoples assimilated, as did the "Ten Lost Tribes of Israel." The Judean captives, in contrast, developed a cultless religious community: no new temple was built in Babylonia and there were no sacrifices, but there were more prayers and confession and fasts and worship in the incipient synagogue, and concentration on the Sabbath and other holy days continued. Then, still another miracle: in response to King Cyrus' edict, a substantial number of Judeans, though established now in Babylonia, did return and erect the Second Temple (completed ca. 516 B.C.E.).

Was this a happy ending for the people Israel post-Biblically? Alas, no: we know only too well what came afterward—more warfare, subjugation, punctuated by the successful Maccabean revolt, more wicked rulers, internal strife, the Roman conquest, rebellions, the destruction of the Second Temple and with it the end for all time of the sacrificial cult, the abortive Bar Kochba revolt that left hundreds of thousands of Jews dead, the complete destruction of Jerusalem, whose name was changed, with all Jews barred from the city . . . dispersion.

Always, however, if a Jew lives long enough, or if his great-grandchildren do, some light appears to dispel the darkness, if only for a brief period, as the Jewish people—perhaps not in Israel, not for centuries, but in the Diaspora—rise up from the ashes, dust themselves off, wipe away the tears and the blood, repress the horror unsuccessfully, even while maintaining the memory of the fallen, and start all over again one more time, hopefully, as *Jews.*

Is it any wonder that this peculiar people has driven philosophers of history like Arnold Toynbee mad? For the Jews, themselves living in accordance with the law, have always shattered the laws of systematic philosophers of history, none of whose theories satisfactorily explain the Jews' continued existence. An unfathomable mystery!

Whereas the Greeks invented the art form of tragedy, the Jews have lived it—and endured. Whereas the ancient mystery religions worshipped deities who died only to be resurrected, the people Israel, to whom such a concept is anathema, have lived that, too. They should have died out countless times, vanished; all other ancient civilizations did. The Jews alone persisted in returning again and again to life. And not only to life: to creativity as well, serving as a kind of yeast within other nations and contributing a disproportionate share to whatever progress mankind has made throughout the ages. (Imagine how much more they'd have contributed if allowed to live in peace!)

No wonder the Jews spook people. Irritatingly, brazenly, provocatively, spitefully, bafflingly, they have refused to stay dead, or even permanently embittered. Does that account in large part for anti-Semitism? A people whom you've subjugated, pillaged, slandered, raped, maimed, tortured, exiled, crucified, cremated—what else can you do except try to annihilate them once and for all? Or perhaps, what's even harder, acknowledge at last this people's peculiar link to the divine?

So, perhaps the Jewish Bible is correct, after all, and it is God, who has kept the people Israel alive and productive all these millennia, fulfilling His part of the Covenant, as promised. Perhaps the only sure way to destroy the Jewish people once and for all is to annihilate Israel's guarantor—God Himself.

Failing that, the Covenant endures, still in force now even as in ancient days, and with it God's assurance to the Jews:

> You shall be a blessing—I will bless those who bless you and curse whoever curses you. In you shall all the families of earth be blessed.

AUTHOR BIOGRAPHIES

MAX APPLE (Joshua) was born in Grand Rapids, Michigan, in 1941. He has taught at Rice University since 1972 and has also taught at the University of Michigan, Reed College, and Stanford University. His books include *The Oranging of America and Other Stories* (1976), *Zip: A Novel of the Left and the Right* (1978), *Free Agents* (1984), a one-act play entitled *Trotsky's Bar Mitzvah* (1983), and his most recent novel, *The Propheteers* (1987). Mr. Apple has been awarded a National Endowment for the Humanities fellowship (1971), the Jesse Jones Award from Texas Institute of Letters (1976 and 1985), and the *Hadassah* magazine Ribalow Award (1985). He lives in Houston, Texas.

JAMES ATLAS (Hosea) was born in Chicago in 1949. He graduated from Harvard in 1971 and spent the next two years in Oxford as a Rhodes scholar, returning to Cambridge, Massachusetts, to write his biography of Delmore Schwartz, published in 1977. His first novel, *The Great Pretender,* was published in 1986, and he is at work on a second. Mr. Atlas is currently a contributing editor of *Vanity Fair*. He contributes literary journalism to a variety of magazines, including *The New Criterion, The New York Times Book Review,* and *The New Republic*. His fiction has appeared in *Vanity Fair, TriQuarterly,* and volume X of the *Pushcart Prize*. He lives with his wife and daughter on the Upper West Side of New York City.

Stephen Berg (Habakkuk) was born in 1934 in Philadelphia. He is a professor at the Philadelphia College of Art and has taught at Harvard and Princeton. His books include *Bearing Weapons* (1963), *The Daughters: Poems* (1971), *Nothing in the Word* (1972), *Grief* (1975), and *With Akhmatova at the Black Gates* (1981); the most recent, *In It,* appeared in 1986. He is the founder and a coeditor of *The American Poetry Review*. Mr. Berg has won the Frank O'Hara Poetry Prize (1970) and has been a Rockefeller fellow (1969–71), a Guggenheim fellow (1974–75), and a National Endowment for the Arts fellow (1977). He is currently finishing a book of prose pieces entitled *Shaving,* working on new poems, and collaborating on a translation of the poems of Buson.

Harold Bloom (Exodus) was born in New York City in 1930. Among his many published books are *Blake's Apocalypse* (1963), *Kabbalah and Criticism* (1975), *The Breaking of the Vessels* (1981), and *Poetics of Influence: New and Selected Criticism* (1987). He was a Fulbright fellow in 1955 and a Guggenheim fellow in 1962. Mr. Bloom is a member of the American Academy of Arts and Sciences. He currently holds a MacArthur Fellowship. Mr. Bloom has been a member of the Yale University faculty since 1955 and lives in New Haven with his wife and two sons. During 1987–88, he is the Charles Eliot Norton Professor of Poetry at Harvard University.

Jerome Charyn (I Samuel) was born in the Bronx in 1937. He has been a playground director, a ping-pong addict, and a professor of English. He has published nineteen novels (including *The Catfish Man, Blue Eyes,* and *War Cries over Avenue C*) and *Metropolis,* a book about New York. He is a member of the Playwright/Directors Unit at the Actors Studio, where he is working on a comedy about King George III; and he is currently writing a book about Hollywood as the ultimate dreamscape and myth.

DAVID EVANIER (Zechariah) is the author of *The One-Star Jew* (1983) and *The Swinging Headhunter* (1972). He received the Aga Khan Fiction Prize in 1975, and he has been a Writer-in-Residence at the MacDowell Colony, Yaddo, the Wurlitzer Foundation, and The Writers Community. His fiction has appeared in *Best American Short Stories 1980, Commentary, Midstream, Moment, Confrontation,* the *Paris Review, Croton Review, National Jewish Monthly, Transatlantic Review, Pequod,* and *Other Voices.* He is former fiction editor of the *Paris Review,* and a frequent contributor to the *New York Times Book Review.* He was also founding editor of the literary magazine *Event.* Currently a research specialist with the civil-rights division of the Anti-Defamation League of B'nai B'rith, Mr. Evanier has also been assistant editor of *The New Leader.* He has taught at Douglas College in Vancouver and The Writers Community in New York City.

LESLIE FIEDLER (Job) was born in 1917 in Newark, New Jersey. He served in the U.S. Naval Reserve from 1942 to 1946. Mr. Fiedler was a member of the faculty at the University of Montana at Missoula, 1941 to 1964. He has been a professor of English at the State University of New York at Buffalo since 1965 and is now Samuel Clemens Professor there. He is also an associate fellow of Calhoun College at Yale University. In addition, he has taught at many other universities in the United States, Italy, France, Greece, and England. Mr. Fiedler is the author of *An End to Innocence* (1955), *The Art of the Essay* (1959, revised 1969), *The Image of the Jew in American Fiction* (1959), *Love and Death in the American Novel* (1960, revised 1966), *The Second Stone* (a novel, 1963), *The Last Jew in America* (1966), *Nude Croquet and Other Stories* (1969), *Collected Essays* (1971), *In Dreams Awake* (1975), and other books. He has received many awards, including a Rockefeller fellowship in the Humanities (1946–47), a Fulbright fellowship (1951–53), and a Guggenheim fellowship (1970–71). Mr. Fiedler is married and has six children, two stepchildren, and nine grandchildren. He lives in Buffalo, New York.

HERBERT GOLD (I Kings) was born in Cleveland. He attended Columbia University and the Sorbonne in Paris. He has taught at Stanford University, Cornell University, and the University of California at Berkeley and at Davis. He is the author of many books, including *Fathers* (a novel), *Family* (a novel), *My Last Two Thousand Years* (an autobiographical essay), and *Lovers and Cohorts* (a collection of stories). His most recent novel is *A Girl of Forty*. Mr. Gold has lived in San Francisco for the past twenty-seven years and has five children.

GEOFFREY H. HARTMAN (Numbers) was born in Germany and emigrated in 1939. He was a Fulbright fellow and has taught at Yale University since 1955, where he is currently the Karl Young Professor of English and Comparative Literature and is faculty adviser to Yale's Video Archive for Holocaust Testimonies. Mr. Hartman has also taught at the University of Iowa, Cornell University, the University of Chicago, Hebrew University in Jerusalem, the University of Zurich, and Princeton. He is the author of *The Unmediated Vision* (1954), *Criticism in the Wilderness* (1980), and other books. His most recent publications include *Easy Pieces, Bitburg in Moral and Political Perspective,* and, with S. Budick, *Midrash and Literature.* Among his many awards, he has received a Guggenheim fellowship, a National Endowment for the Humanities fellowship, and the Christian Gauss Prize for *Wordsworth's Poetry* (1964). He is a member of the American Academy of Arts and Sciences. He lives in New Haven, is married, and has two children.

JOHN HOLLANDER (Psalms) was born in New York City in 1929. He is the author of *A Crackling of Thorns* (1958), *The Night Mirror* (1971), *Tales Told of the Fathers* (1975), *Spectral Emanations* (1978), *Blue Wine* (1979), *Powers of Thirteen* (1983), and, most recently, *In Time and Place* (1986). He has also coedited several books of poetry and prose, including *American Short Stories Since 1945* (1968) and *The Oxford Anthology of English Literature* (1973). He was a recipient of the Yale Younger Poets award, an award in literature from the National Institute of Arts and Letters (1963), and the Bollingen Prize (1983). Mr. Hollander was a Guggenheim fellow (1979–80), and is now Chancellor of the National Endowment for the Humanities, a fellow of the Academy of American Poets, and a member of the National Institute of Arts and Letters and of the American Academy of Arts and Sciences. He has been a professor of English literature at Yale University since 1977. He is married and has two children.

RICHARD HOWARD (Esther) was born in Cleveland, Ohio, in 1929. His eight books of poetry include *Quantities* (1962) and *Lining Up* (1984). He has also written two books of criticism: *Alone with America* (1969; revised 1980) and *Preferences* (1974). He is a copious translator from the French, and in 1983 won the National Book Award for his version of Baudelaire's *Flowers of Evil.* He reviews for various periodicals, and is currently poetry editor of *The New Republic.* Mr. Howard was a Guggenheim fellow (1966–67) and president of PEN-American Center (1977–79). He received a Pulitzer Prize in poetry in 1970 and the Award of Merit of the National Institute and Academy of Arts and Letters (1982), of which he is now a member. He lives in New York City.

STANLEY KUNITZ (Jeremiah) was born in Worcester, Massachusetts, in 1905 and educated at Harvard University. The honors for his poetry include the Pulitzer Prize (1959), the Brandeis Medal of Achievement (1965), the National Endowment for the Arts Senior Fellowship (1984), and the Bollingen Prize (1987). In 1987 he was designated the first State Poet of New York and awarded the Walt Whitman Citation of Merit. He has edited the Yale Series of Younger Poets, served as Consultant in Poetry to the Library of Congress, and taught for many years in the graduate writing program at Columbia University. He is a founder of the Fine Arts Work Center in Provincetown, Massachusetts, an officer of the American Academy of Arts and Letters, a chancellor of the Academy of American Poets, and president of Poets House in New York. His most recent books are *Next-to-Last Things: New Poems and Essays* (1985) and *The Essential Blake* (ed., 1987). Other publications include *Selected Poems 1928–1958* (1958), *The Poems of John Keats* (ed., 1964), *The Testing-Tree* (1971), *Poems of Akhmatova* (trans., 1973), *A Kind of Order, A Kind of Folly: Essays and Conversations* (1975), and *The Poems of Stanley Kunitz 1928–1978* (1979). Mr. Kunitz lives in New York City and Provincetown with his artist wife, Elise Asher.

ALAN LELCHUK (II Kings) was born in 1938 in Brooklyn, New York. He has taught at Brandeis University and was visiting writer at Amherst College. In 1985 he joined the faculty of an interdisciplinary graduate program at Dartmouth College, where he is currently Adjunct Professor of Writing and Literature. He is the author of *American Mischief* (1973), *Miriam at Thirty-Four* (1974), *Shrinking* (1978), and, most recently, *Miriam in Her Forties* (1985). His nonfiction pieces have appeared in *The New York Times Book Review* and *The New Republic*. He has been the recipient of a Guggenheim fellowship for fiction. While a guest resident at Mishkenot Sha-Ananim in Jerusalem, Mr. Lelchuk coedited the anthology *Eight Great Hebrew Short Novels* (1982). He currently lives with his wife and son in Canaan, New Hampshire. In 1986–87 he was the Fulbright Writer-in-Residence at Haifa University, Israel.

GORDON LISH (Chronicles) was born in Hewlett, New York, in 1934. He is the author of the novels *Dear Mr. Capote* and *Peru,* and of the collection of stories *What I Know So Far,* and will presently bring out a second collection, *I Beg You, I Beg You, to Please Not to Die*, and a third novel, *Extravaganza.* Mr. Lish has taught writing at Yale, Columbia, and New York University, and is most recently known for his private classes. For some years he was fiction editor at *Esquire* and has since that time been an editor at the house of Alfred A. Knopf. Mr. Lish was the editor of *Genesis West* and is now the editor of the newly formed literary magazine *The Quarterly.* He was a Guggenheim fellow in 1984. He has brought out the anthologies *New Sounds in American Fiction, The Secret Life of Our Times,* and *All Our Secrets Are the Same.* In the course of his tenure as director of linguistic studies at Behavioral Research Laboratories, he published *English Grammar, The Gabbernot, Why Work*, and *A Man's Work.* Mr. Lish is married, has four children, and lives in New York City.

PHILLIP LOPATE (Judges) was born in New York City in 1943. He is on the faculty of the University of Houston's Writing Program. His nonfiction books include *Being with Children* (1975), which won a Christopher Award, and *Bachelorhood* (1981), which won the Texas Institute of Letters' Award for best nonfiction book of the year. He has also written two books of poetry: *The Eyes Don't Always Want to Stay Open* (1972) and *The Daily Round* (1976). His works of fiction include *Confessions of Summer* (1980) and *The Rug Merchant* (1987). His work has appeared in the *Paris Review, Ploughshares, Mississippi Review, The New York Times Magazine, Best American Short Stories of 1974,* and the *Pushcart Prize II,* among others. He also writes frequently on film for *Film Quarterly, American Film,* and related publications, and programs films for The Museum of Fine Arts in Houston. He is the recipient of two National Endowment for the Arts literary fellowships, a Revson fellowship, and a New York State CAPS grant. He currently divides his time between Houston and New York.

ALLEN MANDELBAUM (Psalms) was born in Albany, New York, in 1926. He is Professor Emeritus of English and Comparative Literature at the Graduate Center of the City University of New York, and he has taught at Washington University in Saint Louis, the University of Houston, the University of Colorado at Boulder, and Purdue University. His verse volumes are *Journeyman* (1967), *Leaves of Absence* (1976), *Chelmaxioms* (1978), *A Lied of Letterpress* (1980) and *The Savantasse of Montparnasse* (1987). In addition to *The Aeneid of Virgil: A Verse Translation,* for which he won a National Book Award, and the three volumes of Dante's *Divine Comedy,* his verse translations include *Life of a Man* by Giuseppe Ungaretti, *Selected Writings of Salvatore Quasimodo,* and *Ovid in Sicily.* A recipient of the Order of Merit from the Republic of Italy, he was in the Society of Fellows at Harvard University, a Rockefeller fellow in Humanities, and a Fulbright research scholar in Italy. He lives in New York but is often in Paris, home of his son and grandchildren, and in Italy.

DAPHNE MERKIN (Ecclesiastes) grew up in Manhattan and attended Barnard and Columbia University. She has been the book and film critic for *The New Leader* and is a contributing editor at *Partisan Review.* She is presently a Senior Editor at a New York City publishing house. Her novel, *Enchantment,* won the Edward Lewis Wallant Award for 1986. She has published fiction in *The New Yorker, Encounter,* and *Mademoiselle,* and a collection of her literary and film criticism—which has appeared in *Commentary, The New Republic, The New York Times Book Review,* and other magazines—is forthcoming.

LEONARD MICHAELS (Jonah) was born in New York City. He is the author of *Going Places* (1969), *I Would Have Saved Them if I Could* (1975), and *The Men's Club* (1981). He has edited various literary magazines and has contributed short stories, book reviews, memoirs, and critical essays to many publications. In 1967 he received an award from the National Foundation of the Arts. Mr. Michaels was a Guggenheim fellow in 1970 and received an award from the National Academy of Arts and Letters in 1972. He has taught at the University of California at Berkeley since 1969.

MARK MIRSKY (Daniel) was born in Boston in 1939. He attended Harvard College and Stanford University. He is the editor of the magazine *Fiction* and has taught English at the City College of New York since 1967. He is the author of *Thou Worm Jacob* (1967), *Proceedings of the Rabble* (1971), *Blue Hill Avenue* (1972), *The Secret Table* (1975), and *My Search for the Messiah.* His next novel, *The Red Adam,* will be published by Sun and Moon Press. He received a fellowship to Bread Loaf Writers' Conference and is a member of the Publications Committee of the Jewish Publication Society. Mr. Mirsky lives in New York with his wife, son, and daughter.

STEPHEN MITCHELL (Lamentations). Mr. Mitchell's books include *Dropping Ashes on the Buddha* (1976), *The Selected Poetry of Rainer Maria Rilke* (1982), and *The Book of Job* (1987).

HOWARD MOSS (Amos) was born in New York City in 1922. His books of poems include *Buried City* (1975), *Rules of Sleep* (1984), and *New Selected Poems* (1985), for which he received the Lenore Marshall/Nation award in 1986. His books of criticism include *The Magic Lantern of Marcel Proust* (1962) and *Minor Monuments: Selected Essays* (1986). He has also written plays, satire, translations, and a children's book. He received a creative-writing award from the American Academy of Arts and Letters in 1968, the National Book Award in Poetry in 1972, and a National Endowment for the Arts award in 1984. Awarded a fellowship from the Academy of American Poetry in 1986, he became one of its chancellors in 1987. Mr. Moss was the poetry editor of *The New Yorker* magazine since 1950, having joined its staff in 1948. He lived in New York until his death in September 1987.

JAY NEUGEBOREN (Ezra) is the author of *Big Man* (1966), *Listen Ruben Fontanez* (1968), *Sam's Legacy* (1973), *An Orphan's Tale* (1976), *The Stolen Jew* (which was awarded the *Present Tense* Award for 1981), and *Before My Life Began* (which won the Wallant Prize for 1985). He has also written a collection of stories, *Corky's Brother* (1969), and a memoir, *Parentheses* (1970), and served as editor of *The Story of Story Magazine* (1980). Mr. Neugeboren's short stories and articles have appeared in *The Atlantic, Esquire, Sport, Commentary,* and *The American Scholar,* and have been reprinted in anthologies, including *Best American Short Stories* and *Prize Stories: The O. Henry Awards.* He has written for stage and screen, most recently for the PBS "American Short Story" series. He has won six consecutive PEN Syndicated Fiction awards (the only author to do so), and fellowships from the National Endowment for the Arts and the Guggenheim Foundation. Mr. Neugeboren is Writer-in-Residence at the University of Massachusetts. He lives with his wife and three children in Northampton, Massachusetts.

CYNTHIA OZICK (Ruth) was born in New York City. Her most recent novel is *The Messiah of Stockholm.* Ms. Ozick's other books include *Trust* (1966), *The Cannibal Galaxy* (1983), *The Pagan Rabbi and Other Stories* (1971), *Bloodshed and Three Novellas* (1976), *Levitation: Five Fictions* (1982), and *Art and Ardor: Essays* (1983). She has won many awards, including a National Endowment for the Arts fellowship and the Wallant Award for fiction; she was nominated for a National Book Award, received an American Academy of the Arts award for literature, and has won first prize for three different years of the O. Henry Prize Stories awards. She was a Guggenheim fellow in 1982, won the American Academy and Institute of Arts and Letters Strauss Living Award in 1983, the Distinguished Service in Jewish Letters Award from the Jewish Theological Seminary, and was a nominee for a

Award from the Jewish Theological Seminary, and was a nominee for a PEN/Faulkner Award. Ms. Ozick is married, has one daughter, and lives in Westchester, New York.

ROBERT PINSKY (Isaiah) was born in Long Branch, New Jersey, in 1940. He has taught at the University of California, Berkeley, since 1980. His books of poems are *Sadness and Happiness* (1975), *An Explanation of America* (1979), and *History of My Heart* (1984). He is also the author of two works of literary criticism, *Landor's Poetry* (1968) and *The Situation of Poetry* (1977). He is cotranslator of *The Separate Notebooks,* poems by Czeslaw Milosz. Mr. Pinsky has published a narrative computer entertainment called *Mindwheel.* He was a Guggenheim fellow in 1980 and received an artists award from the American Academy of Arts and Letters in 1979. *History of My Heart* was awarded the William Carlos Williams Prize in 1984. He lives in Berkeley with his wife and three daughters.

FRANCINE PROSE (Malachi) was born in New York in 1947. She is the author of seven novels, including *Hungry Hearts* (1983) and, most recently, *Bigfoot Dreams.* Her first novel, *Judah the Pious* (1973), won the Jewish Book Council Award. Her fiction has appeared in *The New Yorker, The Atlantic, Mademoiselle, Antaeus, Commentary,* and *Tri-Quarterly,* and she has also written a series of "Hers" columns for *The New York Times.* Ms. Prose has won two National Endowment for the Arts grants and two CAPS (New York State Arts grants). She has taught at Harvard University, Sarah Lawrence College, the University of Arizona, the University of Utah, and in the Warren Wilson MFA Program for Writers. She currently lives in upstate New York with her husband and two sons.

MORDECAI RICHLER (Deuteronomy) was born in Montreal, Canada, in 1931. Among his books are the novels *The Apprenticeship of Duddy Kravitz* (1959), *St. Urbain's Horseman* (1971), *Joshua Then and Now* (1980), and collections of essays and stories. He is the editor of *The Best of Modern Humor.* Mr. Richler is the author of many screenplays, including the film version of his own *The Apprenticeship of Duddy Kravitz,* which won both an Academy Award nomination and a Writers Guild of America Award in 1974, and *Joshua Then and Now,* in 1985. He received a Guggenheim fellowship in 1961 and was a recipient of Canada's Governor-General's award for literature in 1968 and 1971. He is married, has five children, and lives in Montreal.

ANNE ROIPHE (Nehemiah) was born in 1935 in New York City. She has written five novels: *Digging Out, Up the Sandbox, Long Division, Torch Song,* and most recently *Lovingkindness.* She is also the author of *Generation without Memory: A Jewish Journey in Christian America.* She is the coauthor with her husband, Dr. Herman Roiphe, of *Your Child's Mind.* She lives with her husband and daughters in New York.

NORMA ROSEN (Jonah) is the author of the novels *Joy to Levine!, Touching Evil,* and *At the Center;* a collection of stories, *Green;* and a play, *The Miracle of Dora Wakin.* Her stories and essays have appeared in a wide variety of magazines and journals. She has taught writing at a number of colleges, and is currently conducting a writing workshop at New York University.

GRACE SCHULMAN (The Song of Songs) is the author of *Burn Down the Icons* and *Hemispheres,* both collections of poems. Her most recent book is a critical study, *Marianne Moore: The Poetry of Engagement.* She is the recipient of the Present Tense Award for her translation of T. Carmi's *At the Stone of Losses,* and is cotranslator of *Songs of Cifar and the Sweet Sea,* by Pablo Antonio Cuadra. A professor of English at Baruch College, CUNY, she is Poetry Editor of the *Nation* and a former director of the Poetry Center of the 92nd Street YM-YWHA.

LYNNE SHARON SCHWARTZ (Daniel) was born in Brooklyn, New York. She has taught English and fiction writing at Hunter College, the University of Iowa Writing Program, Columbia University, Boston University, and Rice University. She is the author of three novels: *Rough Strife* (1980), which was nominated for an American Book Award and the PEN/Hemingway First Novel Award, *Balancing Acts* (1981), and *Disturbances in the Field* (1983). She also wrote two collections of stories, *Acquainted with the Night* (1984) and *The Melting Pot and Other Subversive Stories* (1987), and a nonfiction book, *We Are Talking About Homes: A Great University Against Its Neighbors* (1985). Her reviews, essays, and satirical pieces have appeared in many magazines and newspapers. She has received grants for fiction writing from the Guggenheim Foundation and the National Endowment for the Arts. Ms. Schwartz lives in New York City with her husband and two children.

LORE SEGAL (II Samuel) was born in Vienna. She came to the United States in 1951. Since 1978, Ms. Segal has been a professor of English at the University of Illinois at Chicago. Her novels are *Other People's Houses* (1964), *Lucinella* (1978), and *Her First American* (1985), which won an award from the American Academy and Institute of Arts and Letters. She is a translator and writes children's books. *The Book of Adam to Moses* will be published in 1987. She received a grant from the Guggenheim Foundation and fellowships from the National Endowment for the Arts and Humanities. Ms. Segal was married to the late David Segal and has two children.

DAVID SHAPIRO (Proverbs) has published many volumes of poetry, including *January, Poems from Deal, The Page Turner, Lateness,* and *To an Idea.* In 1971 he was nominated for a National Book Award for poetry and in 1977 the National Academy and Institute of Arts and Letters gave him their triannual prize for experimental poetry. He has also published critical books on contemporary art and literature. Mr. Shapiro wrote the first book-length critical study of John Ashbery and teaches art history and aesthetics at William Paterson College and Cooper Union. He lives in New York City with his wife and son.

HARVEY SHAPIRO (Joel) was born in 1924 in Chicago. He attended Yale University and received his master's from Columbia University. He served with the U.S. Air Force in World War II and was decorated with the D.F.C., Air Medal with three oak-leaf clusters. His books of poetry include *The Eye* (1953), *Battle Report* (1966), *This World* (1971), *Lauds* (1975), and *Nightsounds* (1978); his most recent is *The Light Holds* (1984). A volume of his new and selected poems, *National Cold Storage Company*, will appear in 1988. He was a Rockefeller Foundation grantee in poetry in 1967. Early in his career, Mr. Shapiro worked at *Commentary* and *The New Yorker,* and then began working for *The New York Times* in 1957. He was editor of *The New York Times Book Review* from 1975 to 1983 and has been an editor of *The New York Times Magazine* since 1983. He lives in Brooklyn and has two sons.

ISAAC BASHEVIS SINGER (Genesis) was born in 1904 in Radzymin, Poland. He was a student of the Rabbinical Seminary in Warsaw, Poland. He came to the United States in 1935. He is the author of *Satan in Goray* (1935), *Gimpel the Fool* (1957), *The Magician of Lublin* (1960), *The Spinoza of Market Street* (1961), *The Slave* (1962), *Shosha* (1978), *The Collected Stories* (1982), and *Love and Exile* (1984), among many others, including books for children. He is a member of the American Academy of Arts and Sciences and a fellow of the National Institute of Arts and Letters. He received National Book Awards in 1970 and 1974, among other awards. Mr. Singer received the Nobel Prize for Literature in 1978. He lives in New York City, is married, and has one son.

HERBERT TARR (Chronicles), a rabbi and Doctor of Divinity, is the author of four novels—*The Conversion of Chaplain Cohen, Heaven Help Us!, So Help Me God!,* and *A Time for Loving* (whose hero is King Solomon)—and several plays. A frequent guest on radio and television programs, Herbert Tarr lectures throughout the United States.

ELIE WIESEL (Ezekiel) was born in Transylvania in 1928. He came to the U.S. in 1956. He is University Professor and Andrew Mellon Professor in the Humanities at Boston University, where he has taught since 1976.

Among his many books are *Night* (1960), *The Jews of Silence* (1966), *The Oath* (1973), *A Jew Today* (1978), *Five Biblical Portraits* (1981), *The Golem* (1983), *The Fifth Son* (which won Le Grand Prix de la Litérature de la Ville de Paris), and *The Testament* (which won Le Prix Livre-Inter). Among his many awards are the Prix Medicis (1968), the International Literary Prize for Peace from the Royal Academy of Belgium (1983), the Literary Lions Award from the New York Public Library (1984), The U.S. Congressional Gold Medal (1984), the French Legion of Honor (1984), and the Anne Frank Award (1985). Mr. Wiesel was chairman of the U.S. Holocaust Memorial Council from 1980 to 1986. He received the 1986 Nobel Peace Prize. He is married, has a son, and lives in New York.

LEON WIESELTIER (Leviticus) is literary editor of *The New Republic*. He was educated at Columbia, Oxford, and Harvard, where he was a member of the Society of Fellows. He is the author of *Nuclear War, Nuclear Peace*. His essays on religion, politics, art, and literature have appeared in the *New York Review of Books*, the *New York Times Magazine, Dissent, Foreign Affairs*, and other journals. He lives in Washington, D.C.